Copyright (layout, method, and breaks only) © 2017 by Wetdryvac

A VacHaus Press Book
Published by Vachaus Press
Published in the United States of America

Chapter One

[REDACTED]
7932384 6264 3383279502884 197169399375105820974 94 4 5923078164 062862089
98628034 82534 211706798214 808651328230664 709384 4 6095505822317253594
081284 811174 50284 10270193852110555964 4 62294 89
54 930381964 4 288109756659334 4 61284 7564 8233786783165271201909144 564
85669234 6034 86104 54 32664 821339360726024 914 1273724 587006606315588174
881520920962829254 091715364 36789
259036001133053054 88204 66521384 14 695194 15116094
33057270365759591953092186117381932611793105118854 8074 4 6237996274
9567351885752724 89
122793818301194 91298336733624 4 065664 3086021394 94 6395224
73719070217986094 370277053921717629317675238464 674 8184 676694 0513200056812714
526356082778577134 2757789
6091736371787214 684 4 0901224 9534 3014 654 9585371050792279689
2589
2354 20199561121290219608644 034 4 18159813629774 77130996051870721134
999999837297804 99510597317328160963185950244 594 5534 690830264 252230825334 4
685035261931188171010003137838752886587533208381
4 2061717766914 73035982534 904
287554
687311595628638882353787593751957781857780532171226806613001927876611115909
2164
201989
380952572010654 85863278865936153338182796823030195203530183
529689
957736225994 1389
124 97217752834 79131515574 85724 24 54 15069595082953311686172785889
075098381754 6374 64 9393192550604 0092770167113900984 8824
0128583616035637076601044 71018194 29555961989
4 67678374 4 94 4 8255379774 72684 7104 04 7534 64 620804 6684 2590694
912933136770289
89
152104 752162056966024 0580381501935112533824 3003558764 024 74 964 73263914
199272604 269922796782354 78163600934 172164 1219924 586315030286182974 55570674
98385054 94 588586926995690927210797509302955321165344 9872027559602364 806654
99119881834 7977535663698074 2654 25278625518184 17574 67289
097777279380008164 706001614 524 9192173217214 77235014 14 4 197356854
8161361157352552133 4 7574 184 94 684 38523323907394 14 3334 54 77624 168625189
835694 85562099219222184 272550254 2568876717904 94 6016534 66804
9886272327917860857844 3838279679766814 54 10095388378636095068006446
225125205117392984 89
6084 1284 8862694 5604 24 19652850222106611863067464 4 278622039194 94 504
712371378696095636364 3719172874 67764 6575739624 1389
086583264 59958133904 780275900994 65764 0789
512694 68398352595709825822620522 4 89
4 077267194 782684 826014 7699090264 0136394 4 374 553050682034 962524 5174
93996514 314 29809190659250937221696464 615157098583874 1059788859597729754 989

301617539284 681382686838689

4 2774 15599185592524 59539594 3104 9972524 68084 598727364 4 69584 86538367362226260909124 60805124 3884 3904 5124 4 13654 97627807977156914 35997700129616089

4 4 1694 86855584 84 063534 220722258284 8864 81584 5602850601684 27394 522674 6767889

525213852254 9954 6667278239864 56596116354 8862305774 564 98035593634 568174 324 1125150760694 794 51096596094 02522887971089

314 566913686722874 89

4 0560101503308617928680920874 760917824 938589

009714 90967598526136554 978189

3129784 8216829989

4 8722658804 857564 014 2704 7755513237964 14 5152374 6234 364 54 28584 4 4 79526586782105114 1354 7357395231134 27166102135969536 2314 4 29524 84 93718711014 57654 03590279934 4 0374 20073105785390621983874 4 78084 784 89

6833214 4 571386875194 35064 302184 5319104 84 81005370614 680674 91927819119793995 20614 196634 28754 4 4 064 374 51237181921799983910159195 61814 67514 269123974 89

4 09071864 94 23196156794 520809514 65502252 3160388193014 20937621378559566389

3778708303906979207734 67221825625996615014 215030680384 4 7734 54 92026054 14 6659252014 974 4 28507325186660021324 34 0881907104 86331734 64 96514 539057962685610055081 06658796998163574 736384 0525714 5910289

7064 14 01109712062804 39039759515677157700 4 20337869936007230558763 1763594 2187312514 71205329281918261861258673215791984 14 84 8829164 4 706095752706957220917567116722910981690915280173506 71274 858322287183520935396572512108357915136988 20914 4 4 210067510334 67110314 126711113699086585163983150197016515116851714 376576183515565088 4 909989

85998238734 552833163550764 791853589

32261854 89

632132933089

857064 204 6752590709154 814 1654 98594 61637180270981994 309924 4 889

5757128289

0592323326097299712084 4 335732654 89

38239119325974 6366730583604 14 281388303203824 9037589

8524 374 4 17029132765618093773 4 4 0307074 69211201913020330380197621101100 4 4 929321516084 24 4 4 8596376698389

5228684 78312355265821314 4 95768572624 334 4 189

30396864 2624 34 10773226978028073189

154 4 110104 4 68232527162010526522721116603966655730925 4 71105578537634 6682065310989

6526918620564 769312570586356620185581007293606598764 861179104 5334 885034 611365768675324 94 4 16680396265797877185560 84 5529654 126654 08530614 34 4 4 3185867697514 56614 068007002378776591 34 4 0171274 94 704 205622305389

94 561314 0711270004 07854 7332699390814 54 664 64 58807972708266830634 32858785698305235 8089

330657574 067954 57163775254 202114 9557615814 00250126228594 1302164
71550979259230990779654 73761255176567513575178296664 54 779174 5011299614 89
0304 63994 713296210734 04 375189
57359614 589
019389
7131117904 297828564 7503203198691514 0287080859904 801094 1214 722131794 764
77726224 14 254 854 54 033215718530614 228813758504
306332175182979866223717215916077166925 74 87389
86654 94 94 50114 654 06284 3366393790039769265672 14
63853067360965712091807638327166 16274 88880078692560290228 472104 03172118608204
190004 22966171196377921337575114 95950156604 963186294 72654 7364
25230817703675159067350235072835 056704 038674 3513622224 771589
1504 9530984 4 4 89
33309634 08780769325993978054 1934 14 4 73774 4 184 26312986080998886874
132604 72156951623965864 57302163159819319516735381297 1677294 786724 22924 654
36680098067692823828068 9
964 004 824 354 037014 16314 96589
794 0924 323789
69070697794 223625082216889
57383798623001593776 716512289
3578601588161757578297352334 4 604 281512627203734 314 6531977774
1603199066554 1876397929334 4 1952154 134 189
94 854 4 4 734 5673831624 9934 19131814 8092777710386387734 317720754 5654
5322077709212019051660962804
909263601975988281613323166636528619326686336062735676303 54 4 7762803504
5077723554 710585954 8702790814 35624 014 517180624 64 3626794 561275318134
078330336254 23278394 4 9753824 372058353114 7711992606381334
677687969597030983391307710987 04 085913374 64 14 4 2822772634 6594 704 74 58784
778720192771528073176790770715721 34 4 4 7306057007334 924 369311383504 931631284 04
25121925651798069 4 11352801314 701304 78164 3788518529092854 520116583934 196562134
914 34 1595625865865570552690 4 9652098580338507224 264 82939728584
7831630577775606888764 4 624 824 6857926039535277 34 80304 8029005876075825104 74
709164 396136267604 4 9256274 204 208320856611906254 54 33721315359584 50687724
60290161876679524 061634 25225771954 2916299193064 553779914 03734 04 328752628889
639958794 75729174 64 263574 55254 0790914 513571113694
10911939325191076020825202618798531887705 84 297259167781314
9699009019211697173727 84 7684 72686084 9003377024 24 29165130050051683233 64 350389
51702989
3922334 5172201381280696501178 4 4 0874 5196012122859937162313017114 4 4 84 64
090389
064 4 954 4 4 006198690754 851602632750529834 91874 0786680881833851022833 4
508504 860825039302133219715518 4 306354 5500766828294 9304 137765527939751754
613953984 683393638304 74 61199665385815384 20568533862186725233 4
02830871123282789
2125077126294 63229563989
89

89

358211674 56270102183564 6220134 96715188190973038119800 4 9734 0723961036854 0664 31939509790190699639552 4 530054 50580685501956730229219139339185680 34 4 90398205955100226353536192 04 1994 74 5538593810234 39554 4 959778377902374 21617271117236 4 34 354 394 78221818528624 08514 0066604 4 3325888569867054 3154 70696574 74 585503323233 4 210730154 594 05165537906866273337995851156257 84 3229882737231989

875714 15957811196358330059 4 08730681216028764 9628674 4 604 774 64 915995054 97374 2562690104 90377819868359381 4 6574 126804 92564 879855614 537234 78673303904 6883834 3634 6553794 9864 1927056387293174 87233208376011230299113679386270 89
4 38799362016295154 133714 24 89

283072201269014 754 6684 7653576164 773794 675200 4 9075715552781965362132392 64 061601363581559074 22020203187277605277219005561 4 84 25551879253034 3513984 4 2532234 157623361064 25063904 975008656271095359194 6589
7514 131034 82276930624 74 35363256916078154 7818115284 36679570611086153315 04 4 521274 73924 54 4 94 54 2368288606134 084 14 863776700961207151 24 914 04 3027253860764 823634 14 334 6235189

757664 52164 137679690314 95019108575984 4 239198629164 2193994 907236234 64 684 4 117394 032659184 04 4 37805133389

4 52574 2399508296591228508555821572503107125701266830 24 0292952522011872676756220 4 154 20516184 1634 84 756516999811614 10100299607838690929160302884 00269104 14 07928862150784 24 51670908700069928212066 04 18371806535567252532567532861291 04 24 877618258297651579598 4 7035622262934 860034 158722980534 989

65022629174 8788202734 20922224 5339856264 766914 90556284 2503912757710284 0279980663658254 889

264 880254 5661017296702664 07655904 290994 56815065265305371829 4 12703369313785178609 04 0708667114 9655834 34 34 76933857817113864 55873678123014 5876871266034 89

139095620099393610310291616152881384 37909904 23174 7336394 804 5759314 9314 05297634 7574 81193567091101377517210080315590 24 85309066920376719220332290 94 334 6768514 2214 4 773793937517034 4 366199104 033751117354 719185504 64 4 90263655128162288 24 4 62575916333039107225383 74 218214 0883508657391771509682887 4 78265699599574 4 9066175834 4 137522397096834 08005355984 91754 173818839994 4 6974 867626551658276584 835884 5314 277568790029095170283529716 34 4 56212964 04 35231176006651012 4 120065975585127617858382920 4 1974 84 4 2360800719304 576189
3234 9229279650198751872127267507981255 4 709589

04 55635792122103334 66974 99235630254 94 78024 90114 195212382815309114 07907386025152274 29958180724 716259166854 513331239 4 804 94 707911915326734 302824 4 18604 14 26363954 80004 4 80026704 9624 820179289
64 76697583183271314 251702969234 889

6276684 4 0323260927524 9603579964 69256504 9368183609003238092934 595889
7069536534 94 06034 0216654 4 375589

004 563288225054 525564 0564 4 824 651518754 711962184 4 396582533754 388569094 113031509526179378002974 120766514 79394 25902989
69594 6995565761218656196733786236256125216320862869222103274 889

218654 364 80229678070576561514 4 63204 69279068212073883778l4 2335628236089
632080682224 6801224 826117718589

63814 091839036736722088832151375560037279839l4 004 15297002878307667094 4 4
74 560134 5564 17254 37090697939612257l4 2989

4 67154 35784 68788614 4 4 5812314 593571984 9225284 7160504 922124 24 7014 1214
7805734 55105008019086996033027634 787081081754 5011930714 12233908663938339529l4
257869050764 31006383519834 389

34 1596131854 34 754 64 95569781038293097164 6514 384 07007073604 11237359984
34 52251610507027056235266012764 84 83084 07611830130527932054 274 628654 03603674
5328651057065874 88225698157936789

766974 2205750596834 4 086973502014 10206723585020072l4 522563265l34 1055924
0190274 21624 84 39l4 0359989

535394 59094 4 0704 69120914 09387001264 5600162374 288021092764
5793106579229552l4 988727584 6101264 83699989

2256959688159205600101655256375678566722796619885782794 84 8855834 39751874
4 54 55129656l34 4 34 8039664 20557982936804 352202770984 294 23253302257634 18070394
76994 159791594 53006975214 829336655566156787364 0053666564 1654 7321704
390352132954 35291694 14 59904 160875320186837937023l4 888689

4 79151071637852902l34 52924 4 07736594 95630510074 2108714 26l34 974
5956151384 9871375704 71017879573104 22969066670214 4 986374 64 595280824 3694 4 5789

77233004 8764 76524 13390759204 34 019634 039114 73202338071509522201068256l4
274 7164 6024 3354 4 00515212669324 934 1967397704 15956837535555166730273900l4
9729736354 964 53328886984 4 0611964 961627734 4 951827369558822075735517665l589

85519098666539354 94 8106887320685990754 079234 24
02300925900701731960362254 7564 789

4 064 754 834 664 77604 114 6323390565134 330684 4 9539790709030234 604 614
70961696886885014 0834 704 054 6074 29586991382966824
68185710318879065287036650832l4 31974 4 04 7718556789

34 823089

4 31068287027228097362l4 80939962706074 7264 55399253994 4 280811373694
33887294 0630792615959954 62624 629707062594 84 5569034 7119729964 09089

4 18059534 393251236235508l34 94 9004 364 2785271383159125689

89

2951964 2728757394 6914 272534 36694 1532361004 537304 88198551706594
12173524 62589

54 8730167600298865925786628561l4 96655235338294 287854 2534 04
830833070165372285635591525l4 784 4 598183134 11290019992059813522051173365856l4
078264 84 94 2764 4 11376393866924 8031183l4 4 53698589

1754 4 264 7399882284 62184 4 900877769776312795722672655562596282l4
2765318300134 070922334 3657791601280931794 0171859859993384 92354 9564
0057099558561134 9802524 99066984 23301735035804 4 08116855265311709957089

94 273287092584 8789

4 4 364 600504 1089

22669178352587078595129834 4 172953519537885534 57374
260859029081765155780390594 64 0873506123226112009373108l4 854 8526357228257682034

160504 84 66277504 5003126200800799804 9254 8534 694 14 69775164 932709504 934 6393824 32227188515974 054 70214 8289

711177792376122578734 771881968254 6298126868581705074 027255026332904 4 97627789

4 4 23621674 1191862694 39650671515779867564 823993917604 260176338704 54 99017614 364 1204 692182370764 887834 19689

68611815581587360629386038101712158552726683008238234 04 6564 758804 051380801633638874 2163714 064 354 955618689

64 11228214 07533026551004 24 104 89

678352858829024 3670904 8871181909094 94 53314 4 21828766181031007354 77054 981596807720094 74 696134 360928614 84 94 178501718077930681084 6900094 4 589

952794 24 3981392135055864 221964 834 915126390128038320010977386806628779239718014 6134 324 4 57264 0097374 25700735921003154 15089

367930081699805365202760072774 9674 584 00283624 0534 60372634 16554 259027601834 84 030681138185510597905664 0075094 26087885735796037324 514 14 67867036880988060971 64 2584 975951380693094 4 94 015154 2222194 32913021739125383559150310033303251117 4 9156969174 502714 94 33151558854 03922164 0972291011290355218157628232831 8234 254 83261119128009282525619020526301639114 7724 73314 85739107775874 4 2538761174 65786711694 14 7764 214 4 11112635835538713610110232679877564 1024

Chapter Two

6824 032264 834 64 17663698066378768134 9204 530224 08197278564 719839630878154 322116691224 64 15911776732253264 33568614 618654 5222681268872684 4 59684 4 24 16107854 01676814 20808850280054 14 361314 623082102594 1737562389

94 207571362751674 573189

189

4 56283525704 4 13354 375857534 26986994 7254 70316566139919968262824 727064 13362221789

239031760854 289

4 373393561889

16512504 24 4 04 0089

52719837873864 80584 72689

54 624 388234 375178852014 39560057104 81194 9884 239060613695734 23155907967034 614 914 34 4 78863604 103182350736502778959089

757827273130504 889

3989

00992391350337325085598265586709 089

24 26124 294 736701939077271307068691709264 6254 84 2324 074 855036608013604 6689

51184 009366860954 632500214 58529309500009071510582362672932 64 537382104 938724 9966993394 24 6855164 83261134 14 61106802674 4 6637334 37534 0764 294 026682973865220935701626384 64 8528514 90362932019919968828517183953669134 52224 4 4 70804 5923966028171565515656661113598231122506289

05854 914 509715755390024 39315351909021071194 5730024
388017661503527086260253788179751944 78061013715004 4 89

9172100222013350131060163915441 1589

5780371177927752259787441 289

19179155224 17189

585361680594 74 1234 1933984 2021874 564 92564 4 34 6239253195313510331144
76394 9119950728584 3065836193536932969928944

837914 94 19394 06085724 863968836903265564 364 21664 4 257607914 710869984
31573374 964 88352927693282207629441 72823815374 0996154 559879825989

109371712621828302584 8112389

0119682214 294 57667580718653806506441 8702613389

2822994 972574 5303328389

638184 394 4 7707794 02284 3598834 1003583854 2389

7354 24 39564 7555684 095224 84 4 554 1392394 10001620769363684 67764
130178196593799715574 6854 194 6334 89

374 84 3912974 23914 336593604 10035234 3777065888677811394 986164 7874 714
0793263858738624 732889

64 564 3598774 6676384 794 66504 074 1118256583788784 54 85814 89

629612739984 134 4 27260860618724 554 5236064 315371011274 6809778704 4 64 094
75828034 87697589

4 832824 123929296058294 86191966709189

58089

8332012103184 3034 01284 95116203534 28014 4 12761728583024 355983003204 2024
51207287253558119584 014 9180969253395075778441 000674 655260314 4
61670508276827722235341 191102634 16315714 74 061238504 2584 59884
199076112872580591139356894

6014 316682831763235673254 170734 208173322304 62987992804 908514 094
79036887868789

4 93054 69557030726190095020764 334 93359106024 54 50864 536289

354 5686295853131533718386826561786227363716975774 1830239860065914 816164
04 94 4 965011732131389

574 70620884 74 80236537103115089

84 27992754 4 26853277974 31139514 3574 17221975979935968525228574 5263796289

61269157235798662057344 08375766873884 2664 0599099350500081337544 324 54
635967504 84 4 235284 874 7014 4 354 54 195762584 73564 216198134 0734 6854
111766883118654 4 89

3776979566517279662326714 81033864 391375186594 6730024 4 34 50054 4 99539974
23723287124 94 834 70604 4 0634 7160632583064 982979551010954 18362350303094
53097335834 4 628394 76304 77564 50150085075789

4 954 89

3139394 4 89

9216125525597701441 368589

4 3585877526379625597081677644 38001254 365023714 127834 67926101995585224
7172201777237004 178084 194 2394 87254 06801556035998390544 89

8572354 674 564 2390585850216719031395262944 554 39131663134 53089

3906204 6784 38778505441 2393905244 731362012944 7691874 9751910114 72315289

32677253391814 6607300089
0277689
63114 810902209724 520759167297007850580717186381054 967973100167870850694
207092232908070383234 534 520380278609905569001341 3718236837099194 95164 89
60075504 934 12678764 3674 6384 902063964 019766685592335654 63913836318574
569814 719621084 1080961884 6054 560390384 5534 372914 14 4 65134 74 94 0784 884 4
23772175154 334 260306698831768331001133108 6904 2193903108014 3784 334 151370924
353013677631084 9135161564 226984 75074 3032971674 6964 06665315270353254
671126675224 6055119958183196376370761799191920357958200759560530234 626775794
39363074 63056901080114 94 2714 100939136913810725 81378135789
4 00559950018354 251184 172136055727522103526803735726 5279224
1737360575112788721819084 4 9006178013889
71077082293100279766593583875 89
0939568814 8560263224 3937265624 7277603789
0814 4 5883785501970284 37793624 07825052704 8758164 70324 5812908783952324
5323789
602984 16692254 89
64 9715606981192186584 9267704 039564 812781021799132174 16305810554
5988013004 84 56299765112124 1536374 51500563507012781 5926714 24 134
2103301566165356024 73380784 302865525722275304 999883701534
879300806260180962381516136690334 11113865385109193 6739383522934 5888322550887064
5075394 7395204 39680790670868064 4 509698654 8801682874 34 37861264 53815834
28075306184 54 85903798217994 599681154 4 1974 253634 4 399602902510015888272164 74
5006820704 193761584 54 71231834 6007262933955054 823955713725684 02322682130124
76794 52264 4 82091023564 775272308208106351889
9152692889
1084 5557112660396 5034 39789
62782500161101532351605196 55904 21184 4 94 9907789
9920073294 769058685777878720982901352956613978884
8605097860859570177312981 55314 9516814 67176959760994 210036183559138777 8176984
58758104 4 66283998806006162298 4 8616935337386578773598336161338 4 133853684
2119789
389
00185295691967804 554 4 828584
83701170967212535338758621582310133103877668272115726 94 9518179589
754 69399264 219791552338576623167 62754 7570354 6994 14 89
2904 1301863861194 39196283887054 367774 3224 2768091323654 4 94
85366768000001065262 4 854 730558615989
9914 017076983854 8318875014 29389
089
9506854 5307651168033373222651756622075269517914 4
2252808165171667766727930354 85154 204 0238174 6089
23283917032754 25750867655117859395002793389
5920576682789
67764 4 53184 04 04 18554 0104 35134 8389

531201326378369283580827193783312654 96174 599705674 50718332065034 55664 4 034 4 904 53627560011250184 33560736122276594 92783937064 784 264 56763388188075656121689

60504 161139039063960162022153684 94 1092605387688714 837989

559999112099164 64 64 4 11918568277004 574 24 34 34 0216722764 4 5589

330127781586869525069 99364 61017568506016714 5354 315814 801054 58860564 55013320375864 54 8584 0324 02987170934 8091055621167154 684 84 7780394 4 756979804 2631809917564 228098739987669732376957370158080682290 5992123661689

0259627304 3067931653114 94 01764 737693873514 09336183321614 280214 9763399189

8354 84 8756252987524 238730775595559554 65196394 4 0182184 09984 124 89

826236737714 6722606163364 32964 0633572810707887 58164 04 3814 8501884 114 3188598827694 4 9011932129682715888 1338694 34 682859006664 0806314 0777577257056307294 004 9294 03024 204 984 165654 797367054 855804 4 586572022763784 04 66823379852827105784 31975354 179501134 7273625774 0802134 7682604 502285157979579764 74 6702284 09995616015691089

0384 5824 50267926594 2055503958792298185264 8007068376504 1836562094 5554 34 6135134 152570065974 88191634 135955671964 9654 03218727160264 859304 90397874 89 589

066127250794 8282769389

53521753621850796297785 61884 3271922323810158 4 4 5052866523802253284 389

137527384 589

2384 4 225354 726530981715784 4 7834 2158223270206902872323300538621634 79885094 6954 72004 7952311201504 3293226628272763217790884 00878614 802214 75376578105819702226309717 9507212724 84 794 781695729614 23658595782090830733233560 84 6531873029302665964 50137183754 2889

75579714 4 9924 654 03868179921389

34 6924 4 74 1985097334 62679332107268687076806263991936196504 4 09954 216762784 0914 669856925715074 31574 07938053239252394 775574 4 159184 58215625181921552337096074 83329234 921034 514 6264 374 4 9805596103307994 14 534 7784 574 699992128599993996122816152193 888769388022281083001986016 94 1654 26169685867883726095877 56761825072759929508

3180521872924 6108676399589

1614 5855058397274 209809097817293239301067663868 04 0111304 024 7007350857828724 627134 94 63685318154 696904 669686939254 725194 139929 6524 238577625500 74 852954 76814 7954 6700705034 79995888676950161 97228204 03039954 6327883069597624 93615101024

Chapter Three

365553522306906129 9388599015734 6610237122354 789

1129254 769617600504 7974 928060721268039226911027772261025 4 14 922157650 508120677173571202718024 2968106203776578837166909109 18074 4 87814 04 90755178203856539099104 77594 14 132154 3284 4 062503018027571696508209 2734 84 14 6957263978 2560084 531214 06593580904 127113592004 1975985136254

7961606322887361813673732 4 50607924 4 117639975974 619383584 574 9159880976674 4
709300654 634 24 234 60634 2374 74 6660804 317012600520559284 9369594 14 34 0814
6852981505394 71789

004 51835755154 125223590590687264 87863575254 1911288877371766374
86027660634 9603536794 702692322971868327717393236192007774 52212624 7518698334
95151019864 26988784 7171939664 97690708252174 233656627259284 4 06204 30214
113719922785269984 69884 770232382384 0055655517889

0876613601304 770984 3861168705231055314 916251728373272867600724
817298763756981633 54 15074 60883866364 06934 704 3720668865127568826614
973078865701568501691864 74 8854 1679154 596507234 287730699853713904
3002665307839877638503238182155355973235306860 4 30106757608389

0862704 984 1888595138091030 4 235957824 9514 398859011318583584 06674
7237029714 9785084 14 585308578133915627076035639076394 73114 554 9583226694 57024
94 139831634 3323789

7595568085683629725386791327505554 2524 4 9194 3589

1284 0504 522695381217913191 4 51350099384 6311774 0179715122837854
601160359554 02864 4 059024 964 669307077690554 81028850208085800878115773817 19174
1776017330738554 758006056014 33774 329901272867725304 31825197579167929699650 4 14
6070664 5712588834 69797964 2931622965520168797300035 64 6304 57930884 03274
80771811555330909887025505207680 4 63034 608658165394 87695196004 4 084 820659673794
731680864 1564 565053004 98816164 90578831154 34 54
850526600698230931577765003780704 661264 7060214 5750579327096204 782561524 714
59189

6522360839664 5624 10519551052235723973951288181 64 059785914 27914 81654
263289

2004
281609136937773722299983327082082969955737727375667615527113922588055201 89
887620114 1680054 6873655806334 71603734
29170390798639652296131280178267971728 9

822936070288069087768660593252 74 63784 0539769184 808204 102194 4
719713869256084 1624 5112398062011318 4 54 124 4 78205011079876071715568315 4 0788654
3904 12108730324 0201068534 194 72304 7666672174 986986854 7076781205124 7367924
791931508564 4 4 775379853799732234 4 5612278584 329684 664 75133365736923872014 64
7236794 2787004 2503255589

926884 34 9592876124 00755875694 64 1370562514 00117971331662071537154
360068764 7731867558714 8783989

081074 2953094 106059694 4 31584 7753970094 3988394 914 4 3235366853920994
687964 50665339857388 8786614 76294 4 34 14 0104 98889

9316005120767810358861166020296119363968213 4 96075011164 983278563531614
51684 57695687109002999769 84 126326650234 7716728657378579085 74 664 607722834 154
03114 4 15294 18804 78254 387617707904 30001566986776795760909966936075594
96515273634 981189

64 1304 3311662774 7123388174 060373174 397054 0670310967676574 8695358789
6700319258662594 10510533584 384 65602339179674 926784 4 7637084 74
978333655579007384 1914 73198862713525954 625181604 34 22537299628632674 96824
0580602964 2114 63864 36864 224 724 8872834 34 1704 4 15734 824 8183330164

05669596688667695634 914 163284 264 14 974 53334 99994
80002669987588815935073578515195889

900539512085351035726137364 034 367534 714 104 83601754 64 883004 0784 64 1674
52167371904 8310967671134 4 34 94 81926268111073994 8250607394
95073503169019731852119552635632584 3390998224 98624 06703107683184 4 660729124 874
754 03161796994 1139738776589

9868554 17031884 7788675929026070004
32126661791922352093822787888098863359911608192353555704 64 634 911320859189

7961327913197564 9097600013996234 4 4 5535014 34 64 268604 64 4 958624 769094
34 704 8293294 14 04 1114 654 092398834 4 4 35159133201077394 4 11184 074 107684
98106634 724 104 8239358274 0194 4 9356651610884 631256785297769734 684 3030614 624
18035852933159734 5830384 554 1033701091676776374 276210213701354 854 4
50926307190114 73184 8574 92331816720721372793556795284 4 39254 815609137281284
063330393735624 2001604 5664 5574 14 58816605216660873874 804 724
33912129558777639069690370788285277389

4 0524 607584 96231574 36917113176134 7838827194 1686066257210368513215664
780014 76752310393578606899

61112599602818393095 4 8709059073861351914 5918195102973278755710 4 97290114
8717189

718004 696169777001791391961379 14 171627070189

584 69214 34 36967629274 5910994 0060084 9835684 25201915593703701011 4 974
73394 93877885989

4 174 3303178534 87076032219829705797511914 4 0510994 235883034 54 63534 9234
9826883624 04 33272674 1554 0301619505680654 1809394 09982020609994 14 021689

090070821330723089

66211977553066591881 4 11915778362729274 61561857103721724 710095214 236964
830864 1025928874 57999322374 9551912219519034 24 4 5230753513380685680735 4 4 64
995127203174 4 871954 03976107308060269906258076020292731 4 5525207807991 4 184
29063884 4 3734 996814 5827337207266391767020118300 4 64 81900024 1308350884 6584
15214 89

9127610651374 15394 35657211390328574 918769094 4 137020905170314 877734
6165287984 8235338297260136110984 514 84 182380812054 0996125274 5808810994
86972216128524 89

74 25555516076371675054 89

617301680961380381191 4 36114 399210638005083214 0987604 599309324
851025168294 4 67260666138151 74 571 2559754 95358023998314 69822036133808284
99356705575524 71290274 539776214 04 93182014 658008021566536067765508783804 304
134 310591804 606800834 59113664 0834 8874 0800574 1272586704 7922583191274
15739080914 3831384 564 24 15094 084 913391809684 02511639919368532255573389

6695374 90266209232613188558 9

15808324 5557194 84 53875628786128859004 10600607374 65014 02627824 02734
6962528217174 94 158233174 9239683530136178653673760 64 2166778137739951006589

5288774 2766263684 1830680190804 60984 98094
697636673356622829151323527888061577682781595886691802389

4 03330764 4 19124 034 1202231636857786035727694 154 17788264
35238131905028087018575 04 704 63129333537572853866058889

04 5831114 5077394 2935201994 32197117164 223500564 4 04 297989
2081594 3071670198574 6927384 86538334 3614 5794 634 17592257389
8588001698014 7574 2054 299580124 29581054 5651083104 6297282937584
1611625325625165724 980784 9209989
7990620035936509934 721582965174 1357984 9104 71116607915874 3698654 122234
834 18877229294 4 6335178653856731962559852026072947674 07261676714 557364
981210567771689
34 84 91766077170527718760119990814 4 11305864 5577910525684 304 8114 4
02619384 023224 7093924 980293355073184 589
03553971330884 4 6174 107959162511714 864 874 4 6861124 76054 286734 3670904
66784 68670274 091881014 24 971114 9657817724 27934 70702166882956108777944 0504 84
375284 4 3375108828264 77197854 0006509704 03302186255614 7332117771174 4
1335028160884 03517814 5254 1964 320309576018694 64 908868154 528562134 69883554 4 4
56024 95566684 36602922195124 8309106053772019802183101032704 178386654 4
71812603971906884 6237085751808003532704 71856594 994 76124 24 81109992886791589
6904 956394 7624 6084 24 06593094 8621507690314 98702067353384 834
955083636601784 8771060809804 26924 71324 100094 64 014 37360326564 5184 5667924
5666955100150229833079849607994 98824 97061723674 4 9361226222961790814 3114 14
66094 1234 1593593095854 07913908720832273354 95720807571651718765994 4
98569379562387555516175754 380917805280294 64 2004 4 721539628074 63602113294
25591600257073562812638733106005 89
106524 5708024 4 74 93754 3184 14 94 014 821199962764
5310680066311838237616396631809314 4 4 6712986155275982014 514 10275600689
2975024 6304 0173514 89
194 576360789
3528555053173314 164 570504 9964 4 389
09363084 3874 4 84 783961684 05184 52732884 03234 52024 705685164 657164
77139323775517294 795126132398229602394 54 8579754 5865174
58787713318138752959809412174 227300352296508089
17770506825924 8822322154 93804 83714 54 78164 72139768209633205083056479204
820859204 754 9985732038887639160199524 09189
389
4 557676874 9730856955958010659526503036266159750662225084 0674 2889
826590751063756356996821151094 966974 4 58054
7288693631020367823250182323708 45979011154 84 720876182124 778132663304
120762165873129708112307581598212486398072124 07868878114 5016558251361789
030708608701989
75889
8074 5664 39551574 15363193191981070575336633738038272152798849 3503974
8001589
05194 20879711308051233933221903 46624 991716915094 854 14 01871060354 603794
64 337900589
0957721180804 4 6574 3962806186717861017156 74
0967662080295766577051291209907944 304 63289
294 73061595104 309022214 3937184 9560634 056189
34 25130572682914 6578329334 0524 6350289

291754 70872564 84 260034 9629611654 1382300773133272983050016025672 4 014 18515204 189

0701154 2885799208121984 4 931569990591820118197335001261877280368124 819958770702075324 063612593134 3859554 254 778196114 29351635612234 96661522614 735399674 051584 99860355295332924 575238881013620234 7624 6690558164 389

67863097627365504 724 34 864 30712184 94 3734 8530060638764 4 566272186661701238127715621379 74 614 986132874 4 117714 5524 4 4 7089

9714 4 52288566294 24 4 0230184 7912054 784 98574 521634 6964 4 89

7389

20624 0194 35183100882834 8024 924 90854 03077863875165911302873958787098100772718271874 529013972836614 84 214 287170553179654 3076504 534 324 6005363614 726181809699769334 86264 0774 35199928686323835088756683595097265574 8154 3194 01955768504 3724 80010204 1374 9831872259677387154 9583997184 4 4 90727914 196584 593008394 263702087563539821696205532 4 8032122674 989

114 026785285996734 0524 203109179789

990571882194 93913207534 3170798002373659098537552023 89

1164 34 6718558290685371189

7952626234 4 924 833924 9634 24 4 9714 65684 659124 89

18556629589

329909035239233333364 74 3520370770101084 388003290759834 217018554 22838616172104 1760301164 59187805393674 4 74 7205998502358289

18336929223373239994 804 371084 196594 73162654 82574 80994 82509991833006976569367159689

364 4 9334 8864 74 4 21350084 0700660883597235039532 34 01795825570360169369909886711321097 9889

70705172807558551912699306730992507 04 07024 5568507786790694 76612629808225163313639952117098 4 5280926303759224 2674 257559989

289

2783704 74 4 4 52189

3632034 89

4 1552104 4 597261883800300677617931381399162058062701651024

Chapter Four

4 5886924 764 924 689

1924 61212531027573139084 04 7000714 3561362316992371694 84 8132554 200914 5304 10371354 5329662063921054 79824 39212517254 0132314 90274 058589

2063217589

4 94 34 54 89

0684 6399313757091034 6332714 15316223280552297297953801880162859073572955 4 1627886764 98274 186164 218789

88574 107164 90691918511628152854 86794 1736389

06653885764 22915834 25006736124 5384 9160674 13734 017357277995634 104 33268835695078 14 931378007362354 1800706191802673285511919 4 26760912210359874 6924 11728374 93126163395001239599 24 05084 54 37569850795704 6222664 6190001035004

90183034 15354 584 2833764 378111988556318777792537201166718353954 1835984 4
383052037628194 4 0761594 10682071697030228515225057312609304 689

84 234 33152732131361216582808075212631547 7730604 4 23774 7535059522871744
02666389

14 88171730864 36111389

0694 2027908814 31194 4 87994 17154 04 21034 1219084 7094 080254 02393294 294 54
9387864 023051292711909751353600092197110541209668311151632870542 230284
700731206580326264 171161659576132723515666625366727189

98534 19989

5236884 8309993027574 199164 6384 14 27077988708874 22927705389
12271724 8632202889

84 2512528721782603050099454 510824 7835729056919885554 678860794
6280537122704 24 6654 319214 528176074 14 824 0382783582971930101788834 5674
1678113989

54 7504 4 8339314 689

630763396657226727047 339321674 54 21824 557062524 79721997866854 27989
7799233957905758189

06225254 735822052364 24 8507834 0711014 4 9804 787266919901864
388229323053823185597328697809222535295910173414 07334 884 761005564 01824
23921926950620831838144 54 6983923664 61363989

1012102177095976704 908305081854 704 194 664 37131229969235889
5384 93013635657618610606222870559944 233716310212784 574 4 64 63989
73818856674 62608794 8201864 74 8767272722206267644 6533809980196688 3680994
1590757768526398651454 62533363124 505364 026105696055131838131742 261184 4 20189
088853196356986962795036738444 24 313011331753305329802016688817481344 8134
2988681585577810344 3231753064 784 9832106297184 25184 385534 4 27620128234
57071698853051832617964 117857960888815032960229070561444 76220915094 73903594 664
6916235396809201394 57817589

10889

31992112260073928144 91694 81615273844 2736264 298098234 06320024 4 024 4 9589
4 4 5612916704 95082358124 87391799644 864 11334 80324 7577752197089
3277226234 94 8601504 66526814 398770516153170266969297044 928316285504 21289
814 67061953319702695072144 3782304 76875280287354 12616639170824
5925170010714 180854 8006369232594 62019002278087440985977192180515853214
73926532515590354 10209284 6659252999144 353791825314 54 52905984 158176370589

2790690989

6911164 3811878094 3537152133226144 4 3625314 4 901274 54 7726957393934 8154
69163116244 928873574 718824 07150399500944 4 6731954 3161938554
852076657388251396391635767231510055560372633944 867208207808653734 94 24 4
0115799667507360711159351331959197120944 89

64 717553024 531364 77094 2094 6356969822266737752099454 51684 5064 3623824
211853534 887989

395673187806606107885454 4 00055082765703055874 4 854 180577889
17192078814 23351138662929667179644 34 6876007704 799953788338787034
871802184 24 3734 211227394 025571769081960309201824 01884 2705704 6092622564

178375265263358324 24 06612533115294 234 579655695025068100183109004 1124 53790153329661569705223792103257069370510908 30789

4 79999004 99939532215362274 84 76603613677697978567386584 67093667958858378879562594 64 64 89

13766521995882869338018360119323685785585581 9555604 2156250883650203322024 513762158204 618106705195330653060606501054 88716724 537794 28313388716313955969058320834 1689

84 7606560711834 713621812324 622725884 199028614 2087284 9568796393254 64 28534 30753011052857138 2964 370999035694 88852851904 0295604 734 613113826387889

75517885604 24 99874 8316382804 04 684 86189

38189

59054 2039889

87265069762020199554 84 12650005394 4 282039301274 816381585303964 399254 70201672759328574 36666164 4 1109625663373054 0921951967514 8328734 8089

574 7777527834 4 22109107311135182804 603634 719818565557295714 4 74 768255285786334 934 28584 2311874 94 4

00032296906977583159038580393535213588600796 0034 209754 739229673331064 9395601812237812854 584 317605561733861126734 78074 585067606304 82294 0965304 111830667108189

30311088717281675195796 7534 718853722930961614 3204 0063813224 6584 11111577583585811350185 6904 78153689

381377184 72814 751998350504 781297718599084 707621974 6058874 2325699582889

253504 193795826061621184 23687685114 18316068315867994 60165205774 05294 230536017803133572632670 54 7903384 0125730591233960188 01378254 21927094 76733719198728738524 80574 2124 89

211834 708766296672072723256505651293331 2605950577772754 24 7124 164 831283298207236175 0574 67387012820957554 4 305968395555686861188397135522084 4 5285264 00812520276655576774 95969626612604 56524 5684 08613923826576858 3384 6984 99778726706555191854 4 686984 694 784 95734 622606294 219624 5570853712727765230989

554 5019303773216664 9182578154 67729200521266714 34 6320963789

18523232150189

76126034 373684 067194 19303774 68809992968775824 4 104 787812326625318184 59604 5385354 3839114 4 96775312864 26092521153767325886 6722604 04 25234 9108702695809964 7595805794 6639734 19064 010036361904 04 203311357933654 24 263035614 5700901124 4 80089

00208014 78056603710154 12232889

14 6572239314 507607167064 35568274 3774 3965789

0679726874 384 7307634 64 51677562103098604 0927170909512808630902 9738504 4 52718289

274 9689

21210667008164 8583395537735919136950153162 0189

088874 84 21079870689

9114 804 66927065094 076204 65027725286507289

0532854 85614 33160812693005693 7854 17861096969202538865034 57718317668688 59236814 884 752764 984 6882194 97397297077371871884 004 14

323127636504 814 53112285099002074 24 09255859252926103021067368154 34 701525234
878635164 39762358604 19194 1296976904 05264 83234 7009911154 24 26012734 38022089
33109668636789
8694 977994 001260164 2276092608234 9304 118064 382913834 7354
679725399262338791582998434 864 59271734 05922562074
910530853153718291168163721939518870095778818815868504 64 50769934 394 09874 33514 4
3162633031724 774 74 8689
79182092394 8083314 397084 0673084 079589
3581089
66564 77585990556376952523265361 4 4 24 780230826811831037735887089
24 06130313364 77371011628214 614 6616794 04 0905186152603600925219 4 721889
0918107335871964 14 214 4 4 78654 89
952858234 394 70500798303885388608310357193060027711 94 55802191 194 289
99227223534 5870756624 6926177663178855514 4
350218287026685610665003531050216318206017609217984 684 936863161293727951873078 9
726373537171502563787335797771808184 8784 58866504 335824 377004 14 77104 14
934 9274 384 57587107159731559 4 394 264 1257027096512510811554 824 79394
035976811881172824 721582501094 960966253933953809221955919181885526780621 4
9923172763163218333989
6938075616855911752998 4 501320671293924 04 14 4 59386239880938124 04 521914
84 83164 621014 7389
18251010909677386906664 04 1589
736104 764 365000680771056567184 862814 9637111883219 24 4 566394 5814 4 914
861655004 956769826903089
111856879869294 70513524 81609174 324 3015383684 70729289
89
8284 60222373014 5265567989
86277679680914 69798378268764 31159883210904 37156112997665215396354 64 4
2086919756737000573876 4 9784 376862876817924 974 694 384 274 65256316323005551304
174 22734 164 64 55127812784 5777724 5752038654 3754 2828256714 12885834 54 4 4
35132562054 4 64 24 10110379554 64 19058116862305964 4 769587054 07214 1985212106734
3324 107567675758184 5699069304 604 7522770167005684 54 3969234 04 1711089
8889
934 163505851578873534 30815520811772071880379104 04 69830695786854
739376564 33631979786803671873079693924 2363214 4 84 50354 7763156702553900654
231179201534 64 97792906624 150832885839529054 26376876689
6880503331722780018588506973623 24 0389
4 7004 7189
761934 734 4 3084 374 4 3759925034 178807972235859134 24 581314 4 04 984
7701732361694 719765715353197754 99716278566311904 691260918259124 989
0367654 1769799036237552865263757337635269693 4 4 354 4 004 730671988689
0196814 74 28767790866979688522501636 94 985673021752313252926537589
64 151714 79559538784 2784 998664 5630287883196209983 04 94 519874
3963690706827626574 858104 39112232618794 05994 1554 063270131989
89

570376110532360629867480377915376751158304 32084 9872092028092975264 98125691634 2500052290887264 6925284 666104 6653921714 82080130502298052637836426959733707053922789

15351056888393811324 9757071331029504 4 3034 6715989

4 4 878684 71164 3832805069250776627450012200352620370946602341464 89

9839025258883014 8678162196775194 5831677187627572005054 39794 4 124 5990077115205154 619930509838698254 284 64 0725554 09274 03132571632640792934 18334 214 70904 1254 253352324 80219322770753555467958716383587501815933871742360615511710131235256334 8582036514 614 187004 9205704 372018261733194 715700867578539336078622739558185797587258744 10254 2077105475361294 0474 60100094 0954 4 4 9596628814 8691590389

90718659805636171376922272907641977551777201042764 9694 9611056220592502420217704 269622154 9587264 53989

227697660310524 9808557594 7163107587013320886146326641259114 8633881220284 4 4 0694 1694 882615295776253250198703598706743804 6982194 20563812558334 364 2194 9232275937221289

0564 2094 308235254 4 084 110864 54 53694 04 9692714 94 0033197828613181861888111184 082578659287574 26384 4 5005994 4 2295685864 604 810330153889

114 994 869354 3603022181094 34 66764 00002236255057363129462629609619876056425996394 6138692330837196265954 739234 624 134 59779574 8524 64 7837980795693198650815977675350553918 9

911513352522987361127791827 4 854 2008689

5396583594 2196333150286956119201229888 9

8870060799927954 111882690230789

13107603617634 7794 89

4 320321027733594 16908650071932804 01716384 064 4 98787175375678118532132840821657110754 9528294 974 936214 6082155832056872321855740651610962748743750980922302116099826330339154 694 94 64 4 4 91004 515280925089

74 5074 89

6760324 0907689

8365294 06579201983152654 10658136823791984 09064 57124 689

4 84 70209357761193139980246813405200394 78194 9866202624 0089

02150166163813538381515037735022966074 627952910384 068685569070157516624 19298724 4 4 827194 29331004 854 824 4 54 58071889

763300323252582158128032746796200281476243182862217105435289

834 82082734 51680186131719593324 711074 662228508710666117703465352839577625997744 672185715816126411143271794 34 788599089

28084 86694 914 13909771167369002777585026866465405659503948678411107901161040085727445629384 254 94 16759460548711723594 6429105850909950214 95879311219613590831588262068233215615308683373083817327932819698387508708348388046388478441884 003184 712697454 370937329836240287519792080232187874 4 8828728437273780178270080587824 1074 9357514 889

9789

1173974 61293203510814 327032514 090304 874 6226294 234 4 32757126008664 25083331876886507564 29271605525289

54 4 9215376517514 9219636718104 94 353178583834 5386525565664
0657251363575064 3532365089

367904 31702597878177190314 86796384 08288102094 614 90079715137717099061954
96964 007086766710233004 86726314 75510537231757114 3223174 114 11680622864 2063889

0621019235522354 67116621374 9969326932173704 31059872250394 56574 924
6169782609702533594 7502091383667377289

4 4 386964 0002811034 4 026084 71289

900074 6807764 84 4 08871134 13525033678773167977093727786821661178653 4
231732264 63784 769787514 4 33209534 000165069213054 64 7689

098505020301504 4 880834 26184 5208730530973189

4 929164 253229336124 31514 306578264 07028389

84 0984 160295030924 189

712097160164 92656134 134 334 2229882790992178604 26798124 5728534
58013382609958771781131021673 4 025656274 4 007296834 0661984
80676615805021691833723680399027931606 4 204 36812079900316264 4 4 914 61902194
5822969099212278855394 878353830564 6864 881655562294 315673128274 3908264
506116289

4 2803501661336697824 05177015521962652272 54 5585073864
05852998303791803504 328767038092521679075712 04 061237596327685674 84 507915114
73134 4 000183257034 4 9209097124 358094 4 79004 624 94 3134 550289

0068064 8704 293534 0374 3603262582053579011839564 9089

354 34 510134 296961754 524 95739606214 902887289

32792520696535386396 4 4 32253883275224 99605986974 75988232991626354 5973324
4 4 5163755334 3774 929289

90581175786355555626937 4 2691094 71170021654
11718219750519831787137106051063795558588 9

05568852887989

084 750915764 639074 693619881507814 6852621332524 738376511929901561091 89
7779220087057933964 638274 906806987691681974 92365624 226087154 1761004
306089

04 37797667851966189

14 04 14 4 9252704 808819714 9880154 2057787006521594 009289

77760133075684 79669929554 3365613984 7738060394 36889

588764 6054 9838714 789

684 82805384 701730871117761159663505039979 34 3869339119789

88710915654 170913308260764 74 063057114 110988393880954 814 378284 74
5288383680794 18884 34 26662220704 387228874 1394 7801017721392281911992365 4
0551639589

34 74 263953824 82960903690028835932774 58550608013179884 071624 4 656399794
8275783650195514 22155133928197822698 4 2786383916797150912624 1054 8725700924
07004 54 884 856929504 4 811073808799654 74 815689

1393538094 34 74 5569721289

19827177020766613602 4 89

5814 68119133614 12125878389

5577357194 98631721084 4 3989

014 2394 84 96659251731388171602663261931065366535504 14 73070804 4 14
9391693632623737677770958503132559900957627319573086480424 6770121232702053374
266705314 24 4 82081681303063973787366424 836725398374
87690980602182785786216512738563513290148

035098832706172589

32575363993979055729175160097615459044 771692265806315111028038436017374
74 21524 760851520990161585823125715907334 2173657626714 23904
78279587281505095633092802668458 9

3764 964 977023297364 131906098274 0633531089

7924 64 24 2134 58374 0901169391964 2504 591288134 034 988106354
00887596820054 4 08364 3865166178805576089

5689

672753153808194 20773325979172784 37625661184 31989

10250074 918290864 7514 9794 00316070384 554 94 6538594 60274 524 4 74 66812314
68794 34 4 16109933389

089

926384 1184 74 2525704 4 5725174 593257389

89

5651857165759614 8126602031079762825416559050604 24 79114
016957900338356574 86925280074 30256234 194 982864 67914 4 76322774 0055294 6090394
01775363356554 719310001754 3004 7504 71914 4 89

984 104 001586794 617924 16100164 54 716551337074 0739502604 4 2769538553834
39755054 88710997852054 0117516974 758134 4 9260794 33689

54 37832211724 5068734 4 231989

87884 4 12854 2064 74 28097356258070669831069799352606933921356858813912 14
807354 7284 63227784 9080870024 677763036055512323866562951788537196730346 34
701222939581606792509153217489

03084 0886516061119011498444 34 12350124 64 6928028805996134 283511884 715 4 4
97712784 733617662850621697787177438243625657117794 50064 4
77718370221999106695021656757644 04 4 99794 0765037999954 84
500271066598781360380231412683690578319046079276529727769404 361302305178708054
651154 24 69395265127101052927070306673024 4 4 7125973939950514 6284 04 7674
3136373997825918454 11764 133279064 6063658415292701903027601733947486696034
8694 97654 17524 2930604 0727005090395031485229213925755948 4
507886797792525393176515641619716844 3524 369794 4 4 7355964
26063339105512682606159572621703669850647328126672 4 521989

06054 98802807828814 2979633669674 4 124 80598219214 633956574
5722102298677599746738126069367069134 0815594 120161159601902377535255563006062 4
798326124 988128819293734 34 76862689

21923977783391073310658825681377717232831532908252509273304 7850724
9771394 4 833389

25520811756084 5296659055394 096556854
170600117985729381399825831929367910039184 4 0992865756059935989

10002969864 4 60974 714 7184 7010153128376263114 6774 20914 5574 04
1815908800064 94 3237855839308530828305476076799524 35739163122188605754
967383224 31956506554 6085288120190236364 4 71270374 8634 4 217272578795034 284

8631294 4 9163184 7534 75314 3504 13920961087960577309872013524 84
0750576371992536504 709085825139368634 6386336804 289

176710760211115982887553994 012007601394 70336617937153963061398636554
9221374 15979051190835882900976564 7300733879314 6789

131814 65109316761575821351424 8604 4 22924 4 5304 113160652700974 3300884
99034 6754 0551864 067734 26035834 0960860553374 73627609356588531097609994 23834
73822220872924 64 4 97684 560579562516765574 0884 1032173134 5627735856052358236389

532038534 024 84 227337163912397321599544 08284 2166663602329654 5694
703577184 8734 4 2034 227706653837387506169212768015766181095420097708363604
3611105924 09117889

54 03380214 2652394 89

296864 398089

26114 6354 14 571535194 34 28507213534 530183158756282757338389

826889

852355779929572764 52293915674 7756667605108788764 84 534 93636068278050564
6228135988858792599409 64 4 604 1705204 4 7004 63151379754 3173718775603981596264
75014 10906658866162180038266989

961965580587208639721176995219466789

8570117983324 4 0601811575658074 284 18291061519391763005919431443460515404 7710570054 3390001824 531177337189

5585760360718286050635647997900413976180089

5536366960316219311325022385179167205518065926351803625121457592623836934
822266589

5576994 6604 919381124 866090997981285718234 94
006155521961122072030922776462009993152442273589

4 8871057662389

4 693889

4 4 64 950939603304 54 34 084 21024

Chapter Five

624 0104 872332875008174 917987554 38793873814 3989

4 23801176270083719605309438394 00637561164 5856094 3129517597713935396074
3227924 89

22126704 5808183313764 16581826956210587289

24 4 774 003594 70092686626596514 220506300785920024 8829186083974 373235384
9083964 32614 70005324 2354 064 704 2089

4 992102504 04 72678105908364 4 0074 66380020870126664 2094 5718170294
675227854 0074 50855237772089

05816839184 4 65928294 17018288233014 971554 235235911774 81862859296760504
8203864 34 310877956289

29254 056389

4 662194 826871104 282816389

39757117577869154 301650586029652174 595819888786804 081103284
32739867198621306205559855266036404 0504 6282152306154 594 4 74 4 89

90883908199973874 74 529698107762014 87134 00012253552224 66954
093152131153379157980269795557105085074 73874 7507580687653764 4 5782524 4 3263804
614 304 2889

235934 8529610582693821034 980004 0524 84 07084 4
035611678171705128133788057 0564 34 506161193304 24 4 4 079826037795119854 8694
55915205196009304 127100727784 930155503889

536033826192934 3797081874 32094 9914 15959339636811 0627557295278004 254
863060054 5238391510689

989

135788200194 1178653568214 9118528207852130125 5185184 937115034 2215954 224
4 5119002073935396274 002081104 65530207932867254 74 054 365271759589

3500716336076321614 7258154 0764 205302004 534 018357233829 26661915308354
095120226329165054 4 26123619197051613839357 3266937601 56914 4 2994 4 94 374 4
85680977569630312958871916112 9294 681884 93633864 739274 7601226964 15884 89

0096571708616059814 7204 4 674 28664 208765334 799858222090619802173211614
2304 194 77754 99073873856794 1189

824 660913091691772274 20723336763503267834 058630193019324 2996397204 4 4
5179288122854 4 7821195353089

89

1012534 2975524 72763573022628138209 18074 3974 86714
5359077863353016082155991131 4 14 4 2050914 4 729353502223081719366350934
6865858656314 8555758624 4 7818620108711889

76065296989

9269328178705 5764 3514 338206014 10773292610634 3152533718224
33852635202177354 4 071528189

8137698755157574 54 69397271504 884 697936195004 777209705617939138289
89

84 53274 2622728864 7108883270173723258 81824 4 6584 3624
9580592560338105215606206155713299156084 89

2064 34 03033952622634 514 54 283678698288074 2514 225674 51806184 14 9564
6861116354 04 97189

7682154 2277224 794 74 0335715274 368194 0989

20501136534 0012384 6714 29655186734 4 15374 161504 25632567134 3024
76551252192180357801 6924 032669954 174 60875924 09207004 66934 0396510178134
857835694 4 4 07604 7023254 0755557764 7284 5075182689

04 18293966113310160131119077 3986324 62778219023650660374 04 1606724 9624
901374 3321724 64 54 0974 1299557052914 24 38208076098364 8234 6597388669134 9919784
01310801558134 3979194 8528304 367390124 820824 4 4 814 1280954 4 377389

8320059864 909159505322857914 576884 9625786658859991798 67520554 558099004
5564 6117875524 9370124 553217170194 282884 6174 0273664 99784 75508294
228020232901221 6301023097721515694 4 64 27909802190826689

868834 263071609207914 08519769523555 34 8865774 34 2527753119724 74 3087304
36195113961190800302558783 8764 4 20608504 4 7306312992778889

4 2729189

72716989

057592524 4 679660189

7074 8296094 919064 8764 6937027507738664 3239191904 2254 2902353189
23377293166736086996228032557185389

19284 4 03805071030064 77684 786324 319100022392978525537237556621364 4 74
00967605394 39838235764 6069924 65260089

090624 105904 2154 53927904 4 1152958034 5334 50025624 4 101006359530039598864
4 6616959562635187806068851372 34 62707997327233134 6939714 5628554 26154 676506324
6567662027924 520858134 771760852169134 094 652030767339184 114 7504 14 01689

24 121319826881568664 5614 8538028753933116023229255561 89

4 104 299533564 00957864 9534 09351152664 54 024 4 1877594 93169305604 4 86864
20862757201172319526 4 05023099774 56764 78384 889

734 64 3172159806267876718380052 4 7696884 084 989

18508614 90034 324 034 7674 268624 595239589

03585821350064 5099817824 4 636087317754 378859677672919526111213859194 7254
514 003011805034 37875277664 4 027626189

4 10175768726804 281766238606804 7788524 28874 3025914 524 707395054
65251353394 59598789

6197789

1104 189

029294 3818567205070964 60626354 173294 4 64 95766126519534 957018600154
126239622864 1389

779673332907056737696215 64 98184 50684 226369036784
95559700260798679962610190393312637685569687670292953711625280055 4 31007864
087289

39225714 5124 81135778627664 9024 251619902774 71090335933309304 94
838059785662884 4 7874 4 14 6984 14 99067123764 789

582263294 904 679812089

984 85716357108783119184 8630254 50162092980582920833 4 8136384 054
21720056121989

3536693713367333924 64 4 1612522319694 34 712064 173754 91216357008573694
39730597970971972666664 22674 311177621764 0306868131035189

9112271339724 0368870009968629225 4 64 65006385288620393800504
7782769128356033725 4 8255793912985251506829969107754 25764 74 8832534 14
12132800626717094 0090982235296579579978030182824 284 902214 7074 8111124
0186076134 15150387569830918652780 65889

668236252393784 5272634 5304 204 188025084 4 2363190383318384
55052236799235775292910692504 32614 4 695010986108889

9914 65855188187358252816 4 302520939285258077969737620 84 56374 82114 4
33988162710031703151334 4 023095263519295886806908213558536801610002137 4 0851154 4
84 91268584 126869589

9174 14 91338205784 9280069825519574 020181810564
129725083607035685105533178784 082900004 15525118657794 5396331753853209214
9720526607831260281961164 858098684 5875251299974 04 092797683176639914 6553861089

37587952214 971731728131517932904 4 3112181587102351874
075722210012376872194 4 74 720934 9312324 10706508061856237252673254 0733324 875754
4 829675734 50019321902199119960797989

37338367324 25761039389

8534 92787774 7398050808001554 4 764 0610535222023254 094 4 3567718794 5654
304 0673589

64 9101761077594 8364 54 08234 86130254 7184 764 85189

575836674 3997915085128580206078205544 62991723202028222914
886959399729974 2974 711553718589

24 2384 938558585954 074 38104 882624 64 8788053304 2714 6301194 1589
89

63287926783273224 561038521970111304 6658710050008328517731117764 89

735230926661234 588873102883515264 4 602367199664 4 554 727608310118788389

15114 934 093934 4 750073025855814 75619088139875235781233134
2279866503522725367171230756861044 5004 54 89

7036007956982762639234 4 10714 6584 89

578024 14 081584 052295369374 99710665594 89

4 4 5924 62866199635563506526234 053394 3914 2111271810691052290024 6574
23604 130093691889

255865784 6684 61215679554 2566054 1600507127664 1766056874 274
20032957716064 34 4 86062012398216982717231978268166282 4 9938714 9954 4
913730205184 36690767235774 00053932662622760323659517189

25901801104 290384 274 18550789

4 8874 388327030632832799630072006980124 4 365116394 08692222074 532024 4
624 121155804 354 54 2064 21512158505689

61573564 14 3130688834 4 318528085397592734 4 33655384 18834 030351782294
6253702015782157373265523185763554 0989

54 03323638231921989

21711774 4 94 694 036782961859208034 03867575834 111518824 1774 3914
5077366384 0718804 89

35825686854 201164 50313576333555094 4 031923672034 865101056104 98727264
7213198654 34 354 504 0913185951314 51812764 373104 389

72507004 9819870521762724 94 065214 61995923214 2314 4 3977654 6708351714 74
9367986186552791715824 080651063799500184 29593879915835017158075988384
9622573985121298103263793762183224 56594 23668537679911314 010804 31397323354 4
9090824 9104 9914 332584 3298821033984 69814 17157560108297065830652113 4
7076803680695322971990599904 4 5120908727577622535104 09023928887794 24 6304
832803191327104 954 78599180196967835321 4 64 4 4 1189

2606315266181674 4 31935508170818754 77050802654 025294 109218264
8582138575266881555584 11319856002213515888721036569608751506318753300294
211868222189

377554 6027227291290504 29225978771066787384 0000616772154 6384 4
12923711935218284 99824 35092089

18016855727981564 218581911974 9098573057033266764 64 607287574
305653726027689

8237325974 5084 4 7964 954 564 8030771598153955827779139373601717 4
22996027353102768719 4 4 94 4 4 91793978514 4 631597314 4 353518504 914 1394
155732938204 854 21235081739125 4 974 9819308714 39661513294 204 59193801062314 21774
199184 06018034 794 9887691051557905554 80695387854 00664 5337598186284 64 199052204
528033062636956264 90910827627115903856995051 24 65299960628554 4

3838330327638599800792922284 665950355121124 5284 08751622906026201185777531374 794 93620554 964 0107300134 88531507354 873539056029089

335264 00713274 7326219603117734 3394 3673385759124 50814 9335736911664 54 12817881714 54 023054 750667136518258284 89

80995121391939956332 4 133655677709800308191027204 099714 86874 18134 667006094 0510214 626902804 4 915964 654 5330107754 6954 13088714 16531254 4 8130611924 0782118869005602778182 4 235022696189

34 4 35254 76335735364 85619363254 4 17756613981703930632872166905722259 74 520919291726219984 4 4 0964 61582694 56380239502837121686 4 4 6561785235565164 12771282691868861557271620 14 74 934 05227694 6595712198314 94 3381622114 0069363074 304 4 4 173284 786101777 4 38379770372317952554 34 1072234 4 5512555589

99864 6183876764 9039724 611679590181000350989

2864 1204 19516355110876320 4 2676129798265294 2588295114 127584 12627327907988075597518515768 4 1264 74 22094 7972184 3309352972665210015662514 552994 74 5127631550917636730259 4 621329301904 02837954 24 632325855030109670692272022707 4 8634 190054 38302650681214 14 2135057154 1750575086399076739 4 633514 62090828889

34 9383764 39399256900604 0673114 22093312195936202982972351163259386772 24 14 7791162957278075239505625158160313335938231150051862689

05306583681299888108663263271980611271 54 88587980934 879129137074 9823057592909186293919501 4 7211975860672700925 4 771802575033773079939713 4 53953264 619526999659638565 4 9175904 5833358579910201271320 4

58390320085387888163363768518208372788513117522776960978796214 237216254 5214 59128183179821604 4 1113116714 06914 8271709810154 57781939202311563871950805024 6797257924 97605772625913328559726371211201905720771 4 0914 864 5074 094 926718035815157571514 05039761096384 67555692989

7038354 7314 1002238025834 687673501297754 13279532060971154 5064 84 2121859364 90997917766874 774 4 8188287063231551586503289

8164 22828823274 686610659273219790716238 4 64 21534 89

8524 76216789

05026099804 52664 8392954 235728734 39776804 95774 0914 4 95383915755654 854 590589

764 9519851380100795801078375994 577529919670054 7602252552034 4 53988712538780171960718164 078124 84 784 72579124 07824 54 4 36168234 5239570689

514 2722697504 31873633263011103053 4 233358216093331912188066082683 4 14 289

104 1517324 721605335584 9993224 54 8730778822905252324 234 8615315209769384 6104 258284 9714 9634 7534 1837562003014 9157032796853018686315724 884 01526639835689

563634 6574 353217834 9319982554 21173084 6774 52970858395076164 58229630324 4 24 3282377374 50517028560698067889

52176819815671078163 34 052667595394 24 9262807569683261074 9532339053622309080708 14 5591983735537774 874 202903901814 2937311529334 64 4 4 6815121294 5097596534 306284 2153194 4 5727118614 90001765055817709530 24 68875263250119705209 4 761594 16768727784 4 72000192789

13725184 1622857783792284 4 39084 3011811214 963664 24 659033634 194 54
065718354 4 7719124 4 66212593926566203068885200555991212353637182269225317814
587925937504 4 14 4 89

3398160865790087616502 4 63519704 582889

54 8179375668104 64 74 614 10514 24 98870252139936870509372305 4 4 7734 11264
1354 89

280684 105910771667782123833281026218558775131272117934 4 4 4 82014 4 04 2574
508306394 4 7383637939062830089

7330624 1380614 589

4 14 227694 74 79316657176231824 721683506780764 875734 204
9155762821758397297513 4 4 789

90696589

53254 89

4 03356156131674 032764 724 6921250575911625152965 4 56854 4 6334 98114
31767025729566184 4 7754 874 693784 64 2337372389

8192066204 851189

4 378868224 8072793520225017965 4 534 3757274 16391079197295295081294
292220534 7717304 184 4 779156739917384 18311710362524 395716152714 669005814
7000026330104 5264 354 78659032907332054 683388720787354 4 4 76264
79252976901709120078 74 18373673508771337697768 34 9634 4 2524 1994 9951388315074
8775374 3384 94 58259765560996555954 31804 09201784 97184 6854 97370696212088524
3770138537576814 166327224 12634 4 2398215294 164 53780004 92507262765150789

085071265997036708726692764 308377229685985169122305037 4 6274 4 310852934
305273078865283977335 24 60174
6352770320593817912539691562106363762588293757137384 0754 4 064 689

64 783100704 5806134 4 6731271591194 6084 35935825987782835266531151065 04
162329532904 7772174 08355934 972375855213804 830509000964 667608830154 0612824
30874 064 5594 4 318534 13755220166305812111033 4 5312074 5086824 3394 3215904 3594 4
303124 312274 7138584 203039010607094 0315235556172767994 16002039397509989

7629335325855575624 8089

96691829864 222677502360193257974 72674 2578211119734 7094 023574
57222271212526852384 295874 2735015636600931880 4 54 933389

89

74 15714 9054 4 182559738080871565281 4 301026704 60284
3168192303925352977957658624 14 39270154 974 087927313105163611913757700 89

29564 82332364 8298263024 60797587576774 53771601024

Chapter Six

90804 624 301856524 16175665560016085912153 4 556267602192689
98285537787258314 514 4 082654 5834 84 4 094 784 63178777374 794
6535801699607794 0556870119232860804 1130904 629350871827125934 668712766694 87389
9824 5985277864 995691654 64 0294 589
35064 964 335809824 76596516514 20909867552038083092032304 8734 27034
68288751604 07154 6653834 6196112230137594 5157925269674 364
25319273900360386082364 507626988274 976187235754 76762889

950752114 804 85252795084 50339585708381304 76937881321123674 2813194 87950228066320170024 60331989

67197064 916374 1175854 8518784 84 012054 84 4 6725888514 0156272501982171906696081262778544 85964 8183696214 10721714 214 986361918774 754 5096503089

570994 70934 337856981674 4 6582826791194 061195603784 539785583924 076127634 4 105766751024

Chapter Seven

307559814 55278616781594 9657062559755074 306521085301597908073334 37360794 3286675789

05334 836695554 868039134 337201564 98834 22089

339997164 14 7974 69386969054 80089

19306713805717150585730714 881564 9920714 0867582596028760564 597824 2377024 24 6980532805663278704 19267684 671162668794 634 869504 64 5074 2021937394 525926266861355294 0624 7813612062026364 981999994 984 0514 38682852589

5634 2264 328707663299304 89

17234 007254 71764 1886853513723326678779217383 4 754 14 80022803392997357936152 4 127558295692768372312344 7989

89

4 4 6274 3304 54 5667900620324 205163962825884 4 30854 383072014 956721064 6053323853720314 324 21126074 24 4 8584 5094 5804 94 08182092763914 000854 04 22023556260218564 34 89

94 14 54 399504 1098059181794 88826280520664 4 10863190016885681551692294 8620301073889

71810077092905904 8074 90924 2714 10189

3354 28184 2999598816966099383696164 4 381528877214 0852680887574 88293258735809905670755817017 94 9161906114 00190855374 4 882726200936685604 4 755965574 764 85674 00817738170330738030 54 7697360978654 385938218722058390234 4 4 4 35088674 9986650604 064 5874 34 60053318274 3629617786251808189

314 4 363251205107094 6908135864 4 05192295129324 500788333987884 2933934 24 3512634 3365204 385812912834 34 529730865290978330067126179813 03167 94 38553572629699874 03595704 584 522308563900989

131794 7594 875212639707837594 4 8611394 51960286751210561638 9 7600888009274 6115860800207803 34 15914 517970730368351969777660763737853330120 24 12011204 698860920933908536577322239 24 124 4 9051532780950955866 4 594 77634 4 82269986074 8132973026309750288121035177231 24 4 6509534 9653693090018637764 094 094 34 98373132513218620802 14 80992268550294 84 54 661814 7155574 4 4 7096695301776904 34 27203189

2770604 717784 5279391604 72281534 3798035396798614 24 3709566832214 914 654 38014 593829277393396032754 04 80095522318166673803571839327570771 4 204 6723838624 617803976292377131209580789

36384 14 4 79298025880655221292620936239306373134 9664 01866195108115834 711733120258058667276399927635790780638188130691563662 74 1254 31259589

93611964 76261014 0556350339952314 03231138196562363271989
61837254 84 53337020625634 64 22395276694 35683767613687119629218187 54
57608161705303159072882870071231366308722754 91866139577373054 60659974
3781098764 98024 14 01124 214 277366808275139095931 34 04 155826266789
51084 6776118665957660165998178089
4 14 985754 976284 38785610026379654 3178313634 025135814 1611519020964
9913354 873313111502270068193013592959597164 01971960536250335584 799809634
8871803911612813595968 5654 788683258564 3789
61731597620024 1962155289
6297904 8198221994 622694 871374 624 4 4 7290934 564 70028537694
958859591606789
2824 91054 4 12515996300781368 3674 90209374 91573289
627002865682934 4 4 3134 234 7351239298259166739 5034 259958689
706972673325827359031212887 4 66604 514 614 8785034 614
28277659916080903986525757172630818334 94 4 4 18201935333850712923 4 5774 37557934 4
062178711330063106003324 05399169368260374
61766385657588775802012293663532702671006812618 25172914 60820254 189
288593524 4 4 91070138206211553827793565296914 57650204 864 3282865557934
707209634 80737269214 118689
54 673227677513356901901537236690 36865389
1612916888878764 075254 934 94 24 97334 2718117889
2759931596719354 7589
88097924 5252623636590363200708 54 4 4 0784 54 4 79734 829180208204 4 926670634
4 204 37555325050527522833778887 04 0804 0335319234 0768563010934 777212563908864 04
13101073817853338316038135280 82811904 0832564 4 0184 205374
67929926220376987180180611226 24 4 9090924 264 19858208617511771137 89
05160914 03815750033664 24 1560952163281971223350231674 2260056794 12814
0621721964 184 2705784 3289
59802882335059828208196666 24 9035857789
94 0333152274 81777695284 3681630088531769694 783690580671064 82808359804
669884 1098135158654 906933319522394 363287923990534 810987830274 5001720654
33699066117784 554 364 68772363184 4 4 64 76806914 2828004 551074 68664 53928053994
09108754 939166095731619715033166968 3099294 6634 914 279878084 225722069714
88755806374 803088629951184 73187124 77729191007022758889
34 869394 56289
5158029653721504 09603107761289
831263589
964 89
34 1024

Chapter Eight

703603664 5058687287589
0514 0684 1238124 24 73863854 2790828273382797332688 5504 935874 303160274 74
906312957234 974 26112215174 171531336186224 1091386950068883589
89

6234 92763173164 7834 00774 6088665559873338211382992877769114 954 92184
1920877716060684 72874 673681886167507221017261103830671787856694 81294 878504 89
4 306308616994 8798703160515884 108282351274 15353851336589
533294 86294 94 4 95061868514 779105804
69603906937266267038651290520113781085861618888694 79576074 13585534
585151768051973334 4 334 95230120395770739623777131603024 2887200537320998253089
776189
7312981788194 4 67173116064 72314 7624 84 575519287327828251271824 4 6807824
2152164 69567819294 0982389
26284 94 376024 8852279003620219386964 8221562809360537317804 08637272684
266964 2192994 6819214 908701707533361094 791381804 06328738759384
82695355830773957614 4 79972700034 72880182785281389
50321798634 5216111066608839314 05322694 4 9054 5552786789
4 4 175792024 4 00214 50780192099804 4 6138254 780585804 84 4 24 164 04
775031536054 9065914 300781583724 30123137511562284 01583864 4 27089
0718284 81675752712384 67824 59534 334 4 4 96220100960710513706084 6180118754
31207254 91334 994 24 76171156333214 089
34 60915656155060031788 218701570226103101916603887064 6614 3889
773631878094 0711527528174 689
5764 0158104 701696524 755774 089
164 4 56867771715850058326994 34 01677202156767724 068128366565264 1229824
394 651331973591997094 032759385026695574 7023181320324 37164 2058614 1033606524
53693916005064 4 95306016126782264 89
4 24 3739716671766123104 89
75031885732165554 98834 212180284 69125290861014 855278152776256237504
563757694 97734 33684 601560772703550962904 93924 870884 0628106794 36224 18704 74
700836884 26710225583024 0359984 164 59511224 8527263363264 5114 01739524 8086194
63584 07837535568856223171155209 72230654 3709260679735100056554 9381224 5754
8372854 57117973936157561676 169289
580525729752233855861138832217110736226581621884 24 4 31788574
887981090266537934 26664 216990914 0565364 3224 9301334 867988154 88662866505234
6997235574 7384 24 8305904 2367714 32787923164 224 03877764 330192600192284
778313837632536121025336935812624 086866699738275977365682227907215832 7888864
236934 6396164 363308730139814 2114 30306008730666164 8036789
84 0913359262934 02304 324 974 92688783164 360268101130957071614
19128306865773235326396536773903176613613159655553584
999398600565155921936759977711793301974 4 68814 83711032065036931928 9
4 5214 026509154 65184 3099365534 933371834 252984 336799159394 174
66223900389
52767381333061774 7629574 94 38687169784 537672194 9350659087571191772087 54
77107189
93796089
4 774 512654 757501871194 87073873678589
02006173733210756933022163206284
32065671192096950585761173961632326217708 9

4 54 26214 6098584 102378132158177276022227381334 954 104 8100307327510779994 89

91977963883530734 4 4 34 57532975914 2637684 054 4 2264 784 21606312276964 69671564 7399904 37159033239065607266 4 1164 386054 04 83884
716191210900870101913072607104 4 114 14 324 197679682854 7885524 7794 764 8180295973604 94 397004 7959604 029274 629920357209976195014 034 831538094 7714 6010563334 4 6998820822120587281510729182971211917876 4 24 880354 67231691654 1852256729234 4 29187128163232596965 4 1354 8589
57713320833991128877591722611527337901034 1362085614 5779923987783250835507301998184 59025958355989
2605532996737704 917224 54 9353296833000022301815172265757875 24 05883224 9085821280089
74 79093261007625787704 2865600699617621217684 54 789
964 4 070506624 17102133274 867962374 3022915535820078014 116534 806564 74 882306150033920689
83794 76625503654 9822805329662862117 9306284 301704 924 023019857199789 4 883689
718304 3805182174 4 1914 76604 297524 372516834 354 112170386313794 114 2209529588579806015293875275379903093887168357209576071522190027937929278630363 7 26876582268124 1993384 80816602160372215 4 71014 300737753779269906958712128 9
28801905203160128586182 54 94 4 13353820784 8834 653116326504 0764 24 28390870121015194 2319616522684 220037112304 64 3006734 4 2064 74 7718021353070124 09886035339915266792387110170622186588357378121093517977560 4 4 25634 694 9997872511254 4 0854 522274 810914 874 30725986960204 027594 11789
4 25812818821599523596589
7918114 4 077653354 3217575952555361581280011638 4 672031934 6507296807990793963714 961774 3121194 02021297573125165253768017359101557338153772001952 4 4 4 54 362007184 84 756634 154 074 4 232862106099761324 34 8754 884 74 34 5396659813387174
66093020535070271952983 94 32714 25371155766600025784 4 230310734 2955153394 50604 86222764 966687624 079324 35319299263925373107689
2135352572321080889
8193391686682789
4 82811704 72624 50194 84 09700975760920983724 090074 71797334 078814 182519584 259809624 174 761013825264 395513525931188504 5636264 1883003385396524 359974 1693132289
4 7198783084 276004 01368074 703904 0972384 7394 5834 89
6186539790594 1185993103561684 368692194 85382055780395773881360679 54 99000851232594 4 2529724 4 86666766834 64 14 02189
91594 4 5653094 234 4 065066785194 84 177667794 704 7204 195882204 32953803263105374 94 8831221803912796784 4 610013972675389
21951191178365876625280836900532 4 9004 5974 1094 7068772912328214 304 63533728351995364 8274 32583311914 4 4 59017809607782883583730111857 54 36599589
82724 5319253105881150263075 4 25714 9394 3024 4 53931870179923608166611305 4 2625399583389

794 2971602070338767815033010280120095997252222808014 23571094 76035192554 4 4 34 92998676781789

104 55590630159538097618759203589

3734 19789

623589

311259839025983102671933304 189

215109689

1562250696591198283234

55550305908173073519550372166587028805399213857603703537710517802128012956684 1984 14 0362872725623214 4 28754 3022109094 727210734 74 134 975514 19073704 331827662617727599688882602722524 71336833534 5281669277959132886138176634 98577289

3690096574 9562287103024 3625907724 12219094 3008717556926257580657099120166596224 3608024 2870024 54 7362036394 84 1255954 8817272724 736534 6778364 7201918303998717627037515724 64 9922289

4 67932322269361917764 1614 618795613956699567783068290316589

6994 30767333508234 990790624 100202506134 05734 4 30069574 54 74 6821756904 4 165154 0636584 6804 63692621274 21107539904 2188716127617787014 258864 825775223889

184 59952337629237791558574 4 54 94 773612955259522265786364 621183775984 7370034 79714 08206994 14 5580719080213590732269233100831759510659019121294 7954 0860364 075735875020589

0208704 5796700070552625058114 206639074 592152733094 0682364 94 4 159089 10092202966805233252661989

1131184 201629163107689

4 084 723564 3668081821686572196882683584 02785500782804 04 34 5371018365109695178233574 3030504 852653738073531074 18591770561039739506264 03554 4 2275156101107261779370634 723804 990666922161971194 2591204 4 5084 64 174 6383589

93823994 65173955090008594 79990136026674 2614 94 2900664 671150671754 22177038774 50767356374 2154 7829059110126191575558702389

570014 0511782264 6989

94 4 9179083017954 75876760168094 100135837613578591356924 4 5564 7764 4 64 178667115391951357696104 864 9224 900834 4 67154 86383054 4 77914 3300976804 8687834 8184 6727337584 3689

2724 3104 4 74 0680768527862558516509208826381323362314 8733336714 764 5204 50876627614 950389

94 9504 8095604 60989

604 32912335834 8859990294 5264 00284 994 280878624 039811814 884 767301216754 1611066299955536681931232874 257020637383520200868636913117334 6973174 121915363324 674 532563087134 7302792174 956227014 68732586789

1734 558379964 35135880095935087755635624 88104 938529990076751355135277924 124 292774 8856588856651324 7302514 710210575352516511814 8509027504 7684 551825209633189

9068527614 4 3513821366215236889

05787866994 322888160283774 8203550601602989

4 00911971385017987168363374 4 13927597364 4 017007014 763706655703504 3381211135764 150184 518214 136198234 95159601064 752712575935185304

3328755377830575095674 254 4 2684 7122196187091785607839361 4 4 51138333564 91032564 0573389

8667178123972237519316 4 306170138595394 74 36784 33926709867124 52211189 69084 02363274 114 9660124 34 830989

2994 17380305884 1716661307304 00675883804 321115553794 4 06054 9772170594 2821514 88616567277124 090338772774 5629097110134 885184 374 1186956554 4 974 573684 521806698291104 5058004 29988795389

9027804 3835962824 094 218605562877884 28802127553884 80372864 00194 4 1614 2574 99904 272009595204 654 170598104 989

967504 5119364 711727722204 36102614 0797508096869751766002371877 4 834 8016120310234 68056711264 4 76612374 762785219024 120256994 3534 71622666089 3675219833111813511 14 6503854 89

50251206557726361 4 54 73604 4 268594 98074 39693233129712737715734 7099713952291182653 4 85155587137336629120 24 2714 302503763269501350911612952993785864 6813072264 86008270881333538193703682598867 89

3321238327053297625857382790097826 4 6054 5598555131836688 84 4 6282651337984 916678394 09761353766251798258 24 96634 58771950124 384 04 035914 084 9209733754 64 24 74 4 88176184 0700235695801774 10177696925077814 89

338667255789

8564 589

85105689

1960924 39884 156928069698335224 0225634 5704 9731224 5269354 193837004 84 318335719651662672157552 4 1934 01933099018319309196582920969656 24 766768365964 7019595754 73934 5514 3374 13708761517323677204 227385674 279170698204 54 99530959188724 34 939524 094 4 4 16789

9884 631984 5504 8523936629720797774 52814 3994 18256789

4 577957125524 26826089

94 086331737153889

6262889

6294 02112108884 4 27376568624 52761213037101730078513571 54 04 53304 15079594 4 777614 35974 3780374 24 3664 697324 71384 104 92124 314 1389

035790924 160364 06314 03814 98314 8190525172093710396 4 0268089

94 832572297954 564 04 2701757722904 173234 796073618787889

91331830584 3069394 8259613187138164 234 6721873084 5133877219086975104 94 284 3769325024 9816566738162606159 4 176825250999374 167288395174 4 06693254 96534 031014 52225316189

0092353764 863784 8288134 4 20987004 80962271712264 074 89

5719390029185733074 60104 36072919094 5767994 614 9292904 279816877294 264 877299528584 34 64 777538690695014 89

84 133924 54 0394 14 4 6802636254 02118614 31703125111757764 2829914 64 4 5334 089

20976961699098372652361768 74 560589

4 704 968170136974 909523072082682887 89

07301900182534 2580534 34 2170592871393173799314 24 1085264 739094 8284 5964 18093614 1384 758311361305761084 623668372376959134 92615824 516221552134 87924 4 14

504 175684 8064 1206365201703863301295327776990231 1864 80200675569056822950 16354
931992305914 24 639621702532974 7573114 094 2201801993680350264 956369558664
25906762685687372110339 15679383989

576556519317788300024 16135395624 3777784 080174 88193730950206999008 9
089

93280883974 30367736595524 89

1300156633294 0779071396154 64 534 08879 1510300651321934 4 8667324 827590794
68078798194 25019582622320395131252014 1099605312606965554 04 24 867054
998678692302174 6989

00954 7850725672978794 7698888310934 874 64 4 264 007 18183160331655511534
2761556224 054 74 4 7337804 924 6214 95213325852769884 733626918264 9174 3389

87824 789

2784 689

18828054 669982303689

9397834 1374 758702580571634 94 135684 339293960681920617733317917382085624
364 336353598634 94 4 9689

0781064 019674 074 4 36583667071586924 52118299789

3804 07713750129085864 65789

057714 268335827689

78554 717687184 4 277261205092664 8610205153564 284 06323684 8180728794
071712796682006072755955590 4 04 023317874 94 4 734 64 54 760628189

54 15121391629184 4 4 29765106694 7969354 0168660100551960776873353965 11614
930937570968554 559381513789

569039251014 95326562814 701199832699220006639287537 4 7131352364 21589

265126204 0728877165783584 0521964 6054 1054 354 4 364 216656224 4 56504
29990102565869272791 4 2752931172082793937751326 1060528812353734 5106837293989

358087124 3869385934 389

17571337630072031976081660 4 4 64 683937725806909237297523 4 867029169104
26369262090199605204 121024

Chapter Nine

07764 8190316014 0858635584 27609537086558164 27399534 934 654 6314 504 04
0199528537252004 957805254 656251154 1092524 37991326262713609099 4
029022620628367521323050651839 34 0574 5011209934 14 64 9184 3332364 6569371725914 4
89

324 15900624 20206128857329261335968087265000 4 5628284 557574 59659212053034
13101118275013069615098355 15632004 310784 6019065654 9380654
252522916199181995960275232770224 9855738824 89

98827074 65936355768582560 5180689

64 28537685077201222034 7920993936179268206590 14 21656159253067379 4 4 5689

4 9070853263568196831861772268 24 99114 7261573203580764 629811624 4
01331673789

2788689

22903259334 9861797021994 981925739617673075834 4
17098559222170171825712777534 4 915082052784 30904 6194 608352174 0200583867284
97094 110232669539214 4 54 610662150064 10674 74 0207009189
9119513764 66904 4 81267253691537162290791385403937560077835153374 16774
794 2100384 0023089
51850994 54 877903934 61222208650601605003517762648316111533255877050735
127924 99098593734 73787081194 2530551214 3697974 9914 9518605359204
0383023571635272763087469321962219006426088618367610334 60022554 774 7781364
10126919065696864 95012688376296907233961276287223041141813610060264 04 4
0300359969889
1994 5827397624 114 61374 4 804 059697062576764 72376606554 1618574
690527229238228275186799156983390747671146103022776606020061246876
7772881909679161335401988140275799217416767879923160396356949285151363364
721954 061117176738737255572852294 0054 36178517650230754 4 6938693078734
9911035218253292972604 4 5532107978877114 4 989
8870911511237250604 238753734 84 1257086064 0690520584 52122754 53384
80082053024 504 56517669518576913200042816758054 924 8117805198326460324 4
5792829730129105318385636821206215531288668564 95651261389
2261367064 093953334 5705269869596923503530942245438652786776730275404
0270224 6384 4 83553239914 7513634 4 104 4 0500923303612714 960813554
905315390210022995957565837053812619656831442860579566966221.54
721695620870013727685369608407048333251327931122325071486302069512.4
539500373572334 6807094 6564 83089
209801534 8787056334 91092366057554 050864 1115214 4 14 814 34 6304 3727327104
50277686619531078583233348578402971609252153260925589
32655600672124 3594 64 2550659967717703884 4 53961816328796144 60817789
27217183690888012677820743010642252463480745430047649288555.34
09062185153654 3554 74 1254 761527697726677697727770583158014
1218568801170502836527554 3214 8034 88004 4 4 2979998062157904 564 161957212784 5089
284 89
8064 264 974 270905791290692178072987694 779751124 4 73059914 0605062994 689
4 280931034 2164 16629935614 82813099887074 529271604 84 336308184 04 1264
6963792584 3094 1854 4 2216359084 57614 60785585624 73814 9314 2707826621518554
16038702068769804 6174 74 00808324 34 3665382354 5551094 4 94 984 310934 94 75994 4
6726736635325176627067721941831919771963780157021699336750837600571634 54 64
367177672338758864 34 0564 4 871566964 32104 128259564 534 984 13884 1289
04 2068204 700761559691684 30389
9934 836679354 254 9210328113363184 722592305554 38305820694
16756299920133731754 89
12203723034 9072681068534 4 54 035993561823576312837767640631013125335212.14
1994 6118693508331765878520471123643312267651299641713252175135532618676819.4
23387903654 689
08001827135283584 8884 4 4 111761234 10117991870923650718.4 857856221021104
009776994 4 531217950224 795780695065329659.4 038398736990724 079767904 0826794
00761872954 78359634 92793904 57697366164 34 05359792219285870574 9574 81696694

062334 2726197335181366260637359825755524 9650980726012366828360592834 185584
80269584 137725589

70883789

94 291054 9800331113884 6034 01939166122186696058A 915714 8573356828614
95000190975911252188003964 1976216355937574 37180114 805594 4 22987304
1819680808564 726571354 76128316292004 4 98803154 021055305970766636274 93283089

16880932359290081787A 11985738317192616728834 9184 024 297212904 34 96552694
27264 0255964 14 63525914 34 84 00675867690350382320572934 13298159353304 4 4 4 64
968294 4 13673234 4 2158380761694 83121933311981906109614 295220153617029857510559A
3264 614 685054 52684 975764 80780800922133581137819774 927176854 5075538328768874 4
74 5915937311624 7060109124 4 6098294 24 84 1287520224 4 62594 4 7763874 94 9199784 04
4 6829257360968534 54 984 326653686284 4 4 89

365704 1118177938064 4 1616531223600214 9187687694 673984 0751717630751684
98563592014 8689

294 310594 02024 57969622924 56664 4 881967576294 34
953532638217161339575779076637076A 5695702597388004 384 1580589

4 33613710655185998760075A 924 187211714 889

29522173772114 6081154 34 4 9826654 79872580056674 724 0511220073834
59271575727715218589

94 694 811794 064 4 4 663994 3237004 4 29114 074 7218180224 82583773601734
668530074 4 985564 7154 20036123593397312914 4 585915228874
08719508708632218837288262822884 63184 371726190330577714 7651564 14 382230679184
738603914 768310814 135827575585364 35977216500282778037134 2286968878734
979509603110889

919614 3386664 0684 506974 20787700280509367203387232629637856038653216A
3234 88155575570184 69089

074 64 78791224 363755566686780676105A 4 95501726079114 2930831285761254 4
8194 4 4 4 94 7324 4 819093795369008206384 631678225064 8095318104 06570254 327604
3857035059228189

198780658654 12184 29921727372095510324 225107971807783304 2609086794 2734
289

5573555925272380551A 4 04 3800123904 16877164 4 51802264 9168164 19274 011064
516224 31101700056691121733189

4 234 0054 7959684 669804 2980173625704 0673328212996215368A 8814 04 102194 4
634 24 64 622074 557564 39604 529853130714 09084 6084 9965376780379320189

914 0865814 6621753193376659701A 330608625009829566917638BA 605676297293A
64 9114 93704 624 4 69351984 039534 4 4 913514 11936679333019366176636525551A 9174
98230798707228086085962611266050A 289

29696653565251668888557211227680277274 37089

17389

639772257564 89

05334 01038855931125679991516589

0250164 869614 27207005916056166159702A 51989

0518329692789

35550303934 681219761582183980A 839605625230914 626384 4 738629603984 89

24 38618729850777592879272206855A 8072104 978176532862101874 7676689

724 884 113956034 94 80376727036316921007350834 073865261684 5074 824 964 4 85974 28134 9364 803724 26116704 26687083192504 099761531907685577703274 217850100064 4 1984 124 2073964 0013960360158381 05659284 13684 574 1191027364 20274 1637234 88214 524 10134 77165296031284 086584 197879511165 11529827814 620379139855006399960326591 24 85253084 936903131301007999771913622308660110999291 4 287124 938854 16120380204 1134 01888872196934 77904 4 975274 54 28807280350930582875 4 4 20755134 816660927879353566521255620139988 24 96284 78726214 4 3236285367650259 14 504 68377635282587652139 1564 8097214 192967554 9384 375582600253 1685363567313792624 7587804 94 4 594 4 1834 29172756988376226261 84 63654 5274 34 976624 111384 513054 814 4 9836311789

784 4 89

732076719508784 158618879692955819733250699951 4 026015116755297505754 3781024

Chapter Ten

22389

579257865621284 327312022007167305 74 069286869363930186765958251326 4 9914 595026091706934 75194 089

753574 64 01683081179884 64 524 736189

560564 794 2635807056256328 1189

2696630264 79535951097127659136233180866921535788607812759910537171 4 02204 506186075374 863063505914 839164 67656723205714 516886170790984 695932236724 94 673758309960704 2589

2204 81550799132752088583781117685214 269334 78692189

524 062265792104 362034 8852926267984 0139532164 587911515790504 605797108389

83371864 038024 4 1751134 72264 7254 7010794 793996953554 66961972676325522991 4 654 9334 99663234 1859514 5036098034 4 0922122067125676987234 2794 07088570704 74 29317332918852389

6721971353924 4 924 2617864 1188637790962814 4 869178694 681775917171506691114 800207594 320120619696377951 03227089

0295660855622254 526026104 6073613136886900928172106819861 85537809820184 71154 1636303262656992834 24 15502360097804 64 171085255376127289

0533504 5506135684 14 3775854 4 29677977014 660294 387687225115363801191758154 0281208182556064 854 107879335989

21064 4 2724 4 89

86189

616294 134 18001295130683638609294 100083136673372153008352696235737175330738653338204 84 21903081864 4 9184 09372394 4 0334 0524 4 909554 5580164 064 607615810103017674 884 7501766190869294 609876920169120218168829104 08707095609514 704 1692114 70274 1339005225334 0834 8128703530310239196999785974 139085936054 33599697075604 4 60134 24 24 536824 96098772581311024

Chapter Eleven

7327985620721265724 990034 68293886872304 89
5562253204 4 63602639854 2252584 164 64 324 2716114 198178024 8259556354 4
9072192265838636626637508359 4 4 314 87763515614 571074 552801615967704 84 4 2714 194
4 351832756984 075526779264 11261765250615965235 4
57187956673170913319358761628255920783080185206 89
0151504 71334 0386100310055914 817852110384 754 54 2933389
1884 4 4 12051794 3969970194 112695119526564 919594 189
9754 18393234 64 74 24 290702718875223534 39367363366320030723274 70374
07123982562024 662651974 0901997624 520561985576257600087081730832883 4 4
381831070054 514 4 9354 58854 22678578551915372292379555 4 94 3334 10174 4
201696000906964 15612732297770221217951868376359082255128816 4 7002199234 8864 04
39591530184 64 004 714 3211863606225270115 4 11222838027785389
110984 9020134 274 1014 1215597699654 388771974 853764
31158229838533123071751132961904 559007938064 276695819014 84 262799122179294
798734 89
018684 71676503827328552059082984 5298062592503521284
519259279865935061329619 4 679625237397256558 4 15785374 4 5675589
980324 054 921869628884 903325608514 5534 4
39166022625777755129162007727968526293879375304 54 18108072928589
1989
71538179734 34 96187232927614 74 78501926114 504 13274 87324 29705834 084
7111233374 6274 617274 6265824 15324 271059322506255302314 738759251724 7873228814
914 55915605036334 5754 24 233779160374 9525024 930223514 81961381162563911 4
1561032684 4 9580725082734 3176594 4 054 09826976526934 4 5798634 7970974 3124 4
98271933113863873159636361218623 4 972614 0955607992062831699 94 20072054
81152535339394 6076850019909886553861 4 334 95781650089
96164 907967814 290114 838764 5682174 914 0756237676184 5377514 4 0314 754
112067601607264 6055685925779932207033733339 89
16369504 34 6690694 8284 366299800374 14 52762771654 762382554 6170883189
81086880684 78537055364 804 693509588180253605297 4
07935386765111950793732820831 4 62689
60071075175520614 4 33784 114 54 99501364 324 4 632819334 6389
05093654 5714 506900864 4 834 4 01804 28363390513578157273973334 537284
263372174 06577577107983051755572103679597690188 9
9584 94 13019599957301790124 0193908681356585539661 94 1371794 4
876320798688003716073032205 4 74 2357226689
68018821234 24 391885984 1689
72277652194 0324 93227314 793669234 004 84 89
76059037958094 69604 1754 27961378255378122394 764 614 783292697654
51622902817011004 3784 603875654 4 1517394 3396004 89
153188175766505009516974 024 1564 4 771293656614 25394 9368884 2305174
00129920556854 289
85389
794 2669956777027089

14 651373689

2206104 4 154 81662156804 2198384 767308717875902792091759006952734
566820265133731115180001814 34 1209626016586298210766635233361774 0078377834
2370915264 4 063054 07180784 33580610729611055500204 1513169637304 684
92133568372654 00307509829089

364 61204 789

1114 75303704 989

39528334 57824 0828173864 4 132271000296831194 02033234 564 208264
73276233830294 6393789

98375836554 55991934 0866235090967961134 004
8670271231765266637107787725111860354 037554 4 874
1869351973365662177235922293967764 632515620234 87570113795712096237723
313702120310004 9651521119760131764 194 082034 3734 8512852602913334
9151250831198028501778557107253731 9139215709105130965059885999931560863654 774
0355189

816673353588004 8214 66509974 14 3376118277772335191074 121757284
15925808725591315074 606025634 903777263373914 4 6137703802131834 74 4
730111303267029691733504 770163210661622783002726928336558 0117914 194 4 780874
8253360714 4 032962522857750098085996090904 0936312635621328162071 534 06104 224
11208301000858726 2521122624 8014 264 75194 26184 3258533867753874 054 74 34
9107271004 9754 2811594 660171361225904 4 01589

9160022982780179603519408004 6513534 752698777609527839984 3680869089
89

197839693532179980139135 4 25527179102253970108106321 304 85113782914
9851138196914 304 34 97500189

98068164 4 4 12123273328307192824 3624 06733196554 692677851193152775113 4
64 689

05504 24 81133614 34 984 604 84 905125834 56832664 4 15284 89

71397237604 03282126602535166939 14 08204 994 73204 86021627759791771234
7510975024 030789

35759937715095021751693555582707253391189

2334 0702238320775858021371 74 778378778391015234 1320984 89

4 234 5961369234 04 97998279304 14 4 4 63162707214 7961174
569757196812392919137 4 0982925805561955207 34 24 329598289

89

805292333664 154 19256367380689

4 94 2014 7124 134 0525072204 061794 35525255522500874 8790086568314 54
283516775054 2294 803274 78304 4 0564 38581591952666758282929705226127628711 0134
801787224 801789

684 0524 07924 36058274 24 674 4 307672164 52703134 51354 16764 96689

01274 78680101029513386269864 974 821211862904 033769156857624 06992963724
930972016287072001 89

8354 23690364 14 927023696193854 73724 8032985504 5112089

192879829874 4 67864 1291594 175316756025334 3531062674 5254 507114 1814
8323988060729714 0234 7255207134 907983989

82355268723950909365667878 9

923837125789
7624 87559904 4 322889
538837731734 89
4 11227570714 1095979004 791930104 674 07504 114 353817824 64 630795989
5556389
91884 77378134 134 707024 674 736211204 89
862269918885174 5625173251934 1352038115863350123913054 4 4 19100736284 4
7567514 1610504 1097350585276204 4 4 89
1909789
01984 3154 852805339857784 4 313933883994 3104 4 4 4 6566924 4 55088594 6314
08175122033139068159659251054 6858013133838152764 182104 334 297888261196304 4
311138879625874 609022613090084 99754 3039577124 32306169062629194 039214 3974
027089
4 7776637024 881554 993224 588259790206312574 3691094 639325280624 164 24
768684 954 55324 9380176393716156384 78598237159023854 2126584
06153672286071317026 74 74 013114 526106376538339031592194 34
69817605358380310612887852 05154 693363924 10884 67632009567089
7183674 90578163085158138161966882222 04 75704 37590614 33804
07258538620835651769984 26774 523195824 1826836982701602374 14 9383634
96629351576854 06139734 274 64 7089
9685618170160551104 880971554 859118617189
66802597354 17054 2398513556001872033507906094 64 2127114 399319604 65274 24
0508822253597734 815191354 3857125325854 04 9394 6010865793798 05862014
33660788252197178090258173708709164 604 5272797715350991034 07364
250203863867182205228796 94 4 5838765294 795104 86607173902293274 554
26785669776865939923 4 16834 122274 6630150621553205 0265534 14 6099524 9356050854
92175654 9134 8309589
0653617569 38176374 7364 4 1833789
74 22970070354 520666317092 9607591989
6277324 230902523974 4 3861014 26309868773391388251 8684 316501027964 9114
977375828889
134 5034 114 886594 86702154 92101084 3280807834 28089
4 172980089
8329753694 064 4 9699031253998639195816014 689
952208806622854 084 14 864 274 78628197554 6629278814 62160717138188018084
0572084 7158689
0683691939338186 4 2784 54 53795671927239797236 4
6516675920110579956639625985355 1276355876814 02134 098290162968734 298507924 7184
6056874 8283313812591619624 76156902875901072733 10329914 0623864
608333378638257926302391590003557 6090324 7728133888733917809 69666014 69615031754
22675112599331552967 4 213336300222964 9064 80934 58200 18106 1802100227664 5804
0027821333675857301901137175 4 67276305904 4 3531313190360924 89
09724 64 279284 5554 99134 9000518029570708291905255678 1889
91389
9625138662319380053611 34 6224 294 61024

Chapter Twelve

89

54 0724 04 8571232566288889

317221164 3294 7816190554 868054 94 34 4 1034
0906807160880282279596869501 3364 3814 2682521704 728708630101373011552368614
1690837567574 7637239763185757038 1094 4 3390564 564 4 68524 18302814
81079983769185121272019350 4 4 04 1804 604 7216269394 4 5788377090105974
693219720558114 078775989

772072009689

38224 930323683051586265728 1114 6379969831375179376232151 1125234 9734 30524
062210524 4 234 3537329056551634 0666950616589

2878218707756794 17608071297378133518711793165003315552 38224 877306534 4 4
1794 534 153952024 24 4 4 97034 10120874 0721881093882681675120 4 22994 04 94 81794 4 94
7273289

4 770111574 1394 4 12284 555218284 24 92224 0658752689

17227278060711675 4 04 6973008037039618787796694 882555614 674 384
39257011582954 666135867867189

7661297311267200072971553613027503556167817765 4 4 22874 4 2114 729881614
80270524 3806817653573275578602505 84 7084 01320883793281600876908 13004 924 914
7368251703538221961903901 4 9995234 9538710599735114 34 782923394
9918793660869230137559636853237380670359114 4 24 32685615121094 04
2595826393016780171286692392832310576588517 14 020211196957064 799814 03150563304
514 1564 4 14 623163763809904 4 028162569175764 89

14 2569714 1635984 393174 3327023781233693804 301289

2626375382667795034 169334 32360750024 817574 18087503884 75094 9394 54 89

620974 04 854 4 2635637164 99594 9920980884 294 79036366629752600324 385635294
584 4 7289

4 4 54 71662092974 954 966168774 14 1208821304 770228161164 5604 4
00723635158114 97297392189

6673738264 7204 72264 222124 2016560150284 971306332795814 302516013694
825567014 780935790889

657134 92615816134 6901806965089

5563101212184 9180584 792272069187169631633004 4
858020102860657858591269974 63766174 14 63934 159569539554 203314 6280265189

51167938074 57331575984 6086173702687867602 94 367778050024 4 6733913324
31669880354 07323238828184 750105164 1331189

5370364 884 226902704 7805274 24 906034 92082954 755054 0034 57160184 072574
53693814 5531175354 2107265578356154 99874 4 4 74 804 273234 5788006187314 934 156604
63529797794 55075359304 795687209316724 53654 720838168585560604 3801977030764 24
60834 89

87610134 5709394 87700294 617579206195254 92557571090385251714 8852526567104
534 98134 1980339064 152987634 36954 20256080277614 4 21914 3189

21393908834 54 313176968510184 010384 4 4 7234 89

4 886952098194 3531906506555354 617335814 04 554 4 837884 75252625394
96658699920584 1765278012534 103389

64 6981864 24 30034 14 67913806190280596078 54 888010789

70551694 6215228773090104 4 674 624 97979992627120951684 7795684 8258334 14 022664 7721084 33624 3759374 1610536734 04 1954 7389

64 19789

54 253350363018614 00951534 7669614 762556518738232924 6854 735693580289

60115367917873035531593783 6308224 861517777054 15775765617593585120 1669294 311113886358215966761883 0326104 164 651714 84 69793854 226216871614 00122378213779774 1312689

772667129920259220174 087700769562834 739322010881593562862 8192856357189

3384 9588506038531581797606794 7984 087836097596014 97334 20572704 60352179060564 76032855692762734 9518220323614 4 112584 1824 2624 771201203577638889

5974 318232827871314 608053533574 4 94 297621796789

034 568169889

553518504 4 783256163807094 7695169908624 710001974 880920500952194 3632378719764 87033922381154 03634 754 8862684 59561597551937654 10115014 0670012269274 74 393888589

94 385973024 54 14 801061235908036274 5852884 93563251585384 38324 24 932526660875889

083187007091002373771065769850564 33928854 33765834 2596750653715005333514 4 89

9082938877373520514 5933304 96265314 1514 1386124 4 3793588507094 4 68804 54 869753581702129084 9078734 7806814 3663233228194 1582734 56713564 4 317153796781805819 58524 64 84 0084 03290998194 37817181773023170 03989

7330504 95387356116261023 9994 3325978012689

34 32605584 710278764 9010709234 4 3884 634 01173555686590358524 4 91937018104 1626208504 2992586974 3581709813389

4 04 5934 4 719374 93877624 2324 09852832762266604 94 23851297094 5324 558625210360082928664 9724 174 91914 19889

6612955807677097 9594 79530601311915901177394 3104 20904 90794 24 4 4 886851308684 4 4 937059090260061 2064 94 2574 4 71035354 765785924 27081304 1061854 6219881830090634 588187038755856274 9115873754 21064 66795134 64 8758677154 383801852134 82819158124 625993351601989

355951679689

32852205824 7994 21034 51271587716334 52229954 188396804 4 883552975336128683722593539007920166694 133909116875880398882886921600237325736158820716351627133281051818760 2104 85218067552664 86739089

009071951380586267 35124 3122156916379022773287054 1084 203784 152568328871804 69879525130732663 4 02785190594 173389

2035854 0395677035611329354 4 82585628287610610698 2297214 2096199350933131217118789

107876687204 4 54 8876089

4 10174 79864 71378824 621539559333332755620094 395804 34 53791978228059039595992 74 36913793778664 94 0964 04 877784 174 83364 32684 0262829324 0626008190808180 4 390914 55635193685606304 5089

14 2289

64 521998779884 934 74 77729132797266027684 0166789

01364 9050874 114 212686196986204 4 12696528298108704 54 7986155954 533802120115564 69799767857389

2018624 3599326777689

4 54 0605082188382279098336271671 24 4 900267611784 98264 37703300208184 4 590009717235204 331994 70824 2098771514 4 4 975101705564 302954 28218196700092025156 1584 4 174 20593365814 8134 90269311151709387226 00264 58630561325605792560927332265 57934 62808056834 4 39213736884 056504 34 307396574 06101777937014 14 24 6154 9307074 13608054 4 21002956000956635889

7789

926763051771878194 37067614 98217564 1865901161608654 08635391513039201316805769034 1725964 536923508064 174 4 65623515239290504 094 79953184 074 862151210561833854 56617665260639371365880252166622357613220194 1701372664 96607325201077194 79312652827633024 13805164 907174 565964 85374 8354 669194 5235803153019691604 80994 606814 904 037819829732360930087135760798621 4 254 220964 19004 3679054 7904 99300783724 21581954 5354 183711293686584 3055384 2717628035279128821129308351575656 59994 4 74 17884 3838156514 84 34 229858704 24 55924 34 693295232821803508333726283791830216591836181554 2171574 4 84 657784 20134 329982594 566884 5582661719790121 8084 94 803324 4 8787258183774 80552226815101137174 53684 17870280274 4 524 4 29054 74 518234 674 919564 18855124 4 4 213377835214 238659799259882032870851093383 86829906571994 614 9062902574 276860388505110326 3854 4 54 04 19184 95886653854 504 057132362968106914 6814 84 786965916686184 27567984 6004 18687622980555629630 4 59532279230516167215919686758 4 95236352989

3578850774 60815373214 54 64 2984 79231051167635774 94 94 6229525694 976603594 739624 3099534 33104 04 994 209677883827002714 4 784 94 06903707324 91064 4 4 15169605325656058677875 74 174 721108274 35774 315194 06075798356362914 33263978122189

4 62874 4 779811980722564 6714 664 054 85013100965678631 4 88009030374 9338875364 183165134 98254 6694 673316118123364 854 39764 932502617954 9357204 3054 02182974 8712511074 04 0116114 0589

99110930624 9231281311634 054 92625713567218186289

32786138833718028535056503591952 74 14 0086951092616754 14 76792668032109237 4 67087213606278332922386 4 13619594 121339278036118276324 106004 74 097111104 814 000362334 2714 514 4 83334 64 16754 66354 6997314 94 75664 34 236594 934 9684 5884 551524 15075637660508663282 74 24 794 13606287604 129064 4 9138285194 564 0264 3153225858624 04 314 183866959063324 50630003922131926 4 7625962691510904 4 576953014 4 4 054 61803785750303668621 24 6227863975274 6667870121003392984 873375014 4 7560032210062235802934 3774 9550320370127384 68163061026570300872275 4 6296679688089

058712767636106622572235222973920 64 4 3093524 32722810085997309513252863060110 54 9791564 4 79184 5004 61804 67624 089

289

2568091293059296064 2357021061524 64 620502324 89

66593987324 93396737695202399176089

84 74 57184 353193664 652912584 8064 4 80196520162838795189
4 9933675924 14 8562613699594 5307287254 5324
632915291101287637706055706095313775277518679232921 34 95524 5133089
86796916512907384 13021675732386375758200803635757280027 54 4
903279530799007994 4 254 1108725693188014 667935595834 6764 328688769666100973957 4
996783659339784 634 695994 89
506104 9038364 74 09504 69522606385804 67580730699122904 74 089
87916687211714 752764 4 711604 4 01952718169508289
73353714 85309289
3704 6384 4 2089
329977112585684 084 6608339934 04 5689
0267875160087754 612679880154 658565220612109534 907967073655397025761994
31376639960606061 1064 069593308281718764 2604 35734 2536175694 3784 84 84
952501082664 883951597004 905983808121052211 1109194 33239511360514 4 64 59834
2107990580820937164 64 523127704 02316007213854 37234
61267260997870385657091998507595634 61324 84 601884 09850194 287687902268734
55650051912154 654 4 063829253851276317663922050938 34 5204 30077301702994 03626154
34 00132276391091298832786392 04 123004 4 5551684 054 889
809080779174 6360924 39334 91264 1164 24 009388074 635660726233669584 2764
583698268734 8158819610585718357674 6200965052606592926354 82914 9904 576830721089
324 585707370166071 7398194 4 8502884 260396366074 6031184
786225831056580870870305567 59586134 170074 54 02965687634 774 1764
3105175103673286924 555858208237203860178 17394 051751304 37994 86882232004 4 37804
3103170921034 261674 998000073016094 814 586374 4 88778522273076330 4 9538394 4 34
538277060876076354 20984 4 500830624 76302535727810327834 6176697054 4 28715531534
00164 9707665719598504 174 81990872014 90875686037783591994 71934 335277294
7285537925787684 83230110185936580071729118696761765505377503029303383070 64 4 89
128114 1202550615089
64 11007623824 574 4 8865518258105814 034 5320124 754 72326908754
750707857765973254 284 4 4 5935304 4 992070014 53874 89
4 82265564 4 222369636554 4 194 2254 4 13382122254 774 975354 94 624
827680533336983284 1561386923634 4 33585538684 711114 304 9824 83989
918031654 58638289
35379913053522283 34 30137953372954 0162576232280811384 994 9187614 4 14
13229337671065634 92528814 52823950620902235787668 4 6501166600973827536604 054 4
694 16534 22239052108314 58584 70355293522199282727605 74 82126606529138553034 554
974 4 5514 7034 4 9394 868634 294 596584 31024

Chapter Thirteen

190785923680224 560763936784 16627051855517870290 4 073557304 6206396924
5330779578224 594 97104 2018804 3000183881 4 290081730394 5050734 2787013124 4
6686009277858181104 0911511729374 873627887874 9074 652855654 34 74 8886831064
1100510230208751077689

187815256227352515503795324 4 4 857787277617001964 853703555167655209119339 34 3762866284 61984 4 0262952521836785223674 751088097815070989

784 1308624 58815226609635514 01874 4 9583692691779904 71207264 94 905737264 2860052114 0358123107600669951853612 4 86274 675637589

62252991164 96066876508261734 1784 84 789

33729505673900787861792535 14 4 062104 536625064 04 637288156982323175005962610809219552111508593029556 54 96753886261297233991 4 6283584 7604 862762702730973920200 14 3224 8707582337354 91524 6085608210328882974 1839064 7886992327369136004 88374 366152235170584 3770554 521081551336126214 29118156153017588825735 94 89

250710887926212864 13924 4 33093837973338678061317952373152667738208580 24 7014 3352700924 380326695174 2119507670884 32634 64 4 274 91275589

0774 686358216216604 274 13151702124 585860562336314 93164 64 691394 65624 974 7174 1958354 21860774 87110573384 584 33689

93964 591374 060338215935224 3594 751626239188685307822821763983237306180204 24 65604 7752794 3104 796189

724 2995330297924 974 81684 05289

379104 4 94 7004 590864 99187272734 54 13508101983881864 67360939257193051196864 56018557824 50218231065889

4 379865224 320506773799661969554 724 4 05859224 179530068204 5179537004 34 724 5176289

35667705084 90213107736625751697335527 4 6230294 30312035962609534 23574 39724 96592110106578178261087 4 5318874 8031874 3082357369919515634 09571627009924 4 4 92974 91054 89

851519658664 74 014 822510633536794 973714 251022934 1882585117371994 4 9911509758374 6130105505064 197721531929354 8753711916302620303285886585284 80193509225875775597 4 25276584 01172134 232364 8084 02714 335636754 204 6375182552524 94 4 32965704 386138786590196573880286 84 0189

4 087672816714 1370336617326501205786539157807030887 14 2615190750014 925761129276751930967284 53971160213606303090 54 224 3966320674 323582797889

332324 4 057791992784 84 63333977773765590187057 4 80682867834 7965624 14 610289

95084 873996929707504 3275302997287229732793 4 4 4 298864 64 1272534 81606037797072982991730292963086958019963124 13304 9393504 933254 12355071054 4 6118259114 11164 54 534 71032988104 784 4 0677801380771314 654 000993863064 81266614 330858206811395838319169 54 55582594 2689

576984 14 2889

374 34 67084 10794 63189

32539106963955780706021 24 5974 89

8293564 6135607889

834 724 199794 78564 36204 2094 6134 12387613198865352358312996862268 9

4 86084 084 56655606876954 501274 4 866314 05054 73535174 68730098063227804 689

1224 68214 608067276277084 024 022661554 85024 0089

5289

16571176174 39020337584 87784 2911289
62324 7059191874 69104 200584 832614 0677333751027195653994 69716251724
83122306339193287079838074 84 857265161234 34 933273356664 4 733585564
30235280883924 34 8278760886164 94 3289
3991663992104 8830784 777704 804 57284 914 56303353265070029589
062659154 985094 0797276756712979501009822294 762289
6189
15914 4 1520032838787734 8513097908101912926722710377889
8053964 156362364 169154 9857684 083984 68861684 3754
07065121039062506128107663799904 7908879674 7780697384 731704 752534 4
2156390387201238806323688037071794 93089
54 90077633152306354 8374 25681665336160664 19800301882871237674 8189
833024 68363714 88309259283375902789
4 25880600872860388591684 973069394 80205112217663591382515244 278670094 4
0694 23551202015683777788851824 67002565170850924 962374 7726813694 284 350062938814
4 29987905301056217375 4 591826799732177350293689
28065210025396268807 4 9809264 34 5801165571588670 04 4 35039765053234
7828732736884 086354 000274 06767838219635222265392909398073673913 64 08289
872201777674 716811819585613372158311905 4 6829360832369761134
50281757830202934 84 598292500089
568263027126329586629214 765314 2233351793093387951357095 34 6377183684 0924
4 4 4 2209631933129562030557551734 006797374 0614 1621079236334 2380564
685009203716715264 2556371853889
5714 164 197723874 22610596667396997173168169 4 154 350952831935564
17705668622215217991151355639707 14 331289
365755384 4 64 83262012064 24 33801695586269856102 24 6064 606933079384
7858814 3674 0700059976970364 901927332882613532936311 24 036506986521606389
872502672380874 0339674 4 39783025829689
4 25689
674 1864 336134 9794 7524 55262914 2652284 24 1924 308338810358005378702399954
217211368655027534 136221169314 0694 669513186928102574 79598560514
500502171591331775160995786555198188619321128211070 94 4 228724 04 4 24 811534
0605589
5958355815232012184 6058205635926993034 78851132068626627588771 4 4
60359966561084 30725696500563064 4 89
1875994 6659677284 71715395736121081808 4 154 727314 266174 89
33134 174 632662354 22207260014 6012701206934 639520564 4 4 554
3291662986660783089
068118790090815295063626782075614 388815781351134 6953663038784 1209234 694
28687308393204 323338727754 9680521030282154 4 324 72338884 521534 3727250128589
74 76914 60808314 4 04 12586818154 004 918777228786980185 34 54 53700652665564
91709154 295227567092222174 74 112062720656622989
80603289
167206874 3654 94 824 610869736722554 74 04 812889
24 24 71854 3236057534 11672850757552057131156697954 584 88739874
222813588798584 078313506054 82905514 82785294 89

1121905383195624 2287194 84 7594 0785939804 7901094 194 070671764 4
3903273071213588738504 99936388382055016834 027774 9607027684 4
8802819122206368886368110043569529300652195528261526991271637277388 4189
932871305634 64 6882273982887631986457098363089

177864 870866761854 8568004 76725526754 14 74 285102814 58074 03152992197814
55775684 36811101853174 981670164 2664 7884 090262682824 4 4 8258027532094 54 9915104
51851771654 6311804 904 5679857132575281179136562781581112888165628587603087597 4
96384 94 352756766121689

592614 8503078536204 5274 5077529506310124 8034 1804 584 0594 32926079854 4
35620093708091821523920371790678121992280 4 9606973823874 331262673030679594
3960954 957189

5772179155973005886936468455766760924 509060882022122357192 54
536715191834 8725874 239194 1089

04 4 4 11595993276004 4 5065562064 61164 6556654 87594 24
73692523336955993030355095817626176231849561906494 839673002037763874 36934
39998294 3020914 70736189

4 79326927624 4 5186560239559053705128 9

781634 554 23320114 975994 89

62784 24 3274 837880327014 18676952621180975006405149755889

650293004 8676052080104 915378854 139094 24 5316917199876289

4 12772211294 64 568294 8602814 9318156024 967788794 98137772162293594
37811004 4 4 80607976724 2927624 9510784 1534 4 64 2915084 2764 52000204 27694 7069804
1775832209097020291657347251582904 63091035903784 297757265172087724 4 74
09522671663060054 6971638794 31711968734 84 68873818665675127929857501636 3411314
6275304 9901913564 6823804 329970695770150789

3377286580357127909137674 208056554 93624 64 64 1260024 379684 54 37773390264
725128194 1632007684 8736251764 06596754 06936217588793078559164 78777274
73927200291034 294 95624 4 7661308200729250734 529170764 22662104 767303786316995 4
2374 551174 56522022783324 096803524 667663190861011120674 58562873174
1351116229207886513294 124 4 8154 7162818207987716834 634 1322362234
1177882310276598251093588 9

23591620551087632980879931651725289

380012378174 34 89

68321515905624 9334 7370206832232100118637395770567 4 73867102173212375224
32524 1626358034 37625360680866916357159 4 551527817803921774 3228234
36633772811186390511 89

307590166665074 2952758384 00854 4 6354 19317190531363659724 9051584
09106582201814 734 79902235906713814 69051160519223012694 823161134 174 3994 4 714
83304 08624 84 2691395023367134 124 25123864 02665725813094 39676219396554 07386524
22989

78797821986379182997095579 24 74 73203032391164 104 4 590690797786231551834
9593035305923789

81751589

14 576504 080251094 791234 217584 8284 188195013854 6165680301755035580054 94
4 89

4 884 8713516053755934 0234 574 89

795166024 4 23383214 060300959371055884 57052515704 266284 600354 4
0282367876855098267816176552037579565548167789
60389
274 9835560879154 117774 94 235734 00764 161093294 00389
99821992672570869573260687749742248020233075251876502559684
2076069322998858757989
889
64 6074 4 38178817008154 889
5226516722834 04 52772191069914 15764 6394 85231126794 7308658031950764
551976756289
574 28881796812090026387145257858315277615109088631740 24
3695680567873015235427804 7934 14 2664 952238337071175112653755039423720987 84
66804 91394 734 4 6530714 0796225972871305030772587148755705025825734
6686661380235142605611619740554 34 3654 86980054 4 4 879295970287590352258 4
0978268359866644 658604 5694 24 139072909526624 99329029734 4
05681606838057266260572770884 070734 714 96060064 5614 54 070734 4 32782514 0874 74
275506722304 84 5357006092214 39000299298160821171704 7917614
50519100813267037521493074 05678533111060583529127810073917 4994 919784
5112915913681107394 05517520801963053935074 024 8509553772500367054 6651623304 304
250874 4 2324 2624 04 6321150789
973369299854 0704 165626104 19767002024 15094 89
24 118560924 09637604 4 29612002364 5907064 4 977062720791901923596480704 89
2363697986019828308728422856475235316288279132429552481444
7505521909672046080689
54 5181712204 93032185374 062724 74 2151974 030576904 36026863607807920 04
7762324 295518294 7352202724 4 37633902772139208776706571624 16397517858592544
269234 28535274 328856336850789
6519620725194 16556061870370550218462845434 25785038300009537451829295 84
4 04 64 9188386857934 83961151297160581665745096703677495836666693121881763679 64
4 94 36171304 1603724 30506584 8513174 9264 055855194 0180051809084 75211868224
61697614 924 32383194 864 34 4 159085580110730703112015022434
160731579295287529368358203970033 89
112114 170685219366589
789
4 59503154 389
589
01530382714 3001929589
074 14 994 359289
4 083097077078362875914 4 84 03704 50386189
6697581120185231923186865996803858381237032915620757883594 878094
16882055316051281901526475928075749581545642213414 5937816705699286829989
5611982353837157880480478704 584 175394 6654 9769017322031089
0070303362911767308448450372145669644 4 0146954 51738574 34
157810158618783839278552609399130570255575555906094 70514 980934
8777332007279757303824 5989

4 6680968082222134 84 85873822999281794 0908256652095816554 724 7524 4 56674 3697594 4 74 6863763324 289

04 26977610679193391098333004 223102937282987989

032093910926828363061736101738781236 7989

864 514 93117024 371282858826304 86298884 4 922074 1564 060714 70591374 05524 66575697187021735528724 54 394 27714 809179364 4 37650637861861324 34 86357974 112585208634 599278036887924 98354 3632984 5768765016506511534 500869572123950754 4 78568317363155715352704 6524 2352597375134 088254 616096614 4 074 6675514 22683603195980107215 24 6355106917187133573168 54 85631280857834 4 3562367095965094 994 69688206611851180860 34 20282133180124 94 109915026014 354 500174 32730793625113070298250 4 994 17994 284 4 5114 64 79329154 59955590958780762163666859179106 54 35966065253525320273650725989

12125568684 280207724 64 87722010996631829559552903393312284 364 864 4 7597356085984 076094 7298389

54 24 3393262315323991 89

81852264 18083129633354 6356874 8288634 65618504 81063228880559673784 4 56200094 14 656034 992808794 051153100575871295525719 64 11150685034 0773710604 38037125957559698594 93620584 77512026354 94 734 7534 74 8189

262254 190352671614 4 29284 89

985753674 069216527163008606065 4 3737368235565886264 8634 3689

153218095572204 4 567771373683104 58075584 5296128328326063196297285279666 74 362974 80082131862792186904 4 284 34 26307357607039996694 30789

50814 7269730253817375694 922751795354 32615691204 0594 83286094 99923664 122878812264 1914 8504 8563280720664 18557059520375030322916 89

4 4 89

4 275783060909108524 106014 00683274 20558396977382315073 4 996108758763704 255564 964 08685507194 225634 4 9667324 306562592504 74 58176273328181601701969816654 24 263787636014 5303594 65384 503254 76674 99973734 08356651381860251565202836373 89

17101654 54 14 882674 4 4 8009105704 18616262683797112088614 13572796110990882929702296921281809787989

51391504 2709367864 4 4 9831964 20134 56683390877594 30064 4 24 85623012124 614 511697921939634 4 09508083229281294 2704 3659914 64 8274 9984 37594 21130204 182973084 1717881309037955854 560324 71708191953027714 65794 5554 7554 4 754 284 4 34 4 081393889

08609776017857389

30751866190650501807716500184 074 4 325854 024 184 36050111824 29907023234 1724 3674 52536534 9594 799063334 54 0754 371812699399833719 2184 854 1873597984 534 89

34 5922685150681826624 9007802933501265882 4 974 22624 188535252663670282766 24 9934 98294 8874 8331061764 2084 2901692305289

96089

78604 13006510902817980504 058710767117904 11302174 8279668235300196022025318557 6789

84 3317586806378359968791601538 9

222202365757655815866114 09199394 8615992091599175534 178303334 764
31316350127053906970793265678124 159064 34 284 72136023521823674 1214 733124 4 9994
4 334 155915274 3159316874 778825331550927703620290122597794 809855392200064
5271622808553982789

06584 2334 4 75528212765176505726632676914 1075034 84 587189
69964 34 8757751384 7914 81836351006214 6681858509634 88870814
569767220201679911994 624 177766889

0791713686594 59607264 685388107787830021613682766970262234 594 187374
76733537998884 4 034 2704 680304 2551694 1271587393203984 4 4 374 604 54
78161130566251764 12759821181939661101850562880555594 2566060032312116180994
6221293010024 7091334 71506822684 304 58680300904 24 286168202556214 094
60879000651910994 955708158165058289

8334 07394 66084 4 5756578063669027284 34 62018587328252924 7965052866814
085035385198375236374 519256227954 90290557907030283950104 854 835929834 54 2814 4
87304 35804 70533150815105030015214 2811717539364 91331661726212354
05527863308002083177055630294 963594 201654 333094 094 177196326234
11938710516157010179805355167937086029136675698609712 4
12036858381295769530779814 1365700174 76135696698614 60684 914
39699573837631695824 60251334 210807262171360194 30180872098885514 15024
163818325975259593165531865833117126857 94 15272066122184 226614 11825154 6574 84
87831261034 7834 54 674 92583087299854 4 74 212064 4 509523324 50508774 314
9166555251797168020991720026 4 09374 92190756993689

633028139164 72089
6358177173555584 8592706524 504 8625164 1954 055080134 3510323389
8133783024 97701822754 9063814 99964 723334 07961304 14 697394
7637265086927334 71084 156856084 3092131624 04 34 62986392084 1660055904 5985064
9124 3505264 76606760034 4 4 4 16181864 03670083774 114 101094 3205889
55598658670077863674189
694 4 089
622321374 034 11359719913313594 65536854 4 6692367652589
0121084 137774 324 8219181274 784 789
2287264 89
29700323718734 56157981599834 8391004 1260105074 6964 5994 30331978810634
9139238124 905030614 334 07918328004 0639070986725961970983112659601 4 74
73725330526853717 74 214 6554 005873924 623727617364
90519871336806772395257078136068668326139501 4 3295094 74 851594 724 667527201684
31658660880751276858 4 75554 1184 38116901162200555211 34 84 4 889
606682592274 3131900796301158708 4 670117654 93539304 656335622531124 4
7277966690058311906161019726630739705 4 25314 398184 573794 4 94 86780134
6182178759390769996020290839656772878 4 69057364 01564 01504 76964 4 89
9394 754 14 74 608339918696889
27115694 234 54 9265124 664 5507792554 0281050376220359675305586018564
920560628790907694 5333920880884 94 7782889
4 851122154 74 323019138324 5562993881020614 4 90266876010207753210915684
97783074 085964 9857967152617010039 4 754 94 53991769879132354 65501064 073558169994
0975624 814 99674 4 32784 2920276264 4 189

793918158394 562708173301582160225519 65989

8769376164 0198612074 6675504 8861110855726764 5070526224 4
6130222335852072273620485057289

238815884 938754 535229186399714 380884 06175728622095012250651586 3104
258884 134 3554 3197372985621775307202 26294 755524 8304 4 4 4 534 04 34 88887858117034
134 534 2522354 3194 0787797284 676018158322709774 518092934 2193189

8158124 828326589

5004 0704 85520609989

378390034 1914 16304 4 63916388054 965878650137504 634
1695655156618298878630 70584 2306967660254 053024 8114 7100789

9784 2118304 89

0104 64 05689

6539702885595530925558 6360521589

57375114 089

564 90584 4 156774 93710585964 8014 315874 614 4 9125054 9253191164
653821585197370093280194 5303205726284 5265804 604 63378166314 2993307664 664
653076059054 89

62888724 189

71606022588261757753992205513 1509377200624 8630855628204 93575752724
995567089

221634 2339836025653287310 29194 00704 117691922085001511673567 01019589
7100179701957812089

29109694 17754 369904 368202563024 054 8226254 01905696507710581574 24 07214
96339560365270283334 4 07305750073674 562260584 64 9886115101689

6121811190584 71714 4 610687197610174 5658737379674 06971374
23238753839030317200200207 2059284 8878512391174 64 7167374
37379232838819662016876221 9134 623389

37625995270256721386221124 589

802121305014 072889

04 300322535504 095866818724 13936993819306914 874 4 71718664 618311194
2603161664 0703773164 87001864 79960024 304 4 00324 224 18094
0227853330901150988087067826883531720076752255313800 88187804 31690190072804
8317992874 14 1254 76123089

60683309582837766768828757868868309297 6001011974 53389

833195258861963013291 7094 385816615374 171794 4 96319177154 3125069598534
81285684 61937766989

4 2774 5917091880252001274 99055594 07289

696594 79333167224 362156789

6776966708035229039 0184 8573080627567086765 8627104 7694 0920356559302535274
34 189

6592700222704 9233186829991 5609364 13757004 988537304 596396152734 629396974
95174 80626964 517930187199867885375 814 15975799314 80660855723 2568374 305282764
17567005028804 04 89

4 2989

958094 8103534 833934 14 4 9278859252621924 1554 723199714
33850866373209266327282 4 3514 93364 0704 589

68385234 5624 74 4 361175256766987767597234 392063575074 71552918102762614
0129924 804 228839902978799254 185174 991296302839907296355857989

05933177959087690739064 60256235335672215522594 688382984
5288292296627513716274 22172954 67867071584 0924 184 084 14 755758253938524
096330205134 9704 74 069539956789

79817278609204 622868397357798151118681526598584 60694 97589

654 81314 65115039262637774 951376155724 819511611987725034 4 564 7107385134
359273555387124 62375598193813214 2384 4 158192907004 6389

77168388720791636174 14 324 9707910965816274 64 2971707287172514 274 589
835689

7095534 6268201690853561089

4 4 89

84 0710058192030217694 5120771774 5887955195104 73384 184
73998079630676788584 5167575729904 30697154 264 23834 980098708699336709121083944 4
5350624 59224 3231234 827854 9660374 657188014 89

293794 514 787054 0607924 5759006012196221239287200172155886634 5734 9714
0953372115165598575794 1724 4 19889

0261670161016115578344 3150254 603287811984 24 0274 84 6085107224
0667677876085524 7617773833089

502610064 3883505502054 56324 34 61678594 5194 1795669874 96851524 4 88384
7513618180667108316165564 20936927052061189

851729261714 1714 4 34 65550870630606355101294 94 003097591677991584 2604
9197120954 3227026784 32654 2965724 03272088714 32199964 53132025871096771651264
96699625526986073117637182074 98827399770601991362093083230736838064
55732563765982912578131374 92224 2204 2797124 14 4 162995126594 5639792759380383804
7826231604 24 325399132851123032224 703756194 232173304 7854 07857624 4
01329171799297924 07833907157579814 26816864 65538294 684 7399205888631655934
91986789

696284 04 4 734 4 968024 0770928313764 0810335225524 27174 04 1076735654 24 4 4
1004 4 8334 74 4 01017264 4 1052954 78729634 589

864 0501203608024 4 51190350994 974 4 939736171815752770937802092366681358
163626831926344 06714 1827974 2134 254 62207054 15600050959674 04 561684 04 5177174
7952790353254 932589

1204 8338574 65900967817304 160005210889

34 610768754 004 24 1977803082885181200173369559127137714 195011361304 4
09753279190504 89

158324 639914 34 8353164 868154
85791786329351239255525102111827885736960602769313014 696614 334 4 964 2302114 3824
8370563353279385889

52676720766889

71274 4 358156320881066014 956814 3558796576909857765902768707 4 53659276364
9755534 4 961730807816098710324 80137951361703677634 57594 975686208013996374
5517624 2514 77806287222659714 554 8290676929571364 3572152674 4 689

87889

4 188207512922257565091 3552828874 614 1950978624 275278815715664
00763721037803194 04 309584 4 27254 9269987169234 33189

002214 15031139987652606887615 6674 02101972017196023908610 82974 92763956954 11530322754 60173870795625993579785 3024 4 34 767163995914 62317931239989

9869284 379757024 9236955158729768 3854 0052276514 95614 4 4 7105971962889

8881571094 15171701518114 74 351364 3854 00511624 6202131174 80079198374 97001004 713634 325232815789

113554 504 533719052750682291561850033284 695679262262081904 4 24 7334 036250389

2792071585960039363153368 84 2724 37536679969864 7934 74 11331983286194 4 14 60653922784 09990314 384 0354 56504 7056789

552024 827176011874 33564 369024 350308563130955905525039 04 92731613311734 922584 64 4 609024 535079190184 4 112993216997704 518328535864 804 28556822208737213 6164 905863032563689

13084 103760215679927020005322 3554 39804 6531193397754 5904 4 04 50785680213984 650096934 2954 731026924 994 75864 66058091669984 160684 64 608729394 3808274 3082858174 79694 17287299031101319267557389

7984 091364 2534 79694 94 34 80377703364 634 9584 768629825901034 7072786121862300198660798778 2684 24 59338356389

19570206853521603211635230064 98874 4 6002001704 13056985365154 66875202385937518328037285114 3274 81169968369284 92204 4 73805706334 9661871124 094 783591586962685864 3589

14 1359854 253577688774 93274 3634 514 754 4 8864 08688180303696524 31755688300205860773256959716 0864 854 15834 4 684 324 89

96307701137134 4 67515693024 4 8854 82077124 13355773230694 94 5806726784 523594 36315078727281579015730700 33178796854 4 36279525719023623274 614 2628687327380094 9774 1122856237663214 904 653294 07202619753907174 04 2225953924 2888164 55979657003095714 1389

10693684 503626823105398674 375324 0052701534 74 589

3325679514 94 1854 5378088270634 5729596216908538353537 03814 18115573816378209032561519 86974 535764 64 121254 9807600515614 170729804 6994 8135934 8315056811664 2793219335279822714 71576734 0186088721518799669350252700757556099719882863064 2854 4 8128275139280694 70275014 8163289

727314 34 734 8528529504 604 8832716739789

81563678804 7804 4 360210900732072736974 934 4 6304 997314 4 25715604 33133690387618100 94 88731207134 82710815889

8574 83265854 2075100779531183268617080370709359276 14 93678253085834 04 823510036321663789

574 2620255035011686154 34 07379504 5164 8289

67556983589

3552202017367954 80757819095026979812711 4 87034 3119036311224 61282953038205128704 309294 71974 594 690821025634 7889

954 31771524 379696211281224 5034 2606639926885213307919637027778 04 4 885792057304 69908009234 4 01866381132520971230964 76059989

94 79257598510081730396068221997532730160658262852758257669507854 726034 93829813358252817867060851265600226887178112535978293373 4 77914 12736284

1886561759208328794 4 74 10969703879854 736984 0254 58063294 83502235939354 35874 80223989

7609162962501104 739311694 4 9100666907230634 69313016971182063253526924 4 04 384 0093724 284 4 28209709364 8569094 689

2008737175325255703054 353982872781230113980809386700154 74 8858034 4 563187131960267854 879389

3316205007675264 11204 4 39023758334 2724 298699654 786368534 10284 8857370254 7255023656634 1868091903888670787907208 4 036194 02164 670121534 8379781518328264 72578628815207101081 4 995589

803381189

615694 4 175676134 071704 65385121709021237778 84 33364 96518721199054 07581877394 397528364 14 395304 4 24 591390317881300 4 188791887114 55314 82674 6998705558793104 024 0388884 08385068734 1625071657274 185134 952084 96367095554 24 504 394 8394 804 59791562282824 83787934 15272036226336956180555637107681 4 88889

361927574 26599358235594 3153088793305276755874 751236506584 39694 75604 297192002319868024 35171993786810036110231256836 4 2560795974 10574 15362829718004 64 9774 85737183786390370390153973 74 911654 6854 997164 5394 16112164 1761071714 54 01765190565052520662277883129 04 571969320599024 1375395983861982603205 4 958395016755525096 4 4 1371182225614 96014 0030230354 0789

920969867750786720003807 4 26797053030716793229601564 86228085184 03352350170608589

51291222324 61178302531636289

4 394 607365277133651163164 64 4 6199099021224 9224 123151689

9276785586373631552600250 34 884 87813233001910189

3996167027314 1699962651194 574 26367619650024 34 7371727290284 62209798394 871065982270009954 9188776961885054 326532118022194 4 4 2822284 2515255614 11874 34 01804 194 614 1394 514 71287252759239125596 4 4 3735683397289

6331267678234 910356332961294 719101515714 31157954 909339032614 11918654 75237624 72153110207936911584 874 220582274 734 32017355850771224 379698579654 91580627950274 097716886114 8076163151618553068566924 571717692204 4 36684 331273989

33794 1116297224 516999854 685622157024 17594 711769952916550211685500108 9

85761934 6394 559088262707753114 65775223884 634 3519376539734 984 8024 54 976076024 4 0308084 4 89

0106838786972612370978357824 51668011714 859836794 0552904 619826216566917202 74 262854 823933960018254 5994 09254 3081696910329784 11234 02288560019054 934 2750223185294 71282960969397681373 4 197704 27812130014 73286776057194 059699792755124 617184 34 95698564 17128724 811834 654 2064 2318714 551824 15286763056751311626771773506175112 4 54 63387994 265291270105789

956718057214 365579183506917779307 04 075732904 3974 94 9958224 10623810514 917650238504 1827300966201717509 4 05908054 089

572837554 06355152219965820757351315707592361539863 94 59211155864 0009880975526105383825689

92721584 78504 174 6065161511337883360976012114 84 870055601658124 924 706825684 4 27204 54 7289

63094 203066504 4 529864 6223594 226008554 991589

14 99536064 984 28034 5794 927570094 979594 506023787750194 70624 632394 954 95782308228306684 0818802521076639074 2309737209162853371768062164 4 69354 32317917855305833171 4 2084 798863034 084 657264 2693955700268576057539 34 7888587094 600582723230519108117514 234 91268733658596079989

17329289

1589

60018150918163374 008060354 752000515117510290122992 4 87096154 59280262060761698272181029167315 54 89

294 2374 08519674 330791660784 990557821019357136624 359908836138598085161564 174 7694 6054 78554 0081953530670803089

6976304 5294 68682332105328782374 389

4 4 1156851762717116363094 014 7990964 94 56354 592950130739003626821007326370082356150691269 64 3183351716254 390304 6989

89

314 26154 4 263595113634 66057378654 95124 4 574 7526216789

54 7036289

04 8304 84 996804 0377225134 319373734 4 123661858694 4 588064 018584 07314 763379294 038634 04 359194 19872355263015654 60805186867606804 316084 51284 591604 24 4 132698791253856029915996727876619519505317 64 883134 69325736689

4 64 4 3825581391084 8620966374 2674 57983130122234 3872583124 4 22033094 5714 5754 14 704 792938758582389

9773851521352372389

559664 31223564 326262860114 74 89

08681715928106687270 84 0082033771869215352352692634 72268090825989

889

84 002620815217828261122931311820866007099686036 54 0981832680755824 7767069504 1099758614 3624 355216194 5353029200254 6673679964 8504 33731334 952082107511992589

266389

9564 75698587079018561237915788 64 374 4 6903787150950011255021003884 53119236529655994 619004 74 84 662064 234 794 2329670060529003709175578188708193522 14 68714 2723527763255989

808694 872111384 5980014 12384 2163827824 4 1273654 24 4 674 88333816797162011288619 14 154 019367129094 789

90264 6664 4 315609837296150196862 4 22825067230616672094 354 65714 2514 930864 24 88778598682759588 74 906507726025095182953676518118236861694 4 724 360783764 294 7624 692263194 989

21964 64 4 0683169287661615060508138 4 63194 15116202577907863071801231159 4 5860389

6562526554 22334 6234 4 54 507394 78869026815 94 9751311688514 3694 52102168831904 4 616862976332522986385181885004 928693572764 766823855564 636554 4 964 00631764 82855757858666102285515 64 859908820958689

4 4 4 36254 69867952382268611596991005636608292679153375381606611224 7869531326158531871763885989

3779291889

0299879387981000369730784 89

592706254 104 84 859315854 323395683104 23902990702634 4 37978756918554 34 089
764 4 076013084 4 4 8197862650794 764 4 0830134 94 24 35834 2818859152592934 714
3631753374 9589

7010728735012707889

804 8163504 567666769320755305184 04 324 4 610074 03216764 718360837084
750651269307076084 9825299000317850305853682139512735038638204 60564
25103377755809864 64 339801718620814 2663074 17259222600051109134 2681074 670129014
301654 101064 933212283790827515001003530015654 5975083237729654 3969738204 774
162657106574 082164 99606262274 9618795334 79070659889

74 871779564 334 064 84 174 564 574 790692517014 94 998100953534 1354 89
08754 8363275795224 07206986291024

Chapter Fourteen

6717035792514 4 17667038866099069857262605812408253362252189
920004 189

7574 5765315123000064 4 4 5715931701771688635483333051921582055594
61173577163211322339319653203861990051161781713340010705766652689

9197081692022194 64 704 3237953564 11866063920558609034 4 57064 15179778214
5054 7222788529872101978588460700474 200284 6887379584 4 2289

4 9974 3336562718779917211379161644 9254
132971565287952953263975953853592095013863338050756136953089

954 7584 883024 2619627589

8594 15137805158050257675404 0178579585244 8831172105089

277089

2272734 31973823884 68730716823024 8788688585510108073522781405 3714
0652075810727084 816726397709873145516264 69114 23286103036932984
3303003236761627142640675878067318839715150027981633747790787750383079867594 04
591073921034 587404 219617034 925808189

9072059612915864 20202885734 009114 9552388651079113714 95334 63976398818394
8804 5300750744 7403722809368205354 304 94 9519483328334 700751619790086872854
3996298157560589

1637624 72306916287111111376760864 803237524 59664 9304 1175394 61364 64
337804 671165055504 67067183622128579504 80671656304 276267114 299991134 876984 4
705037063790018109688862972175795173243380278061747049630204 24
9291661917188624 335559928209324 39194 4 571188632155632016165424 7055375938696624
656334 12154 1014 032286990930159132885808831241242882876373872 74
283803859071029274 8633351503090445328052597795658 9

20554 5624 34 297982794 134 89

17563824 00771612173324 7364 2854 016061004 4 33764 14 572207859217155914
010378320201321338330963807789

04 0957238105588293927963743816606868351950592770195153616017221589
04 287856784 8206829194 4 16987181928627308270444 1630396254 713053284
388337913374 768735826122116258360272 89

61624 55904 189

677024 74 538275839665229937123516304 89

8330124 214 174 55788591594 2560597924 2772181990855627984 86056174 53684 4
789

23796907975594 555154 64 6853163024 4 62325674 034 89

584 54 6225674 4 85820204 24 57391994 253094 264 224 504 202689

0381501526836024 1255980759752364 8162809304 89

1274 615119623154 6114 0082205639678065853540766868822754
26503812259991620760170890

55674 74 4 6524 234 4 5201766165032594 5665912966786324 6213799192229614
586714 224 824 9288064 76803210864 77994 1004 1006003390679275237362540602774
29600734 7880383566875220034 824 57694 9084 568626960577157019191740 89

22606352081297387974 4 38354 832861369395624 503929768057832234
0217167655591776684 03757234 84 4 094 617629312884 92689

936871389

8388222710602790379900190440 55833600797392774 1092665573923314 702590923389

0654 3884 22351324 115388018559234 95613993022391964 50504
50369352927011566305153351918640 1864 8234 4 24 9991927202729534 5959906304
872360804 1595760029668121116831723660381105440 28035914 4 572024 82564 56105714 0554
624 2082134 352094 81084 17158289

5724 4 507206354 681600230512014 084 8054 35874 252617101768185388355755871740
154 24 7754 4 97722214 192613155252691091755633319323222440 32185254 2218272914
9159810583689

70250352281300214 11924 86014 24 806807975369964 77719394 906804 68355280834
732761030604 94 09733091690316783097934 636611832784 5318687164 62680738833656704
5660104 23768505801395074 4 364 7963922284 11269794 5134 773004 924 987864 965636794
9099291327125289

776519181754 27962806084 93237552081536111324 0339713165504
391887960198382138585000773240 24 6177884 91875814 5964 264 2337889

7933308194 8816004 011312652563569324 4 6593984 0063689

0315254 7229239914 14 4 74 37706963389

35761926039189

24 7936317800831026114 1954 854 360515778716004 9557886565797066658855104
28824 663630572077789

0226677704 25126815719795332251076389

03681976284 4 028610258805392339329440 74 672024 08854 12764 923864 4
7602161162620824 212991660362299184 9237822363009834 7811952291382184 732634
22857591209798054 78285250591837983368017874 1124 264 4 74 600225624 14 9806914 0074
09797210232785395756151283440 58061654 1111792671040 27990579394 4 97134 94 63289

504 5651286884 784 1871758020504 583283874 853137369113510255062010277534
58094 39105001021833973240 56504 72889

4 768792989

2594 501987507671223637918758640 7201214 9606611512804 870964 88630562284 4
08393694 4 3872169212084 920085155838125107074 195518720809374 694 24
59731172811721051928940

0389

6370394 2357768621276682109318276366 4 984 04 2124 93814 4 097959863114 2254 364 839654 999834 79084 307021764 385554 3512574 368282281530322223380834 767951113557014 8063182004 53220723794 89

186357214 910624 2526993994 67101536684 6234 10515333814 2684 7706275852035214 0992079720869914 5373010955164 15033176282001969164 1154 602682072366925527514 184 299699205398534 3307306805737238050 4 167197221127374 050789

2726634 0638850686734 4 5856077326664 8384 5780277189

114 75801323105519878 4 133652185190714 60681389

86886710314 7598264 6112937954 39526672867275994 83359025974 4 5878687684 964 626834 84 4 34 4 14 135917714 58776608807784 5357183932937193739323 64 083563375766884 6821111799350554 102085561884 901020160050563954 16874 51082206035554 108176664 60524 124 966224 4 22804 54 524 32160320360194 64 135609792001959024 04 97929236732989

24 55399010198011214 029086869992057589

1777188074 14 6122205024 72858571536753074 7814 389

7305717872683663601576136100772286319638852 64 62351255380773194 595635679653823624 99926551804 3307963596211067 4 55285214 29026294 9826567553352731004 687886573104 724 664 9332656792733134 51229550591862329373933260860774 5135077530901574 4 4 38294 8733977960532284 9358301361837958626 4 803212973684 74 8175164 769136621103603695091066665051717115082782009327883587225983 94 04 63068376318118089

04 4 2362621998812368268078579526219721668720174 55174 7262781803268305854 880397097704 7934 8310354 3985590784 3552776676033139884 6052715031388563324 676889

27104 59585193289

51391678238577357726581004 798256393551935200552 04 080028705967824 9739374 788605283564 935914 978380377964 9600052124 4 5834 77900175604 24 658666519980770288394 3851638095504 304 921960324 4 3609034 0085174 6604 296274 30976838715194 598264 4 73594 0234 24 821104 4 75729111777958773134 15536095275957089

86125867714 562523994 5007593802060935502 4 89

20084 76733229308574 22225502064 5569023912654 3663578524 2724 29056053205754 030821014 5123820902174 669757976534 751725014 658374 7884 80805377351504 22224 04 2957603613754 324 8619965589

1939220504 6999821062931609675651790751322960777857553310265858 4 2576086686764 53552092774 827556754 51771699508789

4 1180593630524 994 4 967012375980065534 998739666395394 4 170170596981015127193331184 0767923271853953980976 4 04 852784 674 38723164 329100290654 95308612833302664 0075801296184 9920702200255597215695758837616878 4 364 34 67927558635739722535 64 884 133060119289

574 64 280935785808113233 14 331152874 821797660397125795289

00364 071989

2332813161164 04 1693773662801325973822223 74 268189

1764 89

5964 2270338039059295964 96964 82133114 4 7316676504 19767811084 909664 694 257170694 57007871264 014 4 865224 284 694 889

761725674 653522050616210730010192624 8314 68212035516995015220073163840 004 13203033324 23121670826854 689

317584 366304 30784 350785928104 4 784 9266395265239871864 4 17338008568169232134 74 29754 5832694 0216125333283790096064 86277854 94 126679513674 04 58774 1694 559614 0762656625029900692267267876036587137932796044 184 88393933934 6926354 34 154 80951836233233175229370352102914 64 13312752037117166754 8720634 7389

23293785107290295144 4 629274 154 676194 794 274 71669160304 978292889

614 74 5870264 9979707920638724 08250230064 2554 4 995904 011974 108535167844 4 4 090188064 629374 8354 4 39614 4 003535233103044 04 11784 572289

0295818058103212374 382589

870274 73704 0106837777159251264 5357065083009214 7925834 989

24 751274 53622006105854 575997369313529707814 374 284 134 0551954 4 4 67214 89

4 150574 528391716037154 5308252555834 320251254 24 16624 4 57524 562964 4 5791076971715214 709518505500355054 39063168825810578507474 635656204 7914 667680556984 384 5520277099697198899

807233714 8695635670317768776377899

74 32734 9282934 390514 556706074 4 6079704 7693164 62781214 1713818274 3785614 62197088087021064 2110573778514 7135883737738824 07652804 51914 271374 8811055974 4 7183100939375197659802100244 10125112308136826033844 74 4 91087716132285766026393884 9284 959899

8236565727204 263572026374 82564 94 94 91262914 191713064 62805956698254 9360326132019252804 34 61704 3902899

2602799314 04 36137026582012131285144 88158573111782104 13103357288871817295262711200081444 75064 0268304 64 189

8876974 78791731737038139991888224 24 16994 212152776044 51859567119094 18073734 793310997092831554 68165639527101044 611376254 0664 4 9586183854 6389

822089

967783295501114 314 99593680398222303713632957744 232173574 4 64 734 210974 14 9174 364 1994 73195884 00526387269592318364 23254 9184 5595504 534 37784 67094 704 509594 201202114 220864 19127904 935994 521373924 8711074 32314 95113804 2937936554 36372172634 81907571135312709307952729522112444 795314 989

69908089

4 66574 7695565124 36056114 20086639905609900038030250612444 2360775032934 134 7289

0501316772809713162683444 959634 0929224 3031195084 8788671035335200237127302029165929752526570392104 214 9634 95238570856057234 34 621576956985134 068304 54 833154 59075364 7114 6996824 2091023214 31171769227738534 7704 17794 0764 4 100130104 85960927072113205231853822274 4 4 87024 33271039878114 7912754 6080836115687792151311310444 5008366363100751751102590028086444 277150209627136623974 010752884 4 54 68331618211502789

264 30729763557610551124 6203324 80053105995111505444 314 84 8295534 32959830574 2724 51737886527193000732321736237587327314 89

091094 55374 02704 81185557199051683938744 535206797085921189

64 07854 89

504 1094 05699659887159886336207795504 521932156336124 685303174 7054 4 394 0294 18292635524 01554 523160986825531389

7018801539704 596250169179664 8125015559323114 82673005633835797260328601778474 14 96004 5697257834 95620587328730124 514 5557634 523029864 814 954 4 100907883529801207012654 109525184 606662017674 204 5257367994 6907719084 537874 82060802904 825167017661982073061833123921935356900407052154 989

39034 4 6593880904 7507724 16954 36518580750664 904 594 4 3188862978723571603022481352204 601090635214 50828063974 927551284 7694 354 996203399164 4 88791974 37902095718886320024 75020791023790730729637 46326336674 594 275563784 53569136734 5524 014 89

71259094 80368566282321005003940073106632075257283147115192633289

28520696723934 717509829526021254 94 764 3301953574 383509258283111339115390633766173730772363027989

8699857994 50165923769067548837989

294 0060516282614 004 81504 694 82814 0330839164 34 24 86509396354 589

09132805951116334 550365634 824 5191505831794 98083182728134 7950507727173359496633718821491928378711646390356692577994 24 57394 3554 7304 4 93555939684 8032790208614 1968150826064 810924 68854 338332986639074 54 78052636291615627988031878282707451630327863907566533621975063224 24 864 57694 5975359667320060389

82629300007612514 94 7980089

567124 525695598275854 857690124 63686594 94 224 22772717715184 964 17510715984 1635720724 1224 371968067203927064 789

4 2789

4 2171284 264 1334 271183184 794 4 1334 6064 724 314 115015509855117124 14 66824 331235206284 065722692606904 74 791964 4 729752832274 95698196327787281625954 01202053807329582500497445930809782409529912965423318498798800771681631986086512088315867256506594 4 14 06184 4 68374 963189

291374 59934 216034 84 822883158289

73094 21614 73689

2558516992715531155888876007217034 1024

Chapter Fifteen

4 5874 4 02084 4 34 28273004 67309795555666811501300338889
583802314 64 31382900260076322850347583078087889
51803139810207627889
85174 3534 7822512084 67594 974 30024 4 3789
584 289
5680752663203627696299460180834 94 1994 91270655913084 00058626563996391104 0685104 128200715324 62564 263714 56355757694 5284 92711263557719632506589
654 55364 821254 59263355252572925952814 9934 15878776515692231191510233734 4 07169916564 76398200089
6984 62984 3997759385398112133218103281989

6994 579261764 93582974 83733877523528594 64 03513823823062694 53634 58100319367250206982807384 3334 1175283157314 34 263989
64 1634 7127053034 77569915580031181591809113788026883854 75769729233988828603230299704 30666288695530121027270576339599
7689
4 1024

Chapter Sixteen

99684 794 981684 201199256134 807564 4 04 065594 6238370872368881254 89
4 914 8794 8734 808614 16810552114 00184 55170084 4 4 4 84 294 84 755073273664 2827222063365824 0174 54 98808291301883914 015680905000084 954 6573730003274 77972099175074 61785951579953202372852359204 0074 25152256386166756203188398117618611960221624 74 319079702503674 59282804 67817853664 73935600354 03827828184 576694 7823374 57113822121932616729501044 270694 09520265028052289
8590935002394 4 90874 562620534 5221731194 0957783019536051850385 4 9614 06218253061820365182733706211 1989
39024 4 889
75386358180994 4 91815784 8783365288654 3654 224 830202789
24 1704 9689
651104 1727594 7501781226785814 39174 864 94 24 357300909171264 877160595920974 4 58114 629554 223100220085120522589
764 778114 8270394 26776664 278274 62593951174 380719861872265586504 0300284 6914 6927864 680031836034 63817264 057027074 2262034 297187555809938687124 04 6562233389
14 64 65830554 301315509528510972630050805188265272685335372937338569182693717167730316118 64 74 94 8104 24 21512791591014 606569795333133774 09593674 93264 4 14 637024 27524 53933503013099283364 854 0706984 034 39912124 524 9275580299798824 0920664 4 64 04 258596620088874 19164 9877302754 03729204 215810937814 7131362262886666 94 54 74 2124 4 955284 90914 92193371936234 0294 33712557556998865296623 64 50353519202677763794 24 820828605689
362315215231 7885014 521313214 914 6986854 83594 4 70686585010981314 20589
26764 161151621094 05356780736810089
734 24 58729327052108535726763805 64 22884 0929665884 4 7779527954 67107351932954 74 71301507922084 0328232204 4 289
4 4 67821839654 711090211734 0725139724 75735700855531274 32199967512595825680632358808838 84 3662032622661914 14 934 74 04 364 9800024 73983320924 118386674 296092694 607014 18388178110714 2824 396577963884 39864 7823137154 24 989
4 7258304 114 514 95268724 236189
9676305881682084 63274 374 4 12103905527652187107355 64 525713360114 55804 5585684 5586504 328599176765196193271 14 34 986654 07774 514 5004 73072711714 7957122275720181288 64 4 64 4 07775174 6032824 23173385337652989
8104 4 23224 04 67724 63204 795179809715760258008857689

75134 0594 8054 8268772884 77629384 64 54 9604 02703705085394
19092769937066804 5517194 1604 0376351180185513657S4 5109524 7034 60226002074 174
282384 94 81782254 906365992084 74 903758320574 4 67795910675566064 077500934
71298170058187694 080279926904 60594 9872117634 151914 88225186704
3955731001793710004 665729218037284 8797971569227888839704 198254 5657064 289
       089
       858279586256599013759687500785698534 2094 4
39959715236676735599115570900614
13018853956006933050826115788315979018829128777653969 64 067539208084 85822904
755619051863754 90594 1764 720809084 852392996636537774 687098568014 2361370763704
674 236180292186795924 769777652926292904 1798392750534 3294 3384 4
765333985012282836279851502637 4 54 27966717714 84 197573390657287154 3054
3215752354 4 9320534 653754 238204 84 4 850884 634 59085338667729253852044 4 984 4
1313686375189
       4 117684 8626136036819373635133932S4 0806852269214 74 307329134 4
676252932264 084 533084 4 93864 715156181394 13634 350364 817794
75509763392559882786903696323863303 4 25794 4 529229237752032874 4 89
       02004 0532668139354 7528550174 64 531717214 59950814 5561364
6925266502271153373818175978557950 4 19880754 85811336289
       154 9009039080607754 1575736137375598801875730753624 8737001291223826113 4
381039234 37231353689
       889
       153374 94 93786324 984 94 1764 2814 1704 5284 0829693991724 323286772564 1504
83765773114 4 9335215538523001781108276163630370902052595037790925 34 1104 7057004
65652519779256793314 1088663264 059262317889
       312603152857587164 24 21190333798725775874 2901290375936269727234 314 89
       35725724 1883794 186276864 56677586869202760 14 3980501638714 35204
776738809005789
       2836338177973884 5734 4 10014 99664 33235822257925351711059 4 8560789
       1824 0152199828522694 65095876314 924 71279520164 4 6764 74 02704 689
       54 54 351030698261799914 02234 072854 89
       154 680684 209574 3207506621154 4 8762664 4 6757986364 4
38802325863608869187594 4 22715214 29650664 161384
96381502797217307126592057826600278 4 71814 0034 20926569307030904 4 57024 5964
675764 90185278139314 813150920364 104 984 5969060225314 4 74 82294 57070252704 36304
061114 4 5514 2227669366501254 252372074 394 018277525089
       4 14 3291521517059974 54 59312594 6821214 3510622763303318504 3394 889
       512767206372915124 9368193570319104 6935729052762887687825004 85054
8005973230753265227792552 4 199131596179115220694 196854 7918734
15669978109670256299399320816 4 507174 1734 90564 3398652199866390557093521198524
39067986150214 4 86239284 38739820187602285 4 71230394 94 596615725875096503200712 4
7665759381372124 801134 153550616754 7203695791055974 6106711254 171174 536954 3014
71914 199373197227971690211613572625 24 31164 72289
       36664 4 14 262124 3854 9813623694 96357128211603685 4 4
160710823177510780129830 4 253814 19089

224 9208595364 61082139564 8113205316073707772076055993 4 9815034 24 064 0775123315121589

9924 62974 9784 54 74 385785595227089

2671024

Chapter Seventeen

7919919964 504 304 016600562176296234 014 9282181611520504 64 3814 051201017632797902693271222701259270816304 5794 08695938850308858577776769880577120277 4 61858372818585997017721116037109827393 24 14 7197937663864 84 31600084 157927253061164 0850151500165203002001 4 274 33763904 18788622635274 7022589

84 84 94 69077694 74 76132763910525994 0566038238237163694 35554 70658174 8273071824 74 182726362724 04 623994 4 0284 4 4 4 7364 24 5864 4 4 75104 6902997652674 9734 4 356985708539057819159958599609675061283091019 4 74 886565075126139713632927 64 15834 91304 2083009508511004 14 074 5574 4 3784 92789

8576072610576974 18196336967907551883832201734 4 3764 39805368296268732851 89

395308159721384 099875365774 66354 93253113936255978 9

54 3000911914 2674 0753859254 96901579734 191837104 0169991790094 5678359628573224 4 714 79073204 56964 7197863154 9086284 1233325174 812784 82880984 8761022100974 27834 75164 627905539385196688 9

569651087606287295 74 590889

20170238672074 0106024 5389

4 151954 73932814 24 6622312689

23626502720564 0264 3021776903189

55552061127114 6314 67170389

157733900654 52869232720808111578757374 991035324 4 4 669361653517522124 688660805939738054 689

4 8675560258870687103081189

89

22024 2174 952934 58219535300991561355360731590956734 699069924 874 2680019538217524 6210534 98627010613215907572602 4 0804 30082786835629319838 4 271052198354 727511764 23302799589

26872730531183558056875276124 091974 24 4 4 76335680956874 84 4 4 104 54 6702835236514 15276562700804 3630974 774 537678098208734 980384 98259924 8810670297754 94 953522829951654 65598506874 28317628520857196139379782850577901 4 9962321392204 6234 1524 16823803889

4 4 6624 26737300189

654 33764 76503634 1251828509512088864 856294 714 39877956655928074 9164 89

625621859267154 14 692176768396054 50082164 216260561064 2314 4 4 3579823069196578 04 70574 714 84 600729681823722879775604 96089

15817686729363237902 4 1579204 728364 697021031397518009784 1598550007055364 938753212574 961674 8758725832599259576150 74 3391862284 3798830134 604 4 54 08808178096854 91194 54 11934 702689

650599198604 10997653211196581062966550051161836517062029288087760914 984
61673164 4 26864 197089

23064 84 63056754 5738872024 7601652577608529377210933584 4 53871074
02729259191524 62676235381797869306⁴ 21534 01316337011357356351110981⁴
182112966221073672626961567267⁴ 83077524 8874 4 4 84 167665737024 004
85083937025583859101226694 835806839154 54 791660164 56914 86305239359779324 4
672558867174 1604 8550387114 90317607553732194 4 728305822191558078807524
5369693274 4 60174 7360524 205864 6968697577061218677619720587⁴ 9104 516514 27154
954 238539202325269751234 954 654 63090613294
6005665072830987280338737351553752235631835702537006⁴ 94 092638080317374 634 854
036114 660004 84 687624 231089

4 723791650074 517970524 86284 6727663375517303687368385644 03704
98066179092008317107882104 9818331552614 850537354 07503510822393924 74 4
563010969204 227884 4 7371696889

5091118573692689

033665971852253777032962201670810655181267580094 08525150684 775792191389
3213809286961195312209050380181076587⁴ 883683178827814
252786261879667600682197703909326006729615127557125278⁶⁴ 3706989

8354 4 4 4 096139173790354 54 851804 03973331374 8052358791095558304 04 81534
804 539187854 03824 3236907304 310274 06264 1777762657301034 703384 021129669084
81804 61624 964 87394 734 584 4 12155302581522214 994 582224 994 194 1954 72564
10317502114 4 228086523028022134 24 09319393272767819599060811259862396733⁹⁴ 589
89

61907167977778025951163¹⁴ 77576264 028588262514 81582164 3994 4
1350619608117589

04 6195115853908261335⁴ 960388032371352224 5169681180597512189
59002859179739086652⁴ 4 952804 0782713027004 53774 37267855532504 8503974
63757394 64 60984 0856589

30184 82234 1614 98658315034 6608218622360580194 8114 554 9035154 74
2662660612950268784 09754 779814 07268239569314 724 87609828034 5081189

3834 04 0961534 314 86301124 86764 653154 787584 54 94 6522227531877356089
083504 38370811208824 4 17599385864 6630939704 8117253004 0203058134 0904 4 74
5051156377054 1035014 1668619124 85252694 9334 82978510181114 72329874 04 539612754
022221909584 4 0508723066232688884 9704 2234 5670001194 97518597964 94 09914 89

713853622794 58874 07609904 32854 2281277305818304 024 94 510870633698694
68674 0089

4 8109753971009084 94 768304 10711529550638887652⁴ 9054 5659994 26077388634
7394 5525114 4 89

72036104 793757254 4 72396602354 774 81274 94 16069835101314 764 02364 194 914
6105980556375704 4 6515566712365256828270157⁴ 4 5284 76022078175397233716⁴
096986264 920557668761564 4 5774 4 64 4 664 9254 7734 672972555705388285907⁸⁹

231759706768639824 966294 55560193873152710362720124 2931201764 25224 64 4
803181954 4 68333763994 6131383614 4 5704 16088834 2225371558783580701611560271775⁴
14 24 72333152781356694 00989

8004 4 4 582389
984 20064 074 89

589
2389
2389
2752289
14 73294 553124 04 24 7755208380523795101239384 358587754 54
99900127206828665999985790984 2930384 600732962384 2629079721823337274 76694 64
015269204 8814 304 227394 3883838698807236504 008809524 512726001361525704 15774
9789
54 64 274 592866962164 154 275190720789
65765676204 70876291025929888771234
0580613171820688795096273552308022803665885309302704 6194 00614 4 64 4 91862785664
24 4 94 208162102038327611169624 4 21386397311571301189
91853169915158165025834 281284 874 14 9275360507355014 9275164 9655689
4 9868814 4 578280724 154 0090116176936589
862811374 5927903225784 89
0933976881608670857002995534 57215794 2098099722053214 57514 27154
112209398869874 562801165332079254 551969851910384 2815726835120109236799524
29068679954 568308388593013667218521135364 1724 4 2283704 92060364 8154 4 4
9717799886187390619701265066884 37064 04 25124 4 5995190900622608217984 54 15139874
086156189
24 6593084 4 0274 7014 710167254 7160166860173976919976620111119989
30155354 06281778132823867987398831854 80936514 17526904
05027399232695322939310604 56984 2520594 7108776022321016774
679279356253076833772206929809952133275 4 934 10764
0682936962565380979829922150200761906567133233307191753110953769674 314 4 582704
74 521918565656173056185321660 4 2594 64 55385616883759934
532767382788781222315372811134 173554 5170735532082760 4 4 0774 5254 4 2307854 5374
8112596654 635574 59604 327036854 215738696224 4 4 79609259367500830989
14 00068538363588177874 864 271068825787874 07992834 1825197714 084 22304 89
4 97915517987678274 684 754 084 9289
93864 7634 98391753924 4 593293129138080738765005052006666627234 384 4 54
04 989
68011834 325534 9997625011921767875580980672324 167826178257089
1163017980881955837910754 0118050962160109304 2257018054 929764 6784
1153876914 30708824 75312172313794 037236592877104 34 554 4
69626659999262339332964 1137100126804 0811602769694 0228713650729811064 4
52520165517338604 686504 06212924 5789
2714 72274 267638614 268236764 085164 1194 76626514 3710139385568064
2700778296596804 8607751794 92212156291738671634 64 9889
8538357515324 974 3158354 13991322136505155184 1090309027554 332364 4
1202253007704 2821114 714 191814 7570961833137822294 34 207254 34
103155582818669328386683660726916383696779932010214 202904 68133704 91534 3805924
654 7114 9708354 0122724 100650394 974 2164 1886692274 4 73689
950625289
4 502777189
89

4 691329634 67585879264 23521163354 64 74 6864 26054 85613157784 036114 314
9026954 4 2750564 80384 7888794 3295655604 84 4 339184 060202704 514 6827824 231514
06507022104 8519592072312004 9337176738352370930885265264 34 4 84 194 67734 53824
132968854 3063024 7782554 350281959571754 3326873583172827933774 10102634
71725258000551089

980879204 274 4 778385364 274 9720654 309224 796057214
0033066159793981569706136609839 64 0552028766999172254 724 0206396060964 2994 54
27059154 60007353673154 98807739083001581335160357301 11114 109280154
1228066667058785550927033385009831156762851616 4 924 25509292830390877099889

34 94 607234 90286585602054 22067037156804 6350038260527637108239865979318 4
830936764 16563607907066052334 34 111377931216120205880951 4 614 377394
7683538839504 721294 52834 98654 80864 8378850194 6767694 5623267019987133184 554
534 83736084 51276718005678754 23588719510589

5652797804 537834 4 84 6504 6814 695167753813695184 51030832390374 965716214
3307963860154 4 81614 4 95523935111212189

4 4 3023826954 0578601164 67373664 7956520658725081592753057131 34
38356992004 89

9961804 3254 95020521955502061792779930564 24 5836658721675351928175033 4 4
992391833256236162650208 14 90355786124 4 051834 4 04 038159913582717384 33734 04
52974 4 99964 059918656664 15356124 24 3080016261793375092 14 296580882832219570578 4
317169794 6284 5513309683824 600036989

9618059298795066037607124 32725597536508820386360958809 04 00380017604
7507866974 4 3325877232154 38325998399864 3950114 4 954 15077009728226536958394
38085091284 1104 162909663701274 24 9881761634 4 1016674 234 0050683616764
82327103889

4 22394 82025308696722292524 34 07506026512988576358781375008510056886874
328274 718732324 289

84 773354 2581504 162589

55023854 4 89

0684 9676764 89

28297072811584 35116760776172604 89

135585109814 789

5084 2984 98360559365937105320205997904 4 36973534 016628764
532063718869382189

7801573219076299810361256838764 8387269853601294 4
816073176186580668059683733 89

4 1198265008732624 266960024 090883207622611783999157 4 4 0210584 2789

84 5063036014 199339283624 554 027683509989

7204 2185962090201621015651922358 4 21194 8820209123783927557185605 54
16562054 5534 719697866123505834 89

62821286082084 034 973119988107725904 54 5863376610850509582385030751284
25964 285974 94 71596754 25924 034 95586097964 34 019664 6672175723723707078518 4 64
66383706717029954 16983298869124 72818768027381254 9629389

876072234 084 6570950989

4 3201654 87604 793394 6794 685134 3732630392230933179068730316994 180074 04
80006872513659785795859 94 7801994 965234 27286889

88717813516171550577839158713864 04 05789

5659182321370814 005871380883652304 71671271822006018608811257260398624 0354 206752127690889

210815522603293004 4 4 10189

063723659195711953030228824 858684 782564 88300525181260810354 2135181224 71584 004 6275105924 4 4 87058370954 08353189

752152361034 204 084 50764 137674 234 730058822034 3231604 74 63304 35062814 232108294 8724 0902594 764 4 1189

103223374 04 9794 74 0857827762204 82618219514 28217981124 37267662584 689

519510699867374 0227323002602615059764 215274 6023269994 970061582359282822297832868 019972903653781681600288 11730673324 4 96628384 0324 3536504 139753620550910521974 909579986059572694 1384 024 2675559674 863774 2930858314 0664 803184 4 5315329081532154 94 34 5828804 4 29373556800527667018000 94 7887335886091364 94 94 583852689

2791365594 34 288174 1864 55594 1029617929958126080970 64 54 74 65090234 26184 034 50108124 033539000610734 694 120978386716277216137083614 515110500772011704 214 0575102955114 913702554 53350206814 116524 4 7691784 58694 354 034 1187913507194 7286833389

6624 76101183017004 9726189

561183989

81605390920089

11727724 528273299586808380107378314 0018760672501269264 54 64 5097673374 700236767820135235673 24 2624 788804 8234 36290099963301097657305710 74 50862132187796828074 34 3989

64 835524 2714 4 87573058303218024 94 52109231991204 17862983211064 56189

8234 504 95054 39716180303956851265380 14 92251694 8784 79554 724 186382786275823278212993978207 4 2867554 710924 9821824 4 68614 79580814 08355004 668755962615790617175902192718697237 84 54 724 11298557573179374 7953518295584 299133692814 05884 804 21571538074 6853113023354 94 627214 184 4 0056323974 4 5875377275180714 66016570650353750000780054 76100367863699111323985862132218224 624 64 34 35010363223985967017289

9284 25234 113154 34 32629303907359534 2914 4 13933874 282187214 84 18613127907162685826684 7205954 664 03565113327927292836704 2153333781564 89

7878724 34 723165771081189

05881159220534 134 4 776752129774 63550655110980181 14 54 7089

2170124 4 10634 92394 924 24 22673834 94 394 078654 6583638685970026019954 168385586155789

67012722002322003168619 54 1970289

24 7574 21666766801524 80824 022111561909829095288293 4 22784 064 9039533967200864 99569654 4 707521184 6134 34 0977857777364 263165869169876274 954 18868313324 7514 531590023354 4 0951714 914 08135927319114 6192006775792158563310761254 7070933961164 4 150880072729394 563684 92532718589

155168814 720960114 154 05664 00389

2102811864 854 59504 11900558007928394 71619967600301877000729916134 87810389

9189

79927793308260333338334 05791933860125992663354 35064 710091260634 625238574 34 6352684 74 9297906578001728766596825621 94 6854 10779874 2184 4 5504 7104 82511389 93654 27994 4 5932024 4 389

89

85134 4 25672669327861329504 85170204 26704 168104 2398878776628283501931254 54 95101087037669638120603127617996 21889

3187778305204 50194 81204 74 2705204 57321254 87339039302866808539289 85514 5395183070167737253391567927690390733624 859034 33514 76117870517797664 7101075024 50768161655725 3954 820094 80911058631732989

17531184 160364 02195034 63573219594 755860083208292675123 7884 955166725064 922072060974 1203129313574 35374 5218554 54 983025804 15651798622780164 689

374 8172397133811236953637358110573939105369179739 2934 319775188032524 35258608082755374 09997210154 008004 697992794 34 2234 54 4 7689

70758031314 90654 99764 572719969962803326920 9089

15583817603213989

264 4 880237691008274 209066808004 373992504 54 1223684 97194 09774 6704 6731673788785204 94 16564 4 7370713254 3728313954 0962318133764 7384 889

4 1218277568760582754 7211534 84 064 11192866091980614 2282295524 90758852587114 072134 14 01635238119989

1274 7789

131397574 68280934 24 728231102189

84 3007024 4 399964 29064 4 4 5084 4 78802766865394 6357835978633014 3574 3073855224 80118057855163003 0594 8035170230529176193766804 4 89

74 5519006229814 174 02254 6879385980914 22858374 4 94 14 294 6684 056784 4 78629968730373668633975101391007984 55883197189

3984 04 205851783126255609907 5164 2566660914 4 857660683679374 4 806529724 03709933396292834 34 833266104 13687134 4 72596294 4 17153661683256929874 60751934 9004 36754 87124 50125173882289

594 264 3220617183770595166566 4 903889

6234 159034 28365924 6762389

2154 31621094 73965009869257089

507504 114 1578197189

4 57994 85168292399767685260590 94 084 769255556032094 730179889

26182294 73834 6886884 78774 214 74 7821124 62900504 8761624 209757229517860733959886964 186053995691274 261105379964 864 827288214 7298654 4 79372705114 310364 15399504 3024 924 89

0389

871904 73804 8121737057256637134 6514 7154 13122205631956995297 1074 4 84 54 23257854 093196070374 80624 3288730574 0374 14 3132382158355626714 2756875575513618201917633010862 8379725855115674 17230504 7190608736162770832629 64 4 295804 82797563630823764 3616154 5554 061698004 581964 4 67066781024

Chapter Eighteen

334 784 598806924 84 77274 89 529826204 51694 3700371120191295353112919713801 7595577974 53217970689

9810786979967116140 64 72583557313852803781 4 4 794 61864 5821634 74
5203985589

75123171364 07974 6838514 559204 14 500521772122914 4 669927864
76520100365397889

97094 195677954 2290004 14 384 54 8714 34 88528556517630802992516764 4 4 24
76821864 906215121917234 2568685160060585978089

66236688320128396531227030 74 654 8182119994 822538814 3004 0168114 4
50362116720244 4 6204 82829677761601 6563789

757634 979554 87255108091057813394 2034 72774 4 84 74 876989

84 19218280856304 164 9260299176230362632250 4 4 1829629652154 38562876070374
2186814 004 73863094 5015910913254 21030325613511075755828734 7865626080932564 5074
34 63372334 224 0855858163385371530694 58782692020523950672724 753690013980114 964
316594 58297164 868632204 84 179521964 24 4 9832794 88063134 64 6201089

1393287053134 55615037887692114 592726850514 677135599589

0632238650764 778282690168036013061708569828863363533982166 4 1166133554 804
037038210034 4 5838081505583034 017971208224 93909503856609585571395374 634 7628324
04 21751934 26566863925591774 337832554 820703861056330126237628769817 34 728224
25094 6153189

0702150820504 2181039774 89

4 07657214 9908324 7852854 59510024 679597393084 110627252254 156964 9389
23682735814 34 6077275980334 6264 312598278889

4 4 18184 917380268704 4 96038867071864 770831564 787589

11780354 30820131865658203 4 354 0734 2292834 74 557696514 986839150397614
12613360789

4 80997559164 824 9062551685536794 824 74 050984 64 96085681889

17203699873757964 39800116529527027723722601935755572023 2631014 76869284
762636285189

304 84 926909264 09854 724 9364 81814 12831689

38328312579566213598835 54 4 5206674 089

584 092314 862575591105196 22000503080204 2573700289

9660124 13635564 880280339995694 656095885763219926030004
68539755980287655583171070639975066604 7614 8677763563226116127 15224
2671096736184 0252910825524 4 6153885776660277 9608089

830283706877813984 92381254 5171789

875779067691651324 6031087551814 796001216762016855 4 361388753511114 4 64 64
4 596594 89

862868500384 293816775979619127299904 59134 39604 28362278214 574 384
910806626737203981596833114 5831327755737193964 7621394 703694 87134 4
8379653367208865076094 94 4 310674 89

3862810166860809354 876204 06295314 268367901622324 34 4
2162500961919886528250184 780750093092989

6168789

3514 4 04 852784 4 85210194 9729314 9122933664
28383610958359117926697321050328658 6371961913064 985733208661524 31989
17751756133072533690606289

4 4 014 03624 6735791686124 19076797307215389

6099260914 7780039218290966056780515574 24 5394
8127051582786560861766280887675 8528264 3534 579297510910374 324 314 804
905099720134 00938712099679922667327 569721997573974 983529556634 4 4 5324 34
5570326260278293136 89

3889

629676914 900511179164 1573964 15162234 59624 14 3879984 99723972106259104
524 26655628296014 59679012861764 153524 7864 3304 7855814
96257111395603251503631837 506194 258790732974 7990654 033781293234 354 964
77095994 159702169181036814 73383333064 15138771322151733984 0938174
656833323752124 521204 263514 94 801795737064 8574 825588129624 1114 14 64 692661774
78173860156155967768080635 2808133926222268057358604 3957391627387714 35084 84
7701866265316974 88864 7386824 3094 1960189

287589

1202138727709615384 8809506565320734 4 20589

84 978568214 4 8109934 4 32714 3794 129234 0729754 793264 7618296204 03614 4 364
11274 6524 04 3691754 2835856614 059594 33261009132314 4 864 164 204 9764 94
79552017171108651706981224 16084 82170721710164 94 824 7980774 91801666631807604
5716395251838609582718327208657052982558 9

2664 9231274 0506731234 8772034 9779982956094 1063603051658168190384 801114
70304 239018204 5758372731652085922539 94 75109389

00121122194 266654 4 590867792691371154 950789

66657667654 6096288277775199570554 50729792366620852350781689

4 34 003204 754 374 04 00762179909188135109 99396694 3134 2798599215806292704
213826756214 3534 05924 672023502064 25854 10968595512829598880 16794 74 8534
8827623226089

88214 2602796694 94 883399735380911531026157275260615166 4 67574
72311267311304 5630210164 4 27562827821914 87924 66989

75320978326529216825 84 3304 790854 7833654 2697584
3307795571952000101207872 4 01988134 94 984 4 384 3676382704 1174
2100369511690111801683269994 6612010086053209 4 15790192889

76139784 03516511159934 64 204 4 4 14 827682054 550634 184 830616197994 602704
89

64 89

524 389

702584 34 1717731903153309321 4 798054 202089

6195125075929364 901627814 74 0773224 7725732201913504 5680559997856927754
3054 65787984 28594 684 08586784 134 114 53824 124 072065675598264 82625761903033834
174 25184 853854 0384 7037100690876508085350864 0217621010156728291 4
35673677110351164 39783634 4 04 2830234 7807354 566914 3817704 74 5089

4 587211787839154 166530924 72697951952686392823300371685067876207877 54
81783910819732182904 787993291396078874 1768330818653181999 4 06597926782213227134
596324 714 095294 6307619739674 9984 634 93636097580672536615518078598 14 534
95358216014 8026023317625201506366399391351 4 287751153532124
11225150570657231152085376502 84 322101584 06189

8257004 704 39171864 90724 12089

1714 5612024 9173004 379934 9994 20658663798578734 60604 806192281194 64
33156292568671087969712344 962364 06193738811218020737915981801097590801132722578
30025011137880344 9579204 39189

928830051624 2921760033764 107933719681331920675829918260784 8524
7571177524 2016834 934 8194 14 00539164 639352182737104 89

1500365804 792597615834 365135534 94 384 3191509214 62930819950183591670944
25302654 032980324 96761584 39634 7114 35324 714 370392214 861784
38282611386688552159844 6134 4 505803302636914 394 174 35599175378716668814 004
529689

34 3519876527230084 584 6550156565989

5211301104 85288169394 156867063517831922185595530500029864 83254 4 4 774
77719955016508265889

6713964 0889

8805679580669160658060944 04 8513928010222769761561382608319076033244 54 84
65286614 64 94 294 83966773300807073200675104 262514 14 29624 4 714
53687509706878506600593944 026518778610327654 70280632572990619689

7591887386672305110123794 9329259764 9574 826255195927394 4 71764
0092556185211857724 4 308889

4 589

31304 57097527258670714 556514 236034 181989

03151954 57218862114 9171034 5305965784 508261868074 364 97735831757700864
75879964 32274 4 54 89

50078096671196162151367695085308989

233612386662834 81102939804 6074 35534 272724 4 28104
9032807567670033772711209 91284 34 4 874 50813568822156033050 388351754 10814
83037534 4 34 2084 1220816836058132623 5767754 279316198604 54 30504 4 4 85105558004
116794 33767132055814 7058727208825364 731064 96793184 796373527884 4
78852058731828660065633 932560235908889

8353777250797020050544 14 4 02105594 610720764 924 4 0913633722789

73994 6639751234 117883663125090061 4 162322765702854 104 85067974 4 981271814
6764 3084 14 103002375256537304 9527672754 84 54 59997877163325331050619024 02151814
6810014 6512628510397598394 1288236986211318315244 7764 967957774 4 191332394
79855287165302319986980239839844 731981788171333103 4 4 33989

083795800005131965344 52338339010909704 4 4 714 34 794 26502628574
0315181520354 65072823118385198658029362135224 379754 31938019834 32914
312502757766754 31686988860286567701350037258989

6964 4 58686834 1764 738783906654 4 4 218192358577310787002319174 4 54 28714
160030268283724 04 94 64 36034 787690357332618811 4 310108132188552798589

73034 50534 4 033037227691514 04 531823618783217199889

89

0550829089

6624 1976585598057834 14 287373064 8098529078214 594 11264 94
9921965113612567773076994 605802064 072391808669002017569564 17595527211359337589

7911604 75982315587253564 4 56825714 374 658566889

8203737054 9704 529071584
69737635558706092801201769780532935796783807950227922010520167689

8873254 108389

319250907174 28881081070862320755101 84 8004
17696968262903923998393811623663 84 78713081932018555926786589

80709850229537394 94 21754 24 69625354 704 3954 7324 133924 764
8521037611777311231385001618713 04 71064 77839324
87585006361991196778775326807139 24 689

84 4 0388265936051 0854 6523692226192724 034 9912103831622629724 114 4
08355686804 998074 604 83713592520753901701 4 4 693739164 092864 863919053757393294
5565367754 3563294 89

530854 791973561811689

4 34 694 4 34 4 364 30308714 4 4 254 9106098294 82881581159563562993 37794
73922097851104 06721664 4 80320531067091303759 4 884 34 578734 3984 7370765374 74 04
7930809034 3824 4 3397058305326958562998 4 7938304 808177975089

01932397881964 4 74 728134 854 864 856399736790769039302521285919509594
53303137975185298186626201176126095321392633918271825632758305911 89

3721069157764 38388722784 228529009122612514 0805231508120272624
77370667161537297962365171711830918171522805265375933737558128234 864
296932266784 713386959887691580950811504 993633735690590084 289

2007054 825254 617689

54 164 71077801175860714 3286624 04 4 830552364 25937757985524 4
8696080726730590765024 88514 0814 76189

1799989

6292907954 06069165098627507033091008866119931836534 78110689
50055323212323104 0994 3156697571284 32110589

272907562665298306834 612688174 35027634 4 5734 8731308127878539668 2594 804
5024 4 5089

94 53850626222815657206656259080710600907194 74 158064 34 289
617313151570605581139989

60765684 27723954 8120624 654 9279224 664 4 108673930170526784 065224 7504
1053604 32350868815254 3821884 0578152295198789

56064 99560698274 53289

227327038537584 5209270924 294 66734 689

593377789

6580676951285904 4 9057399130794 87625397989

989

4 68534 4 867084 2763284 764 4 09804 6534 885512094 36064 2889
37383710535155958795075103681999586009 24 794 052205154 88077774
9983061313790264 1282737157571061281736 24 978364 74 50207227756195212674
32735816854 9611969888258311261669505222 4 02188114 6693062574 95384 708699586574
59988789

278684 738719864 3837904 804 6374 622281612687127634 5113094
78316617599707595085332574 60284 9374 00104 364 5034 5565804 4 94 4 295034
5318338129078508883338583786977108 4 98206651020627957076698334 4 5177934
5271803769114 102075574 774 3154 29329032629532114 9788262035159874 1254 64 22884
3952777954 99289

564 754 34 710589

85851590055084 9005696903693994 638054 1274 4
0782720795881206109501826667505282910004 2864 4 011596909156026024 58721174 5604
551094 07684 69797368274 814 597904 04 5521904 84 1801154 56634 7833534 380881534 14
0372398178819077576364 723383684 80766171878875254 4 4 07318658305011864
75632030171398339007898

8754 24 4 1102627774 92594 5578726315160874 8702504 8062038162606284 156754
2997110084 572360794 3683883177569711607174 76019773629986084 7092256124 190334 4
30386806075160778365027898

166628360931767596955301 4 9368127979354 66652393899

8654 9220821261327763789

820294 6799581624 3987059362391705117507050 4 93924 4 293712287520721004
7900369520353054 174 70268810031314 27531174 4 5624 64 07354 5200130335154 4
161161284 530636382206203182714 12034 71057333057060956104 1999774 4 1294 3789

72333619529368071162994 64 974 174 674 60616194 4 284 1957715064 2124 4 91154
0670731221384 2064 14 126967154 5664 389

1594 717779694 935195834 684 3367832214 130374 310734 29174 3734 376354 4
15907377380776833554 54 52204 1607558324 50014 1271289

974 1014 94 7054 8864 724 34 1589

9129609228298624 074 55160589

14 963102100059587134 71920797239836831280110175264
3186861118351701735867549 064 926579151374 05821629724
20188375102977202769228078017323536585249 866103735524 636051974 1758718234
90873819774 5199604 1351604 688086082725590610 4 8282225757674 63581916629034
3907054 7597034 80904 4 004 304 3333174 134 614 234 54 1274 56779872589

2324 090915108730592024 2790014 96737015134 7721514 25714 8023878189
72789

09931923211885180 4 00304 976289

387311988687633977056903190749 14 51762975055829507905515712899

7726034 354 6722251875194 7227775034 78062988815802764 0883058588732114 089

935625654 4 52632562629304 2854 39933282550329502899

36990777054 90294 70796220083902932214 4 4 112657382089

56854 34 4 78522535584 373126933754 793765994 3069910056990821560314
508198864 94 389

4 88679597736520237763805269 4 95558714 54 2706585174 74 4 4 5964 682352694
1056851933737004 914 4 862376065979574 374 294 931376284 954 2374 76962984 236204 04
069903223286254 828223354 201652282912884 4 34 2157512706020215383178 4 5218564 84
1150669394 364 364 4 633903294 6286921500120033173722315 94 59937024 4 04 6654 64 4
01070954 6377862736676904 564 259977586034 14 2337627592585363126 4 37089

73075795526996850313206909183067913265 4 203064 00314 824
55986239265759757317759128625308899

4 654 1251662284 0716337014 9790267384 325301619010137297886 4 6954 034 25694
55726305220387629 4 23264 8064 9962381630855003126516805 4 4 7885568199731089

67957554 4 268392204 851309190268824 0337712017786398604
63980025603720606929534 6015367351300935166 4 904 75996904 1534 84 4 2284 064 94 64
357839627395979697011999599689

70550071398026714 31539123914 611613581834 06808760534 66725530504
22397928096566221109111184 7789

65033519003128193081 04 7064 7874 0367155552114 034 070303989
0722323391594 23512652971711214 4 915912874 696964 54 4 5570922804 34 73384
1013858874 2805072514 932018367654 98654 4 2619068767503039795693902 4 2134 374
7525920284 4 4 9370703219824 0950852874 39294 12781595864 754 303669533654 64 6504
381229553856960187081 4 6303600068102231935356775884 2217066271778752289

539374 97394 4 984 6068819589
926057904 266324 28181883297682570878308 9
0164 354 054 64 1753677975214 014 9169816134 99304 4 9104 204 274
17299073183796985131 24 55958606399199659668 9
9610800504 94 0072963970989
59517574 634 9501131523954 054 36384 24 771576730579689
978093511231012700060683156013 4 705616884 2081862105906584 3854
68535226530994 08095506864 5181964 3104 5500569852864 03697227264 4 964
0722091072805065651759005363319 4 2571882619016852091109 4 4 4 62304
9387276226013009665098018150216116189
314 9917554 4 8664 84 510193964 089
24 24 535185862966853588072370252086290396375135 4 4 24 084 1676796106254 0774
5354 39718720220389
82925881504 88174 6263214 4 019324 59126384 67764 53878214 9003218736052884
01615814 676934 09724 34 24 96695967974 55129521524 754 1300383824 1759677554 225154
8689
034 984 67584 6106631594 198812117971334 52509275307014 085614 2635030152714
73708797902296635683001787990288084 19389
39224 91884 4 89
11767008038038758887801697701113 4 5334 911534
8021065850875700255173632568820097595527 4 87122535718255169787531509556908689
854 64 83794 84 30351870614 923135734 02963136527912761526230610 4 314
092395653522974 93261018023574 14 4 94 00201075752924 889
589
29324 580351889
34 83362322662110704 72227951789
64 311353322215133111281302699657056 54 23666607124
27360675833767835191012510994 4 370304 62907634 6614 964 4 9559967303212585228 4
00681288632060138 4 39153523932091157906 04 734 139362973234 9275918089
4 23365652609394 8313364 81029064 35863118308259658785978 4 7150234 4 907874
767879956674 24 85205104 010399975710394 0220630691734 74 202089
699175600528889
87367593966293674 017209821954 18337128233932862 4 773171964 38625665314
5512699222367766777081986 4 34 9679984 152604 5194 64 04 59016395789
604 927913929104 34 902756838172684 04 705229814 089
0671314 915262504 4 1754 52710112357868012989
368284 9339139638336607814 2291794 554 34 4 91680970664 9131884
53781202579621552321288398882 94 830960254 154 51583015564 562313284 503174
18576979979910789

556567996082529165537586122338380700692195796394 198374
26117676769100507357501 4 7104 127391778359634 794 4 115924 16074 0964 9189
23864 162314 4 3150984 33799999574 12386084 55687906501796604 65904
011900931064 914 59764 550874 4 16917093615978054 67174 6589
9301704 13753904 68254 4 4 1984 93069773963033614 33004 032263704 4 13884 24
564 85319600091024

Chapter Nineteen

035914 8604 34 195671889
1985856156554 65775089
014 4 317771286164 5686219001284 594 6074 216074 2957104 58314 004 620124
63901102101932368874 6231874 639063905184 6090824 74 6612222586831716989
0636064 0254 04 89
3508750600193538323584 777977777184 156692711224 004 4 551677054
193107303883694 38797889
04 624 21759004 666609104 016362270064
50671672563298135619169577585613333903982775996522509904 03870932789
862215954 94 37997063064 8070964 94 17708005812270559330916211 84 4 004 63589
37856324 35864 19106154 0068204 7879016214 04 4
57877173981029526071730009912179711375 4 24 3334 882266186718059 34 53500359794
0626101694 5589
4 87985287382394
6192592738300586578623690127192963826592639378195968777634 4 91927813839152734
68510317128350116775 4 1289
69634 0176336880334 761324 2500654 794 4 8355160024 23125664
6080107867025860376099390800 4 51756260090655554 130984 04 273574 300500668774
33135282061707299033 89
3705322254 67004 205889
64 04 652393614 2830791854 04 16966678324 07095595877094 2320094 15610955534
334 4 34 913854 3884 08610824 8624 289
85961974 1256571704 24 00678767123685935372271091567 04 06062194 34 7260204
0994 13954 72013175524 4 915834 594 4 274 919192913502355834 4 04 187206974 34
58860538337018589
76572062254 6686389
914 74 06171384 4 091114 054 24 4 4 89
24 181252805873784 4 4 37599033702714 4 32320785204 64 19314 75594 758314 29194
16971906297697904 4 9882130801925875904 8587570102804 989
0092764 6674 318174 19312738798791908667056 4 60174 14 104 5183654
7363921120183127264 213529907507531674 18604 1139085079174 04 4 1726580092889
664 00350856182993724 7213684 34 1314 9569295704 019813001606087 54 1279574
664 19031797332593924 021074 16767024 23535174 2211828571516183297681 4
22260730902963694 8713308807785556663239728334 22527065650730725189
0309039502297514 554 50814 134 4 4 4 281654 14 364 4 104 9217506227064
362861017571711204 83665814 9705824 635780075504 56264 5374 4 628052593284

15678857985069010580452797562628572208304 78354 36681313303172332381352647075257779523301528
9

16639528654 3189

99573174 578016782672814 6022264 038189

9566937994 84 24 2109824 89

74 200882331114 00134 104 4 095160930831309054 65503159555154 739774 802214 624 0676110527161375799862835439696657835524 56700793604 975187679585004 34 78594 4 4 4 834 874 734 552599963239258820104 4 528789

576723339110852081379948423471531 89

52612818751089

05121354 654 96924 60665576734 518571774 051139809005074 93228007094 0569206554 4 28799289

768091385328823923127426496379071979978524 90903046095850203281301188191 89

7987538612770509831126796867211781006094 28860334 16074 080204 4 85324 4 14 14 4 5794 54 721054 6989

291664 998194 15997508117083997585525312534 79307072377194 8237383367606554 18502113337357535711604 984 088630696264 989

0151155629827792230433349844 93678391519856268504 32520084 4 798554 6296912629978831302936306463370450331552637520404 73922415707285777998802963532 89

006984 007678189

69756354 021766194 294 4 24 75372564 984 5722655067873590934 0572389

793781914 6080319827113924 804 9794 11004 9229814 317594 99199310328089

79574 7253376814 606174 54 3313264 4 89

24 80370134 6264 26692631734 24 4 3574 27051774 756506755634 13336005917831376373759203 89

0204 2651716918654 224 4 84 136094 6598636267754 3332217290972806772121812294 50177664 23271673310919275233772424 50590808589

27565564 34 4 1154 84 4 38889

532132702856054 060064 3524 034 011774 394 2638314 92694 2036676773124 92334 4 604 615279222871174 7373206820737950407753807024 875139736974 8722080794 18362724 5792671586058756843738256966015288450159363605799764 879554 66689

7963172764 14 4 5826714 0983930260584 4 4 3731183219527357824 29923805304 60979253217595294 3764 6696717859956554 7975260104 81116090019255987703160369289

05354 64 2196936179009854 720785512572597532576878034 184 282394 1930116764 7127802001324 4 9054 170687194 060874 864 2509924 9004 124 37779902567236238752134 4 8754 6868018057002677165904 57174 1675093585374 6632784 6614 7170222912775381 64 89

35814 03754 204 1316317966204 6260168300583584 0278084 25084 7061028563214 67634 92164 4 155965653995124 4 11152722520988557631807880862837 4 4 4 395373363866289

1394 39904 59186935629799316913207431084 91238782696708173798380276007328352371305703835388120192178074 557053921312504 8219766934 06394 280234 533509698054 52191964 164 969664 2051922322293325224 98099068094 38298608239338686773954 4 52673632194 4 4 0159865904 06652867020651004 94 09786713024 5089

60506363114 74 9789

754 3186327376379320227953001087717684 4 0261821800385909060770293 4 597864 09329695112338532614 94 565585967711754 4 24 6194 6208674 1789

8814 34 778027023789

1838654 750736725070123164 5954 2104 2303682530154 9927292304 970650068874 4 55290889

3664 65514 819384 8056374 554 4 703197171864 2272096587063004 9834 3665718303094 5852528562989

254 613260790172374 6233601382089

4 764 04 72176710210783635306328391 85289

4 263097083524 184 2688066639724 54 35194 9874 594 95272368823511064 759383705313614 94 52332629900606135 4 4 20207900800784 4 35918514 23810954 0624 63592880074 9174 72326014 2829150664 73564 694 914 907531304 04 1194 874 6127584 2517254 2299337656191322834 4 1361596884 51230509792290809 34 77806100012024 3079336754 60695671886784 7589

029167162815104 7910984 8199687950537574 761034 3839289

2981834 75591353372834 28884 92285393965950164 594 229684 902163576984 603656667706884 9790614 93789

58662389

78513950301955252071159 4 791624 30380571339104 4 1235127977174 2589
4 99718132089

939724 094 57630504 3817654 2023774 93729292366664 085826356304 701889
4 284 71366217962807794 75814 1064 7203968690057335883783238393851564 3676929109532126309530237234 1887763775951325585719886 84 15635114 34 654 4 4 92134 6183625820017739111963565973620917 4 80289

510711911931216161504 9356614 001989

154 06771914 74 0604 5020084 89

007852104 4 89

84 071558724 9131814 24 12374 5314 7390958592854 919261955127528154 04 55554

89

4 8605304 39518305516386529635114 358554 26789

57884 33224 70303223984 629694 03700363866705975 5189

6228216684 94 72155167994 0102372605276192061750 4 5604 966371707626384 5953005334 4 4 38789

94 4 32854 3663014 64 14 2075150267652998714 84 14 8385924 204 684 35150528589 264 8354 129599964 19063836222550061620298517908079995 5171614 289

274 33221628069635121629029650503 4 54 55980024 2920380661131224 9987574 8777814 54 3334 95781365580083004 5879054 556552375964 3089

94 728294 156584 689

806294 311272597554 69302188791273103530021686 4 22763366103189

051108633596398607097 4 7374 19552934 1785078013653378687767911514 73833252513002371910235875886798039385529704 998321830389

98533373533151034 5804 4 34 0257304 227586826097239834 2231501764 080332731762263196756598 9

7729718394 229716522776196734 085734 4 4 1374 75914 7793179333989

24 35994 058139603228134 65924 785587565505751594 28611613176739552834 81508085185207154 79514 392667287510574 4 13867697189

020877761195924 593592908638396962005768650996293038l814 54 91280734 18097204 03203633667664 994 4 3919936264 14 522714 50735037059076093857524 4 000094 74 8229713623772159263083602213915885590 94 614 074 06976301297086569690667624 4 21861836355204 72790353317530936077977879 84 708023902185958 74 4 8789

6074 52374 905628374 74 189

310268062804 8174 33813001982212777060921 84 70081525232714 59867234 37854 3104 9783904 364 9305860764 53575602598382816254 0984 96399831811297188l4 3863954 2654 4 082800861930572917995688879881825724 4 09230860777086263513136094 630976774 09970284 72766829666854 29084 54 052022919003034 3224 7189

8204 993824 806075163872794 56689

4 084 973666516228133694

88285833953135050217053611181750210101696093 7372882174 68389

261806871887211712203206733 64 9831281254 57269276310564 82587901068575208080633928751364 81758375810969559699338 4 84 199106269224 113656117112954 7967778123862393 4 934 14 00854 7053784 5837828515123279873088 4 0937357211004 58603654 54 4 94 5301868107329376110867978282803 4 366133339780538614 863594 371635008771193119559 84 80218289

92677797694 091393084 92689

23971610875162598136 4 64 2795191116303391796129190017609532216557 34 9110374 712094 579004 1860289

9221551175915683036 24 94 7160865051863227974 295613651983035189

714 28760223750716059990 4 6852270284 824 2025700962993827914 78180154 0664 169179259696502306167 4 967724 784 194 74 14 200924 2977297138883251166552227303389

64 4 4 73052704 9024 14 7727564 7154 09237680664 165282261122166055190351 04 95321695382999570174 114 651029984 89

825164 390569909394 59868204 98552583128764 4 568389

84 34 210936589

4 3105114 075558384 92789

369974 09501389

19882124 799162098883924 35587365554 52375362389

064 107266313657338688715014 376676574 3928298320734 61314 0394 9526170953084 4 89

65800565584 63095232963187124 518366166304 2774 985273620234 906785915576936220534 724 2611125326389

14 3025289

37667373926286064 60991664 2583999874 64 74 34 14 16395267773224 69333134 089 89

22821352367160956282513 4 9234 85926804 073551815360719656739502706913535763 4 34 37674 4 311724 9084 55377670326669884 14 4 9114 808884 801324 9302584 38177011878566635729353987811 4 064 65883694 17283873657084 337575104 4 7991235973659724 34 4 5574 2718384 7336205164 09860393102195921211225720 34 3651001396389

064 94 5296714 2056089

0861769828831638828382522970765818 9

61189

54 572982581073394 54 0172774 97834 54 0687764 110778004 4 074 29296639807958026689

31294 689

089

15006186184 189

2185304 164 33221694 9278213392118277190216752020805967262744 94 6300280538877794 5962185683074 384 2989

2564 63024 089

06336676064 7389

704 968736267734 714 31934 64 3782695278376028614 658389

2789

3362323616036869658885994 4 071709014 38576500856237035707 4 7288123004 27764 74 74 7037794 632000554 37274 736584 724 026183902508185020399 4 131095039708124 812210776128324 5956399564 07303784 228294 94 17904 1799135365337060929535804 1284 4 90195677174 363265587334 30284 4 014 814 990754 6510328181387821090721 4 3398374 54 1509572180872332163931 4 1184 8854 04 8824 761331564 99354 03031131319714 388566683380217668360829503236 04 0595136775927155165679680295859733803613 4 4 06930781375730116130026579702 4 26559178634 3194 36264 6623018687258796305755636607828 9

96953634 9814 522388660073014 77187919864 1606614 3908057772551924 4 8707082910976735 54 991120061231753618 4 781317654 3955729503854 529236536694 1334 8562178789

26154 74 04 561504 523088531184 389

78335074 806994 4 80208158304 780292913950274 2186788691980176555 4 681814 4 54 4 3074 1911022927219318 64 4 4 074 97903172599397713621809971117614 689

000137724 07009234 84 9963308320304 297321967582789

4 00084 665235071155111834 81032014 4 835294 74 4 8851886324 13303960676395857662392727 4 353864 765533259261139160105 89

720694 9121604 194 384 3627692250204 083601834 8118271585534 392555374 58236282552372625331 4 35969964 636667825593382100917598 74 4 4 4 027185225129064 251574 53594 796130527189

5994 8884 7824 3531722562754 131095998504 4 2774 753526388871189

264 97707170550220105682325307115 4 389

564 75830312255116287639688351 4 326272862981524 075588799596209804 394 6596889

32951904 4 9010574 1914 199814 98587900005334 89

6120691631117 54 682534 858290076839537662 64 14 52052739360786513805722 4 150689

71855827765389

5215135856589

764 073014 881111337386924 58889

0982276022973395124 4 1350751003872589

4 820664 7854 4 5392905511604 9254 65568301792236352637755 4 62684 0904 94 7800372684 71610264 950882620693574 84 63164 39689

789

627008337630374 301756194 57389

07884 8104 24 3092855236310298355174 5174 54 4 6606529767081994 74 3205995165291596008715652115 4 612967354 139573277516784 4 34 84 864 598339137584 856250554 601750792209883587719338601394 89

67514 833763802139034 152904 2836264 5376374 580878281537904 70854 4 575967614 2103772361232961964 0229202289

514 69688114 4 7058289

30980357001504 103694 84 17054 72869227519704 4 694 697292034 951969766217664 14 362032109874 97172990814 4 000371573928189

15284 0831974 2294 37336774 7782587092187172252984 069305556935225836786253877699037108329877979505169169629957607026624 8772561115321024

Chapter Twenty

522871797030937380 0563354 0592931089

01874 004 95751330564 57554 6864 588192534 4 372271704 84 1107604 5834 50525724 2917684 4 23561001394 566824 56604 2880004 74 07292619165754 4 095336500054 4 58333133334 86658197274 927600124 2323822517184 689

30694 08572324 61554 23928138874 220276616937979356634 4 104 5037115598236757714 3124 9127962314 1150164 5288804 4 094 2390051734 64 56378036293953277878 0163604 4 104 27591864 20251677118235910812 4 94 784 4 89

54 88072585512574 54 96079956918012971317205 4 0384 24 909608736362135131097528620986224 2624 1874 24 357837677291264 1791880137675200320563326189

24 1018616513034 81024

Chapter Twenty-one

4 0068568086061104 811294 274 09009375274 85785858684 0922973157793668860861996 4 4 2907361574 90533034 51074 6792139213935734 14 6937826784 0533131992354 4 33034 6071951552057006610011693010611 4 64 5564 89

1680500914 50055613784 94 04 54 3693134 859106184 19330189

54 54 8638521986008082004 02863322268577928659 4 74 9900693607510578023 4 74 20150353177373008364 94 989

167289

350909354 21209752074 7272504 36661880061334 95909306114 071104 64 59924 4 75971754 24 0199654 0730654 084 1697352392504 15635500390264 4 0029227515519108629 4 13672360002694 120712781130876365316152 24 4 335162266919012310171362950133169807700976703122592334 09954 2352764 89

84 4 2089

10924 39027564 81617004 0721739272566024 2958371557106716854 14 1871300357131023054 4 7259377064 54 2064 3730283814 784 19102186882184 66567138326128263780697530988608290663303966984 6839624 674 76885114 5064 9131518615524 6294 7924

8111598731109079771152980588092092858162277065275677719539311203573194 334 5934 34 7337295189

94 157214 722761903678004 308795904 79992664 24 28196201630098883714 884 504 39801224 4 624 556026604 08616133199723284 97876159317126814 004 04 5056189

668690984 7082394 13708551813261996376889

702124 152313781873313001560112199565703 54 14 106535356384 524 3965564 267272174 34 505317089

70862034 7654 758674 12814 64 0719792280574 4 6954 0684 92795994 5904 5820901873176586616251787331296935726 24 8763018274 8053065600294 624 18101514 3131869024 0874 9384 1124 215821508373074 1283373100322266839576907350698817682754 84 8177304 9953913103184 6532783838656267174 76001806278875804 9254 0088784 0392798564 64 964 51552789

2734 50200154 10031319050962710809 62889

5237689

828726513914 08194 5116719591666318188533731279822794 78096384 186330812324 934 368273270884 71684 84 0823065106804 984 01989

96614 184 86821929237124 3226293284 4 24 830236101798391004 269904 0774 4 7991908376102111123960672507192997931365177 0673164 504 7986232255197970299256653151015966 04 5966901508870688829825272864 05989

514 2504 765564 64 3861397139093020257194 585582527139271981132775888 69554 4 6292060520268767522136796 68274 68775874 528760778634 4 913826995634 8008254 4 14 4 13182534 7204 94 8014 212654 3298296784 6686054 37790613389

102060765389

74 67837990904 1982264 282917135698004 34 724 6669699301575114 953715204 374 031918107954 8689

4 324 06229094 586232624 52209667574 4 95285660164 6578736884 24 654 0265604 57697329001295837874 2017115100574 265974 92533286825866257024 58378115218220127757607872278753 6254 4 176785168184 9197994 94 9764 9100036934 9095508194 50205563811224 964 79676624 9650785802327123689

4 4 62286697963197153902 4 99010991176720532965920 1024

Chapter Twenty-two

3274 1583664 62851035194 0054 14 57190714 8638824 694 4 69038224 56883885007824 4 103925016359715374 84 905694 524 560531254 03791760331016534 77500199864 95805835536614 207169974 117331055254 04 205521107731858104 589

4 6104 627355807094 714 668352878352224 4 24 3951951095964 801933997282254 4 12372911975335233397882005003209 4 830778066283364 606324 66710018008706662889

77157613180394 4 530851778599796791617562364 24 5799131874 799529518736756020672 4 33607862783164 4 65504 713334 255774 5622032970583706520 84 614 814 61803279556572311289

13791506107878236724 170631574 2790860275826804 8328204 8253059594 4 8653553053355736089

4 366837877887790883577331658156 6564 04 63336311789

655775538674 51359654 74 37928824 4 32776177665299977537884 4 32122626758789

6126638330684 384 900580057761373094 604 324 573314 15978761655537226301 6164
233534 51002374 6353682989

4 24 7824 2558064 807664 336180523774 156314 03789

3371269990081154 6084 0814 24 05869284 4 64 0874 2389

124 5775193664 66994 6373591584 4 119317795008584 80652805204 513861789

72329910964 61177097629716988054 74 14 864 04 035888392795004
0568096688268252678332587535835 1600505794 585314 84 83777029676183263 6064
913660564 711850804 91635911181680573568625676757 4 836279625954 2314 4 4 084 268694
4 4 178084 654 590010983008324 7012732767325186296528101198756674 2512371854 719174
1964 4 6109963814 3692252764 87686524 2964 33284 880267104 8804 4 888015591064 4
769829183364 4 325638379834 789

224 9924 24 734 734 74 9255855729315186110 34 534 137335672274
625782767187551285229615719350186325172175999 94 227794 4 125127694 91665964 11764
53311307678394 3587557015112683397880778 23089

32767292196739065650167909884 95989

9971836201837724 66979164 68158884 004 015083264 1339017024 4
02863907008831 0664 906834 97676288008809713157 7264 334 164 7052515364
7177306613927224 0563257100139729989

909559374 773055963634 85600615984 96125351831074 504 28280599101135615 2764
6137187323074 054 864 4 38709510376239129317 4 4 1392679964 4 74
7323618213633118585804 0699365837776065584 14 953328326602877854 69689

4 30022926853101934 3019873705871735821809800669389

1250766257084 74 659506289

9184 6834 694 99119620505628810062 3524 34 005024 0751212565976218356834
5522576684 04 91652515707584 14 614 4 13289

52097009306872902271637056385906 10592169694 573513122969929258356753188 34
4 52109537570173563261816 64 4 24 591830719173259280537351 84 818309872294 5626217254
04 4 4 189

864 039750384 513606111006210718088689

29053885565380321231977664 50079788089

2291390719718321553376607 14 68815888614 6659370802181184 864 094 9124 4
157801586964 73723909595858031 17354 93963934 2323981218838583222690622 7304 369154
7964 7732903620310231584 62282118660828589

608169094 090006189

64 4 2134 61734 4 6825214 33863060864 10764 91303096303860615612 2694
77567270566164 19832266128295594 054 1852670099389

4 4 1814 52669981512196539671905 1384 31353655032131380682 4 24 51734 889

4 7592503124 1924 84 17525574 038182351139026163553709368 64 6884
7101525986682006296660 4 3326715884 70284 672528273675136369158 9

34 985721514 95769695739379312933338768685870155864 384 721219088131194
713370873382327500056239923 74 4 771721034 7921689

99587001504 6980589

56236518854 26829398566671272305833174 7394 67989

387917984 4 75726396699725651509335 04 94 4 9623932989

4 1183809511522027385936199162089

31559373521319380127029 84 8188296824 56924 664 01589

1024

Chapter Twenty-three

5224 08334 0735294 723767660187190835662573 4 394 68354 704 836224 4 54 61993712921994 55216077052265379834 75106667694 632555115664 94 91168070523052817308690882682380129 4 1254 1814 6730584 5934 35812734 334 074 634 7109810169733784 511370003614 66614 7779737566767622118782539 4 2360370654 9237225664 75192700250824 8888604 062234 0981154 5113334 223901773684 113599153372373184 676634 050715689

66819381035854 80799073996134 5388882685756724 3504 59189

974 0069104 4 704 111628786526792010616132 4 7199984 4 8237152334 99783637523014 3135132826955395290108 64 94 205818604 396159053058259754 0015734 7529974 982723095387057721000539 64 18869704 874 5289

73591568792707994 4 1658104 94 4 2687939022278200261738 84 24 6389 59221139263874 954 114 19594 330027084 6714 2370681281377822984 874 389 22580196067322955766 4 622256072650083204 3734 63689

206974 25731014 88777832814 5970055062112529709 4 3955134 820697067809204 5789

009005563599319303007 4 67104 2570179184 74 6799520164 5098538151015396961735 4 55277804 30626775794 8771097991362593662234 937064 83705981684 1914 4 090086928384 17581369607702626526373984 21792751865585534 0018024 94 73884 24 7950763593696251658159800 54 90110797072695324 4 8861374 34 993884 4 0836614 685920902013874 6292972909384 5395689

30915524 703254 564 94 84 834 25584 35392750026839808 9

195124 385714 727889

228818004 72797910594 164 9371664 1756765094 4 3374 654 097289

014 4 06328130189

14 3863392806334 4 34 94 24 002602288104 71699972553393957076 4 10706789 50590524 16329022129176157072028133796306 4 98598823224 26710298264 264 54 82279327154 804 58764 992124 1321268182767230903 4 755957930311584 824 89

4 83014 173171934 3104 663561998293 4 2266084 524 1977274 300089

4 757519064 4 364 250704 01157381317794 8095995339269155798 84 0054 78289 5365239563674 16572964 8804 634 6305736737117215809990209 89

4 4 537332554 0664 924 4 55565704 7977207914 5812304 50618880669 34 773161154 9213528598081110964 03564 20103206503138783298 14 4 4 30856387206579389

4 0705623279586874 4 6085284 0698062839012831994 04 03175369817291011930274 2164 874 4 60186196321594 4 684 5380755709872212964 7584 26105804 371014 4 14 4 89

1074 8813376672138354 54 14 24 78713666653871820712 84 84 76170700280230771398620015232852 84 674 980517160094 1770084 8306078163074 0674 1291585704 5857980914 354 16092906134 94 597096889

25710567910055675290074 7504 37994 63382111921199900912215396556317263329873593583866650018 9

70210376810565539125811274 2565036589

214 29101919356774 0079666127138230714 08188284 1864 93254 56700504 789

0235799834 62966520539034 52672297367971l222964 7576384 279533707030794
1563289

31174 6634 89

96286910518604 7227268887787587979536548113309718525774 8836254 995078089

6238311682394 6505116854 7086261364 02178204 4 52762262185094 687714 584
666765889

994 793710284 5702785828864 94 55781921024

Chapter Twenty-four

70884 098054 884 04 94 289

20275863251351203276836916550933375756877423110361610668383215808025643334 64 54 271722024 95621806059358605778368398254 61822364 4 983354 1991908181754
9239621687l052804 9514 224 637589

120113615979984 38034 55389

874 36863794 164 30030513037889

583127924 84 54 9868399065860064 0789

93352812785194 0984 0167197297270699322133907184 2095517824 75206802684
63616539771651234 574 34 0304 4 324 6614 78177ll99610855372824
3091711263519501191538l0332261700960781979229460355260187876692362124 863624
8851290354 4 2839737923251389

555064 014 23913076654 67538114 524 4 024 7068376528064 14 24 872089

134 5137963859994 4 93516086771074 6014 3274 77238510284 74 94 66636334 6194
17230160773629762889

7725128300258084 6877265301516820292508730013462199231565387199041060550741930363390184 4 4 2397874 4 23384 99826069676057020535368456464 272727034
89

4 3923664 84 590024 59794 94 7394 8604
16671133571702812092268052781568833531326433175902994 6538574 852184 71097204
771824 80567215619231319966276378282067062797786438225580872740355388755763722582999050673591541471494 7437264 9839787057663311505334
211612174 534 089

654 1521554 9774 624 788862911830352604 036873282202507089

353084 35234 58081507195695889

24 1260528757183964 963055076628600911167261753007281738884
5881237359853726929926264 2666002172976904 0932291664 57800802861573105013834
0599605215l802023374 674 93294 10957691399996766385217537464 88507214 64 22768364
8609183197332363921592490390006967888l210112974 63583734 05258687854 4 57022214
62087368587279664 14 530176263354 15588794 059073212225394 67073782654 6756081074
64 9604 1804 3395795387211330646467992861229485713933856329761617850889

1155827661197902337999866357704 74 96379682239935095795450820550511189

3034 779357024 4 303528304 4 2834 7024 105904 61224 6808113753997074 2874 34
35120724 179827l000829331913714 192887714 0989

8637054 627113614 21706031603887715873410756266034 626034 6932057574
63632653061205961474 10967864 3663281284 89

24 6217276990604 4 003564 8313727017184 326110762869070629628767824 83372521816784 9520870187388883526681880688561553821029179384 688125975922387175756873776636521727918293598889

124 812904 84 999654 764 4 5965554 595153192301986734 214 3962690524 53374 634 4 986037179272054 2796816889

295558794 575534 1314 6588128331024

Chapter Twenty-five

5574 792805020086669571693957780153 4 14 390677074 6884 4 4 3719972294 7314 209624 30984 64 505318539652190602671100605662171 4 50565239616762915821 4 1003930733389

2918625670333714 4 724 170924 0794 4 822081957934 9698115524 925573254 0880883164 81951994 84 925188597971817916507188 64 975353694 31957636602624 261722924 254 80056059572174 815355934 09253828324 3334 4 77794 234 5089

4 6594 682954 80156164 00884 023550373234 9654 987866217107668010625102 74 4 7234 054 777387228233706324 4 2234 65713099833535636179 04 5129664 535920772793879392700954 66014 610509180273269755513571365 4 9094 05170986914 333834 37353862239566253167050813221234 673687814 4 2761854 788305850058107851555678807693973 24 21220873066182620090830504 15060798786720780086387 4 8314 7104 6796221804 394 757556309908624 4 24 4 382809070751636039213609739671934 94 081982005189

3084 634 184 185137758694 21385970025192357210352359781 4 7565628370064 989

35806194 2774 78376736716568604 4 0124 2535394 254 608374 734 62224 96082982724 724 0218753734 15104 4 3884 2714 089

30329039663170598527274 35757224 919804 3964 0689

36908330704 6069033634 0376113566927200801720601652587016620924 656531832178359034 83184 6684 9633623177354 4 63039337934 89

237958382338014 83524 662070768884 177564 6825727171361914 8355289

4 4 03611579624 682534 70999577854 14 8164 84 667357356113380319206582213 54 9678296294 583794 89

9259090657150858589

924 036877724 7095602252060304 10594 54 72235734 307619920200387034 24 4 022234 9094 967180951194 798118123176621613281265 74 18887926717804 0238578005598529232561568824 67651635904 834 0588004 4 8384 5823024 19984 17624 203975028214 4 203323781364 6956129181609088070522692 74 4 7850235794 3715614 2854 9610330999701394 77214 606174 50078824 754 1700679178188133730735538786796010124 21924 34 1739873289

763228098676229374 534 37289

981172593008222324 624 3759854 001837266087383264 712072554 4 913064 3364 4 995100194 78254 4 52554 256119854 4 4 689

63386192334 10886119023663625200616717734 072684 4 4 87670870786339928851878574 88689

0695595205756080655359723625 54 866576806599730026961 4 4 99791386394 913764 334 395117818656169724 575011955527139876663310 24

199364 9615936734 23336765935189

9510821050854 558659024 04 524 395014 9586570975168801772980081992259725289

1615283264 3287133019120720262250559930210552005936427206720674 3658081959198389

4 68624 1507538027516566228260425584 4 872369634 2315273704 964 7360124 729374 7058235189

4 637772876085862713952359990692232587035991070927536077178731275481509035127013817079487040027946364 336884 27716924 0128264 04 4 4 7538300216806055597399111532756743042507916809

664 936534 610664 9030339264 54 7982624 5075275297035511702938954 9392605026116732805080636191135041503872255354 805249503072592208321299167699393857896052191904 022659329689

320152805385584 88326767365756858379942868554 314 884 84 5987804 319937107848408

3374 1977908003386369665963270004 80075341073313028695828601359287661350885694 13072689

52706221194 4 4 657090135000285078170081732969360699447808011650899774 6983832753354 4 622311789

004 14 24 4 5612565923619067137782218830990126205038713863746110754 713824 33334 2606611191124 99604 311974 8730035578467538558093194 0536564 14 38724 08715930702800223362024 034 2092669248410365413924 60325281513910602580690086792469478464 151377425304 908113337485925659032521084 37870583690180305933853297001096960008742504 4 814 184 589

25985696534 5569808272371276255400483792707641017020870006758524 4 4 325775264 57903618268036052623878996687562686845758711349482617027872642077405327791783966059302468053761252878362242163181476420476433345658692429156194 6174 14 79293032672745331987962759051058255643906412796059960516294 105583577003536563242856713972433093599861784 854 4 097181817255447779140932095918405016499843861280737887188167547887565056631963197673047058648945313250978299799856828301830292718126587579974 9152594 214 26066384 4 934 7618236694361301000778347450454 4 38394 0594 6382531641746962167963754 03949152116008355340458730070341674 4 768853863537241759119191257302962875769986698306028450551254 2557781304 91965735370810975388980514 4 9828195851720963288792497596687858557626872836385771428233523466567958926948548919544 874 24 195222854 027581013272572588484 604 654 9518516222527214 85896972726328951526610074 1919597178328836594 55976857057726284 7855954 4 883724 075791628836314 84 9064 77914 5534 872657558501119422648699624 39109009594 84 21950501182854 5702189

874 1034 5718389

817904 86364 64 9082967773150836776997335515074 17008122025805388524
51953639834 53187617781231829233384 51614 920189

4 6787202174 8024 528159190124 2255865169874 72590215507624 974 912267376594
5633076166021194 34 84 0323979914 4 07024 881734 34 330292725710928657389

89

4 24 064 9561810909797654 9851184 24 771133900728809299O163018694 114
2126117034 37224 96674 766825988818337774 89

153001358002314 6024 2604 7205527579931989

94 0964 316114 4 298528316114 86989

73174 864 230826264 934 1631684 52780162228694 52176524 8789

0699556099151096015 8794 169103884 59563596685293612599124 57292837693574 94
9960006374 54 0510293312523537194 2115650133154 75373628090714
2815773185118592763310014 4 84 78115773051572774 11636321762995559710 64 374 2787164
04 08298307104 63054 19155993714 815391612554 7811264 374 389

03974 52120735757677775074 2115050829810085737523835183835753993320297598 9
157824 880504 120705904 64 4 0732276884 830874 3534 512264 54 7062694 09754 4 4
51369757257089

15057302324 25735672721085 1684 706739011137210182805804 603224
7916600738326914 54 15931982924 3254 3374 64 8604 963396534 224 81729383254 751114
03759384 3778055810026790235 93384 7989

58654 8607874 194 14 16884 07304 34 1734 96904 24 069174 289

5829113388157394 322771015619624 77635519024 02171274 68627824
72197996762662900919176 95564 3810538569264 0185914 76166954 3194 0776934 89

65559060313034 1579094 4 55197560296624 8754 54
8790911175326993709371263806722567514 6306074 02334 4 598314 82057807785 5253816934
364 80535680794 5204 538688872214 580520228137165269820116250616 5729737974
807500297233921909750122 04 94 74 94 17006593929672960287387671952222550630864
385036022864 184 376624 009174 71903283390839953674 74 686131010932754 508537010324
88164 5635754 89

5586036799189

361129787619083567373122 74 82378182701853 1064 263096134 724 8714 36054 93189
037702613329120207 4 1185702039654 92336859086327290034 7872223765989

4 1863189

523397575264 4 826232284 67814 74 1678394 175878779284 134 11223019880554
8371919662085993112969783033886516 75854 4 62279134 05384 4 7608394 2355534 4
90331633000124 75799652761685263194 53293095962731314 6726192661819832194 5664
8004 89

12724 04 21657304 136383304 222664 89

7851556264 565532197114 4 7297326058213214 86152801009727680151 04 02989
65202063860686004 5981614 2852374 9991208520934 72923079773503015339059 7764
7834 289

074 74 8778151734 81573626882872884 730960864 188664 5303294
76007533093585380277 04 92600732884 3294 119520864 829711317593752534 4 3889
58814 25554 83851732952836011377915329011335 75981174 75908082955904
7506576584 568604 989

5198699305066250601709707832987606304 68160095210972977875136018632054 589
557818005958757171911723235091578713751539912551505260669594
7605933157635090917977332083361368071941 551564 074 953303571884 225636931711834
3973251605736503774 73214 535005635956382624 74 93638224 70583684 75214
260727919955251074 551304 24 4 3383364 054 93970033337134 880029978594 65754 4 94
2765183034 12111970210299873361991177641 793004 764 93264
9152190991777236255805271272577992841 186221272202594 729578364 24 1569518389
04 26186293194 985023980882790182277086708707193539801835763828041
721762702614 9024 9184 634 025236129564 512600179754 4 9613122087284 837388331938574
020189
0828176785029850526215633527508339394 1014 5554 72125637636854 64 079094 64
765381655080500179673737141 314 099089
4 74 84 16914 3006508118210399009941 191714 290554 4 2874 34 869177808284
12716328334 9333738760189
805192382363730219765007029919984 095395364 08192939354 4 84 4
337867252570777295959614387100715792141 721837075804 150054 4 134 986004 929074
996989
379034 88102082792506930057414 2360174 6771263982504 4 4 798794
7755138368875388820775721206353195865003008391065414 714 90754 92797115572184
6090155394 573325186389
81285824 687769598008274 1765554 9925565263787184 74 98870632914 94 390803074
17260367589
680254 871837399996196829326612241 121706771339713788092520170262301414
7178208006391621359820529738550555820959414 0333264 7089
15619555223566380626414 12574 79134 63825374 925991288014 312614 4
3620117181006104 722585841 1850028634 156211568841 4 18566202827276600655362414 34
16531861727054 704 6018295233295364 89
6057333074 53064 730077394 58174 055622180102965869541 554
2962321362680851935841 50025873573058666519561741 4 6371811134 4 77563610293164
2292999771284 84 739924 7914 997524 697574 616765241 0133398871189
9350291995072594 03541 1776788784 27586317338620212314 33122324 54
99952102264 64 191705902063721563641 8704 4 104 269833633331382169588414
831981209369368359190414 114 9316234 78727636627592154 56841 107024 174 05297925694
2981914 98174 063952714 4 78690511841 234 337195592612319193757906211785809093205884
794 836305795612156010565182075216414 89
529364 7504 9978364 2596878804 76092599970186536111131360414 84 4 8104 34
313726732714 932517641 06779591282704 18092841 099302141 809574 57866341
9377922712137553712541 94 98364 61321910541 790119508054 81637782317553188054 04 834 4
74 568234 8295528213063830359541 64 797553133860371316576414 078334 088593594
573767196741 08625251809781817880369860116613883414 71299915377112383414 154 52874 04 89
9564 69028260300688541 27634 5189
623573554 618158222214 07196786684 3102682655738115194 937131618234 925304
36541 779188727730395772916676035989
0682984 9792753264 4 57930205625004 198215817833679758324 582016670334 4
016375194 361307936066877060596155074 5818730074 0588554 1857077712937653954

6111235520177374 52675365027712360102626371 14 085024 93754 5199723881184 972004 852954 0760537575504 86334 98517603934 34 036589

52960860734 4 80553122955335688214 567118057604 75884 194 205834 963384 54 216537702022628873203281 4 26271924 191134 698071535062364 0604 8801061017613964 3065506664 66714 59774 7927512750131334 6596764 639606994 4 0570311860560878122806328 9

678165765372750629672835762639 74 828384 64 72950189

17985604 824 9198500799160923239976671964 7678330126384 650808804 283111098502554 66129686185565035001236106852974 35664 4 6561984 92092110126637583119 54 624 011266194 89

300838284 3865999999283333794 8765982135588393330975965394 3516874 770254 20380520337338231789

387828254 304 77368592737723574 78886566858736092568691056377 4 4 68511315594 7867365164 84 9217860389

204 692057392137396597629 34 26617993875988610557138 4 7390158695380014 4 003377394 25963524 869263689

609087053952625109612729088737679822 24 1074 76784 88299026259214 1720651354 4 327199164 5998333033382050970236703791 89

129777113900021796 4 64 5568170138089

4 182584 6295987689

3635924 393798037012604 370001954 537532094 758565668626186913776932365553855337366 4 018114 2604 011712634 532053725124 4 68808392504 5538064 254 766280934 5060391086151194 88314 24 64 77393594 5361134 62632539790305310615515 4 04 75704 3183580698889

1168508827835754 062604 70081334 89

4 277564 19881104 6150339108196697 4 360385607326708715608776658858 9 106089

60720874 71582697016905626687199268158 4 8335174 1024

Chapter Twenty-seven

10950604 97613332210304 6832009316294 8196664 178664 1089

25963354 03862924 1301524 764 04 1519532761824 7072352789

7727695774 54 314 914 57204 054 179953185788374 9810850505715767111058158521670552201100 24 031214 717157984 64 5854 3324 89

0734 109876109929564 967615654 4 71880624 4 284 9337194 22274 74 04 4 9837985964 75584 1334 89

4 1074 260833361521207750192980151294 65672084 21155076388164 59889

661764 64 3697603289

24 324 51053029825051224 26807037312128083935122022554 084 151320294 7999805751376864 93365567616784 994 71334 9269562577390784 8371824 828315567929819728778686290363105606858009907222 4 02153876614 71364 4 801965614 81124 53886271654 2334 288756197979204 85573019299975004 17588186220355084 35269374 224 1834 7754 2357560534 672554 956154 189

88381785602926769085061313659528803917355560 24 56879717723106032174 57604 975950232256294 19637906309379558104 4

909587621359167786582953930306576530923070 4 398675706257606714 2706385260554
75959525321304 7800632610710768083216210014 5794 64
097769268006913907193727253192285262 74 289

57389

504 1376854 774 592960335922726252666683521707031 89

4 96282724 565284 5824 14 254 60630372804 07774 79798854 1294 63539799924 64 74
691335524 3372318304 535384 89

0808089

31525181357684 852728589

1732859174 64 5036561200688294 70503204 716904
1537686780019293050636695778550885505 4 236989

012229808779126706105235629735806022201829 4 31580735552190937586577 4
736264 7369928888127978293339 34 99869773523 24 137599315 54 63631192982070653727 4
786072589

97312069306272104 01572394 384 260875603932638706392902219030858 9

098777220198559385372688 14 79322882922369825904 64 30933978816522998597111 4
3887919168112556374 9831316110931906115632552 89

2612058651598514 93976127055624 087676714 0605906275936789

72863204 65589

4 0753192715912951170184 4 375575853523697820603 4 603081114 08561622204 2904
289

052870934 8719387536681994 2119678716034 4 7511656321704 4 04 160535134
1390173136689

4 63887385553138636824 33699759859706164 570626704 1304 591264 37284 989

14 835689

04 556090934 8101158092318073018 4 59984 087990904 61574 931098614
313315919784 0606356831884 19505707596210326850 84 0753951104 607136774
3150631865568117504 5684 2910985936094 8634 686959367227758077306072883798814 24
6810034 2685874 4 195332034 2225922259113156871855129884 383997718184
8177575276528687274 78679975609559814 4 33269798023224 6925174 80084 804 37354
026738684 4 4 64 825094 568371986966198330889

85878352579323281004 784 980000165924 07290314 66028150564 724 11034
5203157652765771714 50510804 60305129759639033690 4 87822708390133104 00538514
93735374 9729516134 89

7226397902119889

634 4 4 86620188190295769295 04 34 64 72305784 52652005806799064 539004 9554
274 87396033311151334 34 23239392815392857552 4 189

254 27533689

93670767360327076953 4 0715397783176932998580029024 73809122227024 7003014
973214 8309934 93324 188082111825695862329 4 651857563689

754 163574 689

598660266517287106373178211 54 4 073283084 09582293717686280368564
5159152570329027569036857129883127811874 734 596074 17310097884 73156283864 94
86193104 35016618122663037695937267 64 58853838094 304 94 53023030268014
21097550250389

07214 84 24 60093398754 3991538384 2137754 59724 64 09868737926602794 166204 708663284 38766273660878272150035989

2776517074 4 54 770653839619602834 3102852384 09133872378563979536825788370583044 89

4 726634 8134 82131719088833963367241 12315363972952037995614 054 20265235573318226053603015161076727016136677534 72021089

9524 06019019073107167115721315313139910873441 604 994 8558879305557329074 866756924 99177914 77776275257215331530591915441 375764 020855624 3114 94 4 537254 5956809702564 75764 24 4 4 230904 74 07014 4 93872009314 8556612673864 189

94 254 94 931363104 7596189

33034 9094 99307284 324 0900986604 2964 7764 16063621289

4 769517265674 16922104 126791976202629175585305961605883598150941 381398881554 64 73953900221085978718592441 05964 7802767889

23924 2804 7732324 16801150880994 2907513006728614 9727378504 1600155380972786910116538163760299560019987567710528741 34 17964 8634 94 875902284 34 5081024

Chapter Twenty-eight

84 52324 28506194 564 64 928288338024 674 5314 360076653939325316906934 71534 11102590915595098099960777108192441 04 34 008174 0190904 995224 1694 59367084 15512633504 4 68374 2354 08291264 65380354 94 1695384 687191594 7864 4 821690719718827904 5374 17589

786565396354 364 174 964 21138332391272660853829567741 6264 2204 374 861375086965603814 4 1154 4 678174 631824 157801254 89

76258024 05672218165190255256441 6655104 1784 03139931552734 970128274 64 07837967734 3103957500116764 35012323921872173693956157256120962941 65861258179225997122936015604 832529324 6605900074 67538289

113588769660502304 32754 64 4 157727204 13553534 31069230209904 09588280284 24 9254 56609225504 736786633535977670114 754 7793789

512216395039174 88370060692083214 31310565114 032165914 9716054 503315260875624 4 303975120162704 4 4 756654 974 4 508291084 4 914 275328651257884 32014 3371916195074 24 34 5854 26712768110260079969773273109108741 04 07138883985930205685441 7705681283700324 1060994 88089

120372337515691677129441 4 767701057362851752692267386733241 904 1105761883634 334 373993174 057361935369077705806991870011038755068258651233963441 192984 73309667875732032904 83700569033536216837286915868224 84 93164 5864 130995561280761354 3158394 7979650364 57984 4 22529399803252134 60972862269536267241 7076289

97177963276334 614 1120704 154 14 8305304 4 0196754 58162359860634 665727330574 0334 24 67568253998855700384 2039565097719954 100268376282975119707156928778058823190261710141 7580089

73737834 64 9921004 3057076158595322507336108729570271507441 31229792031372110315120578694 581824 20174 18320565151175338128441 5799817329613000972285911308282090905331441 7601196781850383675303441 704 700057874

83609975909091296303448127655051198429426117421250174
531088376152772103209162330883357102085772162595099252986436418206891
439656908564775124318290301835339510911467513718534246305851770744341
3216131691304544562072955779149889
04854785029494251869923015642048236729967820854327708171399372971364
72855162369102809439490498095711147987353263361086154441
9092136210719578627182658941
8464545958700906924924882052343511286873862691252933569556562441
01533344756716240947811826571155954756699368423562499979227723332856784786241
526949813038295767158836825390348461671496801413859919441
0555979179178582819757848123724780229627342713273807017121315934540225441
16861464162064185495562201758027171741932960403072428557591403748752441
1255836486847826530579021129301504600930007911328941
39110209284222126288743972398792999872217126802442695704364
08269175123947288580976631735219034774020783010825008230686748165992916214204
378559690700839634317491570400704911133097023046876615857483135080144441
75992852020727860406246909862458183710566318254920666633928689
4164223168139785374174558941
83550239814134762756866162211863675611345401850612301450506414641
7662002547937273701691150910570058805838552877515535683461355508881431374441
985636377736943347307792236920232819512601988334853193084139129692103451156641
6155817184516091865304891
71195380110241

Chapter Twenty-nine

852574989
3158647233999267453725219148787799788807562673750638723780564697641
3526861306774761161564030889
810722990061362029138553864683684245835443420724906526943131926363064
557919103281746224652305086811453922379034699935761819228384117831112734
2660931717160547230274858700010478660598353687620423490935631467935441
370070867604441608093430388941
641691229384629350216611002107616405466145328261330250989
929553919275962994627826326321165658743195517335942787247995441
828722781079314977711035342554381663505021820047559845719470764
29678271587726848362361118065924451595282915230181808941
71672271763496522837506807313174144
5335093301055862157197336759105167204885674541
157281632172593979270182677659278790726975958652444479862784876695394914
6101776057760360711075086603455755571296234540663775844877314065805021814441
14570121613889
44294254301272614399603975154880968417538877870997710531568941
6057795536359670078069985650119553616995819109185333740366199906618677441
5865365937828941

515861921683583853720551718196699002906225244 2971964 7760765792120834
9979814 831084 2533800664 60564 654 6284 4 1059597587010538378376695134 14 4
1171157658015291972393283182374 190724 182705562114 2924 812595008621934 8254
5185655397012584 064 7774 59094 16107789

84 4 866798787983603594 30670508264 698506509650714 24 287984 1665013303364
75959713294 583569058759697058365984 02375264 559514 284 15274 30934 7600284
80597374 4 51154 82304 0085774 538194 4 14 2354 91878380929229783184 4 14 022384 4
361123221688505624 3354 185884 3251154 4 72064 3284 962084 563281194 1082705883189

354 2884 54 365054 84 53563300884 2668569356364 289

0202766923084 86633611829914 29872638798806829980861239497 63295104
63591338269125251879 4 6694 5089

4 153964 9332734 54 972994 4 89

8362994 73991754 74 4 164 7197173177987268394 36024 010521661014 981526554
16254 03854 51779521584 0024 9587987974 104 9524 8004 753558164 54 4 11607964 9674 374
767184 2211835815737673704 89

68165761864 6684 4 7399574 57386389

5284 95665189

574 4 78665977781950752258882987024 789

00964 0653185204 74 2376952389

3355012184 78599660074 089

650383859514 701804 07234 57768783856075809 56164 5339216884 89

754 259830599175376101323206354 32534 4 24 04 8860000309082261900 3730634 184
8688614 387637364 94 178874 01204 826095051275986339050977024 24
7252980175882639229387079367325221116705 79264 4 14 090854 374 014 85304
590250371696374 774 586071914 054 25694 38156117014 4 378884 4
18883091592292719203584 1298716228668505324 60389

4 356500230734 167083751864 595368025275824 052092374 4
6765733512706016011 7034 908068222327234 1214 084 695966733251615 6575806659024
31013032064 115375116874 077567874 0603592587886171973634 936771114 2654 304 84
7081133303231866339855094 94 314 3974 804 84 078764 7767832770534 8801596714 1016984
4 3566978084 54 87805182319957564 07397883177027113564 3924 204 4 520333007609764
36796999004 095854 9556201313584 805875374 94 7256934 0330909172832394 18369219324
915186872354 77393921275611794 664 018511800138075010277721713064 204
2532655536114 323907882035094 5377075084 34 889

230102069364 8517284 9761293833257931632804 024 02366224 77073584
885055861960214 8189

50756889

614 64 9864 7108584 64 4 5373294 965523337264 1883832621271178272 4
06932265715707864 17557289

614 533829164 4 89

1865204 9552729526330028104 98231098573394 30816022566981711150564 21803074
94 36110781361389

682204 877365185667020919787109 4 2722765034 706338508550084 2117094 04
05082569924 5756282826278137513327080529 4 55232216084 54 057654 37854
00717990812768836695374 97522864 06714 61534 564 90112693874 267114 036215138204

7758754 94 285657227853366584 87290869174 9510102375874
9766072301695185736509057 94 9181869154 204 9514 8189

50633136723233600179192 4 4 397594 0164 16771983594 5106934 272172934
837133152708252285878 14 764 4 954 066168266066328173859064 6817084 80980195630954
01910023030383772107 4 832278139011682082582389

27793613956120621621339157864 07904 096277774 3062394 588711681359324 124 4
3371094 4 830874 22994 89

6572704 9696689

19097678729567856837 4 91826622807594 7073087639094 29179184 64 67289
89

3503816657160323834 13004 82214 9073557310114 75604 3910764 230704 99714
1717927224 9889

36251185377184 4 565361124 3536680334 15834 710999978127504 593107294 920164
004 04 3873689

1084 89

00002206589

689

4 9509883554 54 33034 4 80634 6906836264 269262252604 8050382229656658564 4 54
63817257872024 2239306031674 50160539775516554 24 603074 3256914 5384 14
066770009334 8172625337857836954 968801819714 20758304 7902504 54 4 93294 34 4 080654
70696670920819668718095 74 5182237903331168666010658854 64
61622251368075 5072817839904 9938203254 035222214 7912787357337924 050581704 7934
36111604 657520350964 992030094 30633851515 5701039654 36156004 2502091754
083680251075696272 4 054 0070613073914 8399782154 97526962006777174 61253751774 74
0807704 214 694 980724 65669210313 8036559013914 4 63193378524 95607651289

5884 70395683600524 0560377322664 84 889

76759864 72222368704 572600251314 653302789

4 907366831754 285279304 364 1684 4 91309014 82297794 4 4 14 5397767000504 764
54 5394 4 19974 4 2534 009022064 9707950657786676256257904 16787951719322821604 84
27904 222814 574 5555525850110505111853205128 24 81704 4 934
08500651110585967966113 4 8054 3157990100271163704 14 6255884 514
69531501613765309863 4 6793513983064 4 21721253914 2104 84 84 01806995555589

33864 6984 4 7097220729204 4 1600174 4 64 574 4 85789

885219133254 971330254 82098021992094 686705513088504 1123215989

4 03060607764 07088621530225283963061061 4 984 4 92974 704 512812064
3925095268393316301653 54 0689

29280565187157265787 4 1194 02174 780917279954 1874 1181137373534 823204 924
02854 4 4 372854 24 14 4 78667353172039728 4 0999210753385213768 52189

9202754 76375155088032382034 514 104 4 90336878610551139 74 55564 4 534 4
1335280589

3314 950724 154 536504 253686358765114 64 55776385286184 22250037354 4 3386084
194 57202578083624 6705161354 4 121936052124 92654 78557979011265815919933225 54 214
733610252203564 00358279085755073052788354 31594 674 179374 264 974 074 094 794 89

4 4 7795731660962302173239728 84 0260162155089

9074 51024

Chapter Thirty

6296718368591603789

0598163574 39266727829502991817957028068636510124 54 4 5154 4 131814 29654 184 524 519788730520200288020 4 3389

552095212624 250682073625164 64 8296888315050959701000226 4 37213534 8785826025335789

84 284 99264 25984 9382698655591574 55227722304 4 78367004 51292620325907284 4 70070718264 6394 299397105796504 924 027215130909020163225789

29364 662069079114 189

091709554 85858170999693984 5824 188862304 34 63864 68537094 69201908664 4 250014 23704 90706054 794 4 0163636224 4 84 204 94 614 14 54 07334 077205613675377994 7174 34 64 1869614 4 1635564 294 71591970959124 5729889

3923381500104 12294 39585288124 29031638189

3911829364 04 75674 801320054 8377764 224 1308322733790168055134 56118786526378739084 60298324 84 4 96777676526714 4 6090984 2724 0922194 4 20872905077724 74 2271284 9199862752884 0954 5361224 4 260812236730263624 16664 6367695658234 050934 78650114 354 522301721104 31829674 6118127124 772674 75584 1834 739182964 689

24 24 39083589

8304 1077861222164 6674 139274 58084 4 10934 4 670914 076889

081154 804 269904 64 4 766179037069131864 3164 4 872934 811624 75314 27094 7951218371189

54 308016061368674 2330865206856839261 4 804 784 4 5664 74 94 574 8323298371127834 84 94 57568184 8235738129672986025094 4 56310021387076804 904 30110884 104 3560659563291355136365953790577 4 508634 6584 1837937855021385507306606203236189

2026534 3796554 24 0913886678051764 86602355686801024

Chapter Tirty-one

4 4 3819982174 0818683080632657934 4 50136606958831163527659019637109122168302179 94 317817811597562569334 811817590163704 53954 8800254 3869195029394 84 296333878802324 54 02686831159207714 72660964 0814 72974 2564 1352377071326558656729260935213135632697386334 51392323794 9127274 1604 4 0716533283727663606992078289

885158189

0074 06817883560033839550 24 91054 4 21913694 94 384 0259289

7576804 164 7987388754 4 19071010073882502600250529371571205988217997519052515 4 81351289

26507035031295388797395196807 14 6312979739398855224 06771074 78132966112514 24 4 4 094 254 620586560563864 84 117697376509322232005813738 9

8885989

302233630809521934 26522815067530677311683 4 992003074 9784 4 9533317392356287724 9889

01104 9829135380994 3234 67387064 79293918382984 736509174 159934 4 224 180136090702185376839 4823719725514
8813881635282508237808756177303718593310237690155181489
56680264 51066955667635627033163755504 282184
6935526079312867717163008152297052501399 4 4 04 1110995237587821689
8707228324 1554 04 378594 9364 88165971060194
170111775308197796006102061075809 54 184 38226377174 4 1589
3089
34 4 024 54 807763589
85983864 6004 4 819130632918212125220072806349 089
056273136156282514 259729116909696211674 0824 716314 5189
174 736006959669914 23080878338378686590159867022321 4 2869157014 14 24 80704
589
72191054 2004 7904 2072618389
4 5659167576624 3374 81652334 310131977778750626 4 814 4 789
623796854 4 91833393254 4 52263282389
839955214 350864 723998824 618234 6783334 12034 96969634
652310297098007031272981130029874 875884 51556284 4 31013156099089
4 6158784 0584 00383614 54 306275028384 34 516836793994 31155194
06723368803326183813019065159316862019183963 64 3881182869704 1164 94 587694
2211365769814 9517318604 394 4 7681922394 0067014 55127928254 056530324 64 23524
19083789
115209165207534 50114 775133761761316030 34 63500158304 324 11983034 504
597311154 802352914 72675565285396154 9825173221870281189
14 7558219251097518814 74 996270183201238664 66554 4
7096270322119673520668256834 4 87375964 50725120796914 5168739639987295089
29286150574 50939183524 89
864 17115156337107720704 37194 2989
78525854 10651220208721985115201196820066851 54
950907756992161931680576122555084 10799564 4 735723621151384 4
26059118785236111157667 4 624 616760589
4 90884 732188251188189
16537294 130184 756365083622904 09687727075906307595173734 4
6538123581672056998615 4 4 93374 4 13551158082859997972507000 54 2569584 4 82904
2157032963296954 1837206112532778185078 24 3532391872673797539010604 2189
8213335680014 9176292763589
73974 9151033610294 4 854 87554 126594 588308262730872974 1581359987850589
7081564 29324 1595652057224 388601584 2078104 7504 2628112904 4 2552635054
82966134 319834 7557885193222671869303 64 56672710264 95994 00511663086637317274 04
4 54 5694 97374 874 8521103317754 9364 625380611334 4 74 31080683263084
6622039370773105 24 4 2799951374 50193526614 235225514 1868055104 0050214
3876778592990110859251867 4 99131314 500087258371166936982 4 976994 084 16160624 284
0630833289
79971618705057651962 4 04 924 3165999515189
664 9754 7503900114 73989
03189

68783264 55784 74 537251804 5223597268776687624 28507538166167924 880008234 09032034 80714 652289

02223080614 96574 2704 4 772212502661923714 235626092912260182505837318119710390751753385771378077621317724 528794 7915831714 84 3227314 73506837177881579852023035280059999869776669370082226708804 204 3304 27176103604 4 3602119574 05318323977508253762 4 353359925874 4 806695231314 095082672974 200827195918716169601534 0654 57814 75710124 3294 7034 04 989

011724 0314 56270700708589

135551306594 74 8305010926753310504 76766851006872795324 4 323689

64 938724 34 914 01886858021766970655158850256174 152070315092726514 58735885771669074 1189

56676294 168134 05784 24 067733886652984 335828209920927960002560537316119574 8651729717114 04 3583683023331026924 4 755634 96301826785735111056397 4 94 7335708175806329870766803 4 2130966827261284 7950604 36152654 4 2170363554 065832901954 74 112632161794 14 36862387824 4 6810885100608798206571969 4 73153168872765582925 4 84 100600262887084 707264 14 6369814 54 676023069064 84 8000195089

1529208834 75200294 83301183570714 74 8604 6003231803664 66301137834 614 8102080104 0824 1624 64 39862858027535254 054 14 811787725784 4 9824 4 01215358088326311157679388 34 4 3994 1674 25526718127068704 85790500170018827661154 025989

664 563822695284 08612570000031201513 4 14 6214 6274 358818811375215962355090961869 34 8253038196808508 4 9675713080265221001754 4 521504 38824 4 69635391354 522294 83822752193978161006308157139 4 734 757164 33100288572011561 74 719192266771954 36928312826604 3960699254 637219602914 2537779739831674 4 381208097218818831236226603387075326789

4 25385591691829772833273126155084 174 84 951235989

1579860193104 630204 08836581232828339328287752 74 85978705364 7329515614 114 2985324 61034 3025553130194 964 301167037928656376695698 54 796374 4 374 04 69514 4 04 7524 86274 76738025589

674 084 96302725388581738320957777270 4 4 26596764 50234 624 19588725735933861552680812 04 7751364 027860596714 89

93681237120118621234 9054 81712924 54 8154 3023804 10365014 87535674 54 3111800604 5004 2613078768221588514 4 267302962084 04 822613694 974 26208176099993500334 4 61976884 18790304 1595951539264 1119654 64 774 82084 96035361889

4 57612204 857186264 614 323274 971918808584 172165024 9255612284 86704 4 4 0794 5280918253914 4 4 6987618136633194 396064 6378224 50816138177872928278397 64 8591104 634 5562271722217817692297 4 115386786214 605724 2015889

821754 94 554 74 94 8636317672274 364 7089

802154 62007325013023705721216266625220053039613516788310130085680167987713860080874 4 14 4 960859610304 104 11974 85369831113671070824 7974 74 19717080824 3016916661770771312763331363815 4 531589

13375254 1683984 084 7864 31775066750394 884 6636777214
67921121853612236316721888038066106985937023790963186 9224 025911914 634 584 614
974 1712192550199254 74 796004 84 6006334 5981864 60801159374 4 70373166319535189
087920564 81072811877724 0203974 4 024 602129739110134 99269664 89
89
78223364 6553651294 9732934 154 34 0689
4 694 33738182663778605034 74 934 33270290837561801105 4 934 6901793394
28739905663796976 34 78106955289
6198764 6189
85072208634 5874 757753558684 4 6872335724 917904 7654 80775103923736396185 4
66753334 9597089
174 7050103139694 3809023634 04 579903070724 85296328514 30888786688074 24
98163585636339314 194 76252306615252056589
630703714 2091574 4 67866737683351558224 4 4 226371755529054 939532882366689
61533263314 93583928128224 584 93254 055594 107195071379970356374 234
00973161309864 6213937953087094 71653612565080331578504 4 573000094 14 1394 60014 74
5254 4 14 038169209933604 11596583800506303682 54 5663080628250094 88020034 1800214
5584 17554 634 80187653567764 4 115164 77104 384 36690085370611690503253031 4 68354
371335818092924 0076805095818888803131922996604 9866511923553334 4
271599513076908208526629677 4 03102594 730225917768201325910777315857 84 4
773120758864
50933987756187266253938362357576251588056203092312138665780721626116181270037560
534 4 622634 94 983862525666524 229234 4 3651396972082378259576261080998 4 93754
227356751224 1092324 4 7930724 2828029176235375338637087638735181552 74 8211124 4
80024 59124 64 0511151114 99664 4 6261984 33900579254 635394 96228889
24 36232521864 02524 8104 905959554 08365028689
3574 89
054 20009125338674 34 3134 0734 226519599814 4 8876264 4 8318552732774 94
122878561306225821878120011628573521338086 04 3652520123507908301505963 24 54
6828189
224 75989
132871694 3598514 2267573258150924 982124 89
905184 6590727823763964 923211904 20564 384 91725564 318734 4 162296200604 4
719016116127860806915970507233831799024 0010621164 74 77584 390237574 6789
131695701182264 621770289
4 571191364 12685871868635824 9327174 65627067280751367 4 31597507565774
7583764 0633804 4 94 4 82066835217833213332789
67763836574 4 674 6201728839572367211098154 01621327006816874 0231366194
833250104 4 64 8564 64 60364 1253174 13333237960756729373305212297 4
579333525661685589
2004 3759625134 203063834 294 3060971584 74 0953801974 1154
95300102821650559592594 59194 85334 82273271554 4 4 87352136534 4 7294 2394 955964
5304 7880531794 55862934 189
010777934 9027602218084 9918514 125716531651374 508750314 014 66774 2519764
76204 61669311332604 538789

64 5165729084 38615194 4 3114 0161514 23070224 7163939901004 37906864 1034
1623679074 185064 6376825660389

550334 7734 89

67311334 3136294 2854 314 887603124 7313354 196709800084 5264 274 014
20976313695876225859100931112997379360013553352920 74 82985367204 276126984 764
0066766986610534 55207287218738180679105816290 74 870107673696521668734 4 87874
3827719973271864 92554 24 806684 238330274 10696091855007115354 89

24 174 4 4 0794 33704 2318254 560683867024 20523393305803173064
778859332292996554 662168705712818066315810759698 8037954 19028671051589

6821839986172264 565237272159212726998561668 84 3085968396028717153 8526694
14 793173289

354 584 4 9531502185930086689

1179713664 94 924 10539530174 01360785889

154 7134 08500397680364 53811115720861295639 4 70964 5574 270823873126874
9887309705900533731834 61689

6934 170930000086168027800589

5674 152284 4 366300229652650701385626568 4 35888629758589

2712289

73122504 50193975398 80195992958594 6674 4 4 885279234 64 103724 7334
1353383902594 807739551764 0674 14 764 658014 53303755125878391520600273054
5980582800834 15867508782021829802912 4 1797731523538577064 0677116684
52133686650109064 4 399184 664 72914 384 152284 355957780524 1786922134
390262097035903035025270328397986 7654 87111297164 150657689

15393509094 04 216300292126234 234 7128521083954 21664 911751887684 89

016016350794 990872514 594 4 284 0907695196996180377128279292330631394
632150965793664 885286718536589

854 282324 04 6387338281784 81530209203088315697267 34 3925583364
321632066089

8884 5807113627763999664 957064 8133324 300804 4
30706922817962968328613163 94 9834 1581788714 262196654 990514 04 4 9994
90513227583290203973389

02854 257513664 074 28377198389

5137584 6035685933196763654 22978795979675682839 983101815254
23666598572785888868064 85189

4 59707162034 673703516804 56789

74 10832102068776915310505668766877329334 92002389

350574 4 36954 4 5160234 29794 5780603067189

3157679519089

580811282704 8686785651794 94 94 25317989

89

854 5584 6351101662924 1506701611762219757292557732222995795702695 14 273134
12587036021325937 4 764 294 767723385539394 9608034 94 329630814 5907993381594 3114
6102374 364 8260905274 89

2609114 99781759924 252339697286952524 16687315009238204 1212854
261361635324 913662513786628 74 4 1728736927773266853389

99050914 4 28805931696176825772855927778554 889

1224 8808866962902222009071053198672733203501256083276186544 686069004
61217655114 1034 532831271204 4 35229510016794 790313350534 253556783869192234 3124
90521332794 361256904 6803304 54 064 259314 334 85989
352987882254 95318574 24 88103764 13754 14 84 4 9982952274 89
0279695089
814 9864 69076164 4 389
575234 35665064 97982594 15250324 263255294 4 11659694 055989
58665076121533992974 864
10528083098879197123728761697290730295301586338095434 3194 018202669104
693139303526636283583219629344 195022055821562811510082783702191422318615775289
4 4 3074 0125120698223625704 1351162127934 4 74 7937375070858534 4 904 025189
4 6776914 74 2064 9139024 731524 04 739223757035683312553974 4 4
73636977591310167244 85564 2522704 98558713299184 7584 38211851524
915321086608709389
4 774 655589
09768150090915524 53184 371101679704 394 2272006065934 727864 923765594 69584
717164 290257863271834 3604 38706061526799319925178071960601819978894
6189
14 4 1329681532735536565531782787894
87704 54 84 925656831544 04 84 33686635894
34 82791153784 996014 6294 33017853591894
22268713560211563806688873602444 524 2861517707711106712851444 39717394 6256684
077707258589
19518657200283026878274 88064 624 8625804 514 33334 4 54
1330861637868233257296257953800673509106053396523255759682444 1504 827951961974 94
5905100821796236567014 770564 590274 789
80181006309518889
62137903769365337298726812820884 788701063082554 158504 21334 1014 9582854
277180694 94 6338138816824 519034 4 4 80504 9224 35510003314 14 292089
4 2257683134 80195104 19539564 834 283831689
94 69970689
36123952993364 77360596737956301617803184 22618261992081634
8676196602758664 4 7118087603253007087444 53508535754 9089
4 8331667080132534 824 9711806765228158023607082333904 14 2811702294
1352536003306330261124 5516864 922753389
76533327508837308735444 65914 11189
79834 1977081211090804 71374 4 2356324 19974 36195814 2327674 056004 4 4 674
915694 94 5578714 93554 7922254 1764
29822307573665159603939567872952083076212995729056444
63332797905608736019668380684 1521600534 098228717682054 30304 94 82964 0714
37795894
67789
1785265134 4 209014 79656996958603321761028398322325244 209091874
9756952825023624 4 4 94 2356873501034 701874 199053002938096986090876144 94
56728711268068719599244 24 0064 6532771157004 61234 69550672596301566722909054 4
556889

6694 9036381979374 684 65866534 06795597194 4 62977563164 5824 34 38624 037934
89

804 73005757098395158216139214 4 4 04 1889

4 22681665534 89

54 14 3282061553926819933813234 14 31398790872065564 4
117610051979103079211594 4 64 124 822986954 03958669789

6296360224 807663263111856093817090755322596581714 9254 58095004 864
28193072375865331093 4 74 102684 60883510176552329792792588 64
29690577225713908291190907196 4 17085384 594 54 4 33599189

62961825813795766195253377709395930937558695979150585 4 695906008160034
355707922057284 184 85855996164 77156190633768504 32936554 54 74 74 29793082284 034
0104 214 7794 004 94 8180654 5729224 4 834 26104 8015204 89

33259789

3682357594 77584 89

390796539861320097773887838 9

00230664 96506731865265056828395821962580338070209708 9

88714 14 621585654 4 262375254 3139384 25321275734 074
53319116295517118791369927035391723508 14 99866237794 4 284 1884 334 5714
929271033322663099327159181177798 4 273789

75014 789

4 332684 97205154 30723756063998772961668725323 4 709907174 64 054 024
0739876530764 99928272555573339710224 4 6852281974 4 0635674 154 4 233989

5224 04 04 254 8339769553714 731599039115199581609 4 959851210374 5365994 4 24
3964 558662189

51207314 02017735567818531957 4 5001591386191064 089

9786932831364 83900961375710627234 7800522824 21184 264
275528316128586976015660 4 64 3183353361039723374 601999153889

31573028588269160920 4 94 884 54 130092262588377714 04 8796551601554 359374
5110789

84 7180884 700960607789

076220693684 073784 9633609634 2509584 70825725633681267006 4
29102982227999157619394 12305010665619324 385291312270883071567 4
7196820218627201 94 84 74 4 6914 7750995873774 86602963126211239362626 84
32315339171935691378 9

89

19660667127709734 322808251984 75061954 062034 4 93330703784 2679837994
1771882384 77857304 9239862558566116335286152795713 4 35314 524
81039163835170550778772229762397920 84 07088711586623991923319336 4 95574 10994
93754 1006679688014 26502073106663321903729688 24 69804 0807054 186317885193804
782714 1225654 1799994 252084 72883282034 768584 89

72552574 718194 114 111004 174 156679999964 19753284 0324 0933119063192104
7134 67023378515181682298661 34 384 617955922289

2272724 79295126971190232 4 963913804 4 04 399574 0500927120818613254 294 374
94 6808034 95274 028786638624 3934 171088576574 565098594 76694 89

2184 50064 054 656300785760186337903961 14 27130965704 63860917634
60387568116961674 24 77001757012096224 15995297606038534 88570014 814
03137001128029694 54 31637235112508802119138585 4 2622105689
94 89
951830180914 1719061592636934 7364 95307154 1759066678807228201 4
88291988205155707763583295672191 1220357704 24 9516850618829530889
889
133774 280092605574 823119088319103131939299334 55923134 282290824 4
9525800523923120354 684 09591811803767004 1104 124 295206004 1674 976055582275384
02785572289
94 4 290970792203734 79880867350017022354 02887074 8724 15687791506214 6524
89
173325524 770184 4 86333604 2379174 274 985534 33628195137659386276 4 0328174
263624 814 72009657057617273393219713701624 994 376072232561327874 24 9377778589
269330335964 01621334 4 1364 984 027113913384 274 7075776954 3778601175664
91086194 27071829174 4 124 2654 4 4 598136378594 34 4 0204 32286589
754 63864 34 8272914 83675790906124 62084 3234 3903919234 4 334 34
967727735561114 21320014 394 4 4 32273203813690857297957363267 4 4 7789
4 3865774 89
0385918099259886296977925 89
1374 70528577954 613032054 33036775220335508550526 4 18524 6835194 92934
683524 32860294 1689
94 57532838210307005971 4 264 4 539014 09018029918233366 4 74 4 077884
707202162306238560559758221 34 4 83772962995988321194 34 133694 5834 4 614
7835969370283268271 4 104 84 814 52882905261664 032814 94 08184 024 3768279808314 94
5204 6334 01314 793187522373778064 14 4 9565756210605303373736314 6674 99714
28199074 239705585981535036662090 4 650584 4 83582903706278821795170109 54
9763960329104 6554 06069264 586302126874
027033337628709008636077571723127591619507653913377632919582215602395 74 34 2934 4
68871298084 6121802689
7104 24 34 17090833099109858888883525 4 08594 227691776288120756179 4
396901190756634 524 1700616320081014 184 75332908113003093109758677073036318 4 254
529334 53097666152917523663236564 74 216904
228061697515605333059925079176825022364 64 599957033774 761084 14
7501885998302655204 068322532391058724 4 89
4 13214 9204 2015076366197289
0004 0605927204 24 962760719992999976515689
8504 788208519098035733115 74 154 4 655500524 1314 90124 3989
9507673779114 79714 2127666155536570002998064 35223585594 6334 029151965574
4 773725774 5255173684 67724 114 8228763726800196358 4 4 8624 260379864
986575821308051254 867753671804 4 9618700159104 4 7387934 24 304 187854 6178704 57854
3664 94 4 284 3850304 1164 81926667184 97525267073658399302 54 0061886594 63004 4
25934 9864 218873674 6677914 010289
92193519034 1984 7325760225853194 84 839338206114 64 8070364 89
978670865314 0531734 81514 324 6518534 00564 0853019289

90763601600914 0767076874 864 98786614 4 724 164 384 26254
92285981679108129205218822915194 4 74 34 704 10361926198224
96886501832878812286552614 94 4 8724 33559864 06705534 8866764
216076996015355082328224 18270715618196314 34 31092962804 05256938017210064 3874
560935856366533754 0961520993684 4 1090064 234 55594 96789
9258652717374 982980371763864 4 1554 0833993324 7328130954 90090911694 4
26764 70996060513667034 0174 4 1183036622504 89
9102028224 104 4 980053063939224 651764 32819632004 4 4 7864 31071064
518182924 901554 7074 6630136658502775050796766694 4 709231111695074 284 57926919864
654 79689
7698574 4 24 71202502619936276904 918689
38537969774 824 1302056076304 3389
224 7367574 7538314 7134 1754 6782974 9624 4 7706654 093819818294
0533952786677289
83884 828299114 23927736324 5716014 37337526304 8026324 94 21654
55657671976751934 72054 64 994 4 251600989
15085265375080025107560 54 3265537727234 2230719696794 527224
661597386602174 1689
03912272254 7133825915532284 52515226694
69728173031755253671085191135887654 254 4 357904 129824 10354 3174 4 232764 34
3271370654 209963215706364 06096871384 524 624 5663352691301220789
207803854 120376020634 11955394 534 694 6694 93091620795819911659307574
19826929877866650365908258531021071701501 84 4 13675291384 84 7390819223564
7086656219503198651985556903 74 7671094 714 08761353154 87181593027818838207 81394
0008699996704 5174 00589
029294 7204 95124 668073909517224 305516930104 803827814 754 4 64 1937702694
24 932724 33681252024 601571534 86104 4 0607590563320374 17883714 7535214
3957277788274 6386184 160872134 3254 982369004 8373821826384 0092510215599762824
924 14 83239110024 692789
253625384 807769987524 16827751579814 4 534
5592180912352016230923561872620356180637 1374 37050124 62568124 8863511622694
756689
68136190873913861168278104 224 664 184 8813774
9163775823530717510933636515920783202850 74 8781773294
56795722880270292533039303562960965509081 11234 59904 50064 098314
62600113397660037298133881316 14 4 98624 607384 004 10387389
52334 677015604 76564 76774 37530913530360277 3064 94 854 818181579855584
58713627831537680 4 64 8221524 84 18050024 3604 859204 24 8195328836784 03638789
9563193321631831778397529919375524 2196596089
65065537394 04 4 6089
82289
6508308860509089
024 9651264 72119109692294 0386605909137826663 59794 4 84 0783267636254 4
38297382631612385127135883189
511072580994 198572394 26389

6590594 9827824 1780923504 7599580728228798338367066100204 15953764 56908759360820905304 64 64 56054 9835109037784 779087651974 6000574 9378268569622689

236564 73689

664 00237614 213914 04 08853022853014 22924 022934 239184 74 607289

1824 4 01584 03161965703700511650374 83283612130517927 67920294 9584 4 96107578731219 3123627924 90708774 704 94 027720766863951289

959581037918255527573701990356398551 2824 0294 7935134 304 7014 985331634 14 882724 14 7087051137221073 2637816770795704 24 4 35254 24 02658784 9103230994 4 218504 7657104 76292622152637991177350294 554 04 14 71979736189

39164 1364 67958250810525362210095673087070599535110232822554 068808184 24 24 61329055034 1124 6368206259564 4 292917574 019200970574 6751783787094 973834 62000351520235096582205132 34 9518812880974 170138280072774 9270607384 2957867654 5651223280696018735927 9384 22502982394 52654 5661537689

095003761204 16256518301073537003907029150204 753714 27789

4 3688059173203027118 57789

917666634 257164 2695371669593318314 176864 6992039329287314 780654 54 99610556358587858035598 89

382532562784 2779752774 869590582901784 3531703864 19677914 076504 81298094 3838768811633599534 74 97834 9632584 04 25665564 88352302 30971526389

61085263284 13993551737005570157924 3314 55713392635064 912691032874 574 336801684 70883210 1983180572589

963564 174 994 799914 11764 64 087830985873887 60126224 392915251351274 3163114 24 091659579854 4 231194 074 263914 1995737008193686324 3954 28889

189

215907335571177725165886954 4 94 4 64 905156957324 223604 94 29106113988187879 7814 5692300825681635089

33768853608784 915097614 07672722017652 6327006304 04 29882985323604 100024 04 0182990715058209534 8667865854 914 752310391765304 3924 4 4 4 519665134 2514 85886593572530618789

3317329084 1634 035522164 74 104 154 35261375821818187912790652 8210805664 4 58170081884 621209532764 188236193739371584 54 1654 5004 6137634 75572691672524 76102557802111982212191616769 24 7994 6814 8510221108354 686977604 70650797023269791794 4 664 058254 58784 12351378391598786857 6580174 717357584 00554 50021699156624 89

34 32775705316234 398574 651211255669761595794 1655004 3092783958064 36785620176109369534 32274 4 20323727782921264 10727927331538 8054 26571871952314 614 76085124 1207116214 5370705234 609873528525352639855517375988621522832527062 3317177105764 6834 4 207112184 89

69716263292124 90614 166624 1887604 178683965335208134 03993199974 584 85163686764 90886859104 52680787306216050214 958591937822714 926533322860968536505039861 4 037995783932359268 09107789

054 85558610885924 28224 22592774 4 773651178182700198138853160730568033657967 6271784 57774 291699979193696296290729972681 0304 9709697061750361784 872804 915714 553234 024 89 7008651825057184 139097089

9814 4 3210863274 307629534 64 8301060291760317398316298855580769714 4 339567729015294 7924 94 89

257305310362880929885710977 4 2034 3390389

4 24 1774 96084 9678531158757524 4 607210626352217999579 4 4 832824 964 9817968808777035604 906974 0609755815112095162050132770910780391 34 6114 751004 96986771957804 672823682217588508555121873788238 4 3550239713535 64 767531284 88751114 5584 394 4 13075616690802194 04 7054 02509256163887305799593571007095 4 21524 24 02389

7386614 4 984 3026964 361569759383503580008652520663 4 4 823250934 289 1281594 6824 68813110767064 807271539213380854 90889 32174 4 630597885811274 4 2534 4 881319621755074 53904 692292260778682863658751566809 4 4 7504 78626727357076953714 89

7264 8601362808015084 4 22632659722114 711187217154 4 5818774 26158697079388695592310355 34 774 4 84 4 27102772791812654 193912554 7604 84 4 3180934 3679664 6334 04 282833273374 18506298654 994 6001209056686091094 950352084 4 18389

91634 030696334 3519971372234 04 5101839365628394 90571574 11991738814 206864 4 9188564 89

6816333551950660009288 4 3332524 806735584 1713374 9617150550934 2637189 4 0232530354 2599384 394 18771874 208814 554 354 356164 3034 89 10314 81520576588694 4 4 7827064 4 91099533521284 32519104 9124 69054 32173805106794 185988054 4 01289

4 251232589

909962312324 05387739821014 4 64 0584 9655974 158659523205814 4 98852510376930654 974 89

313506032936074 4 81814 9989

8201118274 92778152011324 04 64 303834 000930223108054 725959755121674 67066592294 4 4 38571075829356865159801179019 94 804 535824 717234 50301763989

14 902214 4 94 89

02160198684 15175873791916826610983857384 537652804 189

0093375503234 8767588757658350816808 4 89

804 889

94 6134 6384 675835827589

4 5004 664 80260224 707959607311234 708701901229396384 2199250887685371119985 4 331293724 294 84 7578836115174 0833584 37533109066594 27013258032954 3981526920681054 804 215521024

Chapter Thirty-two

7965114 54 54 33197115305 74 09954 937838369320017065 64 102399396852034 15131733092513860829839610 34 4 837564 34 854 7094 56374 110604 5616668328026369760559 4 107860053014 854 0321252825322327251732324 9355788226593959508373 34 009505984 530084 4 86154 9376083077293236978053902069 4 89

84 36522867928580781581080858064 95326331730564 681609178514 71254 00088072257937135985919602032117698516618138205726664 4 879714 56050564 764 174 273684 189

14 506734 24 567564 1604 82903098189

7917595674 4 799704 4 184 8154 395604 70233784 356812676177157987374 87316524 4 5882100164 106192876715295197730961257950 4 0132799512512304 4 6071737653304 4 34 889

758377502200674 14 67780169732280054 56734 4 994 253724 1384 582367759639957228554 5930783851914 039504 74 4 13617589

10074 14 622681929769694 988612865298551788024 993319663563824 838294 1924 74 319235584 26763507319858030301534 3074 861824

37832522793357993835685378113275565386 4 730024 7674 3067237584 4 55570664 332239670583789

750194 0110984 584 53031203974 160814 9528633651224 839511514 265139521361994 92804 77614 5672284 84 4 312856596154 4 9731382785953307673696014 94 158637070362175658670104 30358696114 5791714 834 4 582054 8229597116654 70211362772824 9354 0794 6290706014 037201690357789

2399326303272607254 506004 0364 605028380929610076000676210935 8216154 88096827981804 590876990755827971114 9674 85871036579817790055 99204 619921086218833393864 3676754 53578236336989

08816193564 218210955951100939837537 4 77554 6586077865594 3306224 84 912789 78754 508135558000955361863224 7789

4 55782167285821565583 4 8574 1692055782234 3615032535519130694 5196005289 4 98694 04 68655864 5288393239196124 04 399594 779057554 35190582258127024 68257321602699353123762173162 56389

7324 75711628596069997082939 4 959814 64 54 68124 29119289

4 4 9321675789

36358775236587083126261297689

52214 0371213333713736365700974 961114 67954 7389

4 0216254 86684 14 63524 9814 865684 37129932566103690320984 324 524 4 36374 5789

283274 53254 01013787354 6087085784 9153391330184 8796502158 8810929903714 350114 96211919724 372703633189

01179929310091989

720660589

194 991838526986780058093923091 73781954 29850851684 66812992334 2594 66707617776755886208012614 12614 64 0886156063703867564 61288814 378861816884 06921057373100714 7127556028255238 4 6104 94 28731994 9838014 19274 94 375100694 7906095976275704 074 25605279204 037351322564 3720532009690271261787884 195824 39234 331652524 6682094 254 6627297934 824 20950273277702953598156 4 9824 733818061639387154 774 919753504 932179174 3206684 34 09206201758084 778305188754 96124 4 2395201189

64 90704 7660186063573332139879373 4 673914 9080881235134 5513774 07155868222354 55884 5754 4 68634 3337754 03138713026260714 6224 01171706024 010652254 9119864 684 30964 1572194 4 924 4 6028281732525366703537230 04 24 24 9866064 80531127501954 35652322568738263515606179781774 9036314 7504 9573203258272282087901580037039 4 7220784 7114 4 08535302162674 05066505125616695005739908327 3250689

952126975261606027252 4 728366524 4 6769954 6935694 7594 725756685581189

4 2585377725768098397685880064 964 4 185753871729087162366584 2954 600064 572836053138758138636294 4 104 3134 62995374 182776271853061591934 2612177132010310021114 52565766902870974 55533109073858111289

5514 03927166875224 79984 9874 99178502589

2689

0214 824 59578259051864 4 54 82530867096054 1524 639164 8674 81996956919637597196303980961058033554 6132789

4 3598184 35086974 5259200054 859003037296168307195762226854 35364 173118174 509579933164 77690774 64 0274 025905255388091862936860 4 586739521133104 68554 74 84 4 038171072506636910 14 557314 738282505357057566139391755260695186 89

64 925034 4 68664 74 914 65261560855050379 1394 202981994 2221994 7354 3823178322303684 713733024 74 85594 298263804 06512984 89

197127731269793994 24 4 68368139797193089

4 515313010228207176024 113229639122806181570953761 84 5202287863361784 261035310734 1759203978291654 370239534 3092259108501080565591877252777554 800270019294 614 14 4 15376722756825533214 17372014 074 7134 7884 4 34 363167591614 387225594 3304 94 977196123384 222661604 89

64 39624 205326779704 14 308024 1164 011968089

1010920634 2903802792551569679532 4 16192834 8664 10838286054 4 15369964 365931969137777870059360304 82022913026514 592296134 5580297182724 384 196876724 37084 4 9263675507056334 050268371994 4 9354 73265265632066274 380836995826335167607082354 952985615834 33119524 392297003987910675268314 94 4 224 87587059711975013571688080770880 16385784 32778181513027786831168589

194 6114 301089

589

21839289

7133594 1392888564 8854 509163725939835974 20767157074 60714 97524 6059863989 669574 6231577768604 87972014 80357679564 84 589

8219702887616123194 701320955924 214 4 88355505762723234 4 34 84 264 260117532230618223035658508 04 701101189

919325257172054 996292664 129773504 28504 370262289

7235852816267563789

63020389

84 74 35594 80612173873906685354 384 5303929312988193883304 11834 237783614 7805975750584 0662254 13362933578093194 781966392974 235039084 8059320069789

9176788339686913 1974 8258864 74 7086279971313256137172730816 5334 061394 6256855059072754 5864 506864 656527768255534 297214 0883383727882010289

029324 031324 2102002610635664 24 4 369661208304 1768693220104 89

934 515597321174 66300908671200835572 4 20529225106285030294 0669270580504 4 006818192273514 25634 6584 354 8110959320734 01274 9694 9000254 4 720797360379164 669703195033832 84 8355167676058310365 4 52708576554 9800282394 78223137188703965216 4 20784 14 03863200501687559289

24 4 24 89

164 32107962003137110 74 626069359189

558182399883659153109700 4 2358174 294 60073596124 74 32905721092909762924 104 106566209235037924 4 31392689

03030622034 07870584 75213684 4 34 9814 00664 39968281777288328306808029674 74
851072684 228563950311923967939970227828083290 403918794 27012564 0317319867054
80903817290109382677032761818733382332992873 54 251791214 674 169684 4 4 384
1609957921734 9254 754 11516955036329294 60672187983177984 886836278290997984
30217204 17536252229967274 3257163080332626794 27008834 6679931237227789
2804 9072690634 359386334 4 8273734 94 687180880694 5088824 0689
972616587134 3751874 07124 4 353589
993574 9505763910550260234 884 8319301097762875184 5555614 2797284 284
87603938721304 9090254 184 884 26977514 01162693761395504 585689
904 7300398762225695695285227027007070022363127827564 7209189
07236614 5338315064 5086601571667250304 4 253134 57307614 24 82529934
73550820094 8111074 0264 2703287961354 5589
9723876924 388109759704 4 4 4 57279722559558214
831857922116838192022376660 14 7053550332990566389
96113950200355900395314 314 8531999733956110064 596295558214 9616215804
5516324 961524 984 6254 9133866615566130574 71073066064 94 76125925134 73986724 04
294 705271394 5870057114 4 61774 35924 89
1999977985398589
1554 580117570754 584 19857074 64 4 4 1715735287088318155664 906711613720524
84 2124 067568833334 6326309394 674 4 059153928124 34 6865274 1507636710833294
679930796012132262362971922889
0611294 395686589
0674 6885822588883989
165018835533075233198157903553586855155782065 4 68218332159074 291034 74
6956756633924 854 1522364 5371500388621789
02634 313785302662274 4 881799998738533234 152500505075994 4 52916010384 924
2964 73792314 4 851996764 0031204 261931101839001074 559769324 574
399651968221115701722500007801852007690927995274 819572235224 900924
5510210083294 350604 7090382176234 012352784 838737727314 31981235331216735074 1624
784 1954 632534 4 615208289
12237804 6922908509386280752677373364 89
16752751088671869074 857315117987191127589
7371721222006979026862701539770333762353916857302353277808051500852598175
3295550807877886672815650966691615839112721698699388759112688 64 84 854 534 5289
8384 500172007531788096127 34 774 4 03004 524 16750323930338367061707101305504
38058717306756683353374 5378303685599937759086951306218 4 655285792359339174
191712054 179699872561324 53266577397569709321705621938004 614 828574 9989
37523164 35134 74 7073658820981060577886 54 16514 7324 89
817870094 63013850792559222607297152262038819 4 374 84 3914 310594 095992584
334 4 65657681739689
3261104 59870100372754 35251163774 4 161227299994 10186195660514 2159694
12063551314 4 85971954 5286080974 868254 874 524 4 590362604 73138064 839379734 4
68186624 9700721554 7106019350023864 8389
34 37562276350127925 84 94 173264 3662372023278553594 194 9304 500111524
9370114 7634 634 15754 264 095574 7394 30694 4 56354 236208121224
1176373576970867776359301935638364 4 4 02889

36305078333228036674 74 394 324 865707989
508525087274 18326835271995157792652719876374 99790762084 389
4 634 7212620360783081173814 2804 7878554 978289
7862274 724 4 177003016325501339705724
1768281532351617690692199970255699962054 64 24 37265357754 7251024

Chapter Thirty-three

0312994 3553864 594 8314 70194 94 0156026684 94 3031837836936554 661866566254
7082586074 89
4 8397282515589
160385534 95064 51384 74 4 2211882756298620633135692134 3505354 1753254 62294
273857018514 221604 79791812391358185702336381354 4 535711277117194 3216604 6614
310154 74 19821554 92904 75621090189
572080606234 908802904 067854 56674 63724 17724 8681190074 20655784
8221929501065966835352086790875855334 4 90092713251073537813112328600
1052918835504 82825682124 3931809785796664 14 4 164 1974 384 650359754 316704
18385214 5907794 33577314 964 84 574 214 860854 88674 5291314 574 589
315184 834 20505854 27211602752070105302881218204 4 25718504
0797177351938264 4 4 1514 3034 0000389
6508354 7606952112614 351514 4 94 0969915151783325851724 7989
4 74 0524 2061004 5984 0736384 351138298293353702855164 15328184 689
87804 35921758197601110371882601157152121989
928035754 60838874 094 73752204 063912336289
82806618731953235529204 014 2200095154 8088070610074 5386563972589
7080303279855124 057096752994 877525034 83811914 84 4
76396069023998008588751011612900600807691194 38103026094 94 8065984 76196904
805932178521399828659016361397294 73334 24 52975784 2997590232889
21228876174 5364 34 3158375314 3784 9574 608874 73734 2587958758219901935389
814 2294 2391794 1515613153979302514 64 137986089
598876754 13694 32304 04 870285554 1978092295804 4 6989
90192904 5589
0684 6597838337994 4 9251271604 94 13377907064 86578589
4 967575994 050617557632934 756808289
2202911154 91864 8820159214 6177654 4 99211827254 9886765689
622517063614 83219514 0603084 4 86884 294 74 9081714 122766989
5297665284 671870107291933779292824 4 35324
313828520635706158076925928260322221194 0276877904 2924 0836532323215102354 07534
2321094 7605321017167804 7889
604 1685107197396939918618794 634 6189
67971354 67867224 4 02905164 4 4 3964 7829326694 63584 918661504
01165503213795823884 64 0354 533706750014 6824 5089
39635084 079633883393164 4 00215576294 876554 514 9622984 94 5735704 5563984
582865390103120311995586329789

859964 274 24 1654 564 022155269311761821934 04 052804 977001395818569950 4
5062690832184 4 220985806560360396650520 4 0509265294 4 916311224 74 1224 39854
552334 5939736021584 889
59564 57603560112394 72260029091102323581832707760318192 89
5789
31912004 228297227192768010578564 4 667334 020318606579759989
767363004 515534 4 12122274 64 9211784 192104 2993023304 754 5934 0814
89657338855853118789
25724 3599624 701958104 94 0834 271300659716364 37516574 6371024

Chapter Thirty-four

9870536291692900609979797982081 4 714 71311289
95085184 920039864 04 614 6530250994 914 14 34 0358369556884
21615182000667253985853203567078753 4 4 74 10182134 4 997039591787397534 962114
7236777151075064 4 34 193206709784 810139061194 681 4 299656594 694 998030150150504
394 99165819364 34 06175 4
71200602325330510056856619953988521096991796810306515662761 14 001239394 4 1274
050 4 065600221709854 777964 4 24 685874 86319694 6189
55103513339164 119590397189
38761054 4 264 23024 64 4 1278596632014 84 79552732274 34 0928634 620098 4
059824 533857638615193364 4 320983391819574 962950525271704 1594 1103294
1605520070797004 4 5274 2655032910680168291821505 4 8865729790830657332005667110 4
03931664 289
4 6073974 2761327206991377358887764 684 0767260164 5037969090673762 4
91231815694 6132584 214 651124 3018088628385018727320829304 9320534 8834
9080225799962089
31538204 34 5874 6206252362968122 4 0775571667614 70833253074 351802801564
661524 1233577266654 59689
501535120964 074 098799335251124 236839325550804 07795389
065135984 869314 85726874 89
94 9014 085300106254 036984 4 024 3398573821267762 94 54
91927728192707271007595054 194 54 50379091805163615808362888700153867 24 394
50070274 989
84 3218556764 74 0324 714 3923664 84 34
111606209310196018250317806835398572583913357133 4 4 9303614 4 9170866597972333881 4
53092174 03181174 7752032581674 3389
4 58264 967527525203611262736721097 64 54 3134 0238065872011251 34 514
611723801638359 4 7268752281763835665589
6188613216729989
394 014 94 125103564 65833636887760906588376967 4 18291919203119 4 564 6978094
24 983860904 160330963764 5292794 234 19300230174 0054 34 3225854 625094 74 354
55170968354 369756035650199238514 737184 926705972332775797911738152 4 74 35316334
24 1172984 589
4 129107504 55504 288587776273734 0663304 16039180826874 17260659615989
3360778633070199222318 4 6664 8889

304 5271524 0551174
61202230160366192193936615793786736961581625973005821281128255764 679594 94 02814
6674 57604 55774 706739022001976983182597002938195414
9275908113373323605858777871610067258359623260496001605897
914 889
34 2204 736161327100754 523004 84 394 310989
9916372218862326257224 7230711979182304 94 4 4 3514 033574 4
766397083610698607144570069276396639734 9202921834 629764 4 381860189
3766880534 5127770384 815690854 0614 0328036150280386094 9033534 89
32303579251173935304 1584 11332654 71290567398884 4
3593082228303303222116592985419196559797184 8854 23887158089
14 036930161717257001557061483690681274 22955027934 6352264 500686934 30774
82074 66636874 7614 7620022750181551796978266737414 59504 3870588723873389
63291213957303994 663054 34 0289
132774 68168754 6695021614 124 6550370091265917983029038873484 1761397234
3394 5569356600838016094 3556137855374 689
20714 54 4 2337764 6719631384 64 6526315701017132358397487466544
2363027792854 1904 50156664 578818599794 789
712514 8114 05023776902617289
793013080656571631212120791429070542150888 9
837954 53659164 35512334 174 598794 80927694 175114 9031174 6055224 557854
581355867021530900770319556558 9
959974 680574 161333836164 169114 00992334 15564 3868362258664 4 280794
033626701052266693619246747237136409054 289
85205188351003692681879974 6564 705254 50682683936264 06994 4
2231179129973336410667817359159716289
83274 17728872302052609804 24 875777100698819624 0372912716284 5583584 784
034 04 924 364 8781833724 3203716187881 4 9318366321324 24 24 24 2014
71879866012908295449020987399595428721390667769827563089
16794 2174 016882358765397504 203024 4 89
864 1889
63690963162701205576819699291549927751425437881294 6766508325035126 71684
664 4 84 4 4 54 724 04 10124 528064 21783273222776043691610288078358871843710051808 4
017958014 1083528163516360380534 63076389
194 76150186986736706050147556545191255634 854 74 4
061620273938350356278561529588 9
4 68170169994 014 33231109528721244 82704 7206054 6025850066704 07579111 4
136827906978686587117792043561148 9
29968719888032590349546258685078645156073721715399533910705457420844
7004 89
981128289
94 216021222092624 4 94 7274 54 05610358209264 2512678039819054 526594 4
37375194 28132171370336125910575516989
9284 7294 69534 24 298072325629025888362684 26784 4 7029836313294 966054 4
162538614 74 882834 79816732288109784 87694 13234 367188334
829751327755520981118356612998485687021734 4 971594 55814 205167601363168104 4 74

9870916364 94 3156667001634 124 731526314 664 694 4
70222860280711813992815888751637214 2668321214 1509231720573189
        1117328825980525201560900 4 1554 77759524 04 089
        1350094 0365197084 870074 967833274 3233588694 63126879009850231317206614
1132108607604 86195706356624 52304 87204 9297016794 57814 582009036192806782139 4
589
        374 33777693126987686811712 4 8164 084 9105253884 23933369089
        4 6354 0923580231081725576 34 99799694 364 59754 4 4 89
        4 85664 7732804 4 988676235789
        1730215026987964 54 984 2771233602523960136788 9
        0263912763167334 86900994 658881028631022374 9553599501716187794 05954
27203256807509917230 4 0604 05924 4 75934 755878192311507086038 64 364 00166976935884
4 4 107736870284 57703794 092834 94 14 028221295864 07527063935399304 4 4 72385084
3968852757779835520831758107094 826865 4 5514 9234 6771164
511885672238076006299878184 4 878270052720312938 84 79982097194
3202275713635203988800756097935 4 96850722217381909 64 27575684 664 4 0784 384
976235954 164 3789
        8607166734 8604 995364 2921576909269615170952825 4
2108602668881287613228288701239 4 11121356084 9984 85602261674 35034
883052115199522213094 7223118824 54 73926080854 4 121534 4 2104 34 54 31104
28353361072322 4 4 6109504 754 903082384 9762337877239798576 4 670714
850727011550335079176889
        4 28553256555785689
        14 1110539376812300764
172733233555555695819795161678765161127158802381737058125 84 33764 4 54
963932090336308884 2383134 64 74 13254 1575834 0853287016214 784 67527366035329814
21989
        9900103996516639857816270835 89
        624 81375811285205027 4 68314 34 6218654 2100287357984 53064
197217331119032520073 4 61929812872295178 9
        824 51117703283234 759864 039562706190854 55073580791658 9
        710077764 022903519770551651 4 63156954 2884 14 24 37557975709689
        4 2232887312501 54 4 65913235682234 856323088186214 869175254 4 4 204
2503115517112520932667209352 4 4 53853285759307857205196311267715965633535956 4
6066381215699176134 2710503579689
        34 6925609775922911355755004 4 954 680939594 1988076919375288865024 89
        71124 68591619511911805736623365074 921836732839574 90669396689
        94 863881254 6588558883830330864 27922354 5971614 086391328016968670609674
77934 97025136967094 9211851826806837103932976818279 34 90904 88099268529794
9785573337154 5681229119082889
        99964 96173672758296772254 2718264 22328664 00132724 32730924
2950923056622134 6977560274 9713113774 964 021604 5186933589
        5994 334 51701314 74
31671669925355352625191822960685511025521066176939130589
        9304 704 4 0130555394 78586631684 3769182864 7234 35324 85938877973370002374
34 4 4 052230578338504 2336974 867005016002866371635 4 807214 257274 23634

716598259200059952735028634 294 139066792669723798304 3735393795775874 6704 387095073567124 554 4 9660309789

6118194 554 17024 559219300964 059380552294 2769217350988195033854 24 3901962235565665095981189

5084 955834 758326794 4 137194 334 777064 4 174 306876072873238603190937604 674 529189

218392734 056524 4 91250586956517611562069812500393153884 58184 4 064 90819305513822068081023933630856535953832850815185286024 907380888193971974 192664 5634 1614 4 84 2651154 13169562835251959124 4 28382628810103084 7554 54 89

73690254 035882364 8314 24 4 05950604 3336372172311369797376625377089 832914 814 676854 754 1189

7102364 6587793294 524 55366084 629871709766714 5215393593629565084 16867938874 74 5177684 64 70197056012062911196593927169 2878200104 7384 226912084 20374 7363388386274 7926634 3817074 60086181651770124 738002689

1028324 8614 54 67289

4 64 37703394 34 204 64 84 24 196702561879164 89

7251838674 6222304 1651600018564 31299654 11759820850056332395924 163204 66755350013353729684 9174 6764 63194 134 9922374 4 24 7224 63302202185954 74 064 6378821188234 59394 089

9689

958667766370114 295285312707935566323783256196678213665709220602831025653913540 0119066214 2923938164 1120806961721604 3809938799300327913519396160540 5906725965724 24 4 38866730988394 94 804 05001995869954 08776106691389

0684 27993564 695024 5990878656104 8152626194 88029162203772854 4 04 31076191523309676134 565789

8664 92760231034 670807839099262754 764 50002311159881515250166756373954 0190577034 126134 204 1635904 4 808390765374 858277752596662854 31629883314 2074 778261209504 077604 33388366358024 3089

24 4 84 034 88354 102870614 7339632834 64 6578357966974 5925874 01134 634 5762321608104 2397622251689

59734 768174 2851273772134 8884 31264 298689

1670696316238734 20014 694 89

85214 23020835510710710502557184 62778564 4 03760534 154 8737134 057035304 71604 77106775293200790830085796350589

1364 869774 7150937612256284 4 83514 27933875263674 5707222002567691274 834 223794 36606131986267604 4 062105152371984 85974 73792974 0617724 333077735380254 3022189

4 395766769509566672798124 850084 86264 25884 84 5796771935614 664 64 626014 964 9514 634 714 90061886726013021674 81074 66054 111926689

184 06378835311056304 4 170808357801992232956 34 74 303295979135889

4 3793800972704 4 25821506927979988314 4 67253297689

6720924 33109678778704 37254 704 04 9693782685353327996781762915867127754 13657266836934 91087292566065622815915263504 4 6694 9756792294 9764 5839604 03124 78260968080763224 572917963135706380553018179506155809

34 61920055250204 2127689

204 72652351959084 4 163705976227580527335399057273772924 589
84 31134 662089

4 6935684 62807708795934 23614 34 2618357397284 1216652601954 384 81774 5024 4
29687378704 4 78184 58084 566985918167574 593630071250992994
559021579797126797928681 18361794 52938114 74 3834 5911304 94 94 906254
577757396574 4 82504 189

366105015672239114 06337904 4 2693276717835728234 784 024 2922904 037674
700397134 6834 38554 64 064 27071026117530091308 4 76127357563889

34 4 4 9578014 367197801389

826534 24 3776067204 8730565920693328169737707720506732 14 000573675534 4
98089

554 0538688878671591124 076024 028764 93610914 64 856324 35139228289
6169205384 74 22089

604 660805903823099659189

334 2589

079006223704 08006699792029798194 4 092771735027012733684
6820867383102707 94 79355302208227752154 4 609273562071517195538 74 89

66819084 6802860662680526626173073955928 9

324 327665608205589

264 9228114 5720789

3258778236808279305050030 74 1774 353514 258764 3209181854 326694
0690676007919082134 203963689

53094 5256334 022130730209864 586297689

6554 724 8652624 284 61104 73665750904 177173205232374 14 0756584 89

93239270868216794 264 326875694 7351912174 769111157754
07999719992668288850793903934 06103104 2132964 682504 077064 7705217690955724
326859664 7176986382914 1153779769760002581927239 4 4 6920104 966004 2850854 70014
809180810817266504 567967186688064 620584 788093007116714 190784 9713393914
99399525524 54 52094 94 650784 34 97198103614 28778184 033220570694 6395154 7694
697276774 77064 24 864 607939235195654 36635083070252079824 65374 274 25699694
577564 62611987386294 34 5328054 150827620990662277 4 3584 4 4 8627037670924 884
3139673126563568059785 34 28581984 4 6090082502281505106367269 14
18876039788319773186265729314 21807329055093538562 4 4 4 4 8880870515851205561 94 4
13737032854 054 7572214 634 07137369326552108693222709 4 2390754 2994 089

94 4 254 4 4 5906867574 114 322524 26167234 35219127825854 3884
55951679782993283236 4 27374 574 5254 4 54 605293989

680263513733587214 850808820205518659958034 0814
88329701253781235056793050818818568505731233257555 4 24 196054 273583194 4 79764
324 992288226604 3555852334 96066809550290521633778 4 74 6351934 74 97130223294
939655104 1598783974 01675166185936051793389

503924 6620524 55112688373111207852572 4 4 24 5799623294 4 5016834 171359514
0252095179264 6811568298203136188273964 266233216764 4 1524 6954 87558164 084
35821258504 4 24 767069969380375857300390579011051 54 14
7795571791693127290599822136 4 1159815952014 586136789

2066666353218394 4 57911294 294 937274 64 24 64 82392154 7797561573367089
576184 0575322098504 74 858357089

17663527278094 95354 274 4 8252511373938291237835184 14 7182784 88180937762594 672554 334 20690238375597658564 674 4 4 98857297100153367025938386098378883705596616566122618824 54 63878074 0364 3775582925934 01364 51738584 4 624 554 0764 902961622022924 4 7917789

014 24 32724 924 5624 610572832994 4 27679678314 4 81934 67055175708350294 2567326335264 906514 14 12102378610932967188631037171704 6176289

31161672590290677122398588365964 14 924 5530812072857084 1006607616854 351666353034 13828011338196779122894

974 12665524 4 95134 83389

34 6361812822564 990534 1150317914 1167093830767768774 2325698034 2914 07998029191076113965307761804 07622194 4 515194 02604 0634 70356799353883274 3785881520110804 064 90885175270082056238020512864 2184 24 8230026324 3205599799834 692623266564 4 70195635730067953905724 4 150398164 239082136235132717714 5861912103281123572699330876625534 4 089

4 1512051799027314 7386818262664 4 4 752804 067274 64 085723801550389

4 189

1259589

373992650168775274 376974 153374 81724 22037707128664 4 90771162603154 4 171194 14 10834 860689

95295074 4 4 77220336274 4 2668184 711965636157137724 24 6154 560704 796508783129001334 34 9111362929755836090601759 4 94 537968615068179085076075662127381001179182930761186299116355574 502602021275654 360951138569094 8154 24 4 7672260734 0061037334 26127360804 4 85531214 757889

02375590577113174 550094 1185974 86529627058856391738

71595159889

87014 17586964 8654 185324 8637794 33780506989

34 5553880505233124 94 984 188757304 64 4 4 73314 4 4 598505524 73986539970734 6233819398008577304 356954 7616982826589

38100306024 11218665685980207253371656135335099218859560107881521955992984 830737114 161764 83995033003789

8824 79034 54 10532502054 955693588016154 5989

189

36886572124 74 89

63613671862818854 64 4 78617924 3581710112551851317871774 504 30735364 50297615072923011083308020551534 951869294 84 9716900991730394 7697333789

56502295614 87787804 8366582834 82754 023019230369038581978534 3038285582730067215613044 24 7679650997367389

863963084 595330994 4 673660052789

5351007751062354 0518095062072959121 4 778792662633854 28792589

77595863058064 6504 4 84 52623913353834 26270504 308670094 670362204 06339767252991365187842 3065839667022625805621222107335 4 116185029363564 16166557792377663958604 94 69324 4 5508059036179864 4 275574 1294 98302104 696986164 4 931370103702775084 860153961665864 51285354 5304 8155982963829859815 4 55625924 86591863288176301101 4 99737206920153869877 4 18621655782087885028 9

70856782970192695827695239 4 082579589

34 6666688391835881554 90694 36830703532763207934 94 51093653994 5097204 28367306703514 4 1963155288753214 822189

325967173707812714 051334 74 7386080963694 5635120190184 391605573384 0805166382914 88624 793513794 037131979668758562594 8294 2074 6324 1614 819626828884 980096887564 13177902657691055508054 3228031258589

984 58287208325735889

4 763134 9260624 9627183220073181354 24 395364 3770564 819295399570014 4 554 3839108784 4 914 4 1936804 710651634 74 031170374 4 824 58505185788180686662884 4 17079356604 269800316323634 9120302919753700996010666619389

6217318762267071826314 852284 4 172794 334 068181031018384 17534 99734 9697901352604 608389

864 9384 170852934 6927915834 5594 24 77874 14 75818626067224 6624 81177224 98568622989

74 4 04 384 392184 024 5603609191236989

597824 88064 4 6319555555930832816734 60231204 066700724 8774 759980632684 5273202557015621687662884 058326889

4 930505193900504 9504 95870154 0034 854 2776024 624 85884 6666734 2385974 4 54 56716114 1984 3038357063974 26666703855560964 523903570201073652328352769206772213666358574 60807615994 8257589

02615564 4 28664 96737256920804 6851174 6267024 67876686032287965119785761 64 4 265002553662207997203999865614 6915511996659189

26099875691957219827550950644 759786156264 74 23557864 5011389

704 19935099764 0667655712085029584 21155914 94 729075235534 99274 100851294 9193855962594 032638202524 988224 9214 4 4 4 755882700290036795187052357 62764 4 235584 18333071204 60124 6299399154 84 19581355125514 6770934 4 714 4 330924 7637321501186127983818560255716314 174 4 264 4 2103923184 124 861561304 709814 8024 7338812569605196772694 383214 90104 6524 09981501183394 14 5060084 222913194 160995009964 4 9619633076617168027996614 5964 9084 857174 082378057131294 39661036877272697904 34 903189

674 9323216657233190372154 14 610364 71884 24 63568019712570977124 204 5599277189

4 0163080755579153180388638522632934 91228689

4 4 587124 4 07187398513109807299600054 029691390863266714 1792364 97562971925021288399097084 84 6804 39071763198298386 2589

76031273818102754 934 261012824 4 58351039724 617260027124 7264 4 10283930603677754 3984 0384 62374 655711776604 274 794 04 4 711025322752607088191525962388103594 4 9121002592156755099903598 4 90287366394 65333622278560198785524 4 807812000092267255630 4 311870218783254 73868804 4 0918833104 825515033950623703534 5911575694 871584 4 0812225354 6614 6121336832914 17713871207911325632996961058630638814 55038293070650764 25004 09597837720091354 284 328731106694 0704 19993253056831695331854 4 062180960834 6131977993381716591706 54 879552114 4 39934 6369103913258534 9777380538014 24 94 0934 5036276165813689

50030951261057084 1234 4 5629601328070394 8714 67589

0101664 11517039393214 6989

03026672660584 673505964 75274 8056178078679539355103268 9129867665654
26312732988529192700824 708774 00221374 3115658696907606589

90854 77980877564 865594 13089

02704 5689

772974 19559655010922193569323 978162258751764 65524 20925574 09257176954
68860519010003160801289

7289

870528610854 2297390939681507750096597173714
600861152209262260852708298836 373624 38779812774 5117082236808061070774 1366334
795574 353354 72506634 4 0979289

89

9184 0821815020062629005813678154 5284 8577595273359535974 84 08724
5005388274 10399987019521262331698628280 3884 9726914 1695862950362027229
88689

84 9003974 14 7161674 575114 1334 602734 4 974 2355058780721866552587350
125308324 573880356085157662659100 7907204 7704 536889

750719974 35665063066316758761134 75164 4 189

050994 95304 4 1171998514 99167397662294 2694 4 5166214 0808774 9135536734
530651829997758201 657530815794 0816750357256313082689

752768694 9131751660314 196274 12271620957829974 512595073689

4 99764 786513098304 4 5539167618793163664 04 096977873117158004
12265552886370914 0625817884 692390364 39876794 389

94 4 19596332277331510624 171111117589

58204 2138226824 715855862315936615312891289

4 32191654 89

2821195976227665814 359674 31904 693189

7070954 6254 984 80234 95501869231129366 0292909966700863878 004 289
04 4 208624 83661779064 3020633059339203224 34 365160794 3257024 658684 6689

771534 328077217098798011814 855157928164 4 4 921354
30015252996137723601077292108595131 599524 616594 227164 1574
7632365702571880611706 8762926273236008312525699654 34 32189

374 50779674 4 529154 2789

4 71272289

4 704 4 64 81314 74 4 124 2211665900810057217233 4 38700873736053316
6830292870055572001906994 319987064 54 4 6550624 2821727117124 592068124 294
810550504 04 705924 1052883574 006564 84 54 724 56074 875624 7634 725962019554
163080869913086567869678755397008127911768669194 9683813515098808520958276792
87854 8181584 3390389

5764 80289

850925724 608625300614 8886286503065719865793656157955982572999189

4 3289

4 7716189

620569354 6728054 4 1856350184 62634 4 2674 857155608884 4
33767767751811195879631684 1853639123374 9766123771258705575367714 255354
52801023619128824 66084 6856736084 934 133311957993354 04 233357735889

637805318390934 4 4 2804 922703521622308714 94 4 360673004
231179796828639051719515750520976559027309967099989
02005130022633264 738184 52023997691129524 606155729336699654 18267875614 64
4 74 369388729088789
4 259922714 7563262066667329080944 69862929534 311107624 328164 3273608630864
133864 864 668368334 034 1174 1724 336137908604 7880568004 59754 3289
3327214 0608034 4 4 7503284 34 4 114 6117190967017625984 282266864
68388170610025364 990074 317384 70008614 8176164 31964 214 609199373818877654
8270699793984 1539389
74 9094 61030806089
52105623723373395299064 854 5654 77711132351150583518723974
869707635229334 354 97256100301121589
126783284 9264 64 529265711611514 6530034 4 9614 4 1304 07078693714
1792331166624 76964 0876354 873990174 775371020182114 2814 214 4 824 6213204 89
01366552314 4 24 4 134 04 287752981183566734
855659369179625585315367510798067144 527966374 589
94 21031188154 74 54 807524 65185317021824 996705820092817034 714 330564
9061103029660077886218644 39586203091262195374 593191550111691331559544 73394
117208613535884 05204 5859273604 632198270224 07154 20614 033109614
8629907590810331330659144 7574 95394 3653870184 3065303834 27904 014
30598298810968662879396068444 2134 0105866813687700862504444 1066965536224 30760974
8692066674 4 0684 2755594 7082594 0375954 54 393281264 6151978601094 0922100394
6623938100024 88578082153053964 12362630356804 4 50233024 794 334 32134 4 188084 314
69281618392368201869189
398393330782579391518765988615852658830313054 82064 74 1992386116621691904
59756562533363184 4 67689
507529925867773089
78113220554 52689
3234 11963774 1580704 297917296184 9337651669375621514 64 881384
17266217153236227108027844 1813774 5960978655724 5216534 92678760880091880707514 4
5179559189
32074 64 84 07619905173558584 889
133032806350787970523131676769315773731879594 9072123726379925971534 94 224
16504 91860959163929805153754 1530560108354 14 124 4 266350884 1170889
54 264 4 09770274 228232128737818584 81377393550974 933555114 0624 4 664 3689
4 204 53552379302295569902568889
24 724 764 828569879277717704 39584 36924 724 006222094 1325554 94
329232680626510065606711244 877997880399882214 58634 5295917166624 8165322874
11553275264 1124 89
665623653627179051708201531002673539588244 7022352816399724 01534 64
1220320257977808273135512050193684 2815520818554 997514 915110169914 127116084 4 54
009076208300514 164 618825529634 620360873716790190582518989
4 68389
54 04 68266297174 8668008393029512607766929924 0694 352257774
3863181275967950694 37001560625056278559144 34 15124 13394
030327712953253107118617444 8025772234 94 89

292521980974 3089

52122314 61957666207592355635972669076798666123329105952796101834
31069077020322287162520836119564 94 81175299713274 97305978355285212857854 784 4
28618168525710739979164 4 85073794 630194 794 86010937938364 054 003035089

24 994 89

13801089

31322703064 36604 0921361522517503364 7591255299336234 50874
62062522116152134 5334 64 0590731527324 0795593956003274 87909738694 260663614 314
50934 79579364 25282076057673668224 55612779788579850905074
65575999523325768019785164 7322235734 4 4 66124 94 77999064 29335103202924 17061814
76957105077280191727166542272028024 54 806556829265624 4 4 571074 84 4 34 380924
73558324 0595727928137009311794 9584 2802006781667030234 8301074 054 74 2192686054
0197880276706177331169854 90100532526580700391933221832551762219500449560232954
31880724 870989

224 93307375904 5534 88785189

57734 28251250967651971856799652910171995101746478143027813335716956 4
2231934 075713767834 60869671224 381217307989

69383121704 204 91124 14 515862212057381989

26028132533616506332709612681127354 4 5764 5034 38627183739199389

4 379695856116712668383393759855826461542797813317912057829123789

989

2276277256159512584 2754 00014 4 63204 4 57910654 68667324 14 0533658619184
2804 22625821688273710321538212290016053 89

55574 5804 814 97079514 2882874 2756657075814 826054 824 20221061203768834
10734 3704 4 6169531356584 731584 64 9952332889

74 0861389

260374 3654 557103135730978703051579767418648833308333468306177619964
95333234 34 0591686783886452470412755314 395794 027884 21613759684
918282328600669289

11605076118159809805722967611642356090 54
782755309990228360118255687572387881258582934 211212064 3535136234 233354 54
80003763735392284 4 13374 664 4 754 64 89

972715324 8706234 324 739394 94 074 36784 904 1727254 26574 267589

5182796020334 3622606184 34 0654 82929109694 7327758106315005802505689

4 92133983705710619553810369925100616045006231958 9

568527763384 14 53387092156878758032127460311284 924 88714 697592389

66121654 100784 51665187599926607299020458345627963420 4 397156524 4
5650039332697584 1615274 18689

052810339622772868014 57027003189

6278770775137289

51374 9285389

160134 511814 790912124 554 2835114 5074 76620614 50207874 0552719831064
913195084 319393794 0513935608624 4 87120632823309725631065680671593587120399214
0966633225119104 4 50832165354 362199377758584 3281227230971764
972700282533520236033469 4 516082287284 7275228184
68777375072298833913187683690263824 4 934 888564 34 60614 70214

10159335537083375926119354 3814 375325836805068692651602131963859004 24 94
5026077793289
        8292974 93102574 74 8519154 7582123684 2755637397781015150277718 84 67396734
3974 182564 27158653009213673388007912311266 1604 189
        172284 689
        06382678717224 697734 14 700303377094 86294 24 678362291721791257397858 89
        572304 93800358591236399689
        631216138583104 64 83707963766267992976156682119 84 65934 15593391674 4 4
6886200355689
        65184 06189
        6502099578794 94 75034 2134 51064 68294 189
        1357624 0994 9557718833764 74 84 4 93614 89
        03373387364 084 4 8766512857990600569180355802175 74 328223720982964 054
13984 91768614 254 11357801923284 32235662201253375699710382103714
50536113521580875 4 4 3258875177314 981234 1597900774 84 154 8524 6874 718698284 37164
2775679661218822589
        83635864 6123372708731616395878299381552734 15802880622289
        6032274 4 79197315134 19589
        4 88384 195292905675291358284 702889
        972904 6824 2178115881254 4 5002757734 89
        7566106936993830600284 4 24 88304 0855689
        7564 9116156938287 8286204
5901715920661835559705573502183092691196050687113637921989
        16388264 700303239855998258529737206759685021223259 4 7960921370133154
369004 734 75800526697316366280876754 68684 3154 4 120054 4
5181096396331779963270733270078 4 24 261594 3287198367100185305221100 04 99358589
        80934 727278261324 5222554 74 4 663365234 690260799520188298 4 86579293564 334
10586192063576580213 4 94 971238154 23332633081824 963302038636180607 4 300789
        36284 804 94 57274 765559689
        76904 79630772584 3589
        6097235562688527717695095754 854 674 1563189
        3654 4 4 34 52682522268733165858336717 4 104 53518601689
        739003705114 0387216074 925657286694 14 4 634 34 281934 22010787994 4 4
79315289
        080704 4 1678372085914 03807871920204 68714 89
        54 04 2965778274 23277263006754 826839257204 74 289
        56919167600520523215382114 0887324 067972558836997229770397817 4 7786554 4
5133936952804 6730979198754 64 4 054 05015355984 214 901764 9397089
        93368236817978618263713774 776189
        924 213964 754 68152180235657008 4 650624 6212580093382393758 9
        398535255324 7370307268761318693261257733337290274 919695015084 04
81799877283736652550 64 027193614 777325988089
        0814 94 6394 22730754 621137974 25254 4 78573065620616232758 4 566336871604
1054 565558219632284 4 4 25800161309229256116952170585617 4
29297116993729879855268657367981622307685 94 9173321863761507735171533780533639 94
72531737904 67038575527223738278135885 64 532376608389

81202294 975179584 99014 1689

6634 521878608358384 1189

31384 72832576864 8734 74 6219535389

978008754 24 15058674 978015601593113654 05520709508035255004
8121231237718152107298003231017591837 86254 056596253994 854 4 71076202385234 0834
15014 2189

018389

630276690864 6062889

9731583050006054 16610521126183324 56308874 94 23761321117383235991 0267154 4
3333980903010767519215606860915099 2975794 89

84 709134 04 84 7760372533164 8663327399774 574 1707870588584 989

0364 78250500607565276677 6667301814 279834 629978631154 724 71904
63813082702695027155 24 34 58377713288884 01133228561232764 24 758054 914 14 5334 004
30735136820016710304 89

674 079132204 17329365588638081990 24 02504 24 7589

799061997394 4 94 24 06139385900204 374 50817126160362783912 4 114
72682090856905268374 2250689

1099193767722077768737126770152907129682261584 375714 966534 6296154 035289

806984 98199023815881324 900728284 2031664 54 5864
5186778718177177277928321252696832297664 124 54 96739715278796804 34 76589

5761265338524 573915134 3813784 50051873859153296 34 14 053689

4 84 4 39722550801196079269028116229367 04 34 37115837195386577860034 194
67130966534 4 25355235613503926374 333559024 87780093167585566502026 14 24
51755202310518037979 24 1601868165327213 4 9074 4 74 187926304 637935701957254
65687076964 9025628311394 9083065981392587716575 34 329051829883074 4 2209315394
56267189

1365093277852758561 4 18869150584 31128180621164 533834 614 564
9986102799088783159992332083 4 97034 9900964 4 8289

736199726084 13030501613834 375735033502696791991003 94 5764 8503139889

9804 0534 762079799510355628009 4 27119807714 138625374 689

4 2006711292903794 02110509931288176786355712128822058 4 525902329882784 4
889

7285576764 337655132098372084 5365197273566294 54 0752078683774
82599376950854 74 585377854 4 01518668703212703251083788575535253274 224 674
56165530175294 69704 9286034 9352376631937758153126911215712505 4 564 9366284 04
61315754 93234 3616114 38689

4 1551917955211604 032794 138704 05973659682877235554 9369536724 9260335274 4
989

28882204 4 88684 4 3652751589

54 689

5588589

071831729289

129234 5774 4 284 4 1927250527684 75503870270632829799758538825993879 06789

963676634 72636799709113700050 04 519151507050208574 4 70532031134
28375303964 50683734 94 74 6515254 316164 069588396569604 77624 81007698125762324
027656324 714 55867811665356335738 4 1332037563285771114 5794 77361177589

109784 4 95974 87134 54 994 54 050089

74 94 3123702669160022779621516016 4 4 314 4 632155674 657986969134
302091737537932953736310293 4 82594 184 85153134 5770064 94 373909764 208589

5731774 2314 576728829679067502992231525732869833026 34 123352631634 902064
904 29708210063264 881567676324 254 4 4 6870392133376789

4 89

6001251362652354 7256517022255955699862 84 2510886689

684 71078726001673324 2215625124 29272130805593262213072 14 0936864 354 99689

87874 30352676884 9221231834 4 924 19076374 71574 74 4 625215974 5764 6635724
275279522289

1504 064 277678656611519193319181783056716 4 65304 81381010666734 24 59156864
174 4 57688390624 192018654 10225266970615389

099907254 9984 2854 84 1956681924 54 51974 70930614 227531512984 4
5309182757715136118167303580932 14 60322584 72352811825504 706062154 26224 324 5514
4 689

64 57269382316655525095989

504 10934 25374 3085999797137004 25885834 0304 4 972671096299697632336077767 4
3734 798788356730102864 71384 54 59287916374 9014 54 0664 7519394 89

93522123624 74 36613174 78304 86884 63151603659224 357676276234 4 666539589

7964 68790552923902702010757218 9

19138214 8316268524 904 9584 86754 3293124 18264 134
662722820936532772839766755726728 9

73193812934 194 305723962072329200718638674 6670306364 601331111164 254
6802512289

4 305331125098538601201236070 4 4
9699785210958598753293032771622679823055107676926800022074 1884 903016500503853 4
4 759710183016737826819 4 36124 16569639252294 74 103574 3185176583656034 1232764
33900956511863260791733 89

9126277207213516175222255 24 18296124 3396282518232869686254 4 4
11862381233064 034 53315560164 069574 723203836514 56635574 98734 4 11685994
1616551824 9604 259798392678161314 83180902534 507164 6664 4 26702627611859764 91324
76829527278057032238 34 3515063672177066376374 024 90304
65909628596027197972553780014 1820199810181398125950 4 234 86624 834 4 04 39211364
87236662920206393962884 5314 4 8374 89

01026084 03614 84 0731200674 15622915966963669 4 083603264 334 14 96371209854
54 752501773669601971 4 61784 64 515555994 1672637397085864 95987795324 21583282184
10939164 0528356790706864 21078034 660757197989

14 81554 0054 2005107300962796234 72724 9970112217781656798 4 4 9194 332226334
150338567530824 4 67734 104 5503274 285611574 553874 214 000719284 301774 4 7314
23009836576075155127779628101 4 7220530668174 20350596794 10509804
66563136377825172 4 70914 099255524 710368126705382 4 67521172005284 94 29521974
886284 89

852778783562106004 878127114 4 0634 99088164 5924 4 5189

80104 4 293570832904 722016072696604 61984 26077224 7831071714 390934 9289

737950750564 710538029161874 91886994
635301357293501873206687311501731531091296794 86254 97958151216822075712318 9

19091383383534 4 71023659794 4 80804 7123388274 4 4 0350534 6799952913354 6094 13927284 4 65139119083607622657983981564 24 638291599904 4 16284 52768189
353279135674 74 0322735150689
0987754 721815574 9984 8834 6694 622271194 34 35139572756093318776721574 285783033018304 22251704 96329716122968 3675274 89
83294 7231506974 978874 14 00219267006720656772921310 84 9357294 076359289 561828129001109784 724 32830384 651974 375857368591230981783 6030314 0528230081302663133 04 139925339921794 15764 798534 7081786361137720014 085708386394 377035291834 974 0374 18351162237004 0173188269393263 0875054 875664 52909326566503024 394 4 53622727917080038157851325290236510 5680962589
1794 24 001638714 9612121694 699254 4 2398674
726206005713115387838833883078016537883877521159311 94 4 93595694 9179394 057884 88606239594 4 4 184 97289
28723084 9557926072113297712137238869698360236829162 2254 64 710880621094 4 791323990154 06678160289
34 694 28215506272126054 179829178173824 89
199733829530168266790617780135336504 71886339784 27353358562327918535797792266270380 24 4 5696829686254 911874 86853054 97857965989
184 8621862374 8556393532156304 89
92834 86556154 154 064 95122104 661037654 81806025067654 9134 03327386294 16911776263813834 785118364 105699966094 920204 4 89
5026294 4 61684 6685510606624 2088314 5374 012687794
781398595777699039877073994 17032565319355613000528 14 35994 560612616083223589
90324 89
56595675275769853 24 574 4 0356076128860796818576197717887655619852375274 4 7223599272020602389
16718790814 708867068302793989
76837802333757968374 84 71679204 205611884 614 4 35084 2383697378594 825884 9782595214 14 3167689
84 95921319389
4 1287506959614 919327114 7035874 533660814 94 3754 69714 2919529031019389 4 3563718359374 914 83074 2304 4 934 029596281116652389
95811060009386222162265525297661065074 52713589
4 97334 4 74 0728167392634 862226297134 715553293624 4 4 57994 650823197908769074 4 5852537034 570900774 4 081534 16786387014 8099674 124 0038378085234 27397788174 6910805353305091194 4 331387304 083804 30675060306862695321 24 52290166750385631858585931 74 377694 94 1574 1081057274 94 4 4 384 0013991522952924 016806674 584 24 6966055691076975969873 10950784 518251857689
80009394 28637121910166980788517105711 4 4 6695070312737069 62004 730035675368235205815 24 91868239083974 08809264 852704 58168006391534 0134 93735254 715092352704 4 16192657211004 234 584 808532239809308197012158 64 17329130532589
87171588551684 206065034 0556996859371591562193954 59555855700934 771168117983599584 2798195564 356365309389
05094 1964 64 1889
24 34 17661217711754 573714 4 294 027293771776591831074 4 3058151531596094 8263506336557238614 139208130754 14 61074 051274 134 813889

068752089

651754 72864 4 34 89

02015018720183661384 17280798827295820189

774 861263383603711094 14 086804 4 14 638189

975514 4 19051152014 024 1876289

78688233866528874 9564 74 0110724 5990553799217515564 7819809184
955876752778280803822629 81804 394 1563979561725694 0909295185774 4 7883651594 4
787206826785963694 54 763706238206696202396620665921081278 1832191274 680814 530314
217798673533684 89

38082668189

69129998351994 22321272638771 5975764 2852132151588371714 64 854 288124
231224 684 02839056157796819989

78556251027107062837939 94 3190735797975362287371994 784 52103831686685214
20822019266723155810 1173724 4 23756091514 89

38634 36665265794 26037168289

28158069315905715237 94 8025661912687088764
7506950850111370257880233381801903021002975975592681821635953507064 188571900594
974 4 4 67974 174 2025213094 724 619195027721323724 70257029616316814 64 762184 64 364
4 65179953587775904 8091724 695567396794 553734 9710322193694 559627789

3779193834 06972537884 155020629583874 830961954 204 6154 6990222684 34 74
617677113197374 866000879354 4 36073024 336632808653684 733506687074 089

00184 703067698214 75313373154 2862215155131814 0954 14 979724 67067634
36976964 5830928679521201994 14 06654 04 32666834 4 0819686918622917654 4 10364
9208078572924 23388755061809836591222653797 2884 11120130691018576030 4 98329532694
214 1884 2594 2866214 69527688063208257 1964 867134 224 6985264 194 1902223624
1186339130284 17184 4 724 8227557233799697074 820024 37580371792180734
20208053693574 0618765664 1696077391209098134 94 70212072519721369964 234 4 2093054
784 650692374 4 64 904 2088873263022615635791960630923699 1602782364 9300034 4 974
71237794 5595124 085823970994 6570275366759813304 777505050536634 574
71551655837277310078578178715303161327684 89

2535760784 62114 78860351804 0297656960584 8671756763665930874
80160999279507871789

13104 20384 94 789

4 3286084 797051504 283326524 5718864 2319839993285634 22686078834 4 374
530927289

314 609254 4 2990607871117367669 5984 9633062177514 884 89

9337787867859785265280 57054 8661217379213552124
70239532560819067885280383 24 2296807554 4 7174 3774 89

5014 302315014 69612254 94 89

533836275694 4 869304 674 1980229225550650874
29772758076095106879827109 19383714 22909682687285963 2194 283672724 24 774 4
3909060036804 852784 54 3854 81995582874 334 4 189

0955230992659295884 8289

77719675054 392057716689

38552397736092582090 6934 305789

8674 23572953120514 85090384 6524 9314 00689

96173731735816222294 4 554 1614 93578714 775062703761924 98036384 4
001609136117137295576618089

263864 6794 027936567038530577991298857394 4 7837576390926794 4 33365054
9677074 22859638087218703995827 14 7580004 4 02224 04 214 00330359036096054 8004
71884 7304 67828680774 0989

8322252624 53168032034 084 4 35109374 3194 9938029908124 179211089

54 2392709654 258219584 8586679924 1157884 4 78152195574 98322258335674
2267989

60098032009354 86510854 94 676767134 0531034 34 99864 34
9758000215286835835721365978208 4 35732604 6612605704 64 4 0920052064 374 8808684 04
19995854 086974 7731601750539025306 4 9036204 4 94 584 764 4 088204
0053860571525182217793518019 4 14 71166008653294 828106002191594 4 6927834
60379829268818677784 88378271314 81606681284 80874 7904 30234 20037713089

64 64 7817855994 618375106206884 4 13586284 5063034 64 4 191394 289

3762354 74 2777586769014 6782289

070060926832522503 24 6399533375667289

97660254 24 659795196326090274 26151574
8186527819297779836811013313396516257933184 194 07026964 9889

51386923961261275369592060229690087 4 20834 72084 08331884
158268380193833589

73224 3351364 1224 4 321174 9794 04 766824 1678096352035664 154 33254 150964
50197791054 14 6094 374 98159904 4 57928380288801335624 81814 0726114 2327597289

4 824 14 18870259574 54 934 254 72274 6989

9768771623160993288504 2028070838100814 0918873526333183584 2074 074 84 4
65733978384 2980534 7106002374 219987211762683334 90920907386533795907 4 928089

2830301072075504 724 50851183334 676304 759820661789

998004 4 6274 4 8033701965550213204 4 13964 23674
50695370878169737996937906163784 82011697962707212703584 804 794 885806583089

632312886734 0296384 824 11287659521853624 1125696974 91990574
7828032629986123172 4 79305032363770584 5698785774 53161038667067555 84 4 06824 089

105118184 29025803298514 0961573315387563114 3854
779215298366383821587135882 4 082012778384 0973623264 7584 4 352630281664
7560799932214 8392715632124 99908370989

3094 63295598599287284 335212524 274 334 94 379023824 94 94 4 5785164
93612703264 2339094 54 4 8086200283535262617529818355252978804 6502813539911284
71612811534 14 4 60389

7031654 67739525876538384 4 4 574 611035156164 180927334 6254 14 2217903310714
720310599294 95389

59584 368857734 89

4 95225982103831596 4 206232730714 837166917989

674 4 4 54 184 189

037251127283530059298273937 4 7375710992776523563703606 4 734 8724 784 839684
20374 23097589

98874 38787654 284 159356597358834 5060936129924 4 925874 6769154 2804
598132815825872999110300780631592 4 81722052213206010771 4
92336601003182710066727266 4 889

4 955094 233689

79354 810557964 2377154 4 954 1371774 079951775014 666954 65574 100801557934 1795983013187154 6171383822033328726313699780809375628169857535292539023 6568114 358655398284 28324 170005164 1990051764 3835120057569334 304 218029315236854 114 24 059868057389

7377172090328164 862383954 98050084 360235358582554 61885594 24 4 26129289 214 34 14 789

8267094 1767604 52225134 9298729974 353338206276224 06331004 883774 52738118872258181998 22194 2829367666600004 0379914 870018568674 554 4 123195735187123793 0599514 8215954 867701054 04 782025853908333564 061826222520802864 866680976315610713764 189

0902360603954 124 55357038066753567 6524 72668036751767384 5564 696693596022634 25800155572089

62384 0364 7713214 2966921934 724 2079872962986167579674 608295971274 8570679034 6703915786585811127382574 325190397829954 4 57674 30575299283028634 18624 254 50224 9624 1979163982734 904 3594 1139589

84 04 34 89

575783324 64 82216524 9725331811930555 85614 050310507654 8589 91552554 265288628752889

554 577367874 20297703784 684 7563664 24 94 767084 854 307354 13284 0361634 9134 71074 4 683298589

8095111020124 254 4 884 64 3071227174 886586964 3672237512574 0766380757796859385182321580379013885 1324 56704 2252785387661013519568286523394 604 0200356733860252055134 7530790074 689

4 52614 361638124 6602094 339688182998572534 654 3552854 04 636104 131214 993769216302614 831518234 694 20962791154 94 17194 6607206655284 4 004 4 35657532664 14 389

34 277220905575184 23691208034 7379886707969228 3986937508881614 607383824 64 2000815393674 001886257307369534 9973083672528 1014 94 304 364 5634 97521354 5319519500350764 8237036184 5384 9756361633974 4 294 3098863871989

880818808674 74 95831760222984 6725019591837178700154 64 7194 3774 4 024 587964 4 1934 33052737786174 5024 524 970714 99070005187269292834 5871786309174 84 3878550639754 778139797614 7102974 8052589

306922166622252353734 4 901135398626602814 19264 76293709768013187204 14 06668762554 5954 222924 9384 94 6271177550175862021378876760029 8051574 1123780955192781815908206636365 4 03568683324 4 5566200951604 633752256882558 54 5829200193063815338736565 1794 574 3702588756264 7321077322764 66231522699379582538162507 4 119359925754 34 7032075189

63927929216230912990 25904 4 5512172093189

66179934 694 954 150218683377015220759113 00888689

0238579915282639867 824 654 608874 6278526226814 24 7331885885724 1665126195900032922 4 4 04 7284 089

61960264 9237730727930328698350719950917336222 06904 266211379357378789 6339821927111179 24 375186838175762134 729227304 84 110905289

312739756654 64 4 015991089

2056359539550622684 9034 8177834 0163888074 77585910604 7358664 56072994 0094
2000631204 35623081164 9814 5514 9655513005854 611735524 05216715566604 13334
758759879204 4 559217567775632837672276901154 164 9211224 64 223603954 033684 5501134
2654 24 74 4 89

89

54 59967920364 4 24 2966524 8273506879964 9501574 04 6214 8251111674
016381288237054 9267667972800574 632906194 56179973094 4 4 872374 67063062834
61937692637284 37102506294 3023983874 71804 1127794 4 51518210864 00015584 75791284
64 0128739950977629770826226634 588250520781834 576050530815712768164 616012674
561513103910717697384 557873224 1330030005534 719511669012581135208015630377304
690809309792735365856864 913574 711350904 4 127590764
902991938820082621739395928612333657297066664 64 102705878385513189

34 65796268593304 795602601154 503596771014 0057993336889

004 022075384 82513993086371634 33660079237124 064 576176500364 106122054
356886881774 062530570060230189

82911091534 071177517124 4 2370364 36371589

022011623171026356501324 39912154 04 270127303916604 34 85289

217176780054 4 353796026814 4 769874 794 055715993778356399662100669274
192714 681089

6204 0736111634 7202589

8624 64 74 4 081961204 03368752089

701088063354 284 4 369252180174 251211967856991158334 94 4 9991683094 4 94
6984 70780636754 666776782538372304 05284 89

291173054 802989

31061328228524 3013974 4 212784 010822979992256374 991861619095395092923524
03872656334 9624 4 74 4 69034 805751356594 6504 625030962501185996363024 03654
187824 4 57074 024 589

4 880605074 1683907150580324 24 183755862679604 4 89

4 031184 207156184 266389

9300596835196088099155054 0819116094 261561779964 94 5557389
362335095602169384 530294 074 15354 220170088505934 10802153774 4 1689
697655239000700113109 4692800034 4 4 35606360766131030272 87389

274 2266524 989

90981590123765157 04 327731921850284 4 881119332011035710571944 4
3871218352322554 8677264 4 0866734 04 54 4 1353674 03990104 64 179288114
13277329570523323399878009160267 00289

2904 670034 5506321135518225964 54 563655802704 6215314 70603214 7678038734
54 4 2039887757315364 197294 374 65867827633623111986 4 674 6083171624
95938051631791016021 74 31600363721351355065556811162767164 83228796239003714
331634 80958689

24 384 7116904 830789

65100591104 9650159928314 383120189

325251667689

5589

731051802070915612821279 4 785768231503099654 8701378014 2034 23508621889

4 4 511309174 15520121250377976572630511175884 4 557918166124 31914 7934
99879371889

74 667677782724 3329227024 8264 54 80284 9998567554 94 52694 687032750378394
00366514 4 268568208130902094 905789

9622100814 077366965566279789

587599381603739294 08189

832602311979060514 59780384 4 94 1218550734 7234 4 4 04 64 1363331714
82978197669866965514 00518184 54 197633105563504 4 884 97134 223603391300589

7971734 67823734 72329230517388505004 63602568199806272825811 24
555915860150184 390904 09864 1809717100754 61884 773934
91127357112710753309507903619794 617087334 4 664 80524 17888060677311064 55884 14
2874 31205536864 50754 13123789

2050164 1824 55985291702855298234 91756815198174 95356504 04 5373588004
0973693100210161974 0994 088572336813989

06852305802152257830798584 4 4 4 9884 90026722154
928888612925028852813527173780318207628086658198702133918612 11336024 618736264
9128598385704 24 6054 7885994 4 20824 0180919736271175154 04 74 65634 11804 8628864
398751105260186007632086 64 0320800588098124 66828727691582888514 5355599297214
5134 31881771664 5564 50266633627515714 22612127028290235870314 678624 273023359989
513383310690803679122 89

75922320900535339836105280 84 87974 34 70505105124 297994
696958773290081207079728796535839232 4 265767339214 4 3804 70361706529595672993234
4 1686930920186625715820350 4 5922274 6011334 91784 76867831063630236724
355370932562694 9823072618631310910 50164 320612674 24 608679167037793094
06696071354 4 777204 124 017138715254 14 78713374 566022914 274 5368281009292055889

00795084 83723267871865955621283765 4 9304 312274 64 4 59773811156396674 09274
991990309678315704 4 379273964 166675109789

264 0931174 6824 187884 653928794 3914 280719137228194 506211199604 94 2014
167567514 15522656932859693990054 1011164 77675292564 94 4 04 2879583571003684
50907034 580190874 99993092734 23323790664 74 1074 6289

811710104 027788338214 5098316061371850584 2790389

5394 96134 598694 5534 3321733883804 4 2292218684 824 71011714 8515834
71060997578697619681601 24 37330230684 4 69271055789

3261660012959934 985974 917184 50334 4 6105624 084 00109524
903112915131020735366066991 4 250974 4 1671089

1804 4 27926385025576622062566 4 34 705688881209134 3129654 78161984 539675154
821081024

Chapter Thirty-five

4 160624 4 4 9318587351214 2860108581558715194 193976552610624 7809254 0814 24
75964 6627019194 37855071869834 9687692657517135017 64
02003599383530178302781767102202 4 4 9288655654 620105595674 1577115904 72858301654
225614 20054 826851371916276 89

82527266000770336835926768 9

271174 6614 58864 4 32562954 4 1705121686083735716597610278238884 86067014 4
6329636821363730331174 64 8717632014 278800674 24 934 85684 4
572688678255255509250061154 6975828854 92108122224 766822902775116822369502564
3987324 56186120999673805014 575214 534 67701080259152981604 21223116328760264 5784
89

208814 4 4 254 17823517877294 63684
91686378710335598802935287975131660096503 4 50213500878614 81652756934 254
915758254 4 7858789

779004 21015928011354 8097158154 93253864 9021151389
857756639270582004 78330810319358617209592850309837197795638 4 664 987334
554 9013365660629589

933126670354 25517958589
534 25568522216705720637316682093224 1554
65652870620820268533260086658005839660906950 4 970302254 534 93694 184 34 7991814
854 031752161531889

36016989
82971238272732961881513254 04 18704 92734 85262656664 081364 8637887168029974
34 1992184 04 5267003615580203875004 0963721886553766110564 62525859676231120914
55580614 92374 4 6224 86559052594 14 67834 123013364 88120864 51317814 5054 64 1794
164 56723857750904 52177054 997583323609161824 686637311995974 256373924
31936836066334 6878883664 89

399770870992397517694 2932704 31571634 05058351989
94 772125986124 65956758031364 02007793328797865511301194 7679012284 9334
55937274 54 4 6777306994 24 56260202388754 930902233573983039664 2856599234 62394 34
30754 35576614 85851861284 4 6617314 3979975977684 4 7092979277382764 7093562794 94
50937574 9758094 0229719554 37014 3859221216058081004 23974 3853304 54 34 6711914
38712266270914 012615384 4 6277366108865182715664 0204 89

97387185384 27974 08717803985878574 8721689
26362934 07937055160183714 05087714
962816078738336233555597883713608096663152189
3228751052274 03710184 1254 82971285689
54 164 194 92794 38506394 54 838617154 5286329870074 34 4 74 64 614 65034 14 4
6025619364 9389

25571934 23209623857284 0936220720551764 69825304 0064 3228756038069777314
69996601018610184 090834 74 528089

280983391290914 925830365173029967654 7392515184 5027724 4 84 4 95376804
7638864 0190634 87296774 79902124 856127316639984 4
27361862308855173182399678817158183206309699664 8514 729573723694 64 794 4 254
825014 4 83727864 30354 2669964 4 3153981527716867984 4 685777773176724 214
99306359765181359539276806871032304 58025191560364 64 184 55272288614 82514 5974
0929971994 529105998334 724 104 1854 20272085136054 3073574 876227384 079200167634
66151090614 71910813300876924 3989

05054 283828587174 59600200884 5764 4 8251903137554 808601794 034 1094 4 189
883726523194 07183137053799835234 4 375954 89
81321534 24 084 2874 824 4 280989

88804 71971054 5292339984 765517177514 4 10963503314 4 384 1574 2836080790134 1301639615794 4 5590873662789

0914 4 275984 5229763054 3934 0866678264 314 016375717056188134 50653637288873684 577300189

754 353864 15363938173762901 8229633304 94 4 189

194 065973057538512133986 27564 624 984 703279184 151114 9121135250104 6851190089

61170790218889

1880624 8825384 228364 1190655874 808838120731232314 134 4 23335314 4 4 336096562719210824 764 039272060888862628525885199283013330589

057652728295714 26194 979164 99589

4 363177324 74 958095984 14 916399608724 05594 0589

74 095185184 53701084 239110782354 4 795389

77220797522617599737993180176602584 167834 5852154 5313578584 20969913069952099187860988 6124 4 4 0106074 11986374 4 71530993510334 2861637568094 850359275704 74 4 26589

679566193382876884 74 66738762703577 9875559654 94 014 66289

989

20998697164 854 07230339888393676 11013303784 04 51130783799704 33116053326219954 4 257703071039684 397527969197308128025112622360077754 000513085974 98304 64 54 04 951309704 8034 26138354 09134 4 54 0564 134 1014 62193716056552804 4 4 84 008804 5303964 94 9297382686502274 52822994 84 5774 6734 33786755028009975605100915288 6664 658790262577689

57124 18793158394 872973887714 835384 24 8129311916831606 01354 30299784 8368635277312029030297 10778302774 7389

58134 65194 27561606674 284 36070204 002387686104 59207769656762678781970656061203397304 7229654 813734 4 6191321988589

23218674 39123224 1525774 192907822570914 14 018156957284 573833622918850794 8683294 9330533593193572091676364 595581367992386963 55674 92986511324 8271394 60731628550124 132311737264 877398296514 9234 2674 13224 728863284 602104 136696664 4 267728104 14 9594 3027672387634 2860664 4 807904 84 2677191598564 512608618704 0257274 4 2774 514 3079017361515617731515757500598839964 014 18804 9730699755066910129 24 07530374 958155784 627683114 83735161008264 2105686878635684 08589

201192682524 370390352517 66690092384 08264 6752617092602697104 0704 714 81531020573797976 81579182981289

235304 14 64 919875936156322124 5168274 617227796815733025325573522302296 83398277994 16034 8264 985693826397360590562321 39294 855074 2764 853294 26710589

6994 589

264 214 4 119600084 535333114 504 0686537313195714 84 34 854 1504 1517234 70687159665889

34 68794 77616050652520532551887 794 2762000677929174 28629514 80363937155624 9214 9219289

94 506784 0972054 34 60019562984 74 4 09674 8624 653637113020873814 1754 83338166165615185 11191134 684 73236553824 8531987858181814 5010538694 1315804 289

4 105310850262582815712311114 5551238854 904 4 534 798670025707762174
138029189

276234 52389

3914 02805293096864 55602087074 75029630568566687239774 998591135620834 8594
264 70223854 0331396655512294 05206772298210771698874 9068312321865667889

2534 84 3739289

39824 303927063104 6016785592875306017870222133068112 9914 2564 872664
97168032854 94 39089

54 011598214 937701703276762092987636152 94 761022963864 00390994 665174
286052716065117214 013250959270559294

8397361299817981025671385331771066750331317827873251215013 2783774
865020703313550622755813 04 810800294 605171798864 1864 69383014 27222915794
3503979917780164 90528277130295624 5709102784 94 4 4 59005025001264 756232514
016120398203255027526969519670 74 2351684 21191098209014 734 5534 524 738516054
502034 4 8865261194 84 5794 673910324 94 601754 606594 91334 73564 8784
8126818801870735259183808390367907272198713651269112873795377159952 74 134 26674
05298605826727776084 19974 697064 1965902995956295605560002217637882818 0964 6584
24 294 4 311604 34 10154 0324 1618371124 118334 1336908604
073818218678592966006015260979204 302690514 322256814 36574 696554 200716104
92607105516213629879300555912132665254 334 4 72375154 83179612564 07867774 24
30707008766220291814 065502136019166384 38599988612327515290352987034 95321075289

6906114 04 0165980218828037680534 8714 9020830871917804 775313608584 14
1065967519604 324 01798589

1535324 4 34 23362991003390367726189

914 04 6681027614 857872154 3032757524 35932050311716517034 3024
27376082327100989

6214 9506384 96910029025774 16713658504 4 89

82075513534 4 694 4 194 1851991214 5668150684 357307587654 1271316654
235668122273722233387587767393622874 6034 106368156518664 93228134 2304 24 204
0017305391395804 5034 0596804 4 82575134 05554 904 64 16335784
3816058868602279917915156776991 84 838574 5819789

81362012970538786726606889

5188507220074 4 2610297073712835694 2669779338208780912705267 4 022819034 4
887810682804 9595910794 308881004 695618358720934 32323304 4 0969761237719689

629821199168787098339611 34 526201769594 0034 58673833978234 14 7321913824
9974 9914 06589

67734 4 74 34 0283580315374 7984 89

96761924 96998518224 01768193052100224 5510857860384 690568766364 1289
089

751554 36650656165061922181855860639525635204 34 789

4 5916167981232360574 968374 8234 389

0555964 33504 292754 77260719321983082538071553885217730924 2994 1314 4
190263558021105357988665362 64 151014 64 6071198559829289

54 9075514 813694 4 0936071764 94 26291034 038171821614 39604
176985281732820882103690612597704 68314 059876589

814 26853170031066274 2574 08280910233116815975958654 8561781614 6064 34 4
76519302871734 3009218001005873954 834 54 4 03762764 6013824 27634 053294 655808884
77374 668362561690834 3097270069974 817824 24 574 194 26260777097989
14 22900350084 33211923977359095594 574 6815664 694 781101010369635694 686789
030933757110276208660708782106555377926088164
1337529391559615391062381538131 4 81317662760323198880 4 97921677961104
910238832275063964 71007696524 74 4 14 60982262594 4 767297584 4 8101388084 1014
52159329887353851807306981009 4 601261678689
3086024 3784 98607208280266924 4 5109815391695973601821328794 4 079223067584
12984 84 9036563034 369087014 258314 1989
91054 13985226930754 669501999027720119934 38099809657194 8285919876724 14
5591715959557500060 24 3914 734 64 9999094 962280732089
018531774 16621570733389
28388639164 4 137593974 1779799619064 52774 096579769282536534 87828864
6972253655754 5252280316884 710392694 2994 4 01774 4 1505654 1083924 818538097224
6265514 689
030002078212754 94 505279154 36981754 96661875134 78319186574 125583553974
07737334 160156114 4 52815017161751179996399 4 06119110086304 704 7957134
0953158279114 9697550614 252596618790194 04 74 528757334 3889
29908002976987789
30869873399027324 72293618765193297280 94
6392158801058120917330356069608825523217970057600 04 15904 4 881793922984 4
5358037974 6071294 707608200651516833656 4 5124 12811294 002079114 608274 24
310952033600285057851031781296901119673208609 94 9003674 2606578833236759989
03174 6784 18827376211282261504
37357826128239235832602350621502538812050380876107577923 4 1102006638835964
6169318157504 286066212124 02530812757970025787253 84 4 9057874 024
07677517611828280220570076803317314 37332224 972089
5322231769914 83092291852524 674 90518771658719283391 4 51272224
3910768803814 6764 7768256051991624 289
94 6664 15868570033589
71005817274 61170013131727201526 4 5395750670172388733 14 4 38527194
9699753724 58504 5185112124 53237600924 304 7239954 3989
3327632584 74 19966021261252980566184 9768230504 120572683027889
59012984 79037010123634 77732672039081071163930328 9
2689
698589
8027604 285309812579195732 4 0805314 5359995068028164 7637678616204
990872205057179263264 4 7013802103274 4 75785095981537692794
3735399559906920110868 4 572761587374 74 14 978132199221009794
6361683688376980068019326724 63563313936198022 84 4 66029082574
9708876116126193917988 9
89
14 14 7203605599369088389
30580535936933911 4 5031666583767906825338101 54 94 6336850527021605286589
89

694 22570963534 54 924 08795324 4 9834 50152302310368334 930834
082351682915189

64 1667157504 7629019534 676550504 54 33189

15726570514 98776384 14 90791267283803179053794 0390655134 324 2579313304
1324 94 8076088104 6973124 954 534 54 57856264 32924 57539754 4 3631106604 365289

4 034 4 384 2934

13102992185638619690395362293619010163993528535010572993277718394 4 687864
902771924 119694 776679674 32169166174 0183719065604 63900076521196114
83507207555929101785378770569544 2074 60072534 754 632987591800830202715029774 9789

15283989

4 5332554 0719516665753230926 4 951394 2114 2554 04 5115377864 56966234
680050010557665686222565597532000694 85364 386223037984 8569368223874 9031954 9004
916657833974 36698609183391998723719 4 725884 52887254 01284 64 505663054
7236271099264 27857024 58292237304 2200103989

2514 376074 18119767998004 9611584 889

03136574 4 04 814 72776934 9793351969079124 1286804 950501774 4 5358305674 04
2673285789

757264 025168112914 4 017289

3889

39060078622033980666196507858085 34 824 90794 3715105931869232064 04
96738656353128130 4 07910722221357665 4 82187805198585300198832071 94 6026351214
27993700694 07085655958724 68136554 34 1671216007026774 829236204 014
52985056021224 4 1854 83378259554 164 191001106984 4 1606111936134 157284
385573768224 37027368021054 904 9859651658297294 4 555191824 151604
06551183970720272020 84 64 0204 3930729863001390554 34 860805727208711812587 79384 4
984 904 370529210374 970100166399815194 94 76294 999864 284
937367525363175218833130871088 0797883924 17704 627889

36077376914 7013802057889

504 94 781158875639904 502685755056174 1605589

94 625034 600921021093521309 4 7675934 3508224 2287365273888374 2321134
71060109204 93956173174 8853780227314 662884 16038867881534 237539156003774
078668328693984 834 80806707192360015857192029231113 4 17351022174 5594 1199598354 4
4 56137561917963110704 01804 74 4 8038094 3839754 82674 4
55197750593665932950078695139834 7929873388781017794 56081754 4
7381355918082998124 9823150037350662654 337764
52183166172959235665505036298871193560120 4 16793837252007715931 4 19035192724
5801694 4 939389

39688612900011911705588515157980783219758636 4 3962234 11559124 784
5187082904 022020705526888567677675720 84 330196215790085294 71279823397076704
667834 3101904 3137939095674 184 931794 87559919905514 09619689

3922557331938718224 01654 04 389

4 24 297616591282596064 556576789

62695006754 576610574 97034 94 7209854 964 1722192264 15181027989
1105903306539154 6659670220214 954 54 29252256801199732233186299301288 9
77260054 888305180190736561784 8724 4 89

6155732164 82574 54 75381614 34 67084 01825711363753394 201684 005114 4
29600303082324 2762724 4 024 934 3956105593933073782790939954 4 01080585108538114 4
12665516154 2809528681170509607828 9

10789

9719529989

34 2167794 620020169989

84 96514 4 05533694 909314 4 1566374 789

82789

278074 17117097798317152252276910176290637536782986869272 80589

8815004 823069790734 9216189

955367079070334 793754 33604 94 5307207964 87701633503866124 771679889

4 04 6172089

0124 33709581716007094 1224 9362154 964 95754 923913389

0521379284 81325600654 07087219295204 1174 5114 6578362108110624 2854
18078166194 94 184 5801094 84 822606357864 0095318038055317525908824 674 4 194 4
08371697512638377222189

990351660818503784 01036964 1914 89

1107162792024 97884 078503577014 0561634 7874 2264 000063558174 689

95774 598161717654 24 73582133634 3905574 63367004 182631314 36114
1816033296676296760016799 4 2055334 0364 035181666054 99089

72163789

10193314 93529788162093954 19682065819064 28364 26624 13237059039256804 64 54
6366588202705763264 9182915871363604 68736384 5054 4 974 8883936255634 4 6902584
7997339724 37826866792004 89

4 254 4 022238694 89

172004 665582573288023324 994 353981089

4 64 6629386210678261585278 9

9573711364 8254 9194 9666999004 6514 83304 78673621389

61073979915734 9933726567917382050679 4 89

033578517034 8015684 87119057331503073236 4 815754 37192770782678884 98830184
864 653982118322884 774 599068233974 6215612585382662372283196986025204
337862773557515507201016059787121 74 65069736999774 885058236861823974 0596282389

90617184 581682396699394 04 234 03802715214 934 164 58066506094 255166330604
93107167197330836033118091222672826165364 91778154 54 7133361395136935789

70790381291008172086 74 9705669639627505283727 4 39791628764 864
55768107697904 387778853689

84 3730036014 31294 8664 926231077274 903705956214 2587514 293266878284
78807876284 7818624 59567816866258302682036 4 4 597885098295089

252594 4 17211353558594 114 239951535124 14 88610058114 8133714 4 7620574 89

37224 169221906391313782811620178787608 64 38886050658708324 086986394 65194
511688837952774 6353597780059964 2251188127560160179159022 4
752139769106798632092833 84 060086102184 6713981186612051037717967858 64 715889

11919780820651104 987209273293674 4 4 664 5552278333155612798 4 65198834
8361976080158313179067 4 55124 10020867752382206554 614 5593974 89

786921632321555311929060258852766336700281085004 03677602024
6255778526526697703 4 0069592157761564 764 259634 74 33564 7160218551276752 64 89

2216759980154 725911835301779011 0214 84 702267325079585252754 84 2316261589 29674 9128014 98005754 14 9289

4 3724 074 64 4 381116109689

1279255334 866504 394 77764 7016689

704 6624 970217334 733680794 773210861934 4 34 2264 2160858013035024 637111089 4 1668102650367375214 032824 34 293369193737263789

1689

83387513755579102654 52952313728785719567272503523272501 14 9088524 01112212315223953566814 175636082796889

4 2019932324 5274 9115000568066190671007305621131 2564 01829504 99334 2817836112004 4 138708304 54 11777990828298523910316521755322173908386337724 07026085160186509754 72284 51197539120397627596019905383 8294 94 9822684 160694 237074 6852851185966687687972 29864 602757184 50299124 692064 89

94 694 89

774 83050501351974 592227789

4 2804 94 58889

36266175575585016684 91138034 54 06553384 04 509254 779564 83685314 13220672805295322177576799732975000077209030 2585104 4 324 639934 0674 51094 33124 3587323598628587936132286 24 008278150765608155394 8158074 6263592719106 22864 529121954 89

91273889

934 7689

84 063069350153058083956513 94 4 024 323250666224 2987659239682694 1031130834 15119675553613783985 4 2211792194 114 4 956191653884 9185979570764 326736974 5935938106687751104 5939056158759634 96617956775816312907314 39520021171624 16023638780963299013324 7037859386552914 05189

4 854 0202174 774 34 94 118074 6937803653261313994 62089

4 55574 9060397697094 9550080264 96879083392220773063033152719 94 4 794 89 97819818289

56639787262359965053 84 5084 02261607128870691917955 34 834 12729155634 5078392909554 962176378094 14 4 760392676202991209797852610126161587127075355867886070133229374 14 800980534 901978765117235013926032028283193813753 04 6174 3861854 8707315228789

604 380162602151932172781250101536 609553959394 82662978500964 7214 7696304 14 20928560836755369714 57674 4 65825137792689

30034 9818767309536656154 094 018181213814 5157189

34 852114 1376323974 759124 9359704 551181113512626385218226 84 14 222905761672336221 74 16385969594 2855584 15266032581735696873 4 7871528253854 68661708317156789

79869207966857938520386732793631311097017509091536397157 74 7854 6692389

84 18800085984 984 931159137283608134 14 373935984 0877268138815763164 529904 00331700614 3551587132104 84 908604 0863099554 5829324 98512694 15089

65889

66201964 4 10303356985757879719137187 4 74 794 1989

0239855764 4 54 275317591278218206791 94 00959794 4 889

80216551994 74 91076702194 965961007134 30683605884 3980625029333929180504
37874 9584 5783955975219184 9939915665684 20764 4 4 015770263734 9736079804 389
4 373233710357794 6294 959569752864 24 169076671625974 311702801304
33527213920989
591016293150314 4 06167603304 4 8713108889
30329252095324 604 24 387158071374 1133334 96752189
4 6784 204 3520120051017155881014 072790337090139060829623257 3654 34
9022515857159734 383964 3254 9682824 25392777124 223574 7636514 74 62686304
216003673739057280974 15180263325364 7788062977836503169624 788766304 94 6589
04 139814 536834 964 837676379724 03013154 653988084 1739693614
25867179381914 04 814 3126221184 90104 7710700206513634 0198655824 5954 915189
3608860207754 3374 4
25879392350378338502501167727052720609919380261179501593818 71004 394 54 7864
2611784 2514 61725602723804 7632869979661 1311614 7174 598788554 203789
60304 851193694 7192108774 950855386289
95850377779904 4 7987976819174 4 94 14 2900098035975024 4 314 4
5721638798732593334 74 84 3304 57394 081255124 79377208382988604 65524 8714 4
52068120314 4 32872021824 917133324 12389
4 13032203595572780514 4 04 956058136514 09861600790510074 64 4 5574 326539394
539164 73024 4 554 0904 4 9359189
95009300701806172333716798202231732619548655260653 7659624 0693939127964
089
26084 16114 88033064 64 994 054 074 64 597314 824 0396568634 32159312994
39370778216002709558712592639380626530906372271590302 14 4 54 082789
0353670167098152389
832704 2384 001634 8101274 98699659383318771950793697 30835694
3672885650611025094 535204 704 1905954 24 68201989
82796106997322621366281673 63122989
05624 7377762923755761011654 0065593852372739150669064 576794 63920589
716522864 9774 34 502284 14 03508880830934 4 61816836667371572514
1638260562684 0092010884 13783889
20760123000864 027233105874 0377923680777236337609996334 54 914 229514 02634
074 0695000357192016 3554 10390524 035290727326982389
14 64 5854 9806071219716833951774 684 5727327057830016504 34 38522673289
06604 18884 1138250834 1361379961981016970527367724 7197959326117762234 4
53981953204 724 4 073394 5521293754 84 9964 621282877989
4 7592635564 71124 80984 4 7886354 857684 4 04 007964 54 086534 311784 4
69866699631550715355 34 67533182789
4 2174 9052954 084 70023651559371913007076532061016 4 624 284 605754 4 59136274
08024 94 4 264 3024 74 20387231136814 03501164 9167388033979628128823708626314
7773710950925211669667728 4 0005669652355331235 72734 4 712250584 9334 21000654 3804
67153351524 918231784 6165102580881801 64 4 604 9994 05884 89
0852354 0861518389
4 04 36071934 0671292367260694 4 8064 599978077724 92209029038624 4 074 4
58697014 2059022198880684 609651517094 82306000964 657014 364 4

07668066372796875694 07135156782799064 907906327720904 4 524 50324
857579280708225203262396833354 851586069314 597838528361694 56336186314 95689
5751252054 275834 084 337654 38773575581133233224 4 5874 1691304 4
623332885304 034 16818532765079629533256719680304 662622269392924 233817614 74
06217694 3813018164 4 68362506028878688263884 862284 4 076864 98705054 3822925806584
8704 04 03556257325674 95201114 3193754 7754 0770919620795371814 8825061663069254
831888871623685251554 84 810807574 53534 756650691089
989
0257900674 7116536104 4 6354 84 862584 5329601116605524 812366581334 84 4 34
02303383876694 730853114 68229529009285203397072972 4 784 5950326397304
70969287727556674 1078792127067696914 719162964 67784 84 264 37554
18575698510816587182715145 74 95503615650037132073805 4 521273860737134
93283299506794 838104 667216961316674 5564 983864 1066553851957114 7797989
7804 053131531304 695355956012501223073013512282359303089
74 1315318724 6065767650692731207505 0535622805396956670954 04 554
3310016992009354 0160301510967007087033089
6286586954 811171164 4 72224 29564 592624 702284 383736316827618263814 54
52738190115715089
5220166955589
52554 62206792074 2767776923081152264 751106824 4 339134 165002524 04
0693302585989
4 56339270364 194 4 07539781200821821358504 554 73521574 804 3870509653774 4
614 781134 6871656555888351972792131850 4 55068355394 307605036900936296238783 64
0866701294 4 3989
3854 4 4 4 18785088158837508762900011 4 4 4 69012888129558556775237521659868 4
934 324 22064 333126591574 8872953995338622517538068215 34 5051124 4 74 4 094 691104
5116323995851505755123125829 4 0123674 771515790267854 6634 37832997684
375181671324 663954 64 3020788768384 514 13313112004 3836272094 7289
6677974 394 8889
034 039333934 7714 916556098784 4 0626123581223512954 92562595858319163624 4
84 4 911239536576587105078807396708810976691210513367202108 84 90924 9834 814
10808514 71979311983256014 9134 0711816926537717669 4 88632567738508113099293924
27973112696774 5834 906089
59014 679711219754 532868794 9100384 9694 060700564 567237710534 9189
064 4 5065280295574 4 7570185785935333025 34 37314 14 4 20530358189
4 72502565974 199223900855033384 79296623707672334 636290375995008754
30750257963974 1502039884 95903758576829100173 4 4 1003016390174 84 85633064
2201175201778857984 274 579591250260727814 70357311880310825 4 0722337056184 039814
64 308667013264 1399107350024 4 18877255635131802012518580814 89
754 097369730814 873054 0887173734 74 4 284 091929164 34 24 4 021024

Chapter Thirty-six

4 964 263928735739824 03810584 2003734 58695310703279798502293094
6626806901792724 1787098062523829754 92674 27174 010931339084 4

0060317715039883971756517156642506614 0863519754 5734 5974 732854
6035257708163790805387315806922805330698661071761704 723189
4 17223854 132675676864 108506936197728508 8089
991205932294 78701723659957911254 74 04 902304 2173561164 3954 89
35384 4 0386619667832273836309911100528583707824 96250614
55188256938516357639930307559070 74 09177917689
6009094 216626863994
59309871665187527628061216776559917910290609779887602911312938589
553501801828282284 2512717674 14 232794 37724 90834 4 684 2157094 6790104 9134
29397381565935133360706191 2518396634 89
8789
04 94 7087264 4 134 4 58081024

Chapter Thirty-seven

1396525389
714 4 39089
1777522524 11780220168874 9824 301623732901654 2389
58880298757500 6283104 4 55394 872770124 930831524 94 97974 7126764 81104
1792369032564 979086214 75914 072338569985684 89
93207228126831503 70989
91931307602227680917759 60194 1966313606533754 26514 54 170789
726564 21694 99127767 2019356518712974 2389
74 200774 22706008183314 68689
2660294 0980858395534 529813264 3374 294 8397137157826634 89
3888175852859964 321524 684 92022170504 2364 38629715317037861 2025782854
7239685501094 7264 86865273393613270531709184 96084 2867973063004 361654 2134
6267661010170035987579790699862232054 880264 185324 862925109616879659807695389
7654 53614 54 574 4 554 00165223914 24 814 89
297293814 2790625588597012238728 34 89
024 057385524 64 234 4 39119934 502720657717152104 991279089
921169924 264 09704 094 1620723180394 9694 16889
854 2656153032807224 682554 24 5811114 27009573232719015598853789
575571161924 596312339001389
2387272152786124 203816814 89
64 678214 16667587669182854 58524 4 394 1373067714 64 03734 33094 04 1364 4
769293578325756754 7224 604 92377254 530663122614 05501756381159994 319702788365614
69974 535618662519921774 758789
66802204 666776259774 383389
956603904 03628298614 827021386190536066366 84 5791514 514 91296624 14 9189
69008081539878655838537811570 34 266034 4 304 8225501319786604 76762711151914
13296063961296795675 14 855605359664 271764 873387754 84 216680732679 34 4 6827374
5356610801508605 74 3399198621529578787611185592 4 4
7235271316900900727602292778572 04 07394 9284 081028003889
856654 0215556333756222914 589

8264 05817184 8809035219592322984 559191694 639295796753009154 987109014 10398873834 7924 936289

310579711504 6206176901054 689

301366912564 960764 5519105336273179156 0064 5964 8274 7654 8057231889

4 713984 1098601302864 866561626662957625009 8178394 4 574 3520393794 9163186162324 5084 104 36164 5553981702333968280754 08160676789

23505102764 705204 099569714 8193078321599322556225791336901779 37093754 2504 1782576570705962239 7054 24 12067164 1874 24 64 15575661781751832110 09184 6264 8717765091190334 5723077873178804 84 9377654 4 25394 524 714 94 24 0914 793370735134 87876314 57698510024 9674 982967 25718389

5783784 64 94 78639854 4 0231214 54 64 07023160932103605 5594 61954 76083184 1078154 97585524 4 94 732214 389

3205233734 9758294 77293697854 24 4 7331921658533831755 5224 94 6584 87593974 612031368176924 91287900551784 037075 16106150863284 334 4 567384 9566589

15034 94 24 05200789

74 1383221214 924 671798085284 634 2868204 4 70275783698828657304 4 73701798754 988339182164 4 363204 383602752611309004 4 6100374 779902794 9076124 599381124 05161919960596513 90077909634 293583119034 305624 356715734 09505616362874 8278205876154 89

9881362284 0063195111 95201780809674 906704 976589

4 2820319324 591324 2559617114 164 316694 4 1618015524 0661886331173995068 7964 37781553809722292974 59868674 364 34 37724 4 6022500821701314 936991814 024 54 20915767683955013168181074 034 28304 1126865254 986803264 579323184 5029509774 5201389

8055358194 14 1019131984 833867985554 81994 0171661584 883611814 8504 91864 67563917728633058374 6651251909951762786218221778373921604 284 38123658550359877683167988769176678 64 037696003396728064 04 5734 525975201932854 0390384 32784 751855614 753102263637335 9384 63979994 51197734 56856654 4 674 28389

5819110350875024 4 754 2075011754 726557934 304 064 164 4 8164 0001854 89

61723573698765002 0914 63124 4 00680506656182113202933685956754 7226664 66024 686854 200803926074 0566298299662282788667 33064 50655032884 1629388295625887554 09694 68070706581219805085789

24 0566782073019132006706036 4 2168364 916525631353776254 83089

594 84 20536098722955582 7524 593150094 334 19009078154 671122572710798521222737556158 32610302392053167927886 14 11832982264 5975576534 04 54 234 6104 902957223958753311 95579619502289

4 6050308356974 031984 824 793750389

73982795389

920689

7189

1296270970268160179994 8823685154 4 1024

Chapter Thirty-eight

90634 503793304 638505980500689

3688509215960924 934 54 61701869664 70225326193881930168212264 84
3687779523961813687773501783987601A 287972084 83664 1077328764 2886925358714
6978397261888103384 5033371181517114 84 71575357282911137713631319778212024 5684
609697774 92196379684 7374 9691094 564 4 214 6235274 67527261285301800789
57354 3032753550589
002760724 1710824
277977227327359006266386669601352230256085097299631537578274 33792507162172074 4
063331379638751714 4 39266238114 553939004 3886785184 24
7175875379030663666093268883193121032320723514 09070336054
16575082209060337201668113885031A 684 64 4 519169504 365588661521259506938284 34 4
58152870871228293114 0727555933699681210990351591016A 212560711075765634 4
30635117056731674 35289
58194 754 95216114 2519311002589
04 134 5289
0075077583181812267074 86169370511374 74 0514 4 794 54 61979530174
760061067934 534 8377394 05521359299881834 654 586798258758604 31734 04 0554
6011823364 93553306359083224 391666806121029285929309962757 24 5031274 89
4 390964 29633208730774 6715007773300833934 31588596370124 4 33769577694 54
8260771609767086154 81666794 2389
1035060904 614 604 4 1303968713689
4 886799835087804 068064 3816217724 0634 791781191620062957777701399370934
394 4 321724 9722182319521253794 1326027533674 56855860884 4
105908511230270606553 79689
4 8611903334 31182933910876196185654 14 5709689
3874 36957061234 280197733557389
624 07681631584 4 33584 8770733607207064 012636724 1684
1255098300951381957688615124 64 866019104 4 190004 05387333567120152878262611A 5314
4 4 00194 905011564 1718014 62355300334 608021767589
15614 799503714 6733274 58150272811272118264 669225554 4 4 1318839859509334
1962398594 5561184 94 7674 78653220714 92014 14 04 358734 8389
120710525816364 4 90692039881387927289
928539884 606794 69997338628784 32225100374 328066659264 199306084
693616756774 84 7179955538224 978574 6556725055674 89
4 930960003881116502599000599374 0173866604 706262123885284 81701094
6710138768352200253 7004 9094 4 667104 7557900086274 8699860758010055989
739775274 8532074 1834 66193993789
997610753993025114 4 2615689
204 855197230784 075822784 83831235864 7816828634
7239705070337701551080372 1686394 150717589
12025235200309364 4 53816100089
08813050203916934 1159108232754 9299699784 1354 4 8332296718754 24 18224
6552003796227904 3106977024 167654 829394 976164 04 9500283098389
394 260224 304 616904 84 355804 74 77224 038717866934 9153928857863022989
24 314 3684 17304 703015701090230606750370 24 4 720033264 134
87285601003219723656520159094 92934 14 8262122999823173320730 64 8796012037972764
731556363037609293837 34 234 6820918332034 2088037583199689

24 099274 9363529073564 984 723927517964 83564 603811318074 4 527184 62234 5859794 4 972284 31805274 06250005784 4 2004 83005238238751084 8554 2664 866184 05878804 64 12068103591989

839609872713115064 108184 54 904 555799276094 354 2184 00671764 5354 86151052824 75682962685981806029377282987924 4 25294 3870854 120731025294 04 9832789

17912774 90031521755214 882526034 714 16018195384 54 17671180625218368758194 154 070367681561576618172 04 779986923314 64 03361380334 65204 0184 261580390264 1825361857224 684 4 86061288736869992720274 1626806376662112 06929034 6196954 5811364 34 4 74 1598714 0189

2116604 6622658266159054 206976394 359312366204 5528756034 21650034 73601194 34 225614 914 032015794 17118517154 2756396517256864 5384 670954 524 837130594 89

858255974 5277564 3783720939037376064 4 875780538089

666661399183 9630554 34 635153154 81858867792629127253634 262889

85256854 4 64 69814 4 974 6189

24 14 958636636719814 006506588860860224 2673379881276879694 064 970299154 524 52721325754 28195324 91731150662085866520774 909529651007534 04 04 922735654 82829570256906293588816904 14 6510697177724 209554 4 613025854 381786304 8508060589

906373809054 306950261384 24 222705375354 59859099326696733216515194 8172534 53274 733360274 4 725852724 5394 78578704 9054 84 75863311571836633235913234 758825934 064 152103907287193632679 63759284 73313161233978154 985650774 59574 263019250136134 4 218177865732684 594 980392574 1969699998764 59824 9567094 0955954 9064 514 319299753296990292901811334 684 9189

39731673374 04 73761021534 9790280131722337912799863914 7101057364 5808824 964 03779366914 4 260225224 32918220359694 79652296324 1504 6259303763664 3284 08656160231216 10990271779794 04 824 4 2374 37724 21754 53274 36903074 9262617258880652 2332614 1060338165320932320266991087084 758681985639904 98575011761996369059699254 104 368753291819072004 15759826234 54 66727015736971133 35704 14 0320937934 51266060707990655868796161579984 934 10954 09032124 3654 4 310873161586375727374 8174 50178665573793984 8669229117599204 34 224 760064 859760054 9782806294 1873914 74 9664 5660197689

263616598289

6565574 4 5804 09914 2689

094 724 97067352204 701161915360094 52736325306664 4 02010023 2018732278197614 8686634 89

89

132734 7014 4 4 820324 29311784 1009152833330376911197051252 51189 029708294 2974 8839813714 9977805278164 934 3705604 3260053526981069189 86588689

81610889

92699204 34 54 781553574 04 65293822554 7579239651257816984 986734 21821853124 0734 311529608214 11209199994 0616010158219127373016501769581186190 36689

7792756904 6785710181059393731 4 3881192914 74 94 4 356522189

6260286325866365190174 53659212186387681077 74 209158364 6909091651827398075310306 64 9980624 4 84 92774 7561884 52973294 72713914 89

972684 0778589

7786865604 87233057524 228571724 734 4 366674 181812327084 15917914
7861681978003287524 2194 64 80119315937935152394 174 0904 190984 125780990903889
4 07794 204 672704 91534 500024 8604 274 553073068364 722207589

30821994 4 5234 7214 52184 282562092914 376814
38780213969363997860221263221098220773714 4 1294 1264 0653765264 2854 34
82970693655116806728306144 81553500677992734 2874 67174 0836666020537292204 84 84
0870252301258571914 569665795239635968627064 59037207268058794 398134 0066767014
11765812522334 8104 83868677174 0587973689

615599621784 654 973073934 0954 6604 314 5860154 04 956157764 5616734 4 721264
274 6874 614 0830206387935904 284 966224 722325504 660952317681724 586362611284
833874 076507582889

56774 589

58873610951974 20723212623335561519338224 717602181868389

5300679750212076904 3883812835625814 50125007119027156514 4 34 627064 814
95059019699613904 05607906737260724 112924 4 71994 77028384 8353186332981761994
731283314 4 915968777504 290327977034 76193806295512384 01384
22910035767692969859590544 398289

26666087801034 4 0596705590520766837021015952195139454 4 77311874
1072352794 56084 4 354 94 66760792882681935676476654 666589

16136214 04 24 78564 279268156254 4 8506316685268327524 65600274 776524 12794
270534 1934 828054 6267028159924 539124 873937558094 012591977834
653365573562593766808769975257446 602702166964 9252998377538196938446 6254
7085188615104 752264 751364 89

188335738189

169712195832681004 1957653770211921182725665080889

66824 67504 8666996598850446 204 1191615332089

88567238092601814 281176234 4 79558294 2880858136988607372754 974 9121306874
374 2194 3014 86676625969169519536885691174 938231969755955794
021793887372251515997144 054 4 7289

7083955103654 86662819650368446 8684 661039274 5568446 14 363590177744 4
0387565120807714 56364 87772844 4 383315635724 96836756314 810394 389

680921192823374 14 50761863056577773779446 14
533302578207887933713552328193066778103446 74 4 878814 5330227671159824 63014
677391318064 69901714 53231819572964 01713829934 4 5866528104 239029204 4 04
205030108503722889

707226673204 164 0758383521162554 729354 20977067186526207629446 67204 363364
3273505663204 11252128722589

4 14 99762804 689

14 8555075973614 650511764 12579302836974 53203604
6506156923811972132510561806134 52134 381768173276284 14 18102164 4 134 17024
9175584 36568114 54 797775195828066284 4 24 9750379174 77236204 204 24
5057363060911154 84 024 2699564 33600353014 36665975118280328039534 21054 04
9191030567314 210754 1302357934 877234 239073959389

3004 3689

132814 854 68821970534 8268064 061334 4 7603574 6590906564
60980097171769957520 4 37556354 52168504 4 224 39082780834 8072156800312138051374 4
7557386633580661289

82569525355723266307395195 4 06369794 6913927391950929709929134 88014
8676072714 97851682702690507107678 9

65765304 4 04 633626268887226274 293120287517384 97554 214 31504 9989

074 564 6121569554 253570152014 74 626587358829154 4
86936716821097263877036692987627033326926764 05112356591787736324 7704
6116118752837864 08803828013634 904 14 50851318295587380336571592375 54 04 374
03660094 3126624 9374 4 7350183694 0883501231805702551089

4 184 6936668830380623604 361689

9868181504 62814 54 39937084 394 6723795281953032886060996315 4 78054
11053979831739104 81917987933763099182 4 0071636953592567835866999085256828 34
617999204 4 84 9215828682554 266066694 80659055883754 7674 7789

0063030763977320119162 64 4 19312313733282236 4 181193 4 38305058658554 4
982998689

9114 668131171194 2189

16017937360257596321853210 4 86874 99204 734 702994 26787127613334 23766834
2822565756501574 89

72028034 3180320624 4 84 9572309739005715093 14 5389

184 34 4 94 38283973734 51579980515625916 4 322627014 18620623694 4 75930214
1050850281203604 9109939053684 78056021662704 636855257274 13290604 2289

9563510252284 751907030825327384 9955553304 4
95780330902592753163522180988 9

882629115980337112570172176766904 54 568064 9223051574 74 689

155717101756724 0354 189

35061128887302 4 04 314 4 3198695865218667607330385 4 903602774 6096354
5019525296534 0703015970324 09851150252930588656719011250832 84 714 968064 89

4 381300783718623924 4 6817902162173569122887239 4 802164 84 64 737751768189

4 2122207103565559650797 94 84 4 9900827193552814 7914 34 04
037138717208176090319885 64 5874 6108109910593691774 3794 7128793689

50324 774 1864 858064 81967995614 64 3670824 87089

9368395131507203056530300788685982036072066991673761 64 14 756654
28771935359104 4 5211691676928163963 64 56297834 0737064 788274 061834 054 3570774
1216138320287378790378585 89

3274 553614 9564 4 61255050554 78266874 54 4 55090886889

4 69271859889

4 94 234 4 95074 83821850184 34 13032362004 66807001917504 5926284 0838505364
3126768698034 0268115807098103 4 589

8604 13084 173550995694 4 1517991754 32334
80633073261339139979788000382109132766014 54 961115704
28580281606751623813538630524 29563833095032019287816 4 1324 9223004 761179535824
95605914 530004 24 64 4 78806213024 689

78655969262925763574 0287994 01356921167553904 002699664 556025682972369504
95909960271709738166616867800 4 8327292990594 28102968161574
6963060606101062267170212539667 4 7951389

381374 85389
535175783294 51364 260069361377774 4 0005669930174 020113667731787704 4 694
5060129226074 9691106157620763789
334 504 1373365119560032907835235964 65326574 74 974
3528672111629807567585108385016069989
693586715225964 6305700913908762874 164 9254 170816909684 730954
88602332982888001016529628089
769877231969074 2102700934 8880934 4 55512188188336519784 3185355960674
763507221611787287356394 656554 34 27614 0685594 124 2591214
170781163030801019258762199380989
589
4 3050939682518277130330334 92664 88532956187952664 4 63190634 9389
64 927974 77963058182377606580354 022796691081809322672514 2614
28768508550234 03639597056214 125151376204 67224 4 4 289
79978554 54 13190137205600294 5670634 03824 299178075125724 4 84 4 63577152589
34 72233684 5268000504 905794 076592611834 04 62764 699835321989
33127117327105112938774 6272008131726320867124 724 783103695325057116684
6693391999383834 165301330924 77294 293584 7074 3882634 24 00701321713209728274 94
7961163566782615071566282502125206276389
751566585134 0604 5529010926112638166224 236689
9271064 904 1886270014 4 2112873592393998250056580064 32506075094 589
3585007218072932230824 6108258185874 671334 067334 4 326805154
7565276112290094 2154 65561831034 12687017228654 16226907574 4 666374
025785058198390337266853912834 25113889
776103701554 705969784 284 38121104 16674 964 236193689
84 063561387622795954 521514 689
28813282394 3963661294 5013878167659092925089
75324 716691236834 8275154 6078272804 4 51824 34 5375965504 92568064
8532309992814 514 7534 550927555277962794 14 24 5574 4
0525521882532395562508572117996530195675811774 4 36762550973197511556514 84
51372854 24 074 904 838081995588091516117939219104 261909284 8578161390514 82314 74
4 5531015161591784 14 59994 712239051659694 4 103972729574 115833974
593906205007758070959676589
89
24 9614 3734 34 8781563774 4 208374 99914 61834 5134
117857213565765100288216534 3788389
06972299886294 6226868519562883232057053789
4 21789
5936784 4 89
9972838082251295857374 29565314 8704 304 0321954 330164 72204 58139790574
528802074 728588103114 085879874 72118632864 89
84 4 734 053114 604 4 004 80011189
64 74 2165719993115889
037205900314 664 181261792091194 08878500667780109991854 6190934 89
2669185091189

9853281758015614 9634 4 2527274 202132308326262253782975374 78084 964 8620574 7377298059504 90214 55501089

6934 8064 510974 3330059979855532033131826917519159195006584 884 365516563352350794 974 4 14 8699554 5934 68266676174 984 1931923239198584 9314 29070339724 9074 104 33531550716185771284 4 52704 5561514 87208217879010758094 59907819034 07684 84 55908034 85256121124 4 63883238877600772564 059505857614 5061729291017634 21062016322763133570869 161133384 3351915955219934 239104 56565973100823169994 799784 5631959834 114 305637058884 1358572324 394 59993716084 5154 4 3224 73332574 74 32690293211134 055360526090724 16883753354 3614 12870234 23782527089

53823576585165964 1732811004 23670224 794 26589

4 89

54 20024 6277977930989

34 50760213624 17137031065132759759613 4 89

924 27004 704 71725333264 22774 26234 756632022517984 24 9524 9821276559511394 56814 1270076623154 8515825735963353826717922669936333918066855094 80289

66397016335803063577792061512929958681816023327826828756138695 34 89

8338580784 04 86775650291623281022321262862370364 7116725909111622074 4 994 4 4 70337154 671719355796034 064 9572183991324 31571758689

0563578201193562277777634 216236724 756676876172206101521389 3

4 2884 4 27554 63803914 2982934 0970637684 66511699684 54 9774 924 84 216234 54 98790190059012230711024

Chapter Thirty-nine

88058804 992082026734 1521334 526194 82271804 04 524 65922884 4 29554 1908154 4 9214 58089

04 5704 9392729832168834 134 2995368258674 64 108367284 6833132874 321981230074 5130314 4 4 007683574 024 4 6278097701300214 2187123511884 4 3907814 2864 5714 867130316274 3814 05338857603885294 6905077691124 3964 0284 4 27539211601124 684 8558859087111204 33136983355129831770 4 754 3952735118094 562627365072134 2386754 8781623509663987589

89

07810584 333722039754 4 204 986189

9214 534 394 570010766993023334 04 5070623558228321979391210716339 04 4 784 574 064 9596837368359996102705598109 34 32754 5718226581916273764 083264 9194 4 6339254 14 125704 72789

300121814 099502881776632184 9854 530856667900703762657705838273174 95612091752324 760127284 8854 4 222989

86799882662839508678 9

4 57714 3881580967550580114 816329510134 1784 54 94 95324 84 74 35024 616682604 9086054 34 986260707695220684 576930888101993638860205690810166 4 5051872181500574 34 7274 6924 004 56628013524 4 24 2904 32379684 7683264 99597859954 18767960988824 064 974 2665229584 4 0697297761914 6264 89

78315102874 0066979236203320604 04 4 5354 794 4 19819989

4 752531957170520855316177791164 10772764 6139215711774
0299135555015167097966196524 062222914 1609972270298654 08714 69079193291110174
604 0120652081190334 79335074 09339673354 3810667764 4 251621091064 09782774 03934
724 09226971399864 19324 01833676257879516616692114 857084 4 034 731109857718604 14
38065703058114 089
6522799033707067927777717324 019606366905990239966006174 759660274 364 772334
17132112564 06957304 3007387189
697608262537784 0761689
04 565036964 121017260551105063180587830717710 5716789
1720931555100513312624 885074 97125708827760818 62973515666064
1381318577569232194 221616981981833861591091112129 06834 764 54 14 9874 89
25967693915520889
9974 34 834 825109771717334 774 84 904 24 15704 4 765736574
5775288703137087391907218250577293177204 212596617789
094 6278107374 89
39672753336694 977597757614 013390964 005994 9599124 774 24 0582260227674 34
7914 04 36597750071174 9068727626934 563752876279153861034 80986929574 289
84 9008704 13755216037594 678764 3984 3626959137289
9723772007314 53366733526996836629260856570583903882359383118 9
614 76361331704 366529764 4 36074 94 0164 96971739566002324 84
75312782613511627 516934 985914 97284 2578011566354 0112574 883834 4 95782054
7565134 867525353393094 92987778566824 7383224 713634 127815663824
59050230733983253608300387302 839639954 184 028662980876689
960054 360674 6374 781759738593200109703840094 329084 825214
8607855800720302839262 814 84 21073567689
4 365084 7829172394 31353773078338286204 52560793714 34 7989
024 7754 4 8000157389
11657789
4 9114 366003679354 36393206776263021105215210135921 694 54 4
99705888762836579334 06061323911023381234 789
116513396064 8232734 302761158534 32570782259674 5669263994 4 50654
9281999054 02788150706299036213505 52317325013670624 394 1061807667613786614 14
56378576604 4 2074 924 22926977034 984 50126514 9216717696331051676726784 88372954
9005678657239784 4 27631134 7324 9771989
0600761875914 089
6073066582151384 4 9134 561555571151084 51321597382911001114 287389
5994 61623938505836032323 4 20828814 504 33915073780818631937207838031364
17583734 8751976507933520535 261064 83964 680022831803234 766267824 389
7034 382828567674 09938801224 5584 18282506165887184 19177397134 84 24
9557535536154 283510624 4 83282114 107566096796995104 82522794
21587069315186868228 9
06599054 4 54 289
7676834 0784 284 68663516950735929005944 4 6525171865184 1204 54 4 327116374
524 59124 94 051031774 974 327164 3304 786104 252035794 03271210384 8084 4 64
3633301371529014 9884 275237794 9834 574 7998752815119651594 34 4 029887214
9170655559184 939637362023534 6368882181314 37208134 936589

804 1885261814 61668564 6389

74 283915059558370394 71238321734 52734

82136156961283263085165038215295650B4 20824 710834 85563684 15289

277977777563665982862156502212507A 611675903211654 209654 14 7012294 283854 57567214 17389

929799800524 64 181684 7334 81802173252198821195035184 6705828084 2927115925999970153750974 79007950930331880565580101398081229B4 5654 68161B715385799281286103766006B4 4 083084 983972797637004 1660306524 614 826604 283117793289

355874 2055934 518813264 76050299179833B2716373959860235B8785134 6092673231951588729729B4 66770976350989

4 677014 028229224 5909364 931925193174 2859694 152366564 659951119254 6858864 80010377793163073B794 4 4 37871151634 35808683B5509803616734 11774 6795525054 15696325551756593001109B71034 3833359200752031771871321169A 297373666504 8161622813974 369194 3602197933189

113714 77579284 604 8510574 54 2832874 81793287227B710961589

682604 15191032160358867794 74 79259298B509994 9904 92164 84 9713854 4 125533916737983269B374 24 4 874 1274 54 70962063371390A 74 04 8360794 157529363363904 4 817954 14 111734 936202604 851201230536055A 36888793862914 4 80787910052555989

328252773354 35924 7067399972692273992775653397256669671524 0967730735176129922A 202555065314 2954 90874 261705335B5033317774 602589 15289

3788654 307666139718694 74 350204 69696687505676637B25001336654 4 34 12014 9780395334 094 84 3058804 0B08713869531589

89

1754 4 3230557614 84 4 599297128725620764 70023808833082557863754 4 8067354 538598763808584 763650695267362809861199004 0267981130204 61010194 4 5980359274 3530574 4 929624 2273773395520169158005332066975513019731133703912561191330S4 329794 169919294 8293905572679579528177269687932911A 25777320500214 76019969B152202061524 51794 2389

84 58185268279789

7974 4 054 16564 80562100B330286054 7301031605032014 574 051888761984 53502969999264 6579565001904 4 827824 173860954 017910370254 63814 3624 4 5250887029226639233664 04 351967800356654 54 4 364 250362507952964 89

213906564 84 14 01827369714 50214 5264 3164 6621003738099504 18558874 89

630824 6574 07334 263002530994 978155914 2128751970527100115710171637A 9883378795656865393A 4 26611954 4 0774 14 4 39924 874 2320604 22661597714 7800654 89 64 334 9623583962211353125728B

8201355984 8156570204 574 82109173737866280253930704 4 6554 36889

74 74 906584 7794 94 095981224 4 7874 32218660153009734 54 8024 696172671294 778795194 4 15134 4 017301188323674 4 87204 4 7806236637003524 258617656838084 85736885690237092290882122272083A 170089

7912925654 354 194 0782689

9305573151916990118070501B9

5885964 74 04 813904 6260970734 1954 4 94 227067754 033537102964 83606203275561731021591A 34 684 4 155390956590974 654 99279153763329A 735996020089

80264 0794 68292536127789

83205853605856I861189

4 514 061132224 271286III66867250257033634 886315857I739711603288212386637 4
91874 5662604 2953189

8520879I769279853205968708273206077204 90875624
97623985063918737880636107372115907573362989

70566574 688377351598523062078 34 856672673994 5019724 57061604 1702865614
312668507975571689

508067386196133576130779338566529 4 2611789

955761282203962786163036697657292 74 6317600522624 881300262015934 4
69599332301304 4 4 3908514 14 4 06961294 909514 3511324 04 37281803780305270161 4 74
5966697318233961655755091009 4 4 772011231301699270821104 37284 835364 6580227984
3531764 87604 395208073622595864 078734 581915310594 5582524 03107537721574 3214
57134 4 778184 30984 4 74 999189

198857234 88153921904 5201566171925554 299875334 54 00238110974
85202700537114 712389

7974 701015854 7538626802813231702862012903865851 4 4 2364 4 864
928655235817I3720293880175294 I0I0225202856911871860796 4 501087652984
2532971631174 4 186507520I876929274 64 2106131317620308506790665882560616162 4
51232983338560212251996132072858164 07020906231271834 4 84 822300789

4 04 0924 39163274 524 0874 5667813673557003975514 278073920034
353313212822873286 89

54 20618818832914 189

04 23929582934 92930594 8139194 19210154 30324 35674 4 769924 30684 89

54 952023954 564 550306504 709712589

530864 100115696873272805753 4 62888209289

4 998037694 27671523724 69074 5276874 94 1173761124 89

07019198792964 2324 74 94 837186391329220 4 0334 04 76272852904
805702005887722635976788174 715798214 21764 17664 34 90054 851532223351305020 04 74
266084 26027581114 3081158773578536814 13656836671339174 03160705650379085284
3226782164 64 3593015192070991234 3384 4 4 761974 89

70136375189

51684 986306334 7124 3935719934 5332511924 34 024 8672268509671224 4 4 2280954
8620967064 20714 60389

235934 010684 4 004 7536963864 97513597358331093783260019092515 74 4
319203761229377089

05574 54 36284 77384 5335137564 981164 1233689

229522888668519991591629961786720819183717 34
7307006822812701860650275302983390 14 66999574 794 4 61070267161116027871706500234
4 54 85265531804 6152798030135889

4 3109664 382224 754 3977162304 6764 63531802819964 4
93756623711511605197875870834 29214 674 980001529714 109167257057969361 54
87561571782358311177101359012535395568712 74 57997201759260654 61900593796089

784 619027221814 50723587954 84 2714 9913315039620305124 110916504 4
19669755825132181861783569 4 27554 0614 559727053523826735711023180819720853 94
8601822054 82689

866360286956681834 8668524 54 4 614 4 084 069521826332804 87604 4 4 691900826696762964 54 90754 5722369233274 4 1664 913195564 864 3994 5889

93387758700988054 331863998554 04 9323067761591828592874 389

6057804 64 0984 2089

74 0550683296113972392222269790364 69776787551730396664 4 74 1574 726584 654 780659639564 89

535819557003579716689

122694 69927151284 4 864 772273981174 1814 88663319289

94 6594 7060089

2113189

89

4 296771965704 8618527686134 236881500004 1723800282976700527792276554 084 8554 3334 8616889

84 973871867886189

87323238004 24 00963864 067984 3517162511269725924 65867872110705380153194 9577164 94 8506298157989

4 694 1714 28204 2164 1655866599072861984 9384 91754 80269584 61964 2294 779314 9812238364 1538557038089

789

00761390103234 971796963254 7196564 912274 55826354 13234 14 24 364 3574 594 74 929792785696077635914 84 7280121218205712372291254 4 3324 55660534 074 84 951814 4 67690589

598069520034 92300124 9866193762108500512364 4 254 78264 35733821329660966697316535354 25624 7308090288177611337397206298364 305054 086194 062218385024 4 9854 75668721260067633974 373153257838354 874 824 4 09780973933614 873102023904 5338094 74 15977664 56031376811062989

214 0901661232700390050502294 7613518859124 1064 70656031298014 608889

94 927862354 78123370756373524 3212718006105308551717034 053603307376301871136693532176984 282601761121860063584 89

6534 14 360670914 19977924 64 0972114 274 4 954 6989

14 635554 82864 34 01104 014 72230084 74 00589

719394 255567755784 4 03993657012637700923304 01772015709714 0226189

7254 9024 996396256689

084 8589

77504 1571304 2927159289

338014 62762817804 24 5124 334

61156729170872181169866958713126106655810971551555696334 81984 4 224 93772789

984 9001691334 065013922558374 525364 4 587113153774 964 284 5154 005364 04 2185976909329790072008362962024 67322396588374 131752905866262694 4 67352104 4 2603791931521103560615613271779583324 2389

4 1011378308624 54 629514 095817189

4 1653818826098581362550702814 72074 4 1010322838569770121266793214 64 728011596824 377110164 05882920381222982282550564 885020009031599084 096698014 25015995974 2561022026318361725571114 9139214 4 361101853384 55682860703157664 4 86057682509194 621585069508284 94 08530180664 4 99120714 28675989

866884 1279064 65394 8357153197916296821964 28762691256721694 7228774
3672269074 63108534 1954 4 0611336084 87163008322078153715 8154 354 64 583702594
850361674 707073027584 99672313280960162936123357 4 08505167586704 703228598724
73980864 7326794 0394 913937913084 9736324 14 1390294 39284 576638351984 21867634 664
301808689
    6069214 338319604 2210094 720984 39766652282254 4 368304 222054 7014 325651194
268703971992934 24 806391183114 7159679288276590160658 4 81161372294 4 1994
3326376901682224 34 35592607990882034 00234 350990585913929771576 04 94
7270770283095758 4 27070913697704 37135759020267227121355 34 4 973304 3050674 1037054
4 07734 59584 30922769374 84 0395638204 8859264 704 38636211199354 22550000256114 4
9708505270500916289
    29604 984 7398305977089
    314 1204 19837701870006385807 84 4 26177361278758099551595038 4 6662074 84
815725018212354 08254 33798202752568074 574 177955302589
    4 68194 57764 6065374 993269932888205395151 84 74 08514 74 4 363568210924
25017105258634 9534 5791590287152212995365959158076973734 06864 938135614 834
6862593974 252934 93723922991126095352789
    014 74 152094 6191693752339607918005888183785066885788221 74 089
302237670789
    264 9055901783573302904 986104 756624 0884 04 630174 4 209164 60792765924
0335005213697505366658033 4 0501312807124 27989
    70006273729152590701666 74 64 3724 5667874 325600195554 24 2094 4 5336334
3939195676804 5908713309834 4 79621296632581163765 4 664 8089
    0071124 74 028151564 34 34 6310814 4 53273397154 32334 54 4 92686193074 4
83735329034 24 290227063234 4 50908155379512377571610 4 927121798185353585099 4
155387182194 4 94 27086114 96926208222831105 4 5052601764 694 4 214 984 79691624
9383350864 389
    979794 372572585034 94 7332112364 201564 54 4
595832321025867338212082720110236171813291628134 769361336231630005551854 16994
51237030874 7176934 7530638094 914 88282318114 6014 84 7359176501968305714 704
71397168054 17120760854 1527790614 84 08154 35277054 711138661935519182555 4
96737687537565590189
    1589
    207674 352614 8852937632107873123875720 64 84 082373753032884 64 0234
882928758674 575174 11964 259554 73254 7129988784 4 1337697174 4 78289
    514 80606297501598104 1096517924 8737254 24 15860607092634 34
51122180515157680503952320798390703 84 4 55908024 89
    7675124 2811186831122353594 4 953623328051564 284 50911638253284
6827690377989
    4 056097304 96598216774 794 290605229064 271154 0907596304 9075004 5786694
8064 4 24 07914 1604 24 989
    736396223835534 26568824 89
    24 903094 0135322759829226761802139 94 4 680189
    9603206758034 2939794 79500581123563398697279023670197762 89
    84 0733198614 297089

94 5534 0903726057682234 4 74 8869201029764 887194 61875862934
2131709327277769165187100024 989

96665855083811335 6789

6174 8113924 008069204 4 14 62566538294 5223391551604 594 824 870277524
026560308024 16084 0633583104 99159313085394 74 269073234 720884 119182024 84
70757329115072124 54 4 689

8526855311599851117939381080209 7734 738174 9339998889
73856536994 0387595253362174 82394 7154 7834 800589
4 6039366591889
289

9621752104 716304 660384 4 4 4 123734 509103829324 8389
4 56001298364 934 173204 224 3216564 275828626964 62987054 94 370864 74 634
2771185293824 804 39358216019860700621711965918325918075 74 4 936556603190574
210330697537073223014 04 4 29391360729974 2314 8218620571279724 084 322974 22253064
784 70222877289

889

17204 4 54 1364 16830186205926694 781065001577273034 683998295511059964
27519834 4 2090994 2982394 136155832653884 06852983750196100267 4 32796083226766089
824 373992304 58381935994 4 5520364 7109590825189
91662915931963986386099 84 4 2524 559194 4 4 2374 09807650556117505789
614 64 35919925564 26759631196277837512874 653796523866525681695700326964
287850720184 716605737922725209523210990761127024 194 9139628074 81696514 94 3204
3193064 89

96967523523778013360171535579 4 152722674 4 04 38354 774 7834 6154
1713610807197104 73088602374 503121389

0081325624 317204 97688680228292550 24 334 939599178274 6769594 11554 4
30985036164 31316394 4 2573259674 614 175806634 24 4 9250604 023220280294
69873751829312706554 137782988619584 8109350266364
52075093196152508201502395128106961883020837 87779175314 24
73780066613661071255613809568754 9097630224 818254 7336957774 4 2501363334
65052729624 1951503070016298234 339909100061555024 94 673712884 3219723533994
529380672234 1962170161634 32924 7937574 4 5914
665771562668285110792098013823602779 08524 908614 0613238204 70296033614 212396789
1694 99234 23217152888329 7993911294 66525384 726864
0531873197932267770276017871517 11271319022168364 1694 532904 5195204 6150335534
734 4 6978714 15224 4 7087707084 5614 1208314 98011066671652074 655536718787287374
6904 9871627624 680530857583522804
191995607327665917569577300287920706287306356228290 71093172254 124 4 10289
96562194 393033935979312729824 901885059982075302805818268734 5362620769884
288389

289

63551772699775527089

28071198383271264 164 98135850566092974 668194 14 33220376360160317023864 54
0103804 19337568874 559351238398276056529937969 4 631115736236765803515756 4
368020797909806973589

289

503336310275094 784 78135700064 70316765317984 374 89

38593199284 4 67970505014 6584 2227782696067591977 74 314 2284 89

834 622963809575224 5329234 35922351304 4 12034 59096101274 4 8589

14 05058274 767759110361971874 81126259602724 58667655714 72754 9394
12055513362289

16904 26382083573995206157 2394 64 5174 4 4 989

912970211065709594 4 985564 756710539101364 04 6559061659117790624 364
59573934 6071857771170611184 51700154 54 508099885004 0593155875095120616554 56314
62007387394 4 33274 3915654 0822226551667114 98136135073739954 89

339174 8086374 19664 80932781710026395502 5914 04 77751934
7205269361172155291 9289

4 89

1128512312563105277097234 938677089

309885624 7973589

327598084 634 2321851624 985305036273164 5550860024 4 801128794 87089

02187528734 539294 131614 66208814 826808614 16201591554 912204 1986025984
88609910010089

35521986004 274 34 0573101214 2734 0294 7594 35672697762854 27772767597954
067832154 999870802605838132869028183862100061003 3764 237919800194 4 23704 4
20633319989

3214 6516974 334 576991282231826114 0907089

8614 4 154 0819914 7374 74 3368164 4 9824
325266081666966973361969533212777691297726357984 301509710815856277 9524 1014
0312197253995009854 837006991572638174 9334 231984 17086784
859633091293669773835628870784 0800239223578231036122923 1334 313870871375607264
7955306878567678 7614 086797853884 18397508504 683509284 14 4 7196834 3566924 53914
539697267038657031729624 18389

792354 536870706291053584 09586252881729281692 4 7104 63959137654
339775103303861869054 1627854 067967188564 52314 62534 6834 64 3002030663624
300772804 1839150504 8399774 63906523527004 766822033701569158523770139905 4
1263834 764 84 66384 1179107634 16394 509626576134 524 834 091389

87537934 88871084 4 0822515024 794 4 7198768883992003573792607 36576854
93015534 302684 384 83889

314 0272196682038727684 904 06507864 14 983954 8386239914 4 327100354 84 14
285714 663675814 10868575684 974 964 24 92058856984 374 594 686574 4 80184 934
2280279582356377564 388268232624 1877622162260709 04 51984 593267734 77350182854
36069393524 16589

601174 507376114 064 0689

5988292994 4 64 538186860664 74 728889

919098229601789

297804 73579124 79632186915368703655952 94 4 4 334 9954 25160580908304 9273594
0881012512804 5910650504 7664 96267582224 133933158027094 209234 354 824 13754
5730590871565675676701092095054 671117837732104 7597669794 36357024 9991724 7764
0990996184 2234 2259389

6684 699154 4 188772094 653007034 4 371831157287057320673987595782140794
0736334 236084 963832333591790227712682630327694 877532004 680184 757705394 34
300795119666775243961591663082780839590538322951127233820755074 4 15307889
77762867716625188109118753519733009863771748 786188154 764
1160222390303195596789

8153733333258298360045 1889

734 131385796009297774 5880614 24 0104 5915014 78206797394
36362919935582276023675103478275564 8662712188255528531782535860103510822581 4
502611204 74 70924 01718602564 6900684 617317679905734 901100727287689

26194 527588335875822194 7384 320834 5786330528075574 54 938289

5239005984 568272914 134 64 3234 881714 8584 6067830594 826014
5359687621596708124 9553230576378156 4 934 4 56525782552293824 9626575117074 94
9886687654 4 103827053374 089

89

2104 0368677365604 54 28584 516950314 0223236337570264 1796577852081754 4 89
24 655709924 0813236655786985264 53538880111889

193286251925592221355667681557609276306155759306626 4 73926089

8327834 7680214 60555713159391575134 1973623814 3794 4 978888581196334
3728292321966320335780126113077010857215989

820280124 527014 194 4 0551082110912682626167070806274 271062080737562374
7391179018806303915191 89

82517186661375757275971038 9

8114 628132094 11824 321201157828817875559190831284 16589

81012959939724 58282885034 7090530282922251789

724 313294 8789

7374 32150734 1389

531992364 5094 0330089

4 4 4 177994 9785506114 695615294 8565531122294 62352630605156014 9924 64 164
694 1653581717906597534 64 774 74 75189

4 4 903388637694 54 91013384 75379570124 34 353283214 4 9298275732064 94
6005703587974 137284 7308556850024 14 057806994 94 4 4 2096564 54 54 206704
0671269177034 205589

354 59214 7513994 6586563795324 4 989

394 80729634 53595989

77325035224 253669755202625966190223911374 4 64 70151563774 94 681734 4 03794
53288595394 92677763875590864 79724 78088680068172355853131 4 356329754 3176604
3925383854 0575689

974 2985095171277824 8854 06609203265598281270195713564 28139254
0661309838725191388287 4 3230385070066019921570688871565313698 64
58667179283657355256586271881 4 4 014 4 31714 3679374 8105969137093212168062 4 24
716237296617153934 39953368054 14 5698679389

71784 889

1015986030954 1293529874 616910919252380974 294 4 5514 885583184 994 98594
7959024 263664 2554 8655563314 934 689

35615034 14 88374 884 631294 6530056598074 676977360194
5598152863062761262676635577359767581 1384 21612373314 597087298604 71384 174 0124
88889

18797133273636262511311334 67653762929984 089

037789

5200008539399763584 74 4 281979857678072104 89

634 59907780154 26697174 56754 26172384 022032773364 76397551754 916653384 4
727336853524 96691562976924 834 3626504 74 61988233594 5593854 238873901364 17704
694 5395798118752712 15977684 4 251179958071694 54 6686174 98200389

14 1367574 25295199235363028 64 099584 7738080667594 16971558083354
26239966791371918 11974 565095014 21574 14 4 5024 65594 28230866854 834 54 75504
1753280904 924 3969757733834 0692003659626982380632 10584
21 168311536080639600030298 34 8698625014 189

5196159770985 30989

34 15906918264 4 74 62124 298360754 34 64 4 624 34 64 1837589

126993823538014 384 957364 3323589

088034 003650356294 50989

57173 182 1193875360604 03375025733 1 182525704 66934 4 7027575665724 602024 34
35805176179804 30500157661220685910711 9164 4 7836787755287555765 14 9553864
62900314 7784 33524 20182232281862889

83604 99556710094 713073625117504 656828874 9334 51108004
37057008572073227508319673684 10921087264 6030862698701217604 4 0904 028069794
9111839 64 366052184 314 923073516315889

04 4 4 54 80567978322555962857732503063907386237033313393794 864 907355954
6851796504 29666182553105264 59824 51735375632502837394 355101805927205309010514
290924 33527312786900151513055874 0539553595264 90302813127589

26687850268380277539808784 196954 24 4 4 70759826527714 763680134 4 5122704 64
69658616014 0500059813554 266004 555304 12564 538564 89

931603128055964 6970972771764 77513623793 186953564 28514 304 4 56301276104
28264 94 0367974 8029330190134 4 3998609284
0586881002688328778606907005752229 1637884 5954 2951 127 12364 162904 1724
9259287033518121777 24 5720634 74 4 4 14 07104 579870116834 865389

4 086087934 64 2885814 05323722052203338827824 916065507514 284 9889

50267304 7338689

4 14 66577151917067007154 6284 9334 13054 595326178257624 74 55778605289

07055681209392 13636020794 84 001904 534
8227175019919985035172 181982915553 7394 0524 4 74 8816084 01 14 286829854 2198154
173994 615194 4 675665399 1 1086257026617289

15721 16167086 12807864 4 225968780654 05524 084 0769809262297989

089

74 38864 87188124 121528586210714 4 171314 6827394 15124 54 0231527184 64
1602104 587509694 837594 3180736202 1929374 001190274 7502717656734 3594 24
7367066180398677673056064 018589

90535751230023066083708711686914 75791336384 0862325384 34 926718606613904
6684 33787965 1679007095096077004 4 54 53556313624 051358161617384
39970087207800572797374 7669733000195181571665 14 4 8215634

06218186569555569523059973209613527960436084 9164 64 54 4 0098534 02960861674 5334 3809689

982394 3693824 94 955094 716954 167064 128394 24 51714 1260191624 73827086697693118069609710155725814 7853194 62574 614 53503976260554 651254 350214 524 14 34 329824 924 13812177132034 03237186715206273592816337 4 103154 7104 63963111770834 5350154 4 82594 576086659775717391 4 57660958775366724 984 051724 57008259582124 54 852196164 3789

3131098824 81700384 223320632885004 3254 2084 921594 4 23734 706930124 6933339188876395624 14 254 068324 4 2961396568624 03164 1284 03058782564 65234 28183365665189

585503699094 325953094 2506080824 684 14 255314 3703739066510989 676539808735874 993770334 589 530194 9519517021752264 52073203602754 6394 13113711611622289 9004 57080284 754 03614 063814 77089 04 136189 639814 6793609058294 82054 185806765374 5684 521520114 14 513584 74 004 24 91714 1834 97910852675578692364 6084 05102964 056854 71629114 79605166051298601164 2189

23584 706774 4 78369791634 369220302198889

6384 901524 17264 83510873673134 5839534 4 2150224 626155336633614 834 7864 3233561380530074 966762084 2875753074 4 84 76761221295204 64 02684 2561574 021989 84 9634 090361092184 7604 312888296926638081824 774 1624 3214 91805174 57605165276714 85956723605854 4 814 854 4 0213290753231 1933789 7054 213766925989

4 14 624 4 37580625161532179973 4 6963717964 554 7335354 924 90014 056074 36631064 74 176679985725698630252839 94 4 4 34 637993051824 25984 12579835864 959062789

06953651854 959181602825231129 64 88624 54 6624 74 14 98780234 89 619904 934 728196665830714 757725320158683554 707783672825756239924 3554 6393774 54 4 779733829602922395391013639 24 84 24 5799089

5204 65639804 5121789

1118683684 611173674 956595237321588319222 4 769664 29594 9694 0073685050284 0377689

0626580850024 671729589

76399152885528712794 692079212206720132052809396 4 5226322708682212314 758006603178586184 106934 504 552579097773956618012334 1874 1794 13622157860500783390 34 591252524 54 04 85754 363277089

363734 813762506583880204 84 570153291728775365851028 4 304 303738094 64 582794 4 6317034 7696134 4 868288054 93874 74 207836072091819669560779780786595574 0709604 4 302978609309079720730 74 9607010815586850159 4 8097534 35305272934 1161714 83174 73396610051752170023014 799010869034 52297704 8775984 0572862989

4 181021529690074 555659724 334 83618503777150550860330 111 5053176164 169618772366138127227871098651734 5203857378730216612722258062394 5634 2389

511827106389

99382819394 68089

089

1714 26867874 88703236974 23698254 3558888324 6084 5820284 0234 8362623588364
34 932664 801755904 6034 28215172195639634 95304 30084 84 1662178271514 4 94 5954
09011794 4 885259504 94 72655691194 5792036793654 03761138674 937619135288389

7654 88612131811530304 7160619686704 364 4 2884 34 98822552331296875029163 54
58654 268660889

4 604 69293705964 951284 4 89

74 04 856780035852704 03993562604 89

828221525557199699352 5794 54 526174 074 327085989

1130014 2906714 0022594 3274 6902189

829951795534 4 274 871811164 21174 2934 34 6618581259577501754 13534
1180155914 0012523994 83939017661752161192300632039269350 3074 4 08005564 85321 7364
81168158330203170589

764 6782329202381824 76764 4 909239971574 84 66900662684 870792697974 54
361050266597917187256 54 5818722599567184 7189

539689

6356398273911694 54 0082867722083973564 85201960596067264 5551934
29252306818637594 67716574 71639851037580102664 51314 90589

4 6532011702593902980926721553261881121687059584 164
729322719691537323315514 9878813034 739889

4 89

6254 271704 631085200203089

34 976074 74 8096952314 3814 4 85952336287596393157034 764
29000525190908752531657 4 07924 4 9294 6317614 1128160500604 332367814 9217024 4
718104 0900025235729074 5094 008754 19094 4 85013234 277377902820376877759883889

10224 289

4 65863071885783632584 0114 004 029582015157277750552204 9767174
180652296812814 4 5359630774 683991974 3615077556084 9014 8304 88152662261688754
968034 6283304 0684 96724 884 58314 4 89

61089

84 11164 18534 724 67904 954 2984 233687929502850535622738086930362906 4 34
96106389

02734 2398164 4 4 3712989

67524 622134 998071790983253853751824 514 318229817014 9804 714 74 4
05208206771734 829307574 24 4 60717784 72524 594 618574 89

04 930509650979539054 22530692123607017038379108 5714 698302257724 852517384
5914 5607910558853704 706629305268611514 96257016777566050987152 2189

311993190860804 09589

3272714 652003159911804 36374 064 9554 4 98522211631107924 0253084 12085874
327508302573604 67355905024 287620096058217825 4 0707253588194 24 274
82290612611565067099069000096 4 6228666919350261335698 04 4 84 99030606977087917964
2034 4 94 70664 734 35831304 985932397059589

0765212059389

769761799954 60990255750129252950517564 633281937784 8179827289

21626883979150390284 154 89

284 84 050101832934 30169393085976918820760983272888 9

2113551698234 4 564 4 4 7333253072962398579923564 5767684 4 4 65574 0788184
75328003206204 09124 85037907903369696799857569854 811754 81183866884 9282624 89
3373134 6365620962364 36017604 7562884 825574 68798352316689
20327581208311926727387077762830879194 4 164 0602074 62803182215764 0294
565833974 7608798691752555031704 96291961917121507124 5277331363754 7286304
9900375024 5934 8596003211514 4 99284 06621582574 3674 2274 4 75501063912224 21889
0391206885714 99028125033222930101962598793831274 82079514 574
66369086901110213105305738750610287625824 804 72978297597037886652702174 4 1124
60837370072764 091503713333614 97174 0090516021354 28701865990605537125909299
69887572687800067915869091084 574 07802739901018725834 0250270675234
9279084 5564 584 7233838793694 8393212193705663102735811096309 4 234 629357335874
3954 61017150974 84 176032594 835362175167124 9004 82878786934 4 3178634 077789
56134 314 765304 4 7271015873083591854 4 227533506094 5004 54 27094
3829595234 5006179508154 991222606770536954 034
708723167037735800385888201853606074 078592030910013073668615332051 3094
83297128610836602524 5559269732660010329761 1119174 374 276782789
74 7510302954 650308104 0604 84 2126629274 92258713195804 378325583814
279728206104 67164 4 54 5396678275066337611956154 71808114 106637289
04 4 508607112165066033989
2385555376753205387993 68505034 9218586536215611625607737850783368139 84
5092505697034 6054 311689
014 34 56562307724 317804 51284 4 14 990211879930904 82889
89
6661964 4 774 2952614 8689
7574 573204 68170131393090511705612968133624 6565767032752997884
25636726104 684 5139557876174 554 2614 0794 99278851594 193234 5573064
58553637676662779904 565194 68752359050707029026 235937689
2174 11258335714 398554 72717969334 71669904 524 57385765734 6363234
02095801122354 4 764 4 4 1723301996887594 84 11158859193880265208 126254
15775923953557139009 06192578857624 3834 39670825359850867717 5203064
77125971687162927198110872264 0716731620311995057 4
95353350785579058055280567687094 0035886214 5084 19394 51102129664
1803010250719004 14 351802625839184 1696334 2871083924 4 7011217284 273032774 70134
37984 117330124 4 6913775974 88172808378086328358 80604 10924
22086576772875220996324 00804 2994 4 929304 986884 989
84 5824 99837138589
16691314 11594 8053797704 20015970689
34 7111831573389
0104 74 64 7987808156521926 4 1124 175366266821681770769 323814 663364 194
8679086382584 7134 14 390786785266254 202550798750059834 4 20864 33532034 033854
071697004 8589
54 238194 164 63202364 4 9921869693519762514 87589
5364 4 751634 4 4 94 064 161989
4 1671134 104 4 35014 824 84 379874 6391600009785800714 88654 1351357234 604
66234 792972728314 24 155920800251034 6789

54 54 2752194 24 1325704 02630697694 654 0161354 854 687985714 4 294 8680303910184 4 1086389

04 14 4 81123754 4 3712853308239937328366819623130295691856958566274 11377033885853664 62274 71931672503361104 07331565700765207124 24 0797569995015171682190064 511788702874 6352292980881877100729033972992256664 211305601375775977190139940 1236326728084 5389

4 00319096154 214 993192613364 112255536011836627327838526740 0198754 78187635393573394 9284 7102958252871038099756540 397325671294 87558224 7836268074 52739034 90374 5390658115194 1957264 5585878826961885994 74 9183952654 96354 4 757136504 122860593117832774 704 3171702175554 27338113164 4 612205777914 60736577914 630762301569877794 27994 708000666933390808663128520372580 4 2871394 552756934 4 1864 3828321630754 24 9357674 34 06689

84 2924 81754 07624 5634 84 358599789

4 7995073584 089

72112726010980185913187269858204 3602154 4 9353734 22820998321512799675 4 77151086725568882 1989

76906794 3231991850034 564 659754 689

4 209085865186885 4 15650053017704 34 7774 4 794 3867270393095250807174 8114 3880667694 4 04 0880337002762289

2294 0394 954 64 568694 6736562765121574 4 4 27275561854 72729709231607710083303276120 4 64 4 00195010882554 3666118384 0175064 330798789

60184 9572564 092270264 53638384 87828264 4 37784 6764 67889

4 52186137353554 36563776064 7667817089

84 5054 355114 6912314 274 14 164 83679764 5974 96100751751595807391 64 79931951112693660164 8584 82939073318797391690878819561867 4 35883137351553906131 4 0986275515212954 4 4 877104 58089

77219105827633989

4 74 84 91027833916995225 4 3776814 394 074 18668237567124 4 23323514 8234 6586764 9964 5194 524 763308705364 4 068714 14 568326066397694 54 80193094 371008679575123989

119060859807956189

7702861704 6714 0202639004 0755211696790396797200717133559771 4 6779184 571361114 94 079667124 6292299933 14 77634 21654 1227783574 8258627534 9900679211197806030788574 954 6973284 1964 64 4 8724 8154 923884 504 16874 884 4 0326562774 709529606774 81195278592514 81070284 9070915018652287534 294 1836314 061123708587326294 024 3390981983868089

7918601274 6208189

39502098874 88319592020920204 19914 311024

Chapter Forty

32886184 04 3867214 6984 4 72180588274 776118855314 334 54 77594 9915708112154 724 304 8811098267530850187927122360672654 24 722554 9511677834 99513760704 930313675989

22164 57674 1761560889

4 882995093114 2765681879504 4 5739072603866015581213816955577713584 204 354 934 789

5364 2023389

74 64 954 927668535362013175286570550588094 4 0977166826187785035656 9324 88370061916868813257 6989

889

2153770164 294 154 770352800561194 84 224 729851874 87774 95354 6599864 731283766810231684 783864 208035715066104 3760802759009924 1762684 10207319104 116864 75234 925060364 563867772961804 9536610561814 53874 74 5364 7356295576007682838500265390338 2204 2359255398293284 19394 4 94 20500089

988724 89

180621128704 90391300294 8556514 74 954 34 4 57524 4 8228715834 0654 54 23074 6784 94 274 9309634 7001514 3263124 161298211097657797 80864 62089

6364 34 72088059155364 232264 831264 5150216051965026584 720667061301204 93386969922060721205 5074 84 6983132504 4 56790361979375114 5105610994 0597227061024

Chapter Forty-one

553164 34 184 231593135390530727 7364 3156367264 58013226763772668618 6334 792960994 124 327001774 4 953982304 3204 00254 4 9854 4 64 125821814 92056014 9218878884 85004 28184 18295383774 71703679191289

37630870104 27207210527934 076159095560569028 7884 154 3593704 1294 4 8706773764 271263821528379114 6308614 5996881385154 9589

6934 94 77753009109089

564 50628879874 94 99879189

7733005539554 996967223113032996223735 74 3856778002884 7289

64 2133583266974 725834 6061528037126274 3221724 325293392575924 924 4 74 1154 505859760314 253954 019027327179534 824 534 4 711818326753377256883131935700208316178318579 34 69555062509874 14 8085073837262014 4 83584 64 003533691270556211 9589

062989

35556277917839908857 64 95624 0379714 3088390971110264 22589

74 6293176689

672234 04 012789

24 9994 4 003014 64 6792202038304 21619880771734 664 735164 6810982056584 4 5677184 9874 9974 291629569527774 4 17095631284 59610269014 54 2233395364 4 324 79089

88275294 5116320992753074 9937938189

8314 756794 4 4 124 595963726257884 8779824 592170128005575802716 14 75792168773028767724 14 2783904 59073912739294 267884 3857719239680522994 034 05334 7073573334 518367251554 26582639619999309836730795037 24 4 86864 6114 937304 95761294 1570707066203289

1811072389

15527538336663817 0804 30330556707275261677 4 194 6306060870155565 74 4 5230874 6558396124 0503014 8057910614 581630901314 89

8861882107938274 751304 764 124 868278016019084 96784 4 2189

0111018392559678015888 4 05085393976838736014 191230960600868884 84 095875909397988754 571250989

027721154 014 4 019262217279654 6564 989

599214 37569114 29020204 111157924 87312650807559597284 7278699682789

16268278694 911524 7674 5851922811086526770098192794 35337913553500514 689 857938237138827353572717178 9

383014 22164 8571714 1029006997282353232884 84 62192811289

4 081707974 024 4 219054 4 36930380174 92997032084 34 0110873321114 53684 23599993209089

515669085964 9152277667229639694 224 24 234 188318035210991164 028064 34 84 7354 4 37983200003628081909768558 4 9256117523929774 1658204 184 4 8109089

51268364 7084 624 74 11739612714 8810193294 5586738194 3250861265358837368559920259078153960821287907306065333 54 4 90598834 74 70101680869637317737325829139 4 02014 9923292096927067831675968 14 766966752080774 82680711116784 9293584 61984 18626172110925322160685253881591855988062776872164 3818351604 955385279364 2109031310360781624 389

14 71254 3316537004 92954 3573131191804 284 19650321615780904 2520133124 8560532036085914 4 8176717054 9766907392764 89

514 05521520609254 13291657024 918171664 4 37203666136857876733251108285903819215 4 4 766528622524 6359219175013034 284 39331954 91229727926976395317 4 862232078789

202684 4 50835204 124 96126094 7859764 764 0505134 4 6164 5779957974 19209394 1387311276724 05794 054 104 6207559701574 18271819156561183209665877 74 0814 6769169774 837664 1838608175254 78596851524 694 80775281790629399270652523129308 9

4 8664 5014 7904 54 71076151553997996389

54 57354 9956164 20964 604 74 74 598537724 05194 5204 24 4 695155110576014 94 2214 4 598507856289

800520015014 4 217236030394 4 2834 24 4 4 87088873811175695 4 84 586881015884 7305082029360514 301370104 5069902681581989

4 5951504 5374 857234 879807161323689

9889

286204 9934 134 7784 4 5964 8262388689

34 4 9564 13068869396801624 022569609725905836903591 4 4 78304 64 0969184 582654 7581534 94 5007765160758195664 124 0074 3361172866660578064 097906850684 38390865501366034 171566121774 13653524 6662924 03852731631584 2924 75107182073761997 4 257005266362873 4 24 852769709124 14 632604 391164 6825719384 4 74 9765274 12791288332764 7534 004 587978756721972850802515877654 90565589

2204 714 96205252104 012016698764 4 538174 93876153962176209981866956 4 34 93775204 0786704 55027574 954 2082834 382652727990664 04 04 6308555601579354 15801838870887714 052300577774 79101336075834 63708160374 14 03358166217105237795 4 7780310828789

311389

89

4 4 795861169392281377 24 820976622315374 165551870724 3003784 4 6838734 4 4 6101858764 96624 830235355290685620889

36705012914 503374 7129770829859205524 05187831056216521 3224 6122880034 754
7325593257117509161 76594 1664 82394 97291335237054 38862724 084
8370552817002962980905865 0804 794 954 624 58224 0135714 1584 9006733084 4
5738818119674 4 514 29115214 34 2793926996556225719864 39196067753038374
68667222170355689

084 25034 83294 766784 15036783681989

74 75626360760561739594 95904 5378728870880119654 18789

24 7653078202554 1234 215275554 653752784 851164 2193002104 006960154 4 4
2855007174 370354 0070335935650539865178570700658209980 4 19574 4 9512358764 4 78124
86104 14 75565904 50055377874 54 2573276631373882502017264 89

6961612910104 81279326374 5673134 73871166387709984 54
206702700296011172263762727 2674 5210181186559105258614 5338819701289

91196384 7350290174 000706806314 623013080539754 5776028724 74
0990975069178826192831971 64 721284 9587379180354 95590854 50061798813211982114
29825837530563509789

9123594 054 4 860179024 86260767194 835184 4 234 9058719075337294 4 3395924
09185352802957201038394 20962334 2775620874 7723170117527568724 101224
53028153879584 509634 8579839104 51921318634 95690303912564 113905964 1254 0194
3629294 94 9192135307171534 4 84 09684 2071064 2282289

811864 0267635071607969350 4 7021002318781098561356791065930660078 9
776255319789

82500663151562983354 4 39164 4 4 92580570078010616280321 0220195704
75798656581168093324 23000560664 89

673694 87624 261724 1011990759620694 34 68594 04 06164 109057115534 54
53768092327128723539990 74 4 359195398397372110133 4 94 9165692714 2993028020314 774
5605054 4 66184 5753230590170786156 4 4 3038197017914 956765394 04 594
35606066050701739389

3132134 6258503810731950386 74 4 835560194 91822805167730576850268 84 3254
9589

089

560814 19950752565189

3554 022636610084 81614 62038654 4 64 7710712187951630698336202 14 074 6124
327385607330074 172908534 13714 6764 66208233265300757784
5780127550787262783016182508700 84 2818774 5332078797789

4 2964 8585975819284 204 9964 8296204 27354 073385310054 6993954 1254 6194 734
7217039952702270357793858512968366 4 4 067889

8374 65656361354 4 4 7806668384 669765176614 99961854 3989

6235023717671102 74 089

091939958314 514 68723612871384 9724 20690809504 4 22367855102876286804
25188163584 02616298518072115283322375809709057 4 535691784 01938160024 39654
325782504 54 4 519694 034 884 0924 34 085789

9982771915123030 94 7380554 0308231556081860716158 34
33955617281063733110606015264 964 14 815684 04 3194 6235604 3630174 31750920771304
9088685604 727385517309538084 75014 4 86517604 9756773607833154 4 72292534 33596384
5630215217104 9873859253102039789

5814 33366384 1559299255089

4 4 6027807017962274 5210555067119131632626527993669635989
23830060969816001670881344 3002039117719163070163778003830037112641 1824 14
6014 98704 1714 805662603384 977517560384 954 919157914 1792953684 9597062863297174
52214 94 5264 364 0004 01168512758738794 34 866688375722889
96134 29938664 02364 0589
4 4 824 529124 28201658004 7816694 184 780636604 784 8381761856515584 0174
6037289
782158565908314 89
306511779198572317164 764 724 189
304 31531999088154 99713774 20721011833196861968 94 4 05184 7134 8051037624 4
8875818172772334 4 2721570874 0008524 939194 9339810308319995228854 262630851814
5514 104 9674 89
64 257681720314 5774 19760554 01166514 371933763721881865065 24 854 4
5039993766092267777074 793998014 22580866214 98719124 7013874 6989
5676580981634 24 07951357037334 8683994 6074 0014 8381880910912278504 9874
2256394 71028589
0361789
24 8694 55199904 9171162317092974 08195172163625062371 4
2082526119071317918763800373820 9989
4 1551673629031054 94 02905372537989
5773700088178658870 4 904 3920910261127811112935519 4 2277819214 70074
36373735190083294 73368732239654 94 76329928275318351812624 0071189
2034 56588554 6809503026304 2519219879777374 4 326372609289
11109005219868755372281053055764 14 7614 824 639858637189
7727977619373087670 4 264 9704 4 115114 1289
00621261138853060373672295958161170213950300 74 14 176611284
83328860167367167320358804 70158024 784 864 639807999576764 70792331064 4
566260337307361589
9226178752674 260135360072952785114 4 73129927914 524 5062334
029096397175923219795801119 14 66992839606609054 62007982374 521224 50360169104
1156322195329726954 4 5551518284 094 53955078674 04 09371853236603877962805 14
3126766274 0364 39823983188176059785281 34 66394 6956055581184 589
398070501135751682068069 4 89
4 3855291350882854 4 734 82815176097154 2385952213273086132204
12923307765655869279095700 4 784 303955681994 015964 223359594 550228105654 3779954
708624 4 855908003706950156080193072 14 64 89
726731639389
255381599586170220591397302709006385884 14 9534 6162764 2604 4 2837389
12519184 78198500254 9826303585100634 1034 4 376334 07334
69903127035583080112 4 354 8158661164 679904 704 09954 79238128789
7186780109815204 9788060504 766682036629672509369396073136693374 72036724
3003189
666204 997506525201754 71357865734 64 38364 6763792685019584
6151069676536390 24 4 74 89
954 32199723190611693296228778 9
4 6122656683064 35189

5616389

9574 5077221094 5127991885324 4 4 93764 87789

04 054 4 224 2334 70979587265217693777637079604 0732789

7024 55829538696164 126324 65754 92104 4 812238089

336380764 94 996719634 861554 06090914 1594 9767808774 619122770828684 4
605325727180192324 6319994 6676789

2603035979578118279004 71394 0921719399874 07600099970695816 34 4
792336051061664 60077875593954 578581356191179734 84 724 27564 3954 4 4
6900185370303889

94 721998308058834 058367204 7301059337164 585377733373826188199786074 0674
509062922554 889

90834 4 3584 4 707186834 62839079294 70801169686394 851185081164 38134
60281234 7712665009370864 34 980810611925116998390691124 1127884 922501074 04
670010024 987554 9803524 056367371564 4 04 834 835224 61021967504 0334
226809019609191836769 7539184 4 8889

81030769313603684 64 9075185192089

98079674 84 952064 252815039882199294 501631224 4 4 192907905821755002124 64
1564 38780114 7363534 860323181769769925 6886234 224 36511614 13783584 86034 5729184
564 59731014 58014 4 23391034 366190912117514 14 3224 004 33814 714 64 9570280368174
781573399255278767581363359753605595393 84 0176867674 304 74 620112279164
2138790162717829363320257354 064 98294 3159500554 714 114 4 066372802259064
990772972153184 835396210592075094 818702230994 8254 672970184 837824
611212322639194 350073177762 0066954 059960374 037654 4 1062871924 17866624 2088214
64 82782794 3811361974 4 675884 359564 0054 3384 0353292127859574 8814 0007374
970832504 832785755627877386652837788884 3093724 219594 5555354
36816532937198863634 36817907518019612735 0934 5804 1094 4 6551725884 96802612101534
6697273811614 985607135933184 212517820869764 4 13662803131959266 2998008004
99938017991534 4 9183914 1860014 9176520095550574 294 39030632354 0512913272285289

533183861280090024 201859206830124 55768851599860366 7088214 4 03617994
97576930101581684 04 89

6369505707194 1618192298699854 618110664 31624 2154 34 388574 4 834
33888071994 76674 23092554 14 252204 64 613263330219254 123326554
225179003962370011877224 88012189

97398674 54 02327831011155813888762532752 34 66564 979284 5609117583939724
76956922958164 79170577534 60630170075274 314 0171314 0934
70826207580556365138365779777856686672314 3389

9715854 05128381753951728867267924 33519324 2794 4 64 04 274 84 5572204
271370383384 2824 335856314 2551037569101814 74 583564 14 6789

534 5086856290184 867609167706199880065923053 4 4 36395717282508884
25996639289

7124 77574 013093554 3924 73324 07918204 5553817663723533222093512 54 01324
815902989

0264 2974 259278789

4 54 7500654 994 69212124 66620662608214 34 93200208055224 057223984 38304 4
93632828192284 54 889

3289

5874 0225793208207774 9921263608591189

02964 66098389

5888100292388204 924 62297133229297037751993136100980352670524 4
86853226374 4 7804 6384 32564 6301000814 4 8629121994 571564 4 7900994 4 6084 29368284
7965274 4 61276533324 4 881103324 2025174 738622234 4 906972367553788033399596664
0307214 3753602331036965733231523777229874 4 269056689

61779628232189

87189

0962510009667381607994 856169911256164 664 51101755971637994 994 874
517358658677084 04 71684 4 74 77084 99097699794 4 70710722164 62801394 62754
5923362533618584 4 5760238686903734 04 0234 29979586621889

714 158804 57537565078504 261021206974 36970969214 4 094 1134 689

94 2630874 378569318126994 04 38714 594 89

5998350024 8233904 352960214 104 34 79871030683534 29770829833207751880715284
808828337014 59951573669234 089

522074 67531109020004 0877667734 5208304 1072554 159390052576034 609120814
0284 1774 2037713070084 24 3715867293605934 80664 9256089

06006214 0073524 622034 6694 34 04 37762973714 172956577384 4 3594 0054
75357783364 78717385883199572538063980996026 4 54
0532720562873151122978157160862957374 684 56654 23600829004 30576533154 1271689

89

74 6228513385107670664 2751110612635113161609 24 24 34
6656970070932995217 8094 757112910514 8114 6984 68163620994 9121191573759093 4 654
66617608592524 9964 2964 904 99530084 9587607819636004 710267394 0074 0732084 3624 4
20034 614 4 94 70324 2395176785324 24 534 80993775280280525924 04 86576284 6714
12186729974 0770308393074 26174 014 500322104 972620715170167184 9128134 389

8195596976652192019081370003672782082 54 8084 4 4 077054 889

4 97735290074 093964 1152159281309852 4 327606824 7595225330802824 8314 09114
55034 964 805588336314 3637808692685098 4 022754 3561095303877707012120002 89

803251790104 9232507788502590832634 14 354 85168772200998294 7719960230524
38855804 4 8738331603586172269203006710187874 260694 178604 0706999025075004
9323362692993214 094 65809964 65314 28589

4 0295050759938374 24 671389

269904 330889

69689

3171221522509329615283223 14 04 015224 7200696225193121876 94 8328674
20029173664 4 3568066358210533280 4 176726151562302124 2888554 32501934 774 7162804
3834 1939284 79334 8612220573524 01287750089

4 115331923097650828181118 9

6355024 9584 6710684 529264 4 84 55574 27712134 74 28588612865531692904 976784
56625964 1824 72669277834 4 00266072794 74 14 4 4 08370664 575851237670920004 8312194
034 83729208560022902779773086 4 854 14 74 61858811157024 0287314 904 23374
710220512254 21059966070353839506 4 82334 5926097124 4 250184 778080977172673924
73194 0165503960786701230 4 7395765332806585083 4 84 1252600889

4 6584 67311915729174 574 224 17794 93354 97989

19007820621308610803865516223758124 64 83554 0650724 32929291154
50926671318592967693090324 380500504 705798029574 71634 654 6186859666334 8164
73756375825302952862923734 36789

4 94 660108835291361314 6663832807119837174 914 5500064 29820817274
50617511533164 317850686055995804 14 4 7050514 5134 4 34 661354 34 9132377733690004
775758504 04 699354 95286508212310688552096189

97124 3934 34 1116809879539624 81708529338557609002702279 974 124 17974 04
7571783589

1513010194 83114 208868324 94 3314 817802337650953324 2995528594 4 36834
35519727318517804 94 655835099194 3093702256819318024 684 4 8831867708730934
7278038059155250231204 064 2236094 7098853016075837054 36778374 14 64 4 1160534
2176004 593264 89

0125101094 36888394 9375010807823551784 95090823589

954 07264 74 6204 374 2888105083964 55884 26654 869276504 84
03283121820919225254 9114 72664 0636220307934 5506603988385724 860051085280789
8750922954 15205368592926198779 1689

22159220522055198532014 792614 7108591884 318686574 115963789
931121609989

761109796335654 4 4 902734 3590983289

4 7867883974 9661090310579656789

884 814 633779378097206339058 4 010251514 80018804 01230886131297554
20721536964 927058014 55275021614 67808691366074 9812251621634 354 851006334 4 34
9103534 20533934 694 524 974 76955086265693627621261091572689

1851277303763839795715936693067 94 929864 838663384 4 54 4
86312760855100518189

4 581104 14 64 7084 54 015362914 582274 572901534 1057988169354
0552831867360382508835230 4 73920214 607034 933191067272651277179914
1383722670503004 2889

5154 9134 8029236323928824 220795773086577354 4 30078714 994
07960630325769589

9262392059660138555 4 18034 1966989

324 3670285104 94 28362179024 24 4 4 777381925654 5997264 4 214 164 5880183324
2657385618786789

598523634 784 2353680905992711999559785 4 014 4 8359660621563295 16389
073004 27568254 0019235888320300191134 9752328613006510978769294
55311396689

555834 764 370807033156924 64 77056683170873581839 4 804 53887530751714
783371195076879764 0772884 64 8664 9791823184 5023153810551758734 07189
625387985376214 371724 368207104 68814 20524 9239365508704 4 89

13554 1655626666713154 1921763666664 4 54 6134 197065884 4 04 8039586284
01161360336854 8134 5505093590314 16572525760552586987870305119319075536 3634 54 4
025154 52339582336587160381608528218500714 10354 9936084 662784 075061236838764 4
6214 589

192177914 25930064 973124 1854 636559956751295850203082278 4
10326137151135198390612 4 15964 633398239008789
73879933716728872035 6789

4 869612784 6918029884 00077024 04 614 1684 3570964 611623794 84 580024 3691534
4 6231929702763704 581054 66861864 89

20064 81857884 4 704 61376294 2820614 2107034 80363084 4 11167800614
815023913690139665758 03093965904 4 1591251209695297358127 3097903258329274
79399692824 38314 9206259029330928601033239174 0383834 274 57113513984 5774 7832024
4 88386021968076716 3316534 98673034 74 54 0139992159822111671115 1254 4
25853760916734 327699904 00584 4 974 34 75905564 206307694 6934 7283565064
9910777679589

26507983234 81084 018224 4 89

117074 9665104 0618759184 74 8576972103674 32681514 84 2019569722074 734 4
822087928699608362935 8763165389

04 7839004 874 274 79351515284 19727078614 3219658284 170693904
96815772568280501220207510923634 65517693151572323810501802258551751824 782234
1364 31788165206850661394 22626534 4 697289

35978057557926078321 66673889

80661251923880001695 34 32522620052889

95610861328799507595 73554 74 95524 74 24 308328701918030564 770827367014 34 4
53937593763155017509 351851587985050694 639052319582925230975 14 074 05254 5956314
0074 36631365318598857 5773788784 1902614 118689

54 4 56504 2160337064 78625262724 70854 34 175977950069264
90269511202750263 0954 3674 0580164 721315926794 53794 3694 9752610184 4
660858000783127191316021235 0913829704 2587023364 1604 64 4 84 61284 70918634
315198653654 66090267618224 74 71801225355996813235223866795597369 2580689

597530371264 8024 4 8204 581370182034 328690863716598337757108583301036874
34 65774 110621814 31765563396 21006385831674 674 80918871707737653 5589

866220294 998738274 4 4 2554 7924 11634 654 6794 060365024 74 6024 56189

52590934 99667359512271273 20524 0111113918523027067614 277230922294
72881013319296333997818 5503182934 4 326322064 69801012951704 55704 30063250156 2504
31508365762832674 12300204 9506 3971736784 1889

100514 252530524 96886256738 7384 77796628662164 973624 0288369309617354
37337313667758358357 01794 4 714 574 708124 9069802297768156882572257089

4 989

089

9120660554 02520608013224 504 82512081375674 376619867964 264 129860594
31128300054 088818812331334 72974 731212674 4 4 4 311867594 320910668184
178102655733532621387 7374 7375534 57827904 1511593132185182858877 74 4 17722966204
6913866020934 9694 25605364 5066213331732596198768258 8594 298794 26709380114 1054
1539939189

60836361924 874 18791693064 635784 4 80721565839931203794 0118324 4
80201556714 14 285986372785984 697074 04 7554 3618234 81587960114 136623524 54
80672034 5614 75693978012289

5658521622561696712983690 08539004 3834 5103629959 1188765554 85850103824
200072825738319153990752 70712724 12720139581995535663 73551289

0906976251070304 89

202794 525915565004 855304 667824 94 374 1234 171084 51112727160221094 19314
554 0157999752575970623571 19650920779653514 558284 9694 64 124 71272627520263856889

880768351634 588214 74 4 3822121862964 6612627082674 2263505719504
7392386350754 1211664 8302620097127671004 89
8267161324 51910352783620701 2854 4 4 4 67011130523252269301508703063384
51974 189
270634 06924 54 588091376803729575334 68067793504 6864 7874
5877073762192530 52874 813619851138575784 54 29291076654 292834 07134
350225088281889
291524 4 5277839874 72190081314 3807204 3020724 54 679317587784 6662665684
65288615076884 03122321218733 2960724 4 2684 94 3391394 8234 4 004 8794 73181001567234
52617702576708867907794 884 35759761351817722330324 69991166575966356154 88804 04
973201297560095265988234 9602233294 9604 235511787278552924
08028587766780633702288000221810 3354 70733819373826226757192925 93356370954
06157277805724 4 14 8311164 04 280200117378104 53773569712267028220634 931269054 54
98167184 995028115689
01079688029001 1256589
17905559234 54 72292137852872328218 12125034 518205954
80967722776607131017786034 388295733182064 235872369934 1009810617234 963824
68683009133256534 4 9234 684 068069390174 7353201504 4 4 06113834 7551904 2887754
060775819161781154 13003992574 037864 4 359130190784 611315598122874
33383309853783972802072728689
23202989
4 3973394 81981775713924 74 91694 64 6666789
61234 29109370338793251233773971 3880254 9835070664 6550164 35659685314
58265075610705724 702998374 0904 8601724 3764 19814 22704 314 8037384 52936874
36005363912672650761 5680781314 2004 1224 119594 94 039297701634 28124
0787208085216663064 5923056703207098161722529026960230630812926 02279781774
357161381029192980622509729 0234 214
02721191693803271 329832008372850667961 6281592358286686576099904 4 1599158720394
18368224 7309036694 969071774 570121777 14 4 672683511194 5799235764 3789
4 693565354 20860629730104 67307198227660774 393023094 6886154
82810951520215970525502361564 78355794 19688175556091385778521 92225964 776994
1023057003836674 76235506978823189
65569824 14 6502867863189
21131224 0606180938604 883264 5173084 01695014 2082157326064
29222886911152502 54 99360218005104 19326096907384 74 88323914 024
15585332601152850704 3066093224 4 4 24 82524 14 4 174 6074 4 4 884 4 534 18552824 14
0376224 64 30116084 9294 8664 582998552054 26715174 054 54 4 202062807034 33294
106933727264 29706689
108153584 84 014 9094 5693824 621684 799297070687378774 06289
283254 5134 22604 088371872199038355 52674 722094 12312676596338155725024 4 84
61126959274 697523814 4 932164 04 4 4 689
89
516224 00692837095862738068883362916 3724 004 187595864 55204 6374
6275695830507984 5381534 715230664 1100725692362934 92763936710913135 12704 03054
57696996684 553584 714 559181928377124 625835214 124 4 58120274 9660784 77181056994
5704 3360508168509589

4 5374 630795183950034 71725194 84 4 35994 94 854 4
6852681297359019069065 35989

033569560310064 4 79682631204 57319101154 4 4 965551122684
173251522773863030813597582172290597661 3762764 17661634 76909125070161 99955375964
3211557534 396621688271084 0367511929996000 88624 63219998754 18094 3600530874
1339626929982076296680154 880905235587186807616985560604 34 175392524 04 96799964
65176000269269165516987526525067739508 51304 08053884 4 5060926010964 36881089

4 202685615907389

98509908250154 94 63918220970064 84 5536636689

968589

22863821597110767 17976789

7501154 2808723039128878869961 86789

307198286754 991974 326270934 100026851032592963268818524 14 89

579124 4 32764 87218014 5298218574 97714 29294 366689

378364 382229658591114 1794 05184 94 207357064 5283259884 5912259394 9274 4 4
55714 66776515114 5692903139525375804 63375857964 15811636218722766151 89

824 122053513224 224 8825616774 24 5967654 1254 0331784 4 988384
11137607350077200856972776264 873652783389

163614 24 964 2106308834 93089

0332084 87794 2864 4 04 9722268286185994 6689

34 3794 851334 855905828206964 612394 64 97574 12236283139773381 90874
55803316751727223 8664 736033632294 221653127763584 7730631534 297372774 92314 97394
27339168139875171650178103261 3174 55063776577097886959767574 2214 93716352884
56874 1975606953600393373320206 5164 936970814 92295834 3311631037274 09098662574
7050514 7022723096296228767689

36937738712390204 65167295592539637 5704 229682701372159784 9618036234 804
337906397035855824 22108823529872394 9688535770504 518289

50991937634 74 7320351938281114 4 209254 6739336782292584
965322008001526318029 14 0864 688824 84 51312773062679808155954 764 828504
17271139264 0315538504 058354 882187206324 9822568308378114 4 74
9672788833320028717670034 3696901126333771 4 06814 924 8560992223709551854 7384 4
57179054 1768739279171785165931 96828 87564 1818677687684 101914 918079399611289

07075158854 5524 6994 7650821767567721164 66364 276819985224 1009652130504
650834 0727574 4 84 96619761614 6084 05906074 102214 4 4 976223667994 4 84 83777754
6120077234 904 834 6804 7995536374
9200222871127185135606616822912 32392180055827814 1858159904 4 0624 0526254
6367710924 4 3831733984 76328514 7065350007978 3184 915824 01175965590053502 7064
0384 0870712334 1254 904 300589

25526833691094 7101885680630974 86389

4 07660730095765914 62156505019760734 4 889

92170674 595990100871084 361834 4 33277876536825877230822334 4 34 54
329275264 50350827510368852787696779 24 7529054 351634 84 71778306004 34 23068025104
169270984 04 294 2326154 9283137612187925615980554 96179934 882234 04
32228376565318861257502 64 07804 5152954 197194 1954 779774 061554 624 2676714 3364
705108681554 0321664 4 52516231071226012 3089

37104 755068250860324 04 639086714 4 369077324 4 134 3984 9284 14 6788284 714
79332996215272656768340104 00353802720252754 184 352253722834 4 89
70658115608571059933666774 519856604 7220084
1601908600007880595268182669131384 1734 181990559010582359290201354 0514
610372925984 089
24 4 4 05799629261209829819631751214 5353321039055651854
357550155063302303939832174 24 16388765814 18283754 9573824 8135795353764 1564
8600199102097635339207540 84 934 83886928161124 0904 2860516889
724 15625937579583189
89
50072924 59604 67988554 4 1909311233298527184 4 62335677735993334 804 074
7037205328034 70697637002715728202307305769614 14 8719664 204 255727504
91950366323004 6513954 1814 07251089
307094 4 39783121107332766875928037765071725136087557193764 8563674 4
85588882578876613391844 930211918822927090195001454 684 234 363699275319954
611567138685704 5074 4 14 321633904 07802999234 905814 4 6565204 4 962335154
3572010554 1820604 4 0262989
1318181183565214 801386554 84 6503939174 4 227689
9832095994 734 532614 851533809088184 4 0673726935784 293194 08508180054
11125012034 574 4 53033313973804 4 694 8852770989
980569600051914 114 14 22794 7762969039224 1524 4 61598136812557513984 94
0301589
089
1283903969068237159676228264 37559056160300204 57274 56152794
59651918250071334 8715654 510175277234 4 85087001667162208134 714
55957733125187680564 85291054 07392802221120032862781056 024
39800380701905697739652978779098800316206689
84 037215519624 334 297992810095608616020 14 9108819115097937929003694 4
991206217653774 82371955324 5806361501300980865 04 4 24 252934 7835698514 94 2884
63384 0196508628261926818181314 535227102216178688563979618 04 255727094 0196904
19527822189
72371157604 6001639909088872571825104 6884 2834 6189
1318120296964 1334 89
31760054 804 6104 950927989
7517631114 74 02264 219675764 51984 88724 5324 00325330251824 830774
9123252566884 75616954 23934 889
7784 6191575794 4 227708558205785410061634 8798261398555091924 9337634 4
19693864 7024 154 34 328232827684 5684 14 26994 38372354 0254 0939373073804 634 34
382820719655314 032671584 701694 14 83313914 99674 10908125309984
316312073108505016906329319101821105395585567039824
19629169520765719992723071763730813 64 2389
4 014 823262654 7055090384 19616639574 5836874
7626735252555811990719183623735 84 36871834 30590922179954 4 9969222330034
2870822693305654 4 676836776755877960837571832810682555956854 316804 574 7689
684 4 7920124 4 4 3974 874 70057375724 574 0874 9217827564 24
73325859338271836011855063727116823814 24 624 589

04 5907602969214 280818057785601886552690999279221 54 7127089

5924 01794 7650784 4 514 4 14 64 5517172724 54 84 7694 16076624 783260657354
1389

4 4 6198858375674 984 767805369839295763266022 64 72399204 1365216237363614
6664 03231551854 15154 81118581084 4 3398551504 36734 8070980163062524 75101971504
66954 5974 914 14 10113086616816368604 2103388074 5651994 9324 58611604 8711164
862799838024 8125394 189

9013637727311133834 266778532592324 53334 4 853759664 7162083385374
122635553089

374 4 390195154 157567994 24 532380334 0830721684 1994 789

968124 268884 616597060833397337177 14 4 364
986798767187972512615063197288554 0631915126103864 962031374 005154 4 134 572104 4
904 4 6705194 51569227393667324 9768573916031054 3114 81689

22251592576687809534 6204 8818191351201284 1625814 7210278096597999194 4
16034 4 384 1823262314 4 80816732189

1237994 65974 694 4 7371994 734 4 754 614 4 729069858854 2010162523064
196805972372284 2337324 5114 0654 028375526303970784 269804 5973210194 934
570025250559594 69814 54 221070283690676511133800827 19704 304 51924
780925117856272910352627916974 2580684 02627307584 190214 6284 4 091789

84 4 256162986739091005370029788550698582319092885 54 4 09934 577175078784
9254 7917137854 3226314 655666153587021 1691604 31720984 2652323139660654 889

30853830196834 01924 13686714 2069727633671975814 778723614
3301726125552055830024 75666557171155769559720731 11366164 764 92124 100074
3253672111718190269864 734 965813010136711373222930768214
6982330958626017552721672584 24 77594 4 3215834 4 8325166771795381374 4 964 4 4
065673813832664 575174 4 90574 8004 6505684 021118589

827064 600254 984 22293207274 982206974 76980622608266011096184
8556935211806622929 94 0380157261010384 282960889

874 60656304 6798502292990209291 9324 61771606160384 8014 22508869123734 24
85864 4 1731267184 74 6634 51214 908085532127581189

4 74 825178594 017584 4 722914 25938199664 79033908751036666615 4 164 68654
7007202202254 597534 80984 23501364 84 8574 94 788554 74 592133750963767821654 27914
1354 74 6700628127674 4 2222991188279981357269073785 4 690911015568104 2971730577884
24 76385374 0267974 15237094 624 6394 34 60512163924 514 8210507976032685986609 4
00873234 1564 2353566766637531227634 8010107704 54 89

0510324 057956596674 130831157927974 80966954 34 7260724 74
1069201533920909334 5827774 4 73396165009357524 71124 17075063503208867717 4 121934
9514 666763871263737284 611604 08770630158376001115336 4 92121902033180685003 24
6663792217379792680 4 6636376195583620 4 719574 5588172551120008 04 199114
6136339555201130039 4 23915975356674 1136702232551901934 1764 557314 694
8220222522954 833329774 5560513730774 2517709774 4 4 659807607594 54 660659310312734
8715553264 389

083383702773822074 314 5689

4 4 5864 371754 12106604 933774 54 24 904 70014 9039594 6574 594 377123789

72800584 293962105526750395663214 92376729814

06635006120236079359507250026118822988170 24 4 093230606654 0097229824 335376524

377994 15918514 933904 17225014 69974 253353780504 36214 10935772354
90088186907390269514 016697214 83626167233238511176389
7273755722811689
9199803995729374 60322172819284 534 09332584 4 11696304 06238300354 268874
290211824 298564 5124 579520734 7984 62734 6195104 5524 256137362994 33014
9839372911108705299695191835336505534 84 4 24 284 804 63104 765220834
20859365173096584 4 96130285833654 81954 3598186756220294 161384
3211632576859825629672018289
06781124 186868784 59731338714 04 1872970071191986770129310629309694 989
9354 813921875928804 83984 513874 075864 302765615714 733518354 4
07350625531234 3664 96005310914 8813032384 4 6265204
3513629026265933306812051158885104 35856994 564 993886957070611192357275710294
1969289
94 1876554 36884 2569280638614 351303106384 4 4 334 31339619697973356152324
26664 1706639024 0362365593574 94 4 251038356824 93854 306636956562838134
9757831909024 27704 99094 4 514 111124 123020604 34 2232889
25974 914 38231575907984 4 23517784 54 1128724 2594
9353333098571097875538683981754 8252121751810308218176505155634 524 2994 84 53904
577562674 4 657855175914 89
162251178070532881704 5974 059759864 583008005610322325384 300750981134
3101204 508331904 228654 685877994 4 012296561656389
081595922394 034 392226001019722176573621711635990257575290003386602274
92594 219355961294 7551851369939324 9692786635065238826769
4 11676389
089
82314 6190959683386123118586714 9575727057568639974 54 27113036591818384
71780818084 175201006556621304 763267524 94 6682059974 6393688064 9990764 134 258089
308204 090236323835178306322176172064 3363201104 034 4 0994 091584 0514
68783262604 7756804 07126154 84 26034 6833880268094 04 4 793089
193734 2390363864 4 0254 924 4 8115739076316802664 67996790175567187064
1363324 02887050874 571658713959164 29253614 4 0259784 029087134 3774 4 4 17589
56655811307376296889
34 75271737113137790003100827293871224 87986914 124 280084 50272512254
63527219920187624 2350802784 4 796784 33702368073614 399285904 811111254
193110135095931272766124 8889
54 689
194 535563621879329974 884 5867834 814 4 86269804 7039900916289
52883689
11374 6167315617024 1004 5157757001603778370339572539261354 053250114 6574
19224 80121824 316985303536394 598857504 113262224 0054 109705194 916292574
379281916876204 92675684 7774 86034 513839694 6799094 3530558615004 2794 4 4
831120630905934 4 324 700093753671005604 4 926556034 7274 7780790783639504 5187624 4
8392697987313535284 34 84 638881332304 39792774 80220152961923554 860004 734
2730950786780625307677364 33322824 1961324 27056557794 52266065695016189
262562694 823800569503364 91504 711624 28579689
6829089

6905836375827828389

289

55203632239309604 204 62287810637658111178274 276253234 0505564 58534
32873936828810555823020155 4 34 0256660561199160833124 527637674 938321952334
956317862584 22134 166574 826288774 4 717933870329083625039594
51591113255050506004 05519331067854 02214 0139289

30774 7103178334 105594 829183713076924 56979522064 14 02279584
670586885775784 68725289

4 70075085185004 530687570783974 666384
5073601953573707378535670036258558206673724 3338623835066357323527255029874
737157104 95782761939356350167592836 74 2308538385735127612882617320094
87808731297810994 01372087532187962176750723 4 3104 204 09830054 30754 54 3089

34 756099996705300626089

39587539803004 7816817127195093934 1910683317924 294 515954
3851121090917226732183211816227957059 54 4 782253612682950954
8622172312363166507257218634 53174 107239765038264
7261206586272339002819509088574 0960057687874 5913537314 6151589

76810289

4 4 6734 608601099736780315612915571 89

2379694 13783512316274 0751694 5694 90868054 4 1787597920036554 692634 4 4
6181773732271670034 4 4 26677604 6094 924 812058797064 6584 973528807924 15315639324
34 4 125789

177935725901786375825693806 34 2504 4 3054 588279581374 1075602287584 4 4
78109654 27651767062223706972 4 197918021522914 54 8339562562284
6078386629266810605263766773584 3824 87337825864 288501212332924
7207096075960682756058028 9

3569806800904 24 7794 14 4 805224 614 08019298274 4 535914 2613006731539974
2203980804 4 53750119539726194 4 84 84 4 95199114 02819066003262802697095 4 4
8716577923187991552650311232353639686684 53024 30159619734 92262352274 323053604
2233756064 17777316238560718050 4 055918235089

4 14 21612604 389

37320034 97532633969317683963974 0834 087614 89

660534 676500201801809501790152 4 757381590514 4 6684 04 233204 62519585964
7960289

53155907754 7204 187516804 22104 88273979524 827374 9674 2588221229084 184
267327354 05062974 739562518609784 5807013227661151733251592801250066103078 4
56552279339066119554 676984 670693114 4 54 34 1653858729999 117725534
0758362673072059819231864 1581968334 4 077561735876011585 4 1062885902514
859706630256627278188193 4 3204 4 354 4 0594 264 174 72874 4 4 638 4 9708875389

24 3654 826954 25677051955005030 4 8573967192593691831322 4
9952382903951907875007 4 774 1928834 12833931514 36054 56554 99274 0034 000514
75286011764 91368819754 05835181301064 2819185 4 277239798889

1155654 4 20613295214 834 03974 65595374 6931767971260593262273578 89
3694 3952814 0371554 9812562291836028 9

709884 4 835199959092724 7614 2927384 761134 27394 270764
6596586099675123050324 376092528374 5354 4 759855871927974 51354 5604 09284 4
6312383889

192976387224 5094 8694 664 33164 58586117087884 0725956634 4 64 887728389
814 4 8069759334 634 89

2092084 74 7933664 114 7691694 8304 37595998302984 4 85104
6697116761180315756704 3074 8683191350151086626814 8110806626764 4 4 8818763734
119104 63014 864 339513331694 3864 86719125305119771222260512927206628882836514
6022194 4 708196954 63197824 8180623064 29591934 38031910707567289

113034 16669390683766514 37334 009829176917783350235113772378070080134 4
9375124 805050073219738123851625063208104 96669536517392868858139774 90771907824
529794 1956168869722316752104 5066713791920865389

3674 9986314 8664 1017004 4 4 576299589

4 532195598663958091794 1851056008686137283520554 4 64 20332754 284 59604 284
332904 254 398613235909889

616104 91104 0370538129550774 68163875576813162991902508157027190764
90775784 360216977227904 1728321524 8311154 673779867534 863300970984
071885291772936383789

686704 54 4 9380220171574 24 305990922776633024 2974 4 1704 50074 589
94 4 75150076574 278290259389

6377634 93531594 7832002254 24 326725184 23005068820208254 972129214
05633725581581127104 74 1570185389

317829398787712798274 8865671504 63224 664 38555534 84 8878687664
135561276104 85824 20589

1865197234 3533639572360994 808168173974 031190309304 510004 396180691234 4
770855514 924 72966785089

5219861090165524 89

83577004 96192037386165583736313265234 59824
53199510591605837900039799695177706979524 69522983676074 314 9900854 8564 14
3327220034 989

03384 04 2853124 211234 021004 981624 2918589

24 2224 34 95753608082603067624 0154 695788064 72961926684
52751116009590537854 8316367124 54 84 8677882017252054
639855865003582350020215085164 236635007877607151985614 5256264 9515910555074
7727853798154 06327168195111754 1022889

29837822254 533675665190251216823016918198394 25989

997594 117695875215092794 637661963360871925094 4 4 685902213621857104
072204 9966386358712990530555270284 104 677262021274 4 6674 54 52154 577237082364 4 4
53357064 522514 97567870517194 800500802567824 6078181854 8758389

225888164 176204 9036112904 31281674 8320766934 852285776067934 84 64
58657669095206610087879064 301681675339162115205681084 4 6789

4 159123374 14 636821138833757732614 0274 624 6664 5150989

2104 4 0638180830560804 0137010089

074 1719376629584 4 4 216912279089

3283198267723332127920076809166102683872384 324 54 4 20686797560394
82673658206734 515504 267630881815558039319161732754 4 2955764 3651620151664 4

66855759372594 09711518783692173299384 15788276602267092529144 74 618234
1866367219311226984 236086854 5204 18831280199780334 878756588271058702370961302744
79913234 82258137696121704 62274 224 961016733754 788010634 085514
86622869956915271626335017894

80339827364 4 8774 2823153814 82900134 3256788832287607165110115958718714
501057834 76297528874 339274 5818276860004 52775717724 788020989

6564 385294 2388173879991874 712975874 11654 133239155651089

08775257686286616807192109034 326503014 6354 274 9204 4 74 93124 652014
73231975770361204 501174 7939862821525354 9720267179089

50519508590979562153894

12180564 8789

967857306884 99639032778132294 0152073050520209607654 68832525175264
10135506514 5029802134 353365875559161683674 94 289

4 4 1214 804 865998225611198797208669302128494 99501664 79523817064 9564
27351552584 684 6289

20014 188138574 3510670806803934 0064 93980278204 084 50155974
31112977796802358220494 3997189

18274 081952024 523016175994 797082805860032889

288674 10624 7132869094 694 6684 3904 201205774 1066994
62157238511091569237592785586844 93977360688001922934 914 717580163165254 74
7272854 04 1117825003154 04 94 164 9532114 74 50754 96654 8023101855184 4 74 204
93368214 986786738789

24 957514 7069024 6623904 73966302006615781093579204 6362771350394 69784 34
359174 14 264 377803119021954 7522692089

54 7968878254 8564 57071355666985023275494 6123988230278689

0131757321917167894 9301636501389

55291315901174 224 89

607374 94 6020294 851279855924 50773793569081333869744 70374
15739655825885737494 134 9035827814 34 074 62554 2355164 39689

04 607795838664 99664 94 4 5074 7565796993514 9351359732001330337208116628994
16765098694 807294 4 032991761290723011144 04 6589

113824 272726329685176094 284 1879398026052395654 0664 593300789

6574 1576697086719209294 525393155274 37352828004 8234 5750914 4 853354 24 04
918205830211736693760494 97384 2272159134 8355204 04 2576169928064 2854 714
01936855614 110276582808570494 034 2325875865694 650092023084 9830826784 3272774
86927795504 066111004 359764 76867865384 95502722558854 224 986136573631739614
809989

36084 74 0971764 954 7154 334 06237073265869752764 59213374 29714 124
2070511225644 4 94 99079144 4 19244 4 4 832839379138044
20636238002970028206239318075619226494 85397394 933083251970873138494
58119857017100244 9136525227198684 083184 04 784 69364 290251112927517669939886203494
38789

175172675722174 4 214 53857611002834 874 32190524 3332939928094 883906152944
0644 1101879375394 11344 3031719168526355316735298536398677616350661196822494 72344 8644
0344 0968103858504 6067296014 76131074 0244 00744 265344 0244 3680379210684 4 615344
197080808812207680711064 389

0588634 21578528258228774 36754 7014 083100311384 298534 9352824 9358504 036234 59239266883114 4 807754 67105910694 0654 723734 6587789

4 1924 8732364 37024 02024 01751759704 682954 025507967730984 4 4 317986354 134 64 5953902276574 320351884 3111559754 63523304 5235505529285063611524 081176784 64 54 714 132798134 0659274 673208354 5282276634 305953054 734 30938175037787231764 64 89

0964 9104 4 255879694 04 11705277662970232569524 6367177584 58788220284 6053053054 66181722096550981839675 4 4 4 011935670278272108335560 64 4 66575228098058628703330757873821082112921021038 9

61652312284 8792032803766538720195820518561825014 4 24 096283660984 633225284 1101574 173614 88234 14 602873774 984 914 984 5904 629889

03284 925608395739914 0591024

Chapter Forty-two (The Answer)

120684 557624 8034 5904 723595368839274 61900635300602528684 4 34 54 6600578574 568725002887974 078126995014 3596964 94 764 14 9318504 96255521694 4 4 5285574 5294 8072324 3302773655574 56104 2966088356974 2530736111303108238000315853873628688 4 92109174 9180339054 8285054 627864 1000131694 719989

4 889

4 209530864 4 6502679610071504 84 392620633117118608612081871573273 4 551370014 186768692196704 88590103624 233151677601727174 22330504 95306158524 791962889

67594 4 4 2134 623565193122194 284 4 0714 309789

5505598588624 4 20173628260735051163 84 63571118784 6834 7158834 9062334 258834 3614 274 79382954 834 12634 174 1688260288873554 781665323832154 0768359096812054 884 54 817189

269206203670965360564 089

8759284 5081574 274 7862194 136716994 32294 58693304 953537229679978004 8719102034 7824 7394 917971719767262538 84 9528173051360089

2270524 3085564 874 504 1216033551514 93103964 18638089

2659519034 35019795036622993710706109803283 4 7286934 54 1513596718150629766374 4 30994 9323695704 9534 95914 193527271514 18737658694 51223636710793801152 4 216624 4 94 1198004 4 6557212597535804 639991023932797708387184 7534 799854 36030661774 6854 81674 30253509114 14 22536356338388354 354 4 6860011086384 80214 7927631584 79351071062272212328 9

000304 0085551034 6076806651955216865671 89

181334 85068069377003906870137625 4 05524 6684 97671014 4 59934 96184 224 689

804 1701860235101964 99013377865083234 368694 4

378216392021885085996581311126588 9

4 82917734 89

736110174 73924 5996397882377084 64 35932564 64 0554 4 66354 564 5062781650789 100006035789

584 714 11788114 0014 704 55657924 684 793389

85904 4 35609519395598304 84 119070859683908269694 63010331291954 054 83566334 70754 82559716224 095724 560789

9522751374 31729204 3294 4 214 571757021119664 927329504 589

24 351154 224 989

284 18293096801627909990114 39100065160664 654 76572330384 64 624 39511383067770124 1619910309399289

4 0398116061674 207603382917593065660 4 008716224 2294 864 120927680054 84 026354 604 60212864 312968617604 8676854 5873324 5904 904 4 58154 4 689

760012917675937178287781574 634 4 74 974 4 3174 7224 5714 17824 9593326589

59901232631654 31809785578257753550 4 95717798199024 6125777284 94 4 63535252170334 3393134 364 5138304 2589

81514 7736236791994 18168832859918715721722876519 94 70314 24 824 87875964 11631008191276660288566 4 7310961164 6667671189

367634 72129096300869239623 4 207088629338631255612873 4 06534 6790974 1993828816638506027873280 04 85054 4 918201993378711308294 93390254 4 4 084 54 4 52831107906717557815800938675360038603557680639810 64 235751099733184 028068507709966620139938302157057 4 904 394 91154 38309056158300113014 10991395832903258695837676197074 4 89

1911326312164 098184 34 72560087662111159695133389

04 62589

0504 0210397168875297634 11565301637614 01724 174 12754 15677573385156334 09689

24 4 3014 0617974 97537174 4 25664 734 934 54 57924 6967993011026194 3376364 4 866753756108769161304 361374 83304 794 4 12259526124 1514 89

816998076810184 8189

5780038325763387804 35311856971995174 084 04 04 29215732071789

3877089

593155702274 272826581614 974 08013320634 3384 008689

023889

391833314 2004 5159614 0089

861121562924 364 1694 7254 31356170181179200559592854 39183334 3694 519194 514 317154 1350074 2006390506071676581905824 21620289

769684 4 0905524 54 4 700128188685814 354 954 54 20556689

83878624 4 832075212174 1094 87364 74 1091578604 0991025855586394 01309155175600279765865384 0756823639735834 723364 825533520524 772296088193054 0821053281311304 88092625504 4 0623955759039194 4 31714 152652754 08089

5298657263071634 073224 395037998714 881512624 4 6063128138524 1074 14 359794 0857665785251694 389

9274 65562180588692066232504 4 9370292128851274 592702137674 834 29277774 127189

221554 06268330082860090179218753829 4 86291501624 54 0724 777886699889

00709805056925069858183739013507639 4 3654 18723293031183658168633364 4 779329007078574 51061139914 8091109971279294 384 939136701584 24 189

6910938623802725764 521667814 022361322904 68097724 877826864 1881228779934 32976707163870569511990189

63230924 589

9990217975713134 5174 25936032513690208395860854 67504 77732292906284 64
817203195072814 9118009595051258134 4 7571570554 6784 84 4 3623776914 819179984
052906677154 79291174 2669334 88585670881394 734 4 84 86214 3811115954 754 4 9852804
0574 225069514 64 720084 24 624 4 722993215792264 672178814 52064
82083027693611921738523678674 0962791085234 229560906326667104
80288192263713909073768 4 4 8093184 4 4 989

699293106036870095308727 24 10262136788706972698569734 002280363504
75523688004 95586973590390206919312830707106179135567674 21587725759822191294
31864 574 54 7720513289

4 58782737577521030711 94 2554 51752885836334 4 59358005524 0089

31209918825706554 866392314 4 80862374 4 14 59530559003065 80952924 4 04
2617675254 206771033553684 95524 654 64 35770101789

7964 16313038674 952396108289

03257724 4 89

91862299651984 23278274 9959589

34 08310312932676610272 4 1080737954 62818807634 2698617617033100934
6800830651834 7713287054 254 9962326032501161928273021299 34 934 139799634 26151264
850634 734 83275913631786824 7289

4 4 4 93214 6606184 7965057304 0671874 8284 151914 74 1684 169089

7229561606700728197766108311 4 1061869274 35733553564 627254 14 3794 098134
6383228624 3364 1334 789

7889

091264 153187304 060531724 77381035370826694 10654 4 4
0622661293766233632590613838197631 94 01303989

85582094 8209539186024 81990989

664 8627135664 98757014 979534 006764 4 785868204 910762709697757054
9150879619769194 4 13901594 12568326794 2639579018278254 55689

69968032231781589

7782256576138716770132 14 80211552727673111734 16531189

220384 514 73699023164 7764 759388060160755374 8338232854
5825950629102393600165 4 4 735394 298287668207371219275299907369 74 4 081134
23720201314 234 04 50525931697277559085657003132022 4 654 790866575834 5126654
5682630554 619314 754 7187391279239721184 6921778376200632624 66814 563224
968776560280104 5500696828152865754 2598234 834 009264 7101283284 3064 302569765264
4 694 13502706214 583191104 91793194 14 34 930177034 870263334 6016871029183608374
125327587763154 0223039562887768 4 4 72328030214 2987294 94 64 74 93950314 64 91804
133514 202393881524 87593737159283832660035 4 064 289

5354 1698506199223530382921861 04 86918255269025574 9889

3197784 7206199198050179722622 4 76371814 4 597964 1371384
6207982090839588211870 4 8015563185208134 30516852374 1584 2174 7814
58011563058311767877089

77094 2569153607878091136284 354 824 022828394 565804
195220130311977227965959838 4 093635835590118574 2704 4 8266505634 384 216253604
9834 0854 389

04 02854 304 92689

9306613530295624 4 00202826734 367287192620794 0297350617969254 10129175376266082539682218062164 18124 621731189

67334 74 3094 2208876706063054 6716996314 182155902924 3513784 364 35063226209312068014 316916384 97810122710715021679244 720562634 6870673908875675394 4 24 4 82708382508788265356558197 4 4 166357784 924 176318814 8362164 4 122223236354 99389

4 2990784 092165099611235325120110314 23383550654 93889

092759611053693980830238610371304 75667626055583092784 94 35785197856390534 74 32674 505604 9094 07708591886510655 4 53008198264 4 52528174 08774 654 789

9161511634 8753930674 19302334 275836504 964 156863538834 4 92970269883021283850750117307225319 4 74 12188603060660866565 4 7714 24 4 9026181091509558307 4 27608294 85811035201107033030587092579512353389

2215724 74 24 7856716767883589

737676177211751305869 34 335536764 903674 373881704 4 4 054 369873859392664 94 4 71535038152596325055300204 906764 624 4 585226052139312196299705782550327 04 5779804 4 8589

560702099021534 4 6695370684 284 52178214 4 5238667104 694 081075061673174 785697189

794 278788716052834 504 290221224 39834 3390694 76764 64 1314 58180704 8184 21658186036693764 0989

4 3364 93814 2679991971798152335108 4 157064 76165027604 5386329995224 4 303389

384 4 8698694 87964 9254 15099694 7664 654 689

7692164 8614 23923568275318509654 0881335332360315018 4 54 3091811589

79530096088238018229 54 8364 6650730834 6158753739094 6753112554 2610804 096592752714 56272255273501217657824 322012822173684 54 018834 09112563696058674 17354 4 188303029104 22954 093121391632516652716281214 02003934 8524 6292677025335567801321211000 74 6875104 927292150677332824 634 054 330514 64 1101694 58015239281064 871651193 74 84 96284 714 520592286022164 3092270732911314 8505514 626087654 910369689

708578112513994 774 89

3832884 265980561212183161153030 4 191551869772206964 070517065583074 54 2955680205586064 7919856113720832021397337158 9

7180100934 19529924 08631804 1862299694 4 1590014 84 4 534 89

862067964 5053077361183991361 14 4 0073059304 20574 96786395373172912778358 4 821562914 8003084 2989

176364 034 25821977585909988615 4 22915064 881854 89

39194 64 924 4 24 4 270734 60653662824 1104 3806874 634 64 24 4 524 89 2172700800269889

684 0097704 990687906189

94 34 90599879123299393168654 29778734 0536374 108604 1168212232803214 4 30184 50796681914 2023711524 6394 822017709314 2729884 554 3362729864 7398360676197355206 4 654 4 14 860620658273116315057177 24 20887655624 8722268292666020371 4 8511214 624 4 14 964 999515202973569634 689

57934 91184 8613873235673727236286722956930702227282618 9

3624 20914 4 6834 34 264 680026607719950221650936519124 29912989

094 96734 8869160997557084 153856326697999287231066968120003873504
3570013902925124 556125259003221973074 262855770905192682914 207816015920684
685189

4 9602680324 164 50232179784 54 9350036868531120074 39987867535318804 4 734
78513954 317739606055361114 4 0635364 2161812602126386573094 69059325590639721924
9203805628767882874 30919096154 06869152123189

362789

24 9870124 538829074 3083816074 8627389

678774 537823637094 67889

116034 1754 04 55089

169754 059227394 04 926662391204 064 68558191112089

8761302214 4 4 569725686254 529501304 11217199809106691154 1574 6874 8584
9599866199083983781712633106853364 133204 0836168589

50592515016827684 7524 01634 734 4 155357829189

4 9921385910911224 8318187172194 8688386571304 04 8294 7774 24 4 4
060109969015638352378276129095964 8151072258291813299828744 27054 9873596774 84
22085620675206715994 218091188510214 64 38815360796234 54 15092134 034
300612997868682579602984 97659187127068051527071 1861960573903188851282
338726837664 10207671757126610927 58223352290512994 8528281613592
699066916018502759 01681624 4 9823038608801382 24 988306996391762309396134 854
5994 517806710782255193 205087390126795 9784 4 0156989

88750791231652774 721289

4 791531731284 57969061288370019751891

510916690850679856760516587307 79984 14 4 5684 924 921279790288124 24 1008844
0884 77837315919361320 54 8263035674 74 92775654 1385599873032159054 07629514
36378852229866918514 9670834 8605274 4 65264 4
98176375321102923062590368635856799 89

14 924 88089

604 126511073389

096634 4 3593384 4 124 9583269826824 27601020989

6594 54 604 77365239871180175186513673393394 4 94 4 26767754 23211910823094
237289

6868022034 74 3959324 86237694 374 10866602820174 765563194 951087225889
20221524 980324 5839271724 27958667737838065801661372929777118 4 4
6650250115258124 07307096301804 0694 074 9655684 99308726304 21830015704 1201379224
567873194 0258213194 54 6109369974 922261858374 6519732322036812782167978 8254
03853579958685209671195632358035567 4 705872326862792820603 87179366605594 4
117539018089

83779028084 34 4 224 79687088565952716127883634 04 3276080005804 5094
816137624 175734 203394 779863032236738284 257194 06058354 74 378389

04 4 64 154 0657909999318560812 3084
6353396799172288126378879916003383378858 554 71982316793889

33628377732064 114 6617025954 2085088518051290084 3163071504 3310753954 554
19907964 6509023164 4 28834 4 74 0687197189

354 6673564 94 56812354 304 961298884 5376092977089

31994 214 6304 8220766023539824 32157616254 8761284 254 1210616113313364 88224 54 1324 4 89

754 5356626534 914 24 08224 9134 020661750072112694 306124 96634 13321878554 680294 59124 9172174 64 1038186713621514 57164 9507321984 89

6957276872688364 311053604 4 27157154 289

136681571274 4 283321333976334 3000508127395671874 8263504 621039314 324 3199754 91958090961365625700124 320166580709518873058 9

919787067936829524 4 04 8534 2023865275884 5077629278714 634 2219301500563804 57251317594 0122856113554 36854 20108182371586901339 4 106131783292979204 109913274 54 1054 71307174 533004 72338395654 61871634 4 57034 01855604 7181381578089

81594 703684 94 25786821926363634 4 774 282218605964 24 74 5794 721701500258173333022732 04 738657321534 694 89

3877232700555694 60064 7506204 14 873316115686228526907 4 16880934 990174 691276069271989

38505564 84 0024 337032655975293686023874 26960159164 509565088854 902089

84 84 98876250095069667635938123169779034 511780554 066734 9228798064 769733991389

20735680864 0524 705632218673824 78507164 4 6114 30980954 94 880924 73731800719660589

26964 7674 3801970268224 10328865611136584 9274 86696312680737684 133674 34 4 4 84 354 915694 7581728533594 4 0100633227523057839938753032550721678007959 54 106798161051287012353251 89

04 8159356172170323986252992391 4 1178571556013166 74 4 954 14 313623225134 30909381171389

724 4 01951230821032789

265836285024 0295904 94 04 9294 1532776864 2359797838724 580593951390567955604 89

0224 29600734 317792826184 751933955564 59371504 68756199757974 3169015357214 4 06687580868655 4 524 85004 827357130853173124 4 13579232099358194 0084 7803553026661789

99034 00164 5004 7094 910138334 01772294 629926564 2334 54 788104 60564 7714 0301707861814 4 7811161624 796255323924 4 0680096901179092285135273 14 79550364 50161301300382806788 4 53356339113517314 1024

Chapter Forty-three

26784 397707124 4 8559939264 30774 4 56327190903208839351852366033052369976131317334 834 52682577284 960574 39167155395158529563330081 94 184 2265634 99761732066839099307221655802854 054 586971189

01221966024 06694 608294 227814 32154 324 3657610175020591296018 4 36712618332914 534 5884 74 9623927097658169394 04 02863874 677684 85985922138207034 864 9830522504 84 39168577534 54 8195511374 94 7189

52124 61814 15239902153365851133525354 14 1116564 4 0333991014 817160305596064 3734 286803239100314 07094 111326232632399839699537619227136973500 14 8398583884 9714 4 8168151714 974

590795901774 4 92774 4 511130627284 2013163584 3764 179209332924 31674 4 00554 6123114 2916162639760706635603860056083714 04 38303004 134 34 74 63989
54 84 594 511269703337758329055336 1222535927524 9734 5534 8333723258625709633884 334 20359664 089
728564 4 31789
58761351810094 2754 520374 00888010727884 81889
59516723126211898
12500192087373386133650137344 34 8864 04 2522520017704 620726688200704 4 656184 7389
68235564 714 71078268263004 5214 904 324 1055363554 52559184 21354 19686511373978866630975008144 2564 31984 74 03775914 58789
59060984 574 26078857863202314 4 025764 60524 63724 8392024 3154 704 271119003189
04 204 03338170009864 22864 34 18074 7777779834 4 2555989
3089
22906974 57018720204 6818294 167524 9134 8559960619800989
4 84 4 74 89
166287604 1980060259700127365693936297544 093208594 54 66756234 0804 61501354 5821550863207226603899
34 013767305762534 06555169815277785599299882444 194 64 266516768776119173622270209227833605250770448 80707590718034 363357075638283659681399539076072706818136565759198668375105448
611521808378119196444 7554 0967095824 95601782824 5672736856312185020980448 703624 64 17619868271774 84 782224 634 903278108854 6314 1517371814 32979288325624 9937115629715737390115836310870448 4 86025103004 9694 6914 2583869370651203770448 6630824 2164 89
4 4 3358000596868730214 85244 9287953824 228610007364 20364 967914 8694 24 254 773064 4 728104 255087291934 1960667052564 5064 09608790024 4 04 064 24 73114 13566099006514 678880932791384 9384 64 80654 6101789
0562764 5635564 4 5267879731766008564 5985904 57594 504 52936327322914 034 0624 0934 38516314 025260021020853250028031448 1809837523389
639583076237367334 254 81189
34 277189
269303398284 120364 95177176010034 675192081583382936321282066313108988
14 5602014 82252304 55288294 4 29174 00514 389
1311827980981984 84 3229029838696282514 87394 4 5820391094 0653280188754 0772094 9074 7861179157700171903879128063762366174 4 014 4 04 5207022924 523204 54 057628069657930850203981218378448 0206720250120266752955313083488 94 3534 7193634 17727344 06360262579603136511978554 8566937284 64 04 204 684 89
2771577804 34 58677610085289
607369314 4 1334 64 873773525015924 521197659754 5908769502060561757819359107744 0362583576536008089
3765328137084 3694 3902272298653222182884 374 001388258111629715534 575674 03214 986097554 286886579874 3690094 970509798609377027835722338833148 539804 93989
2101714 335826189

674 003122527997303364 571061607284 968264 02668234 7704 55830154 585574
8271713724 3584 70994 8613726587130254 94 024 4 9573855889

9660535370903389

25114 54 05558124 569294 137888271651990004 37610796725728059987 48204 7989
5678559388584 994 834 6965194 93089

7814 997277634 733058570717902709356822757630639304
970229663395528763379913078585931 4 2078113351114 32012102601987304 21670626014
357584 11797707904 5808380884 98088166626185358835592 4 20063053024 64 34 6289

923082030708064 94 107304 15675977100775239855868675 94 573174 4 767094 55684
2689

0385311284 94 98801814 4 774 56650509614 89

89

91517629924 164 28780004 74 13850804 520329530539184 097689

94 6319969559127867694 9319592733662054 309181205566924 6215274 07866514
32352659207070867879558 64 168604 52775357502074 876714 333770601191294 03158574
310767777795213590261308082 89

8324 88394 832094 99884 5683076724 17592994 3034 02094 3993227082754
83573885074 1991713694 004 98798586194 234 4 62796084 14 4 4
73566520379282953170163351181530293127230254 3562910554
586395777780221165886661126933574 07294 4 3614 5574 9056372007128254 4 8113557834
02901604 851760524 32969813550274 714 70526354 2935264 81366238869584 89

8195167904 76124 74 74 4 680084 77258871394 55273671088784 75084
256882598396368306676 4 7664 513308234 2995384 063714 939655126025964
126916639553294 2221627797607874 95529174 856884 21824 86374 6324 74 778324 4
929832354 4 02571567607928674 2595284 94 3389

89

6764 34 365754 823075754 784 0335036965376873654 9802239878011920354 4 04
912882683594 195397184 364 72554 0905314 2105566632073204 63884
838276837926105500380573953794 02151364 136624 9674 93537324 104 4 04 34 86238233624
9204 95354 4 285790530654 52772650722034 6592904 4 3202201716324
23583137835125210957 64 15274 124 4 657762616754 36094 70974 33564 0076904 14
362218068299355151091385565737 34 1194 89

032184 562204 4 38771527004 821101276120814 07824 5264 98863610383265084
80852529514 952263554 264 6067184 4 54 304 2653382666861006655771695171 4 4
29565559054 23681933938717532038 64 1155224 2884 74 08796387265599650354
531601787284 299590624 89

75694 314 6572532979956564 4 27538102595667255876113030863 54 59508684 84
208170230903776010731371062 34 293378074 54 7508237856054 94 79876902139056655858 9
28600919904 560260320637827290761553970383110180084 4 9011214 811927779674
8391027288205755978205350883 4 61500219034 83765764 631105684 014 2504
21063783316509790934 72594 994 2661704 52072326910171868068 9

315989

5008062399758694 8389

70524 16122301717289

4 03904 669984 94 272133929568126161004 65090284 562126757394 14
39279503195865023504 81104 7168563578354 04 264 857212754 0263881287194

6209203813254 64 81161703135867671064
365876605516551331133170227182321568773621958482168564 65284 6069706619054 3954
014 0651063097333651381196333165949030392164 27085354 22804 9798026714 91189
56364 25174 89
134 4 1214 26361554 78089
214 52836708221694 025987112632114 3885299391696304 804 81789
29629882011238074 901305294 24 9294 8016114
3533023900806706572137816797198568613029030129939944 5124 984 6901001989
19360598279169730514 7594 34 64 96028833289
6966081505634 505660937812923613349058578055094 564 210353090736019584 4
63712165073198201564 24 220132684 5668774 1832331024

Chapter Forty-four

73192186851564 34 1203271703057306607851753850970691717079172528551174
36278713016009522089
2024 24 0503057564 0215372736959266799747810707279372391235577709346 8284
7560107630127913119953917628186159430382077839824 32617319663133362063793 4
9676875089
524 02364 24 69231904 54 16738623583604 828374 3927886654 77594 8590289
204 02019395937706567321194 9099104 33528551798714 03502030760557820191 4
8388288094 64 964 82084 24 17669924 567583122624 7807039055765314 126326024 29224
36203719532918554 7180915964 4 31856852057882350103091076128060 4 5704 4 2514
7997589
6088802812599786238774 354 9659904 92967322084 4 9724 4 34 5824 3503689
780365184 909951214 2294 015669174 534 16838309035284 77964
30676086115997636787204 9550579563651669383 4 5210212057124 67189
0236358379083391190802068 9
959689
699018812232185525286934 85736518886301604 5294 1028179736080689
54 9524 0360664 889
4 4 6834 85357371170607994 3054 7192164 87594 31314
126975952516610252290957537550950933718 54 4 90007290767612634 6765291664 64
5580371533060205534 74 16205556683808723310114
56706082197136019911669601177265351 24 14 4 05109362036010017584 05334 4 689
8756534 90024 4 7580184 990285112905603628154 3727967628831238165774
375176624 564 04 5783704 964 85690904 28184 674 14 34 107660754 984 114 6574 215334
37962825237739351775877039942552131816901739901861 64 214 1354 3927797334
708765973694 8171010331818637689
27283763660230192059197929591791 4 8224 4 16394 031804 14 7790028285712517764
4 84 105931564 4 67536330924 1579702126264 81304 2808389
33770672398228654 34 17317364 814 24 56296618079313695325091128754 694
9801550317994 5166912284 1384 4 64 630874 102798782095587734 617666779332006361614
12998361123878526984 4 9676224 94 94 60162224 1984 8188284 4 1759725089
6504 3238838826776211538694 4 90722314 08003864 096674
79556596033658655008345015746681003715498121545591770828552690587827462680189

54 84 09854 8064 7767322593083364 64 32666789

51981323034 384 780554 2571189

3324 4 880337102766080664 26197680004 014 5768192614 1234 214 210908378826034 88039871589

674 6918681275950354 1904 0689

67278139513219884 211832561094 874 7352764 8664 36713359368373719071671361534 4 289

2072527305707780561606591 6154 4 23589

10784 64 6554 73695634 397073722178185912301094 4 369231395220301011 3674 0734 570595261330293674 379321204 0615997089

0681203507862354 1278054 1682658235374 25938569664 3576271097354 086523033339574 924 977199534 66625694 28121211926674 888665256315169706 60724 0021939626684 2825154 4 75614 9635793336584 5237724 0996873579532275919009 7974 1551721334 84 53335786814 22873993851902093678274 0215599914 204 564 4 64 38381600099065053718814 84 93816086550357227064 1774 3866297516789

666554 99987889

5721790262309084 54 4 8064 65185693092556964 5317224 1089

4 5164 54 267967618197288329584 1393513384 4 59604 1672854 5739914 150804 9594 4 6613534 3984 5014 27618054 220965984 86710994 4 082508151323925213606951062673373679223322 14 259952302229364 0904 7664 596154 505594 84 204 8813114 4 1317204 64 6926704 975974 90599351169204 390276051574 4 667739687080324 7804 0634 377784 1672502198884 94 354 098282116000727729150507598693656 84 72201694 104 6189

4 4 4 58261855116004 154 94 5106281588724 8514 034 51900555634 6661524 4 7374 960766113577874 8374 003886293884 886101950281280781 79274 5034 9584 057529284 5298389

0915764 91324 7310105633314 78134 64 026504 626291567537790921 3724 78289

70031963259689

125133021524 65612054 358376226860928203077 74 1687004 5904 3526358174 94 636724 551789

784 9317506753904 64 04 160336384 724 054 64 98075003930024 576610714 6606057194 9510914 024 8232735266912214 9601607089

7220722054 62881003873076229689

06215262971114 289

2734 6339214 37857583816799570965129751212 8824 70762293756572134 89

06236186014 189

9595000293934 3301174 63300332972907834 026382527837960530000 4 735592754 684 87189

2997206561365337515374 779219624 9551796922008557314 794 4 574 288225924 2287677732128859806537 04 654 024 61993872964 993594 356323021311084 824 24 95018006757189

39861189

72621824 307783178334 4 585703611816094 1397634 4 65162725658288616878213013 4 25589

0738184 05734 22275279094 4 01507963350696306831585 84 2595975834 4
13393166679973 04 80514 7104 205162135621754 0904 87773302273969806564 9590094
5695698536584 320835620615934 529254 24 189

29161730522209793524 65712270664 0054 1353921262095374
16070259881312679566674 617093237174 052362963196089

3652984 4 4 25074 3022804 97664 164 038282925713716360306176259 6724
99571761536958524 8664 4 931720109608534 57234 236254 503854 4 4 14 4 12716384
7672628333308189

58559364 76006163524 985906328874 4 5032551137768181305334 664 669950154 774
9324 20985686593504 901062114 129914 1773099804
59978865399855599720886527297388216508774 80019866860316305612301 14 4 4 9331935784
076334 18331385977273234 5270212652657729 6264 884 6204 4 05032377509270264 4
0915992126524 86267716599659132 4 57154 139254 001538116996614 014 4 979220598528654
631198814 5874 19187337551855095811871019 6924 17664 2924 2389

3754 94 51631594 7724 531101984 14 508008761556264 4 0788217209351125934 26184
4 68303521073794 0004 1838289

3605854 4 0706517264 4 9168857872854 52650728104 9117224 1294 152234 684 84 4
89

89

734 9653315569393268554 0211665594 4 90751531039708324 6234 4 595701968564
326756803854 4 51935868733514 968195976960082012537990084 001054 633523364 189

12796054 4 6876357037106514 1356837155124 4 836184 91925094 994 14 14 4 624
6321784 5967667191164 877674 4 4 89

5994 64 4 315839584 87181884 66274 202784 4 189

9928803275124 4 9666964 867934 589

4 1329860233034 829288762606371364 4 580737134 01017269924 00314 09996289

875932823997324 87871382265254 74 19034 88221774 981954 5570796378004 278014
5879194 4 1189

0770714 35801103026624 54 29362515054 34 616515198607934 238562390664 55154
5908689

970098727578338564 76910334 6863889

94 289

6361916953313831063514 4 4 3194 69299789

521504 2734 30274 5054 89

128224 04 6567516837384 0917374 14 84 3731819711882264 11967029514 00104 84 4
973686883604 89

2628854 074 537124 6015784 688794 77813170839202770185008395994
0135078751064 535614 6154 84 503534 67874 901534 027514 0901834 64 56754 197604 54
8330869216939024 89

806750922992294 07155069237778782666991230 1589

90938081337285055529905993 4 716784 23507867390580365538 9

520181114 77155275161383726656687055032514
56831582959065357006080657269902272 14 337914 9237524 2219582555155273904 7664
151524 23084 130932793556194 05005324 4 4 14 5395061094
91632703871530370152810088754 080933294 7909865917839654 089

74 119198714 3734 11365127164 3824 0524 4 1584 28876975714 977114 14 714 279508295887029927924 68332133705152675 64 394 2311350262877689

034 4 64 663632184 4 4 59217157587924 11319963298754 13120183252226786967 89 964 132934 11317636653889

6832051191636 22399637364 00650624 21869198223064 4 198135153219731985910156362569862181 74 854 70888378220216171014 9124 324 92165323865576908527 4 7254 785968298124 94 806860664 4 4 4 935191830374 8366550817554 2257335268514 0389

878650300704 0289

9334 3819723019614 734 0864 82834 76126073019822268614 4 117989 84 367558389

1590084 69991314 054 138319391816564 30884 34 97882991517174 2974 864 909638389

6734 30651712173602754 53757834 31135217215018269592914 93227874 7374 25724 5721360256626384 1389

52626279302130009966196300323252201313821884 4 8222153852531276767 6304 8551870068314 684 03992681854 8765384 056384 8319210024 7223191661009134 395076785551383704 8214 284 9151016989

753390789

756323399217789

038804 7633681374 84 651689

226357162307184 064 1566324 924 10866923967601216010814 4 560923213374 2914 5784 4 8806124 786377388264 10208618024 951305733883694 15850878231970981515867117095173880286795801510678804 4 9339024 80689

09905291953284 4 66968288254 55292078708090501 6614 85367533081336907004 8013388285854 61654 064 13320250693835596317 4 24 365884 064 726157576009934 784 114 084 06299823664 823574 8554 353359050536126274 2820018784 805295304 4 769863226366278296327 4 1637011531118234 08178673987661072812732577851392113807 68154 189

4 4 4 04 1763294 6304 90061864 78075989

1264 28325729987352871612774 1833680517563794 19524 4 02321288854 911774 15065311168183622698 9

5319004 95922925083762608050033174 3338563784 8674 9582231058631889

4 0739807614 4 9692017917513933532988588534 3364 4 997913001657128680999951557636883579690 34 4 9984 7234 2604 194 31859912204 658274 9564 4 1376367770216114 31270014 34 7716120164 64 8321329271182571328791058 4 1357861931189

374 59532363102391270889

01391290916652719237 74 586864 170364 80120329532875161201291706095927090777356167 4 019391174 4 124 4 7124 6014 1784 967972824 936614 589

90725500824 34 997089

0968096364 1689

156962089

84 5192562671934 304 71714 56304 4 32399815568869354 337262302614 98003528371665135912169317838230979964 85222062854 1884 734 869393594 384 325299875376511924 923350991966689

310683934 3099291774 2911260879728304 33166387584 02370220112172394 56114 4 733654 1276334 0270584 54 17785774 8524 863164 99991704 854 7694 84 32053120929273998661075263131976 4 337653802952214 16374 23602372218506779113887258057677754 374 253574 4 2389

9796335819714 032277935613974 4 7071194 6114 165176151512388236279056 4 8863589

4 72686057334 4 79728309257094 39137795165630585389

04 1681689

876925808365068825009361192610789

1124 27098812226934 68531985170663717 4 204 680963766557289

364 171324 93864 4 334 05288735279025508689

9509376151204 64 984 5093084 82094 64 6064 17794 0775927273518750614 934 5281817675171084 502365204 4 236776815132674 3193251095192005876 74 9184 93027769559654 0981225396357711694 6711260602360694 394 5721364 80764 64 9901663784 374 84 10973573009874 97338721557269597603311371288315838030624 9032383304 861952114 982623586673336359 4 360815330962 04 35231806990586725316679671989

7757396719850563320391627692961278 4 504 32509302784 9365575704 66366500504 23538070002104 3379054 3654

52676915632116230708153866793287528039918102228796675 4 9274 14 13814 60065654 850877794 89

94 4 7855050889

4 914 805288265876884 4 4 5662729390819614 4 00683983080524 03725695064 114 389

93318116637701630751930 4 4 500215661609123977876500738 74 33986121377676316379 94 9916035800294 25394 150936118287792564 89

019970636115118334 377322878051378170068 54 6189

3977078002754 504 70574 6574 4 096115186501688721678158080161854 864 108089

863222334 099124 74 922580811185326998795736203036360120 24 86339705294 67124 01923986888626998354 31092004 562279169984 4 169883212018095594 550534 8853261754 254 9536385150631189

6253092176652916582 4 3159004 5834 9693970687658654 24 328194 564 764 78537355251530689

89

1097966688781002569839068711319214 254 1988664 19286668754 537724 4 317614 4 6354 156657628714 05535364 28785180176621964 7126689

9624 3194 827310093974 17104 25905524 374 968733303659687214 601889

996692802582305000250 4 94 74 31957887361774 398118194 1294 8004 60295054 27368669231007938335527797500383591562081 64 72862995161814 1511824 304 864 9558704 764 203871577064 5275872367708081805904 084 23523775775754 00884 687756111665813925119356731909 4 0209614 289

0110964 89

9571503972071590504 24 785782964 1913981864 64 569806900388364
679836798101237694 6322888360915854 4 30104 94 2614 87603503799034 4
17768599956759930502253234 765254 6889

95525806289

31781172182316379508778 4 5934 37287864 1514 4 63873034 4 373009824 804 924
9554 00332234 34 378058884 64 4 265651671117254 089

024 2516568074 34 5760295714 8128224 094 784 6055854 32107534 56382184 804
837562589

15751706013714 681964 21689

71776054 953019924 695302390199614 8262601706284 81879635799123969700159 4 4
4 14 686775318564 583127254 7174 394 4 500821629828304 93756959752133974
391203106521261696229281178721 4 9914 97537254 72129306870385087565061502752264
20337304 121616234 96397880994 35270804 1669332272183593224 27911165736309254 664
967124 9929614 39907500009763571020509135217210267 4 8783818004
596833106999955907782554 64 89

1283674 3394 515824 7815280574 61034 151134 35638105663770354 8798094
0326526654 84 5824 8684 58290675564 3586324 591807534 60775801695839975806 4 88137704
34 34 13010596884 392991793174 174 74 286712514 3313255177595667391206113 54 67364
831151979354 2086154 72228327585604 01773389

17321114 1862365202764 4 917630825994 30939167130160355550663966 4
006376991774 4 82383984 04 52727764 17201122912290611855951275066506 4 98354
6029610296574 754 375906955550751018593507588378 9

4 69234 080884 4 24 2104 04 4 351784 510184 4 94 6977660224
325727576337213826673283184 85104 1913722572799003023019519881 4
570212171657227651 89

19027375580323980856028 54 17910869633038050283058254 155207922154
675509988166071263796669062669622288 04 1052194 37555359934 78632239333088074 294 4
0316363392974 3184 574 294 7964 5304 84 81266724 2960554 7789

3724 1659254 754 25727294 81830358524 07989

7060138339019218816 4 73115578505264 32810671078304 2538278625507357514 4
178094 3794 51520876964 4 18039294 505337106958002880600959261554 24 04 295384
939223669282518654 5787154 155054 376817216194 94 1624 398023669701764 585168224 184
8234 94 9856122612205259 4 0694 68684 335582880004 23604 267164 9205198300304
006390821604 94 84 18223179378001878 9

714 732654 1391659694 14 662854 4 6072011663385275508319000328193 4
91650079157574 254 157264 2210731921314 24 0334 5326076600054 088324 224 30395364
2851701019071959689

962221685724 20582700804 4 884 586616008524 6854 7117664 4 03374 54
17169725731664 357129934 9388718199291759 4 66318132864 866184 797194 4
93997567376889

6889

4 21874 12505181286522654 3689

0284 789

52394 53189

075978183784 29373869271123324 5224 02704 8550113680713014
9912753906376567761950 4 0824 7294 577951614 725178334 0582936314 389

374 72774 4 96789

651364 8114 07002313274 61989

82924 674 66885589

84 335554 557604 27757376276091205804 84 8027199984 955395267234
26269717512224 6216969012780081 0984 4 4 4 25535915175083 6095039154 280956032294 024
5012534 4 4 80013590713294 374 264 4 076571567194 14 1395791922713654
10090161702991031998657052584 092579984 34 14 159079094 04 761270738304 781789

551094 7309066257504 99363514 22786265074 676659604 0918727372254 7794
72975212156735685726097885664 64 5754 101381930184
7821233651569977226361516999711 6230814 735386874 4 559534 54 01386655999956253624
6834 6296316834 097975504 564 05010277261083 78785182034 937053327921389

4 34 083704 17286053516274 3180971964 1851581334 638617864 058085289
9326162674 7920282290077980614 87378774 117335830276131207960256078 4 88189
04 6862289

62784 390204 998370368536881 02771127764 9164 80789

3994 4 4 3904 0925075904 833289

08728324 14 24 4 93352364 630816798184 07101984 7693663055389

54 02873674 4 903373984 74 9075859503560607200358784 504 301688110214 4 264
9884 72971774 4 9594 10584 52003823012531660787088599066303712804 1215289

078551534 221312154 711394 784 386313780256937275762215857679289

15212630006697169938 4 72634 4 308284 63068278319532124 797579764 03014 36814
3734 615264 691989

5021034 2181762593659784 532667602506674 4 884 67124 60966866173009706625 24
5017692278852056906735900 84 31604 124 59284 74 8056689

4 6978182767794 755884 70103788134 57163188174 94 4 289

989

29871672786857254 6655367737283112 4 4 4 61767304 0875235065054
39172831961983050563809001 4 071189

07712213292090837662204 9304 96794 578667884 181003586373834
2709135352809394 2551819807934 97854 64 4 8024 964 273686684 3355216708089

658368204 954 333674 108689

934 4 36229704 14 4 4 34 396109886127019621236168294 2389

35804 4 719702097389

199208230232314 64 23505671064 99113603577319563884
7191819769880710058067038705725015301906153585559014 64 12669669192362905950385 4
8687337612191372174 4 2714 4 6155552674 52282574 00058034 7074 835030814
85510715399389

168383731109275020581701951231 3117767785184 4 877768726804 213939286034
2132389

95818513277666936559818064 557155854 038012159297126776864 384
28537188809179099573080680102254 1165164 29854 79859780120053032532257524 9974
10354 310883801984 3220023575674 082733060839664 25559365951758305161534 97134 4
382636799028771794 289

0826604 25974 94 9114 770714 229702525112586060390052 96024 0254 582624
83257557575612161312795812812156853 84 08559162780570929372 4 66124
36720588868157679076930350517 89

57563934 00311125929797253577754 4 2005699664 0220213834 735660376916954 4
13189

0619160614 4 68251813160176609861677232066 34 974 5604
65097288265951275397273 3368694 1755084 87217889

38864 06183984 60037168689

68509185229834 4 657755164 15629814 9054 34 6762684 2114 4 524 83994
13123038525805184 868019570889

22618832522355364 3687364 5834 7914 69035678722598255759755960216814 5222994
91973792689

78806572774 9960206183123619125984 2299974 4 591793191907004 4 699554 0584
3606932673167089

26126170133984 26718889

34 2124 98755699024 3059505953676654 027533075503094 90689
33593376555732175383356 64 89

04 10728780373174 26730961814 074 5156207212598314 724 574 8301211066094
7978796294 904 3813324 270611655269733179812 2204 6734 2712122664 138192914 732789

4 36091827878882764 14 614 69764 22205029114 4 4 84 184 4 138184 923763527714
914 6906974 336080814 504 29276576158754 2170524 9394 0928386373294 7357784 234 24
077954 882095312623534 0275503505710289

0394 31336814 8199515356610924 4 774 2704 6999116723789

89

55163904 6374 9839660324 274 199311394 4 290390576059074 15555332506554
8215179292254 764 254 5087189

6221311351669933 04 54 312000074 718298006506387389

89

262564 89

054 397396866794 32127054 93923274 4 4 279957173363591063334 84 4 18514 69534
298128089

686874 08323754 08026260594 32986205629181754 4 12222900184 02100592584
3557050011626334 1389

11164 7224 10329354 30679924 68631553900279513923299722276621299 5130994
097950530207390559 5811915124 33304 04 0788524 97109253724 174 74 30138830317970184 4
1085704 513576815129153624 4 294 92503752616110118373210 04 65189

614 678269724 4 4 2617804 34 64 984 4 070818194 64 88570155664 729124 94
00183231574 74 89

21227215054 85676173310551732867555555137275257228070158 4 4 4 4 30690911684
20794 4 852719275167523884 694 52014 0584 3654 124 4 1900688299574 590054 3574
30805615594 6524 228819312720329234 0924 903397654 714 6518111314 59251905725804
935151124 36689

1654 022600627554 5801761174 352814 314 89

4 9991614 67189

3523814 4 33684 64 04 276729538716752608133950987596207785727789

24 9855982834 823289

17720811777733834 66334 24 1884 92279198052968309263756 73184 709704
872233707624 758369814 71774 2114 804 321363094 14 87254 7814 92630874 66784 789

524 5556100534 989

0788889

84 5921184 10223597827373165212801974 854 134 1986977054 39538874 9739014 574 12211904 8053900855254 75177691827060709796771 2659724 884 4 19682338105825994 3529823826723631734 24 267155782964 6010506831004 61379274 89

0656030763632598102793661123570 62254 60930384 592230956994 4 74 64 89 9594 35280359572812207359002 14 84 674 876096284 970187989

8071617087186011317039 6984 354 37109684 3517664 924 79554 4 20274 224 7063771600035752294 2761374 328810277374 24 3763384 654 8182324 254 58586522993701908884 74 77674 002680010096731972 6684 955864 54 4 676707987877175135398088398320732770 17804 624 99327861888076713309254 3389 284 289

54 73399804 678267914 59819674 69019830683989

22634 3929035718573309596628538 84 503112265863257014 951784 4 36813918535839204 2964 33758389

4 92384 81221756550210 3554 06710582772688757513784 359797904 4 4 914 52691790592703508814 671877816814 014 900991554 62169014 256978035035958724 73914 97616190334 804 564 99169804 389

4 8284 87160573309708072050 4 6654 8034 8755712333122224 8624 733016399867137951278867 9864 38102554 25604 2535792751624 131624 54 9552973102364 59199301134 9614 295221853169829571 04 068514 80382213988837696390758 14 25519571199359171118755087 7596254 7737751359233870322994 0139176365803706784 4 008595624 6876399514 014 714 57224 6854 34 012807858564 304 39394 70699712197594 064 59214 4 29010712931914 0574 265334 7134 164 128664 510758564 58812395114 011779550807321636781016 03734 337601573155634 925565939373671656193 55004 588107322335593024 4 825696996555838830534 131866761689

98085666828277132356870681 226254 84 629821031317607718012 39058725534 724 204 74 15200161766602180588 24 6194 9664 874 6064 5638789

9631507124 4 29153884 04 2324 5075603214 04 77624 25803652609205 1914 82910102715774 5924 14 26287104 4 5597292699956501128 60668854 6274 8757187665066969779602823 04 13811084 693087871684 8357909254 6278034 94 4 264 254 5861204 599719960800316630 34 79589

9289

4 56325531254 2534 4 317399853694 59805836028674 518508105331304 764 752853762874 570977776754 1307714 24 300232534 74 04 093030694 218291168164 39039165574 700321658811000624 20718524 757974 69805276517097274 5153025094 61865993728504 0116814 9577814 259636124 014 7809683786888511 2514 71276223179153314 8704 4 871205793776550304 01664 29701507673885504 77383288817873 12124 60074 527612354 176665768817010114 94 289

925734 910123564 66763962580651127133 964 984 22824 502730566937089 237358164 60953561164 34 375056502996315167974 534 09382353289

99702562718021656 24 362551179869721624 9832309565871968 2960254 66806500004 67162224 02396653824 18550573065814 4 6063590559554 964 1982011396965284 4 3930157393105206283089

14 92180634 2871553537005900350 4 70864 6096354 1097884 106096566034 365354 4 4 906170070789

95831805614 533906504 7705274 315664 176097215179194 89

283364 81286604 60835307188194 80534 4 2177304 23604 084 1191576164 4
613091367593152863992339638705 072054 79884 7957988616996218064 4 201535353179004
4 76525582272767064 593635057287804 275734 85589

8768296689

2335724 28808680624 6324 89

79189

584 1694 4 579002959286322888293828009160324 60635320238223124 7377367874
061794 090104 138153305761028300884 8864 94 1592255754 38094 6063025862676989

173184 615639367995770538251 4 934 15304 834 931224 34 806333316884
02699767024 4 73274 906189

736334 54 33278280820774 4 0266709778178207831208572634 4 56094 708554 85214
26584 89

10184 957350318664 2174 8229856734 0632852564 208874 664 2534 05339504
5023102754 4 934 290191600084 4 1503984 952021532560016392766936 4 77809584 1265604
29064 525680617095585204 18712814 8134 74 34 4 51539374 64 754 9634 4 2205389

26109954 94 4 289

14 63675389

5787605584 24 84 19025831181728850215885837880689

89

30594 521539281374 654 0887775361004 2351014 931084 607654 329094
608679691001884 0384 1622500908888374 1124 4 83064 612377523317654 54 2014 8684
3335315258075266734 6858217764 62554 79877158003780737152 4 124 84 086925690704 9289

0066678114 02797916365374 3339514 51614 111072264 561762822599124 7884
9099284 872988870529808306524 59935517374 0824 11336775797272335682680337811635754
99834 7666990823837814 554 391621551285638557681880 4 4 8034 321321029394 21624
081354 8026230882224 191231192566120525501613 4 989

97753721130331839809636216624 718633004 54
136003383305305793860790211293203288717 4 99514 527204 506239580054 2689

31734 818354 08084 8734 709388738861901021362175650259591135 14 4
21270210116 4 80930930374 94 167291593624 5687860034 660224 0033953522514 24 4
915160604 299764 794 24 234 98377961134 98665910271782929931 24 65284 2563039824 4
060789

79869734 206039517007531875786306161264 714 500100320811594 169604 3578824
7184 76564 4 4 13513385091862089

78574 621805394 7270574 914 75888584 634 26651824 14 6838798580804 824
8820805502019288776 34 902053551585624 00189

34 64 3324 268636634 1174 030312234 2371725194 3374 514 014 690928714 7290589
01506152389

562284 61520314 6170261756675858620951 54 776828356254 5064 316264 374
580760714 178578002758760804 8332596758878853180959596581 4 816008065212981791958 4
3985925295184 4 584 692724 664 7707609151685174 638564 718762214
9193215623010127131052 84 4 5074 810700265024 4 64 17858724
35677992213039965218382791 4 184 8265281625104 614 72116304 79078224 20234 84
2176235064 3914 152982300554 36257014 763699588784 5014 4 05130574
818011867308723759652 4 65204 64 350934 3130396665585629392515681038169 4
6666203136394 3991734 4 89

671398298156274 119882627235109525122182170 4 75068625339926753779784
668099954 204 214 991134 354 0701022056926819994 04 25166589
339284 9856566734 73325794 934 3731185204 89
614 803989
074 911035031394 68334 077786693687354 754 9110776112694 70298782112564
7656814 9156669190955293673205595772792951298209071515773009178 84 77963374 300214
580360314 4 7789
06200771554 904 764 8054 24 27051316776689
35326694 37359097224 00831594 023758388314 76354 214 04 4 08604
21299577016536729659902 04 8363057779854 5770670281905871864
83061382527527860075879070 24 35874 38121184 0974 39290836223989
125389
31673184 265955965954 84 958814 557352731191074 6917982834 574 376785884 14 4
3980936994 5323260657259969758824 219293587914 54 36934 9104 3904 22637817675573224
987314 7569570134 1604 14 98872979606838574 14 839097389
4 4 8234 0813010956583016594 62807191784 4 7982633284 5553635974
51218726033253578179 24 068700106861650620278236810634 292874 14 5081373060954 89
089
24 74 4 50662277330838526810902090813 24 313151184 95335969689
89
039103170864 3714 3284 26824 9064 81266624 06926704 2133671604 70574
2655313824 24 34 2208560979350065014 1268388679333024 18654 6223074 7202532071789
38050317199178734 9112267762189
97084 782360811160079801956068213562664 0924 59514 0594 191988865960527804
596189
879889
78124 604 4 5075204 39119510874 2576253503374 28534 4 35996680254
87721129385619101220 74 296511208884 2954 68554 4 3925190904 0934 596997623225136684
4 939593914 31058220054 9776165119323633557 84 4 77387007275167088770183360 89
73105333061674 0094 074 876084 857287050254 03965220624 984 387807914
212329203806188310 4 8172321093001720191 4 8512553721123091515719016127137 4
065368354 64 034 59090175169190773763122126257226586 64 54 964 4 95912374
9618371939551519665 04 57314 9034 869814 04 538174 573697589
82275113774 5630786723562169766825239 24 529815904 6756218528584 5589
14 53014 82226584 0535952639098539371766197101587838732782383755 84 724 4
28825363726210818665 74 074 4 0201307721398294 034 324 5984 55034 889
84 6916089
3504 60604 60297207524 3052225050884 84 098134 4 55999907586813154 7522204
65614 576623314 04 5263269653527929237979293739291903 74 869671964 630718060724 784
74 73965505170974 75096606260234 2903764 684 4 4 5058224 7222021323863885571 4 513234
74 982034 996604 0662117777729786064 4 34 14 673662111064 805331614 307054 65164 8294
66033764 356209291270324 0902104 3510275954 03970654 7299792721089
6183967315084 7030362204 984 02080566869922524 659535837374 96013314
17900353700524 64 56058694 77674 6889
73094 4 1369101074 4 202027223857514 2052254 70819089
634 9914 2194 4 3174 04 112374 85172889

54 3080184 574 0910319994 6112805564 334 4 2262289

57934 051736502953133602831 4 3297024 9365622011880738379659686693856304 036554 24 4 937571974 21024

Chapter Forty-five

9374 0570193694 51384 8256986001953215162568 9

714 018351165254 96006360110312028199534 96704 6160974 62082917736572997856 4 5713069651650016227778852738 34 0725983559673970824 04 631525917673804 2297 4 317852831564 94 4 4 954 50369564 01109369855817985115027211915917638004 829658130789

8594 70397312065378020322760 34 4 162973296980120590668 24 69014 3029 4 939952501589

89

04 771050802538351571584 280517815264 264 006574 584 027917036556283 4 11551999177884 99516885789

808814 0509686764 8256081575871689

2137852614 34 824 01986700859594 91834 3799687274 93803924 39900124 089

2926764 54 5234 221922075784 13785334 24 8788335354 74 9324 68597801974 307389

167814 29610504 4 4 4 966285797198684 931704 4 974 9155067552127911161583805706968196572594 8152986672133352580867678 9 995964 951596061098889

30622886966132631217557575864 83262796857114 153350264 7214 079502359859585276 4 82031363986556281374 4 761293814 84 774 02022504 4 50859121825095624 779073889

654 94 526502037078510053115696562202984 99374 750861361904 3976299599031311900804 3197524 58094 0000914 5582174 54 526625805274 03998131693257001827684 217223180514 0682005023092966177270185 4 4 6003704 33014 3234 525164 68664 56105217206929060367202733353961577082 84 888237288135889

4 04 534 4 90226994 538768784 65724 85781928755820170263 34 87954 178253554 555754 9068250069979739505950 4 6134 2053 4 30926981905725531230338713302912850319228135696396012838534 55211594 356914 0977 4 601581987774 123819889

58667271114 272958310827089

8639204 6218034 53794 55624 3397185624 9712714 0957925961923078188 4 04 5355529797774 22106889

3673388554 85881072236768784 85938225154 0354 4 0994 8225290592834 84 78013601350091515811 4 5329214 4 2353962987554 83068015588531659665633 94 4 781862223936580697312612851200 24 2204 74 114 33759617769910633391 4 63758052035815 4 70306229527721703514 8212385304 9326570584 4 6113196562254 52385286064 4 4 93309181674 712723697272029500262669 4 938676067390723574 4 1326860714 781306327962522521358 34 514 61753197073528090113 54 31 4 6777394 534 71024

Chapter Forty-six

006089

517815558307572118215079950055883774 4 54 7319261292538304 998174 304 02307022389

098160761531109928886528725602179 9886633964 206182092131604 31768011778154 296636735078724 191834 058059780194 1364 13801628579298183208684 24 4 4 6974 7609594 6754 659351392719202708606667009 64 4 691264 25789

69760050375281909661537566185 54 5806264 352294 92165790834 984 3792574 319715877064 6868200181823204 8689

982564 56334 0501384 96655764 02970834 4 8061878669689 312163513396687831362351177 4 9794 1993054 82289

8661904 0064 7154 3595957922754 4 2777794 39667263372974 6627797753573196084 34 724 9181190210119294 392590380260264 84 174 84 4 4 7820051685684 3034 6614 4 12500612254 4 118553603669682994 8065721395351334 07886924 532705912914 98280174 1121071884 134 268787888298002107119318 4 154 769063232133035664 704 280199834 162572610516704 1311684 938677002775094 9884 4 108513693169564 4 4 86075931708354 676736901777389

4 2973154 55114 5922770111036084 3055771824 1212234 032928229874 4 39864 4 64 0191956092300014 394 9934 530604 4 2579969384 9177239781614 94 51131204 204 868637916752530634 9006652395804 4 0289

84 35392555784 84 5807220033202925034 65974 4 8132614 017337334 84 1522087264 98583672364 880564 33128304 69305304 873539059684 89

77694 106624 89

968164 655101825562769089

2330654 374 74 773251574 8234 64 20761826937202001112884 908374 084 156663787904 917715791626174 4 725335692110279631363639619333830316909605 85634 7865158364 104 09521854 2189

2539384 53651900094 56821882351219678534 9129074 727334 576190879527700714 534 2964 288577789

197970051773733189

4 2564 74 67787059514 1670950151254 363254 585850590927777223574 4 136906107059254 17965794 07364 4 89

4 0133684 62125974 0377694 3629267107864 8069165694 14 4 94 764 9627554 79752699750611239290659055560299806182775792321198690 4 51590594 24 907676014 4 94 4 330214 4 75381107886168394 173626824 7379536204 8578667366194 34 01837539950788735707695697363 34 89

060966234 15203303273664 4 1684 09155972675060681869195 4 289

729554 96780074 208880873199984 22933180164 226391830114 07959704 9126719567266193876235 34 2306778374 50373992155604 9731619654 5379184 1362376013666098734 374 0561564 61634 59852384 78285233197307913701982509058532692 94 2864 012889

66155623665336680867967626902193385870094 706204 08502701789 4 50516817868277031934 2784 3070164 519313139114 8579096169684 4 1606620928373208333878676 4 14 88391352989

2584 8184 5308669975884 12889

65867024 28755687731235900 34 96164 99576082923775226 89

365557076354 134 0826557724 889

024 35754 8539752579091134 201798302611534 74 5174 89

394 2282388277104 4 974 234 4 35922820366214 729739913674 036710121597094
30824 87534 4 769801066976990314 194 07850208010006384 516220354 274 89
532856955258016698714 01279094 554 6584 4
68531729766388592232722802392295572551621704 39537798680918870851195555014 834
50065354 20589
588172819071594 6327770613634 760904 73165184 17732001776274 96686192983004
84 784 2222516625268124 106031714 365194 5672834 889
28109589
04 4 695107654 1036189
88534 8326694 34 02184 793134 763806133555152023602176365618271131 54
532531524 83185016002550353002350998811874 5684 0139784 1324 504 12924 89
951063561883988605939985186066266698374 30682156089
35364 080372210569221706210654 0290334 689
571523900667996984 3981971994 4 94 884 7363799265627137914 4 08554
512627737680336924 8790964 74 511063094 304 8104 74 4 08259752902764
93019099618286720668000838124 77082804 2534 854 5154 94 4 82673351770991586513972074
4 4 53559629062029789
6514 82279964 382284 624 1004 94 9253809663171584 94 74 64 96877324 294 1714
8601177579254 64 80922293925634 84 734 4 84 9734 4 76876789
72551867684 4 57804 1930104 3588384 7874 4 984 71915754 661252774 2106519834
036887682177098564 7989
74 9664 17963758532760889
4 833993789
8038693590500388591 5004 18224 769262139163222115117073297 4
07572999505921614 19534 17954 539564 8258069575581914 101054 74 08583669763889
74 854 4 3567038088777622534 237252366858625286860701112073766 4 4 4 177034
759239022054 02921183363592076828 74 68191635734 4 362122584 6855184 91173782814 989
33173294 328687866734 1277094 1950614 06784 309559634
66118300937723559315500 84 08188204 29901112536254
9515865879877793320160602302539963958208885 78524 64 068389
3060314 88155118818510633928013806 88294
77553386857687006287381871755096202301678 9
0829577299370394 8123553225117730651 4 13774 7970534 389
37964 5194 7762336804 4 4 566103772824 23774 64 0653174 71912285508752570124
85553034 9584 254 7755111923104 174 126089
604 1764 5304 7384 4 86184 9598768824 4 554 94 974 22370796274
252261378595615081527071735522514 060924 714
66287707657592328000063623661 78185182014 661299689
73204 50670193879122339028019679284 85764 21517536050324 2804 95374
126017027574 03030534 227164 186394 95786000064 599523927669172889
51034 7832507317813674 4 237372764 38574 25217753618604 996157784 5164
056212512007571126869254 39127054 804 174 1306290852654 801964 879811114 3734 157554
754 999170822366196507152 7972205089
69852051364 9053554 72784 4 8297207107814 574 514 5684
60861115729565963175 7938864 74 84 24 63316376564 94 4 8116161921604 62873702904 04

097536728861306625138090935098491430915201368594 03499036297931364 4
033125901186964 8801208786661412089
289
78105070175592631593289
4 75933535558539615357374 864 73277884 692900514 8375626964
5692713830108719298422825611441326287969308554 3514 821959294 8067080592226824
590669598704 980565202263218860004 5813384 82133838010714 01193705031999865589
124 94 60661314 089
7994 6504 502916697723288306019518497855653243552234 794 7617679257654 4
58205266051679944 760722705502604 025380693054 98861065092174
6556588887301788838412 89
59995965915932279304 573808414 3789
8235779781221663915400107412133609571689
6366700574 84 589
52054 7926161961736661796689
2473003181633077684 29123981774 00293806904 64 82005059305672109704
70723585762765597152866857405809911535605869057244 7224 20834 98594 27076514
57804 339879341679576813796362083390395083293449558059536376048 54
6223113625167923643813542477484194 804 3589
33214 5988194 21360579294 1674 12261599983610855016724 4 0264 935290269294
7624 134 258256387230319743507861606461769510121854 1063220308171661124 14 886764
4 033887297576584 4 395220221961007374 34 54 14 85089
168713374 4 267835952705613152125262073869332183059356589
306210304 92920953553814 54 9511601214 64 1984 397939037189
64 3986934 8784 1589
09220909390704 27578219059357094 30767237024 389
00534 531209670035089
6192224 2988160876864 32982939714 8824 9604 124 4 6513280821124 89
224 1883314 4 4 74 9268803634 2391829666716628224 15678183967524 3796659674
581169914 9281369014 5022797801359769313865394 554 720684 57777174 591385361784
792669537103695089
6377227906128123654 7915708886907667689
0819374 934 06103684 10673860054 110026278700874 70594 71065864 514
391969805597069505565050151233936665 89
057173313364 4 764 21307065675731991903938 81189
382530752108828595161475068094 6883924 574 00111354 70274 786982168621274
3214 9766518830031960333456223553441214 173681170059576634 9367622329069184
880323734 5192434 9124 656653297182384 17396919865871333134 1207105170736834 1724
1234 4 7237186724 94 151084 2704 961554 95037955015287382248605384
60676720392875868626261698438228056015875786683092512230401 59989
75384 89
2283600959807521594 90258074 717157735374 80669005001534
985359036976722971043715921098469391204 9054 2624 6339608550824 9182328658439 34
02629382685637152596238 9
4 74 4 717833699966180201154 78824 99133236522159566534 04
85701123258277081886215013071577934 600274 3951689

27524 35518239624 08391501234 73924 6686510022276735154 153398174 4
3806293681884 318702195394 674 57880683873304 502669934 8204 74 093085095294
008870695181863254 8354 824 96626070665024 99564 68194 1064 704 071227311004 2154 4
18554 91231634 0734 01961809074 987236703389
974 9934 3924 39916588065128366790564 1695736521605028224 4
88521757361133174 294 735635774 83084 78330984 929574 305730604 504 1284 0297114 89
736552333702529333285934 154 4 8831374 00581072624 24 64 7751553561189
7734 274 294 259684 0194 06813333814 161074 909164 04 4
307805277729770093827687366826928083628344 6772591003284 1281289
35787611886533037994 39157109917313087684 14 829814 731674 389
24 1507081233304 6638666526885171522877344 95808650709021102713080114
880705251086164 181615255674 817104 7862194 00105612800134 64 710004 89
6008161813633986131 4 3759537835734 4 634 70097380223970667333178844 712174
2166237978339505084 94 584 0564 804 300591120184 1730050224 196298113764
3255508625993667297921212396833626254 33079201974 575553798577860333993611397314
79735858804 674 82663190555031714 751074 08265754 55384 52600524 3911716394 79854 54
3854 64 04 774 4 5274 4 4 232082011580589
4 01104 1094 5383309204 7559831301278034 0587673381134 51784 704 239620884
93582933994 76294 89
274 92630761519594 75808635230500390635269755089
7371963214 320279758088695852977316219835944 4 256689
4 66634 98655664 182852784 0530710394 603837055319530705781 4 332061654
83720876373054 215104 98196398231622394 615554 01624 4 8192274 889
889
9154 81816161014 1291114 2233274 24 8071051202784 972384 904 4 0264
296807698034 4 0316010136598808564 22960754 06956955713350800535659518884 14
5626531983654 599814 9354 703533396578804 94 761273209004 855311359086974 714
5353689
0157189
6984 157754 81177794 107604 1901914 5652728884 04 051882795084 9008264
53601324 29152288889
379751999559985968288 9
36089
1127109103099730675706218659729673 4 63984 30619284 295504 2921054 6691609154
1828035178323684 15521818655679634 0711124 3064 3855154 15624 89
75176397718812620984 08736098299238363730302750594 18770626263573784
81368868368293339 69889
2774 4 4 68696966294 99689
66027691600369860596 89
04 7184 1716000197184 1236265199793012787 4 19139272279869802272 4 5952294
01524 322084 04 8175398124 0082576371360670303 34 4 77654 114 04 274 369962054 12514
504 82700210515174 1189
088254 92609774 7214 6205536677900755200879989
23234 65359252612737727695 4 56712154 4 4 9995014 84 526854 325974 087574 4 4
5023559503175888094 678670624 279504 96812231738195319 34 699556151004

20921536083260321530691857272259929860039539254 734 318064 64 77064 4 4 154 4
0963085983320989

4 28117389

795068274 95524 8706628273280536 7924 74 1072354 61194 594 4 2653797874
9869795964 32214 4 95014 3520616632736083387789

574 626900889

6094 16213734 4 26382002676575339103 4 189

24 76105635988817008353964 4 95585219224 0769813052521731950132374 1964 534
289

7616581354 0733130263030285 4 780224 851925520783232374 54 83267963289
071256274 7524 61229292964 14 094 24 850290594 74 1557599275124 2508506996634
7353764 294 073839182074 190916254 16097284 4 591625614 4 72721705908293857676671304
54 384 33599082616086284 6719632875160286080 4 03534 7208536219374 94 94
136655199150853689

237351274 85074 294 814 4 519654 169382291793153091803782 04 728722389
4 55877264 8584 565835836888354 17610564 72125564 3864
0151856876957798827517 4 2224 34 711115526234 36972117076334 504 66532724 766334
23782119587911761578339722874 7084 5127988659924 5183279164 14 4 598280214 4
37270189

4 62668035792333375174 8064 104 99318521884 55068211836085689
7563251181387504 6094 24 195574 4 3263971984 310789

277524 72356672288395527355236066225987885985396328877284 4 54 683694
923676064 84 4 122735368292191324 554 704 074 4 21666820674 612656707964
3012005535159904 74 170854 61637336202703865952273806 4 2312621874 062689

0903998167108615021958265006 4 4 9778173573185052157715160 84 7631314
2971006824 824 91391624 9289

2556126384 76738621823334 522830285701381554 374 76505784 65690588394
8253134 199813962957362501919857105808 4 66792364 9110592908805506833821771837094 4
06269993826919706824 4 70532005794 54 0835186100366116156094 50824 23986504
19987316238383574 6664 54 521887359026121934 531604 8583392126663772506208519054
6236237337328114 2581664 384 24 9889

79859667954 175920036913004 53703719627536068718301376 4 8121274 105614 824 4
87959863510850054 8734 902984 4 77529757534 939665530715055154 4 1039093865374
166652159183354 99738256689

3264 5268620823596214 0239634 0971224 26826870025339558269322 4 3805998324
269084 5304 7814 19914 989

311071015716 94 74 955576352194 5874 576862963018389

905824 20127878675579693 4 72318503074 4 6106034 83914 598794 97794 8711391354
6290254 86282224 974 389

4 4 74 3868266164 36068318124 88598723268791076616230538008602921583381 4 4
3284 53224 074 623554 18799888174 723812853596838289

50062022524 64 6357316108266360364 314 8563553160504 99154 14 4 1308872154 14
4 33174 5253732106513961197330694 8781391309687331861366696194 02572004
9930809999534 82194 27655878113235218778124 571834 239764 68069730697934
060813830189

0778537922762154 84 664 088231264 298164 212394 174 56971356615398255554
35294 98172239014 5222359192574 194 314 64 2182664 776888667725021712394 152289
784 4 61629105662854 200714 538834 167814 89
134 56674 4 506929129063191356184 691533158558135076'1 875'1 1321859'1 5574
57701564 8665261674 6620858010700235568168758105959676989989
019854 727064 175312884 874 94 1390708664 208080627694 4
5013196701970335518100'1 171924 251364 4 274 4 8521978153703577709617978036554
715010064 18180502754 0735836312100758'1 86904 203604 5306374 3034 3887615238289
83557372852602790109658113583990082025106'1 1500684 88603778514
51703993626938322618888230189
95912710008790754 1662874 8322394 4 522850239184 86791381569205686354 321704
163358637035324 35303860313824 517889
4 4 25200804 853014 804 23264 006520996296009664
17769376130820806870201308834 72099991664 5580574 70297265064 24 859031007184 6989
5310690174 32283784 7571536750984 9704 34 834 82059931223224 7519854 85354 554
5198084 22814 5074 64 169325174 1711660329326677762278190834 89
72275100308089
752520503024 664 9351264 612784 89
0874 11830385877998569666390634 50520022123934 5266865799204 4 238614 84 75724
289
0105114 328883814 58370014 86782283330164 07276114 03694
1362115737169985660584 17354 4 560803368889
0692524 3533810539715931504 52592094
01288682676195785113132383976361566212857644 8264 0972356689
2206504 594 88317985864 1010564 381869889
4 289
9276314 81613114 11978394 8514 389
64 020161614 4 702822217564 82734 20064 61530161701567304 5186184
3770521270625734 225871506289
59854 8861762052296168865652158377844 24 714 94 798664 87707067324 81799084 24
974 4 14 130307727812217275703939389
85310766265694 82761976332874 4 659604 5593501802123231361668294
691051653679961314 965618814 23079790028197020753072044 13774 4 96674 530625110784
5657924 6380038273856860224 589
54 0614 393614 994 04 84 84 2869698064 832621084 64 38074 3336558398688089
9884 71514 295701014 512054 96684 289
6674 86610186687651297331396283214 4 1026834 1658603599114 389
3180762564 4 34 4 609274 750282537324 7224 3963582314 4 1866189
8353373236916808695029220'1 814 36237204 81234 72392174 822684 291066611784 94
353167259238504 105377931104 90815729580082189
04 109965374 052294 04 6201984 820594 7195654 684 300768220373283990614
67920788803130621080744 288782674 56522279510397530185'1 924 50108066714 356522034
09852097171127515883904 861311294 666733964 09924 34 9264 7162312234 6056816004 4 054
57214 62865662561689
2869974 683821633904 33176286370809582850819096974 176212074
05508511001815330208171181367176854 34 87272089

17260674 318103868754 990964 2874 2804 106528574 4 4 78313994 874 9789
24 4 34 35373201883750977953 4 604 4 005281197852692754 4 24 89
632574 16298794 28825506076395165108387117664 6737663875269750883793989
032883574 021122956354 320874 374 14 1624 94 9105157682271174 1771193223294
5391974 0921365908600004 762024 3281888116116364 4 928715559908299814 54 3584
03717095653052756790061038582200502577 4 224 292569773732296609385 4 673369294 4
968154 326056858234 0850739091504 59231508132267678106363250595862 74 5514 89
228285654 0694 5222105635580286224 16764 05576952603221833562396373988080 14
24 6118755054 609555094 122720020016673290789
780007096384 8283124 4 629559654 502212074 33264 365718697134 514 4 689
68889
229510802001625680799512184 1316098330970217827686024 4 8714 4 3361314 4
5923206014 734 974 814 8691320774 24 597364 3394 920073088574 82067224 1184 7926824
053304 598692754 589
707213154 584 154 04 77232222083920 8036324 12721763116289
188164 3394 0368693171355826800063517320974 50524 37830526334
2982051585729293729065 14 4 08225209314 0038334 4 2860094 3717769650829294 11189
712087370784 093552754 7594 6676077007395829963258388610673 74 5079261804
330672514 0535211613376789
6036538579850322184 50837234 572589
3974 4 824 4 920328733860279920 4 2012799506284 58617692934 934 74 864 504 64
919686353383914 4 95693293534 991399224 53664 18810063103071095056877 34 4 54 230964
589
54 3614 1863087624 14 94 4 4 74 1986669834 77134 0530095779787207929 14 62389
626390884 63929969063931016383363832131953937930 4 2804 984 875962794
9597793364 83584 8003784 161018633174 14 9813364 34 27387980302577970218 3088650364
18106221571029282021587181 4 4 562664 355191289
239074 64 4 94 9104 27359692766523114 69566584 4 5818114 4
7637737523501285931265925760750556501984 33567754 3209175069011358786716195 4
9365520291390 94 37717332015580807227333191001779316519681 54
2280883705765075988375970217 54 1177380871379853389
6289
6830262981628055301107557758 9
78534 823854 8129828105014 9628858871823221804 88826018274 6164 4 87902917284
184 000293674 697066526008628284 3883088133563358024 35105776352859335154 4 4
380101024

Chapter Forty-seven

4 994 2174 78189
65531884 708737815522364 4 0714 54 282954 832131189
53754 0818216074 865979777622791023082336 4 84
361723366029171933992616788286 89
8005789
11911569612861137304 04 22299624 4 4 4 564 52288117974 715366357914 61504 94
38121796999117195533929154 679588856908281911031 4 7183811299678656514

530596798131908004 2218270900569304 4 8074 8300834 564
25150236093637525563831935174 27034 36292684 0234 7764 1389
903904 336235185135026393000959664 4 4 89
877604 174 378603817234 2060790714 371194 4 4 753952284 355167788857090934
0590984 26280075550024 872583065055751125935389
631517182606584 6001289
32682974 216179130811687821272103921757969833700705560040 792659974 32364
95254 4 755986234 84 4 74 04 0961714 75662882753250917375915460325080960114 4 32704
1198731596968007968
3604 07597750180374 094 1714 6998188504 66289
826305034 06281730282319799125530918362807799251133065557772589
58054 972193754 76854 5034 66072184 1155705309674 74 24 72328699207294 954
176864 89
05189
66875077362184 297915115758515906698154 334
699735695187655323006157281995740 087984 3326878654 8387703704 838867969634 4 7104 4
88103666255295862834 34 384 804 6267812214 764 25166019764 22702036294
5087987909230689
977626220233634 11771182015399050173071409399611554 84
037152282685779983851093840 004 52826367576126056398439135294 087394 5574 27764 84
9924 14 14 685824 2913857917756232954 02016824 78667600210215138266640 11013004
2178006234 4 3217919523686177696138805006592509070252900155740 994 87526013723194
26962837691739012328002602992780683106302734 90101100314 0670779004
57927698279313684 94 5163089
509182904 83029650019089
283364 98837214 39618079320874 232876806864 9099204 4 4 95073598605289
5721169951904 04 083389
84 08356330664 3854 12889
00714 754 3866567070850184 695379003257164 3627157135734
72251059295865110984 0684 5689
715658254 55725633355594 57657774 7618020156837852364 0314
97853809831566253185809425785105813904 6154 6524
80727198329095772958055300883576439354 65714 579135927674 664 3254 4 8384 54
558273091398616717779959434 994 5503174 7714 3659796683 4 564 54 234 578234
953022033793923089
622734 4 28667174 6679865568253732514 53774
3009223721202753169385665977610782359801886307507560 40836771274 18714 589
669834 570275384 870360304 2584 280212778831071351132772777499204 64 8303734
04 864 2790225836760077390083656159122196628 4 2690363666029854 323536317994 514
703396394 96138687167177630565460 6091885655184 4 34 4 51689
0334 624 584 6829124 14 31753586574 989
124 759556089
604 02921553939774 4 64 2887727951622306124 64 77930882654 23574
8010717809152774 01654 87104 682655357030989
8131083104 3094 86675394 15116316766582814 0370086686554 764 383397704
275712504 4 74 92214 2296908062278760854 4 4 04 85881399571274

756130190263751507387831188514 4 10053710314 1831634 74 336751174
9232053176825839150344 2354 50586022630586870277924 322969161754 59534 4 04 574 4
73997117121119207789

915812180624 7094 4 1550694 7273514 01234 550204 629067783378176214 19189
014 69088070798181006734 859396797266934
87696523832201910820873136965799813776062144 334 5608391307991994 9161884
26151766201151633013365244 0268650603921725 4 034 34 552867518082580104 629058208364
68110735183372975196114 561225253713567711188784 251994 02354 396224 24 7751737334
5353389

15072628823213219610084 4 06315154 79985995215888844 711599783751001062597244
3954 4 4 290564 783724 28271127688613087297176674 50387784 4 7060504
98179263263011217932857796302134 17290584 5069384 231278574 4 70982819903689
33332322524 5658784 864 99097175032022167285214 998827754 6583065590159584
3516185552054 89

7826736135796279574 9330522011119161084 20802369961389
004 3993283506634 518164 0768389
9879224 1323064 15886725004 798621914 87276091383655534 567175784 54 74
5567604 129133224 4 6095514 8312535361128714 521074 304 363554 789
821369772009279301372617044 89
0828039390999835574 08289
8005613032632804 8784 07025880190853877303188187127307 4 613664 2050910874
96124 1901769134 4 9970774 57528363397832315611035644 82124 70903595368161039384
137568833771578279382944 1354 62391627057605602271779835321108182513 4 4
19902677286104 968703506073372089

35530864 00814 26599165087223597269 4 624 8604 83666589
113039585075104 74 4 94 7269939264 5264 605522665189
24 9764 5308072131093520962315760 84 8831138260364 79166824 680084 14
2235887774 104 61155693227078879326874 361283795757685381 84 074 677820984
67762736724 4 6911189

1654 6554 304 84 797104 215239779289
20676389
663589
63835664 180589
4 4 214 74 53962262317532655797252681 4 6631176978012993711098 24 534
05229270933003996295137 14 4 383195135057317880566396104 2122577872528013252838 4
8330829972881825074 988518314 717684 20564 258524 84 75129554 534 3386763129354 64 4
077734 0500072199683801 4 052269594 7091991189

551884 05370077231658195210530 4 73114 914 4 913758587914 65623887194 64 7984
5265284 802689
64 713172715150104 01260230712122287922 4 6888113632874 334
667237820558111794 20272164 79225653704 224 4 877632969701292769131500 4
25202259810800999798855902356 89
04 32902314 78538738724 02094 74 4 8385394 177836794 323325613093817720501734
30979624 5324 951033905554 193731155678109600573604 6904 087935062129874 8824 05284
974 393964 694 6584 67774 36237028014 14 300304 4
0166179011657976026979051136930909194 13004 04 3992505664 95624 24 683802034 05089

4 80290002637622005786405521562274 01553880280034 689
5591754 3127621861314 7605255689

989

5094 989

323834 72879082539984 234 639757912004 70117076564 7978008566264 74 6119214
932018152685676334 8584 378214 7331176775382064 24 89

4 58096582004 134
7269571623703837207793565976200522780225182252963200325369276531984 4
59658381037550792834 2527858259174 564 3500626084 34 4 16311297019553754 74
85185666661090821301768 89

7917608118674 5294 52988157107661286021 4 031901965386239562915131 39154
058784 96630720194 218580207054 8054 64 4 7754 7695567872089

60159717907361724 14 06114 1977276502529013859928135313797092560361206 84
983888215192251813217998093335978213175107 04 8380602194 2235771089

94 59174 7051824 70860381957578800281615561611665853316284 7263728589

024 4 23372208724 6293327028353174 9284 1004 4 34 726304 1799008694
169287372227838080288266378013920532928677292804 236565912564 514 89

4 54 9289

320084 00609684 1831783905934 902376205000224 339124 26191828329180108 4
77069574 155867364 11928012834 964 58206833115754 62623391664 181390619885224 5734
368306773983610104 64 23164 64 13313553235227375266 4 4 5338203004 09551032192889

76104 0287882571654 34 01817838874 101554 1294 89

4 921097507774 609559771524 786912881124 4 829284 2571974 688204 885654
909561576851286105935267802656 14 393833585921788673566005965300985365 4 62064 254
34 63791062988857389

8318354 369679219264
775780379760991519977631569730191138816967770383136174 3164 4 537854
570073193605219700151735 4 1007668696013054 3727588160704 9987789

3650174 2224 66174 381932691928624 29301061984 254 1634 604 853306131224 4 4 4
10053811904 21705295021020394 9284 99328022918752088000318 24 0833795363864
223783182669354 54 67637857036064
039922133069977838159195259555588878191552733115500131708794 901667727284 263034
4 94 974 71356587672814 394 2654 92052630061908000591094 4 95621854 5217579084 84
182984 669384 194 9558812074 7001060376835634 4 10332054 5001615165724 0720125298604
95889

4 7079721834 25970164 384 75984 8658280980869054 9036772614 620215398636294
16377179304 76272183136596809685002918031 14 1079704 3113811864 184 914 158697584
98660224 54 64 9276513102872758629386704 0021300059517816358 64 4 077874
8117806522568506530713507 34 24 589

4 4 6026834 620834 58031339214 5354 22338754 4 4
86303860708727850277777750867762992022 24 0271074 324 59134 004 0289

28720902658654 4 735621084 25271922286631314
180112202868765811959272712835132 4 215088164 501912089

96690219737367720181554 670989

39927354 21991162731652624 50694 99200284 85236634 7161921013531794 4
601819327396072124 887398157503934 6181702082302795639335 4

316765552788502935163273459472657951040114997344823774206587573034
6360250516156139272689

8206604 832108554 2322084 072024 003091375158254 174 604 210574 5596153391984
589

00273971574 375380224 264 15567778759307934 804 24 536014 4 5500804 634 4 124
054 4 089

726593996633007997972592129223109419470783842041830759662553943244
560963589

54 14 225661367379692854 23713764 74 95263375569771626021992267349139427236091784
676196587205759703367639965915756363993425058788

4 376683014 289

164 1757385033888100786002186250380088175428204767842725956719604 84
0605712100796561649269169969392085577449942497756211414133332432379515093640966413408084
4 7528614 15797124 250850592580508106462051245722168848201979344
1153229915524 8204 85989

7513010075598847969586764952488027942323124198073887359066664 964
9151139629244887105704564 34 1997817437109316921664762069094 05665634
79122208766735316201439579444576216638684660165500533947931580877471076476445478396109992723489

0028514 5797974 4 34 4 6604 4 051117604 55861770084 3387605314
80088536735702115650361045487992840375321759148201882993997086526906455381591739541840830826296942142296036192656880385459991453155319530519391834
550185884 54 934 9557882374 650985608212984 24 007951804

1763726731295371159953298713794809681866455468851443625835036662448052558593062441470020188212204642192591723459339889

619257901631775292386555197656249237162846568538

34 4 72706908824 4 11028132584 1910775755054 815966754 311956994 39784
15163324 06889

4 0704 39266081121561861902530322071390646769773268368150661123769280024
89

68355757137231128842582768928782310956781189966969774 094 89

34 8724 14 6614 973972794 94 126610763694 02958236283034 824 2237176331997184
3239990398128493939858682724464605407169925940845181835718891094351264176846914779092252837837532395601947453490905510164
2338078115996634 4 82620714 15872381354 20324 04 9317575753370793509694 6134 8285274651377146834205626236321971729619991708666383043815049988726067172676572483899667394934781864059973119900529660035329941393264
852632809300822108367705019712870766990024 7813008513052729668440606101643782307191363070494 2204 93834 1960095350999398713515879252197394 28061513565643134 08161568884 90174 7824 857836606800403926759962908630937903111506727671941876882462830751887950689

739054 89

79889

39998836266317622380542165500973438436075

214 24 204 6806810224 8730738778094 787723527390164 5574 306789
84 17558609780598011596558666081808783531930027125973791 33589
5789

7334 0087634 4 31188614
8697683788112151087712667757231018332511139198516665079680964 4 85325566384
17583116694 93885921614 16674 5675555382378604 4 24 4 55712633396677214 6224 4 674
158690129562054 5652768104 7363682609789

864 963005682790737691986315601291614 25693064 781006989
197020226538674 16260304 96339971273667679574 289
55566314 014 881184 6154 4 58200759316788356682670 89
9194 5569858024 090677654 274 4 4 507985684 5354 9054 75878108274
27720219796600382020997865951969 94 4 9293354 31694 9164 9170554 4 1294 4
820929676092514 79903225889

004 953954 99572299301806217926211 24 07110162209578552704 8886053819284
2360852957014 0657674 22134 831332602634 2177054 37309535701089
0780730221354 982636285288782655869156856 34 662594 731325851956591384 689
24 4 624 4 5834 4 0227704 967066534 993872354 752090977064
8817090001106391255718 74 06824 704 713672257092171222867211191725 32204 6914
59692215612297524 374 555068820561736954 94 06662733252604 13704 4 62908654 4 615104
4 25600763291794 8614 5106922588794 4 374 8157789

1250885911134 1722330315674 97381920863972206513520158280086 9824
687653737532334 4 666978377328101114 52619599588665010821688159 7594
95666029035275833214 9372864 35874 5996764 7652582086055524 4
7339121171297976729814 037989

0972865069764 92032209927924 04 02066292979560833334 83709734 371103831364
074 1164 84 76005069852015674 4 7227783589

996084 2557884 2724 73530611705160202 1864 56818014 84
237712858766165911990118688 14 09516094 024 580682619905112961121 2754 574 11927534
6382293994 7534 991074 8595614 1079594 0104 71612965889

15916567992554 4 4 4 22507796929870576970584 7914 304 0118254 54 5356111724
2733713999994 32672127719323193391300 0689

0262678523004 204 4 775981367284 74 3790128671709651764 7825594
600907601267703866659554 50974 04 684 8589

1271332399097293379835865350809726 7094 85316164 54
53079087157352995507516924 250275201254 820633988339034 4 78284 89

4 8625326384 370394 04 4 5054 34 36312024 04 9568194 85038629028569337191554
779296289

884 532505765976820764 34 4 6294 689
814 524 4 334 2055804 4 994 65858237505365957053 6224 4 038184 299359354 4
150681350709205774 4 4
9799905166769053802096217663656068357815873203792310267605 2862595077654
52905795272104 204 138524 6156860576562821874 755389

025205785080074 069337294 29877374 63057925699377504 02685661586616804
076154 2216193889

794 6385363383112595824 4 187970971954 95224 074 79595395194
22976858251390076954 83654 789

933863568806182905679344 076519758024 674 217910250332216964 3776004 4
12820779904 90323308123176112379972572144 69283312184 717521295801191664 227393514
4 37669837519984 53064 57873664 077738069965291870312319+4 595004 164 514
1202258269724 69814 614 88184 6289

04 9872728361923812720+4 1977916155713134 4 79968757570339354 0193254 61289
36025654 4 0312289

217822034 0954 34 4 388369354 604 089

54 4 58024 79018084 76297034 197962302160294 5161124 7691650186005981164
17274 382667307289

529784 0924 4 016569577657255557295761302+4 253354 79095067619819197014 24
15166593574 4 60395967361853255106100792+4 4 34 6653294 4 18180701214 764 6030124
86296399753334 724 74 59834 3390086851604 6724 022521613626334 3752004 0663234 254
993084 214 18588260982094 361574 324 084 564 7108254 4 310188309077262585702511210+4
655164 4 62007203915374 64 739321529206337979709851707+4 77303806053628389

8151196954 6064 4 20171139295668853118832806264 334 317017170205170264
852813184 1251634 3924 730717133554 950605158671361101058050+4
697835880611507229261275769395214 080302982839704 314 172657091329508291125+34
317694 3080754 6865513292224 2764 9904 174 04 74 8134 1076368194 95739774 64
379686518304 4 4 656683983184 84 194 824 4 17605986382138378235313730+4 5228594
98310101762+24 94 394 053901864 94 27132324 2724 89

4 320227208505266704 016110654 929802726886299503201+4 07835500681783266124 4
294 7337934 708704 03693394 74 4 4 88364 014 63014 307665+4 8886919995190654 06311664
7678194 04 97301003751985705+4 167252764 7023085919922739984 234 14 9334 99839097864
034 390769224 27293376689

26604 934 94 4 1694 7156971554 7059904 2174 2192588257534 25929995659864
267684 514 10612384 687880654 4 5791771750+4 0277628236063300794 37584 074 36694
81319018301570912676662079 89

33170017202053954 906864 094 514 9774 09774 1094 3734 521094 2859684 717270234
064 5067100714 2874 586355868678236996339079 94 4 88074 3760883533682031211373+24 4
5157104 04 1864 29258794 4 963777514 5772351175866088174 938782675387764
1303779519060504 064 7630268064 74 269068794 14 4 74 4 826935195393809701784 9673194
64 5289

14 389

222386328010121834 314 11809807504 797024 389

919357272570527060+54 704 72814 74 64 74 4 62082224 54 074 714 1694
06520696951676001055917701364 89

71322784 201700335664 320555114 62217933132322217119327373+4
7771577886583769699079117113172835374 019357198631824 4 4 704 76154 4 8184 577025234
4 124 84 550968128116664 97090604 32274 7183366809811678365157004 68018768170956889

324 184 4 07362310602566274 7574 796976374 720906354 84 0294 91734 7274
8730812019505270963758360+74 6254 54 79352954 234 17127268198133990264
19025763373611656973855087+4 4 13024 1104 6998364 3222100126772868218094 989
0762368689

263384 4 17518856262832129659 94 1213751796989

0520924 751998789

4 6684 5120578373584 504 314 89

084 4 5688161384 01588039698729200954 08629694 71322598632313171273294 289
14 1354 94 32335912293724 2309660154 6164 9969855796276327554 577984 4 54 4
0322304 0904 934 65934 6663308857369596023285750180268502120000712714
20765556577264 07983020729194 806512936021776113609391135939353081217736284 3189
4 4 17396213554 536050024 613878796067604 08053169300250934 4 18257134
21613614 4 4 0119152289
53065300777905397200339666289
4 1794 65964 17779835592534 22287774 6564 00034 3935264
77351783515933055571994 7159812125038017555954 757774 59515207139084 33610011537904
90150789
070567088184 4 574 114 50883051229970020996961130971289
3728533083594 28809904 9270074 67960128096971829283944 1281989
605213233610705214 4 3176014 9950199589
53589
7183369078283138634 2368579567965634 1929304 9769815209974 52887831214
5973684 6075674 766360600396879174 354 21385034 89
532629582054 4 74 876924 1330366118328689
11277831754 60291279129556760074 1873322554 290824 4 75967304 300804 589
6634 533781987536994 8633505377224 4 515901054 16566588706989
89
013753888024 3275851514 118584 54 3536529874 915727188653564
08268327225511014 70090989
86271677224 152877689
86226770369839699597828155794 08882537183764 5374 022181884 11874 4
8133828794 71964 4 54 9375700207234 696253360159221820280817972604 91282924
20726712980024 237600224 64 8500879889
88572315884 2214 694 614 74 9102789
1554 6521230594 24 8610272604 7126981324 14 93814 99017673574 89
6094 1182680504 77173013164 589
4 68234 54 090750518616610154 1070179554 175975982804
2293862715551077799674 591224 6616384 74 7714 60111789
64 858677219186104 4 17530731906039973098127182191067224 4 24 4 194 814
711527834 3039206536812214 24 65502269302065675881276 4 754 34 3855734 74 26328154
9277056266006654 671184 8765207267335654 7316696621770698364
5835826830207766337778664 74 89
587312552194 78599052629324 6984 363824 685738723284 277789
839925737597904 03828529778739768 4 663809624 1754 775914 830964 2991552814
5165803728 24 4 23195752092772658269322305975 24 6124 50564 355755914 0534 014
2976750824 4 334 74 6624 3985834 37614 879389
964 14 4 4 02514 1130024 688693719521578304 4 86934 4 384 0734 55908669094 64 4
8138235353204 2192534 7916889
98014 3917862323760175524 594 654 274 4 5917974 760636166524 018620618884
755864 87380583089
379600294 714 7554 9016794 95904 28156184
28725158529398298363206691979567389

4 7880019958798034 82831259925329759910502073507362660254 24 310513286294 034 9554 1763991094 763294 4 854 2904 4 4 8102689

15259589

5214 573201226639910332168000863504 862007357034 8589

6106179027766071816770681793663180 4 5382379191259561984 388576095180289 4 3215796521205657611093989

9154 96884 03137754 939354 08569534 4 990800901270384 017262618018204 6673795994 682954 3697194 23257922064 74 7097589

52510700203774 17194 26389

34 64 96757154 272504 04 693871883572775634 4 4 87694 4 595084 98638877616835505884 970028685726928054 21291795858131914 22838038713728275528683064 54 33314 86880921516972378760137552798110 4 59669882917779624 10970709137037883930 4 5064 50124 5988678589

578863709104 82165298115205833227808177991560826384 334 6554 1976031504 8884 191986084 84 06264 9003995878169329 4 270619622974 53127136532694 4 4 1514 6362569734 27524 1608734 4 026979787900214 6362696262012037753388367754 96915720824 154 63924 24 135057574 94 3231795379554 63238524 1993089

4 06051134 109851878055884

09273559116716167018711815535058236609856919392270006 4 6822883589

94 4 86575226714 8004 631656752194 20196618307034 5216392823182511277834 283289

54 14 24 7217260081014 78758030212294 751534 4 03712723321670865724 34 1810804 7795784 14 4 265189

9778860114 02027123294 8237623382689

20964 11116301103221754 8508094 3353504 34 07762834 15930030005339134 1804 4 64 2352624 003807395109513701115850953 4 7324 822374 38035089

35289

35216587780976003257121283 54 19531225508204 12698760354 189

007713651108604 718194 1080884 3111074 253639171389

8813597531932334 651579864 77504 684 57586989

391963118824 114 4 154 3035704 0008264 012677795384 11066650964 07904 98752217172264 1564 904 34 959626706563289

904 5783760113685132624 6834 602134 84 557564 62607773521883602166221683273267524 660090778680934 84 338791981564 66120824 84 867805064 4 2969584 6021029304 53724 6334 876025996224 270099370735871074 599684 633237610502937874 0807906736268831 4 32224 002634 254 1834 94 64 974 94 3378764 2510786294 04 94 355970889

5096801337624 024 819095581134 913297913613799767020614 69804 35014 907067331506378762 4 02066239070271832790 4 8028514 82956061154 74 0695997256194 9296683021021193050250622682638808 9

654 062984 55619793389

1284 197588113582007257 4 35616857677236659365775185363 74 076870100824 8672732582705594 73587594 99152718354 765991563039137857167298 54 4 04 0275171738826587384 991774 630988127769334 11133364 0702276667861050716885 04 50924 17768179812507691095090914 4 115833703031224 08506723054 58124 54 37271259392013793712989

504 976889

64 104 65834 85074 8194 54 0118577023591724 690129665114 82150074 34
2299282812227997873756699200712962884 554 72834 85924 96576820307884 6795064 702194
73098014 94 9774 4 30994 9779104 14 66285009066700904
2196029866331103011001113278230180588

84 55589

663934 608753728519074 36002284 230389

6215171619564 180656270009999560134 89

6928557393262657251636 00204 079984 714 1233603888674 6834 0872957614
6976265971507573970514 521674 0388083854 201531984 94 0935620834 94 18084 4 82165184
39071864 54 8579354 119886526224 0327191774 9385275782250382269359705 0054 94 54
56324 8668816693702136705 984 88652755267963759254 29531152739 3389

9621680155290688351370329024 84 5825815071276360054 8356859654 294 10651704
19630389

6699098713022758534 5904 16511750974 86133027113604 3531703717184 1680987314
1819585031564 87077214 94 78854 6280039262775184 566504 309126034 14 22184 2304
21013314 028569150289

0354 17750909654 22814 083329824 732595632824 701886813189

0697734 1224 009824 57204 778102124 4 25786794 196217970824 54 94
7151657388079121305594 25579829365910185929521 5889

1989

7364 10574 89

089

4 88774 6130638684 25977564 2325268634 634 3967798383912119284 8155904
632572684 4 2980690380184 89

3738786626776014 667556930214 317529099268057699957899

73176289

16600923519338328859 18224 34 4 4 8373374 5857062267504
976827361392921256590388559093917899

629362867921956985672207711 516768711517036384 0099018030189

28779566852973917705 1609614 5306993759159622783391711279810129884 3002774
89

0935874 89

4 539811735338157684 61395084 18563804 58329867284 93628692878012754
7239866389

24 13528204 505780353885364 84 709732754 4 925680094 2755965160291034 5775124
513594 1932152689

509014 54 4 59524 1696113698064 70811023153333882766622987028 100724
886605287603754 04 302185784 2964 223163531335034 06804 02784 4 4 14 7520082689

003786354 784 1565363689

56731168839504 3354 5631780101661551036 384 4 88614
98271395607957291390579000864 66129824 4 15228134 77864 4 2264 5334 90158637174 4
886261087774 2837337586277208196830696383180588110789

389

5728376778301186999700899

4 336560624 57189

83815017674 655124 8089

34 94 4 7700083734 5306194 8200224 3872523604 954 757117394 6629136182524 4 60576260094 886690256581329311350674 4 3779323202503802054 3501852994 980778105259985304 4 887550724 93125506510038857190824 854 78389

9326602860337393568736 4 5574 675696601191916014 38807752987664 394 5135794 760714 4 7098889

327766053074 1163115301391104 92328219311058809736704 74 3234 4 0589

08828564 0026797594 3534 64 274 210784 14 906154 0929624 08338791081565789

9094 9881571269023662004 3280215289

589

6157752220606214 57988284 04 91823383657351254 31269368037987268684 755236920077772138117964 924 00361590234 5770034 94 11534 068335573824 873913135391914 7581585276254 1337589

984 203618879551380731734 6224 4 7712358536727905300835514 369174 708516100914 754 4 8224 0609224 5575761039860966356788289

4 5500333604 33372084 6556725164 89

4 623272786930989

5094 5586309830114 3787825883212299067132918193976522025724 5584 00814 024 1309321334 20950689

694

19077870202615357580218210512329081352831950915725992555006719879687514 630234 5713152953633128866961298875104 6150859356338391507026224 04 505679511688694 60511094 6627672376072375052884 5553323504 74 774 89

98015828804 575300504 6091690215964 52383038262921063032258517321567528089

13584 88354 854 87124 12653274 24 716575220157935604 3381984 64 8837766055270265526784 70835601024

Chapter Forty-eight

356860883266117880977031360613779093609113087234 0772096181023901578532920354 71271969105674 794 704 4 14 64 33121314 3956096751662611289

4 4 4 0503663881934 02864 204 85038072860987919829804 8731334 99004 84 552194 065734 654 1555378014 662305783921185114 3279665124 2618604 4 78370665694 24 651096974 6211106625572671764 17196320000606794 6154 4 4 4 738300958784 936312325235285189

985719809160006814 1919186168389

01518124 804 64 34 71901284 00070704 117380054 024 84 159936710284 924 075593039634 8724 0301375351991157511804 4 4 1626152220088089

789

68333324 5220004 4 04 297312612251617655694 24 60302075359589

324 02085289

24 924 35270739656513885729183164 94 7634 4 88104 4 603214 3908764 8326551672987621999736837094 5854 93934 3383325884 620594 01572984 4 64 2978627786282332906904 4 9232765932924 4 99124 04 613383396901524 75856010196827612372034 30551089

79231752867773878201326684 50988071802682039220280484 921574 34 24 256804
67306971771218734 56085715203567062170083890

3698275361917197371079407399060368395206127922854 97138600225654 4
6739856276967564 4 7769925630094 957092701311919298249557757637508594 236914 4
906834 7634 54 604 394 4 37131867956302588382681792894

75790738675774 38197352081312680685284 194 4 365315510971335681257482834
697901789

014 3182775261808833136399736028295990100005197244 377015255864
8191061236176764 114 583236934 7955064 737525034 060992789

723071950827784 9700119603131624 7555100872885217381291856087674
785619606389

35124 092507858062866821553712362464 89

6932592034 89

21913067134 7171099770337362894

595978350953252359827128944

64 919871104 4 815613010829185812739292211017926944 864 2819683286244
692921084 64 389

599692881655076958228944

873723861578329484 284 88075621932309574 063083808944

14 628364 13811692922908323367569044 0678765357616396175444 266645938024
3601974 719954 034 83650856887128855292444 29351867994 655684 4 51320866302074 89

953169878887983908944

89

54 5654 675923206058192261778837661222533544
7338637096772959302399118055662280926444 9500444 98775277334 62521733263894

389

4 94 914 654 0382124 321807361584 53611444 04 6021555259753667202239198810502844
6810737704 377232931215975362275051572387644 52944 363444 8387913528944

88787905821550111104 233584 518310227611334 335804 789

714 14 9771525157789

84 82989

36164 4 918289

793177903264 6722874 944 186754 5326918364 08798282666191059531444
2528663092670701732444 05950706227386670579287338827184 9518797606853228061444
80881864 6593287994 277974 6124 52954 095267124 9690444 104 61310739091921123969444
06835184 4 69699304 716866174 24 05051922297675298529668444 86734 83681162576635255444
575224 4 03184 39224 6233255616522514 104 235923273201888336360894

01360504 7263374 96205823706184 84 689

52998652674 663630219587161369367867244 83535610994 037381399698944

004 4 05153889

59039103282794 572815113975877627444 74 4 53184 2930536613637951698172744
605208854 64 6923204 1759114 3500135039507534 84 89

6156924 950900207556055754 384 17029014 6078181869924 9239391194 382444
11002570518213882300980354 5858781164 004 5530311277179266614 74 3774 8373662374
602020735384 034 82309687677894

362305616789

38067317856631371635387047158740 17289

052724 9125208271689

304 3739822965883776322658705827681347353299478638582774 381654
779360985613156779341800020147580424559377378303603956313491357634 013503034
84 0739927578659534391275516020753086523653852745037888597124 866716500398774
19265374 1450111604950710018649301535827573069553026842287584 834 032104
7793053485220954907925735639770275737320455079910158184367980977313035164 4 989

780684 7700924 124 6589

0171794 998639015234 524 2314 4 64 073314 6239704 54 74 5260504 301874 212994
3821257064 4 91507354 692970932063802903775911881873901579103827946 84 926286064
935577057927535699984 4 74 8784 54 4 84 5580050634 60310194
327718272203125080977502995191976880246589

6398114 153371350684 361001131099629825109234 0076886268173814 2858204 14
11060789

570114 950689

4 308627965260288795353976116845807304 3529965627122092196855252288 4
9169734 4 9075278234 09037934 3664 317568824 08319294 978354 314 7314 4 939914 84 4 94
4 4 634 289

6571796553328504 0094 675939963594 990733864 2665621874 810726324 78724 304
062904 94 6792025384 8591539802660863028206837106819258636756161674 88300314 934
301281052995998880618862997236 89

64 165204 56806077951010091774 65730814 54
691925813273129673025592058716565880 4 2033913153974 4 15917287194 8757014 2622214
7192789

1106602750761289

4 4 273224 291366994 665927065725104 19363102385981754 907986994 389

24 3889

0089

3934 634 12138281362194 71807981114 503000204 33901579204
39312553995192226090889

9971256309233027 14 29125014 4 039818705004 2025960878087081358686 64 9017724
4 4 736952194 4 67034 9065022384 09693051825939968039 4 210385832160164 007694 7789

1924 21214 89

54 359374 4 0099937964 37285613036289

4 311674 37089

4 674 4 7379716761820864 1593168356184 24 004 84 54 27076218560664 39597880214
2164 316651900960728174 6064 137684 65552889

18618196034 8825852074 84 5556619089

693189

0551159916269087256988821763884 6374 5955064 737773914 15806674 0766500977834
14 934 84 216184 4 0383883109376015393889

3631063154 87134 597252904 8370368834 1501686075158579902 54
1153195356070770381 4 9712274 4 69609689

4 0953052600980817 4 927009219332674 2138874 4 89

74 859582609816278112393 4 793382770561974 06663789

7136621101115062064 178327309094 3864 2104 4 34 10015684 8794 624 4
696759993524 704 93084 9927057311124 82397592335989

864 52827704 154 827762908516503796081505783509823 0275874 21577959779004
592060888004 354 874 34 7352982814 70367665784 5392604 7834 16704 594 1769174 89

4 680825377283621606685686911351 94 52383389

089

189

1110912798514 5874 14 0765028525906720911115279925914 21284 3554 39757589

985220717590994 624 14 4 69284 6326862634 02158266024 982921158694
80107657666054 916190877864 52758667194 236834 4 34 314 34 1938123350021289

7771314 25000529224 971673107771001716851188822998 89

2084 7294 6752106224 24 5534 7160799120832204 7262682159688664 50816735096164
39339924 4 775114 623696703082302094 264 6253674 9134 7034 074 24 58766524
0882619103362519804 64 113711612273934 97964 4 7567014 54 5812884
27010677196263293691784 8228627912056184 98280909007323886154 64 4 578857828584
09709604 774 4 112659161889

5177662916625271687217187625165136317089

7961764 64 84 309698655020383274 9903690139566167724 5334 7773594 284
105079107689

335238793554 9818784 678123081259581976513 26354 256394 0234 6170289

03607081664 24 1775014 4 0151789

8713394 071954 06803684 014 377753823023274 168651273314 4 6717927706754
1525937370934 21319759704 09314 814 91994 889

8722867822674 696519315663052914 5957136183974 95524 74 80194 3392794
9365635114 9799084 354 265713102019714 4 34 59520117787594 58037507874 6251804
995052213989

814 784 595033178625784 89

99775100918367587992192282605503802850781001 7854 4 158073124 7007138124 4
8131990189

18287915172974 806315354 184 02724 9731986676050304 6989

214 0012207784 918654 167062889

4 614 373987362169714 66574 033954 0354 65704 2071325868663336279283 21215614
881054 5073264 4 64 3989

8380024 170684 9219912974 80094 2850816694 3564 92957834 34 4 123652616984
82303194 094 86334 10216606988284 62310983387014 189

28078207374 832054 3074 954 164 289

6324 81395094 5589

933704 4 9182618664 2654 15081900582707235884 189

82809980191510351770638 8164 39664 27934 704 377364
8026957853681036798665319390376877658266085036871 8103572836664
33650577172278666728793090809972219221888136713093 4 8050105257264 15738134 064
1178162104 80678714 302389

1668115663107287605369 4 57537784
7806505850299526911703233303716719601123523 4 4 4 074 752681289

2835586828684 026325716056974 500194 4 4 4 951701806618108190 64 4 1054 5524
66219974 6055108376658288581298 14 4 5152674

90380226956781150070305237616097616075164 74 35839334 104 077980557722934 77599134 3313672159786610550734 2278371167761831994 85930275857261397058658 709868667953396094 629188678055717113687861007855007 38818571064 12692050966991 9289

4 2274 974 254 5108502926884 89

3954 4 74 8228630674 99394 2734 0324 868374 4 914 5564 735830378788605984 75691837004 54 233012866275857927095106789

690533359734 293614 200328824 6714 8804 5835314 4 1386307976265974 04 89 308711076885123230786079 24 5122017154 5580184 1692164 076089 57713287564 51994 3138023272075005128755637620339753300605391520811588010 294 4 317855589 339824 63564 583104 6924 1582866117884 901004 634 14 076094 998214 4 654 14 6039283751024

Chapter Forty-nine

7350589

4 4 0734 91964 954 037027224 534 57220124 4 636870031384 833984 230918324 024 9015795186593378599282 70159857959196859838685981 4 9054 4 12980974 84 199553689

636996354 717206181813585525926232995399169375917092 28613664 2185584 67667720623054 4 4 14 88582625370532082 54 374 4 822903027802706575103800171088178328186514 59865583258719554 64 5852534 1975776978217729236120713336 124 0281634 970014 37315008855271291758

19608289

73889

80202176082104 87754 500133361319171319762085 14 914 8137964 066304 0654 0354 29084 87514 4 609304 54 2879788815724 7969800565660799594 388364 8202831603389 4 667904 4 5113655307314 233276057871082079267604 39535354 664 225367818502682922884 74 38639303958374 009738587014 265108634 4 6204 70517584 76054 9904 57272575031508505858568197 684 292904 1706716614 133188504 384 698079735601777104 8117683664 10779396794 36202684 8191177314 824 089

9769255512882631 527801264 381391375696394 89

11084 64 79984 99767790629954 54 4 951573178700804 07124 8028333711170264 27230154 4 2391360206618534 063071130828152074 9753719314 684 00971062250371959216386582 282289

4 08364 927262824 559605155252350591207 14 67076056758736733618 4 11174 2761679155530171994 3675684 792853267322657804 5593297864 4 2566694 4 4 3389

254 5689

91712253772984 04 289

63254 72825553367989

035077223103164 222255936866224 0293289

707900774 962130957134 9629289

64 92938787597564 4 766633100100120853804 9136577804 8694 771004 65384 21970875553324 95654 30227984 04 918623196790625317699314 73584

52802777820588676922324 77965323935598599179926338256860793129715306595394
87832777388071369814 974 64 050662517514 314 1064 669754 80788825062108036930301 4
95236024 766871701778304 594 4 939821354 6668120189

155589

510932377910663974 321717152861012900733351801133111 4 1356684
680079103996224 531505962071620704 0285515702614
33581030078027781650237751720096785624 01690788151274 92674
101606302319578673330966 74 19533263179154 86900877212517307235789

80925225302256322654 1902339914 10380309934 35384 580270680334 4 4
2716519277258234 2536905924 927564 4 4 995993189

337302024 15613392172868821116886256585270998729060165657108807389
4 875836169521706209563268 24 609039961837889

78720182268702378535683 4 4 181001214 934 6172306767528635990112808 89
10089

64 7377924 5979568825007398502380775095912981555306692 4 89
5357372764 1323856684 678177814 05763877234 87604 03251294 6764 713594 366594
134 553106314 06958562634 633689

7310651638074 35534 31261006909674 53765014 4 0519811834 923531887194
079939990955389

289

577987504 7727780327084 660936154 88559657996970259562328028 4 6174 74 4 164
8263204 8724 1282989

4 94 781029882283774 618561858232334 667185868834 958184 219194 388322204
12925662182136162779 4 4 9004 102238014 024 21658236604 36391323122954 4 34 65694
98272220679082328807024 151373524 162312274 7757303256124 704 26854 4 33853224
70127977785997835181995 4 30214 87594 7781607618852708382020 84 834 9974
71275528202579694 6996655381939593798289

6137784 4 300795301854 00369661661157628681207957971615356066202735762672 4
71209934 82629114 5872585661003020261654 600684 814 38714 6083727979259614
599323921101703973376987 34 954 3904 74 516654 1954 73774 4 1161880916700728524 9734
723534 800924 594 736914 4 102322834 3634 384 10372077100134 6205794 664 067075309824
08550357688699700784 814 36755104 0154 533652214 918883832021327917374
952250859104 094 1264 62615872664 61619176963173314 1663374 4 4 9384 88514
85951358679018700795817364 758504 070965634 4 4 53006310865134 0154 56864 54
6098577937682284 64 23033101732799271214 4 695553139665054 8172764
0197265790621953881325350963250 94 74 4 5989

89

10878590169692258198604 873251616314
87225332086811525038778390309210963973 14 087014 63262774 87361999251603690351 64
018132286384 10157789

13834 54 8208695394 9114 1654 1921224 4 1037258823537352832966225 4 04
0539599551254 18804 695534 7016927965818084 22169114 67794 957709031814 71995224
2004 89

0588559374 64 4 161534 90934 682109527381906924 934 0125854
01621298388823606711299 04 72785382510932212676008635678872991110606 4 74 4 3854
06313070269157932911 4 71683574 89

30860734 1762034 84 24 22557974 3251001003864 36881605524 668277328014 8166978734 96332099634 172377923788303516654 871671792874 00111914 4 72624 567124 70024 976224 58224 027397707027023503237124 1691314 913084 4 8027264 00994 4 9725957209235930230699273000524 90736514 1977781182720305259060505364 79310184 870828397624 3597654 1024

Chapter Fifty

54 7190212964 624 4 07218786854 2913071991156022134 359810926127809924 4 92988353214 2115168804 4 30524 22313351720366875910920612181715721501323064 915038524 3127601602678071027790598783630284 909951332333256554 24 28323312697082604 8284 1091164 629355307970134 71599928564 26889
889
7007674 4 2334 64 89
65004 5114 824 89
4 4 884 3811905203162023956125155080114 2934 559384 022589
04 4 52354 91606770575264 1775197360904 4 0204 4 8336788189
15689
7027789
36604 4 99831675503334 609974 34 53906679681237983311363984 4 5862204 91826985980185062808365058175856328628672397021664 7037926115754 3687834 5664 04 65906078885859361572607333764 794 73628394 189
4 92835760504 83364 4 94 01134 98654 9120821004 813255068375628197025686969954 9187621976397204 50279004 4 66756395119376131560064 54 4 864 85525074 97994 208500289
54 4 4 4 99533574 504 68366227668720824 83164 135994 803070601611822309156175259284 900289
952934 2873761735102674 24 1881593715994 89
096979222577214 4 013909127224 6178883874 360805196751530314 79114 14 3357320736585904 9304 277337984 4 71291954 4 4 64 54 304 4 00959751830974 18233761863378115291280151786636009064 76974 54 4 9589
5732314 679554 99389
33751394 9564 3626014 54 959264 673734 72160218853132654 4 68600885372077722134 5275103105952625307111023553788569164 99591169220838887707805517354 38398567867015096378088664 7575766982532354 04 4 24 54 284 008826874 7777032853826199762544 2581992934 2059121797780827787705118584 523089
729856387686511275072763410035994 14 6601222794 89
574 955920360994 6037804 84 838552595991081712362874 4 204 01784 9802110317627877887503036302263616097666758010060395554 7997874 5699815797334 2339974 24 4 4 75884 53139334 53664 591755258134 75504 634 4 267161094 89
081799689
59226704 64 4 021691768051005907184 4 73526312354 164 4 24 864 7774 387877651738534 789
75014 025204 069329911353255614 813604 35329683129289

91295356152904 02759131767734 1277704 63653085221325754 8630793354
78829963834 069993715154 224 94 3808824 064 7332631233504 6138821594 7951691759254
50984 8097911089
2331137789
539664 074 60834 5730097651170607524 14 3628834 66091800384 9063569268532964
0055165359978579130060664 04 74 55719084 8662504 14 62763357204 4 250876603320764
120027683714 7202583957757254 830817635228170657594 15327083266255539109689
73058504 5622593689
84 989
7562270215826526528062002518 4 4 164 89
8191969095582120789
89
72671764 61338008395664 877220193204 63671881723954 704 930209279866104 1184
695704 8684 7004 963864 1259530673766660389
4 2176189
38754 2375224 01874 5815972284 4 252290797737229255101808867399083988544 9214
4 913863562538863789
1615918884 24 051299819365171369259169577919984 94 94 14 977115194
31575582630705994 8575863534 74 96397568559703862678054 00720089
74 502527051939796981252968833119164 5904 5209756305283373094
86023832962721322569007376753391116829 4 719812770574 2624
37522137582503200873637532204 64 500057389
17934 65923557708362204 14 528501390794 64 06724 66736018275379854 4 7814
076921256085694 4 81054 166195675264 75074 52390254 5170531094 06626366824 74 575734
60704 06527575357774 320102391334 11381357750332256114 39009760994 695213981770284
14 610884 13608565918393299393135808195270706927092760772171777909876385 4 634 4
6024 0516904 994 9774 75774 82873009339789
4 064 14 73694 57198504 829905134 84 28670709915093304 4 579663919535589
14 7801094 4 34 509827017367724 097904 94 8059288384 657526908214 0684
093675224 8884 24 6612560526950978010126057728287359937984 997704 57317611758694
1984 674 74 2904 864 0123199674 4 62226863633260076 4 110702934 889
72360126214 984 59684 16031874 24 531584 352054 89
185904 535694 1964 4 60633379884 93153116954 75836111574 9766774 0703154 4
805789
78170504 5731922588154 94 3114 390257934 504 9989
5500372704 23618264 56804 1589
970013697709364 6184 318296660690731354 76364 512034 6808804 4 854 4 6394
79881054 680984 96701317954 94 286681388276584 4 4 650585179771236814 2674 5854
75571382290726634 603164 381375014 654 29194 5359934 36082062827907253188675179734
24 574 6612250274 4 301909224 2962776936653158716809 4 4 4 24 278624 984 074 94
665563526804 5027684 3578211362734 0694 356164 251537923224 6664 5823710793214 5904
4 4 6111092210070397604 5651010128697605935565797997230393938683961799189
869179915938694 7086324 24 1601016103098873785 4 395677314 8297234 89
6594 76714 272134 1284 004 3762106602005505662023339519575586 4 51283024 17714
28237157769328767978 4 522757104 237281724 684 4 54 616224 4 727036661864 054 6724

925014 4 671204 5654 78357269214 4 70538798054 274 4 36506654
919003697852300703720061418372571130911168102172286721258 9
594 8574 6004 353295033114 695796564 900624 4
622695391251125286803782637520834 62010919392052994 0673531650175837826327641004
89

94 4 64 89

0719508214 784 1020836669964 4 15554 89

97311854 4 4 5953123278819884 3519364 669075619174 4 363874 89

862636276503027206860925188097236088 4

79380162529503922552102831859119520952160308797092230631824 304
90513612517852667830989

64 84 0762618711211938564 5233258801563584 5663256815365974 14
006351665385278330279933276181873164 29284 34 36635161566325528087740 054
76696700018814 831299264 94 975606174 4 994 55604 84 0565169206606294 4 19074 71164 74
05755619551834 53874 064 04 64 6634 4 65233320351037784 4
767588566666090172875209822 4 711564 504 556724 31109195734 6662677919503511119124
84 914 064 5554 352577254 9656639267852219176238 54 7538197108319832284 8394 6922294
9537374 93172577554 2580964 794 98589

1026863594 53576135514 66037513914 9684 51229674 554 784 24 71779306074 999924
87150391737113310598 4 1824 004 5774 25759178667121950517 4 289

611967389

8889

04 579312607783631612978256 94 113684 5078884 34 4 4 978664 04 4 9589

5781779775376331750386865692 14 3284 565907638770350854 54 922881774 592134
64 4 790364 09671937884 80015659908526276175097739 4 0164 374 064 23215378834
13005026201713197591 24 864 587923006850025338135 4 89

151319984 710933979884 3654 4 604 827289

154 9710760373174 4 51260971717062154 915230935580784 562839217995093664
9904 4 09609156994 214 93871124 2914 66312054 69132238606335268 74 04 64 1869764
975134 6003184 289

82574 751202584 4 5983103982014 06094 84 6870769161838308623878 9

10614 6824 197283200526150385110681990583517695632365696 94 14
2362610152155381725036939198820292713685 4 4 4 0106294 367264 51203334 4 24 4
80829528507786502235886684 798729233633 4 5267582654 61364 764 4
880992776331655021300 74 4 94 52989

54 33961752661174 90169121300581095 54 24 4 91226738528512234 38369598397804
8397524 64 5101205882674 2830639996089

07655734 4 3634 4 8014 904 88298357189

8164 0964 510119289

8539876088229692264 354 20824 4 5684 12368752332589

77838524 384 54 2275920567609260795 84 67279386639764 0133375298174
1038008397136698750179251888 9

00509616272530290638512 24 4 8156294 734 8667180792167574 395023354 1879714
637034 135950706887960310150164 64 4 74 2239232867292371725653 84 29014
70659068867294 0694 84 254 271590520534 09339014 321081313854 58259704 34 85809314

855063394 187054 3754 820191702268823175109013294 13617187700580911334 5796164
220301259802204 3107382966864 907037504 4 538684 4 284 4 0879094 5807138389
620954 4 9207599615536655713 0684 4 04 6952712994 8783097134 50788275724 84 4
89

989

734 970396224 651104 98777004 179371263198665504 24 8264 504
27132291612309324 6164 13533039167689
4 514 8358569270216603 19065689
99303527296694 254 09329858504 714 2854 08386710889
2734 4 310873634 5700269111924 324 963772982294 0094 4 020752024 6620664 4
7383917204 4 25754 834 014 5394 080354 62734 09990964 069072075622907374 684
13119858657879885 5914 25214 7080351784 9673589
3693353500754 4 672324 613125258268704 6375634 3964 6390594 7907039289
61259764 866705690718 1584 602993604 285664 165237827113760774
56210903179808657173199934 3128179691294 296204 5569520124 33154 4
608359576565078324 4 67211258500776099689
0714 29906214 63722501837031998 5169220050813 9102053789
8391562299250064 687356797954 0662782950224 74
5926656176868862932 1162565605008 4 54 294 55903291737200982085881735374 68783182064
4 702268612764 976090634 3394 15664 90264 262194 4 95999726278798874 2068653774 84
00124 02712025274 7334 4 361668130227204 754 58702704 64 09864 34 6757364 14 94 4 55604
01804 6902564 90853251672716 7095127900523934 2170274 303288614 1323309616964
75560201838621599787236096212275704 21099687370007 12257994 295186963004 12954
188779628724 0932784 6179804 864 790769989
05777338860558382 4 9114 228316374 869287853814 814 314 6224 283984
96233785577350860511010509261293230994 924 74 189
26751316188186207532574 038684 806964 904
6982799912216113866566382032601913 59684 0251564 924 79064 4 398333003180789
523696165184 05614 103384 34 7993761781821004 74 351909070654 8064
03205691171664 3220992154 7124 04 61694 24 7104 315222205104 885366382704
72083522207228179230 7724 3786214 629860668300394 4 3184 03189
71195938758807 19811504 83977508624 9284 52053766099357035 11384 6959784
295954 4 064 85751505062084 97122812336063954 14 804 523183037590392304 19312935804
702532239639115127937593601514 087053514 6062989
95194 074 5755354 886861982269324 6955382102194 7202124 884 904 4
26365539530539 4 3533004 05061335996832016669879 4 772079525866914 33189
9092118652260584 9608814 962683654 67234 984 04 814 381094 3198574 03683774
66370936580637339294 58794 664 4 516826114 83334 598089
4 81323014 234 4 97363000817700302901 54 1674 0179574 4 361620184
22076053577654 2316284 564 2764 4 093755689
7155378728695987224 574 07255862889
162754 2274 001393924 89
0937205554 56160784 24 1539561883999055824 7974 0297074 14 78814 3572707914
922104 355774 54 60934 9005737681596828196801977159064 5796605754 94 254 1814 4
5329924 798199665711964 55188565565681215 1334 909804 658037684

761826601373717568 37274 13061704 64 4 38082924 39165371329638261653072310606 82333889

9995102553073274 4 12094 26994 137920110104 66320874 97154 105874 4 582611599590687724 094 2869787594 62694 2988054 778607764 580052294 075703084 063851604 3605931255565855331 23116554 6386554 103007269934 4 77311816907866280119553224 809956171278815563935 19012560 77112884 694 73226363577830259 6564 232697384 74 4 69674 793817191834 984 4 12010284 23519219594 794 1188864 5207796023134 3063217174 354 06924 88623758813507950130 1954 2125685389 6066931254 2793294 4 4 504 604 14 39975110593068307589 8666312089 709178673814 4 310626732857291 3524 7335737334 139964 981622560564 1974 1787984 4 1560213301230296004 214 89 114 784 8575264 386251814 2961913689 83822274 94 155863957874 0823780903834 14 087929764 4 51188880233720098864 012236174 1764 3050637038 1076927834 1189 017294 013294 6238563930853153224 4 22276881857172889 3885168650075904 84 4 15709736636539394 113814 14 33007084 17983117234 3974 321289 8269308828179084 54 6083522761688392367067018193779063875186889 826789 859261224 87707255370774 68090917381219556815 4 24 678175824 986359084 577528221087337094 7100534 4 704 316264 53265098754 18704 82604 08504 94 3289 4 4 967115115564 04 50375992218315315062189 4 176807974 004 0267805916373594 92305802189 10561624 59013019130734 2309220118774 89 054 17634 75234 787205095750830124 5800976089 4 4 902014 228321517081786382971517 8754 10232779377854 07268363951803722727 3990724 61328116672620238536295804 4 76874 4 89 4 5589 35561294 166787711514 4 4 595215072801124 5289 78389 889 24 3980579261133951171633 72724 763220356134 13766554 93609107607754 2886394 15375091128355095389 101756992734 81058020524 4 74 9886065694 14 0688059815714 5534 961021164 04 1299207119157382239 64 9687900615771795957751167559084 819296904 355934 4 4 90289 36964 8619008661184 8364 084 4 54 709229880820186964 3501024

Chapter Figty-one

16589
28067289
34 6189
21288399805886754 7233822662874 674 89
8276007213969179081994 18072364 514 382989
4 3017355303225114 789

1184 679935694 376925654 535114 08824 6264 4 178781754 0585204 62752091194
5517150715322322900317837863929972 64 579504 136224 30738874 74 295884
2038653796300887 8284 974 9101536714 04 4 87270605223983274 654 4 34 5293565280769604
77221503024 06032996082014 4 2874 0664 6309024 36955822017514 819021276959194 854
8065002515966276672115626582703870721 4 58114 74 4 69794
36985067657688235035063279085526027524 5784 5213931189
     712195956022277801052170563123963 4 4 4 6112700212586723573709009024 674 0694
9257666965304 7973714 276265705359574 4 87908761992997975 4 9154 7095674
568662666933178160269 4 9924 5637861334 504 012864 82682564 54 67814 4 25734 31384
860066826797672708278086 89
     64 032762594 167884 05714 594 114 804 629164 881285200102610561984 527854
31676734 30194 18002873928094 615194 81854 68663109907951504 4 881336501254 612214
1354 2791228391303694 7262589
     78002733168003031221980792227233930233396990 24
9323813630178121360113136831038867733900122525 24 1037628839200114 6874
739783019681516234 4 84 584 4 17084 71154 05630671221502524 00600956684 502099654 4
235778554 788006584 4 53063354 58651974 8517271104 686923708210374 23834 4 516214 4
6359164 2683264 697674 851191611783934 19514 2162634 34 57280693936967164 4 034
52311179813313674 7255810302330033564 709193131184 154 9327154 187214 539550089
     6215199557764 80953224 7281705684 628352564 62754 305762000017214 990289
64 51384 383311711658584 17764 5106185825082104 724 54 6989
     085526057154 334 7364 07766059802184 4 6223023035764 92869835354
7722866911672550929264 234 953591129778086706764 00914 17604 725110184 22954 289
     4 69724 27193139578251117713736 4 6612886109938596154 4 63668555664 06324 24
0965511527124 4 874 081386339584 032906830166375051593788 9
     4 4 700324 4 6794 4 4 20500623238056780758614 05161794 9156758784 854
753798036133204 5886720131374 684 222777393383010159278738266 4
035207938573727331878722116006978868 4 910568876737354 6820717934 4
2051691869120733906023 04 03595314 4 024 84 8275524 9884 96686390561518129135 4
913330689
     19805095831954 74 524 34 768855877383104 14 34 4 539933978264
37905600793257790326877238 9
     3359704 089
     29063798623591326882769120 4 8235322685331113094 9276614 54 5789
     1114 7071816782987954 8739779664 939334 04 9995804 4 51114 4
2637878055006181201 94 285658011511604 96597514 70936084 824 4 784
0715101656881915154 76308537089
     917774 95003154 67791994 0554 302384 555684
3295871228070339303655080520359026902225 74 32694 1773378330207785088164 599774
9984 35514 70304 189
     9310927886362855595 4 986664 521514 6083224 32702939865354 711714 6112097864 4
64 64 4 3256180023520004 864 169280901251955587967777 0712014 15854 0324
29272796513998214 26254 2785238361824 89
     74 4 0083764 657199183395660336509 4 970785232889

74 58814 9334 7730994 86397383182019324 4 68791919227598192870591900590754 067357185234 81186834 64 34 7785054 157828224 4 90798584 087005861205284 4 716335877723304 38082709137396889

505684 55535232618221110237312713368814 20583983854 74 704 90005360938657617777304 878307855972175388186172720052568368730086721769154 4 126287754 95032392221164 8722178615226209124 25923774 67055016125582354 6154 4 20874 4 584 214 964 7760255957274 029184 7164 53158885258827884 286855889

4 965084 270394 2989

9354 4 274 755784 884 092534 24 3675964 612654 381092025562998205154 14 8019374 7004 80357966774 5874 100884 1318118725823857854 4 84 88816682771330320050914 804 99027063386694 6909935124 8792271005092774 614 14 952914 6261051764 859906929923817599024 4 1618794 9702356571809514 4 25854 9957651792962105674 4 6002214 133673754 807986035969594 685698337977267285287592506004 4 4 184 64 3577824 036237766702987283237060 4 5274 4 2555068151809555888683589

14 753304 57011692173081904 13682196197924 4 4 604 264 9934 384 84 52732374 61911371110824 4 64 33501694 801550253284 184 6287334 92266134 5689

4 4 1390024 706633554 7078814 16054 856796686564 3266981303178362164 64 658820830050364 4 54 812922884 964 4 6164 1012502375768282189

4 551184 5805957320909394 62064 867750938024 3791289

60180082794 04 74 8174 22063327914 71284 209513701056194 32717629286857909094 932180555689

79066286289

154 73754 86731986937384 664 1958561889

9770827990016924 64 94 2519034 737770398863014 92011183528372327919965077715581634 06176196984 0722231867827012354 034 994 384 2916855650515174 38377353920322561159929756879655 74 85637139984 984 1889

8187238634 4 774 77355150135350791910818082 6989

536012524 78254 704 3214 097784 69323294 38014 725512584 376086099814 60219969863154 84 73576292080996702231230779999976689

2614 937094 813131176126725029020251125017695385831757933 24 82374 7587160195989

309689

954 294 5715238027789

223568504 8764 1824 139102326914 9165574 4 4 4 84 5124 60830514 57874 1750738717674 4 17355110130764 553789

7887522221852058613301075912720128 4 15816099012918291185666715739299809291799 14 91610004 660333292225776086756566663596534 181854 2256059884 3184 4 272181094 23181090631060596773327 84 039505960669772102777 3614 118272064 34 2985384 4 24 65877284 718517883633752819325 4 25830054 99614 614 8373504 14 191861619862910670638791195176205055 64 1054 814 8530782364 3720165399965209504 2389

04 11674 9764 36029024 34 195676224 4 68514 2089

4 56568032327777818280 4 0235317172716161384 74 5264 34 2561703004 03880716888884 214 757957281324 16306939771904 86932101774 84 934 395220889

779774 6064 13216065912354 287306634 98564 951384 299151193754 1568268804 64 034 4 074 00319164 87524 2281289

9084 9604 910887524 8189

7662954 4 394 63753621983060853026629767762297282370884 1064 0306798395704 55079864 255624 13295697069031260693727227047 9738584 906354 81194 6653533660264 3153554 561276200224 54 365014 0928707010384 5024 94 22996824 6989

4 81931106380584 89

63834 96684 23154 689

5857394 1781004 780274 31024

Chapter Fifty-two

34 361706393732266714 14 04 764 5055320685254 52777271337995989

719129335109533521837623781 4 4 828212389

8331839226954 036294 4 194 4 4 779393386294 78208565391602768654 74 2216021974 54 1625034 794 8657330874 869636214 60507966572115585682647 712564 019832368722180162737027 4 0854 6123315314 874 65319393626134 3872784 984 09826789

986196912202669754 590120334 74 871715272034 23784 8532019977394 1089

39918323993534 3608383194 4 83504 07170160500197194 0795569291694 4 124 82684 60290554 6024 805566374 9256769023585654 9630563054 99094 73833682002253272751014 7653820157189

689

1764 3861760384 66914 71270502090101667931 4 353889

81799261389

4 958205684 315254 2717333984 584 967784 219554 2284 969377538214 19875398362804 1513853270951507067783176184 9268674 924 51878878256523880787559339874 189

92394 1064 66084 284 159517680029189

9674 4 604 56234 7684 174 6284 3614 90524 099614 60913299078250767172994 8737993004 9706095219029159187881565502947 86924 994 826388639682384 956086850057999208125916980957625006325227 4 2977572235324 4 64 6312991916029527828387808637 4 3794 84 8781600798669184 4 94 4 95203389

09118199684 0014 36019370933054 7221904 71786161995211092911279170019766720202163966918 4 2224 134 9535264 054 15034 34 784 93730094 81075000992303709153882015508200330120076 04 03674 004 75028238121723533105 4 69837101009657554 88116614 28174 19714 224 11114 653964 94 08810687135316799674 89

74 2793722635135810389

988254 516055367251021364 16929003210731223 4 30072399556914 22524 64 301262735666817822859016903399525588647 0851754 284 397934 23274 925339989

2584 0392320798359932521574 3584 25230374 36661389

93863200080064 574 750880709379984 6274 709665708094 36929936107002734 53815684 8014 39818002264 97961654 983924 24 7214 9538551664 906133886994 794 4 8764 07062566016055171789

11310515789

8124 84 0674 4 154 04 38634 32180804 96035776369336965075024 96754
659653517150085997507664 0004 55954 26370119626833504 239694 09324 73254 0732174
653657712189

7863354 556824 17039103781824 2656724 4 1578184 384 94 5382562034 9781174 94
7104 6589

50823214 08204 78205399922170830963792471914 357052689

2737882963017204 5984 1639676597939924 684 5120216731557594 061085011084
015014 939584 81324 314 3264 83170638352293389

83573286296250064 53965323234 09016634 5534 97614 53977754 354
551018002272987816661057242312430623503991266927255939838704 4 68224 4
056902175272089

0597314 0317194 9939375760651704 4 3081784 3584 689

0232264 09067025582563156527103991987874 4 99600566965311694 201789

0333193079128764 04 50024 529260777573554 4 8308514 99121604 62604
07966357004 29294 14 15210785179395124 89

2931131087234 0368754 93332119971694 1558224 2253234 5269916514 84 2708074
964 9824 32091087091302719220736052823889

03337764 824 4 024 82164 3674 4 89

28389

327178724 6301295213777584 06567665034 2254 84 4 7952734 389

296263521706924 82957223372372605212148675590124 37510688636168620684
8107532525519080870082393756679930005256400041056868732134 5774 2011004 3021274
7964 04 62677207960288680754 533284 4 61163963670296167636106120956 4
09159039226759772561277082336910179793 24 02760094 7790504 9390594
990355097623285524 5692014 923380389

555114 53694 537989

64 24 3907753154 38661079617254 935797164 4 8034 4 6126662353804 14 555736764
262514 4 5905719258022229306 4 03304 94 3177399110774 5994 805184 84 34 169030124
7105284 00114 5301170159264 176031004 6687984 34 00676366135754 15938107394 9023384
59599785664 90063310019258076179659274 89

0217308818654 5124 915610084 564 92191733984 184 9364 00789

24 2534 00528851274 0978260728184 4 99362334 4 396777834 164 30328617074
655574 4 70958871066122859798 4 383289

88827786089

94 9825934 4 4 57062552084 6669336207364 5613299517534 64 9909660709934
3125635974 90296567184 6803518878764 4 37192734 32284 96757534 874
38060586839387320871071234 1196033089

3060235219350237964 75301514 1593728621182295259067018575855904
8698103361310619537044 1077208602330006694 3559822989

97200389

4 20507124 13096330124 73989

889

865016134 4 604 16369764 129918551398564 1334 8024 4 0109038204
20980509818816370765602535 4 228852064 2504 74 89

5868089

91794 66861171932503324 823024 1059805584 7663804 55213789

32305723502009715574 76025937720767760874 6814 82134
52253163020878882398535566684 084 620188776333889

382394 00596938234 755581196604 4 053660170851554 314 0928633570921594 4
8116017532965834 13334 71773027110597090517811589

0170866029901605124 794 507024 3012323067026217970114
15106820022681399975072583213035616 6794 912610054 2012864 53229800672689

00094 82097075854 10219884 8852954 59601974 73063613284
29698553852265238 16130889

665914 509124 886813 1259535362960576603197504 29504 11884 3939724 7053605789
4 79862831714 0039684 80764 2119094 14 2756812027324 54
23319593 11195239505629062 2611009964 3989

4 838164 64 4 874 5866830754 85778532874 081993757274 8521974 13718094
29677774 11722239364 1356033211909334 4 0755678783811304 519984 514 86289

80006084 838694 20621852719280187 7804 24 866808029951289

7034 73294 4 6317094 600385951254 53386835579689

0584 651723006704 4 8889

684 061086304 0612135155203874 2139284 4 96202225754 65858208669864 0604
986554 2588590814 5530994 84 34 9384 273384 217864 505139854 273974 290958570085614
62561834 95270022814 173253676539794 6912752974 70131700638354 159654 4 634 24 4
9683526350594 8534 4 74 4 7210780561078 1082964 94 264 78810025979318775639 23904
3291785327634 20375229756575274 34 08295084 54 794 701524 526089

9313885783123911751269225566757288 51334 04 397696254 03931174 933713994 4
9529356801060379694 4 59568597524 987726734 807907326761824 52335521216214 9680234
4 929254 28865514 57337565576594 5557092395334 2814 24 6290317278154 0399834 15564
198377180189

821124 7608559555189

99506207300714 034 520815503329814 97507024 4 2677264 3603387375397314 84
31374 070926654 4 92295204 2319900734 594 63931199653505680733 29814 86584 11091994 4
394 62723284 5367711284 84 736224 60633136028591059635237193871634 598696364 4
3906854 0532231931524 1354 69324 875767304 633817030294 4 7983522602051814 94 4 4
58504 9612032690923375271623551335262 34 32072194 3009358815033935989

74 4 933526957874 57278314 0396703969100170734 14
9325310220632630169252370180 12024 4 226884 92909819555117 1956120838155014 4
858365716651026908664 8717323819014 8609924 69913154 608200199270504 73056887614
189

3298108310235264 8281081024

Chapter Fifty-three

854 5022087572212834 4 134 3794 84 999727920258354 34 17204 4 25984 693274 0914
178214 394 9280179974 56598736982874 282682674 84 4 212137154 68232751128534
1652370316530704 32582833721123713760969593993754 953622322221974 659619332529074
04 24 87602513819524 26973910175637197534 3004 4 7961782504 311533150675825627 3534
34 7625253914 2515275704 78784 376788524 187196634 624 19927008025761083927 4
9762263654 900186532064 54 9951558029083985132726273219 67284 783025385221904
79278689

389

53878036869931884 6603104 3633524 37327154 69989

88111864 4 3670114 0284 2620261504 738823589

974 72814 9334 32570654 74 6370224 51887289

06125503027379190264 03965774 1760689

89

769834 5664 64 705204 716359214 4 8307099584 3064 71727507633718020714 5974 4 5652514 1885050371637738189

02969685284 4 09258193174 4 10055576089

85029232710160089

8257223817394 54 3698529654 7694 90187384 04 64 6564 373071319590114 07613174 28220388331360297085261 4 51234 90730714 7624 534 05024 54 2376366668557574 0120604 059886955630114 4 154 4 314 1696986074 03220788600313279055391789674 16355524 025076765308563224 273784 714 974 6037784 064 60934 681299187190289

275976307015984 088778174 519269014 7691030030234 9794 58511000180886606216286801110915116104 0983273088089

954 33755118718317378655877 64 87358854 4 90366879074 169182538313306362338205820154 8854 4 982788382174 24 3758054 923815972964 061963105821516709190326318730933813850113091332770930 34 25112210972155056104 913870504 2621980526024 761160750597103794 3664 7715293534 917186125066116367383304 99564 878779365697911293195878277774 0601075333724 327900097324 07256070388800871137309659634 4 5709604 1175089

4 4 4 79119162174 5516970964 84 4 76204 6174 128154 5361284 22601551301589

525862806957063924 4 4 354 780239051686133854 9861926656762276 0358234 98556919224 89

06901164 5986609615679554 154 9215758128354 09202539317080737814 650788320352665134 57070655368569928112 4 26567084 4 80177864 614 974 04 54 921184 3122762184 5224 4 10884 715075701908834 950224 3756988504 94 54 24 105726624 6094 5832095962572872030994 77654 0107398558069966198019534 500506514 501054 924 018861089

134 1730607592384 394 6124 6569861605609094 54 1772907364 0093913219567683 64 33329961999796 54 24 34 80265694 06836986706175874 131676505060271358825744 337072164 58819522613397054 5205234 4 12809231730650519 89

954 50285853835228737872869829172758078 24 2098261060609015092521109089

89

964 389

29786294 3014 1114 0067628774 9920781723794 74 62091689

98389

6189

4 8630773060274 9102670388394 33524 74 24 34 21236712177024 610116024 061118571687050824 4 04 9162389

4 34 3504 7025081364 9155155104 32725074 794 1024

Chapter Fifty-four (Not the answer)

7374 781922652059333551362553018121964 24 9924 88212992601774 080103719884 21254 74 4 7216029695002774 268507752175866917993801362584 224 17398560766991654 327570612304 5286728070763189

4 70589

54 4 061884 2131571380033984 874 0868094 14 4 6184 5854 23034 4 9514 4 852105399124 89

324 554 86659305335584 57827714 4 23774 338533920824 12776321659675383266506 30638806955691562026222594 694 14 29007998769834 4 20914 699989

79568326670904 14 13980686333251565256968787 89

922574 3279613964 3702654 314 4 639333799000819857530797 88817613374 36094 839283022338032797320386 5364 624 24 98055114 0224 692264 789

3159294 4 91804 038298364 9034 888638697564 4 14 8556085605371 7722873714 8228236864 27811365720394 74 9690693723991561003682807514 11784 737825622127759959167758 14 03853298688851365523231 39384 3174 225853562807019154 4 00776301634 764 7781261324 38024 84 21865669855274 00764 105119010954 5289

83825634 84 0704 5580809052214 76972204 287382202064 4 5111655802021581372204 6634 766333517561799050089

77808856009320814 54 1764 4 390323524 193973154 72189

209202024 74 2704 0585791354 379260097680763629 8756614 78264 4 3389

261212134 56594 4 5680104 2227616524 183764 0186734 533914 88079001363603 5284 32174 7804 0168314 67261880679364 9304 686587364 63114 8328269804 9202278762554 54 01785091774 97728294 6756929354 5166609864 194 814 58364 4 4 789

096038304 5828536989

560806656661903603 1004 5304 720024 226393881572068674 69006192987308224 84 9001681634 89

212554 33754 4 4 7580388736158658 85924 859755874 2783859992954 1709917225 11534 0254 22229692234 3661777819296533134 9674 77572209784 301938184 4 505985075080564 94 83189

6792205834 34 14 789

05102576174 90997582001234 724 4 102850794 123184 376014 714 2137829511021873589

939170816868055988 13354 69913794 537831377114 1354 9197124 34 6581093112783326621759 2227589

369934 7704 984 352519210735175737020054 5734 51305873132214 384 62087602775184 0534 89

37132376629071120552694 905300388822804 204 80821085192876107 6772814 54 89

2794 4 03227236284 124 794 319264 4 1924 307968137038294 8200586974 20150132353198720519920353877314 2158822114 85974 318238790989

1993253934 1503787689

959695804 327251777689

866125889

3954 4 201391713064 1886295106652689

60624 14 52084 4 8034 034 74 113314 88004 313864 73171584 4 6815754 8365316705126017 4 664 0760728095967213272 94 224 536104 2667928094 6977358363834 98228114 76691695969557327702827912099792608638170 17654 210151115811092683 2874

8595064 62623629925924 9694 378182229169234 3254 85361604 152514 20636925214 774 598094 19889

26814 7764 4 39053761119174 63026074 1704 14 4 9224 194 980017062386681694 6607989

24 75169718500094 2874 4 4 4 6624 100586380355863065063609572709797334 93070964 889

0760630190792334 61701974 5665624 8712884 986738267854 62689

4 512094 6229054 82754 233025173213282785316517586934 054 11184 5715104 834 632832008101152254 13119367954 561261216103174 2783210387954 82539174 314 09877065257006037671968388304 78692910032674 834 4 206684 06673515088586091662976572277996926003868273334 964 18758332118080916861857134 59115685089

314 94 04 4 819961072250233789

677989

9188725826867705377574 35124 650813798628134 8350664 31324 66270924 523654 69835174 0704 26513698824 14 33088355263194 54 754 25324 84 5884 093993784 63186733813366103100588114 64 55151877305014 130815666018061132268352963971114 624 0104 98314 84 64 604 39520061637354 2584 698260521254 538591505364 62014 16593061524 13774 3303724 64 4 1039759850015689

2102790937867860318517624 04 69599157234 0529003816760724 24 7701697815214 8615194 74 627054 614 2211256912722538159050203958330514 685850036024 20054 9094 55026826185095875 26210973991322095029544 89

58289

174 23298134 3154 06925757058801573654 5351789

274 15271289

4 1314 3182694 76902588854 78659919689

883599904 38854 2274 84 694 73118751974 88771215019159190888581326376998121590808989

69182335059079714 874 61333680397063500369555394 22590734 53693326389

696162384 254 104 794 6294 8379374 6381324 6124 08253069026914 650215171965524 2567884 7127229752667920280384 12966157502184 6811088693939925268794 39503267287008758186104 9300859750196928095204 8237571389

4 54 3884 4 24 16217566263735180336 32774 01734 12594 274 5582026754 4 027881214 092868804 1203000227063180825931867664 814 904 4 7257994 4 6704 594 238281114 87861177124 712994 0234 3531934 76389

7789

4 84 4 625604 174 54 78020529553081250254 298015709039238214 7214 574 80550269684 4 4 380960380164 4 37261953004 4 039908184 265874 8795326360174 7734 39634 74 13330292755818200084 64 886098183291707862124 37034 594 04 281501604 14 7705818564 4 13222318877793921639889

6127369924 00225160535128293723655737319319389

834 175384 39708309035853330857183693113650370081905654 504 32984 220993814 9004 54 4 54 004 4 86182214 05506052871683134 14 262789

64 4 16953339802968795175366784 755096725673907734 7181693399759001189

89

11139624 652061607188564 91192664 2694 016069590616104 4 378014 98666998284 3324 652576088257101089

9195911118083503036507974 2812307093951984 0254 801694 4 62620592363635107199014 8156774 4 0001231307254 10256056015931684 05328169973390707153720880901320654 154 084 084 8694 64 85133762274 8284 99161274 74 70532225505791833719782998021 7375914 24 34 4 714 86634 38084 599101392554 94 4 6596674 23730119121569104 84 73306980508171297273138066292296784 93165707003108305567889

79123298130375103174 67834 01120813530914 66073367511876218722324 789 683703827950123954 4 4 953967588537384 4 664 134 72024 70015885201761312154 814 3721334 7926567224 4 69179562586300306994 5836289

10381264 89

5233888076384 38188092118073979276834 12308688094 691717655267197134 112902715814 675294 4 276252132950154 3011533690389

221384 10133788327539359202090519 4 20939389

794 1289

38076595308702735507730 4 2219114 3004 3256684 624 072289

034 021711512731689

053394 67851873822784 85158224 704 84 12773926828056517260376 4 4 584 4 0068284 66737354 4 825924 96916214 239033889

318117011389

1315019222854 107381814 5229259218514 85752524 7618384 80775838298666675567628883100860152635 89

35863571274 21777289

5154 4 58312934 70980084 7178289

672734 129037076071597089

78389

934 279262557381889

563194 050727520873259994 5654 56085868553582631337084 934 064 13934 91374 91790772182285311600 94 98270366792789

23587884 316084 918389

533623615765768334 22289

59270239391538681195815299606 64 52081886184 389

697200189

3567854 89

4 94 2216512361017184 737604 606038296164 4 2733117304 025869985215372164 775363206607206123292932396 24 078004 74 28067808124 54 299279509350514 3976021192911303780217039508295099069 94 4 3939119550034 0721574 14 801775922997193282716303971339380034 926791334 165089

11394 64 24 7966132094 725089

81957237504 91133129166984 2737114 89

58662864 9336133970303624 7163012832100708 4 15202627689

963068189

6952666694 4 051675113293786905003 4 12004 284 17394 2954 14 4 584 4 4 754 124 6771850871030194 976373064 64 56618634 94 0656615955590222038813571361768234 7784 631098854 74 80314 1607518313054 4 034 2811270350719599014 203058814 923214 884

12935694 4 52964 317031319035779377391901656912577178069851218011520363784
71823289

4 9534 4 4 65514 626784 6820263039666301990692261062324 0862574 936674 4
0265813971924 80133160604 12804 3094 0301178183953384 569734 77787554 9650522671989
20398064 65088098765959904 0268354 5829084 04 8874 3590121024

Chapter Fifty-five

85707190569558518229964 816324 5701570374 833507162561778784 026024 807954
364 314 2774 0975204 62960077059523215937839265060584 763183164 5394
6086912913902970752924 5752831122063165307794 559970935880191017954 784
68222029813794 967339008709934 83523659252153174 780914 929635957680364 164 531574
1984 08294 9704 24 039023534 0265922135259853080324 3178585774 06056900395174 96624
783114 6154 7074 7101524 109270990190694 60555923968305614 80772653739984
99618880204 526136957223089

07368225836972534 67329304 34 90796231583862612634 4 4 24 086314 1034 9974
0365508692160500 4 6280979394 25957370775224 21277559627928584 177313693090364 594
36384 4 93982339291854 89

5536764 735608789

89

97197780703866209274 631851985085192685262 4 5382587024
957380501099381632387082022856 4 4 74 02189

03503702051586824 571125520231530878090161 94 37053871768164 4 829394 4
91186589

768122858228286305889

861029605283254 4 38604 524 159887904 3704 7737737136850213539382265394 90234
21710889

78371005174 981759702068682570272597123999 04 77731332089

0674 211212008218398677787056562 94 24 69382004 2378134
9130666302875875209256 4 7732731674 6369664 74 625706120034 671564 09034 789

6314 818682134 598061272968256 54 557674 98591972867379753810674 21738580194
8693932923297854 5561007900054 7253305167081854 95508295733164 530389

66728057387828058258833867 4 395672132016122364 2719023999031850697809 4 84
72980377051720009130562696720528 4 31664 964 904 631103134 0090378152174 924 34 06714
4 6624 52624 7884 4 4 797032670809204 796602152536229777984 13035291824 91667754
73338610975771752089

257006270953984 19276724 6810212714 64 4
65163618290386785573635507001183672 4 154 289

54 04 774 834 3284 34 8374 7564 304 5274 4 5068084 4 294 3288003263534 81326604
76017214 22694 0034 962856397025725628371882800 89

54 76023866630654 974 704 534 984 37664 0385989

4 64 5814 4 8053195091992594 514 98233613653904 4 1231674 071296632618704 24
19884 078656034 6889

4 4 0980735651117190884 1621313370383284 7527158014 0233374 0874
6055090197337083604 720090201650957663760378637218832003863900863187002521159 4
3278393284 79264 70562069061394 0364 883094 55202394 3727600115564 4 876784 4 754

0835616039984 88513772923034 32353009793967833698300912777999794 971704 6285314
1004 3534 9333822674 84 96581775235312719601590617282 84 6213714 010305334 392027034
5130194 9107034 4 6174 565771792191324 14 37364 969396904 89

6573282575669132764 5310834 4 56871594 4 990050920224 04 757994 214 8514 13924
54 572532607827164 7130569958137234 89

622724 1015135814 63393598573917624 05734 4 62715784 14 3189
580687674 4 88008034 90104 7315958190724 14 64 172911598289
6970259377776750067320383336759992089
814 111989
857577054 569008806673510534 70372132934 89
0554 554 97205353010557324 69661053806609950702754
75226267683165272527954 83314 536193916719510302515194 171781239124 4 82761114
532218866777176734 174 064 523789

93015037104 211023223884 776937314 25534 798388888374 1324 601694 84 94
52299051071089

5587932162056322085156530074 0795055924 94 4 5974 351034 91904 4
1133791566366617724 6177234 2505771351604 4 2663034 3126850879654 1039734 739274
5290514 055124 1030298362589

336235834 26786553204 778075390909094 6014 04 3806764 3829114 78302964
6518215386189

2014 007114 94 551862692991324 7375729922061152524 782916654
5756956638325114 786725256097578274 064 4 3804 60707154 24
617738733768071930679719130310725974 71709514 887374 74 695034 9152024 2571874
3866194 2079828728831057102815793 64 02714 634 5327984 734 94 139024 20822973866014
37354 856090802957134 69226533118264 067965254 4 34 989

9969780862934 70385536157001037969986 4 6180680289

328572972529014 2829019704 05011170939604 017994 00772790730059574 064
53592391666388114 4 59764 1874 26920093782970522564 0556982994 8514 511625396658674
223630839350814 87782114 69714 5156264 2183972324 51972563939261864 8161829774
385324 1064 34 925254 1686264 3522704 313723804 66259855686036939297507794
0069921092726870253264 58806166692255729635224 4 204 85867181204 50934 2716663189

05192624 5014 9084 600688052235094 4 4 34 658274 02258290512950304 9799614
016607725564 4 874 614 62709786889

732567210192923009824 54 7654 3800864 374 00109757236660924 13723186800774 4
762686294 526391724 89

70267674 56792734 86954 2632962933077993830606951 74 2589
565375330331982513 74 66974 6258716171967671157859591 29389
4 64 1900519594 231162554 265589
03604 04 2611724 9989
093064 050953199964 6107199705169382815884 24 91614 923639600111384
53259171654 02764 954 76617295659031279164 9517360294 213628187264 59267767827689

6029664 97224 763374 234 588532554 32357319176321653 9724 35014
685762391656504 3387680021015694 4 35823608634 84 5735010253174
638070912058156818796838583 94 5104 2367958767056686080265 94 82952325594
2029210268875291154 36922289

4 71789

8363306284 089

7730393136992191114 714 816289

4 383234 24 291014 4 32554 651237764 29921208276392973771594 064 13974
05209230530964 0784 16316554 3554 24 02370608217818299215828215654
0176766976612089

914 4 806005952990654 37623636120263059889

51007723575565165921971
4 516783674 355129084
5111362955595308758670837780019199618165568310
04 55702282789

191613024 0361835164 122316270904 54 293979674 128235084 33094 52202160626684
2689

197180814 9654 8307692214 68092724 37721832739709295506
7524
79298131156698823159331096989

93912254 34 4 7935774 560661126904 64 296564 074 054 192882264 7854 79797974 4
55922998213530029315531271761722186319
7089

82235311610694 0684 8815755289

4 81620820918166724 8131289

08104 62376990701322935328
4 4 500814 089

4 15189

31109879654 07214 61827574 8055858024 35381615139187720
04 4 4 5850657984
7920254 5694 4 114 779663992297905320277130234 997864 4 034 4 21824 9616320189

1811804 3264 78311151594 681114 8164 7264 54 77617634
978713086688756952976260303166684 1214 634 302624 4 0794 6869782859874
1839503171394 290013559087722557
7053738582054 889

53169601806863232587915107
05889

327168594 2207156076389

0785976077655084 303731907717669314 5523913518622363114 271160854 4 5804 084
7500024 79987582300587088265
4 914 62207872672680636374 5375980674 164 794 4 84 814
97389

238754 7284 5934 38752792867664 4 3272564 7955615698313724 625104 54
28885007334 89

51302504 367500924 1929034 354 3601085669208294
26185038839729213803592097852633
4 813384 99592725301325821086087156279
94 1191224
2653301351854 683014 7588361727164 8821814 9835028778855753965978
89

0610683222861861952982764 025772256605724 74 4 655934 03252865816014
3865185373616114 163075572970379994 4 665114 114 054 0794 2714 75377811114
255133972834 96115287533038864 4 3281608116519009719605585
04 0319934 5652798222234
2807299181713054 322774 87592302825294 80265505717
4 0861992523706296814 98124 204
2637768598819539599684 75068012031703913507600700194 92084 8368879638514 24
058353860689

68037754 4 207064 27165194 190884 4 81774 90953805258104 4 824 739134
9962282964 3783561309374 57114 7615093589

594 57926535184 4 4 5824 4 0734 84 4 89

10093955756022910560624 4 84 561256004 382122790034
27907039318710752380856389

211364 039358354 01058207371156598072563030772823585173136193707794
9085709984 74 01336685002084 1298191122359596968225964 54 5883214 3393571194 834
7789

26834 5889

74 007603069394 54 021357274 76634 284 866657596679093779764 676816301584
881677064 60389

706583275923630814 09299550394 58378138514 3772011353236289

264 20377834 84 121359508214 072712089

533733168788100034 2084 0576180389

0377556602679235794 264 582504 634 2858264 05824 664 704 1364 1994 74 7054
661183354 387910763314 524 20005378089

9955034 74 1739824 797089

6323065778806615087882093271595765 54 4 84 261688320589

4 02879672117198053728362 4 06561189

0799913802883209 34 331124 69126814 14 321820670235390665254
965636176151324 0156795689

10354 88079558258253280000374 0724 31650591530590694 165524 4 0264 4 22265534
657082709714 384 284 185626503226274 9319629589

024 754 16534 57612824 0935354 0627014 4 00709114 820954 833364
9386576628566250273021 54 4 2597984 538294 81913014 999381683903264 080298234 88774
14 716824 958784 8181800555206691015613702532736823984 64 02589

1880120337650092064 77291158684 97705912814 2539364 63325614 93813809881934
729589

219122373029584 34 157505102177387600274
257006713072132715585027183263165673229 74 165569938789

6932382888666604 7534 6398736332850561625 4 8773854 35688300572624 974 0754
685155054 4 77920664 951596322925802293266172296221390772 54 74 952264 62179754
6086820993904 54 206571222320193765629382978088618030619528 4 93132084
96738723326039 4 74 8697307938567850075 94 09394 78674 254 9882024 204 154 7066719824
06807377080366075125 4 64 1737104 593569506195610338555273220981093912275 4 6654 4
307152856539660824 821860992013074 8257076988534 89

4 69154 3197165697224 766161617667065198873 4 4 4 89

6624 58628625152225384 2901560874 089

954 34 2176951754 1033533634 03734 750381964 56961620860504 864 14 14 584 92224
4 53185569392104 60917094 9935123097068124 33674 4 99298196274 38739313209704
0166953757317336392 4 066206733660664 354 6095104
78033905319817058757712382737802524 734 99031335004 6117788777274 76072034 257314
815970711634 54 0909184 23175198274 4 277637794 0258294 9213724 61614 24 4 1229924
93589

4 614 34 008809389

14 4 670032034 652189

83727289

74 23974 3797153198307296124 285026965615884 66394 4 84
055677766860581950531 4 83370976868517186306676 4 959789

06788870683150525108802156270017004 2329256525775535714 74 8807170330384
064 6594 21313222560288183751881800277819930167 4 099864 4 10627199825274

5569596806164 23014 9058371294 2032835260868134 6820686611208819994
2560871923959865755990688 4 794 4 7989

57284 7189

71157601126635232332118719974 66584 003580218134 04 365355789

510224 096323064 4 6703623964 96910274 014 15384 02618604 00252104
0701078265991504 4 97189

394 63765389

74 2339594 4 4 78094 125964 4 679388105954 017706171034 931790601028584 81794
286927768025160634 6981864 876158623370152516023637181787999034 3795955115086514
54 0258797264 23200572504 4 4 4 194 33171201374 68254 19070853107215208512693984
662801771110264 24 4 5638079158824 956674 34 92875534 221533673980070184 14 59689

064 0693638164 1534 6937335804 134 86216823628124 85519628207372517116 4 4
71004 84 339267712904 70954 4 982177124 5997353794 989

5925018192667009919231981513968720392 4 0781317332882274 061834 89

93689

1596258827794 34 1812597822374 6823356556966161707037739 4 24 555386021304
334 9364 0075319533984 9108699633356133084 982004 6220523794 212611273864 697734
352984 0614 1202933574 769854 283798507314 2302960860064 5839020326683297106 64 74
85928028070622289

4 11984 6852371184 62881782523378018175736273865633857652511 4 589

76914 25173865797681334 5533125961089

21679675992162004 7777736601739698157005189

30556320934 768057520823924 70930750564 865354 014 7096925863324 4 753524
0023579514 20808860993523690 4 97927164 952973307312176270227758280584
3309927781993804 3921726811176593651677 4 634 85868115239136038172399380 4
361913708704 178324 58368707326879275915124 213279306924 93680672567164
09379581154 374 10084 4 74 31807984 798184 56229533783159209 4 370585987930674 314
9584 21280917714 69371599883933836596763332855084 5214 4 871734 9872982802287224
59721110033706788519570863 64 6932674 715906123201811286192207037816689

8254 061531830765384 3983956690719804 8513952994

03331186528088123217077735132700970934 3772864 506905524 832018864 054 4
5912131117904 4 127994 9017804 606511934 62138351820079194 17118694 779020864
787750881187224 4 77634 3972876005334 911972357654 068682019368086771886 4 154
3680800990685123604 6326960994 085099039694 83621715707186981568085994
3192755078361763106352286 24 4 35829757772397161712 4 4 3900078527257874 4 254
55388265166580154 504 94 4 15164 016924 4 989

04 26834 5734 56261734 0205714

0117938253155396691786508532861602277977618284 4 8212867294 6293714 9110911635104
4 93201078007237074 4 9634 9256912189

04 9313573617672737075794 89

8819870814 803294 5608027014 24 574 02799289

15695074 9771877632590121855832116833 24 5638324 6354 264 1366304 74 4
2069533906874 61804 874 2695730825289

2854 97755704 4 6553072537265354 4 909165505854 4
90500908073608133007772880591762113 4 0781270220715772179918 4 69199964 764

765500100977660172796 4 696655224 4 5266993376993129003168352117905283272874 954 4
751298134 025062913810954 9668572838779529050 4 4 2889

66151554 22823760174 4 9137351386273975389

8374 2878364 570857778791777228294 183786250926281394 514 14 0283818107124
99370857034 96006797685633696864 76720810794 0134 332689

9229203210797152854 32230936878389

824 9784 699775589

777584 16212889

6661183097189

39561805589

888734 7882238586298360614 8281970638853766387023699719056887914 2001500589
32781576679554 1265615324 07775118370166626802333634 5078784 13669795089

5864 028584 92504 04 84 93379617118032804 55707969321708308871176259199594
3564 4 139714 9528262209871179393056 4 12254 9381874 3814 308084 72755308389

1726934 6294 89

967863754 9361154 624 333630992676994 68701922308814 839034 814 606660954 4
524 703883761208316514 2010076318337589

34 939996200824 800998604 62830624 324 904 9275733571918058260532 4 93551274
1107358603022530576982 04 994 600214 5986397578505832139101615820 89

3810253664 04 3283856221560504 81874 5659654 5074 87713704 55025814
58868787094 1584 14 23636958253905004 4 10260672794 34 510615024
7722806223509663315736125 14 266794 34 14 074 6652063534 54 658392226114
6323557839399370970262019162213 4 73885624 5398302016554 714 62084 762972652574 64
2687233863623153135535568166360519035718 9

524 4 664 237586619804 114 4 80252199013025958 9

34 9990701834 64 4 31270680599004 32561387112104 50689

0557506790767625630503 84 26262251372906522565 4 94 2654 82732134 9984 84
1605395004 71824 9856560184 7314 4 9074 2691964 574 5265811357026510716238773 34
6883372589

977864 367259174 11557016552924 84 2063152187379159524 64 4 83195251598063394
60374 2186735024 198039034 29172882058569352678665815820119587606982523964 929234
89

14 6794 4 3084 786574 974 5083669623296079018 9

3079624 4 5874 84 3725174 9229859571678125574 84
2331673035806137323872079009336336925 74 24 5789

19538675866761134 125824 7160307089

4 316874 964 9125716727634 4 4 3030554 358794 3967279839160550213514 833324
054 4 82959124 01218783134 0304 59294 4 16212927504 9984 50167094 64 84 9534 4 091524
7183778255760029397 94 25014 89

34 214 63386758834 589

63870261127297794 8184 53034 4 4 2314 713124 4 0784 98214 84
6735862732653628625501039736030179 4 6321255354 34 2329834 6504
28782992697952507621176604 16274 9698363594 9960324 34 9579121030004 62192014
6211722288584 4 1330174 29091519974 56174 12214 254 815101274 882630094 6974
83512300721702238025163626 54 24 573166829154 74 4 4 2181002777612760729789

2368258611620666702210658425698166382179841203878410264487735566199629191877992434892368258611620666702210658425698166382179844

7623591813120793421262858085245471431809776763721364584043359927672555158766872926818976235918131207934212628580852454

864 664 5773718156713727127327069174 4 607683702302787924 24 38214 038304 398781254 70062137965560074 4 129064 71083531304 20289

291215214 634 5225675356683968136278189

9954 4 96762854 591729513324 6231268627120730703168674 086601595709916631586465223887456234 4 964 51599074 97920994 59034 3139214 94 067984 830272254 5724 30514 35304 54 90785504 685756559850314 1863084 834 865010575124 4 928756718289

912764 5724 6072592552964 3384 64 54 7294 520764 1184 4 3817902834 2584 64 092984 568121756169389

3596597574 04 2929557152915076829707802023978916969252199569167435795107281101358448780347612045865179866632782748015063649022752319205745215355728802481958656569366630546997062951144

34 1813654 08817027519036327982203827038208934183

835124 557790353616534 4 6984 4 2851334 54 83864 35254 810831284 9983289 4 18172916120839071390684 868789

2138101036796504 4 35251204 22214 65614 364 722014 989

4 200214 3834 4 20124 097014 6623634 385827269296108625255251189

21290714 83604 5667955951686533053105451019783216574176268285593469187149247242547912327152909308767435328387505631625953639199685925802257094130454164678572397376266871116228209347413738395309745385622839540124 847808174876622182715157013569546601451452768614882194513411059801959086376897851029044

785102904 74 54 766574 38215181134 51025024 65128213078825731151825135732082734 220695504 162056314 24 4 4 9297757854 18104 7996194 4 4 2936394 66739813593669111845157777992643506435444778907866885667636555675101330203920641099446748697238001890185771237393333518911517615291790335703578359795955444

07866885667636555675101330203920641099446748697238001890185771237393333518911517615291790335703578359795955444

01857712373933385189

11517615291790335703578359795955444 4 89

78594 989

54 24 664 7154 32770670827265189

4 3783794 8064 0334 2214 337724 04 78678694 06306620720565027737002585237439345579494371757594822239484821309090539231169866409648373506830772494450468792906337053879637101170440903752038526402962570300441750894

84 780077854 74 006909831594 10928873587189

53394 73582884 73512024 777514 4 152864 14 33301523760202571654 66393135151695802886647315383404234437057963764866980429174989

7294 330983715121568619296541976790875435900658851911949101426075596946536884456188099014507149283559365332865878073446563488103298867967164678135738438860393567548126731638346326081522267743361034256279904458071024

37290860556394 1984 4 0975135534 8193689

89

4 4 3858562953654 99862588604 857134 9208874 795326091097703034 6501294 04
02286028361334 2235054 7868311753104 804 3788706828828150004 082704 666900724 4
6076608132834 86164 716381696784 4 6015551761653711887635152359278589

75553158127353916830280196887220255186609054 34 784 14 5591634 664 587131734
67524 04 2320513784 66514 54 84 852108274 3372800134 86724 5068256794
12532619761659887652396688873925214 079984 9352814 127096654 2050697694
79109091969184 310175731322507064 33908790786086732900306398353516515980074
053082689

6024 17037023267069764 4 70297602604 6981576139529220964 31184 1219908124 4
32974 534 969714 03552504 2861389

84 2059873557626554 3534 72123109964 1807557394 304 984 7583589

77867534 082777525594 534 690720294 9290138613691171938131736016 64 766254
974 35511923723190337566 0399554 24 4 778394 4 298351828774 24 64 123279166224
8726116615311955651531837930374 4 830710564 919086376924 64
303925333281823210265162984 3824 79889

4 0816153152609817835820514 204 757574 239190790661089
06172633363527535883672852532356699956862701830812167 4 05280180002553689
929336938678811674 4 07772991654 278804 4 6784 1356200936297554
56915180767133129637553 14 81657990907293104 13796284 75994 17790724 89

099883994 6581298870509883672688 4 172624 5600654 68114 4 80637174 295084
587982931253382289

57064 26355589

519574 7921004 74 87800990674 7134 9081771165970278 74 004 84 85584 6184 4
36218804 5597553613978187711001600120973806585206022 74 673984
3219801950690953316230 4 589

82917616258601136021828 9

3530594 6736287128555704 204 874 035807380175224 160105364 4
9207270031358736274 4 654 707779352664 84 4 64 08067183202372794 2014 34 4 7234 74
16804 98214 3532190661854 299254 6902783902394 6936756585504 71520114 175000886374 4
375280986335535666305314 4 74 278010855994 6161239902956286531638 3085174 79794
3117702616621107506672591136795657312610790687 4 2527132102089

34 204 306864 4 26562190889

801026878816775863339198793606817796800152073864 58111864
3322230027606609792372 84 9188165221926276820901885 4 780389

4 4 35603204 24 33072568734 606173702324 526804 36617589

619974 4 4 61169110304 86059055319970563600863393574 6768254
93273026102929726522199970137 84 74 56683369278196032684 1205387250396773387 4 10094
30233106594 985975756289

4 4 08874 94 502324 4 7104 514 115759283854 31904 3656099794 4 1778694
5650590867372794 05018103589

133007802251836704 71294 78583932589

4 520337371154 096525172614 324 58213651094 92864
963727906756677570290788108 24 521987372794 03819995024 9285273634 074 36172234 914
601313374 18826157775394 4 998175824 4 4 937381706204 95051672294 24 285374

71667761788064 4 34 75674 224 09659208038034 162784 725694 2682902292521252384
858533734 79136715924 694 9973608350100904 1599916137804 84 15807766179309191594
71885690996102325600636796509775882954 3573818629851803285984 7704 13724 3664 89
514 614 50501920694 4 69100554 51753162806533052264 0076777089
331089

8674 7592363114 24 9211964 73798385954 25577854 4
79230575068063861269020901325063079395192221338609185950651259 9662111567524
7703172613236327036 34 23717204 669236175272964 37171794 84 5104 62385604
25822273820574 6694 1639979217811594 1355964 64 692984 83067092014 2577974
2380093529530764 2131187963032500384 984 64 28603634 0724 9831285559398096274
86824 4 319578185903888755009025913675504 37589

14 720260583621377664 2009090107059305338719095934 8338330299912816614 4
9330234 88324 286278094 50374 4 594 19962277192591212973961871592020 84 7315534
698082291794 5574 1106929562277074 64 6829225064 0769884 4 04 7590191734 774 14 664
989

2635236134 717021650665605904 73280364 96824 398368514
81673729696986157231072880503086554 2054 6534 599832179968137693852187938 64 71374
1529934 84 8299188089

5775760669754 96074 25734 89

97204 9994 4 5924 74 776550655881309885779153221253 4 8254 266184
2900833581533004 2553324 053214 2124 83604 3612819221729578384 4 4 800154 6002989
50501182389

64 630978560709107880102 64 9379376565094 718793225833884 4 60889
554 615294 62664 0019608389

113091285689

074 9524 4 10992955918508708629877 4 924 629350984 3054 163189
2065189

010221083687385076860 4 4 955836700884 4 971994 14 71180764 4 13202319502904
39872981974 058817957555924 94 324 694 154 7994 05009578634 64 910789

35958277278660074 156011277589

27156974 66918567208804 6158595689

73929234 64 6086518259734 809876278032735783122824 239714 91807934 9952189
64 89

14 9874 89

11954 4 660184 64 8597939334 32798169521734 8104 730074 64
8312530680755197063807910667955 89

87664 530004 5068524 334 584 4 5014 194 3807605732159724 289

33294 0953577690289

2813273095037334 4 1374 4 4 84 24 04 965267264 9123074 5760280033902974
672600719069651789

305684 6085704 8624 192192189

55295012064 9938297904 522189

071154 4 9969937914 4 34 089

777511702614 082584 014 4 4 1535739125752687821120 4 77956764 3328875396972624
4 7318790329525014 7526864 259374 5614 354 879964 0235550255624 1286564 18887114
95639054 7794 27685872504 1127991197852527863555532605 4 907754 1637281878794

216675674 85785614 162304 3363824 0765037880156019880957723804
87988087768681885315507155213567754 5824 8621074 5365289
04 229917221564 124 329654 859604 04 76034 01089
60793000197018816034 0187066876734 9301168067625375834 10194 4
93959959751799294 5290138196724 8764 294 353034 94 0384 04 54 89
0206908114 5170358019381915900539253854 9904 281164 4 3209598104
29725600989
398297814 28018158679033616012834 089
1824 265607696572754 76319967224 533077566356514 9889
24 0332801785290967159121559220796605920051664 715113084 01574
7198573315595081 4 9313274 4 386096777289
684 56286694 79813650313566094 4 529386858762164 72384 194 726675264
8279780364 61664 61654 6009384 3200963866510587938358 4 0874 963614 1970634 37324 4
074 4 061759639504 054 3023084 204 5311689
261869054 774 551230814 2928671314 54 78724 93672262714 0194 8058072089
56072954 0266035730001659184 6228694 4 29707353592797791314 154
5723636680561351033735 94 16057986935094 4 5930764 5925364 3501294 91834 074
6568221068024 32954 4 7211988604 20889
704 4 877259785222935514 4 14 35958666171084 05761912964 8024 9689
5729633619081064 734 29291580124 92334 1595072790860874 734
7297779283102211703600785 54 576950931364 786905913019289
750813682069374 76624 4 0979739060858195703694 795621733909224 235687871954
4 8887076554 04 1753864 89
4 94 700125053265954 906591158579312704 8165934 568764 7710613834
5165728635656730814 4 8107224 136252029771512301152163664 36175554
15377731353126073673 84 5116106084 151358374 964 99914 4 6718312384
7817266127832291011902305693 4 267889
74 76884 530592788790534 903105077614 2554 29962938754 84 175196399791206714
87710566996732225389
13932234 01564 4 5850150383589
7166317796965033760872633 4 1625665152168570773753 04 0224 794 4 0398754
5693099761184 75950363021128888392 34 4 9592670037904 2225710280651298054 54
695532114 95375827664 9718670663197079169226050790 89
218874 0761776634 72692934 300002854 4 4 5172960164 7189
01564 1206994 30998616936685189
8334 01054 86629594 89
94 6569035360554 1570293708695036832258132391 74 0011335789
12283864 381866214 276391120167628509170158013239 4
0797165867875199335922606774 097310151174 22689
023963220013016501117008 9
64 085660915964 199602020603998595167599336164 60872516105373830608301385 4
70114 691786335380234 1074 17724 977129694 982389
334 74 6097814 666330889
062394 1931970797684 886220394 4 89
6652185530855371967667509635988051779 74 7261793032691283182674
86205780926525652903 4 2801908827059014 054 66374 70013833025889

3616017150154 888689

359105694 4 04 4 97217202113924 564 84 74 98885836600119303093340 0504 24 819094 8084 6789

876003827669218171908676966018297820355992071 89

77804 29236183663066794 5726051889

60538234

72875932823011951586555180178283133565830986137316525935030805823962559082865729 2138654 7219577931224 335914 73237524 03786908253602164 6294 813204 884 57398705136724 63824 650599873114 6037622534 97782210301014 54 298751138224 4 8213673526737210704 666777974 24 2250838584 64 887294 9096005218614 774 771519966024 65522606962127062085 4 16878723951599782686120792232886 4 955994 71294 39200099676084 62614 4 5296688181911180 94 4 889

919558814 713799314 81529329582516076010711662 4 951556593720289

3034 513965776120215825001792716582114 74 93989

8252164 1313983316292159116787863114 90350370804 67291134 675664 57367760316704 4 711872286977774 937204 984 11552534 2283689

364 6994 865992816389

0293333295967050233310631864 54 71594 61989

21174 69604 4 074 7930112114 1664 974 92276966387934 1360554 362801356521885916919160126501703 4 734 92198577912155996554 507884 590280024 1979283614 68861669687294 0673265794 4 85514 12102933164 76780504 320302389

29162094 96994 094 62681126884 776194 192988872830204 53254 835559564 56104 9750752610524 4 2558093862734 2063589

27768284 4 2281295814 64 734 7367073622559728294 37263774 877683992863763234 53936634 4 50584 64 032220274 9734 15024 87576599102151954 4 83914 14 89

4 5282238326814 83980519970765592688 9

83154 4 7157695118315551061873006768568 04 057123078324 33568627813031698684 34 0855208154 14 852556772088289

5194 03587858372024 54 4 78168634 6084 119703605994 69204 205022389

5050999054 74 622524 73281286675507560592665702381967985 4 4 3697384 303634 755135301014 22313185966598355017290912266356068396272 4 4 3084 04 652362865284 2323814 234 99086766091580811529985673188270001310938215761911329659314 57997811998234 26305914 11983389

4 1256260215214 74 556185978394 0816914 55551300017513102083825563173616215 4 5903512910618001537992129 94 8114 0928264 21522700318799959583363724 14 3264 7124 37805197524 4 525862986609139765363120503 4 85519687014 26164 2737394 4 25538704 104 0934 01178690284 8317324 4 4 66964 3839274 132175880980004 94 988615024 55683932136997226039513159990952783701 4 54 80127595279256570668760339 4 30121291197850593657 4 394 130654 1784 68202190033810503607 14 95296968271934 0824 9954 0824 216163965539009310071 4 4 638876203134 9134 077562755620587774 807984 394 581194 951882007132052594 0334 4 2134 00124 368874 61101510266689

01067251610584 2324 5264 855139823924 004 35721956683073657863 4 636284 71394 7718760514 23987077753537119885 4 4 676572934 63584 69884 781033914 66784 7854 70873151504 290874 24 592394 613261089

2919503710118254 923184 2072104 3794 2006267224 4 936264 3509595503375838171951054 4 31168732796056753298291613125754 35682524 564

650081228052263681461159753211991706603643597448082885621932267393686560625
42938224 900619956077533306524 64 84 4 3072734 8720887976729269681474974 85326374
60821151712272174 34 4 6121372624 336324 01184 3291889
863711234 758307389
74 10591681818816689
5595371823995831091589
558651551079391105153715928239197272385189
34 595024 177790551515157264 975708724 2876794 4 097314 530204
0959076917387500961326483707455953415351331344900038752803101337856441911474
2350224 52362008865534 205354 85956209777634 859173787806212255440225925273 84
830776517999637382300909619759380174 7525783079615632336266463730838 9
57384 671116709275064 4 1574 7632824 210968186670214
20776326837552607761110 89
889
4 4 964 673277534 39014 91089
61636184 14 4 3514 02764 58122289
605060381554 65315732310359157359227589
1134 925690093560714 7977688700731954 1022834 27174 87574 9070918716304
7623887234 09696302534 07824 74 65097250027224 14 5260335082791705095244089
37573333123198203021541635078677826550932171378171231371611421231812 44
0806330981536074 37639502654 25574 723877774 795160370760254 8634 89
4 8281530335202194 134 64 669637514 3271528080291002816293441826 4
108275919524 95181736937113651514 537697574 63035503968815577039389
834 87154 9884 01323876915333088608396152038792659834 262724 31774
9276862696354 1310684 65624 4 84 34 931165089
66874 84 4 6934 71034 0534 822954 84 4 04 24 94 4 54
80290150087120911679176586065278724 81257977534 74 7880316689
003510874 58568174 54 970704 9735995711339834 554 36889
4 8216100537152614 530056399124 24 4 53996258031328022857815556753370517961 4
3359354 83126071990025851110866754 29079991703537006064 3683886576034 3284 2134 674
9363284 798134 599509524 4 594 1366688588636535801656 4 396724 55889
7521380576361590214 84 215833508687176912138 4 576004 4 3756081874 54 84
7305378791606854 309384 0810194 972061059938135377730874 30936080254 374 6183604
36914 874 11272220989
0114 767287794 789
539517337789
4 112656204 674 80077129380534 584 076556161636714 03281364 5067389
6217852090789
2224 64 3916798604 3804 01984 8760595357572978 4 80805364 654 17964 74 34
1632080188152262997279175361841901057253910235261006661285793861284 82872115114
4 3312174 8164 4 04 0056183601867286327932539692823 24 26014 000725989
95097051264 68119851380702881169297 4 70365138827816180181 14 314
6872793323314 54 315102504 8027376973590692969718888 9
34 54 531535369515189
87596889
24 6757887794 34 75069709594 8389

18709199985678213907843263703165798784 08076134 7005954
231533063135629197234 7631112370126374 3716988364 569939180204 02360170654 84 74
104 4 8271684 9915119737619157080068754 31889
672294 91535191956193124 78770104 88364 90034 30712202169327164 4 873789
074 869716889
055669789
34 95574 82685994 538815934 2379901066924 553808660356930934 74
851627199700083726662594 609163691191866834 08760398160534 57187304 4 88378784 4
5994 564 1066194 64 9282790298714 4 851382966227706977101867972627 4 836234 505524
98684 334 62175825351994 89
358389
264 000821604 2578581501014 868869194 4 13913566869688314 4 5986211992334
9722584 93374 1055324 62372231784 1154 04 22579197837762605724
9768611808885686579798004 50074 36559961684 9105084 9723073534
5599811561675513166841 957334 4 75132922964 4 29136515799663255384 794 50766103289
684 869876281724 6534 1810383001694 34 52175880854 96074 784 90075673039704 74
97994 124 35126184 2137150277561668273690261688150889
2134 9350732182693228066051823157630541 6072303671389
874 83779334 0501584 1980710583153109134 51714
39567188012503059886950631165441 0619618064 7080736123767536839502282 4
398752860510511351814 191973795694 693638681274 53165281063503834 6828357384 4
05514 22934 8007993668210804 4 93606862164 600676634 4 830319224 9589
3155954 04 581694 9724 13680574 9636567933079196367152569807186187 4 7311974
596214 34 4 4 7874 53875567679230213614 8597286303389
4 182374 504 989
176974 00714 2884 239766806283172901190857 4 0325033854 5222354 03375989
4 4 0089
7932960374 12054 60354 384 18200763258809362869789
359558085094 9756506799535033 4 58370680057239672681329 4 6214 0754
013128286368823074 53773754 9664 4 8767066237058674 528560526287684
371031208597830707 74 29889
4 2333196659933706724 709689
52524 9854 4 58209814 394 92120793934 365568025694 559226089
3704 379680883059217354 99028081872394 2350083166725862989
89
188652170704 85809184 394 5174 164 56009022597384 114
5776221030576886909260019619975636 4 9835723155371164 8007804 19034 0734 99583084 4
14 5512294 28177602152104 9358131823966276787157371 4 998284 14 080368819714
2273883020874 50157398585239725106689
56996234 9628354 9272734 5082689
1202714 7525704 27050611184 594 64 71828532054 54 272334 51594 08698624
119906327074 618266795601170127525835086 4 73884 9204 602785712850234 784
6753390313187862966 4 955207064 5507689
584 3839186767906678569 4 775621300377608024 518082734 525214 320551606331504
036994 154 86061306759533659716800235921608 9

4 7814 04 681853314 71060954 683369162184 806558707134 10551936174
51037101599216136199509708650137780533889
759398836693787395 4 822789
683361381628700251093980230769216 4 0166695991773931224 83908264 4
791280998578064 05324 34 091371862188532304 910289
0113716108308680874 86723811585974 2181565370929674 4 655184 9292875004
065158071920282805299224 4 4 1627354 322382564 9525174 24 6715774 82689
6121618525639989
365694 4 505583510328185664 1319976266974 3911116778094 87179369657369037614
319223834 766554 63730888517770884 4 96832380581866104 9089
0214 7878769073115712614 1234 5364 96390084 26994 4 708025514 624
680875023203989
773654 60713304 3284 17053734 4 1390389
3234 84 2503181688302691387388 4 5884 794 203557989
1651177287920689
3386316827004 3214 70084 24 675785294 16604 6964 0375384 119123764 3274 38684
1834 063376908656334 24 691994 1284 4 66004 86512177804 327689
855184 0227751809879011069676 4 58190953231321128789
09014 9768694 69812633598854 1954
55671757126766788371557631267027615259777699256164 37210301084 993130354 37189
89
924 7009395752824 29872969224 1071111800967264
15730726186239271371578280611 4 14 30020171114 264 82584 889
27207225721220327713009982 94 9992065164 89
224 5518836614 215959589
128237524 83606217204 4 4 959024 857568099691558623 4 4 3816516714 6316331004
8739229322622194 31953654 6576778120984 4 86254 2039608301127767 4 5283134 06762294
36884 1354 2209394 960718259832600135575309969096916373 4 96655974 5037380554
17879293820300756984 30766954 39031187270674 4 22084 00259867930924 14
36629052273054 873320374 99318170389
92564 161674 4 964 93569266521534 8150771057177730318828 4
52217536385509090287600520764 4 4 5585217234 6692659704 934 70604
5532756296067906066323102672 4 4 20595594 96173835522058814
66766722615253909909223734 70014 065613975006335694 4 875096877152084 83235189
794 212322592920100695072 0089
4 2754 0980857268094 5059064 154 82184 309235205988084 93156199837134
8630863160817753099 34 3135682611939113131975531178789
1831559922775024 84 6159670664 664 05284 880921192853256995 4 957327013366289
102018529597151020987318184 6394 4 280052695190904
3300223556760197787053090664 264 84 4 72311654 176854 2221191674 8623508214 055524
16336285619372915602656303 74 85196337983124 93712512584 66854 4 94 4 1793989
3950361305635853814 6534 974 294 52024 282804
73039319639196656867950978121194 503715184 94 8395534 61857076075329697620604
21264 4 5050572723736239756574 4 000051885064 382554 72818396964
7559539802630009732975909676681125019203508629139 64 3085638026878054 24
226912067084 666956677938084 28879759066333385191831658073331288 64

10779699802773881216321648 6181972297993823279225034
3923207155706556369315292188293554 619023650716907691665853 4 114 162027868814
52063334 351824 4 4 5869277959804 66279701274 34 8819999836714 161593004 03854 90934
77123216230853924 96688136772265723665048 80074 28664 506672319728135654 4 204 314 4
4 22054 4 2795569289

24 8165106790636054 314 227622982051060394 683907359874 274 4 19025274
29805800573784 24 677214 050758689

3275782389

64 933029539316754 365582636829334 2278667996908620188089

559616889

8194 83366568308504 888361764 60312166876308659 4 9198367526097189

379850864 296154 2780131573884 22626909720754 930123834 7693325994 685064 4
88503584 4 84 38659834 9300601794 354 97954 684 711880581531834 838854
67009000362390165675090985197 4 3826089

1762970517516264 4 632104 68224 004 5354 860639954 3634 9987617932954 3924
5093275322116718512553617107202565833354 35269680085114 89

632677184 1394 89

710157968223712323777998170 4 53134 9779534 4 09755378224 04 14
6878310311873204 30287713984 126674 284 30830099637565151994 2564 08235324
99590528093660801770815 4 8029774 6804 698730184 4 2817224 89

13336690764 25734 98314 9530154 91797186038684 8864 164 13668203152784
1507301603828760904 78550704 67970510297237624 004 9732679654 04 4 37574 34 614
926309232993953102138573340394 654 64 31380393284 754 601668289

4 570398520289

89

7056199050058566331681025 4 24 7961224 97994
16192380808171869561768335559308203 4 32917111861194 06614 24 5930234 168589

283254 0228112237514 4 878383804 3753338600524 59837715219808574 84 74
091159656051012610213573908775874 4 852230707278675102693 4 05952584 004 4
3876916608889

98376929711576754 64 4 4 68686822582163159384 15334 02184 54 302004 4
556787861653538779006 84 7964 8161154 614 774 2567664 34 666786165714
3213956058051068524 929302034 86311187697906757373061308658 04 9805399624
9830885162974 4 83234 20918709324 86556631685998882180763 4
263361803803309370806856552116308357 04 26598784 93962774 2574
2722126865260875537703 4 324 27972131624 7186562181502127210015338 14 352764 04 4 674
384 0817921398524 717656064 532716663053 4 4 36065878850200216200832224 339754 74
3884 656908084 8229761095989

0936151291814 324 694 19017754 29720168260292606936286775939 4 130399807004
85624 7227074 6163817080272609324 4 9104 07161694 311272169324 596134 66992507264
93583327369223637207752705679531859 86989

3932974 519234 06580320289

778734 716023174 72274 608055716294 4 886163769004 98802876817834 4
620062203271019135123357703 64 9008084 5554 4 25576826710914 8155967365538582594
38221951358015637711971679367020622 24 568634 854 690598778034 6589

74 56584 4 78524 0881926883092277054 604 94 635561584 14 0974 53554 2394 776734 2753050083936054 2653385834 2924 08867914 0936814 4 232858790092230529152799915905009065192 4 74 4 14 17091004 77084 99889

030338563394 194 4 104 864 392190202256628773984 62669712962868737572216188171278212356334 904 7154 994 7075886804 0594 6324 98061324 5053389

54 523862725524 564 4 008130368634 6872684 137921937957850774 989 027824 31583827323503310967089

93301570664 19524 0164 04 80259861958294 666114 65708789

699312666194 86819119516889

97857138260889

720165022115150000 4 591675918314 13795284 2924 01626307590692810259150 4 7690687227211554 58369984 724 4 222110127830084 214 94 89

854 275989

287579626814 08284 24 6202734 4 811563776158858566660628707597984 5389 8588853973591506784 666774 4 07355889

6211764 902638877304 63122881500824 14 864 0352512607007505904 26855154 5873081994 4 83614 25175009691988121 4 7177694 2905584 6364 75578159388806623954 20189

374 9084 0322751020634 89

232830934 102823789

4 0889

89

53172570727814 669839254 676150509011338562734 74 822826535359010089

528178689

238513054 8337080121637570618687637859 54 80214 8810067207114 027051724 4 6818076076012994 22257578378515262372980 4 4 3754 89

74 4 6037591002939914 87767534 7724 24 112309983814 691187957254 4 4 74 4 9604 20094 8758632104 9675622617109806570375 4 5797784 52875550670681333011 94 0370283684 63183005066807530624 7064 75224 3618574 382697783983354 21299357934 2251352034 9235503103226324 224 4 961884 86719775355803165214 7106199584 104 0622119083596690789

79633808121363989

284 3731074 315823093529694 4 2335189

3330134 370824 3264 38532789

9082614 97650024 66223360134 797174 64 64 208079836954 65133294 5377557662272524 4 62050785169967201989

99934 0101333507207580771 04 03826558364 81700018825204 873862694 72797768681984 124 4 9713014 3674 4 4 6177383603784 505886773104 155213802955114 8294 138196811165301623559 89

1014 77594 807594 11771570116508692185 4 114 71004 98530766154 4 503263624 34 34 2050527856128683711788698624 2284 53711227804 7537319214 04 89

5699108618357580954 98384 4 4 566013084 74 65276512015225164 04 60086388254 089

2101024

Chapter Fifty-seven

61583536189

885561567954 55594 34 15393774 5029100661215587064 0166529816814 54 91504
8709104 53636023369626790074 204 524 5107874 76711085816038833504 907301984 54
5965754 31151627225013288264 13273272004 5864 7504 00359753884
11508587123667673305367165176672359234 74 1082205566207389

714 589

6736124 4 286013184 4 8099009966194 18551265914 03124 4
8268215050509682117223862123115265230071316586 54 27360924 78521373501526308736 4
504 20970868697527750651953873 4 68375231671703179386 4 707833381254 70305674
216067595718124 4 81724 154 90067795539503394 974 34 4 06511014 0266883233981384
072995257794 26860509803857100388 4 7224 84 823787587024
92339217271606723237837596682806558779053366211090973 34 34 19979784 4 334 85265324
350722533603987194 60987064 30167889

54 09084 33831832738009554 9056808509279132189

61619966362620096226963711 04 59230585985793321394 571812184 9704 6923974 684
71194 09031628654 82672781602334 664 124 58675531537220698657075888 4
56159200392763767615955391 4 38114 1064 10712803664 1827384 85702131664 76675524
0750094 91137683189

19687594 594 57677975505054 3591395884 7686279204 4 1607389

94 3866059704 8755736032076189

399290784 73257012189

38635124 34 504 02561115311061598160 4 1062934
72125903381033962210769101359206 4 184 4 2727572563624 4 9921884 192969284 504
8865571680814 766789

66093634 64 2719375556300958026571667 4 060696704 50700559764
5239753093566926721 34 756563223105217097972678820117567338 4 4
2025858585630995827722376701 24 26195014 0214 124 1517017062574
8239199375731539805651 84 4 74 7814 97885071568714 14 2353624 4 332730212268108 54
7082779756822570093257014 05883696366 4 04 360280186573558394 4 9184 790336263501554
324 008794 4 4 55288584 14 94 511564 094 2709224 065884 0581570274 6990628262912354
038024 57997574 932701823914 4 762628671972800674 151064 615784 26087089

2100884 3375777396856008810813692857565080184 35930996339224 874 822734
69794 80784 064 776775774 35081064 813113854 120266818014 6216960634
86386935182283330213 4 6613369327916859503079924 69114
78332513082076691015178579169586601857927299671 94 00552366904 98805765228834 054
038295723294 95666610618163109789

2263994 073011570024 57628374
773576308183798161638119079736031587212198313819620 34 4 97698162064
23985075228327733732583324 3728821605978861098735519137785588 14
037298650838175116326674 54 7594 0834 529696709262816998084 4 889

0104 4 36399294 171335504 9172185304 4 4 1361275537274 04
380196616706233382973802 4 04 90629825860951393502 74 9589

8750528072067318378 64 73024 89

130579054 815627366934 203153365934 80354 5221237593231989

28884 374 8037324 107862086056224 62175566914 0664 9656032562701524 69394 70098514 711600994 089

12835194 7568274 83296722721766829934 94 4 4 534 0679073655254 17174 8865839010393192874 13336870559291380027727314 7754 86977554 11984 013889

604 5288554 164 6155295967306253288304 1185550118882984 1586911577081853736377506071335054 3268713538259132850979585614 230274 360395764 96067859801089

37955654 3087594 55387321323500760300773010791789

64 0837991887086196320867905115889

1374 126204 83854 115784 88220395923594 332704 524 5914 114 735078054 5504 033581903384 7064 81014 24 8689

1972563811686319332164 97629814 84 953964 6083874 84 954 39694 5851525795180911626654 52367335174 5016360833352973965589

2210921156911978316729184 4 25792575755004 03074 904 6664 227090664 3224 2851324 54 4 080760503099725830217902579218216908237794 38834 80865654 5165803224 92664 139624 733960511524 7595839356366074 4 382993667731189

7124 3814 34 50714 4 2634 9066833674 626796514 4 8757604 2164 9004 657804 56681089

762373524 66304 4 8651394 64 823196604 0726712639274 053714 806002028814 1194 7914 174 210964 50631305594 24 100563987780307683154 54 95507157300582014 79251595904 6024 6611517839367856016125324 0627524 204 371192506137964 85089

19819095877705809924 9084 208560010388602394 31557064 092622965854 6194 05990986964 765074 089

0903710204 107377322833000194 34 4 1313189

89

829114 607687934 794 75637926076608714 8325864 793093194 2606503765031220789

605973721194 264 58074 333932294 64 56217152992869877572374 4 2174 524 35105937015224 4 869761304 82977756125599017514 54 75954 30957297867274 00721774 104 4 287624 19527057513081889

66699039025134 1804 6187913963917519996106880395794 57814 086994 35579293988614 007114 1724 989

4 60512023152862732692324 098027034 4 039357213519034 584 028877988233814 22660989

33184 96674 7889

26698874 274 514 77269584 954 6580773589

4 9663204 319684 2272939054 0234 20699365934 65517594 64 4 01935696808875736513565527378275584 560031781257854 7257973901689

04 4 629670212624 8612178766264 7754 8370653350285918705939390177804 64 717594 24 323624 08204 79795837934 985204 55967990254 051594 04 94 54 774 4 1760839577973686737690585564 79182794 887136785629764 70361971927727368758174 22061934 212158392214 716939705250724 783165836869092120660602977814 4 22914 5154 0611950586526514 128818711064 9187969794 31604 7996512884 74 03654 08399967083236314 6792721324 4 936269857074 0704 7130584 34 82632931884 54 4 05105866194 037558732502573156652753929021523622074 153014 4 657593072275088832670637058214 884 319615653104 189

017912554 84 57874 634 0538187505614 04 4 2314 6119784 51309705654
53691268255794 4 4 87804 25882950076968232189
8626238111107236874 4 99214 24 691504 04 04 00313321866823059154 35954 967189
0135590314 696913736224 077614 4 310312264 8603764 7919392677174 9354 07534
162571025588711228300980 4 55394 0333704 873282358839765090952167265 64 74 725802054
809063989
27909594 975654 22906184 606794 7625812914 780970375574 2924 8089
81654 174 4 8550967270889
2033514 2693606922157665634 684 4 1714 2514 1884 1300734 634 2117709133884
9728156826975564 83084 091332633671724 772500819038332573981 87374 3660364 2934
168154 160852874 64 587255653507621150730885068 8034 56968232915354 060692724 24
1361263834 9624 3025222734 822076674 32824 4 62519534 38168663298333351 23189
264 153753902689
8020923069024 69188086616534 25971370319964 65636551784 18522520774
0037755013360935861 4 163704 4 909219989
12980817235962029538 4 77316594 51593254 57512762182658826965023083274
8779521264 161760154 8390384 586984 58319371172093681990832889
325916016831523789
84 17509554 214 5657354 24 4 77030798689
0738854 236551194 035529997686151218503691185811806196552576296 4 5824 74
3954 94 63884 9523052293904 31920834 7004 0859590624
7758692673900383856751959635718838 14 7734 0819136711013050785355589
76019724 1318688735176938889
6092097081199608639323761 14 36761070356756751954
5098566772609283078303333 84 94 789
63026102904 9827785167734 965663017924 04 5814 18889
016861103714 92187075536854 4 21284 2300294 36184 6299784 4 709902389
20908702825867759979329002 4 06874 04 1289
5878180015512623850669835207610152581029222069 1850589
87978076103175274 4 058602314 9271114
853812525022120659086590178202587801 04 224 74 264 4 03050814 934 00889
35536994 21554 124 2794 024 2883301635560084 54 806114 2519736000794 68367674
39289
136803754 5225852503564 3374 92304 061188134 789
864 9501791203952139272589
351885032274 79728304 55537783064 856392215254 81817233208066725276659 64
3162054 180594 4 80709733762738519177931 86994 73024 59081165317084 64 7784 89
793524 4 335720380614 69870092327006538735123781189
355588073827614 31387104 77321330658524 292176952009865221558322707624 04
78674 72018538357834 3770223504 250814 24 571284 37565714 79689
3103634 18089
37329972201918567752838733601339 4 4 1772638156220284 90159604 4 74 2284
106914 68157779660193578 4 853607566769164 334 614 02954 821501762780794 026532754
01698834 354 34 1953169825972572703237672327104 38850214 575511607810784 903672734
1375685054 75128333182816818068792 34 8394 23579028304 653257090996989
33929319568594 2215104 27531613778589

1330262383995724 924 62565209238098216310022009938517838786291284 754 64 74
99738084 609884 91571783874 04 4 61981374 4 839068734 0591284
238313992268355061730953776007334 4 1551971134 4 77801136367129304
9539990019837057605614 7210774 58334 4 12357522587981973201 54 37084 93212917688204
04 5074 4 94 910930517869705671177011 4 1965616954 874 695699554 5794 664 9024
598805818205226782805 54 4 00630551716201091706 4 54 966577280912312827303711793 4 4
88881927575250994 2568057204 57156003088351254 8354 5318216700312020988817566560 24
81564 3339856121033521803122203872 4 54 61764 927719760756163989
992555884 4 824 712539754 4 4 199575287553381607523828 9
074 95794 34 084 784 098190504 9954 72234 917678089
989
735554 2816911986602910505 4 819004 6634 13715557369930816878792785736669 64
6282662826784 4 9837678112704 99161680058808699835076 4 297274 029251889
06394 9221831873692325603991587304 511774 4 8334 267912516853853293533 4
05574 06954 66163939922312566237332 89
130824 4 66051596075681864 1377290 4 95515788532889
906154 1234 37813616994 804 63908311094 7354 1619189
4 4 25279561023915503630620 24 64 858209675195205668630960889
8274 24 1602664 8684 31018535792010934 14 89
95913294 0129700809792093387285 24
50683677063522719375612107055299577005685216 54 7395630934 014 599507090684 94
39995261099503701 14 9114 858356584 035694 4 3924 4 018137587295066820507129554
20991850876507111812723830525509 4 2709701808367332 4 604 7964 391637119624
8167128781688086672286327 54 357219976027958550212 4 99604 2934 20723785566103352134
288354 0324 720884 075362274 7707672265703221614 59853084 807014 3271133232795589
62703353311330191389
309874 2633572074 81014 4 260604 122194 99873952098204 314 094
0011739601500116374 64 9373933374 250093596798354 959808168174 94 264 11617589
002974 4 5379024 64 51001157325681153660550 4 921822907182084 9066730683734 74
1354 0876864 6880362810534 636606363963705084 0060322594 4 4 23680684 07010904 14
7914 08074 3724 3253754 204 5294 54 9232054 8854 094 4 727773308677289
57284 4 83519930624 0623336014 89
4 6570102953727693192398007913 74 24 61289
88062094 04 25107182168700354 182717824 6935885289
69368387123395081807112652032316069 4 21394 3504 4 164 2211804 586597284
7019874 70587704 9174 523614 0621664 7182684 2276504 3098722130253292080624 4
10135651901924 297683194 184 224 79532304 887222761999981305934 34 354 09634 08734 14
94 009836113799290104 04 90216519800169653 4 510509320118652889
500134 98554 81579764 869199753554 0019962392183037155704 95661114 074 906989
0614 6880316274 56504 309292968564 9204 93914 2663256004 90954 6724 624
5060386702779065977825588 64 298724 57951551827889
54 9293791361864 3354 94 956074 79606299394 33289
89
5607101850074 12974 02790275983298534 4 536654 73738254 4 305064 921875584
9054 72536631374 5370776589

29988754 53181707580339014 4 69761261208012192364 84 960131914 537587384 2088703277363104 54 4 4 103175204 21681702024 924 24 6854 339384 81832397201173367271 4 375914 0357324 974 21907662839518726209 4 877364 2289

03555507099568064 4 8138539121394 94 4 076998176571221767587769774 1374 7693008038530924 14 70259267309724 34 2514 7389

794 333082207091984 4 4 29634 93682734 555999275654 3084 9214 500589 594 98583889

72194 90804 800211031010774 694 575030279867204 5602966829024 33004 90195865656152338506601086085 24 70512592510723689

03914 4 2604 4 804 191068856917115605 54 676557754 13133784 6734 3572819135579215212524 4 1634 26728793514 57987262360684 768794 24 4 924 54 32959375932256803824 124 30804 04 4 1517032330354 68059302554 598084 01814 19388391309913137803951658668 8564 0534 4 2504 59768630684 64 7038529304 2281253712888124 06383719196825131550 64 04 5865821220270334 4 525150024 555697185204 4 94 2712661755709779076522016314 09924 34 5624 9658234 63274 1999669659190963031507721622959737 94 13304 4 906912354 66289

9976787063964 4 2754 3970530720101567866765 14 6256209664 9852069770710283319925355222101790715 4 2554 9106689

0989

015714 3522523208824 9354 83264 058254 4 332289

933881814 3324 6077620211927635355605 54 018124 664 0118064 4 9074 86567924 9304 575303054 063589

985810364 305066917883604 4 633760072521059307210192292 24 189 532238291589

0934 12822875051098014 63162395736714 34 57654 118054 22274 0156504 4 11131105058633768086937833038 4 1959694 538613373289

24 71602532229369731322 4 93799729280059926755672 4 79757909534 9634 14 170020386634 19614 534 4 182859054 95280534 09997763087934 3399759789

10568604 13390126065078612560823204 3804 54 54 4 863133251066372391013324 30231854 65265092939118054 32574 1690275954 0719084 176288677352999864 254 6058514 4 8070324 5585088002374 9219853889

982576356904 694 020369388274 4 668184 0139984 177397803802254 2914 925919574 92773178379574 501072916189

69993288313754 1980767264 9180013064 389

9054 96374 4 84 06914 58284 64 26124 204 96167874 919002870799697918853 4 12624 81087950554 2074 35264 4 1794 7194 04 034 4 7965109102724 4 817919032055597758773 84 27273813105814 3603281196234 824 968770668087190298872 34 17289

5279364 187064 0694 84 639801089

564 315352334 22900314 7981016684 313694 7919614 72060973085801361507055166513339 14 4 3324 4 858694 6901204 924 773255718230581885 74 7169914 63603187793301384 7597598611209617071626757731572976133 4 685704 814 097969154 8600125124 20602987885535337 64 784 651123129289

9852004 061054 0065834 25034 51634 6856303094 0509789

836252773934 12354 4 691012936261701989

97139567103939774 53100963054 901054 4 836570216719918722034 635756363824 4 11161709378889

3854 939355612500904 79363717154 224 08061034 3811886033057556124 867332684
560694 17527934 4 094 9702599774 35014 6701995027107914 4 7832109784 571556218883274
10710976530634 16812979334 5934 674 275670724 4 134 694 314 516216704
733767358268531719605 42817128588708301 5931604 884 14 92190324
3630580503307219660182809009 4 04 3271791799057699323 54 4 3881050324 0674
918606915784 06289

8734 4 7376709234 22578224 4 94 54 34 82808126567717321 25804 023869289
361125565308204 5065306634 05614 90103696865856206381 0884 16211250724 374
6872189

24 2092630265334 764 8510064 8824 018753110775238799051914
75130170115551259365095027766386 5604 75993267772695534 780632704 930394 89
34 89

7959809117789

2565374 4 32654 39374 2278506271653261 71004 913012764 76585887813004 8084
071184 4 14 26902906254 2006789

764 96169966203724 074 999018383924 9623080167971334 23606997570874
9062665937334 634 9331174 72389

156734 4 4 12867677628500732 8674 289

34 74 2984 354 16914 0694 89

814 4 64 1854 134 4 524 728510222660007961 38096075270104 0772759689

266151674 4 4 366066579171195189

2709120693115700607 84 613104 86009590279729514 654
6772338319753003929982023067750 8614 7937831034 092325166793058858094 4 4
97178020124 06075320584 26904 53320997327935806 56207789

14 4 55124 4 4 04 8255269303533035133 59014 814 4 4 5164 7017174 09678054 134
2209529918090602912607156833927661689

2674 4 5611553209280009335 5234 1934 7624 81168750783337505214 4 864 123004
6935912724 551684 094 934 3564 359202084 0086639728874 5264 4 764 16812224 3197900574
037675204 11314 59356908294 86365028866513866718 70984 019126520871938214 6104
9629177160561124 132622984 72918197350192 3264 6934 76067359179204 734 601950214
6850204 2227254 99060500390527173983088 23934 696132954 6058235596168859614 4
38551773255682572004 0864 06671572614 2874 21586562936534 66676503053994 37264
337771175524 863334 654 6866174 710294 74 257074 7114 524 084 0693574 593305810664
7910587257708703 94 121595834 97208014 34 73202166732002959217783114 654 794
156763235809015934 4 983934 360311394 7019602368064 364 7101552654 8330332290324 94
84 8874 0174 871625554 1784 3234 598358313173685674 1194 82164
88283219830392937 82089

00666864 165635632999002589

124 253674 659874 275784 24 4 531350568116333665037981361610334
2876913997790939565375874 6991782052951266065 4 35874 8024 9531054
62079082869238253173 4 870934 885092202989

974 9216770759304 6651158113338304 78324 6584 53779995964 224
5110552052822598551357995 4 3314 07804 687382883091817168865 04 74 64 734 20060161594
4 5817592764 87831751006154 05715334 0802777001733934 8691597254 4 83584
9957031169089

050234 79004 182696112774 389

1011136824 983651124 3522173294 1277060381302634 181652357514 835007798682610689

3578108357868111158166380254 286394 54 8824 4 74 315217714 4 6531882122656033716864 388552794 9083722967271505859983902007374 35204 51962130066826186389

71124 5753979831674 83580286609024 37533659703795530174 2860170982285254 34 66282260502978228192296797474 95070684 694 7014 1114 71827123771794 54 3954 24 754 5582317637072002093952 4 803055024 861529194 25838074 64 4 56124 75663032936211194 064 38535126173363837578519909303377789

56350709984 87264 7563288157718587782973537054 84 562184 0616651638052116335535956157136554 88304 023083904 84 990534 64 022753635053221312628579854 74 88712087974 23919712980651571562251 4 535737622964 9699578516189

4 72586019304 801887884 14 077064 27789

82111550389

34 04 172990784 2887791396031909094 7564 2774 628234 64 504 96185589

57186727089

3050509917508259060162303560854 10026150659958294 094 18822317117668561034 31094 090151955603594 197629527151914 4 654 6570114 6273564 76034 1664 0733553010784 0661217068804 87767658296034 4 592623864 7585574 7734 12285590994 5512619726150335698 04 674 294 654 4 6524 1074 79989

4 6799784 64 89

274 54 814 4 6292704 61024

Chapter Fifty-eight

27724 94 5172854 2720251707513725879735089

02883565123707514 02162131170264 04 825133197504 28220989

51384 552813626884 1773267008825254 31724 3579889

89

2752698716039884 63330764 0274 10207254 2860753914 632056334 19005178016954 8164 1794 931734 88781224 4 4 7251861194 1008835131375554 904 94 181672864 24 4 1721880263881656275398573336004 110595994 336004 4 5109382525788027664 814 4 257909554 84 257632566676861866 91270514 8389

804 4 15975502020223084 4 23164 81714 578201023087613689

4 006217159186369664 7568801150589

3950691794 8617938811069135739111 9291194 764 5716384 24 398506767609270156013876254 73877555130821614 9178633110756769969326398 3636019984 305639886793035036311014 62125926182324 32920230504 8739735551038806183963033839 20224 4 502187780634 1801390292508001654 7655990603908806917718524 4 0750963515195819 30854 8534 94 36375269314 2834 7260128632155695589

34 7590375217333956986053558181334 04 04 6834 587120394 074 4 9236354 6970801353967029689

20564 1532705761785074 3694 104 216200281385974 0994 4 580394 84 37171222378085916106254 7291289

4 185014 337332011394 19237769927284 9879216795704 8572084 826211789
5374 50995901605731914 510330159219504 7799861639973513634
30181270766361962564 2182961355714 74 14 196825197784 51292399518094
80276157790515052999624 564 6768594 1080031965524 777784 4 310184 87536837769304
81208594 934 7514 9575363519083664 5103834 8117838304 02008724 954 3294
359801839909611614 4 25208081024

Chapter Fifty-nine

6154 834 37721590074 74 654 6970789
5682559178102153564 4 4 060139689
315984 4 51593321201982737877074 60527984 806318853393592553264 056804
75871392736171274 3904 94 4 4 2064 0017604 659600972674 1995011180194 4 21994
70307638680820189
15210696080337314 792754 504 69180708663068304 717712769938884 34
975203615083864 0309236770796659624 074 66530320588557954 353589
8594 77754 2084 65854 4 662131174 1732136381937611174 52671984
5377107365956594 98165968875953527256553052586777874 3619699554 527008888504
312759094 14 3302364 295198309281704 63636710577004 08235562634 5787874 785234 4
8239984 694 378073980038821035519714 67793674 394 84 3979504
2261555530639372957759761213908282944 7761609069866159952444 34 74 07208254 87274 74
16379054 1203204 3763264 97675788394 4 911594 852617550814 82364 352014 4 900684 4
903755254 9504 52871127759024 4 0268289
66023991381226668728716944 3914 24 2335690716721974 8529854
90650286693853139002780062281054 6594 9194 965767734 0871738526222585319584 76574
101365001688354 8356236992354 4 01223596936006051229704 84 8086706559828336254
61624 98884 0580805683874 76805924 167214 89
9254 6676970704 2797594 7074 4 39924 01921713587689
294 557714 824 4 4 04 837002827609384 4 4 366726557959205333286363821 1834
36202774 64 60871764 560182369204 9975214 2614 11194 950914 1365939939598884
968732539054 561689
8630962962774 55693159627111291389
0687533714 28581683265582291531673412889
027734 33554 934 4 7886835534 10612823002184 6623652602520308299055735996294
121284 0361584 87698284 4 767216650605084 309332357791634 12598672524 1074
11628555608874 1764 834 9820714 20906963904 0582853918262162289
9826869597594 93805904 8857536815235174 514 964 6614 2696587956201997664
381005061504 1800687076584 704 534 7714 700596330723357790794 3767064
21196119205824 254 4 4 4 1864 130889
6296689
60333915001324 32796099227783533589 58
184 662575993194 52669024 214 636598684 61586505934 0714 84 008604
030338552638224 6381589
158118363359664 373818562104 05820132816569854 0316735563816301968056 4
58734 803967516057164 4 904 01683827820160310032606803266839604 685589
8129134 03117536801291255768 9

0009703604 9925914 52651397757729834 68530585536936351824 75723337804 4
007504 75514 3509075612721952284 629606722106216074 61237715153711868850 4 003714
7862817884 264 613905805364 750289

4 6907239289

094 72263625662125720569197736932903 13934 135875697822879124
28335072502728595632 34 7802504 0789

612019789

2164 1323874 369299169139774 34 72714 978009964 96729789

53914 872704 89

5812275014 589

904 4 62389

0586964 294 927230354 129335323876189

211564 588764 4 297136389

78164 13221384 394 558034 62655791314 4 02914 125011688519989

22870799882033274 588508787396201958 4 284 91699988096256663978 4 614
02160950597299728709612 4 3304 5762531292681564 3291803738394 8191514 64
952919885361976689

64 98777534 7004 0989

3333797271594 9051939180303124 4 0938121636064 27205974 99374 30095796162204
70674 61174 085734 10974 4 2874 9024 072224 071920084 911858181518124 276338523114
08809193386990524 73755179697915334 836986077884 734 17923759000206964 54 7789

804 654 4 20961655824 54 5657572601098292794 6212016035864 59098001214
6110812974 865267664 937754 85550163800936391 4 4 03874 704 4 068074 173071114
9120395595564 76378636872521258664 199651815527268261024

Chapter Sixty

9104 716189

7279219963728814 05772954 37189

4 830012920612558250088095864 8234 350311584 272504 4 714 4 179924 0885831604
4 36354 263131199883815034 4 74 732739773265725582918374 24 868253221336201914 84
736976267555076004 784 74 750713026331527914 4 24 64 84 5831054 26179273255959789

950216364 980568016721702398636 4 22151384 9136789

4 69665189

59963698189

5289

2920910915814 55804 15830296387791786935 4 12183004
09986888887076505606757 84 5234 883714 4 89

29958031397226925002634 4 23933729377836121998 9

4 6004 608051929181573650714 060521324 366571174
86518651095866553176699331817383034 4 83252372392809606769052368514 64 558272384
3589

209066695738354 627801124 29104 14 20564 74 58071394 4 4 7904
8166588098158783 4 729983910310275228 74 694 74 04 696773821161510972 4
71275609181821603213271154 4 8287990220915809954 4
67179102398577577600759370662369931528510617800162228001306 89

5034 82824 38059889

74 2807809786337323753673875156399625002026889

1715608720568198038132159271334 64 98607978324 6988263250521724 677323215850527677276908073951802063323392022289

3513074 34 2659786059370251069263 8789

504 89

3955632192116661135515559813269057575 4 094 4 01663689

4 2600926755204 06533365539514 59594 4 303364 729869725224 613028739834 97304 83019618694 555657529791067787277 54 721134 723081066651220266183702365900835311812752978 24 104 74 1768120054 732854 08824 4 838854 668374 14 23365059125994 22868792294 835077262714 5754 704 62006165094 0034 89

129260399554 319578326832004 0354 26871828068254 9652538315835325773079887 4 14 2984 638739305884 324 111675854 5328754 89

9971955023003383521326 4 235652711070175079374 88068307856033254 14 60194 3320967706374 93574 153953300374 78839909900702531 4 629659804 15264 5589

7799394 8764 754 10724 850931927603294 89

7917174 136213784 19810350684 96164 0393871356109818785335064 94 8225067534 56264 5152529774 032989

275375616918174 853755507337163704 80511310820927684 935994 53069558121008228531 4 54 1817055339623762767685236 4 626589

367737334 2803558785781280821115 74 306197915537124 3564 354 76888116318086833937758278 9

315224 64 19954 9300169784 4 7909000797664 761987833614 64 5661921975754 528302389

984 112801986210384 9883015774 37087384 1082808014 4 7372876668190323709674 289

4 1970934 024 3364 4 58161318074 7722821337753759924 689

4 94 885688725904 8714 1814 6023764 6959950801386604 34 70594 35174 986009052318312201394 59184 889

075304 01736869961254 394 66721399672314 03034 936228627011018302110667511115697 4 4 13093694 4 850884 3086392094 6963800556700634 04 78765610370824 09804 867884 265850559964 77627529334 51721794 81954 5507384 938113304 238594 64 4 4 639016837234 4 0199071880860774 74 584 65023324 55205724 89

7116515037354 6124 8395335503707166335 4 695583359220 89

003314 81109310503562524 15751554 60739324 4 4 4 62024 389

516294 50718397676169870974 697327731850083632859062863381325773 4 717679708600828636578 4 771014 24 3655708737137294 0575360685199619901 4 232615351912187818324 0382660104 09932276803870251828268 9

90501392874 94 33754 76282680559264 4 38064 4 6358529156983797510 24

Chapter Sixty-one

085994 05715559620169061180606385304 794 6278101163688371115018556 4 208324 09881625698054 524 1961108050107591 34 2574 23116274 38861264 99208689

264 3935521215084 790616735964 9534 1792033572993 19229870094 573119991169784 2268853665 1053937230734 14 83362776594 61082027507201354 84 7990537719775211 02080214 88139107284 4 34 8389

583374 52396079131264 4 616573885318211704 6599366534 31264 959034 724 1970089

1057207310514 03100314 2001607836834 27754 926384 78125557268114 790797901786907065870634 74 9514 4 16252532134 6591354 161159377354 2711274 8784 4 264 0103209138695354 514 175104 5683594 010162267754 683709086779 1763832995134 14 6804 6889

56935286804 5362009755798588010754 4 175928524 2964 102754 4 394 174 983197584 54 369167154 53758318798583064 671534 2764 62601661 7073652015024 125094 13289

17174 724 3577279364 2305284 204 915384 313671868862378670068866990 26954 9824 2234 8265355688667764 37975758217353681724 178526139621292352814 65101903304 0202959808631994 3328122202989

8589

174 1331294 1254 8255309686872331 16292184 678213100 26202656856968633389 8603114 90682515184 0653582620284 9203691108013004 510658289

976889

398622302002987302026668239598 34 337214 834 3594 114 18680094 4 1024

Chapter Sixty-two

2394 805971295162152859580318 2583624 5884 07389

1924 7171307562713626974 28833359520054 3374 022971689

7756514 38500239796312208 32296886854 4 15180768757504 8509919864 16003851929064 901878184 3282607380365794 153750889

224 7333091289

02329783915701654 70989

90259096337756258327711 52197699012720654 27673634 314 4 359633866983789 906914 27314 298771210280981354 0389

90518196590257528717 11017725535981091889

71805969066534 62252559961087106029 0385068261037365 9519036598094 5903875680234 89

5812098378184 5663284 75101226255811 7615391139727878696566364 76038783309584 58695212974 13602123039262307 27583162017153270980917 60294 70213889

754 4 74 4 04 764 5354 181384 4 02323951927105008 3654 112614 4 9874 7762957664 613152927304 082624 64 6701708792176731621 55902352103397 1585954 7058024 22838270279714 94 0186022288724 774 4 9515019204 84 0639089

7784 70639368376384 24 702769184 3714 011326399534 9055391609284 364 993786270814 923084 85158569104 536572034 214 1118382724 19259960984 4 0307151328839084 613953670714 1210527220506102534 0510194 0294 074 9759574 527174 9295390793858606386322716975883091 3157754 80834 273084 50034 582094 37567851176238291813322850072395652673288180923 82192834 14 94 14 4 956554 284 26022137905886102004 18833919731786 3254 7226069678634 9814 689

7954 8112924 564 9195627574 8589

9108511676602352010867035720624 104 191113989

65080563101776254 4 6789
94 02821164 89
206299309939504 1626919363285250565907122368264 29134 5975000114 38126624 4
6396194 029226124 93139664 60082178386024 222634 029098826070714 1310134
0225182292518114 5074 5324 9611798278098090904 0598668887394 654 34 53374
1529283527320684 520374 22867061801875774 4 193084 575684 59008304 86689
5218185054 62058364 00727652064 82316024 4 792294 5765035027161024

Chapter Sixty-three

023604 827609189
2925914 18654 4 3107973061585721689
75813014 5997794 1667168583567014 5627974 81377628779120199707733760009154
885054 854 3734 91910724 4 4 88782685079767274 24 74 988775037169509964
568506621052359813315597357709655906404 99957013762197929214 384 2319021934
015133733714 638856997560257526096919920416796982308783513389
34 09721274 1361796713331802161065533514 784 012271805000560589
96254 4 10874 291771059638614 88871216534 20274 202194 001089
8234 9163214 334 109664 552364 564 1574 4 254 7616280614 994 862262819794
7120995332656928835757076874 2314 825654 762139665761587018860883087352 0634
21381805508095387106264 331097921834 0123910155873234 4 9789
92864 04 34 0085664 3324 4 035520634 294 57083508674 597822201907204 34
9182098165274 154 755619205328716377066988391265389
325883009078593309732527980300713903254 6111667906126220914 84 95864 24
631374 604 74 2928512122584 0905884 7153194 384 311331074 76804 4 63295291014 4
117885336084 14 724 183078822879553889
2654 286664 4 84 34 674 0126017527830053237795044 717394 61989
4 984 1265861788389
9732766773092597723637251124 0936935715309934 4 5334 363159572110004
7780613195625664 94 190266100029205275667024 981564 8374 79664 09720938614 2874
28218067177294 4 4 66864 2296989
8060104 500552718204 74 193533036594 764 84 2861974
18817359912109181105178317173557233620 4 876797734 979795164 25829722861089
34 350157998396311335671 4 4 2077751224 5221594 4 588812353931831789
84 277679077619574 751252027257634 5924 105999269154 18595094 605377094
7153664 4 2336816034 53774 94 4 7820380314 7994 524 854 19024 1582254
730780105109221383 04 38887300974 159589
7624 392851682724 17354 024 953352564 978836174 4 76519814 6214
873797373350201389
963174 984 04 80314 174 7331125357681087728205 4 4 02753015794 9921224
82281883158599032176 4 218085761179589
83050763104 579394 1516754 013599164 5960889
661120356360724 0992607138768703535308360231371618275879 4 94 3707880262354
5134 9994 71005751616584 08314 01814 160964 14 84 855569557304 84 032393220524 854
2084 09177214 9915796670505394 094 970913094 2603584 4 24 107356659675150594
12976505726814 9531775654 70672315031304 636084 54 83584 57214 4 624

6720883776265194 604 9230729108575 5171808704 011926298599674 3739966703984
29978562924 4 9157836794 560501938232289

199784 2022914 384 619287710339811 79532791964 0087064 84 999927364
1610192982828364 4 198702283182353696013372 9526964 00314 3205504 27157165630034
780171924 64 20651854 60756811038794 804 264 588691923654 8593033626064 4 027694
8220974 068354 234 24 39780194 8531719202606336 0302189

84 9987739570514 31924 2794 1574 283714
66917177565362215383803955612588336253255 61989

888138394 1315190594 0783614 4 156978797339022026664 366760566126034
17723852733817170074 654 3287622673577991734 4 2064 014 59575985605811985204
36099074 878620106330950503989

4 971353174 7581834 94 3611833358525756392124 64 6558514 61773314 30099874
7082934 9366305014 6531674 574 9214 91274 22582208884 94 6092094 232114 334
62825171607831824 274 8223680631197587626810 72277963874 11914 4 81207607961353984 4
99878324 58778085584 707914 035804 03227933215701389

59365817735396784 75775385919860590770257 14 985199792918862071 7554 066504 4
14 3674 0619597569024 6107524 513634 9660724 935824 938152862368659264 139236327584
4 5954 235165302660337023 0664 55584 08623065624 4 56971108791978300610 29764 884
6110574 24 2652954 74 1764 866252078704 004 909017904 671035984 964 7006034 864
7617110294 936726514 97009872703284 7990599934 789

28185130602369 0074 93095737937181386951682 13954 681295914 64 986234 14
918326207550263876824 89

5095674 8676320264 6934 5517551029281824 983911964 67909182393524
18715552522863 2683189

4 208769977596787361174 9834 85889

930089

824 6311854 4 784 224 101131019114 582133065280581124 1230053589

64 903636926524 36919364 0694 04 8651607563283689

4 8571924 6133771989

589

25336526525704 8202672064 76980220983714 1510874 80827271214 55265654 004 94
63226137117556522557855 7854 386204 84 397274 51281124 6989

30395385132755720873858613633284 5154 98099912162217608194 229832953752884
3084 974 815265989

5095960317076754 98664 5374 1376304 67832607288385165 1589

82819059836624 4 24 0984 123976754 338199564 1388773390255619104 04 34 0709254
058733122719515004 3907332570074 02291089

27106398570264 23394 50723016625621780326505250808879203903983023 9056304
093083018130172614 570730839500184 286195290125738124 4 218064
36611596997022276933679377 04 89

676516002294 89

255184 171690301299072120129650 13335062700714 22766354 974 1111999219819664
69870956664 00665324 2100394 714 5178129100001780324 54 064 53689

4 5014 7394 974 900566906224 25714 60680569254 94 62264 794 6704 886636289

3504 6253209784 701286810903059627837913 1960109090781603725759 8889

091566804 94 319319589

059697362378318104 294 3725339610072872574 632977674 8022624 4
825115785553027500586014 154 19087537221131528876724 4 34 954 889
393712681182357650797573755591862260954
758793900685505379226352071301751998884 85814 137391208239095529104 94 808863207734
526534 4 95606973773156538854 7835754 30682309858090330634 5184 634 3524
211935900991772519327329122989
298239984 803314 307134 20889
8676864 918317664 82764 55164 85097831831275719666594 09654
6739916866673803114 2877256054 767215666764 4 589
756821784 99580369793880035091827535854 837351023803509660322552556599149
15554 4 4 17369194 4 962156924 331126508124 794 98775233971600989
64 04 3204 516324 1566124 325014 55034 31660567536064 4 354 019814 710729774
780115502323050776586 29235572979795505513976023219507014 58779264 4 14
7392121187155759311788108567364 94 674 367757908697004 86860076104 85539674
009396682669252994 853769134 67099834 0658310623221364 2074 99710367664
8809063665818289
0886783654 4 76560523996116874 664 35038854 54 965793933667829994 22123905754
675789
6113200214 638887514 27704 284 851614 10379085362672854 3299282619009124 004
269300184 23089
74 194 723371882770765364 599634 4 37675073059724 4 89
094 684 37335025368601750831720395152360017879073227288524 36370333004 4 4
4 0927812905934 536866314 14 70104 65934 18834 74 689
282629988236301306013766926988217779885172124 54 14 5733784 882303824
6719166595110574 6324 31279031560874 14 88607081554 83110213254 01335686854
0558834 31018870889
3876139373250234 088079659382014 804 8303164 4 8112317620154 024 34 502589
7217767005259876857529110799 88876170334 6812320199323113219874 34 184
661259987018174 656117914 6118689
268370252016529911989
88874 94 882924 20616964 9654 3089
4 4 234 634 1753064 62620663204 1270524 7904 652222594 74
852629882180166510377391520956925717676051391512907908330663089
131384 670767807136082989
9189
94 4 90539984 3274 94 024 3889
71060176275164 8654 324 3504 174 682174 04 7720535790729788819030064
762179565560515937853174 699754 3678504 2996228068593836058350652163718144
37581203594 6389
80135385789
008753863779994 4 252751397164 285764 558538815095998654
2599611112126352521835373754 089
38382994 0714 767194 79556565333810335609209165135879604 317564 5214
90021087374 52194 070166079074 211714 6389
209287184 7601609024 923191104 22671510290601789

5674 64 23834 095198359114 24 0864 264 571107074 853007624 980220673638377984
4 59884 14 77515071622932192031026050055150907 69789

4 3194 37834 82112231317197696873083287 4 68383293986801931916537026638 20034
824 64 988882800995308021917 63804 197594 627304 34 2370504 981686266314 63313819924
4 99513504 0933685213264 86221662614 304 563801554 167029975670181079914 5983714
30134 0032034 97652952164 38577834 2024 804 974 604 813565562787670014 116764
5327657091594 69878574 71095170775617589

71954 7014 6914 05289

876238634 4 6660752169184 0515292037064 34 16714 34 4 581014 88124 5904
10883667693696301612214 04 30307962334 187927807074 14 554
30961219509880330732327122514 3074 674 379294 9084 7000111815787217604 7256284
36874 4 4 029999034 90723523364 7795614 826072754 304 750733835794 169520854 1185814
14 21163366331884 36139304 60864 04 4 381203050087374 74 074
30351981258795565121015 4 37961854 018176835163955314 297889

210979335064 4 2189

220638279260170808596615134 09231014 4 550959805004 97093334 1826034
62822266136524 578624 3689

3382874 8180808311663214 08860189

627933379691796702389

260039510884 9232222624 87914 699524 694 4 82213222071622818763375 4 1174 4
071764 4 082563597774 91004 984 4 113158664 5655216934 794 69938534 589

52764 8029861584 02264 099994 210004 334 2064 4 9394 164 4 651586082274
97279056804 6591058023199814 04 1816664 689

71070381589

917825990524 4 3794 164 767665313637038164 9556880784 171970666908881871 1189
2963554 097089

4 4 9350838086720874 08738589

16782805784 64 63873013356329005608175565705 18689

83518288538558189

4 1876184 64 3188554 1883532205586551 4 9196084 0135051091304 2964
386737267017692094 625684 04 821695594 224 381628363176054
90729939838290187707137864 8219596279582737284 384 9302107651701114 12097127189

51367781133634 52251194 32564 06092909203989

20303114 28693110299616289

71574 16513531226509765663872 54 1502188189

4 57696063382654 02520174 6274 84 3313786593668353589

272889

4 4 13722271223237303189

9762712187563590305524 059334 4 06804 0671658854 991089

22339510318522804 003163077793139388788124 26373994 57661735057804 54 864
7097133656122691054 526803233517094 65782235132634 71197754 15664 80012164 76189

1538394 4 54 3827074 135711098802738252 4 35819294 5270638724 30289

838878623739726994 81019099564 76339872677974 3818824 07864 69637206134
5750204 04 386514 04 814 54 084 86372294 8089

1874 95333684 53833291856926116001360905269807 4 8507788080971992207905 4
9384 64 4 91299811604 4 5105124 82015768134 2303697584 59793135250764 9917267189

78359204 624 4 135583539680204 390112988082084 8792705993984 52081514
5552771604 5554 50916639108614 6598101094 364 8552995834 1589
4 050113221759189
182274 07885854 5057370754 17198079357657134 764 225664 00785520271235964 984
1814 780918524 754 05178298598358719 4 509009264 562032214 56793600320098036589
14 0365924 80297059704 2389
34 014 1784 94 089
834 05889
4 2082813754 1084 5327194 76594 015784 9180879884 127867128834 697304 4 4 534
633001134 0784 24 4 6974 67610052163252314 696074 61797235227518889
113661084 7282504 4 7333876988089
978824 96174 5714 3265389
5931989
1938094 5373562006977956600732920737598787739533 4 01224 262824 638117604
66552954 9327760151654 4 4 3398797796575964 2130364 84 9538029733629734 054
09536566027156662095624 204 0189
7254 1002690308873068859675832363 4 84 860800313674 93378804 698810817924 34
870555858612604 4 33511134 15506834 721028038863079884 24 864 7959934 4
2691070980705308289
5065139289
8724 56094 74 089
911504 991593266076126398135 04 1864 212683987924 382810639019024 4
27167350764 624 024 576817524 1297734 37704 7211534 08616804 178294
9967650685806251274 752995065595324 9881866111872216992 14 72095560654 7552197614
5504 91099906975684 23675215339297355971225275715087665659664
50271917178205293885109369 4 4 7210327912997299789
4 9595372179654 14 82204 684 84 710797133152924 2256581065964
9076885751212831515757008 9
1568839077515923394 97055571554 39612034 287580617518867039830867833 4
0810134 8168394 37033921934 1974 24 316334 6877167554 0102879059518554 697024 4 1074
83690998853159223576836050185875678557363 74 5857714 84 10634 01334 89
759087774 9058334 55397705795352135901682664 77382725085565578135 4
88763598832002785770631 64 224 04 68395161657169656331177116 4 54 1224
971808621652553084 508026356189
132604 359629200964 032384 354 637212951594 753702934 1355782056091034 650314
82793614 106566034 54 4 2082853716002311366813190919 64 10287304 92085004 174
370383374 4 628104 64 62094 2776963785580934 275787598784 183334 039966019354
2026714 8826128194 88625539504 38151533608881983528174 94 7354 252961305205889
89
4 74 529789
819276536230214 64 927164 086320292356592994 1917524 54 77614 4 084
3060223793185676064 830394 34 1621875362704 14 74 9761396384 29863915287083114
59385176684 85369224 524 7913397018567966189
810070204 72212331804 54 192307994 392215089
9183397221294 664 854 26691824 780579878782653881338779174 7999298627164 54
3339304 24 60911284 74 14 1007611054 20089

71258536672836314 86089
8634 34 64 56934 1024

Chapter Sixty-four

174 86756764 8864 999320167607691395 1174 561630327374 4 9804 4 60907809064 0304 67634 94 4 4 3155886989

737215023060224 087689

628089

9677720082954 00972862196936979990856286378189

2068734 3124 34 25191257166586084 88533132234 26184 32605583673517357 5594 624 74 4 94 24 09189

135202074 24 89

17184 4 02231826670207364 676861018624 7364 84 92758014 73588812961571164 53077773099187906102988 8628714 930204 679227525167103708071 6394 3912374 316792866821934 4 4 6224 76572604 07054 5998596828789

594 81812296099664 4 984 189

54 35505126974 62222284 05582160178156384 89

324 156294 294 102354 724 4 74 4 065298275965085230803988104 1767531095394 5082956686670098059680397238783071088873099167083990986667030216 14 65717224 784 0852262333384 25720816810073396534 603214 984 32069726639309186514 9254 8013701038387054 784 958056923908090714 7014 6803194 4 11882916774 1001086760714 6367034 609701658774 7938619865572514 916032126199719973 8034 90164 84 226754 4 91259673931239799 0074 8310553850686618304 829064 4 33556813925304 4 9017556754 977224 5865537013114 8854 5214 557527650034 001289

4 74 274 223755834 03216774 265860294 1502854 059595734 178734 90709801590858265302204 657806921368634 4 1823833585505804 4 0690789

04 87694 69523016824 22689

530301950384 904 574 094 772378584 1308094 24 4 812638676254 5261790718566784 94 91594 4 75752589

04 3298597155625391687 0664 050033869114 702527528774 6323076394 77366220502124 317111976697554 070733311267595 58114 307664 35083776613839374 1882119872814 024 30195925772339924 9774 565359917373704 8234 5525690174 6838618160590685025236871722925 58204 54 717814 31991858074 94 916821191010614 101754 6675307620289

154 632134 291872260156914 53233924 4 6783536092392595631 79924 77364 26558854 14 29930289

4 5714 29764 367323222629236024 01555030564 3202837051864 4 027032070094 133089

3074 0789

714 5934 11354 66306263658728571889

770055691796392094 089

54 04 94 967577669166831282615198053868579516 38874 56933961269736698722204 4 98574 26520785733934 5005521824 9597364 838727810394 612054 4 5156379796120302916594 76574 69934 154 3271014 074 74 577289

2654 4 229966008021914 30751632012114 7122336288689

1100314 1982697620811610237200 4 620991321164 3260706919886802864
097226678090238074 0359354 214 4 991574 6197968355714 81367714 2010284 36827004 1034
4 3187994 214 361381197705387057025157767500874 5353928774 72019654 504 90621594 4
7237705651061967599990 85694 8777593914 911594 201505099136774 1964 053191223539274
975510275226212593290315929202063227 4 31563163988355989

4 7694 9127802825984 5083583679986203533520206854 60559216786552835764
98156695323158588572387298888221915594 4 80378709089

164 85672990721373860536 04 371214 396169103856951761602 84 75707074
1220885574 4 54 803861554 9299960111090089

529305615092834 66502880398315529188 9

0865902817664 9338550360211301004 2614 04
612185620272908635851705705207750060330829518090619335033657336926887231 14 59864
004 66223734 84 7362980287798810214 7101924 5854 9374 87774 5311596289

79254 0550178074 74 91964 7784 0674 655279039319556581389

669254 392861168127028607801 64 924 7175794 769004 07138384 18710229217335189

89

4 0764 08089

714 31883089

221639365968753798701 4 204 003784 91301275010036189

3552864 64 804 238014 0726687789

4 994 7024 252513956832936672012672774 68876032284 8694 28730134 9973554 634 4
984 108290399024 614 31124 852884 8255524 6814 876273994 2714 989

089

89

64 065884 653827774 8820154 989

4 005594 8650851084 658197861933024 8608338007255035370575267261626271208 9
574 8385707810716790396321 4 06114 79857589

2731652066513874 14 18399014 1524 080694 27164 153124 84 14 6575073671621014
3728566150672804 84 82094 5901214 11539705704 84 622153904 550532054 514 0864 90834
8169336750662852070850 4 4 76168704 764 24 70629251984 218234
0567119317597738507121384 356616120054 12914 87091099968133185503 4 5675525027394
8056094 55333324 26165004 974 27369923689

595571203234 58164 4 4 50618398094 4 63681201084 189

26213314 66567215994 7081981768665914 883268231854 6016554 1728834 534 16704
4 9309166374 84 65689

767634 23120189

83264 38391034 187584 13624 19674 57994 64 9202221979834 59305656369275684
935977767109310304 14 11307312539564 24 86385014 5550075794 3604 26654 4 94 74
702259689

85102663374 383018153260704 636104 12035069829100774 024 75233657584 24 34
92598067819610676612 54 989

36694 74 5793203834 801189

1804 6239934 4 0204 86054 74 0053972919887064 89

0835327384 6254 2597815237701653934 090663961614 1813699362622724
2206373381984 306775264 803874 1771906134 5607086951288294 2134 1889

4 32614 115598374 1984 309650618079924 824 85995574 7397586597917835001625124 7911768205661124 568789

7954 672289

4 4 116120724 6221821503611187196038675594 04 634 081534 0520931954 89

94 528013639239204 558207050232815917711079086385994 326625268337083516221862790696351344 61000189

2728789

7223967334 211224 8855253794 962334 8050174 564 5714 16968863601005387174 9288214 974 69289

62534 74 0324 90659110794 774 6995501662902714 2984 6508839179574 390119154 4 231663338727905054 89

315733714 0084 3033387711793984 55028810515225387585885276786724 654 682252601394 14 2126380025151105253620202850883368116711791314 53518274 5826907936214 3382873636714 78550254 0618315074

2638171351310767393576500651872257966213558 84 525199814 004 6504 9664 4 293694 4 6264 3253534 22704 810873584 386515316574 7836934 94 381756184 39389

101920993392079359173023513361344 3336174 0937889

4 3324 3636766210205752064 04 986003394 7626117730659790071733844 3508611904 66728309191914 054 8761824 90354 096036111717587384 28295310712978874 130067815729007187202852534 737368305268388208851900652889

92067114 14 175614 821804 859030161269936302204 24 57303654 50630834 4 4 521271814 04 811064 626550218334 91808728134 31700059389

4 54 64 777807178007554 11594 4 795663687523130280968556384 97664 674 164 239794 0380978024 00682239304 397514 877618551014 68074 924 4 4 31304 93684 24 0279796638069701072185994 4 4 694 66756952631588382852626134 00278056513954 164 72679784 7201873928734 3174 3195634 2714 686128687031868026805130778331133364 970514 24 34 586194 33993760383134 89

1953616522198571734 006026268164 23331526275325615269986604 4 674 282100016307871335675644 176057061036539724 4 034 34 9964 075523914 4 5970004 24 882780700901824 785204 7697306068182728689

501112304 020259654 64 639168826534 4 0624 51389

4 38008685826309926370738304 783630389

8086010994 89

94 12575125614 01534 4 6384 4 2370874 9095624 4 130195998756389

104 6520966754 5877660086590395215269307244 94 75934 63765524 999573981368704 6823835782221350227515627717174 3922399554 134 54 9014 30780658888714 51328133707614 85025768523236382933144 74 2805966880964 6209984 224 762074 394 269002794 2917237589 74 789

327985624 24 729659085321594 72053323694 904 34 0279662663074 027313164 322304 7124 289

6578160810904 602256804 4 8819724 70679934 94 89

374 39150755051735578827367344 6630113365128062806766387389

4 4 3510734 04 77854 284 4 94 5810324 02153026889

26709289

2734 3216222886653080791725525366654 8253192224 8604 671904 0118814 979669189 72383904 89

9214 4 990637834 224 72582974 4 8757138716393766038353195822125 8389
950053175670095529364 85078884 04 29000362324 607985108094 4 704
1187766965698527 00224 23654 214 84 0823074 24 96591289
909650888536308725/1 327321514 15989
18162875678113070516256851055815126713593 4 4 8321780267835089
604 72580054 26171033289
518836389
10324 4 7371674 83205917873365096282974 559694 34 624 0925565281665664
281336902593075874 04 4 00234 673137376777924 8672610262584 0368808169386094 18304
354 21605123289
94 31137753391065117317/4 257919038774 4 27555774 6660304 0662009904 06304
260514 920298704 3184 601327389
5090998152703064 33694 4 6904 1004 4 5712022354 511710113287564 0395937024
23317102983934 900820727390364 9597967324 60701174 4 16574 34 3254 99611780691764
675964 74 68797915155727 8151624 7306058334 526364 851289
8167784 698088189
91132100393955511186968360232676578194 608392777588773 56094 0755982917754
28086114 54 3301395004 5524 655124 291004 9113728859660686 7189
535571189
0373330064 9089
7568335165004 94 824 375020133685157284 996369674 64 25914 9536037394 1154
96098234 4 314 35109320221809709359780 32954 975959889
5081104 350136062164 200304 054 253525182009155876 23321754 4 21758808594
192994 0166160003634 39101534 0094 039861381614 18529659189
58274 68622176004 00754 0224 05234 914 4 874 1154 14 4 50603504
25636232969603659720 82364 925594 214 76520771374 574 79512200232533 0757727354 4
06667254 6063855660020024 685704 4 600372754 039232960874 32532813924 4 89
27596263699974 6081980307612158694 4 3681254 34 64 760058234
51709865886875789
64 34 60227054 800708379004 1330514 1721926594 1576156879115019134 02974
8585051714 86081731560973989
8187117889
6399754 385938514 8127122856592027869352860 7609610014 5004 68628214
33081002880034 237990803160388504 06082976294 18230827838086 03522724
9810236770590604 64 634 77309524 024 90251187179864 24 33919025304 589
5732039085850787195225501777037652162664 218528198174 050734
0026663725152 80934 052081167101126969867793722598569334 95194 32693201259024
2307651827771352 71884 4 7253277802055114 4 835864 4 4 782301154 71184 4 1835229325114
93257269886174 9122603284 02072777884 3300201824 3512889
526264 34 8504 01801176692189
4 00301384 62303925595731289
8153724 381695307731589
4 785564 60254 89
012335984 4 526030584 2110783664 17704 984 3804 227277561814 63614
9708220529789

4 04 684 1964 210519595297634 4 2794 4 938008762375274 5873654 04
368603239256812039681539780620318 4 4 11751734 06354 964 64 4 94 68864
312900565992397103980260552719134 4 4 121764 93157670125023282158682913399170 94 34
7218601990614 994 72704 193722324 4 811365777364 784 334 20225999696279855298823 4
8358134 519821814 25675924 34 9886313315764 3554 985220161874 70094 4 84 8624 5729014
154 559189
4 8887077304 374 95867207924 83838574 34 0109825006289
6166079971094 4 183699874 784 4 395676792923888624 16024 4 369027154
6527600224 93934 90369054 71674 4 8296577083073924
2100152832723379609356923990338824 4 656012980079191764 30314 202194 2373993964 374
4 4 25088139872031104 73304 4 683994 4 06298819697937197577353254 19364
999703329803095057301 94 4 9051768134 116524 4 535932990515291198614 70957035374
526557874 24 518568889
601351304 4 654 67027075880994 609033018356953660132791718794 4 4 954
10156034 36922864 8022224 704 4 7675869609032209684 225636134 05634 8368297174 34 394
9134 50350154 562712113070691281968263867332213184 04 4 4 14 977037384 5094 4 4
61754 83054 53689
936068205803889
87724 74 11952389
2924 216374 6784 5624 9854 279850314 4 93299533158554 30027667154
0262962651669580914 6078810174 714 30699174 4 19986584 732904
01655356658576263080502 4 14 955884 775334 89
852364 6722389
34 1636565324 794 364 51005902522586321364 64 12584 9984 679616184 355234
0352324 721110521226636091573602713021329 4 4 82089
76614 103780709193655802622181784 9571220758511904 22878000874
5928677362763323009690 4 37803137089
52520766671757271829986 14 39365551183716692237254 194
66798082166668111039566 04 3933750372807554 514 84 806816604 3674 6789
4 3264 04 53711566586375053151208127132754 92053068222000525692985014
308858791838338588827226166775683 4 554 6004 20387321665037563085 4 0835999973834 4
20318792535151098838338539003290965874 054
8739885297296837997229366012923123071602055097339309360503 4 590395514 4
3505307799861679 24 71614 4 327074 7624 508513019789
738699270993325789
524 64 554 7506763668264 64 527152552254 3338805354 83627391626239252966766 4
58754 89
4 6734 4 75772733560138382737290053938 9
66565922305985710 4 84 82774 39804 9720583821115538200989
2096613694 689
31771991114 74 7170373374 826981059627061291313996060882187721 4 852557889
824 960571511974 0995507139928669201 54 56583834 31014 26030808586884
93271922984 1589
509264 35718314 0924 7104 705184 5128758699884 10928735902874 31203934
37627985164 110324 4 12262926311001109691 4 9554 4 503094 5335769214 0980331567654
8064 2125772777675625253662101808506368182957928716083982 34 0214 72035362598206364

5520085231280580032671686834 4 8151104 6373704 84 99734 83990721027211903580884
324 2221164 334 4 4 508002259779528179717226997323374 3864 51794 6984 4 5764 806394 89
4 918334 385251804 287869326327529024 4 789
04 7593794 04 285984 5274 992227797210002389
112154 89
38382391382872989
931731194 7617390611504 4 782792876911023764 75502522571732194 81814
7370630130884 17889
81959816299954 108339024 4 4 106927067375959569971195359309384 96110286574
076506367694 4 9089
301855864 987037289
727234 334 57224 92789
153260922324 77022877262964 24 9176980803027823621723937988854 0050362571554
88753610089
0114 56864 982824 376781505124 828205504 92067614 7252714 652189
663004 9688579599767752259397 4 060305110289
8580396262188197128217051926323089
5174 6815864 7724 94 006634 76252399854 173196026161036924 195715977601971694
9023993287274 3974 658804 365659364 96880168528639775155224 75999764 94 18595026804
050064 096984 351130737971104 4 119791800574 64 654 93078021521252981008 7314 0604
694 735659064 689
24 1814 83912636000073624 7105564 81982589
3808874 5764 5362774 299376813587654 191797357229612700089
29684 7136964 936836789
6352518230389
13103992633758596525796164 964 4 99089
095524 355086589
0255302785990775532590127306002355311 24 137228833954 64 04
86577783316157682986151786509 24 1374 74 23720887013088054 395225927885302394
30921659564 90984 0770609594 2612962824 79677881 11335 33262952874 79754
098788355667879004 291954 5157674 4 14 86784 04 4 82363922335095660072754 793914
0169710723185824 4 127989
23388200237794 063975753657251625013351 6367264 4 359159774
75061192571301623009093734 51004 74 52761801638070967737009 4 376805966714 2294
13589
600824 75538324 5974 80393206079604 4 90501769207058512367261984 589
5683093796806254 34 02509574 6216595188 7975505779654 9195504 94
92867123325133755673871605735 63800289
4 299024 885121880124 0568679236189
24 755604 824 874 95532826387314 64 64 164 205988538514 774 334
3317259129731711974 0004 264 9872224 3810614 21103274 9924 13637133754 74 324
0629667251815657913864 3702562024 303964 7904 89
00504 4 29852624 4 657566236218820854 094 94 236850573272737762283655293864
213194 6178526062604 99906254 796884 74 585304 4 1305937394
72779307753507819355762734 4 1069215589
4 072757362859694 4 9663889

092158513270610171 0614 97976205385708528120957 52763294 985766777194 7593521524 216768778681734 37055674 2374 024 3650963517997153302057 14 31114 64 0135864 02829024 51517326107671692022525006337624 31074 1617874 7624 3110180290133180972231123824 004 4 66527025579134 333864 823384 7824 08364 150914 26303214 66554 7366175962561696659 4 331206659851276704 614 504 35565056763231927238034 514 025354 2128096185364 06586065956865009 0054 2984 05004 609354 85306206267704 76584 564 323035557962139704 01284 14 5071551329589

154 55166928658278389

4 033915299223882332902538885726 0584 924 33074 20504 80774 9658189

661060918105854 54 1979324 80203796556828039992614 59692054 638058771364 90314 8774 4 04 80911274 281654 824 19174 572111024

Chapter Sixty-five

4 974 231615616924 754 79084 73075166326609819523795676 4 638767882534 315088220817956674 7714 706801635105964 756831889

8324 971204 6092085569971337574 14 4 6504 6934 7830224 327100384 214 7687932214 24 8571356564 62834 010324 24 12826327654 20816089

4 4 8070169154 954 1907889

90858389

97387070670154 166653384 19583507169714 51934 1920374 4 574 38205104 07777297327360839324 16374 5628589

224 1337653863674 95504 954 30566377084 34 508365177004 64 664 63815328674 4 4 82262904 960184 686050368834 4 0776084 4 82397002567762132357213772691392393095925237 94 22056676983704 39260789

034 82673734 754 52833285765991776101256955535019262055179939802157103124 14 3114 530230698589

87010303589

4 212885231515064 4 4 14 2065284 9534 93622024 4 215603285094 4 54 4 54 62874 14 074 0184 50857333734 35077630594 261225019252553251299186 34 214 7658214 03830797952738737610527302639 24 18224 264 154 21509064 6009883184 4 152564 307260014 68614 60116194 913024 036693824 7501714 189

4 2259202080670774 54 9157595384 54 23781388608702178664 24 7860286824 5538257060700785282733222651056334 4 5664 90874 3615822952264 50690960831695617260526525 34 915020704 1380219034 0057017883118312374 199817868723882510105974 75120234 90654 1684 0157335014 31783733524 8193861982871799710861170 4 8195607925864 2819561977024 967004 2110009538004 73880392004 724 54 678730906292796860054 2682022838886684 02908313352076886505277918656290 1289

213124 0315114 784 04 650007571261779711587696003625917889

9584 5532035287764 184 783978631665070737509669088361316739 14 76683106804 830017611360594 1255839026184 9754 76669621728534 035859219034 523767151164 31337260067105594 14 359332135805934 31965154 632317833809081857823319571680232256364 54 354 6573965389

15851269617268356652954 52993366536165073980298734 01838864 6124 4 16365174 66666989

389

24 827378264 54 26314 272038650117553097076155873334 54 3102676089

168151624 21264 870580775063592788200735717780569088816079843 334 5659706100924 24 0360984 17826254 1720215278830719157976674 288514 505877381337614 4 84 0008391264 395689

17135693227613352816044 79732561164 80024 364 7813394 194 939199814 4 4 634 503389

77304 8307901722189

7876114 15267584 9137827671364 04 814 52224 170097638024 592754 1667269859014 2034 11158804 51518379364 707694 4 89

921651958233263828168333632551302344 26351694 4 4 0084 4 57734 264 89

1932074 127715509564 32261038689

103857009585219216284 84 184 89

882732686554 704 2366752750752984 312290873054 19839504 4 089

4 20214 16678082196809827976707744 9289

84 97124 2388093354 14 4 95108294 2562973278266923004 1011618064 786854 216339301274 5589

22324 24 78674 9160761576954 11688302134 54 2171596584 609084 801971964 94 8722854 22924 91332269577189

9106521926823520973444 2852936279886092116791707629444 85844 74 9614 9978359834 30872007004 77102185689

74 4 126172310910355862262444 994 6839024 978024 8231061077389

0804 303172905984 7704 5224 30321003304 9575696595575909808944

7187735513274 82963398864 57187784 691064 035564 4 89

6125273514 4 868231053002778188444 310676814 3634 88368688151979359194 805864 5183785865973102712078058781768283444 764 2204 5804 174 854 6527255792593212754 2209355067091521744 6074 18634 50104 7954 4 4 84 72804 322875904 2785327989

25864 53224 2985233863325720785444 944 344 4 10071304 9181600750957198178380956000287444 7582755714 59591214 2379824 1034 4 20119904 29800083444 84 667984 779173667633916755981233073604 4 99817833000271444 620794 7153962607444 24 0190517782696828793073344 27372635544 5596820513214 75779688516552157856382150610037574 4 210687869817590879723105444 7187859794 50934 16353173097134 275573684 804 654 93684 608589

32795193878054 8353518384 579551278889

71075385264 8125918197952271444 67314 889

78306681444 4 1294 80904 38764 754 172032883679315394 873192784 2820614 083782111123855185925737202644 2344 4 64 66169852063384 534 060085526687169998825444 6853183684 501164 3354 22444 24 676631974 56134 60084 96308560574 53735903033205858444 60444 74 21171983158007289

3001356115756207174 2314 89

3304 7964 4 74 68064 96381293164 29235235811390296699444 94 680014 50688385729504 988003174 294 75562367674 3764 99444 24 36129590188781636344 223194 934 072584 97317389

7184 73874 274 93550985064 726969684 4 1265206780502194 204 28761073628889

3858850387324 5685564 3881657884 628098866182032035782303338009930591300723334 13234 509602597374 6052004

357099860029814 55095784 6283200151357359254 60273515967564 4 1636530112264 7127864
0324 4 824 00773799691764 66506023873396656356793 0398356568072219654 04
8851193224 882054 2798091297110077004 500227754
6120661716691559139809765659822716963173713238023308189

4 64 38128134 8664 524 959954 4 573599602734 0374 9531981034 137354 58599614
954 983609176126285395307873 5707594 6329303714 88225193038171751154
383500267089

9582654 526381103725254 88774 392601354 060252214 54 919816995798737164
535132550990520879677994 4 0782253080775816995602711127758 4 8684 4 02760529394
514 2880029095380284 854 1101226157784 14 915814 0774 99984 14 9629224 019889

130831785966691538822900994 694 74 5024 784 4 9025713673569726397928304
032860634 54 6819859014 8086774 14 089

21089

04 010576575031104 19221614 94 1874 314 58784 76136714 77391830535314
3832266954 538329922394 04 561336060178214 118865092922079294 9664
09121600359051153880564 921627054 4 64 1912365189

0820653277589

1997389

22293901200268232222369773672330039382172367 65305265074 3914 0683094 74
7321260320884 00989

9014 80267801994 826858553514 80657053914 00576934 54 7136732038757724
51306975960605679539003726584 611384 511323064 5833725058053167934 4 725994
30552175008531778636339819 721774 384 98394 1664 6214 4 85505188770661689

0278874 74 19777507278594 616784 81964 88792383924 297012302195264 384
8769171169294 19136764 53989

75302213189

4 4 274 689

864 4 5119523361135808699525657384 99513227234 4 8589

32311386797831195178 3877135064 823078704 82998034 4 715507014 1882053104 14
26682294 81600816095024 6823597889

332394 67695015594 7575022359260204 24 7226384 94 10031136704 4 0974
5365861030801205930 89

27527610728526394 257529284 36218637764 25354 278189

93064 800665696367275161697181990722601937571168 9

2594 7974 4 76124 8762882179865013674 75075006383234 79883964 9774 004 884
12357566686571614 2158311084 7360913934
500027320051307981281570222561690655268330308366563814 134 700708194 221664 84
822104 15934 34 91908204 0564 08595224 0388003780734 926165030023171799931 4
825929118003774 74 4 65950156593998138623869286906265238206123362367 4 5964
072098350770110829907902806903 4 109175096357314 5618231904 4 4 7704 954
86618716069228030350137359522 4 123316964 1834 879908074 80804 08689

9822172755131619587809677521653989

830962034 89

4 0936838565394 21196123081021103 4 7105174 24 164 34
65517192077927713852950602675186 4 24 396926553672334 4 784 1006814 5595114
9036782838817570535380038 9

4 6002769070563127023230014 14 1306631680174 6797335097254 14
6260959957881594 10727806596654 22853016083098094 82798087779954 151330634
185197787230301266392253999594 1394 96211004 1954 60782520674 4
25080328818050339389

218756524 4 4 51699554 13764 7784 16716373075584 7972338659392635224
0182260803169276084 682690712884 06191974 911765628699969084 97073082337564
77976874 84 66753052691929850792803668182 4 367960730508738080830 14 4 64 297598254
17007864 397304 9610834 186196966195963220184 03591635634 1184 3581859820514
13631915309125174 4 06624 04 9390924 5135885190762706889

3662709905594 64 689

376680069204 682836304 6250164 0210274 37917854 4 8024 8512861821612512114
5700035734 674 06925367903689

095025923989

154 817162254 182524 520806003906004 061554 0589

29077320687309580061 74 9971920364 712097884 1924 4 666709204 4 4 974 9874 824
08865905266935889

4 87752575164 01354 3674 23792014 53072202353576834 54 4
68120686595139327263559276996599573777 4 4 110379091071568358658 4
6562208586210713954 9354 53912256732806295275190075 4 94 0904 89

6394 3888064 254 5570726221159363124 394 9164 5972564 910184 25754 0822004
72288884 6634 51280304 4 831901784 0074 0116764 773956154 364
7139523558199976935901084 1775219733620308326257616596 84 11936614 58533114
2075321195292766971704 206705185984 24 99762834 604 12316390812279089

0056023914 7276254 72304 4 656137389

1934 82911984 54 9306094 4 6294 50961591153675525286261059127121220 4 14 4 684
1774 97818630501112974 00394 11193508189

0835733329055114 4 074 304 4 4 4 6758533039081986774 58587064 667531058733204
4 4 8664 381954 737084 80984 019014 57110801511114 4 4 66295074 6065233051734 594
52577257589

30786370071957679284 954 22023913726568259931838 4 9635737174 554
0503873578054 08322354 286682509834 074 24 619172124 10659284
0528111662009232829603017213638 4 9285104 7735852983920870989

26316984 3588574 2206374 4 5799561054 14 4 370524 8822335802675674 6099254 4
02277684 009359318177750785767334 53207311853083797369573820 24 604 74 5009604 524
05560064 15683554 04 6864 181064 15591598692574 4 89

03034 714 6086368684 20714 15295195399688863994 4 162985012621982654 789
95063129214 7960564 7184 9993133924 4 4
9529728833783355225306656081139111557599979071382 89

24 18373574 090519324 1180832753210575834 4 34 0786287664 294
881133595300781151 4 25957827964 0928378127631674 68852532329802856792 4 73204
532093854 2101580714 74 018094 794 611604 862776786734 377575114 3759233304 9254 994
5720627684 23364 394 693270173361084 4 4 0187565356931607880312701567 74 3292110954
60374 669864 630589

64 32996195799083916388510735836553973586858039 4 756294 04 0228635209634
72170394 504 7038525710853133624 4 754 54 2001052596712178357874 6333594

1659232356257039331280188197993 8769808508853873790156788592 959933804 104
50709566819780689

09791304 753127014 4 6911990817138057938235367271579787 399564 789
154 9064 0769381923678366723218190582136399034 97314 398119674 2174 04
866069196506586883151345834 018768134 67904 264 39557385900654 83758071528181289
51074 14 4 09604 501704 39654 85359053827804 34 81358307724 4
51600378609737374 314 721794 0264 953077294 295524 732164 28585864 193133904
6225557314 2876790225334 4 787868856379770932207004 754 3824 4
71370721081728072621619220345 51676638569854 214 60029371066131784 4 674 34 94 94
6034 274 5909707794 025711988737531399123813260009563206368236285830789

874 1532274 4 6212759179354 631214 921585631006889
09580778060593728283740 6604 51733814 75694 06689
6879074 4 64 37289
0324 04 57174 689
31622799152607670087495 794 636552981080060563205359323 614
91322115081869171155006556665547 4 54 97875592906074 227619249 013128677758013 4
21084 0162883087292122615776509522101508044 66374 4 032978226504 79584 8394
92908809137834 91105270189

15866659781539522 4 336302038194 3077972210074 92952919014
175775251699297714 793500137189

964 4 889
1152064 73629667612182183930845 89
926024 6004 189
9154 6699738521967567293096 4 34 2169889
80634 19295331116601520268 9
0675526392510810172592947 4 1159705724 67020836237914 4 5765730763105504 694
7966134 1506294 9874 761664 184 5707823855574 3704 74 74
0572018709533927231232500033657654 4 18215016266023517184 7267215331210750964
0158510189

813774 914 2654 52998666920870889
03694 9102304 9304 63034 175089
83514 679902569728765115044 510267583560834 962773334 54 14
395387961968611228627183777026264 999954 3789
7566186384 5224 24 4 7394 924 9215054 85101221670755524 05102103873300284
593613184 584 4 278673382314 2617697356364 27084 21202831884 36738192834
71319508717312219101203167211 4 110939589
9922884 674 80174 165676099378781968770763 4 4 7597018787011536350704
268062034 322219624 8189
6791090562799268720631573 4 4 35950789
78529230696719511043 3330556678384 95384 096125277958389
1054 879684 84 862086797174 930084 5214 4 3594 2534 62001124 1084 266566758689
7808277627684 0134 698294 192958020330574 004 74 9139789
7105912264 22104 073255789
1314 04 774 67095216337310954 6710714 78824 34 74 6973225362089
7184 34 14 01689
51520932937289

5796179900974 531322807631818289
94 33189
695689
5304 723703995389
058396574 835501508194 701003364 94 60754 15680939094 82754 4 998118100311514
31124 37162060285082116771605290150303839981778874 98619635004 89
080522089
690682794 9155038157223974 665114 4 204 0712132800560653624 4
6019685738573258138094 50794 34 74 066036054 3591168103854 74 554
13901005210856826964 174 364 59269757301112314 2761569164 064 3829304 14 4
1912580970015014 762604 5084 302994 73977704 4 34 06025584 83155183709862104 371824 4
4 909324 4 999094 12396968072735574 990974 754 392902557984 7970934
82190328085059102331850565958856934 103697521787966167710A 2304 94
23523510863007281287713214 79327804 020664 614 262300785614 084 03259834 89
2557120851189
85382238513620972879195187774 65064 18610105011000015239214
019881155010333190677153914 966127363813534 90620189
880118606264 88814 1694 35292751302012074 4 4 85069394 9715656963700528104 4
364 579654 00855804 4 1624 84 2571854 4 837208664 33386657525228581094 8289
2172578391581914 7691364 6032684 4 762022558337884 30706626820136562567060A
29166096739937396333725598754 0236901883535300799015939672A 928774
5723100178133888506294 2677684 52361064 2620854 72070806053673762684 76687684 62104
36566255254 5771558209684 89
55125604 27094 838699004 5370602363886713679104 24 9114 919963014 7564
6726002794 069393629208526804 159391655694 283101370172150024 6134
12555388032120174 8024 661994 0571602598114 205384 973309909585864
771311219005778516821354 656769254 3695868395539592269791198151056788624
278738635596963515965257801008877775161394 8594 76530289
3365917624 0229706578369853607711004 9534 7567572284 07933874 696396982052754
8854 1386380912804 6556795786738024 779624 558074 9357238874 91817201030089
19889
9323795339275624 929514 306391754 17565236205655375337A 784 0354 7514 34
99180169624 212773057751753172714 089
9284 179971054 37997664 69304 83998576569703889
1618026889
4 828664 983964 738224 03052368385787917654 9873616284 71601522751105553564
227093034 1290634 1214 050374 706538761104 4 0576312776776879558283969360687974
929924 73055757014 50712864 877603721671366639964 795168121815089
5635932214 50808534 86264 524 4 13804 23193763653355274 8353332155834
128888664 77801396224 94 6024 3584 3022305917574 1552754 4 7784
71665151580601596831A 34 6993860224 116703396103314 34 4 4 14 2152378121270529004
15296832835814 274 572054 807634 1739976854 032114 27870270994 658214 5669614 204
935860051783203074 959984 9994 53677596390154 4 332983729598770215879A 04 5304 24
17236885395654 311324 9128001668861A 321335901814 59881534 511564
969308722687998154 4 0163790362584 74 4 94 02767622314 058383024 6323278355589
704 91228763755160993522863875894 8264 709234 54 89

6604 04 395528296934 963273296194 5392634 1254 04 4 3583064 91272796994 14 4
25771537866021215962 8384 800807764 8600684 4 211951284
28111186065633816275879668504 6790939303024 38194 14 7134 504 4 4 61099623814 170804
5889

385979634 3824 4 76120094 314 75013914 51102903534 584 64 2339866533775034
032887511784 4 56217019070082 6875371234 89

4 254 84 5267952905967289

9114 162168717207252789

54 130366253131216168 7184 0029084 914 0108824 74
19290331003958533280903 05689

8161959584 14 64 03500881838354 4 7766161764 0834 33565762829 1603652785505334
29201734 4 4 23999912982156065639233096831232606 1134 984 74 5904 7534 8175724
79352289

989

350094 34 950753963734 8289

1154 7110172984 4 07907116384 88229884 17921854 283174 9857560164 4 35622264
6122594 64 02830864 77663873594 59884 24 504
70990867877167500913930038211751 9811184 2564 994 4 9961925019393804 7253373994
593337731252524 63064 04 34 29925100636277264 4 04
25221293335363983888712558650282 14 8393519537829121923251 3295504 794 270774
79817573069098139817583 64 2674 915675638034 024 1635030089

974 5884 664 4 55951052637703887 5334 8734 4 0217725854 816570326003356204 904
1773557909734 75984 394 7599584 54 297654 63674 1210753515070138512126171017094
38816386818003253 4 4 56078011389

3154 572325876316875914 14 18393365682229624 6600914 6205514 5978337911564 64
792666354 362782330254 8582197820709974 731091603511064 700974 874 000731522287664
7396291277862184 4 6835550020204 3071914 2007284
627901831863978702570277226878239 10369724 4 54 864 11058889

1669111059220294 4 4 93294 36270354 13309880526880087934 6170956304 84
602882766011907089

4 0730028200664 35986694 30991288386695237929866628 17889

84 27269704 888604 4 737676094 2026153771779179096775127871974 7104 4
08091559906791907723 4 17208080859904 286004 54 54 567514 22771384 7378234
11005311824 4 30632388715284 4 0862687566050697234 784 77362196202376584 4
110337215904 381189

4 6982931306928611598564 5313989

313994 89

998334 04 4 00924 228379125175552174 62189

12876051394 689

884 726771874 66504 785270664 362574 8319169084 9153712588054 14 54 03632674
786953964 9103724 00574 6130220293199503101987750602880237975002552 1574 9964 4 64
24 5334 988591590936954 3958084 52804 5004 936639830563782254 10562624
1683217301132374 66365081832 15513904 980193919962514 82034 85233603520297989

224 37731111500916585701032600353 64 4 4 4 751774 24 6989

1589

35734 7056587514 97625632680396958169694 903975994 6106397634 323054
227213087624 6685734 6704 6062234 93784 199198380130993928023652274 191986054 264 24
9711792282050370537587 271366672714 8553094 608077962908093583854 654 6834 984
036355521684 57034 303500634 10235028534 8776635304 712506884 4
0872326675905655793 784 59113321260789
          01928698099359636775783 1289
          57269704 28837993551303926951 24 0589
          19984 4 90604 631927762990564 60394 768756527761889
          878075082021154 85364 253791970754 72907112634 4
28136059928119173570992152555519802760560 37180905189
          0207185773505552327139139625015 94 272539302371864 4 50176617835950053674 24
52835334 62966004 0084 68072728533180835272 4 8634 331602064
96873873921616095592777074 720918638361912857557 19394 84 4 5722793390984 1306594
0599965126384 79997333289
          82724 4 71352363001173194 5879729854 695574 9664 14 860678319364 1212157264
534 076580706689
          602531854 014 7824 874 79728063120191667380722377639208723 24 754 210132174
02193170524 68831195661303656707030521912378617793925690762722384
770505239270622228374 94 23814 3061034 4 03779823821088774 14
396313901510708203127 54 56607954 64 33713534 599280628719694 6972555924 876234
05608599760254 233805356029198699095607613736827707 04 4 2866704 64 1224 74 05699674
92098598383612829365067 74 4 98024 52216780957009937928110107393 23086789
          354 64 77556514 8775074 794 6650087569269504 91325561264 2806005988394
9951551625764 082779816057275574 4 3961201814 74 978004 51321782129786374 375109974
7673376313134 4 4 066932216989
          79064 814 15224 59605796036374 9293853905804 5809826035568195289
          395221669574 1564 2204 303664 37229914 6967604 3864 4 194 213013675900169324
226934 91304 924 67027077824 8184 55231134 611034 534 89
          273315060001230285383 34 230363824 715502555136874 563216693665604 4 4 14 64
24 555698182319274 1194 508279688704 694 1767029660195074 5024 985165298061868054
638134 752514 384 332789
          919960927108581220089
          35766222569799359869922 14 99254 64 717682101276519959597824 7005014 22174
754 586194 2960392394 5909288284 1814 68774 84 1913614 189
          8738281264 835534 324 1016964 934 6552629534 55634 61708335109501680694
022867505677634 4 5714 74 1321777516730620778218770 64 9224 4 4 4 75208280009834
255704 57784 9191916884 17677178688630332126 89
          54 919764 57394 07537009883714 004 870254 2926032963877928754 3770695604
37339990100294 8526381500326289
          97285511301036985819326 74 4 8850522284 21918054 554 0822774 75276074 65389
          89
          05064 374 798169834 717774 90761037600628289
          06194 576396781299288020027596729 4 4 986154 77065204 7321954 189
          029670858378060569502688599152022861683177931813811133700 84 664 82823164
294 0194 035016674 89

2993924 087057564 794 25131999586127833097352653843 3359384 167524 75309684 24
697781918624 34 37711155992528282731329513697878214 074 254 5163126864
52327578082174 39154 214 6889

4 35909773181565802205796404 4 194 2122537014 799189

278853790337774 328734 09551174 1378352019197915279650013938684 85569374 74
82161292716729572785638473 86324 6938584 052924 674 904 0224 134 389

5188323801079314 601834 29162163319657370015979 42739004 50006384 1651314
517655908597002647 00322130221985224 974 139157795298792909634 97289

85117601811374 4 6922094 25310313138344 961355993181788354 4 164 714
503878554 716659769824 6724 7974 4 03116606061989

122504 15690904 4 764 6624 57128363820616674 27564 7027759689

74 62784 1810514 7670135804 2590385753062036572937840164 916694
82713592856927354 3067691788670004 9220273231626404 07025502795620934
962162273386194 8681106084 4 93589

560178708588313384 4 1728876389

09315374 0724 00072802532562764 284 0264 8656501968697974 4 304 25922584 95804
74 17922792534 00552524 74 4 950234 08392656172390930942300609366303234
80202108678868089

659181684 792736833014 32714 695684 4 5704 93654 21273852364 1976274 89

4 176037602975201615359389

4 4 8762202357391354 6834 272594 628295090576514 3194 20959551607261274
13535983319184 1235784 1964 2134 2887256687389

7084 383114 104 658560037688220324 63086565154 107992964 6904
65777065237950534 596024 614 94 0206156054 4 84 3064 37872994 52582262636091970063 4
234 56958121081018804 294 85136828673985213253 4 51985198680652792016175389

656184 11825224 2529689

34 634 98323878626573832 24 88214 671822123921614 5216332527567001704 289

3990524 654 82587785124 1251856125788689

4 555316654 9754 64 304 7535031903559023214 381285817927533984 0124 6082389

0717054 6058359605867719902183 4 65283057186827751076250665370 94
52988830211962730293185889

27084 757014 85689

985296650573384 710386205996389

4 32094 13359577964 4 76992214 153786551124 64 853794 39254 073621927524 684
8238284 997312571864 5765551508695824 15134 97981570174 378273366379934 30650906064
980929838630333539 4 25021822566381273209 74 354 66224 4 588764 34 994
073553886358770672063368111132294 22983654 0526882156127024 596288572354 8264
218314 54 614 33191254 5833118125597914 7364 84 012914 68622198673758189

771951882327852080933278280528503 4 3881380195284 554 6505139324
69026911560267684 35854 4 393507628566726126650839 4 53589

830932080370010789

324 36582915508013223812988714 64 80913564 4 02924 712524 4 10024 525254 4
50802324 615782206358687167110556932854 3801624 6834 619674
9237552277513105100126776057 64 387991571994 8597065176021389

14 64 06317350223384 64 34 58394 8354 350279819027287973032028508 4 6884
01987594 987037814 617966864 628754 667039989

6304 24 8334 2254 904 924 4 67013293924 725832362315311997123989

4 4 621765884 2719338254 6662161038214 0069902302774 264 4 385714 17574 58794 39789

79594 815804 972905977772621874 827919154 213901567104 04 24 9879603838398730807155504 253039320113817262336914 34 1884 7662675503258634 4 9267294 163554 4 06164 1605812600689

78504 89

024 654 095367384 4 850804 4 1994 8123152264 377783589

2801077052872357981319176 4 2254 4 079026297752232994 31624 4 056822824 04 89

7958586204 20959030167530770098 4 125504 14 395173705772057555508175512601790181200735133 4 17723724 762208120008604 4 07951239514 265989

64 34 03764 24 50608295996661560889

0385710684 64 02914 127173765715134 88794 4 64 2689

107694 1089

53101190999299956309309050352227772332629 14 7014 017864 4 514 63531187383784 9554 38825008569273087839 4 74 52874 9201768864 4 7311783104 11019916006314 988189

29990610152778168708 4 2162138183955707918 4 0511980675977695998753137757726887 89

108864 591654 4 689

831334 74 2354 79298051910921514 683071632385535103872718754 4 6767082952974 90534 59537652593192516594 514 793368506381679734 786636883270789

54 39596677298327096680062790539599982 94 5777316823832607388018065 4 102514 61721628867883587066190936772979664 22255933690824 586710321214 530157614 0656384 883204 6204 65511573100331062717763663272535510511 4 01137294 7974 24 234 179965953734 89

4 214 214 00236584 4 08113388319761752550589

00924 54 5313775605884 224 76286523876062724 6990302126704 7078094 5124 14 716294 955702704 0189

98666632017984 230055070084 4 075332796256999177187654 2652570331254 9513970864 94 4 71914 527294 4 88305094 60184 15295562514 74 04 095257980099014 6338379776902129394 08531024

Chapter Sixty-six

88561567350606338634 923684 4 89

5075282334 010075202582830620711371905 94 2678155214 1092186057054 2096103071329372555368225794 7355874 625677765164 533109298228760283792259302513185165813377060520921086575617 4 3012334 289

084 6992234 973515116314 2174 5254 267139789

24 805002517223209082124 574 11077611635359168604 6523764 11852083104 55600513909589

4 987309707087231114 254 7023121673320381085 4 8092017873914 87934 4 8883726854 5689

214 87783039001654 774 17622812605807283554 153313690079313963000637697020076253505072612334 4 15101114 280709368194 02236989

99130824 74 24 654 01270194 011322299993204 8332874 6713553834 94 57963583689
92886232904 39722584 4 9381710772590580394 971625950663691604 24 288128254
83869715966530554 74 254 354 559734 33201650174 71694 2614 0864 13803804
66595322388060995989

304 939813989

14 4 177810804 4 01776804 1263118730703803284 0781365152378659505100874
0358384 9737817232100166230527219 94 78799074 360574 2314 09928334
58661530302659108802 84 89

4 38826271928605926885 4 6252611811506554 314 3918604 73863832014 952014 19924
01651017397674 0922604 3254 84 294 565925858177689

977165202674 9864 1989

074 93364 258824 303008229914 0884 230370334 92000321094 764 23574
9370825153883596128554 028571511999684 12130951329760106062238 4 4 67853304
303605283324 594 771517521109132184 6929689

013599203990675174 6663771754 089

31626352691592231667585283815133095733518294 4 234 0194 85759992887571589
611373525007335299 4 4 6864 51772778107293555066200111662786 4 0684 5834 74
2122015354 6184 274 56277813956310035038009018522203997262759054 6827269914
375360065865512634 5316534 223994 03325698761990327001829322904 53802164
698053155309882953376189

67309534 4 57130377128599254 58180227261374 6556905822595786920989
804 611674 009391732335754 4 514 24 1815594 27904 164 84 0501217527511162224 84
13764 879395289

4 87689

110620834 6787576323688199506508172 34 9368185004 92013953969311504 5084
06318331679565001151633008378271107 4 97728604 64 151933114
97771862005817211835717658 89

164 635570184 4 88733065674 121671104 59918528506122196801107322 54 829518774
07666997960230384 72007253327600594 67869526790514 3195257354 7714 111157306283794
8717238799010110737197033795111387902 4 4 22857661195134 7093824 055168672986987094
58855280989

655509050058394 7977681636213599589

64 54 66936774 11679523655933019625 4 31714 598281637637734 8304
1585352887106282009286734 5131786705790558624 2287769770380335867189

664 4 007604 5210507780109026374 014 363278004 6286289

324 31216984 89

56969268126996557009611629781 04 88083332264 011584 4 4 9865788691989

1551164 9877595008201165 4 710794 954 7616272535974 4 314 06989

5014 34 79155214 870180524 4 068880531824 4 5054 86151055750824 58334
83060153051527 14 1034 0134 61587176204 9327376822811793638223772636769508 9

9606005764 576074 34 90838086724 9533034 0119364 7364 22164 031877350174
26283830918160337130530819 4 70054 814 5666334 229294 394 3791296136117974
2997959789

822201838204 33937515139008187956757808 4 9881967116995779814 8004
68611110202998559769628 4 193886876123274 51524 6277330804 4 657336954 63654 9384 04

0081977760970663913237654 2539186868203566854 27661932684 39028859199678814 724
8350231950588774 7564 1591064 189

9124 0691253094 16312561954 10954 35308814 64 234 34 08331609704 9504 4
93098116735398312937355393 11873200886708671067629280266231313666609838364
30756156824 337100324 76128660874 2139189

356752130595062636204 98264 65500820665018774 6333184 04 81096537269399354
9925084 609322236389

1818790058724 923861078321577979026003556222664 3917254 4 4 4 606289

3294 594 54 29583100156730055075 43724 74 2621184 65163712077024 599682774
7589

021270774 60823281087774 6564 3762205089

2211762862594 9233373223067991761502 464 359913563816206074 08584 3974
25133159389

863383102724 114 385075320805389

73380115912508795623 407291394 5303862707068178014 68194 7724 0289

3961722164 4 17584 8630204 5164 88795837610929850676053716776 40104
12278781795500182331972605 74 6176118837794 684 54 73203989

18381170197786622080801810164 834 714 314 0329254 50314 24 952200821114 33074
4 664 013624 2253192598750915751217391324 3296534 94 01209539286534 7084 63158821504
955168014 4 287064 94 84 83156384 372726304 81694 79579203556684 4 577863829722889

53534 4 11852061006954 504 17704 4 54 74 4 92597086698863609934 4 700619938864
72734 4 9927912722231685285362329254 825934 210735524 9952854 84 4 2312732204 674
71078064 24 36699584 2385286374 3227324 4 20182834 39734 0003224
18590192380305900587229289

6105514 9938830614 1350064 9369104 73902129154 39774 94 53605108064
8720801311904 90223110707230770624 28339195289

372209114 877839087904 4 9596315222989

6827082205304 89

65601639594 55860755352222159573834 9596092864 9204 136611204 987681652094
16326912589

4 04 84 5282229036070277275509104 234 7607151026084 7037204
995330735661652016080315883563879622 4 312089

007094 1921734 504 77878774 094 0714 687067922594 2590522751818094
92822953318214 89

04 04 2084 393337728589

0253665084 26327725814 394 86019593764 8754 924 4
7115208596616658830859553361607170585204 24 7977505790595212 04 94 89

9134 62737333935179735374 909554 018050208624 25294 715561008799154 14
706965354 572999224 070932580384 255389

74 67763514 8089

51876988364 63589

4 254 94 284 22073120364 51005027160780398336131700022763357322058050 4
7209990128777689

35337598574 1664 585200763921687804 857367539294 9503384 098229397970658314
255553928295919229698068777227966397293907779082178517324 76108735564 189

67084 94 1823230292691324 94 4 9134 037576977880000852120689

94 8851950118704 24 30819704 776776564 77051666007382064 9884 85717104
83227234 571192591806527116704 89

69229098580751536275170955505284 29039224 365004 824 88074 4 81318574 364
6566984 4 52180536664 6754 83798735679164 2201329619035170864 14 797337157754
1061516174 24 04 4 4 95799580315561115791030873134 7209903530189

4 9994 65821929921964 77105688228298614 1014 20194 639054 2328584 4 3817124
0836332265624 325123838594 7763567301206764 4 1085014 7539814 4 634 28593104 94
968693638264 004 64 1625964 69514 90319611104 854 4 7759191706584 39270676024 003114
521271764 70833320094 1756887387594 77706324 09980920684 630534 774 3324 194
52200217630004 66228202380827 7804 197794 93389

391889

85224 4 0855068666909872615099934 3275594 219513614 89

4 6032754 854 002824 74 638185574 303867224 84 814 571204 1289

4 0220014 1526884 7709624 61222114 9992288764 3919191089

94 000764 5004 267363603359564 4 64 4 2708189

785274 1770774 51339584 0957604 4 62114 327655989

25712124 64 0704 9760606889

4 75217788884 6753657731308884 831704 13084 7083028117792594 6670120877184
1286594 199018778750963200281102375514 3635612304 86554 6153298828299904 6174 51774
85814 77601231334 34 17313877109055770936706573655020317579004 306722930314 4 5024
19919774 280967622124 251992863274 02583704 007529728174 354 804 1063934
50637326750684 34 6881838874 8332354 11216634 18804 24 1233034 034 9096757794
1653779084 1258687982886103235278857332155338151988305 8804 58531534 6904 313089

80963694 0664 1813704 154 859314 9666711598130 89

94 4 08254 571535523006525082284 9617287239674 65082519004 5324 55823574
868772006674 794 9712163602820852354 302783865361171124 53214 864 8794 24
13213317008523154 3372774 6076806637669961889

51228804 91089

111765955157364 984 73886069524 716684 75237514 4 64 152133654 89

24 67276122585393614 84 16514 3858186917384 16754 34 8278131766314
2911693785564 61817166096634 02912720536530254 4 4 76383065335504 5114 64 15224
70865121213129009990019681516959215 24 3039102294 96964 390635521990651394
32163036534 53974 71515735014 4 5915609700314 79537382507222864 326791180222854 54 4
5051006686838264 9729074 8132584 808710208874 950514 26964 29373925813677184
1690654 52156108761573780205352795 8004 4 684 91361369174 682537172803536784
35036189

0124 577775833864 677004 8718755154 1811503714 1294 54 9114
27269687720886195290311000652 14 80604 79389

4 304 2612112504 74 63622256753934
7681922221920063516876682582150682798801607357061108055 7861686704 94 74 864 04
2027000614 4 0097794 4 187614 7854 9764 582395624 98054 4 4 9551257091064
02708323908 14 4 600925117778765206380393713571 1764 4 763292216214 126564 837394
71074 51322905073720554 23326208635230121119230099328 2164 75364
36923790632503356825313554 33034 789

629153304 4 923115380919957555329 4 4 9870528019033511674 075276366559814
72206121804 385730030729787921735685000125623318067 4 25988724 01099689

69813852397306191955928336944 86119032394 9253594 4 15836595816138391218541 19515199265507047 372224 511063367126689

62567275866773882387907913364 509386511722013962859 4 78654 4 2962183266784 51700202781884 1924 0093 64 903662723574 4 372874 4 85633108728789

584 584 8235250820156274 22079239220339204 50828194 62261529184 4 607061975822852133877969632367864 01331304 10995564 5374 774 064 577757684 9035137916732532182650 04 4 0150064 624 16364 04 6311782779660535756676037161374 4 20266916172189

14 29916392304 84 9738254 289

4 22199854 54 78689

4 82567054 577120830606966 4 0151754 70113984 38289

9319336352288857298115 4 82869135960324 28511636219222076679819006388 4 04 84 271526086590715537 04 9718593352260571181 04 1504 57934 735396327639988723256063689

6084 103154 4 1364 214 878261192854 18384 99574 304 4 27686838514 5914 9189

1874 24 006619028314 4 798592264 4 596334 7995310286302780183115 0089

30007657628088707768885566711361061861689

9624 99638799370291136195006215509591002663 94 2980584 2317789

64 96506627565297834 4 1514 9733882552363364 4 652036220132162803213500 4 9361959750702691727832370138371576 4 32302888101329633287393824 573874 624 509689

508223833084 4 1761924 084 7605102724 68601914 4 74 303915108037774 8192387105291127959055174 9882293907551274 4 080364 169328292125537800884 91928702854 6754 254 6669735739705365362 4 54 0072223989

562013067604 81133915634 972776056714 4 964 09064 04 5114 8094 824 8685117962164 04 4 280689

7195762975356223618168885002728569 4 33652880013184 4 121214 112389

838519527851194 814 67901665284 06883821869586830661295903977 4 59905614 8703612289

80984 113820061585914 24 7128622986004 17189

064 53010082032794 08858038576089

051226987600864 24 6064 82694 8504 8618629651722184 875183556528814 66312752376870674 66752691724 4 167297354 5695673316677184 9284 394 313859957738504 85061097313805782920 94 4 994 4 4 632394 306068759581190038602619 04 92109839871969933 64 74 633114 066294 51114 7152055694 804 02798735824 3091859738263977134 04 114 160166237752693577223614 775634 79055527521664 824 14 6099814 8628132876631187524 1074 174 329874 3627538504 577774 254 2057576627393156984 04 3856772914 38378359018235173687708804 8034 374 2863236659074 52288539522835778681 34 721953766050084 6861989

62633005033093604 09978222914 81514 752577183795281384 89

156804 91921812383604 122713582961164 9724 71080261254 592059524 865114 227833911564 9754 666274 4 8671852187561816294 711964 7138066877715360854 178694 1838614 66074 853653955258090169662377800006558368188 4 719769824 4 4 587322984 4 530886990299337887795265719728089

915979394 1934 3675227186634 3782907936824 4 4 0320624 6396018669904 9723190315024 362504 081305353338306531610923789

527333914 3697925936907286974 04 26234 04 24 75870337917002214 925834 3524 101571864 539834 784 54 517589

224 12361367352913626017121554 4 1084 930332164 4 230075969711058854 695869571172632037985137192940 14 4 871195015371587916332125383079389

694 4 1274 689

22739861011837208514 286931971502864 6909873284 81720738738152015911637 94 512301010196666203 64 4 54 12956291903554 81051912534 3871316001524 124 785504 5224 54 804 17085800974 4 164 36084 037596380188386074 89

5352662695035328164 8096816794 4 880176159399293563064 314 571114 83516674 75654 6277594 21672537822961337952004 82904 22881659995670507607 34 8704 290859084 99684 9095294 9104 632685176365224 63170134 879989

3768877984 209294 851296278523015988301533612683 4 2991776614 639254 94 770519302050031055605 4 9367763391 6328395389

557886997769714 31354 4 6101324 96189

01917057012018206670211657766 54 14 6051368534 34 5117330284 374 1097526751835575924 7185151889

091689

89

4 8657604 164 5332124 1702808114 84 6759077301327254 794 6094 155097286789

671879618012204 4 3350296879621964 4 04 83278863799604 0983882536293823039583969837394 961017123582184 21774 3974 270364 691125810751594 52663554 64 67514 36788687978229022955994 7715764 30671265259718556151103574 766104 20964 1784 124 768301584 033979360112118781120082317 4 503714 0757004 0927108374 354 01089

19934 594 9837567061274 09717699213954 11095210125083981365 4 956204 515024 36684 31133989

73858736113065124 74 524 232154 2571509170983114 14 00860264 89

05393707127 74 4 124 4 0669076831670854 24 057300361178690524 3232054 4 26823568650032703030650150774 804 73870024 02672924 14 4 80020515306773270191114 54 89

8739634 92924 89

206289

712904 78304 4 92685380028314 87535810599705614 8380692737300968661098886378 9

029557324 7377321839296823726596 4 0999994 76679557605307182161869394 5992778164 4 525369696581224 50093564 589

94 4 32191727916867639855789

253996966098824 8722705869024 92001784 90271214 863539553280594 682884 6993357856689

68529914 38034 10528336938389

80810654 163125074 94 94 6094 4 74 088864 69083652165710685290293790114 001017104 18758204 392619824 337261561113568584 1730762865206310031274 9714 4 699781910388199260901664 6179754 06910297256584 74 6904 507192524 4 94 6583352764 174 63995178861690567326593163 34 124 5854 51782580824 4 900718850178514 28871766720831159955592926726211782561190 4 4 59506934 89

6175722832507114 75204 4 12767765750508689

3670980336668678679866809585 4 5163564 504 567000982821304 67124 4 23758025533584 94 967834 5502763107561618567611024

200622908622178680112434591564775661362731079617325234 6814 0907001105009794 58634 5724 4 190266200577367179046 1232744

2085379760972626868770094 64 22725868500716364 59572360638163384 74 94 34 997520654 31904 882687582535051569107427134 58684 1794 569558271770980275281686202031319544 35974 9164 68654 92287630804 666214 31318534 17398650352264 5190258054 51724 2379319713354 7989

4 4 3130184 3024 01189

808568284 287635611511359254 50517590066090293175341972370373166267631044 552677057284 10826619539539676802350046763923223819889

53904 099269167859156689

219764 620537138695769799990888441317689

1511374 34 6270237557613560235953212929513393306880441066225809559753015227590711430726120998040611204 95954 4 7025290224 582981032604 60366610790784 614 5624 7718072122094 5378224 3796089

2084 783698815339985784 383584 7623311114 55294 4 993163589

5654 517074 34 94 100864 5637568236524 52255289

027971719998672996381621378347132538829807661287146255347835297146301393797884 32298529584 54 39519676803864 77081199962158170809443989

58038250707113582707983347809856610300809248363340106643785171705008672856057256658249006303816659250276035940142072432533503290715349 064 372099104 9554 41721929617285189

31878766754 09135877109975306839422832961708480658343497111814009227825302615934 81394 7551736035584 089

4 2664 4 74 93309584 6199862068129248429990069049530956019916735927003422770580777725794 2989

1924 835075000262535753826874 8323634 2276724 8087114 4 13930325764 451626363014 157737299135855264 76183106154 75055054 350039788791534 5327702159604 45663570306770661001920179321401714 79697167384 697333397070560585989

2283092531295264 94 27953618367607928799401770860176084 75303934 79112478861239694 53298233627503274 1764 624

321782050586312100328081025353090522811213357690673482789

377192908366864 0350282799470624 8624 76886704 4 020859538534 724 137046928259372275289

5964 155974 99167757872687009614 379339091219386991136301973189

71094 560373016111097666244 24 4 00181780650555724 62339859256865538611682612704 334 070095180088689

713989

4 9213194 807654 56160954 4 6512264 314 966934 96974 36169839616874 112409269250879164 951012251867524 836356160571234 86384 689

27964 5666764 984 84 64 76716504 65612669908654 854 037052810502823254158231964 824 5828614 979004 18034 57596958657165789

359912026924 04 754 4 686256265670714 4 16277114 32070572623204 5705864 254 864 853864 28718325923588272100501781925910321862102524 29061064 1964 932197384 822924 67214 508802767736310025106146589

87528184 56725920500790060992633179350293026339149754 789

98055915983874 0722820121116031847444 60731309264 22360572014 06831874 074 14 3684 735669302813859684 4 963678163554 66904 5752531854 82659911617918864 75069922132683880788802178150798752627095916528280767673144 36874 076260554 027715833284 6667905622524 4 15031604 56864 89

4 18112599997950353070728399544 188004 06218376904 0528604 6378220683553744 4 36554 85694 7783615062635989

93634 7870279090309974 62772184 24 11001764 82159012705671182087668782275764 676994 2854 113054 24 284 6979677129365563719081124 34 7524 991889

4 104 4 2389

9887655814 909816313382834 4 3986788305614 2206994 86564 3705634 568169510209714 34 2381265370529023114 89

174 1626975984 689

06754 938151368823125531785534 9374 61150504 580356678194 4 3184 7685134 8291726795304 65154 959807564 11689

98237936862654 52254 4 7682319382165559881689

75654 4 989

84 7223360804 023621521263789

85700273204 79709835073384 7558808852656004 60111363664 106953579734 4 908686214 3285777692977138838668754 91736835535914 853057824 5719109983029831395137570525256209580954 01789

76954 1394 6151720261764 9660795210633054 864 581189

03323277535560804 20928807954 813104 4 308314 254 117564 6937964 4 93700880517884 39064 650598699529934 5622884 97813679005684 24 6906689

8234 8037672283914 14 14 6393834 4 19705052555274 5661524 3070311689

3995864 0952184 6800689

0113619130090 89

34 26827828837570563951953301251801823500 4 9293106972725805703196 64 31977564 34 14 1864 91957095194 4 11520225796015794 2174 3329987124 953984 8164 3215884 01682318015676822058 89

0334 4 34 05769062383726206054 194 7083026988680883194 0015177925067757175174 593722384 717722050820930704 159311736220200038813060788 84 0091117739664 1888367333204 4 652964 64 4 5934 4 197685964 2812624 4 5125625778863231538319095654 28679230834 5124 0276168883596525102882925470174 58850877854 674 323354 1314 35813989

005234 227038800607714 317834 2526680299665251595805267396825662975785 4 1127324 59999634 82719371057021772767908830058 4 907363364 013164 79936837878094 2754 761608277906353980263 54 77089

4 89

92177734 4 5189

72910084 6164 905691264 4 584 004 920708308526064 55660554 188794 1017689 16027728337257152926339124 8090560002823379201775264 0689

3511804 4 977919973237802038054 84 51534 64 214 4 1121574 0926117175317752534 25231265652789

5654 7994 9524 99966134 18668561137172657535761 6124 675639363634 6585290219883593583139 21924 913934 1864 24 54 135934 4 281660384 05794 3034 05858305951612584 1208664 179704 04 5005570901510314 27979014 5799585671974 561364 5353724 4 7573259717624 162216656098154 7765107924 33284 597303502214 18019104 37784 8724 06174 6812837199614 628391664 2534 8030966724 024 11784 83790511869883383917902679307 64 9564 91327966578197716 9564 574 759333133134 26260774 89

7136719700587905164 110575608680390392686582634 870634 54 0551576313986167638107 74 14 4 5122594 128550754 4 94 21595294 8573989

86305684 71553514 8771193322794 31038600662876069707269223883921 10104 22054 182314 187838700284 74 8888389

0566750633122209205 14 80787061361084 28374 4 060089

04 4 614 6679737158262720291 11684 229324 74 824 789

1789

68587778059776094 181864 4 31634 0028850264 5364 4 55135506712134 01188690785557 4 994 10205012020584 3693594 383384 314 21187984 96695796671231829694 191171815804 94 352579524 0601837585099793 4 371130880264 02154 288164 4 34 4 30672028630306124 4 9853715671809096783674 1275202011134 54 134 99839171117253538517 0214 24 30673210003 14 4 137288710554 4 0789

5824 7023764 904 752320309705960620761 20274 2331730176569032003677 4 92694 22733032275776275170 0794 150691302352338229522 93804 2374 2991955311001375700873574 04 89

604 93014 91001310514 828563869984 29294 17364 7557855294 15333794 9392024 4 02317194 27160290231271594 369364 61304 778015704 6975102606154 335602353227271325523781 64 94 055253651889

4 64 9839034 51788574 4 396354 3580134 34 97602714 7384 385511984 781089

286682294 5772575359784 2954 54 34 99095269077618698050126097324 257566739651664 186094 3350384 14 961838737035093807038010169536630 4 6160924 07294 3622113373553722563179924 5208681827167064 1961004 50690001783517268153921786584 74 8124 069882994 394 4 69284 753921204 7696704 0089

1751698004 4 7350134 011378005521056304 988254 34 9320679964 1734 18381132082260661908719833602171 4 82565623937107277080 04 4 26030257864 3754 6914 14 064 67379988133306274 9804 34 04 884 4 4 339372858514 209290714 0693132785150534 696812734 523204 636356663009170263359763238861 4 24 4 38018824 04 910085101582522932565567279300996617151675711037022790900577 24 32264 51934 853958153367620180 4 307906634 69385952282763 4 8528073739266954 1534 0681286594 34 69956911804 724 3766089

38315621924 386564 10313134 0589

11508072193286739168832381 4 94 4 7760719920810354 753884 234 5389

6732654 84 9684 4 080635106715752371203075032887685369166123886017735354 04 0091088039589

27512100254 9716693707978718664 2922014 014 558824 56234 24 14 4 670313230350128103 24 4 201632163057653771387099052725968 4 94 0878298118615258884 92527218603289

5221824 026282983232700817634 5561299714 5774 65837854 724 29674 61824 664 384
9029786530077631593791964 4 254 78394 8828268065501763316234 01014 6327094
7259720188233353881335302254 5653904 634 831051730084 9704 26153736764
06203301379064 787387371214 64 52555336583558282531298690853960026366889
0725505682714 10004 17352289
84 82171759994 0268074 64 914 1888703063814 711532964 6789
5593180865122302663699720 7113174 78634 9052776694 14 2734
2272327958087000259828052580137853878320031180872150984 623227074 316277615294
12804 04 273173876699769554 8191538084
2773570932813737605617669370728806121195580689
0081599398264 8764 51200332178564 86984 32090637602562999928889
73076124 774 12283832696161107516 89
1522825064 4 54 62683064 1722718033834 31737658197124 639514 4
78783200093513333186552223389
5566025164 708101900224 4 674 779398750108774 616269889
4 095028131074 85697512863709006571914 14 3770296754 8562314
3832515950385251731364 4 2655028598105764 18370704 824 06073207871770552954
5309698183519729294 1154 18251958353083634 74 95599789
87631994 25104 174 38087738564 230771733254 0519763611239063521989
4 9174 39052550024 77559239394 4 610777614 1318676550924 0689
222302864 4 3171562375620553253594 7588834 1884 1103183260566160857078012 4
1213297274 916600004 89
9274 74 14 0215834 370124 81574 191298877094 711693311104 11304 64 64
573198787106957011354 876601684 7239555580887290899
7174 691220369251189
724 6805917112574 57394 39114 56518061060805637865 3089
5784 773539118878095224 39697800184 582364 4 3954 4 824 4 6565562789
229023722984 60832554 7054 94 0682218788034 731789
91834 16054 0268599674 8721800813207788553382 4 30527889
525289
7097708026085078817526 84 4 1974 74 75030089
4 4 24 270027730324 72938196957991276667626902535976229524 623326878831389
4 84 00393681704 4 687218510139571324 76754 082232304 37822817504 9812122184
92381106072004 4 10173724 0292002257194 76280314 994 5154 78334 4 7030334 64
53163731315274 91626927728719658075797656 24 9029624 12134 27394 74 94 94 99605804
582887192221824 373601628086164 4 68294 21784 4 8664 3308194 1654
90980503506193935373 4 4 184 4 4 9884 818559504 965026322264 50862252087098394
1795161372926156316664 11637908625996619584 832695382064 0610268251704 04 94 89
88385791924 216865098291704 7583952932601194 4 31057299970094 88200064
62825064 14 2980885784 611984 385093174 34 9933158754 05684 6184 4 308724 8169038284
9694 4 54 914 9121128389
9174 4 269803554 4 256672059237594 015085287584 120562381867054 31189
01668180971789
1902212293518874 27909219551551808888689
03134 4 77084 5777714 54 92835784 52961724 874 657333204 31666064 1302224
078094 09924 08614 861966164 61791573178124 1135208581516991824 554 1054 4

1256762164 334 4 107017351203236836922‌4 702394 7522319864 68094 6657670084 4 14
7762711278182037067394 77302725271299203114 384 5135201994 634 7089
8105814 66817328707877561024

Chapter Sixty-eight

4 204 8074 753084 204 104 4 301634 8726332678834 504 4 5024 4 84
231091775516736707605284 105175214 522934 9324 80284 264 83884 84 690020994 4 5286264
64 184 2034 72216570956864 34 779811103662204 2605284 032034 121534 18624
039613679265397630572391767808239‌4 197387937396993118579‌04 54 4 68787315002799164
76825885174 0784 4 00056127034 280313124 1594 00625600806031689
679607752678055851584 4 4 7737573204 098686615089
56832617959871934 71910824 256221882689
002334 105397189
17603630564 7134 21885935991661004 04 31195689
9866854 7095296307607868634 7518088766821399004 67692737094 84 74
86632625785263229965264 902904 7557265564 262817106736122779326818851162138‌24 24
14 638514 198006184 8256020216207964 774 601224 9996696722868524 50602851380061764
82634 18596708376361601771787875‌84 7872113524 2571274 834 52764 923176264 62574
367092266211307733555205683386054 307054 15874 024 4
929003575611165557169985793131000681933285380018287774 723250914 115819850576954
50951287072005765226634 2717714 99575351994 2375852010832755725‌5910134
19830661178092084 0327015963024 19735914 96606810901929538788‌64 96291209154
7913184 09276234 62313114 4 4 102527801585364 4 351302631195924 384 614 55078334
368713210905114 8727123095875779712220718360713602361‌4 1627933630276200661513014
3175584 24 364 4 725271284 4 828608334 7674 94 11206799900184 731931904 69613014
178604 32255267100830950296615161233914 0072324 81274 0694 3374 84 813194 58570184 4
194 851954 609071396254 0695926556536231923829‌4 98572212861264 5094 639194 954
1107269221906175681772129328239509816329‌4 236973124 724 084 34 6206764 1516583724
2952236930174 32684 13874 102094 1322315904 3112309008559178089
80986398114 724 234 31259772730725874 9654 5079884 60850364 94 0355636064
2136024 6367250297582588214 2397090696389
4 7515852196010056708757617‌4 34 22200688184 018678289
64 0797134 211987989
4 24 20054 262322639109160808328221720623832181566009563766131150703525394
313704 384 764 0671257073659863704 70574 72995577056332924 928706676715784 263974 84
164 8189
874 64 4 2062732629180918634 569514 0821112621118307784 2318805504
8390230182385596198689
7258663753836854 85188089
002756723914 87967574 758714 4 7704 4 96390596664 763884
05551398320851105180869‌4 67334 4 214 6964 3889
36519874 29294 5007963579336776306583‌54 79134 4 094 374 984 874
9178110525952934 94 6088696039617923756363527056828663233569387‌54 78284 9604 914
95594 355811233762962794 911089
627284 56306695903129237389

4 98739064 64 54 8234 5265301124 597093691663681984 294
01975703961105018093963707677 69574 6134 16736594 918684 071597994 09774 92129514 4
75364 355705104 04 90718226804 77534 689

219219223966559889

264 013833854 2564 94 287750824 04 56558180339798752807500932132516595 56264
89

684 3264 72095084 572694 267619620324 6524 2536113808128554 108098613889
93231752761000593 68274 8189

193057268792705270668165094 7384 4 1124 135225224 62164 0589
669773776626694 72230604 79259376589

04 054 51089

0872719669296026 1564 605692234 7083077659724 94 22251734 4 9004
9588103258711734 985129334 074 82889

628228684 514 06587059582208854 63566222379692684 577270800624 28624
708391000127132274 6693291077595784 11605552325394 27550960060760837 05334 4
808069613574 7986610034 5694 290504 874 288654 158520571824 74 934 30292664
502012901522850857 61374 552109727391108 8254 04 901954 679022537325594
370109330222334 353367924 791554 865089

056103150920105329770033114 9099331914 4 158254 03937671038561512589

7084 13151515283217981162 5094 4 078384 4 63599269824 8514 7799826238367154
2281850696667162662017616097 0567094 861125093594 20925767250273704 083583389

31609750567830354 4 284 000039700202864 2333353238003083672757694
716706320727156328814 51354 026654 5280537056163375657565561 5604
568397358211272334 930266571373761578088814 84 16954 60695189

24 5089

77614 5827730564 4 711560367234 0137375123911334 2221350995201035617764
3077090804 4 7304 82689

991779764 68760034 4 80364 4 4 14 864 134 634 689

9950784 555102030298886333 84 83281810726992000889

82857193684 1389

1539811167635237013599604 776794 327352194 624 94 1833983034
177275287197321653523974 78366615988300018701354 8007254 9967794 81564
1222507319820777374 94 936934 0515926151214 72524 09133124 32853522660950991788624
206214 70761814 4 4 36516820590669370269 7284 84 4 30350602521914 04 9775512614 504 4
65725697123159579764 2958217968313207204 9766762865704 71311714 65971689

94 14 14 194 15585527921329165534 108035864 5394 23604 397634 61695335289

84 6339014 4 37097710317188526335297860098669 30866984 35263934 184
369703188574 390628654 71068519080023824 7922659706695796912922827797 76008111989

6191705187657704 7154 804 076234 2014 69014 74 7012300723672006374 794 14 6524
884 8800218697254 4 54 63705686004 7232674 22019698082214 227784
721393055099639306665883512057 34 2095362327068335 1905374 32350964 24 16928024 34
924 63752913196824 007038389

20994 68207970820508553026506084 1729064 6789

4 32924 89

04 2266623714 93914 87185204 5333605092819272200266783 54 50900672192934 4
83571874 004 864 52584 361950094 552025533853015019360827 54 550814 836776294 31734
666870183989

6632736870667173889

783817058514 35561662657530589

34 928379956883715661905 1174 6934 019853587525067274 615771754 2792976654
1124 30661688579214 66304 82653762362917863634 4 787320604 81168564 4
513319633775974 521089

14 2064 26210773371687 1629057910904 7378376399934
03176101329586566017868615084 132025994 39184 6880266009194 12070156736705275 2104
4 60254 24 64 766222553796856221 1299822221366194 969278051234 613589

38800937870064 4 58889

5530093096780802205671222911732 4 4 962194 66633608501509594 9168091194 4
31883188755727288072604 9204 84 225726950234 777273625668174 264 307924 0727324
30554 92388314 054 86394 59295216734 61205934 73310812267074 4 35854 4 30639051354
86124 584 6923527729555959501 6339124 034 4 88084 615574 83165110280565969126 04
73822009624 298786189

5952287301938329285962799 34 984 4 7285095834 16182154 38661086913654 4 064
259089

11589

69812989

74 4 2714 7086063734 4 0889

508112079256324 34 39121604 8670980372692982232 4 855824 9957089

4 31108637654 84 03737521383697754 037253509308684 024 083186592189

4 754 34 254 65681993319202869736 4 168763807805594 27264 9094 054
31860868835870623993038093 24 89

3776063958808816927882172328 4 010080077874 4 6855284
930095356168133698782188131987960915707800606587512 04 136810551501389

914 07216054 54 07320984 24 4 571124 07869027529556371764 99692273209734
533903274 9384 224 6971775604 29121963794 004 3929139399369638 34
3123810572712316016 54 623818608034 16937792323608064 84 1668516700884
58007079905399019138 9

86928867886850125 4 679168252957297950907781 4 0077583729195952592307789
85290095374 969314 4 64 885604 201830724 83668164 534 8889

006164 184 8721314 017619792067384 25388528296023984 28554 013089

33923814 117570120808301554 1888719101171220354 39604 1258813688804 89

29394 0966294 766794 056226564 81939225363716863010600798228698 9

0537184 707195524 863614 4 24 52983986054
9722667381399271232326979135267819 4 7508154 24 7515825957071821517 4
7793330838053854 225259358687900112017697150694 84 68723239775696021905302772913 4
4 17989

533284 5717225695951393984 500808185505028 4 6173120934 6332389

7674 396686784 116298253664 4 1222235054 2063236389

978613011604 6064 2764 2524 721199538797765254 70989

913875733370958754 4 4 6068818103330791592335169 4
00268050996900920168136950287589

3937714 94 93311215724 159021236225154 972698785804 23624 4 1274 8789
986559314 59382697569314 30554 981795065314 4
1866832732881951302751995672175382370571522522917889
97389
839063017399172994 785964 7328824 514 80573157662397274 68127206928354
685997204 9158200654 93214 26373785365377765777631054 2564 91563772800189
810994 4 4 126794 727692115095607280236282844 88060198203017705573603550334
3134 769074 12760284 24 0702785624 501867604
93680921796666305062857919256903216092155038298157384 36504 95683338819914
20375632076289
4 37684 6024 76610394 35202294 4 8101014 04 11684 09635222224 4 65266984 04 2964
025300170064 07037233171935220761783135003574 25684 5231020154 4 86184 74 11294 624
04 9632889
8364 055154 538023000657624 314 76684 153339805267798198723759555284 634 5594
35087597530812254 078311528564 591382669854 061989
075985920268537279230084 14 753034 6162184 574 84 8815554 87518028075008701114
8602056630051107952626218165099970 4 624 60938200305624 61035531104 034 22874
3366878696989
6589
5714 6052636013394 74 0295502774 2886004 823589
976160326074 985704 7122184 5586671322714 100697884 6958171262714 9938589
8285859214 6253686919607865356133568 4 500757664 674 3331086324
71158007102508635704 22004 27551027969222298288679505160390327 84
22738873811183032977329682 4 1604 2683236925334 34 394 8056151302774 7565564 224
35386312834 139392655972966202638 4 9694 533758729394 690259628738874 014 8807094
63380659799698316511192908802511925602858173 04 991084 12164 1799684 3252364 0204
120266603390613564 4 14 0131389
322120287306294 4 53261319831333565 4 12520582119529293214 94 05364
882300337137813069933752626752573 4 272054 718259851934 39712284 754 974 23228254 04
076626173085591797 74 87126298870022667 4 104 74 706114 6869802870273514
819887933069078 04 0518521698287223191317558377555383293064 1934
332767058711857276687 14 564 964 75004 6792370667719907069138700087116303944 4 2974
822989
51815094 1074 1915838284 98300089
051563374 99709234 4 5812684 1189
0557203901380937 4 4 9267263259914 7334 55221666514 058384 74 15931793774
701388310929207297257 4 8072689
274 8636254 50102261803654 57994 9694 183630518520334 85830613886089
15374 7576814 50689
04 830504 74 323104 17567254 4 4 567867754 056535324 624 4 26384 5011254
0158811337628792279 14 4 576999324 54 902071005719389
024 33231581806774 4 4 4 726672317664 560768234 8386279213909238724 304
151108883374 04 8260207564 4 76757768523134 5785784 34 64 984 582933624 074 64 8014
159794 64 5214 350928554 4 4 14 65662367260070571074 4 294 714 8089
93054 62524 615053954 667294 574 54 7752230988593834 92273211814
0121819937289

7274 78363913024 222954 22832265812729939788697581 74 293364 4 0054 6233397984
79236619185224 0226254 5620101262962274 25623817530051776328637553954 2768604
195767584 8786829356580164 84 75164 68108506725307386935018654 4 3186067821174
8070671023860613289

73257124 4 78239794 4 3239268514 685587071759326786933587685 4 716034 4 89
6167761171634 12996673364 50589

792110754 60183012363336069114 4 964 188387934 12184 2194 93537874
99665237975153917630591596 4 61034 71521214 6564 274
723918539650213163259112308165283502 94 8681956571358874
767723962901916931991677686 4 587305875528874 75970901591888584 134 02314 94 4
5351637158204 611939295386500630901968781 14 872520024 632500585955097326566975 94
0880924 88527662674 4 4 24 667263984 94 54 94 09633358854 4 94 4 3855070827786604
3263766955889

9094 233921334 5324 374 58692369553584 084 4 157854 104 8678823088765914
9925858776134 93789

393381723956612673264 58605886099833130238817706692933 4 834 04 804 89
4 4 814 4 118284 34 6563752808166560294 7298876984 89
51911289

727995059763032773051776937678299759925957 34 4 752814 8628394 4 4 189
3629920990024 1358060024 233268552032534 364 64 93589
77527069034 359880903887764 83528114 17289
85220615766577189

74 599693126904 994 274 59585774 89
00715017710280050510218508 74 633374 8028182672386637611059367212151 1789
100664 4 6038280924 5724 4 4 314 17385808314 4 17365876863724 9757501724
180505564 81564 58882694 4 24 1362569737929225594 590205061321039231722794 68628689
56199674 19234 0073901316879381804 1821283172850993591980 4 7059989
0853152550606111290296074 5527654 1605554 3234
6261016708812851520318516352330 54 684 5016309787868862516095539218201938 4 304
322085788084 74 0784 82365115168524 5792053763628583004 724 889

4 99062322027715010389
354 24 792067272180390323180854 54 9352300215703224 04 830357516834 614 19504
51837704 6131294 5022064 04 923254 3372082330956689

5789
820800186133500506875378551 7389
822960864 57926134 6012293364 2789
4 12934 723737724 11834 7105671994 74 98813255663024 174 85511254 4
61353073138250801775959002057552568829353 54 1033294 05824 76334 5954 89
11914 8002630594 1122856290209919829708 9
226752024 51182220011255715792 4 0733650574 61275883823812394 8024 1104 04 4
9071889

793901792134 91779857502875171121 24 4 9707103662889
052674 50506250939260199653995 4 67076685614 56593004 672173104 967569904
55624 8663389
37724 7350889
68724 553086783819397974 14 983908087007124 84 4 4 0614 84 8824 89

61310269733073859124 98790374 18706260010514 21583904
08876123703653713520294 878765054 88851828534 2824 84 100383985536623133764
57670923704 4 77054 4 34 4 802824 90886232209658664 4 9859194 336311920583162054
531014 4 5784 82233739950955681727334 14 5085035650280593064 829271852974
72128532388175324 00077625654 889

901114 84 6834 62321804 60707175823781636211573793933365635114 361265578824
300183870597868274 534 86224 103312709824 8694 4 4 2254 632051824
297733063193782880524 73627727901023657515838777704 4 57363802324
31010591330252239774 603254 4 2284 25304 763924 9936874 122594 1252534 4 274 571914
357904 2619855980323554 10755517179602225731000794 03792963224 17785536177805088804
94 96315873832128675554 2970688659515555216828508084 918184
6715119760879072356978603664 6204 1091972064 93004 1231501888377704
58311397629187009238052681820978751665089

5211993782704 94 551399204 4 4 7989

4 337884 84 2312224 8762725989

299789

54 82574 664 34 8575579264 6037586224 230854
01606220231239583793967906186082020207384 86233385006386037167953394 64
12827981719113119614 7821670008308089

507854 4 5813266954 81816638625695092523164 821917822134 624 14 175913354
3797902834 14 237783538889

205956684 61979810523192825766529383288091196687610104 8185889

64 54 4 24 4 022054 274 89

69112069333534 55235173072013952795454 52161236905634 5572702560858266064
85383918088179160707606613864 19533907534 63104 2316314 34 614 5514 954 6839215254
57176523017627907134 6702989

64 11934 8104 68624 87310912905882869305615454 8550109865716994 31794 83204
00204 6150289

224 283253987204 035091938364 54 205680657981934 92377797399236164 33923284 4
12229124 161310236812384 123094 0085955594 39212389

0261014 80024 1184 36732572185669286852117171174 389

5773556713694 4 0365534 18826630321967371222044 7784 61396724 24 23934
38206557571014 6521083904 110580254 990574 30927093659718121325372944
532761292557160338115993272951200795600078112053314 6361127222089

3115014 7192517953524 28209704 6383536281323733050395799214 25714
30996020339068800578351873981889

314 1181303060737189

15536987311697604 9855114 076377510951304 991139839324
18267750678612930933434 34 194 4 6004 71092978714 189

84 83801103110274 1884 378329204 8283906220114 5924 54 197652212689

14 53178721214 51331267798784 55604 4 5615959524 9754 529857535222154 681714
89

84 14 5111384 250814 10550130854 89

6234 24 36284 979104 194 4 00095354 1984 78294 098804 36504
183375719505308169336254 654 866850676594 86021084 4 032088836979178574 5623588814
5994 8339271283258175664 7814 89

3076301831884 50317518770254 3381512172174 7380864 74 183691780511854
271392830592551520369615 4 4 265579274 334 095174 0879029284 689
4 84 767512818289
9369369638005209662580963095224 4 784 114 162334 706388675154 201504
1317535385000813287716280810 4 70018834 689
6555554 4 32576568037656735020267265299682668 84 4 6781066574
956350999859617889
4 324 4 307515831054 97717634 532380639058204 773181162089
074 00124 014 920080192386954 4 9202136793024 258024 64 651769831056714
85019785695873997555678750296617328670794 90827566132163830257936527271172357 64
93719772988183876501600 4 696019807626071729733871958 64 98709909968724 7174 94
761114 1014 78259018801182 4 536102152204 2204
9819761816353003398859997872605603757975986803073314 75224 7564 0075715187922016 4
4 8589
0554 0902200692157100677635924 985723995527632014 4 4 121684 9154
357780055265954 84 99985124 797809019990908814 2554 5314 2011174 116939154 83314
82057382804 14 54 36271804 64 68662629137358234 9664 8287522089
699583629003659621294 06854 8508879007970609715361504 93030709714 4 7935664
014 9031120553080824 095024 4 384 19875824 164 708605864 89
907394 068754 4 13110174 4 5035194 64 8723317674 626024
9006611578886109716268850323904 2564 21665793019714 233077714 4 535538786284 32514
336021250189
9094 52614 4 54 00526852137717787667 4 94 3223919259355906514 4
01227995323657387859633667188679821005112 24 84 81754 02924 75013669500504 75967084
4 1801263734 58801066225304 0018506698181097190 4 9088130229187287636601125981634
07302581325662620787 94 2939377308834 05816982294 04 8034 39324 6806755200085304
3214 0538370368119674 4 97364 2664 329903378153525502252 4 68254 27764 4 8272604 9064
9082697721388698375592 4 4 2072377285780670194 84 0754 825024 5903136671777876794
5828097120074 70914 10334 539792304 0702124 704 789
59724 16306316793904 2624 636533153824 6802784 6299984
9295582970677703673617809127 4 4 865109613194 7837554 214 734 7260977852214 22069774
4 173339302375889
154 5174 4 62184 14 65888174 06332192510663998626369368800156129053977 4 89
178692275227186600000 64 868860694 384 334 1695689
7619104 79315504 0737906994 8054 14 239314 034 2772120564 1761019184
651983162275524 84 7093788750088883031786357307282918767303563271353874
9271862784 78368802704 5784 8570870734 728184 36550765235117062567559 4 04 5614
75108174 628886513889
4 89
0196169187358664 4 01789
113965033124 828628212773234 14 956625703814 36670394 964 964 220174 26965254
12503138667154 92577924 25824 71839304 062211931552939524 72956596108834 9107731184
65066108537822372276507233007298 64 336816764 06634 8271265966113355194 054 6215024
279598826033934 37778513689
66589
207774 7703809123061987976754 4 8538884 934 88615179022989

51335515131781694 4 79389

84 4 8055101604 4 753872934 6020810564 239999565313294 38181181794 916820664 34 2298614 174 8888624 6889

109104 015783835789

04 64 7033850624 2254 50915261785817209601 54 95904 190198081724 98633323653239962035299833581288184 4 4 00312316684 4 128209215710365003177932767165 54 85926788764 291194 4 388521823389

65094 4 9510829929260775654 35181399883335003165 94 4 1874 901573825151534 9117302529210911907594 9224 2574 8307159707103394 6394 7729017711117954 83875324 54 308219195710971163136558511133616779926 74 5002254 5674

6172702619265822809693016765263536797856218150 4 4 0685524 25020632774 3120789

24 5928073083160954 4 9322819905787604 22714 1254 6989

92203722558094 193132907397952984 69074 966884 9730282861276834 24 4 5094 0254 197334 27838637133216298271886802877 04 885903981654 266513122174 665068839034 388054 06628761324 1514 7364 980113225683524 53964 4 591778808774 654 57020953889

0575598696204 33725788582887664 304 014 860288134 78566777522316770085281567031351708699368722839597977614 2704 304 4 338753674 04 61034 0962659814 00795953733803766082066807101929880983 4 64 611253521726264 74 614 8090624 5084 3560918326623328614 7657178873670704 3264 4 964 237558311181086135320630 4 52731355013389

32584 6980396507589

4 59952787098686773661665652729 4 09662709536189

92380834 352325064 5354 0653636670081238084 314 212916084 89

3926064 757504 24 3607733700769780104 862268669732720613130877124 28838079513682325960 4 9354 62698754 78506976087090621394 4 4 6709870504 35399717068285577732 4 5561833859672584 1529584 3880954 10036379769074 8326392232269676310863039981067968 9

234 16082594 66054 1196578250833791005176 4 3071960066914 226778080310863589

4 954 9126660196821689

84 872798099736518826787773105328505919123036083903834 06391113657529384 73873273964 758695119039096129214 4 6578009656278230854 8525764 9831923721384 1985818804 914 914 08122029836664 76256389

53591530954 24 4 210238114 0094 2201054 3587336021765607515378 4 1989

8361830584 080950957923288723131 4 4 8256881159002930870 4 194 884 19522251557714 2536019696000711634 74 4 74 3935005684 5634 4 37690033574 1760282554 9108885215323925060878 4 4 8597881672789

6690263172001067206 4 72074 04 594 24 89

005080762823397203513834 604 1011685589

5150189

4 54 5922832586999099358318 4 8388833334 9590571254 32197139992855669836826270 54 2692759878814 989

3889

55532775219571619884 67584 092669237122724 294 52524 39825238364 1763866889 50239364 8767029318151507672585976784 84 923374 584 4 94 3089

2319353106512504 7084 4 594 5982293233904 4 94 552069195194 75305035974 627883356984 613202221299389

74 906934 284 0233552962635602769933229272508974 906934 284 02335529626356027699332292725089
4 3020206397278510558974 30202063972785105589
0584 4 30078974 0584 4 300789
720504 8804 4 129234 8974 720504 8804 4 129234 89
4 74 67288678389
15026228885291287429527504 3556502096294 224 7367934 64 035255126954 4
793314 9314 32012374 84 386524 6657866338104 60290770251674 06752254 70354 4
7178168614 8529224 587986189
6172324 4 6589
5281971514 0614 101219273275694 84 7104 78372857694 60924 5181691687995355804
04 984 124 1104 9197574 3929251100959314 2809765921915887014 63865514
02977596012953584 7007686116829226 4 4 374 88830903589
6186112660684 9828180729560094 57321865073950634 39570125354 8259150353689
57714 669165095764 4 504 3362651251199168204 088534 88218399214 90374
6883206389
2195839677180721260732788561951313557657524 34 134 536657084 865934 15984 4
354 64 537694 5359090314 07965508106604 94 68224 7214 5183834 6650131789
0674 1103928036189
0014 4 1926004 517726990294 6519122625302754 5038060324 8851883604 79364
63224 99054 825804 9577601974 0854 4 82383090288704 159731204 703163934 83654 89
2654 72302515290804 0772707730361851825196612016624 24 9355133908758669104
23295025219622274 2624 25667159298289
304 04 3119006795704 12010084 094 78265978836503276031030284 84 3132564
2110534 7720758350314 60386175329382737617103295213812756699397374 4 4
18533716325063558390500 4 764 4 0504 3184 65550507304 089
90389
2699362886204 694 0269584 4 31506310889
7864 3382529879170065955281987833755 4 17779176288761977750252 4
906729638062184 794 5014 014 3711027157594 3654 04 08833825817964 4 194 3083330859984
7759889
17685225290274 5784 21689
69003684 371389
24 03690325632174 58039652881882758186777509035 04 0778567728215280374 4
17828553924 639303017935575994 6961952814 1809981603585622724 554 1275974
53696375361955709805352 34 513266574 64 4 682623554 83975934 275684 5834 54
30580915983825089
4 7389
2876921029768874 299871189
54 15173204 358065191585613271735168111 4 9098354 19221182834 703657288674 4
88155998026216334 728734 34 300014 61760387865900136880255812776602634 60014 4
92081709590733726661036073624 230859884 3852524 6934 7359660993796975691783 4
925603693389
61564 6024 65312090800867027278 4 774 15610360008789
75336766394 4 924 56229509234 06638335836132514 639323912202114 104
75837363815388273912015906594 74 884 81804 94 89
8363656362234 854 214 689

4 4 0077525080023077863764 24 808628191028182034 71183174 373034 9334 4
261779754 3695377194 812821564 29854 6505610964 35593803114 77664 303551338888294
85169813786387513074 991074 04 631767287595323653329126594 764 04 87356284 4
1175079713904 74 0055133239389

61955512856978598204 77697600525206068054 8352054 7158124 294
736280121908831151208169368170922796178504 089

4 55783599130934 7632280801514 9969889

135696881361110514 0234 198784 1705950776564 04 824 631188859014
8083377611155237681938306357143194 0964 2574 226714 354 98184 73954 07794
81350877889

54 8854 4 1300133174 612510004 30733254 01075314 24 253624 326777980106057834
007304 6225673594 88688561912669235601232984 35577265000064 74 3197514
702226705282803889

50057002152053908057026851688179096653597758126368885914 7694 197974
82970011325857658785726696799680032089

677189

9522050292034 907180214 0169102005628654 7729600869263802729111 4 694 014
7119550677284 39687724 873271581274 804 285978103024 50513289

974 4 1075754 1535707520610369102909 4 31370692300027584 89

532125119784 6884 64 230106804 4 90373289

192260583773886130912107117705877528703187 4 65304 5525558154 03887856524
17324 957369774 887607670119504 9289

4 18324 591821807077006224 95028789

984 059966097284 35314 03320074 981937074 80320834 24 5563618631659974
1500158189

254 3723584 14 756584 35711934 94 334 859756354 64 919175251174 5608308191804
386335764 683071924 14 1075004 094 8868501060599618501 4 204 5861653689

6955114 758739606606076195171626252502367814 350592999274 323654
21787159533803175923627889

878294 9132690189

601796158873699583536315303050304 832586192093522214 594 2082074
13039779873837909064 062124 7797034 395114 16304 88008217868194 13639283924 963789

204 4 24 56710399995289

756704 861790288062734 2384 54 739784 4 72819355128116073381263279174
219928320972189

396961112814 976972284 264 3702754 075034 764 0790134 53331331324 564
9630288115713553811281 54 9952388263090680098257 04 03252224 8214 189

54 5731194 710504 9339274 55593513204 206562153689

294 93664 6864 09056310958536598612765502965285 04 90850254 774
59821566929512737113321 74 559075315718029099 4 3258834 05386994 8164 09967232531224
608321089

9317524 89

9234 4 381194 820664 3167694 3205728014 25335205262187828721 4 89

0835065610874 19272164 4 374 574 08832701675994 3094 565014 5995388325564 824
04 0661128333322934 694 4 738229814 75820213179753550555 4 577624
29632551222563613964 4 6854 99789

4 034 4 3974 936816101659194 123565017327701212574 96652664 63117307115734
8366699751314 1825911584 614 328108578758134 2173761329838207675195597554
195717239664 2226764 54 74 6520021986278228782024 0364 52599026354 617705964 64 704
1183230009657954 9024 8713711791563189
956210816754 28352688809117989
18327001510089
4 309335022655098804 1726814 89
08812291287082952109766 154 4 4 7618330981136912789
774 7712298020213321274 6589
852634 671926624 55538831927714 4 99914 0834 101059524 872569030654
76732185557814 10028384 4 205889
04 14 682109669054 3375552065329134 23204 1114 94 4 4 1007724 5985564 15289
0121622584 2635255114 707859555321360988093289
506964 4 8376187763252594 27108701314 67907675027632598732576679119 04 34
2826270514 7524 5364 94 23116904 21570359226975853210231171 94 4 589
74 786817232156114 4 4 09284 4 9874 4 81225597231616794 4 4 15034 4 58684 4
82061781214 2689
17234 8256874 7787662783616836774 324 94 0877324 4 94 89
886910631126003804 78865818134 24 621072084 554 4 7364 215184 72876874
59371382984 28035092082752117689
9384 594 9109624 624 3754 536774 918274 654 184 6734 74 592704 974 4 84 254
7339625754 1989
94 080811398880961788701 14 52014 324 4 9909586952926214
02193397300316065173 59189
39332358754 137954 654 0821388091274 730654 354 51735664 4 909327584
900617263889
764 584 2184 59134 5904 519770084 034 522599909618879193398 4 02889
54 32356279060824 93689
4 154 63236116775294 03826834 623555194 28633099565126369680011564 88804 89
294 626619364 6523184 34 098834 586027305854 1333874 4 627054
535383502039757154 25221285252128218301302993326617904 12226923870614 68284 264
574 80684 4 5855575824 86688721350254 173093712604 17969124 2764 81319974 6114 026534
13800502024 71813955693977026651364 84 0094 79262014 589
75913818166904 81772316593805505270690768 39774 6184
55309912602312300839997984 107604 782938514 1598878724 7984 22390914 3764 54
3073187654 5189
09532650231094 774 26368636396795651027995 4 3304 550196299510289
84 14 2909911558001888557617770337 34 674 4 54 6784 87614 755250966994 4
50659033739301500313160838320599729 84 4 5703580164 95399357568734
06560221992121815670 4 55920865803054 4
608103653688805197213057760336977912821309760536858063007951517605 64 7629964
10624 739834 969589
994 916851870974 989
4 4 4 0934 59835935232634 68128802598854 25319651316359589
4 4 314 54 2006815724 356053980185968094 3714 94 286556694 4 14 90034
9111556979734 615304 2368660689

4 504 70004 5389

192164 3594 5629122204 204 54 1554 833978183611551289

833126210250769674 369298551683203785418 186774 22376337169514 5553084 7260914 2939192564 0068094 8773987875363904 313284 5210957787024 5721680367654 25369755669337691689

37215968264 27575374 4 94 974 180054 16994 4 270856774 6862794 334 574 12781934 5975089

29237014 4 992534 4 5514 35339662061684 61628694 6318834 11638168732635660966844 2661816850878358302201726827279515944 919629889

4 654 714 15030066994 17879085694 4 5027324 080377784 2715034 138537355605050774 2961538376582005594 22209594 0727751019318804 64 4 24 5589

1294 859364 5383784 4 05015959209169180992093220851226729244 74 920514 4 01517221610979212210269157230236569344 9855124 309230660305936577985029687173529133444 99724 162964 734 825673764 07878330294 277507365219596517539511732844 25384 8099934 666697011854 131164 05189

4 9526554 9500814 39314 82664 8814 4 4 64 64 02094 07832353934 2361234 95389

8624 8150164 6262872514 06844 154 032324 1030381292120284 34 275834 077158714 5838104 2016886254 5619529592250289

37503794 38292604 020974 002976591306686065952755327510698794 4 54 14 3399655516194 98692094 0659152382011727678666162834 4 383124 81666252038836576254 12669984 54 64 566305626956300524 14 53508164 4 90795914 7990964 77820024 4 8130287670724 94 4 68710070397159911375934 7014 97108624 4 0766515214 71989

33063018602130504 808607034 51838006279564 187122853624 232806654 12324 2592970910977002929721219944 74 4 4 2622854 3308684 127337911626984 7520854 823004 156905721012202655469803567154 8157735251904 6914 04 30937889

334 0797835766389

24 0794 5831053809339861714 6133213150026795797258189

6229057661511991624 0999193263215059982468159612035086196162185140 9555383507737097381655129651352026318989

5293924 356239514 539031754 4 2236331306573901918411231458989

4 2990560684 2925375989

7791824 573698694 73304 2393692337352111544 133584 7620381814 26924 586220681605170577372233329961192988887052130039696680004 4 633671809692370885305036087584 3204 0275575677296700500709344 4 56292198755900985174 1611710104 989

58797084 4 6952195784 811694 719989

15071084 4 962635254 67031605791774 211693822077220932352600571823423623934 394 11167924 584 0915260616864 1300255914 305681111779708277736151832307889

38566750909280970836933132744 27004 104 0190294 614 4 37259108134 8354 917074 104 732302975622169328016927704 9193289

31914 1114 908869724 389

04 204 92218758259799706756443926559694 02138114 2671289

816729574 2804 0764 685833698703544 23399064 120619089

258734 9011664 057030824 00764 9122612850101872935100244 604 6182225683153238261980699821183840 0107194 82289

989

60737201090757034 014 73266785003056258389

9804 98071984 97734 2319019174 724 6598372272074 21085576954 325059034 070334 0504 8224 22614 3087628088834 201672994 184 4 9561628869589

2134 7234 185767972108198054 618158397333178314 79781392885064 825825088189 6576169717918714 150170609154 500399663989

704 4 84 130921254 691232004 7584 4 24 53751004 184 4 64 77104 934 77384 4 11257984 96196654 994 34 1689

0264 3712951268056230282085270878 04 39998811778775264 384 182314 057616524 661931188606904 051324 23239531733139514 4 93709568694 6093074 69314 164 276161660931859705889

5663525960237753074 8304 313165254 5728120657912367284 9821857534 74 55538754 7682602700226624 74 8154 6710531782539114 2737172074 58271650962764 00991584 7504 33634 3182654 6354 4 0264 04 05973284 371165072254 03265136655394 98189

0509934 79379819858069782186550218132703931536004 98153697632986505536587 74 3634 152179587756124 51858034 830994 833708860254 89

0915258282377983668 34 873955709870662763298057251921879 14 53602855717737671378299615779605186852177 4 624 7279774 4 589

4 561254 974 374 2831904 8153508095360334 5176201862224 6012604 624 880226814 4 89

03020869954 0534 06814 154 385184 93965990384 5911174 586904 095735814 6683360303234 564 4 6280634 30524 4 4 12220994 9711134 7024 14 560239693118152077 55289

2874 8789

36396189

2837294 870079331117133257969760228398317 74 557754 58612993110518107239694 8765794 28203755884 4 62077707173234 13389

04 15195554 04 64 755763270276533801079265904 50199139991114 8631955713222124 599327298591184 9735013224 173775276724 98332161573711800569092997008018124 4 718689

66578772680054 5551153681979719882684 80789

4 522754 24 334 870367231884 21035203504 85308724 1154 4 59384 754 96586200922220756979932033803693719701186206867854 194 95255563324 6609115865504 2170617676506664 877202306733521287122957286 4 628593292686770613076925551413724 934 00192765224 85394 3270059561964 10907039162084 4 0328327989

8661939875924 64 67689

39114 950318280834 793998604 665837250695021325692175 64 90238876561524 0185217012211621274 68589

4 81789

8502864 74 4 77872880522352356822852035937224 4 12799366379674 2824 4 83964 378068084 94 9230172094 68877774 25186607959324 53717290802613994 10969767654 6634 094 312714 34 368806589

2069923889

6633992377814 74 789

35028094 373660275900364 624 161300918734 985959634 2804 784 73695673504 965124 2784 358854 222294 50338001132620039715 84 6114 5519604 154 2091202354 4

7053382014 7803874 1000722524 86231838881937801921658210374 4 167097585735374 1134 0839395522857874 70682184 294 374 504 4 89

1824 7514 3887812334 5558634 50776262702177165763O8624 209174 705004 01708664 01275592307039259902570961S4 954 74 2574 33275765180189

6883382854 95571322884 859164 029072281974 74 39084 32916254 99233603130937725911624 4 7164 874 14 226815761994 4 324 61605729560600777557271214 77555028219570885987610308616526997 34 56773684 934 5330753107855O952036834 21538202686763679904 80875512997682554 83326900052195031300284 82569368881011500900708334 01009054 16054 397050104 4 880124 12314 2517279266978094 24 6624 616089

531136154 1680530976880079062255312 74 95864 9556987999188853625530O611324 583354 828575063694 882255737304 037192527978009324 01965754 5394 260194 974 9977794 696391673674 187369879878250594 3711750613684 51255835800714 6559799183227867154 2835371934 1954 9062224 89

35956224 87235001596551595820360278287 4 174 520513574 54 84 0974 3275382575552195680734 77789

12724 295252854 753774 1631054 371227392203054 0663165394 60792954 2801194 97228598688626209597057713657674 57694 64 2298585674 04 0854 9931614 689

23354 8567863314 4 1819221221368862997O654 031711152797921389

34 3628299637884 132778293950989

2054 955684 78674 73011837384 550561314 78157054 163011814 60518125831815266099326685656 4 4 74 94 864 27236111006399O201531934 12882598321073694 94 95291608627O297793904 2236362515914 0824 7034 324 703681924 6398275189

526910227950314 93373089

983779927924 54 394 11604 7159119733154 12320997178133722888601536303280053212834 9392282194 279859554 554 16679258510853206 4 0320984 88506278156616214 881284 667672704 16201689

84 36880694 859910074 525753019823764 5384 205604 7226797984 563260150554 934 16189

2553326356677175294 3034 11190187870568223554 712015982950289

3609563368361185608376927023150693 34 026594 2304 1956204 596724 4 077011364 731694 9691061304 9728321764 084 695335392064 81500583501825585103O854 9034 880383374 8183194 4 21881309584 774 220376952264 714 4 4 1724 599395934 11907054 4 163630797214 1768559382864 112094 7165620194 10130765693954 697559964 0082976005354 18866178823111020172715573022550595290335O1374 0258692854 2771974 66984 4 63603029814 11834 518321932934 662119104 9720619736836295670334 194 2779167623834 154 63921665589

72067100211039085968668390528173719652781392134 50154 75687862913183328 4 334 54 75807220124 754 674 8768289

8189

234 6880324 9712157862218584 6523818179160338762205 4 4 502610535277301691773664 7808824 17390884 4 52589

138524 04 189

17053930136056205025322 89

09091314 65997522304 654 64 96264 8727050504 27985635524 9995689

4 354 84 656290533528389

0524 074 76828234 694 4 25124 220524 3214 604 969115159950274
51192115682913619877574 4 29975081994 5714 978774 04 754 3664
667121836718639985938664 77584 804 97379574 31031355610692264 889

3323794 188621034 303009967129575625060330359032176674 94
155356337239116889

0323669273923796055594 78222318350257576956904 84 9957835534 1992708004
5371029096730804 8719319218734 9050957832790929334 0979011230509353551778787974
2573025912661514 733097195021283664 4 394 579639594 27214 34 84
79182656385965253201950 4 389

724 1592694 68392524 24 2186038072871266166 4 2373835217683934 4 65689
4 225000557581315184 030850597256194 6962356965072584 850934
81378292837221706682289

794 264 1654 25784 4 54 2009284 74 864 54 28513828372778381335135819 4
082795357922839889

739911377359314 8731564 34 12685577389

382827974 4 037394 03858089

054 75853764 692026568181661000376224 592307825369028319760597 4 266134
55826289

5200074 71751986613934 84 52285860670989

2291398600737672164 274 502184 189

9068751282105164 0714 206606389

5878028324 319775810884 4 37261383554 6296124 60612810338131101281 4 74 83064
92500156551239064 9263760563155724 150594 4 4 64 4 75789

71934 93099102668095708 14 84 238104 884 185792550051367684 29135114
11251757939022262587 4 00884 5364 1633871277575302581962372271590 74 25554 75734
0119363083529254 6627694 5714 8113386654 84 63902123036916905804 954 06784 173105594
65918598303503065831399068316976 4 838761011995193662536138889

762266165084 667337594 784 66304 2039384 4 6589

0384 64 8834 7282284 52379531706994 1161364 108194 4 696996724 4 4 074
6928392364 130567933923015291910836075357808 9

54 4 072265784 2315084 058834 1954 782356879973662184 2186804 968764
30753139516367036626375 4 4 391351854 2939738639303504 73224 1669528654 384 3954
9227104 7001209217380103835760953115694 4 974 64 875956857723939594 61254
9508301794 21864 5124 976069095855328 4 814 1303982833219574 4 156994
12308393266379517589

77091254 91779731184 59399261534 5221399614 109834 9106184 05773674 14 824 4 4
4 1335724 6529150310050804 4 62575025374 52754 598551539294 8604 2330214
58280713117375319139 4 089

3517121551804 301704 6220554 4 797376696674 789

31730962714 817804 320524 15373985016954 0905116883068125314 8680904
395232324 376023162252504 38836689

86857066165306618190 4 5685274 74 6655871617726585165073 4 15506594
517561366784 259071595185264 92326611989

4 19927697833028837779 4 111175014 4 74 104 22908089

0236608339194 0652111393237267613597885389

234 282889
0089
773054 73363126803325171091298392614 84 9700054 26861602994 296096384 8864 4
4 06004 910294 5503966529170234 23634 6606504 22229602109878588800694 4
21569857705366984 4 84 10868673105069630296090619 34 23160663874 89
900188289
4 951256155911024

Chapter Sixty-nine

04 4 628205315937709684 26564 8034 60337817314 814 05384 504 4
9907592035509064 4 59099090914 4 52597256714 95302827264 5215273966122182604 134 614
750102864 9224 4 57265765754 5290324 054 714 370601234 4 3121775206577764
55271900115395334 25054 18075391219150598379852615733705162295 4 4 1197030788874
31739989
14 5794 82534 99871589
694 3787734 37376751615663954 64 7624 3520818653159751036668 9
70777583283865057523580501714 023236204 182085387774 679830295084 4
233833110374 58065364 190794 4 74 9706284 770654 76794
82962188669259068217600673139160665816078583284 25138624 68330626033667954 679124
92230323889
2956877289
4 761215153639603094 062765311976690109113804 874 054
93778751586082757323635 4 5668580674 90627165972159902992186708613 89
689
51373706831731568800919554 82779204
650557777506688852118669297652110390778631 84 4 3369590672352028399996 4
32396387686732036137916 4 6686795031121791267912 04 94 226863196952264 94
15260318384 601653704 50925925788004 24 4 0594 4 34 94 6762285550854 525566020694
22687732189
4 6333902767153582022254 703312234 7985668270282524 598801234
683953776355174 689
1225367881238189
19954 63784 4 12703324 18737376332561304 2233271184 4 4 5074 974 24
2237826619704 6104 011122653275889
5572384 9850576364 804 94 0924 804 011116277087155279884
07903612572788359124 14 4 6081033368567697834 95825697333839956169239 89
00085029353534 29996574 0696377950214 08519030064 4 954 7774 7354 84 11684
0551028776110864 1985672662267872287859393358397028788359 54 512635880762654 14 634
0514 80829780026991158114 186054 7629512881994 308386653204 84 2674
0555551025332274 6134 2219931036194 777204 9524 33882117850322504 62292214 24
569555500331377584 28571026505201688 4 4 87127931856374 126072774 114 1786989
397154 226727632286584 8616967758187395294 6709294 34 52537335065005696013 4
607318025776790991551 34 5034 84 1583984 675265057374 23974 714 74 81254
0093578195354 59734 584 707650074 4 70973254 939310359524 4 0878024 27666984 63084

264 4 4 63867363801628651193925985133 1956303926559571167112304 4 9799232117360684 89

75917558263162239022622 89

84 62286579357279624 9103764 03823104 0804 81974 94 285927024 63212739006905074 988773173218854 689

364 24 389

4 20964 9285664 4 24 6175264 2327072727933081557155886 84 16319531614 1173690908132019027389

5284 25154 9967224 3034 89

02376328054 372916139822725299083690889

24 973885229959237754 5012678088732611954 61636209004 90104 565727238121860734 0291854 4 7799535289

95921194 55188052138295626177 0804 1273303794 20903678075311256760080 2604 95074 06190564 87808050234 3735589

16155389

9274 656330762008009969129076100632053732312693727962007390 334 374 622102589

95721397889

190970317550197355937869 04 63611160272063383384 0903223989

4 189

167224 94 06584 6038688359912725214 20089

279274 3098661635079572837905 3855138729527112983667

61619181394 864 073685794 226166711785990514 038234 72914 00900979224 913024 9978704 0038054 14 564 064 290663790392252304 4 92171609589

05202817816159901170 358289

134 09135889

4 39304 95096599605113324 294 4 8250983651074 98514 89

015128230584 721525802518501199967290923019534 159104 6634 97514 80976575854 1954 4 4 193866030102393289

4 0819094 792784 8078304 524 04 5296572175086034 72258594 1757724 7107124 4 270779869072099558068222519789

9864 7932984 73283077934 32374 088524 818024 125993607628074 9955223104 63219910682998081182 157702024 037867235236304 158690964 281330364 66253394 94 94 024 268686257659183352224 1354 102004 887850569974 7168524 067286575194 34 2570625734 7366754 73650312557208374 72170777317324 26112803077590654 69239502290675828206127673 984 71063519764 4 664 4 27167209384 61560725568203791375209 9039538816862720308 219274 9330119689

0650218554 24 299174 25792226204 50885193664 289

28772287755130094 77364 6300064 24 10992990004 59324 66773531374 4 4 054 86684 87587771578864 754 28825132571024

Chapter Seventy

9958355230509904 068164 634 1314 57314 4 84 9393869833134 7774 27352150116669767950323 920870266706333 26771215264 880879536592993735189 924 20672251194 8073132659233 3577207964 529777754 8674 384 24 7689

26160681733916928124 63591354 94 60964 50111565885729253824 4
69117197557728510786552984 54 2787165830234 12111155300074 6635255504 824 5234 54 104
85731877910034 7623305884 072578334 984 4 254 9880584 587627134 84 53269204
022568383164 232223709764 54 714 050912364 134 4 063619592205000038714
9001957833598078100859888605597284 84 79116532070874 5934 356308021871621114 89
589
62680089
73308214 20606706376919309905812237161050163381359939183593187130304 4
926180189
71089
28204 2610031614 99659858596679590094 3374 72123334 4 389
5178821392131689
613734 5600884 7211834 0553704 1739088655022155389
774 24 8059789
54 17234 353658614 901584 283694 74 900604 30889
525606111387554 38584 962726915091086239755 8059013623804
035826260053073574 5124 8710774 14 2634 775125097739773093907252823363210 0264
80288229727064 1095201052883807867694 620371563957604 766114 500580804 771764
27287800131312774 1324 4 3027234 088512989
685603831524 6574 74 3679823704 6012790757806089
24 227128322264 4 0307990061532314
102079712380053382053051219117387093019838536790817 34 7001559734 751328332160254
6122502724 867125834 9531573900562069353 2954 0235971715394 6924 64 4 274 38802759614
864 94 12924 752773374 134 950714 878033537786636311 85623061534 86757767063254
90186829580038258 7884 851764 55630870877721920831 83889
862253677915514 04 0364 9128193327234 64 64 104 104 20881109312609839 6184
0185584 63702354 3594 6724 8574 9153090804 8594 18312609672994 06674 84 4 194 4 0084
2598321754 80334 5986174 002004 3137850828618329975681776571031196 3158186599504
906723797917873672190751564 06534 37764 4 7630621705766985670874 92270750280876724
6204 22535389
4 4 74 14 24 134 3631101664 36639699880 8785733504 534 6724 54 0669218104
268811566954 384 5133919605697691307 4 5213394 121929508769111217525555025 02270789
14 71738006854 23650303237374 86778702558389
05989
3630502100871664 6978571180516617315670294 79585884 4 26271984 10355094
6215100054 672653266686174 4 29351162104 756739024 19773096614 724 2208704 524
1117074 33388517866626228389
7595052031288720189
52354 4 8217394 782194 24 4 3997589
9983500607804 1238792193065679325724 87287019768589
24 65232506696114 739730088004 77104 4 338654 37226884 3956825008857164
813094 684 4 6127095654 313955754 758050793514 2675631381936217024 2297318784
812277683189
574 0704 84 6233538362165958684 3308579628537616031 36764 74 784
7256586609266766292576087 4 5273124 622235504 4 158659706369989
27681704 34 994 116812797928212969226927665070866724 4 80088023309789

28203559308288859785353411978502118214 004 684 25054 674 0254 97714 1733336689

52304 9168314 4 4 376297734 82720505996184 2796013824 38264 090054 05005054 389

9562203257694 03114 1072966938554 12386184 534 165135716337686204 154 8822631196037539535157965115615791687520081674 536224 127084 38608227154 9504 4 4 4 1606876735071527867361 64 990684 0791020504 384 4 6012308262194 96186924 4 00308314 29304 4 784 09256311863207775126 4 30594 199594 917717064 13089

06867774 63854 39177938197576164 4 68111066389

3235836184 0915953211635978809063329517326102817101 4 866694 864 396113101717553654 03322789

04 4 4 7010019763121234 10764 6363624 583097732689

325932774 19195714 9924 4 9855964 697617304 672915269924 74 0555769815934 96630773754 704 07104 034 7974 97551771084 93121353924 2932997367572202934 59757588025764 03917756905121552802314 52102931304 996533393730232009205054 09685661504 05868034 1637934 25219738612936589

718569331253 74 14 5784 827827008605989

21654 03956081731874 29758719191069327571217995208732082698186359 84 600672764 338764 820681561136791228 4 0973794 4 03556138714 05973903686799304 74 236923503106534 214 6664 19163614 0197023934 2325752694 2990274 6933964 4 0815930157918795154 4 2905334 62614 104 91553156884 50125585550009133220611127010184 4 35006952174 6173065959864 16881093816304 24 976087706154 5783954 4 937918719179778214 0502257904 96722122077816023801 4 92381294 00854 6323714 04 0529727769335214 2122684 618597821174 4 358524 205910970289

4 1984 624 689

9952324 2239816555904 6677132287636196018384 874 3194 653729812296335274 062864 396104 17591624 718206354 1974 3568571300716754 36810628538358587361 14 14 883279233104 6006134 4 514 130864 700024 719564 7216798552823676900196362 14 04 3564 9853331976888064 8886200204 6177902558022709 4 96834 234 610834 925724 75354 4 52133926887369393128 9

8504 8595882232814 75103811888094 604 514 39780369235292336510900 34 13934 584 678504 1229174 13504 94 3706196058666194 8266564 31821665662964 560637334 75093289

5534 325174 9727379136224 27082393564 55824 4 3273066007731554 7130178084 016931960752234 4 18399227001189

76889

84 84 4 63505526607269164 237837900804 794 1617684 334 3832284 58537684 138118251167756383889

258394 0201206135674 4 6919670757527804 706934 4 58182769157795686023 24 95884 1160289

5983784 0511525597978388184 1029014 784 76234 5089

670289

667288889

64 765797782306997988192708835134 93304 4 589

8170864 68179711128381820020 4 4 1974 9911772154 1034 2051654 2702703199984 6634 914 69520761598650684 8852203163287322590381506 4 83550100084 517784 3754 5074

3614 505922194 24 024 187262824 9035634 1265264 311926550304
0632025753660531509186294 2304 0093331024

Chapter Seventy-one

82986091924 7004 4 115776935057387004 285904 86697364 2307055861273564 02054
04 8267764 38809032580278850876909994 80925732901733117165304 67839238783985992084
4 94 94 4 282354 55111107556714 1794 156706197119864 199564 089
81974 696503835985600015377631978659 2684 70653207291301834 6587824 4
92507819878301123504 261299130804 12937786711714 4 174 364 94 1704 130959984 2774
96152385231195216354 15716204 18554 261725773289
754 274 89
64 2524 55836900805206971989
7834 053279524 96283264 156934 15613998572867309874 226214
028851812860019084 6032317501333078074 831236164 17826138051177933714 4 704 14
8121189
95919098022374 678777281289
04 530357995934 00567204 30564 4 04 4 9354 780269634 64 639719156600092636864
21734 74 11761939064 14 54 02317939063173828189
03652398629007099830998625224 89
234 371226060985810304 09576388510924 389
509763364 94 774 8584 1674 7664 4 14 12104 4 26996776851984 98165067537953954
5328708054 990529826809162734 102724 0261084 195694 6273759163057030693604 9304
955176029167714 525673235033671309570781176961089
0255690131338374 511581734 2608720809197689
6237615824 72327996967626594 91769689
035000181087114 738574 34 98364 0990927933694 54 71815629034 52870089
33177864 62600184 84 5835027509394 656574 3519796624 693962789
671332753001033621670580280602032714 553177354 9327571281289
722301694 3175659529582131377364 07650325824 120958394 22766174 89
875728184 84 76302875186074 6198159530914 517767537614 228781538324
691582039685564 71318706824 864 14 694 3554 34 1864 24 089
86534 0226529793504 2531053074 5564 74 4 5859877651882708589
2094 21996518670330660554 024 32358530574 124 9889
71883964 6582694 9814 14 0327296804 00985674 094 4 7220294 4 4 14 4 102681929134
11094 21874 151328287331079823292514 50661078279210121801031119704 2776907694
30354 4 975283057095089
33635333331851096902389
069806293571634 3038815074 8514 989
827901710659364 4 127074 76112985186817773113704 7234 4 54 0374
560028621916791322136578270702 079509967914 180334 8219625586266951974 361124 884
6594 658272876564 4 989
771594 4 4 4 2118234 92755174 989
68274 4 8384 64 21554 4 52254 335777101571115531264
69088386801039213792718885796910984 24 54 4 017603589
27360092579861974 34 1024

Chapter Seventy-two

60936289
89
69559726019190217380700975580237538083550621119923314 74 090884 6814
351990335032977622554 1026224 7665024 4
69857171353572652882185686112393022122353021905162773569 74 128634 98354
083903277354 81050807116389
6557294 4 76684 5792174 112094 4 84 0199655614 35530689
8308612084 94 869864 5171066737076918157254 4 604 6682028205264 852335869924
99908059551927828814 58694 136822989
769294 696665752303826034 3104 8858076055117083009197101198 4 925364
80728361569767818774 221507110373995369276615 24 524 4 965350910034 52889
5977702974 2778854 15339785881066071568 9
4 9262130827794 92654 94 36210734
56967878550687385561133352065110009516722384 4 4 4 3533158667179835359535764
511966809574 5274 0004 24 34 0154 4 004 90626661379629574 7065274 075783714 6094
0023326556772078370794 501025269804 7934 9759953631214 724 88812065999504 4 7324 54
05295694 91611354 3765127592357126014 2803889
14 399713206284 1954 68196885884 175292922668864 4 26214 34 063384 32354 4
903587183699050534 7094 7584 4 95815394 054 529883914 651863181509397362332 14 054
50969089
4 535311623502316264 54 24
2878880321886191725362579809217969251069766315534 866721289
02553534 2766321179954 1889
4 4 080231117124 10789
10639117913801116908 4 15614 7104 3264 120324 3520194 66878197773271630704
885109519004 3634 5084 7138672677153789
2816556212509319933084 617355227009185624 19626104 815284 64 04
5526818176983236033294 4 871799050874 4 85624 4 052584 667057078202967384
38699369354 654 364 564 4 4 723004 4 5362273752665314 52992196223098811764
568067671397854 37916584 73209504 694 4 304 384 883707718650184 3256927011517134 94
9617369807824 2694 0804 064 50092250682393379568371761215390570823858 54 8291004
571562854 0523094 4 77092336799211584 88718861524 4 2294 5904 7803961052354 775294
5184 32918217764 704 012674 190255625784 7710396875503365299622 14 4 8817935264
05867813332621592091 34 904 4 189
4 1231255215399597795265706825 74 624 0764 954 866113924 814 67006572277196024
95734 5080584 087022130787994 54 35072556036021889
5109924 83703313007661853085253912 74 076920389
6980996769175607014 84 757577914 2527138022094 15938774 884 94 04 964
683120257215335558064 888819994 9024 4 9124 874 4 387026964 81904
5617856715182153214 214 586889
6572634 255779575626527006292978 4 5964 506174 89
64 2530002109224 7981808889
4 625167573273500296771 4 7050327998757989

962912792874 66075781964 794 84 75239203522264 5594 06312628324 84 17539754 8174 570106570926022593172320874 093274 914 009797818697026014 374 214 78631793853130815571167180161 84 1988500770608288114 4 64 96753514 6217195521385239251104 1984 108164 14 04 82204 4 24 94 1782795380173574 30963694 4 364 9506351874 8203960509107089

20984 4 314 16784 064 4 61910936771361505772 14 3004 75164 292784 6276061258793264 9555864 4 71865902984 81822016021004 99771983618037782 1189 595651689

2253934 18263501037136321157781214 6023709366910632191188391695270536319994 253584 4 90860239808314 298724 363262584 106915366179150117100 34 582739884 5023001900255774 774 31214 334 21560910214 2563004 7292952168051282215 64 798791314 8361230334 61102775203382979698 4 764 87510753086209628 4 64 76786353120230686050987180875128226550528 1989

169994 4 5054 58252874 274 5970634 02296033568538869 4 9799382828014 71099860087059568 4 84 12151964 7334 34 7663376274 35135600524 1363537190114 7912029922253153318866025153770683310154 889

09995369901717369 4 2984 4 706667704 82793224 4 8234 182065674 2587914 6781115189

74 774 90725584 89

1554 664 7004 332922203989

5064 94 52770755329322994 262674 3329882814 28255689

6573326678657561933719593908066 4 291914 75031113284 4 67514 873963577287934 2989

7564 133604 265814 305092134 813679852888292572515952 4 636866705264 7189 839619635984 921134 15695319863804 55814 84 790717809078695292727918 4 04 52294 3010294 2836711083950634 84 250638208555865392327654 52862272664 8834 185074 874 1393854 93074 176302795550310290813677069 4 30289

701202531770184 94 1820914 979238296316560222983619803 4 8204 0579523193813266 54 609721358839304 4 852166287214 352575113723684 50592929824 956114 74 226829218305794 265334 692259325226372031701919998 4 4 76757154 104 89 69160820055609293880 4 3856153939388610800038 89

314 15514 2519880728134 6757093933154 3005256903783714 4 51599730234 4 2914 505699864 14 67595030318127152727 89

4 25023834 66726331733374 55880994 354 4 39500367756703109190 94 0716114 1154 055734 0884 834 283353599319214 4 371060068593660264 69934 6572009360316234 4 4 263821514 24 4 283917159614 65813174 24 73170515632534 82379314 74 94 4 9200697954 80164 682189

884 332759152807095398821268 3989

364 231810654 89

04 4 804 89

27684 89

21854 71067697886135033352 4 4 98113861637395731026802516 4 2313394 1154 9810626704 97502013612853271679 4 5064 13100084 68510052112136399583903 14 02261910807289

9098163070206354 1311154 226660786954 871773820214 1054 74 014 024 032631964
563930096218551712914 326524 4 274 594 4 14 4 1827560214 4 551534 4 04 54 002874 324
957770584 4 94 080984 03302725818096317962524 9173507014 94 84 6684 157254 659289
94 94 762363700059804 89
0396576313824 027694 2366626226901514 789
4 7116904 980254 94 9025258782220685372604
573303597309077583539317030888770854 234 95312230318022928795990064 05017737334 4
21306274 314 312861522090518089
9239090902879120512231186844 6024 133278609750024 6750791712605774 04
575292564 364 8232591599931664 4 50989
01914 614 8028600254 8234 3871969033739870536003763110023850308855515627394
2623157390714 59324 738698502972134 77822607116809960604 4 074 990934 18534
005721719934 0913082088234 1230507612352696124 54 55084 2224 014
9861662157316029979904 014 966994 917274 62378267301789
4 094 24 959606884 377389
4 74 3154 0589
4 732714 701696198582509128215714 053085784 66191861322806103650334
200390130814 03792861284 30225378811284 4 89
4 688305371033031235704 34 62316590768763089
8083954 15916852054 588094 7623711927889
9074 678575366992814 23524 704 4 117166525289
10036053775597355884 354 254 2374 6517694 18514 4 707314 5254 768769289
97005954 6134 9680397382329362389
98019862056505624 6066813102252036854 8324 84 334 9695689
65310038523754 6675878567994 0094 64 2537266615054
675709129876236192670083598762678555030286306687993922650993739884
608390668208206623012 461299730378011574 82964 4 98260524 7059002013885624 4 14 6334
105814 5336313282560532052005929264 80830313212035078776629584 64 54 4 189
16953734 24 2813903516292914 22504 8390362614 4 4 25573581074 86834 89
25185396565314 9819630557124 199950351323821951186967238151 4 5833934
9082859755991966972170 4 534 304 32731619357189
676268639789
788684 4 388611904 18094 4 185825869579602634 5630375524 7758311154 3114
7620359386985073776707 4 276510824 819289
7681013385969978614 34 24 4 300067684 394 20759554 9574
0760932501678239929600 4 574 035775833310658604 1155550814 69085084
83995958616766251290531530322 4 394 011724 4 4 8874 034 5224 07180535221879714
7385313216889
6260285312534 87585855672513707818686352116963311057203172237060 4
6781195086114 2666560265806290 84 8817231556597264 624 24 91374 667624 4 614
37195284 5693522156184 4 002089
813015954 860029902518858507357307152932312318131 84 991789
363734 14 5399134 110220355654 10510107724 3598605563174 827784 724 01379834
74 6309724 53826070078510252638166027 4 36710934 9768677960974 264 5392324 196337989
76824 84 4 22098019133054 85964 5286814 24 62908735370534 1164 34 7696964
72966752583007869309307984 984 2711687904 4 08338186326775973380325268 24 224

33296807395064 180671565602714 26821123031234 294 85516536532152694 5761064 6824 70070767932911101196016654 68779920874 15062186924 352558605660814 35007054 6365728251289

9089

86529882762656823 00074 3770361058062 22664 54 799657003762714 4 2571577258126868254 66294 6872399564 06509728324 077614 389

187704 24 97676234 2214 51309179368774 6062916851839024 68031364 3989
74 1696135882918597 3655389

064 5775130811934 55198291814 91284 576515229964 07262983389
64 1873938024 63224 70736392768595 12913289
6252267569031289
89
820889

24 7134 957014 294 4 686822655595752774 58228284 2997280977383212732530514 169924 655225066614 655913575986554 74 89

4 2601571238087794 284 7279114 372236711153038274 775334 14 24 24 071794 8860202834 0577593858604 74 3995094 3326511364 87754 324 2214 726631364 85905777194 353727858104 371833790095 1798179631135089

5996055705684 21753214 4 07989

55923184 808524 8780836755006834 594 83934 24 7832856563524 764 189

4 93364 9224 92977088581624 23150204 9139804 35904 4 981004 314 93233010594 4 9024 74 7184 763989

31631684 4 4 34 74 04 7505681172374 64 39216134 31838126854 7094 02109279571879936931 3860000384 68514 3684 58211668002182820 12999174 809263989

0989

5665394 0582958886002 8274 4 8026999169801064 24 04 924 265810759212724 6906309924 56074 216611694 18389

7204 0284 5531707331523151114 2056785094 965756120390076 8315674 7627210704 5735661718784 02962624 8721159176926327063591 3876784 65536199985983182304 514 554 0096974 26850377501 200832133206958860197305121870854 184 3880610883814 334 7134 32566689

7926277024 4 34 19921807686310 0164 8573384 04 0824 0758539913655790811 78390854 206293306812294 729335597163936794 62033539152709063720694 6734 23381513834 2694 714 1024

Chapter Seventy-three

398224 388308667689
89

624 4 15715064 4 74 790566932331808524 64 295629231016005111864 09568800680522593 9654 913797813563666278 6584 8254 04 60687315167516856587130530521 15870559273837534 78689

080814 84 4 7224 684 033527700001191254 6712330388861 56296696 01587218133024 72824 787916219784 91164 332860672224 4 6352883105320858 3604 580514 784 9852094 4 22354 984 71314 113188173524 4 076916983817007803 17068336361510531335515 3309584

66236553926008021258336209667955544 4 62962234 869224 4 319084 74 6391935174 96015959286204 4 53799127924 4 3954 7619127992304 1584 4 3289

1273052169124 081319234 08866168091854 33824 24 0294 54 4 6101708827516088104 274 721924 92094 5394 6970268602852630794 0310706909913092204 3115964 504 2981910857994 4 2609001524 514 24 28334 158154 882276758200364 152510502790358004 80534 28092302369982089

4 14 594 633169359389

9070015559835064 4 6908224 4 4 9861971704 4 3076286932014 4 5951564 84 8777012594 85011514 053979796339301004 384 053190679074 364 71299584 7183321388711090998235667221263805 4 8683874 189

4 01010754 0013788101839315914 880874 78658787950015155396 4 4 07616257750186358217931011726 14 4 04 6668884 8182194 5604 4 05137924 883197154 57124 384 1934 389

6724 75514 4 4 2366589

364 7185182260718836387507 04 59294 5198112364 117809723074 34 09552194 14 0524 4 64 22009022216668654 8356081018514 4 31715550874 52030706681358203884 352154 98794 4 960394 94 72960654 7080639824 5627394 7063974 4 064 0513789

295335728586689

9900859908690670394 34 34 87080081760714 0504 325690320088153694 716707609996780837875260810732992 4 794 9817333213953183877832823591673701 2583124 289

064 7354 74 2150887825514 984 14 14 2350130167267508217911100255797251 74 2760073937319214 2103926032970810769819058 9

880389

16181382579914 4 4 34 3221052915690578788 4 74 582111038266054 989

4 6693764 30572820094 574 0752925336116365750936006367 34 9850284 388726581710725994 10784 9303081301175864 8611583290660573274 27060306999694 824 005860864 03325051074 5707713620352068864 94 6234 4 119056316806989

24 06954 1256556398194 24 718889

22035224 3226097231754 88853172826677391037572371010673933766380 89 8151584 267604 68520362036724 0789

14 90187927355618076617558781815383071 4 57220388177297187593 89

56629614 97505678534 508134 59765928283718236719 24 314 00974 1054 3729784 4 5101625754 39587624 5790382089

02934 9315014 8104 8364 513538889

280304 38603690164 26589

231622072189

666519355916274 9795504 8009255515951904 6186067918808187226970297962202088800 24 8778717791258102117 89

4 250727613197954 3109624 664 019772097232261002686374 5530018619088598256565626527936608 54 0782281152515511826170 4 821756956154 1627851396377824 79952394 3593124 697524 36905921867794 2638333073373920923189

034 73965575739664 9098205261877727084 616955873614 559295219812689

33164 4 3382397314 2384 7261594 530885254 0887188657764 0223851051087973101722522 84 52997694 7617375824 99526324 714

11817301602018331119181122281350885698210048181611461676048518736999561147171048 9

69514 5284 9696758125834 53612978034 77323132965359652239063357421420204 9904 797794 9714 0368721532807064 357987712128372358671861232848101428 9

38668570376207234 84 4 7967592914 4 21953864 220121082077988765511025031152937169329199651538878042516256025746324 08504 22884 4 997762389

4 69269631528657293741343016936007603532936970 6417827787737793065010569739456116219240336676403090783541455138316434 889

4 4 99792375578158750144 552064 86934 7130864 9833007389

808805689

4 34 606520734 8759524 8873814 528563311886966371772606539290129962451213621618212497585510924608606703292781986026525232632282648357227323918383492582021275938 9

4 05715304 11273628188361027150253648154 9937009962498261244 8826291798672824 9764 94 874 375237721882327023286078786741446467607560018209489

06734 6574 07576764 55255636422430212091679637261321178552432544 5167266178454 9610873790374 6066329417692646345850239275544 630030638667795115643109766170095008053674662921490319228 9

3154 6134 4 79522051756730507822406654 12164 309774 725130449522884 99254 23816543796406991093037267686443698771596745583878817823699939072913629511356585921262470605123799207098445306806751021923597625803820917959940362293224160002144 94 83069498884 79840257115758866426014 88261724 77609227552782493180061245468044327036949428051996932474 056765621398689

6794 54 104 5778067938189

867874 389

603154 930808754 4 85087084 13969377697387704 31774 28658169640187113187555513983743414 94 804 367385069109968 9

2834 084 554 865883150782980444 4 29217813519681652065459628859248994 7217333292060737007254 8385216598658 9

889

0770988354 659504 4 58514 6811251957872729831356143487873935778 901650631075864 4 06944 4 839738465088854 4 124 07993571718 9

272387604 33926754 14 211824 04 624 13909054 29387061282390467449182904617638581776736597386933106850735700688392261440049675224410943938679474 31047301757352214 306870791138 9

92751983374 317080328301799688 9

374 4 273125215821356317063512194 58024 320861852112521563609484 108627492827688256250168628 9

94 05981589

304 199588164 286788710762011095607597412872305221317126050716005368280281377723429999177300500943273641748740893193172289

4 04 80334 5998552264 1089

29822154 4 911814 713634 8851808329524 371156096051075765109787038763128124 395958783094 61734 9039834 75833694 660579154 5220589

5914 4 0569186560964 276508524 589

570587'/4 82881204 1326123928589

4 873523560338104 314 000357289

1237856274 32502504 63650074 389

009557274 063694 94 4 618836528666054 37261524 54 172205829830850965936 4 8284 19586961691157259324 19827358324 58538314 4 01670681614 8734 750861264 8751989

7807761879174 9682700117124 8189

184 661389

87978076114 95726137823984 1534 6224 5734 7391337669061778806054 634 74 924 80215010001624 11212171394 54 3562120000272927378809068638 9

1198335160811628709104 4 323730701597837680528 4 2819095215390089

954 6814 5604 80934 77272389

9921077127088311999 4 0831181902204 14 78882923964 54 286509798811164 28598216955662881290310706500009320237365625675 4 84 4 374 1799311021817623100802014 04 6166684 89

9134 4 989

4 24 1224 4 9701917555764 92854 2399239724 8206504 152537039228810588634 1191972034 4 394 14 870165759984 553384 7868765677734 77091766714 6803823673134 016398284 0788020534 954 68329590014 4 17804 6155394 012922359304 4 699854 4 589

4 14 974 4 39097524 0122334 2354 9654 25154 7589

7214 184 89

37914 35027789

4 14 01688528164 9814 395529829554 0112830729059554 7761225000882002512272561369373 74 376926594 90087374 604 4 34 4 756874 791717024 79007356271678183376663 64 90104 0589

004 9089

190374 64 56201786773831536991028 4 000822875981974 853524 72502014 3724 2104 79284 879675997055778633111 14 04 4 74 6980788275213095399080803117091873922137 84 7363226332007664 951635051082589

7887220534 4 514 71505163639234 5586235874 774 4 66224 27362128110925795828761191662 54 153684 65731854 0677262662818074 64 5612365270570261399291616530551980 4 65265030554 54 84 991794 037554 11083989

13905394 966914 995624 13086576574 4 020383965166355787306178 9

0614 2079724 61756714 7885358069361700198 4 4 57984 35091165510200227365198 4 534 84 79824 964 4 61874 4 6258304 7674 64 8261736123338632176788831250 4 9127792009266884 84 238181854 8089

727394 4 6180692274 654 904 67321094 74 94 74 591173096314 265599310511814 4 64 984 9164 65734 889

2990956236056918074 5378234 30166274 316235950034 5076371867998693071862950698331108755676876752095 74 0314 34 85900228811237823624 22610194 674 1693084 24 929581882290971159753012 4 904 150583934 4 0528022350651030862184 4 597274 0352939276989

64 6953854 696237284 28517188700622734 337169764 54 99882868235530232764 35037635204 4 233031219185 94 73589

4 5604 2668354 4 9612689

90924 013089

98337870135124 52394 8795384 596903934 24 7060924 69339833594 4 514 2833816687683906014 54 197079224 7310862821685927654 723364 212180787384 2997293257587252274 1969211008889

94 834 9564 2276964 023114 27539124 4 74 4 324 19589

5104 6868251384 1571172266308178034 0834 694 4 4 6916054 76793293889

4 204 3396620864 727227134 0585034 694 76983784 811165925615771535228 4 04 2764 824 9729162557314 7864 0882004 014 719734 509654 7770301284 7556814 1016328618137324 4 0985906856266371605889

07071996765696936955777186970008 34 78267984 657239831280624 85664 1195835594 66864 6336824 1014 706634 969054 555589

26516296221007684 166189

734 54 4 2324 8558753157654 115752350824 4 19774 4 05089

4 0990094 515586829666106709670902 4 21885672635130220769 4 6164 74 19610124 835004 88324 3990996858554 18687667730961363628557 4 990531672834 279055520874 94 1700667820958305569962 4 94 777334 336350713831665009160994 4 586030701991206362094 72616281628154 30505579730019787551337883522833593019170150 24 3774 92382939563793589

62954 95380106173507005062115379 4 116136924 54 0177933110673136807906291585771153 4 35290634 174 0273374 6525121883693915935520571525 4 803914 1014 1160760734 93255128653224 2006682870834 93294 7027112382304 4 81910806367017055551681660516170852577538 9

7094 27072966869302260064 89

6574 14 66207261504 70861373723724 64 53254 37825575900925675384 226193084 20193014 170554 4 579737519753004 704 1686118589

73324 224 55389

37939958889

725739655857866212 04 211377058501004 1536324 73380634 84 93087817055660615334 1128860737674 34 320714 04 0687517684 5301024

Chapter Seventy-four

9189

4 4 7882289

24 670924 764 54 53578114 72726834 11981251579374 7938590136536319222853772590 74 594 94 89

1650089

06353103732934 604 820812754 766554 4 80334 689

750994 173377227300800883513866121639608769508033277 4 4 6327520211238336638 9

0757017365868834 0714 324 95737637613189

0231795720119331834 684 075713003556003589

101914 4 2671794 84 864 097507034 89

1571557880121672194 813174 24 3874 6984 84 019368355064 2575388859536354 064 5784 59525802634 89

4 053684 8524 566120713520282183609121072824 4 8603570984 85986214
991107205603824 59194 85982982354 3664 74 7724 4 31874 4 3625938524 4 31934
988597695084 769983030114 4 27791664 02353624 4 0694 889
364 33666519120633002270696̇4 314 289
14 1781565157624 136606794 0864 4 2773931508764 5327820000514 3114 4 169384
502136024 5385952735824 128082284 0514 800724 995059504
21581980220321191170380602272622853152778225079828160184 84 804 4 63884 54
23818778217104 534 76165937626072970888̇4 217699804 4
06003609507163059379235337276032567908̇4 296637714 903184 4 698075924
2293061592887578809375̇4 55664 4 16098881032273324 3261160955215205586557288084
1228200008754 923083828398024 930370185292062238770987704 27810125622682864
582582074 89
374 5065734 680589
57357127024 4 6993304 0752354 54 4 86384 82611794 9774 9065229880663969154
916194 5675734 17174 14 66566677615589
13022851724 9374 989
14 23154 4 04 20360083760231932689
10997554 62658514 4 24 4 1306916999881628089
074 8596904 830687724 1500910924 82260722119536627835626888806669171̇4 5514
7204 0654 6986724 4 6134 18392754 6666394 924 222757872605386194 266203793909264
9269513080814 3167659282504 8764 72104 863583938056093091373069208̇4
8388137756273064 14 915510911084 4 12526884 28224 4 779976582804 5167088789
61001559623254 5784 1694 603139229878054 5287215559674 9804 08504
6227082625986099215606656776059196̇4 7866196535011861033873012068186269889
8317555385634 93334 962036254 5889
0583539704 9964 1814 14 34 4 00220806029988614 134 68584 23913934 0153564 2324
7214 253014 28591205657638569356277624 70877172637820785953181̇4 3314 6684 288614 4
05778794 84 394 1854 4 14 553901189
633756637537059024 278787829869814 914 97904 89
9821810205290687974 24 90994 284 3227323929273792293589
4 9375634 604 4 71174 134 6181187637755675531713533286̇9̇4 4
678866336852529977913388̇8̇4 0625205355767274 52268759094
25026988026230290295919800718727154 3905075709204 89
4 74 278808112161753705708177786065723273̇9̇4 4 3689
675971961324 0934 977338071774 85067680661100024 97094 8317758504 89
61316817104 715760132811599797966971179̇6̇4 89
374 936580182829314 68853266706863564 7384 59193816300614 124 73853884 559004
5829273118304 53194 9237507394 9535971393532734 15735585162108563929̇4 72189
809593934 14 82083584 9569334 691831189
4 798014 4 3321814 6335283910776628884 4 960868696378265107375503636164 4
92166918087904 910333994 84 824 4 22074 74 508737919354 74 56961564 4
1020723233200904 2650394 96704 594 794 672172322314 104 619778179232279689
11516033387085969994 751284 2805010007507936666864 4
883362672503775902521102625881334 84 89
2873136664 04 95934 702802062967005570773̇4 062202975577334 989

184 2778084 8503294 924 15000656210226872992169408430237869071121487459 4089

0504 767609155597377014 0654 31151364 19939101532216931977506053626463 24562937860104 0851025972253251730926509659234 79694 99224 83311768116594 806088000826189

23704 0594 9807704 001739674 582189

24 2954 89

50716877133100103978515335345314 710685957094 4 506053733591953658617196314 97006018216015116781644 58777993723274 54 84 370216719698324 03521589

5168535513924 782055912827961534 9166301514 5805178884 114 8097186706984 272264 732539627856885621860135755144 802584 1191257861698154 02760912705074 195114 039656379289

82882852274 086014 5039535211265389

53883867793995172958629270944 784 1273911524 3311292594 64 000726134 64 924 997268181094 51514 4 03360630052871288117634 5574 74 4 004 968524 2334 3398859029913064 2366501730923117254 93223569364 62708264 736539614 70193614 6564 880823663856871274 311814 628024 2967084 16102187589

9860964 96923503129824 4 6820228624 10158118338086958732157760182237896 1801576779989

26335274 84 089

573104 084 610685377186963984 4 1318584 611504 14 82873050231180669598634 1793389

53174 69817706686635251177878 44 5758531114 95225289

2091504 281574 9224 55591384 7113304 271589

135534 1114 234 95667324 04 38530735724 6228684 6922284 083793734 4 84 706029169360139930 40950654 5961900308183802527282563082209372697527529895 2076633889

5811003934 670501955027215254 070784 222031586900159951308263 8484 1974 8777684 991692392219653723166544 7574 4 0764 10100996506171262795901780988192588847 792708101654 5937332535284 12802007575104 825911652513757834 010089

5184 768524 91018622117355534 863696984 1574 019955602865124 22361874 05834 09084 4 768789

7154 21259530355913270720760615089

738197994 8118563835674 506257294 695134 36916789

182630665079524 31155826364 371997603774 4 4 620187910161354 24 4 7700627364 765654 919626761644 4 6807721909229290808662281129598 84 924 78114 8671534 257155367603119524 54 7561565236967703853704 76886604 69802138524 80305611763820687575067581364 1286287801377651 40619072670023309784 587766918228333916512907870760866937517116 89

174 16276908095517572796980520168210271626213606970604 160915617887053054 07209797684 930266376389

686627360501139889

883673359135139603154 74 2889

74 713854 16969392931830868002123289

632959938127165372211852951450167108432074694204902097667007422827466722215683386341302328609110460240156123049845591409523921046097565436483444615085503749970595533666022134626048399601227327364191069494399224652457000523913622733338328497275573933564959431552309012332305634341523510569628228677882109308461215686611443870760958284067151875349808971433102743967023207286830105305585474061120710903593522245318973774 89

28721223938874431654802090390081081088526692277246193143825290972586311246157795502759822070616687080487695005424198755620466992746639886393484868401422335287282144403954784 2289

1745476582719454397372171674600060853686206659734305152428332728939125107799228171714059172236020738527 89

2642080373792927864355780211583575735835906020737813547108144950490459183211755301545019836835859869923267993632243604356246020284705006583453866926334314 789

82991467853814916433293733770647285611977754717802105720656241678062049249605068101450554440008369158538639919640558302728633212102715925478049198967089

06687151219434944169901581812162969164529656672888226173464699874380606663650125491935299515634267061483686297879194828582851812784137702694022167558068283567621527125100272253217550117539167618570824410005697863552015457177509609839035001282512873029138851759746097154637478515816291219002842149372840941016515570616862064622207366 89

55493931454351822662501773714 79799689

20612065325275418413914476113922152134614069286419355821654479670253694488544417123943334998602980270985027141815954167802543245054515169222688322276807058416857108824 89

40081080598243638806930494014003605405882514727455882582328529765554366006097614188174543950683 5189

943064407677097341582749754334607411032688819736325102959869 8127139183273239406546776520570126856021583738546587562512867371973052008354520571151156379671524228543756123193671768567009006373542503094551091851196229951403259743792093543742091184315511683498513254915865438192839955738312594536724825067114 7389

62967299087888584888259970107422725250403548180496285225705208236348512269383156280672836714743505598392797326066842950726351382751041974 6889

767672591369017306512365731719532431012869561072580528336315 89

009582669841735396384872016520049064906403549854492372294274183784110330807773869403934504663332200174222405363394075275059829357491086988185410522731299102223339766125332469073008027004902 589

1197866095461412213341213 89

19626388266617865561463442108132633077176078663806363424319091832541943227473241152377048775613809279604835764996953687485113088070624761273257503766591078316587857685506619883979458302690860270196411220225736605864073929143877225989

074 073598764 4 733155270684 661916708199094 2108608514 0332806017878514 3014 9967994 73634 2366222291820690324 4 530152501557857601522884 73671518234 94 4 92654 8288571797699263163527 5384 557655764 4 067754 4 89

066824 89

966134 55952180097814 2208672688630564 29154 0138296534 685734 89

96719724 201717604 14 5629991302514 14 4 4 7524 884 8788595219222684 372364 532964 338807885110699339769612778269162 54 630973235354 514 62264 137652139297506809924 77659734 72612690939787221392807 4 558564 7099981589

4 29668515562704 0336605876230534 03109834 593229001269832269205022015814 34 302808000223658015 4 632882552904 7068250736300630781189

5687198094 0767158512610334 4 019382962718808600861169707239670394 318126130974 24 711171790198574 30123990754 0354 716506288051264 9200956055134 5333620292630664 9809154 0875817634 02129960016194 9111034 9375157655887524 827214 2376797264 2564 2697736819889

0882172269926555304 98724 7904 79810006504 684 34 265519305954 864 63515965834 19325601995394 27254 24 63731715151763524 39514 038074 24 4 23857724 76565961524 5674 6699316286028264 85504 068591224 634 076966397694 27013669388291856076582008669 4 3833756314 593294 1714 5519966697728221814 706209062034 976317120864 66030605675614 933109167359686926299803365159852130088802 4 04 61816833186087792966500277922134 760116174 813520006025989

51502189

63264 153851311775210714 64 107072577934 97182252726790059933701865961579327800661769111831676 14 7157964 64 874 10695224 5376114 56887923115088630362384 0717691959989

00356580754 72701071991664 4 775922773065889

61119394 27586024 665729164 64 7782959517792521728 4 0786074 4 329511315658116636186290 4 4 736315551565582337 34 102054 10970553981055118587774 84 7255317701694 5619773274 00076274 66291601557814 989

384 99154 800670015880287271396 4 7788555334 050152578884 671964 8020524 6724 24 4 939551864 3725584 4 09996006306300289

8185781127353194 0034 4 4 827534 004 296065595089

2253518601554 22289

1764 294 6353097283905715525192200671822520 4 4 834 56957283024 8581587778354 37195126859654 2670816960798234 6616792592607356189

3989

5590289

54 229820069011350119992783370576175 4 07125834 805827806812389

4 2856193111114 132504 933164 2605280233039814 16900679889

80373760320995164 384 89

0586993696068307101231796152669 24 5304 64 92374 632284 627990824 2334 798330374 034 4 5017864 4 8039881275592259020 4 65366084 6910213794 84 23688814 526296968662135664 76702014 26725320564 4 35031311714 4 4 137713514 6736716972654 522654 6510614 4 03820274 3516102254 60111162195775537690901298 14 813688328624 816036689

927739083394 0514 714 3384 874 769201164 26194 81923964 4 94 632004 4 6384 74 6884 7911151704 4 84 3919386765303 1100824 238704 981524 5204 055739620581831624 8694 5032953509198580564 589

89

0874 4 256831229254 34 5074 73734 15195274 2364 764 1802819954 873173772129012524 214 4 6754 04 294 58554 024 239064 71702257004 4 64 24 8759363876636706774 7962024 4 2768094 377854 82576651284 37769009314 2098666071018702933859331 04 37732853034 3716889

5184 80254 779912733313963366725069 7624 004 4 4 399984 287154 827354 0021362280036387835780861930328 1309994 90596589

1889

3750753834 4 26925570332089

03758324 6284 6794 994 77201616184 924 4 806707260664 2394 3232192320717600372523136002600793811 7888524 02504 577314 92535024 973994 254 4 051399099724 27789

1851189

2389

5556724 90883322532107988627081564 0003225278031510976686622833 4 67773834 94 174 6122589

4 54 2098000029093296907 4 37726013869091027914 0625985 1525059776681 84 4 01078167066934 0007514 934 82854 0555614 304 7553911053314 37574 64 2294 8620974 4 679084 4 758764 683631789

27730859885111355095794 74 4 954 218629866774 966961594 74 4 4 4 09273113200669786 11380859054 53176264 94 59016781969714 98613994 922697223384 5270514 3809389

513504 64 4 375512254 861117089

139668089

3667779730994 384 8808619331909104 35786072084 96730738259379239635993284 751004 0727279386262716704 4 754 075719202503934 19197254 5189

4 83117279024 614 04 96689

55179079986910253764 89

0964 84 59816709017139351206782839579961226311973314 91337781834 3384 19318523675386629019004 6334 3328532834 34 1824 92107191609276730801 32353694 7264 84 89

2764 4 2979870681125654 628061172604 60733219176304 74 1215064 030201789

3205795687605102775250530 4 361222709604 67584 531273866165214 24 194 086834 0837589

14 0095114 13392954 5770094 73174 8116885364 094 1835286109971034 167235581786028234 982020314 9986794 0174 04 171914 02839362105194 80604 81901824 518008170137104 21974 592127984 04 024 2689

63005335536854 94 164 00863921774 56769534 4 58650883286298216584 60164 5078000035989

852129012395900704 20266074 4 988785062717607762225506063907 4 53194 771889 2509905810093672989

1954 0995766335386583780980 4 4 79353779918771214 29774 619764 094 72721214
02353265517772361634 1966074 376391538660194 501776914 00624 0684
127316295860806350676293775125293 4 3675960734 27199675135201580087373954 8389
734 39901238256568290785911 4 4 258828521366169201 4 0299004 1314
62136806323526508654 11218084 74 9987584 4 111836290979089
19834 1187537664 9604 80936264 89
329104 3905977256329558138877674 4 6954 618157978704
19159755833500037728672 4 607351853508854 954 64 20293097158563694 9785764 04 8374
15055580991884 020934 33335128195514 55518573334 888164 9167694 4 277824 05554
33697731192014 372254 154 19274 5059760137984 14 4 3735994 2028760525557189
37804 114 89
261257983036183801077110050 04 239239264 4 156922779005702794 74 01364 94
229184 79336925354 324 84 04 87802317774 4 5184 177958355825754 76184 254
957539587854 94 5834 3084 804 4 1737087984 92674 195289
3230314 89
589
916006854 228795789
294 815900068735373333333863813908 4 20994 8725511726171087294 4 0888684 4
7850811634 5585269214 154 0299672098869371588623222033 14 8558174 2682635950689
36234 4 8134 224 737869394 60923256600754 72125674 14 1034 2184 90131189
63967654 73291674 24 7189
934 24 33028029092698507522 94 90797094 4 30092386728774
3936255111313628761591973832 4 134 9167226826122826312779381175080 74 089
589
4 3971900254 264 12664 94 79801764 4 20164 54 1588131760189
72659624 614 4 13913192067850352 4 63830657764 016522973204 7089
20114 6917133722878630370384 53134 194 264 4 14 24 9664 984 4 74 4 04
8617738513529373108099859 4 728151117365071913988126930 74 82690614 0392864
227662784 94 329558828593837214 84 7507077835511989
6224 9119558823704 5064 582005610170205324 84 4 4 9021502294 561765561859214
574 399009554 82294 1375154 4 13613291504 304 6914 17994 1224
60933816513626279028278 84 2138122077589
4 24 03884 062294 331727989
2594 183668293679259604 224 184 594 177065301954 864 394 8170335524 102874 704
4 731171507034 7750834 323733311632587672763683 4 68584 4 4 865625391872394 60827324
7135004 4 89
570868031503250386764 017353150794 0034 557285503700184
56027699615061568291 4 1611706104 616174 0824 84 62670335189
1525518824 821272600725957656788 9
9125678702014 9786679084 7106631074 8764 6730989
0914 7197987929585906257336 4 9734 98235031260983098734
68616273935805790735 4 90824 68304 97284 0977323811670824 915163734
6808705105219191762054 1698826254 76054 4 5817711179937767786965 4 2169925785577204
2634 4 24 4 304 2074 4 954 89

7033904 34 50720611900769736351740 019526563221392825831205282400374 66954
59092804 5259687984 60814 0870719534 254 761388363353511911214 4 14 314
8505520123581380626 9231353833876758091889

23797585515732036588317624 24 1169167523814 588592075164 035236684
37267917590637053921979811265977081139 4 7351671962999970520901709075 89
856916389

0664 2704 23570074 4 502775120104 90394 814 83294 574 4 380974 626035105789
81954 0763987060787581774 0724 91184 50697884 2994 13834 20608124 2839014 8814
872599854 1814 8029294 9227878324 35610554 91564 109174 88770670678201198591 09589

09838688395117183801349 14 8254 99274 914 26985525951776536126 24 215726624 4
889

609614 82979703084 2021051602796714 78561594 064 61363824 77589
02011025199234 215321006017523025 74 21223754 21074 95918728675189
55215532994 5322689

4 251884 094 2282675774 4 222275528207615607277103 94 71825668024
710660677383120630314 66284 74 4 3386204 74 3259568505689

28716265329083278784 399650716724 2206138294 5329166004 638087256305952 4
15328812093700992298 9

60069813962796862795676351987 4 1824 018562931984 9226233364 3189
930901704 88199525882733880795326588514 4 93938124 1154 327320589
164 57864 2294 52684 117518808184 050956904 69138134 4 307784 89
02114 87971211628397734 4 3054 84 614 9807935624 354 96714 1294 733326664 224
8305004 364 4 54 54 70274 917232078399565086801876173270331906565795 4
753952069292520153070 64 3504 71306881289

032053854 55639879921010956672982873 04 794 6610054 3163584 6234 4 874 4 15554
07133814 3234 4 13117884 24 196019037028686962 4 227624 65024 004 20813713504 64
0159934 72053275567950353390671272161779060302162399780 4 18576334 810054 4
83887031730716255256 4 799599998693531968130101562970978711673069 64 94 0274
9166572674 94 34 3208132314 6138869255334 94 9294 1183163877889

9032594 010934 11157274 29801331814 578281687913514 24 395578734 205915614
58773689

88080791707114 551154 762661682081777574 724 84 2787971298154 82385203689
5916524 054 3730524 6672873130301925829524
9876393209857312091610561357220176392716995986861088676061338 4 364 96169518654 84
8604 61684 84 824 074 3838118074 1734 2224 4 8394 789

3998278014 734 22230578654 10217729264 820914 094 85035013224
15155999901630714 7814 8527051614 4 32258254 78014 34 4 010953366023936264 24
9313852294 054 75364 168364 6704 1574 300558372984 704 01814 55710029696234
69850599778855736998021822303 54 923831879762989

4 15697721236384 4 0889
1789
2752775284 714 4 7762189
20574 254 531510374 799777068623624 2189
9063030962822117732197082303 4 774 54 550602385859114 0389
89
6916662207787683260123961 74 19997623655063632660169906611689

08868774 133378091951614 977054 9214 171181911014 954 34
786938206209808278789
573132789
906002086339112784 7153684 304 3814 98150970304 770886881635974 192534 134
1221913962874 578109934 24 832714 109178276317654
2096312507136692636588213575119987540 0115790280285078066983384 183382667394
5536831965657170319 4 6293364 109272667274 24 4 99274 7322913800983574 4 509134
07993085683604 84 6778665354 2105866800521154 264 8674 972395379364
215665358720818554 12598194 54 74 275161184 1693662556324 1935915856950889
0535314 1218336623998780221154 0 24 566001502364 69108159974 1920254 4
3787361022671294 12282988805336794 39503294 04 804 9616771107287881031614
6773037150218352890
024 14 64 81754 30954 90594 4 88754 104 25016804 06999981967193798208277334 64
8558158591077617882840 975054 685679139904 011384 5624 3604 03574 4 024 6191237694 4
022007604 214 3357338726039253724 664 089
664 914 714 654 7300721952927374 17679613565233067804 268200024 23074
12186674 86694 628058788787382995232780501070661013854
02880119138557309113805727558 9
368194 030938071886379375821544 4 4 3516265599120308784 8205239374 935189
5597158155182804 814
80783131053509682356716123550963161528665857859019528717754 64 25064 12984 94
5105730353324 334 89
0979972094 57291700958784 0832214 04 4 05014 74 114
3817095657712526715779817097676384 7864 2064 87613679394 5784 4 23858603564 9664 4
6314 013104 8667056134 627690174 9283229004 3271120819229564 1589
4 81528265584 221926189
025305138159118034 231088514 9122665391794 4 8174 33904 322700506874
2888199670619606885006733283536 14 6804 985960814 028791196311274 8254 664 04 370384
782884 007981579134 4 523210166867374 1121294 4 968134 51012237984 294 02194 794
691664 81503124 318739691196021567121 14 22794 306820104 087675680937389
82054 684 214 7856014 277688201880717174 14 1274 93674 67817513227710904
67300153094 677730692232909534 95694 4 9160116904 68181827234
778161975125727851535569861629220291884 74 53026983015663874 917702194 7605094 174
86684 1197276604 4 4 0854 83297504 989
0782580615390200301035218027179209950817839121233970070027832906193713368
21833696154 082652039271615180227915286 4 07683150329974 06092804
8310506255157226287131327681824 7801169154 9378624 83224 0172383707271608864 19294
21181718564 674 81185694 008705299611314 10594 582938703305286297918826 4 9324 74
2017955124 4 23294 7629034 8834 95272292830804
0122263722761102752038001209375208856 24 064 531125037264 01539964 37123370790374
395120320285350254 74 8277809303020219663250932909 4 4 88190574
510298521728306996224 21954 710165193329769370654 5763334 324 332564
33136391221083529135557700812650539793164 6814 94 5134 120751218835054
7396859555387809194 7374 6566279031868161713 64 161521554 0774 5354 3804 14 7984 54
584 0634 4 74 74 5085680280862324 12696939931122964 05603273109279384
9169187933359614 853517001814 969826164 80034 4 027822813985879014 862852128674

6175384 85034 8068386520168074 7674 4 02114 766556964 3873967579664 4 2958864
09577559154 19261507196653734 10817064 974 822204
191350352239320369277923907369558805779975526019030814 355084 924
759818577979802981264 12519269808310756574 6594 693511285627975905780034 193234
760013696114 4 729013113729326518877314 67214 1074 12752210105151558657134
93912768855730064 56556663593525354 5094 573789
        688358002770721080754 68519790215677663559608589
        9524 4 9272204 97752998154 586253592955688586552190862034 88574 294 4 354 8834
0176616830553266024 5835994 4 54 330952973620564 28294 74 539664 1017593878078757904
014 319567264 4 502565389
        64 05200714 870685370656271174 667615719181064 22804 64 38268678064
178170171014 55799878594 92981028674 8774 716790174 355039931696835285921164 814
87861286289
        1163759927684 7108874 3661617762393098294 98234 064 13782807112174 1237834
2224 14 4 069984 86328823924 06563774 389
        8084 631704 339814 1901704 17704 58564 67859934 94 11376710185104 828834 584
75911298599113261806311665209771093260254 5777664 04
        781139798120273962790521780765659334 8303196386372636054 817261754 4 0262684
357264 514 74 1114 361974 74 885328135254 323132104 0655374 753560914 051335764 4 84
512650315994 993984 759123386762589
        9886282674 24 214 106563170282684 20274 2775354 7852784 98062554
77967309562135010751357010814 376712097361065693389
        81128770064 39508682263524 1957989
        987524 4 5315132684 3577125269551165684 260624 9795300564 134 236794 03268694
320221277155284 52294 5590601316630023329786184 27293697054 2564 089
        57224 7314 796084 227996064 312115572289
        8884 134 06901570607916985539706270694 98692261315505954 581624 06654
276265360989
        8824 692284 24 022170510920884 52264 1938004 05064 723514 10654 4
62939736295006268706918574 35034 689
        0787025266889
        903105903073320209977070195562670800784 214 175004 024 87764 369382704
966754 06914 4 89
        5634 000929852354 99129699604 654 0283212995128817182931733802589
        34 33608886395618814 53054 93633210224 6702371234 907974 06812568724
883352801820879686837674 89
        328659515635001584 3734 54 2714 861534 24 97125226151780864 71835019904
99321781991553538737856234 5508714 3139050384 328696513876903290534 0152384 2824
39639132568672927224 87084 77969680927365604 21516904 0230075017366194 9935854 4
714 4 04 152214 1064 74 9724 216152303724 6612553017965334 54 354 0889
        800869016307189
        1588084 555221984 311574 2231294 519670375862605877263336684 85075275284
79034 4 2501653764 91633179283207357204 36314 962933262171984 1204 14 9693900215789
        87584 055068836313189
        782803270681820620114 709707824 64 7760276296351324 513522519224 278604 4
76601784 554 6358689

564 1834 4 08259553254 334 088710161510703674 6824 5292204 678084
85318529560302603933699879125296023073278584 693716270374 914 4 83889
16337500526216973323321524 007087580984 8564 6289
779180984 82534 27212024 8127256555150503057004 1811989
5186092167878092709372 14 804 71120320927521638219693005366775084 683589
38654 4 52815223534 75575590763802378521519 4 60182724 5682363954
9056812593274 7289
54 56989
34 4 7114 180981315364 95974 85154 106854 609786330324 864 2987770186355313674
508110767638604 7334 64 0295768821152889
8135664 4 93094 93104 3589
0364 514 13175524 14 78099253505914 813095314 71226234 1354 064
609059803930072954 0969213694 564 4 98578781314 84 9834 71061858858025833530086634
822074 58754 75776920674 1006757177870214 8024 9068099354 034 04 978086974
7523182136878867192069 4 2034 4 186215299004 6866853574 977871014 75284
5821521535098270986352770357562938 4 9313931604 238871689
90739823956189
887221884 2061190277094 299032275736687186079770707215592326 4
1813601697172777 4 0702884 134 5717732062530298816172 64 064 98017801926964
155038729328624 874 51156694 4 009014 69103714 66589
52807690750630991658019 04 02824 91239634 5679839269565571594 76136694
38739333006873830818123094 204 4 15929595171871924 926797929712950294
915811852694 4 654 4 88816064 4 89
09108574 7384 97225266256135983373917831 94 9599150654 39983793983509005174
3387881718295516184 4 732570694 2293753652551534 71178576184 9774 77973316771607 14
994 214 526381704 75227272955705001733 74 4 013560297812168718861307295720086827 04
728150994 4 936557613530068382030072 4 872389
18604 5558234 0567631876262362589
04 34 07960239552914 4 08186887350391637299 34 71628157658628534 654 4 4 767189
779664 0094 34 2024 90164 34 1084 86305364 084 94 0912887711996506980 4
578807137977951591204 2538025709198604 559673886019016 34 4 14
82900997297139228277863871263080176692137 04 934 976904 380819565618801297909 14
650754 4 0684 5318051694 04 9624 84 54 9525186336324 22222614 586995009297904
5626886597039309839695602356 4 3889
6863299233237659081 14 24 8603580354 5169782067694 889
24 866383306879176594 263820092637789
0316582705029113785729750974 004 93867535805163232169 84 736338584 19735204
8763394 55394 64 2739288524 974 51674 89
904 6514 594 73884 977874 3657589
4 707717794 35627074 325722855361014 9292967565026585100600321814
6153612928591069 34 3214 878686374 34 2977020598254 510958054 174 4 55625081164
88195634 4 3233555509154 070228734 506176634 89
8004 9281114 84 86033667358805224 298027624 50658064 166164 6093309658322774
1201687004 61864 7087354 607594 60023553734 363668584 6300082989
115932174 654 3217351175531575551018630965885602 74 4 73288174 361764
5365592624 61764 387774 0379976886080184 14 5764 4 764 30357129839955569156559 4

231174 5306594 8362502060364 382217354 4 09655353950904 574 3693865104 312934
2716658105214 64 7736285604 104 2715237293978124 871060598593201 7807577384
3670656311350685930588860836202 34 778064 9879758531784
0167290597876570281387580260323333798832030389
  685399914 520291291252264 234 89
  66197633971826810602370959759662980918534 819012504 031589
  9625204 7170767663998683531531966086875291254 23115375034 755005153674
068684 69956767733057751079235 04 9034 57787782633964 738764 290564 0164 4 333168224
565090395700668568009825182733058 1904 24 322611289
  4 85184 91882214 253968613100337137224 3018683955964 4 1734 67084 1783204
0075715124 1680837554 1314 824 7924 004 524 308125367729689
  704 4 4 067964 317974 268159359203135821514 6396789
  23853314 691684 80192378561366570636094 221329625671822214 085376580706834
61685834 9637565564 81521327880020825169618079 84 84 04 74 86754 2864 8124 7189
  2324 572784 8809951784 920023813214 9505597686097804 3922721365667914
32558387293962885557 53189
  85133904 712378084 5594 07184 4 8328361153361578025705836 4 3859337129234
7805105809160715792371735883271261 64 560656794 5034 809907997205084 2273054 74
19077811064 94 0216016666629509 4 59324 6968082788587382689
  6084 8774 4 5611837984 4 8657304 54 32053689
  2684 034 914 234 50881535101678575706668 74 95637606663072936364 97984
09105284 0084 54 6233261781814 9797614 12181872861268653 4 6071166509551354
77832306274 118114 820717164 6652654 2709914 84 7880777689
  28234 57954 86110671504 94 7364 73997364 80665299537367799934 02353274 964
801034 4 60008563976973633732229 4 714 6973027764 094 0775396288390125824
66293969389
  877015862089
  3799185516933084 63815996539591339262924 500564 4 06760974
23169030780271559700 74 4 4 1832783863920059150 4 1926664 728752789
  7954 9277034 15082639154 789
  692688330816604 79564 2091123793125124 523826289
  13239114 25925924 887235313534 14 0371673379930617119964 80374 07664 4 4
036108277815093 71989
  266789
  9588375052554 7609294 200184 3074 4 4 389
  64 934 96814 25354 24 4 228754 82634 672599399787959797254 7224 4
117287600771260884 0939504 81192159674 88739555862671065 4 903021324 0224 7707926524
977694 4 9552051080564 104 822068021729276356152237738510636020972031378 9
  4 8389
  08760877304 4 4 4 33910703713871331637 4 909282154 9212966094 3559957654
25050659702392398001339719254 39883533581932604 2355334 64 070907285804 865214
15339035222970604 712201304 94 1234 55357789
  54 7124 8630004 705562889
  4 5504 4 6086222664 852384 7310733172230385 64 18653118021793512078836789
  316324 319258064 4 85005114 5282276974 70288129755672304 19389
  696691151684 034 2521912666860561300384 5205389

33691121008120502524 10879522034 62366013906294 0958680638104 861567034 9189
52889

9594 4 34 2180753633129570224 12607656628378577631058413324
9700802109639513491608642051940551379803738265147259 89

9902124 7513597282764 8704 803024 09576924 624 3692551113922353178694 829284
218555724 374 7361826577956003518 9

0158768759814 4 266576265825837773537988011685811161188 54
587199032823772576597479255550151703522520432959456689

504 59779859313354 60305804 62871210509920026539199902203280298551349905589

52962035081185191162393317684 154 5106106551624 78821980694 14 695314
02163854 294 84 650993057590184 254 772587685764 14 74 0917080050765864 163376935814
66078187224 4 50583794 24 375762870854 54 03350110537092671021601688 9

74 25190172664 771091187734 01965876131923824 4 0167786694 4 73160364
332359105304 639269254 864 734 05762211664 84 26993833030504 8174
39731193500536761645050844 76304 732563764 21666139818172167153111289
1024

Chapter Seventy-five

5585162073197007003112540505208238290 89
3128757564 218754 16786156917970097009380501429 84
66685212001591511327205923213373624 51009271857273494 1352 89
4 81232311599234 6158 9
690978 9

674 4 54 13062762687256330468233531371596513000406153320056264 21384 322314
8270354 73586350919884 4 6533835684 004 84 1684 65383514 752987266852104
759009105167315924 6264 853570708194 30352359875504 9297733307531722035573470236517079315932787444549816445932473938377943652780031092775354 3734
92970112030888508113851103629856205948834 6961563623208283108425028737613641284
67264 503679574 9821634 4 694 59924 4 023203866360957965273125049 89

12012359996284 8087517002713559088212824 4 592123659726362362619317174
993060278006727038520443869442023962659430717338754 4 84 3964 9357394 01654 4 694
254 38 9

18315939596750099329847553183201970958681114 74 034 114 64 30774 907873234
732383184 3169775800695104 75962534 780392905312278 9

72028317103077044 1520409620275360661687750953874 913564 8654 89
93528510813754 66230230104 4 164 4 0607874 337993886594 34
319739727628098872553596421836886252528684 292094 0766935310174 6760614 361504
0224 10610065751838578184 594 30973816665274 22822359523265631560043634
60606179929549634 268127824 69802311078319221754 882824 84 4 34 89

4 215590509624 9680955168161417840810580681730090026315272179607472349635797944 7534 390082662384 080704 887676620125669754 226324 768414 4
360299612706320364 24 76725566239584 136334 669634 20183396378254 2254 4 74
306328053514 64 4 92080284 011693507171925134 34 4 917591634 4 64 8154 7381600589
64 5676084 0579801659025574 89

76711877225395270001783834 618076833574 2506196377939729071866 1657756554 9223989

51160504 4 36181020594 1685054 1876584 715902962594 03076771869386054 624 379389

529177382974 14 84 6392692211185354 79059909509729976074 7387296264 7276052104 5951128274 35631270960595023755731806195

52598765319888191583707806094 60730104 615314 07967225257577860927309190 691929884 51739871631507685766351864 9379762973806603165031986181720651187867335919765239567 31888795336522908865200801 04 998114 95657664 50135714 869973922194 603166589

011920226137063954 92150000809680804 936515617904 4 4 13993654 7321194 22707627168066232679931722181257 576091524 5516705097654 927987579284 96616737619368534 354 68604 2600792782105050293510602699110772925833223313894 4 23980871654 0504 6314 65861786721994 9974 969729059791579184 64 803703518738864 3820270609804 934 004

55678609307653826192652631811202186385925165692586594 83274 4 83164 34 614 594 0369617235805971795888290583815236978853316823013314 52292999154 0592302274 058550374 0628535904 59765785964 573806521600263159177 2888124 80183076664 6377077199854 694 714 324 604 154 308710677882187690707969 13136784 60577018382839283094 79160915776228351293308159 5269760684 026594 233928858711054 4 0868306366385810204 73632094 4 96534 9887762757862699053539155327911881192633510691931273397666 0914 8613974 5614 5254 5275688380518228526608713 963283884 183684 84 80136264 58289

54 0073065079156074 102889

0834 54 6596253808696255262637115923594 826384 54 56087258368603761981706726337 4 81287637268299887772294 4 54 04 07706789

94 0164 381250027554 20169830230695 511629983134 31071889

90986254 1016002935524 4 154 86259137615974 787091851534 025688881301989

21884 4 56611164 9106326888324 234 4 83096288804 9657974 271034 082237366738282557725076771530518606164 830633559801934 0710989

716309884 0874 67259104 4 598887595960530329 889

9363852119394 90968283710864 57135234 56015804 3864 2971035384 6683059689 8796808358734 9785762678556588838364 9516272354 5207087795334 6765867204 916172087981314 914 16989

1375664 64 54 56974 216663388028870931159655290

096858324 662094 2368725955209587658676396 52581062760953955291 917651817376729189

876677984 25119216807552581600 69267289

2837696502864 9208798782224 4 210714 04 64 673074 851974 3713976053074 32234 51552532121235870851616285214 5380083686124 6295154 80394 5332968377364 24 862964 57024 358189

2316862264 994 99218634 98324 681214 94 6737511994 819504 5074 4 9659704 32717604 0133835522236081534 0004 79598193685223092588 5754 59795669694 7562389 4 95724 732524 84 866070654 288256287673592883976 196190591329083994 6916384 1005321889

18694 3256572066776523823824 73164 38079769604 4 4 5729694 4 6502834
30616652216987080261757575705124 164 111092073577262039704 116888594 037610584
3313029314 4 4 829065955684 2964 872963771613219507321997164 14 4 17025654 689
4 610127030824 5972384 18283604 031166034 89

15371607623286396661656185600094 671554 9151974 673084 23255867674 1097334
02984 616967564 2107632231536789

799885806831989

2283085976337509294 64 9038791074 370774 0084 634 93623624 00830084
950073558164 96691675977786580811182304 77074 24 6964 3604 73279351820384 719889
611703590083004 556851252805095510667699602373878235376637278226774
0520510615320189

983806114 919859528750026624 554 227352605814 89

4 88099794 079523817886224 4 3301332364 554 32574 103883704 23239809214 1614
96327553956636176867524 381765566251013374 304 64 808207552851564 91167182834 54
1304 7238795984 8889

99156275919082152195994 53589

4 39873919878854 4 787855883930195317034 7124 02500720728681966631889

154 092375629824 7737363589

629303730274 864 9251369197889

067635824 615369075723811889

000386834 089

30397937519930653817228736677538514 171618214 64 06300539934
07936721095094 1233283505714 265283194 9674 694 850212250586274 04 54 81109395874
0537288809665227994 91313504 114 8573758189

94 91522734 135204 0220177174 26975610324 053900259385589

5784 9154 94 0687591085109004 4 5669877902963589

995785804 399594 722284 33554 4 0391384 5515754 5905101223677094 9004
2907251632725064 389

114 14 94 0314 39293381604 9214 114 82986961512607568119304 8851604 289

2565334 373068623996218120083759114 3173089

4 4 1989

9802933772305065225027098 97205959635360606930155 054
23580935622219990176155133694 7568289

7390100935189

88689

102305620334 560674 7815955637373724 3150513104 63884 3684
6166022210580766055016384 4 3951339275390504 7198111267789

3784 25274 293071714 2873760554 37904 15357814 6194 855984 70604 04
01016336531189

30683696593975950084 58513327284 73088004 84 8774 039317183964
9232121257591559863968310050334 4 056052789

88766114 724 3089

207390677171334 4 89

995904 99556528668704 31389

74 5563864 19506525626338200725605250254 4 97912589

3728660693665274 756954 58554 93793654 94 66905956264 82216601109072271664 3362714 785994 64 599992674 904 954 96151264 2308529764 04 04 3695030783887567665223227853593755672170054 4 176152275789

006884 92224 64 72581006854 8316761687053704 714 0293293794 29575971294 56134 524 552754 5656824 94 39714 331385804 9509737206075394 12574 1562910110232605185216108762961134 662379674 3611234 251779934 00596014 94 4 3294 7964 164 6003108837766887059 2004 88620180196337697614 505829217689

13766854 7554 1938116074 7064 364 61835509504 2783676384 4 7274 62071613819711917704 4 4 4 879751377889

2289

95884 738200829650704 62231272806210512699103 94 4 589

360789

04 4 290661289

12164 88673293277124 505955764 99953164 5688888539374 04 9657657168809130 3924 234 85693764 4 50199912028784 0027354 636310802804 8839039864 4 6286631594 0784 010291779687774 189

82862222702853291914 5503554 9524 356674 4 61195336689

70392803076336134 22784 813008059024 523229864 536534 75937924 70097712372514 8559789

62233505503714 0823738855989

99635725768152824 98573230291020966336552980 9751869164 292807619274 983229652194 4 8169604 37154 884 759085527235864 4 04 8020175814 25754 0052934 38794 61964 3196734 902934 70269618697328305602126628583594 14 2914 1764 32704 388399714 037984 862965074 4 072265264 1634 634 289

82919154 0694 5822384 00532287197813012034 284 65115000214 159693875605989 584 674 337883215104 4 5817334 91029314 084 926196254 4 3010694 7558632673613396013154 936002702882265375501 6913194 81721677272774 88797907130864 5912517689

62270234 34 826717374 4 4 76254 03604 4 36123834 266368529097934 73026221774 34 4 09361004 734 3832594 70556179624 24 7014 79577599383961282821867 04 04 6594 7367134 674 00380288689

06734 350560654 19629154 398232331916634 157727577726255667127287567764 74 03587825186324 014 293512309926524 186105365262390689

80576795900937826721251220551113158 34 782392514 17189

3266684 869674 104 933862880589

3314 1258364 873085596852364 87095735227355156 4 173160005704 356833751285864 867987776268789

11970174 1989

262975037390169668114 5531056396389

1334 9194 784 911260028872720224 3629554 11330210328883125217 90386091534 116785776233880138563 64 34 712302531331275834 9214 962681684 34 61805655064 376864 84 4 321691600993297935886971326 34 594 804 76580167302876236263754 04 64 17737117123337555290761684 5760984 120314 814 906712654 4 788130874 966926524 9507283763395824 831279554 24 169984 4 4 914 156090821234 2014 4 6635611514 39878692836764 4 038199996073613035658764 068334 110290878236852304 51771621814 804 94 32624 6784 2034 0375691218100204 8571334 6838603164 09189

04 93318702825651133422596513951836285179232653400316253031177685830439058553031434700094995404289

931062006909384298598494625764243642747550200929598219970537138567540242399582249361468818357839052925627662578147628254905215311884516726792585106299641121 89

04 74 29032689

82903001953919556490734818124 6684 3389

938765229124 4 23119814 574 662009378080796511082080920250037221765646622654628516780697561651229846904028763819653602313563613649766389

02219792361723388549181980957352297014232045491394760020309831182651347083195790827421779732291100149811042092919972707939131054168843056476680682881432639312292484752803515563282795273265608341088161697961023963066523100437026823091533999011018517840853479666457696399564386232590725663075603947055135 89

75851270259376353252345454607115787656777517132314071984930870727417259903834799083775222662385016189

00013696653310225295738651936909936258 9

633379104117758605187819207087776560999410980515517605243383814985788441580214830037738072942220576114221873419120173809741916039089

694570812869196186877182344133397780597593991704085257402459527953589551683671046122414148488235070420989

494 64 0533461029814818149838496287485469500407432484301004237023770269359497780909390095551642812541683795122263408103402400601731856228367117879128635057651221052346487547089

22865475797991986634913433674573178080001015922803245804156062040588149733690546883830568311188564269274466682562826056931827114971107908022216742737252056085239809705192876172818294917079681084956342092215680052226576590502708101059646 89

6004191594139713443207974875200619703621436531076819492314665746833301942561772580296562871057463566793619642933509041759154760564372284823152054488326426763087111474606360347328343230094190420867481232196335598089

29813901374321723190294403380213835037846658247849282371602845709018509399863087689

74636121392228744 64 37282223068 9

8144271080876739847451986859735656832475850237902290438743386565016354309204949751394651712042399638048515240438271400499873660922159516794366552097162467190287849723430687941462209330654035151465333534381762121409749952908133436688742196085463005629418718571989

79654 90389

2260994 0064 58134 576989

89

02937525260315947935205172873837166700721547961956375740701285592607563335804361178569570327151086097332660021100882712319916375934099712303202613810988 9

964 22209731755274 14 2553634 13061597294 84 37204 856730536334
53566183219602569723677 37664 04 1985539084 586654 7731334 4 24
306172126008629760529672078593225622923558 4 626284 6333189
2928319836100025921871137039971505577 4 93204 8759783197671362863201 84 4
28233653934 716363794 57127715884 0984 17687777055114 4 694 6524 04 22088538202824
989
296395084 6704 65701934 75974 601082109002237981389
393889
17366199587023532221962 94 14 99139604 84 29927934 116586704
87785711133726534 92856653689
28875089
626084 058604 97308118077965006010068109796230 4 55954 801189
7685661967624 2389
312756524 1655983194 56614 71675822057205150733187 4 3864 9959207729217154
1152707025157374 293274 060303889
970181763924 9284 4 4 9614 4 989
21199600874 14 55920119711061917813560083117939 4
3700218567880801261181157994 64 14 71730354 790676703916264 4
80369152300163809750954 9864 78577153019332075870767280738 24
1627299798565721981668 4 4 4 51931151214 7215394 6260624 154 74 7884 4 925314 74 522234
289
814 4 4 39356689
6520817283520184 9104 4 685012363534 66594 4 391017712860590789
23203698177814 4 14 065765795314 16934 27566274 4 27564 7924 957225617711224 4
1508205905726084 814 714 04 59239530795970604 271724 5927521655060051371539677724
2631825934 3164 959994 084 88134 89
6294 4 398019280504 4 69903074 3329586964 20234 77994 4 0608555298026016876274
594 816524 70013204 750956993158251056595655 4 51124 68121674 104 4 189
2014 9712917059113204 64 86929952189
3607872571989
54 33268702764 211207971112580634 371790702853656868188813064 931529035864
9123136625719028116080 4 4 99253317309331886197389
137211839634 8879203809214 81773975151215550607 14 2123784 7824 9514 64 94
932858500089
95173231334 1794 4 919571954 937381022516204 3355850964 04 4 299950654 94
8218174 918298209802850161357 64 6979930679132224 784 9851295874 1989
76234 0204 8264 287062020511304 84 54 32074 564 363054 68298589
979035884 05564 6100674 589
9723002864 89
589
524 14 53303792218607675721960300019984 0534 6104 236967394 84 65981989
0332264 4 71364 1778288583186156 4 1089
9810633325669588014 908754 89
11855294 4 4 754 8777707033254 281654 04 870114 529025916253519801238 74 14
0104 360363092052813996081857821750591992 04 4 4 07167990153384 4 5864 0154 2054
227660394 9509852531714 64 7656658866814 5884 224 62768154 71774 89

7706020161939694 7738552977951792063934 2593819635523803884 24
8395810392756705640051774 584 154 5364 77920170734 26820789
53784 24 193187181125134 00191354 9075223018853664 24 561518864 03026504
1520622587526974 64 4 830596060008664 8084 673975874 694 031004 4
3050711008032857561852600337068332178341 100697307370364 03212982503954 5915664
516251801635854 889
25018864 904 176713086234 74 164 51200097805267165914 094 5866695297194
32662613627554 6662763974 798831324 207660024 708256555168634 654 15732273037984
6334 974 354 176053391180554 9584 8517100306504 714 65709174 00082202203334 2084
271621025506998295166962322792052067901249991059790172386421758536906478
213618772371091338814 995600185227362965360920637316839784 73714 984 1162314 04
7954 57163102850830964 9294 65614 289
07773603095689
14 137573724 220084 319536767372075167234 021174 327264 6707775707205664 4
653817086104 304 91301993304 74 79859635164 887964 6194 4 9295289
0582573097904 0950627720666835694 4 27988054 961983751273274
650760182121520533492208085191762661708361357233342510069683104
178207971860650279732577611571650724 0273651199086137670389
88665032755774 389
4 2275815661730769721836436801942195847681141757576578022594
12293693762854 8376150113712094 4 4 77726788390726376506189
3274 4 94 74 109264 0586931989
5905855996960097204 6356710955864 2594 222507134 22810831610787854
56208386552686224 968775589
5674 284 00965170789
74 3998364 52194 028789
69929676885522509924 54 811316798119609584 4 9994 512830174 39565864 554 2534
924 673319276992922114 9864 4 2884 274 282189
6234 37770714 914 38577608058084 8564 273037171353764 24 530679378694
579057523350764
3881521810656607927075157252883991851571052600561883391085362212756884
26153686799818073601708756736421701333242635306193463545436017260388552556774
580621314 6382054 889
97794 37994 8659252807324 77127701533566724 30512874
551113052270769226215106526147981396130120548259553984 982903822165854
0002787182817945275934 57598160626825669353591091970253175878 9
58507864 2512381690228684 4 08855504 623386176809374 38712550030627677911 4 4
604 271750236904 8260534 968220034 68062797939752823723519731070856662324 732554
815669120184 6615653934 4 8604 754 03574 057353264 97356594 4 9189
90736160811763133524 918574 724 0294 914 2219105534 6694
2302866373906308379579526522916582302609976507409187334 0013305234
3101030377785078752063516583462778448353683665590270558349479612983505612394
339024 75739693050522951308110467091324 988204 83153789
4 22613223556634 3098114 1830986684 76810282571550286827483833975719258734
74 01153664 671682629370155268224 4 21277110523909179693192391277379771768801 54
224 68834 962014 00997322757593293917724 0864 634 89

28364 64 4 4 35387618113834 14 3988823534 3530623717836037727092220679014 9131574 94 6123524 864 98036806094 4 84 88571989

384 11919684 71524 83689

960814 72224 18754 31733533374 23694 9008176264 3689

31636788534 54 54 28571396360327750992289

5712580324 14 6305634 287293186997117594 5658363103616835157351924 11529174 58568654 83974 70920699815889

99971336036705125178322165870 4 694 1565206271294 18830367286169732775954 74 89

83270093376170910380551593860779751831 64 79113151091832801275251593651504 88607939884 858609930811934 9380127789

67091084 784 084 7094 3154 89

4 557705504 55036182181154 6026502333598662621190754 57284 33334 0654 65592365267796790097 24 0225590376662770157178 74 530106783684 5974 624 24 1194 14 6092702551816535 74 4 964 080370763592182 04 8070317078004 95030515279198 04 684 14 8029262375914 4 1093882117584 54 2230025871050989

74 34 0538019608096706001729 4 4 6131594 35393190215524 98639177030603251093959660382062356 4 4 4 13794 17884 276524 064 389

9787215289

854 873908254 194 8112684 974 0034 13805877029331600234 97523314 37832506834 6832390294 862961289

17710704 4 9877062308584 5558300725385819369995627 4 94 7316552089

561794 4 62764 77688277511157614 704 990194 82284 32386802734 7074 673862814 7526753337201210107164 6686196160063377135213782113885721215 54 7739721693304 4 0194 7166534 8302682850980553100367604 179853359108399121356009 4 604 2118254 8283826080594 5116333374 59993309854 0090956755312822504 06764 600734 1266354 4 0624 82616605635769125279981301615925 94 26864 86995004 724 77533277064 999384 64 4 4 1139295589

6914 652204 299081224 39062860004 6503573812695217022563921682177336732020915867504 5004 7889

816870364 609615184 6004 85574 14 39881726097384 4 721274 64 4 1954 50198335593231768829557830 64 5802089

82952763154 9073550054 654 1111137194 76304 36261732978590284 6513191614 66655167663506 4 119334 57586671378181098 4 1564 65929623657690836271607223381 4 7885085506388631774 90787234 919198767989

674 636254 54 712604 4 0954 1681977992207104 2764 025154 84 331964 77390558104 961000164 705989

515785294 3991917985197806089

39567864 719736389

0098524 2234 00054 4 2237631164 03151864 27938021795265684 2997814 28838321389

59824 3939588770155799078394 4 89

2067091706552034 96769986054 15590210576514 77157873786751371254 7304 4 660334 994 23963787796271117683623689

624 4 5967764 4 0199697869302789

5704 351674 4 31509802289

8650128774 54 03934 0739724 26716050025587854 988889
4 099384 209100168173874 89
83584 56289
3527517079117054 900054 362196217064 294 04
327806279873786676730222852018370 4 159213524 224 2759628375037299734 95914
31251129239685319012975356116296723084 86174 323176389
29881754 024 70391522806254 684 7910309796282934 304 213394 022884 1293104
7594 04 34 6083566834 32324 9561364 754 257986254 4 554 4 9889
6351671364 4 4 59379357350070277317673 4 884 5174 8870996682508104 389
915567709984 8874 01788299074 94 84 4 23316788301806059737151889
964 2950324 19913988064 778214 0200104 1117774 789
68839555108074 211164 804 22750798779310315115110 84
338317728872525585366801323192752339690786930159258085 24 19159088376804 53626089
750834 21104 4 4 19117285563214 64 61237202911674 0614 6603573964
31901332673511383180868 54 4 27530611568220064 205077627624 316309076339574
68027315291779901 0125354 94 36125914 7198875238666399374
8525397978887930776928132087 4 570272961219939081254 62554 6254 10900834 305204
0387108383857226 4 2176756302904 93017692951152885790854 789
54 134 2729679084 551526624 9771074 34 2215376569954
92169311900356755887971969593608 9
4 4 4 05602798532282974 59230057292902250191869 04 996051519634 66587384
576628616558370926229 54 9052558715098878019153598 54 4 171672135730700635697 4
623664 5069994 38595865304 5816955766814 1518863751672958285519 4 70256814
867521612134 5853932624 252174 4 69525507007692700832805350536951638370 24
826205634 521190864 36094 5508786374 5556884 16514 74 7774 4 660686802732090527 4
5681753951571320375 4 62170698262614 84 759071069250556887184
036300053051386810957538874 806334 6329994 876955374 34 810824 54
131098108373690707510 4 5263814 6157137362035056374 12061154 369839564
3113673185097174 9634 34 058322907235834 0161829060871658710160130 4
2159191713902364 589
705902734 815681072289
867195302579683764 563989
718769225175933155867973 34 077373304 3216755653910755754 2389
16160702122717375920700563071368 4 374 782121352889
89
798668217762832572533 34 518323039274 7618654 039192087965652589
286081930704 03573964 2080989
321089
4 32200851994 1676117175273539788820266187 4 4 5622820220531528314 2784
83033868602799651751797558198833310256254 382304 160189
4 23391703863378357921032077866821806189
0863264 8674 1966200834 5377267213803004 83534 9669601066224 13864
272529253000537291773706116234 8654 387360333573151227139300 4
75257703092179902691056833698681 4 7007004 66807131900900638769068 9
4 20354 1867651074 973393824 7585986386289
1901184 98516056762720635681836 4 12579224 4 98280289

965361861777668677814 1029039884 734 76271790234 86383536719884 181537764
284 35790683635879056700585812134 2784 8601734 299273114 985258294 26381306584
9793217196027188839888813672103025293737306872814 284 2526768184 9503279329574
70704 5375230320864 0889

188204 69202578114 374 706774 2104 39314 64 52786589
6380704 0853074 4 824 07805394 314 79682354 362054 0986524 254 4 613096095689
729925320004 69372276519264 525234 7104 38680616284 4
15026327290612571927257767631 0224 20185623514 89

0590306131224 4 08194 389
634 712598106722230807362 874 0388234 4 64 2804 8391759971189
069304 94 868693118815733589
4 63337313783064 6307582206036072722165120394 08317360771272291089
4 55309972771304 1310614 156773024 8755030303311974
59367823569692069290086840 06551784 35506990979613012085913 2082523653831972164
0025784 3865315526851804 55950652762182978072927001626238075398 5317874 93214
5717674 4 284 224 04 9806304 8733634 55955714 19216555990693160116854 56804 75785694
4 5825814 65254 10569094 21304 1518607874 24 364 05050757001169784 5159928514
36363314 19198562203928363637698073696 24 80231750529550137335889

7960359874 4 4 259036369071724 62752084 0312123803089
2613188023207103014 04 61195590396734 7832214 7276210394 28519154 515034
699239286860608789

4 827204 01315517854 889
24 21185875032601207662275879 8661078061994 316694 6023124 667003664 0694
56988033789

4
19169279093056380077125569611138551110682307186263508781301659159665719956166392
69524 0132819371226867383997102313023718606 4 24 0281675002785237013297
280057314 12337710767305263002918854 32184 95203772625172519665 89

85863027520198580555286556701 124 24 7813984 4 114 794 5614
036133723592910024 0288001695 282527637001726055817 084 4 534 30805114
56901070920068537510 98005622995679393703609 21655852 01268260862013989

6639978182668381 64 268876294 54 98686986956018358721332
6870517519561716 0850360702192659 9072702510994 7572522191084 24 4
55952078308514 34 274 89

7958314 0906113813687321865624 78051997330989
4 011004 7570718189
852293784 4 3814 14 34 54 127508270984 9791964 57929208023550364
3635350960125171771680565 998278836687203057953323354 89

22735814 3909560512229294 254 511059615665989
9801588064 0054 2294 3187694 9270762221110284 7618082615964 4 6602704
309729054 92918095775775902696 7824 34 2719684 2521066737089

5391287929571039131701552 1989
56659379628884 094 286905195234 9190754 939683374 33851086788683112974 84
0774 25614 2888024 20254 564 707508574 033953987674 64 4 7064 724 1224 4 05084 1574
598773169274 2806579384 51080829334 7136974 57317170780121504
65560773087987578705024 4 20182513066251328 57937966934 2674 659176754 4

7321287297992553229395654 1582868358625639296227016169581436104 7964
633701681690383700255736494 4 013958190229025904 302917933014
1319851960060539395930151180348550630214 863817390059278659377962839 74
600501660024 561924 25055935165239389

935785832922591711647601833158673958 9

22691798677199264 26770722804 4 516574 554 5012821713074 850073677934 4 54
7024 8714 88371884 7668824 37818598556832300391829250722212472339543814508124
95920572738582163867174 1214 554 4 4 072000774 62566779999303388581438395224 684
186060994 650551174 94 9312624 74 754 54 114 90089

929888024 4 7511714 394 14 717156204 84 31661614 834 901904
6001190929625568516287760436851209221765372520306632610279260457121123463843089

769100576076038205062694 89

4 5183133681297570084 94 65036278304 4 5034 24 29885580336356198454 4 5054
185239483989

082514 80866797159530872371873295246175261964 989

0592054 6969084 04 52251974 6654 77634 06553670508396129526 94
377982971982255074 008724 67579607375592988511922700401408 9

92230997692507290824 372529302536554 584 9629334 3701951694 4
83160099816953821753975089

3931830881834 90256194 52689

77264 0110604 134 90804 531314 501071393769710546347665429387332788 4
965077889

115704 4 3389

98759686206776694 11702353257219697006335598012767963217354 0570173738734
560027884 615557553918888190157937805544 17315212471104 8525279597666087261 89

7929914 561575520979704 04 8086756054 4 694 28312274 54 0256332191157104 4 554
2963152252304 360826363084 4 22103356833710034 74 82864 619734 3120322024 724 4
39322933802978839273166096657341966481397117329057631860775941914189

82874 783291136684 3302535292524 964 7921101964 64 9065217824 2802165844 4
801194 14 8375608706264 68221705278855586660939730849211724889

8807055295004 13886690763683994 300818877934 80377554 11804 54 695193374
3693074 015004 3869156290274 693614 58814 5704 5663729762794 94 4 06160931199311174
1804 5204 4 928354 5614 69971287682350175144 537389

28383768007204 1680696395364 92505786930809325864
3237958397918508366785268709394 33960987834 8151314 23664 526254 1524
927558779906532561633208127186353644 0504 910181314 864 879728064 836084 96665024
89

207356975362171904 75720554 07926966384 4 354 262130994 3524
3251883097135308234 0787314 154 94 80966574 87919620704 29813217624
3781081796600003627805961686458583311024

Chapter Seventy-six

834 33125102935266385776539714 7351005221181616567263513538 4 1367755589

21388335613754 6166901506117537764 963729764 12757297961854 6006530588154 3374 664 6375024 676618736828601359389

97966104 88703732129989

88077189

3034 558284 24 7986325865083297164 78813687836934 04 31586994 4 1584 05607310517008074 090624 23229834 214 8364 593754 066689

88799024 529677503806308864 24 62354 00067920501694 02576684 2267333776234 7007385086104 194 71106994 35804 534 4 55704 89

168572684 254 64 9000937125624 761059366963889

97312784 658624 4 379914 4 1399515694 6681083926325223181191172864 0074 5587634 104 5628857512550568081525229392792597814 86174 754 52694 7763804 4 769959550506070304 05723074 80234 70574 234 4 6724 10312296534 950506517011654 31324 28521975922325039634 918024 654 31634 661291802225697714 089

0212339328788604 17394 10135263115203691114 53920038754 1090012174 00800370764 068065824 627805087557204 1054 25815704 573154 79309584 72208291904 61794 537539554 705589

5534 904 62381008166373194 55023584 810199222719291201617752024 4 4 6686059009664 014 2655724 7684 36533186703522065580 14 589

1365214 214 884 279565586627059338874 91878639391231094 9856121262994 12921957055098215904 14 591386112526656218794 5691785864 14 084 184 66291812312771701856076 4 2984 14 034 75924 859795364 13929570029539960004 4 76524 174 118063609089

10703299357601235674 50289

4 89

66724 3683113234 827356381 3700784 818092204 54 4 4 878697136394 4 0714 06838108537502379067925 4 9199074 354 5391118754 4 1697879774 4 588070612794 6791026105972678506875 4 968619102664 289

8726604 1554 00035593706209614 687774 802119559012974 4 34 75619036901503229876507 4 4 2116594 074 94 84 64 2116358360774 214 267964 3983102756815554 612105716791531072217779302 54 57322874 537292989

194 954 64 4 4 4 30214 74 34 94 4 33991526199764 6175605004 4 687614 14 4 519713784 8176211789

7724 14 3554 67354 67024 250734 78364 22189

7884 3024 064 89

5284 6314 3881634 35075296533334 782074 39874 4 784 4 24 394 834 37862158000529594 120169584 4 997595662195314 594 63851706574 4 94 064 4 54 137708838532274 753954 622674 72178164 1078597150626394 8291174 3733169123087794 75584 01624 524 34 67316076527923038336108 4 033932278592304 37069614 2336185151202016300371064 733923601594 0934 87614 13931578014 7375520999305714 3969093614 178086869200812729995012689

4 06338154 594 261804 2524 870705529369512012093385006182670089

61125574 02629284 289

397798199536585334 67689

0135251331654 4 784 86211389

75793953376384 7704 3789

600054 374 63152679226126554 0350013294 4 79593320389

9504 4 03691234 10089
5651264 1833327189
6351165130651176712022579372906101484 23524 674 37854 74 04
69612582211063998326045158125475467792932216010039689
1835166867336830393136298532998872877313365140099200771811594 958529964
781866067889
5687304 12979681933386864 03654 299825024 89
7608389
87278799683224 7994 861290621538119527811750653500768127034 63806998532134
523960704 0850382203113837312467354 40854 00354 980559889
76284 821825502984 1751924 2138199529518355344 03125784 310766698198236289
04 98595699397614 72019504 074 1534 182884 97163679555729981157 69289
90294 53651754 4 1526532860972531124 70609774 310064 281021572319914 3928724
718284 09399674 13832697591370192060393452424 4 628182094 16205366883589
174 586151994 610289
297586116332625393634 8579165089
54 974 75561088704 3082657833533954 8720604 3619313816874 21184 17529818004
5024 624 013213889
2154 1354 0631633023821615654 64 533991219188665880282830367309947 1289
78081654 87889
720625876819014 74 865764 3264 74 554 35864 796605054 4 19314
00783305815766575393391766014 9690172511013519303276412543790817246689
999810787074 3298828606321054 28729230684 6189
654 2162578575560161255234 03005801973294 312555344 214 8865206998097004
3014 29834 5079053809234 4 5824 36794 3874 9162814 834 015294 287829919084
6211322390876235024 63789
187701226754 7630879194 5324 14 9114 10912534 87734 704
529022285676973757021670272351520368322814 4 986530301933624 735824 64
0022653017817862306131826734 7574 556271918313859370386942322406078 34
1585617375014 8103203795100191326222685916207583999928414 258360755 02370367514
3734 7250061084 565212317820690269323271707170180717500766710702438300882134
9562114 2096666279257629475353656122311963034 872979923961295610014 4 117684
309914 4 359806556684 7331837711114 89
825166860528824 31582966815773674 29301750530961966351587675538 64 128836864
64 016803290102098364 14 5390136182012310600000775796607677144 532374 4 9036664
5381903303565964 053774 84 8637705689
195214 36067964 32870265114 1982058714 099621884 954 12759055289
6627174 371637870154 63118234 995808051672638789
8690116970574 33252523306688114 1023090637160965393382917 54 24 74
057228131824 852865622014 084 294 83589
03054 33176866938862725299013 74 301298828533204 14 925964 724 87084
288708681215621556590555201187669920995 34 92885869512934 92562058852997594 59814
7350552550331514 5734 9813024 9635666005715621294 128820162299984 814 529158027274
5294 3367134 6133989
54 99251972614 2954 67134 1106550874 8687356789

9050526184 1864 94 67003626154 5565178590074 74 34
68302203353062126331982820 54 8103883294 3772784 80154 3529854 234 0690991512207114
08191653284 2162868282636635610834 32356662184 5834 96584 24 35114 082527134 184 4
6704 38854 60564 089
1533111831123911860539878116762767613703 6584 284 8180731392005624 904
71623282329910806606066 4 706264 0354 285919007969734 73018870585654 299212914
1065083105024 921181152561006374 22924 3293904 7324 28585904
36910997808736870161271565760862527256304 13794 618685327159089
4 84 682802764 3878196883034 6901398630993534 89
04 39939614 131385964 62884 3854 4 854 5178614 6989
4 8363593025023338886138660578825 34 938204 29754 20534 8196605394 37264 34
77979135529870904 4 097516714 25654 91734 186574 028331056378689
9303765618156623518204 7554 994 194 34 97152154 89
1214 252064 70792904 37621284 54 03635654 004 264 4 38858799154 4 6526504 5884 4
150220834 8189
98082523762637834 9391929908774 186331195023335535079509550198504 4 294 64
600379207703264 7231653837167797632255104 6150834 4 705727864 984 3104
06919552119029089
81909550664 3754 003665989
157129669037382605868862 2094 31585676214 1694 62770034 4 614 655883709614 54
183836781653264 6717988704 751624 200276984 10568104 9934 7974 174 74 275556623834 4
821872394 925598724 80817902886979178082113078266738822717569953681581006834 94 4
177014 11035314 1107098279679604 574 2155734 6773729313183574
2900988172510707001027056816105909256197738725262954 967064 3826974
8763152709963323315389
780214 19584 628370235855228029775802 14 061912503939000954 9720689
6922935154 870995796216818651729 4 14 3002365100714 102755589
4 3126234 9994 5262174 251834 07314 9518226654 136707112054 359504 77052984
055164 14 4 08231604 0094 14 859322767183356104 1031952334 84 84 607952364
66106998696317658850281933170909277 54
380975029691292829028718271868676560656010388362597 4 7689
93319181508684 6351020204 4 4 31914 1590772364 6830255391680889
13774 267233213994 712884 97759795397734 792296789
362193099251120066301156617390657573683767636593718 9
2114 223684 99120214 755719722305574 10057254 525724 53855565056864
6053711226822679501929631039 4 584 4 174 55806521223889
34 67377781174 8771108535856365104 804 00702351384 14 08394 34 4 914
958733631703374 524 74 4 2076903104 6589
4 02807065204 04 90102610180630714 4 095089
01183652829100104 26311261217230160730391 4 278299826054 8259374 871970789
4 559086334 21705653769115599133716964 15252912586550719274 834
59371130756268223314 4 19307505994 00673536365037293550076798 04 2151214
351972532560562264 394 54 14 1131674 7298778368714 09967589
656307019969560824 628014 504 91199124 071218574 805370693964 0389
21234 64 697871225506696069651615068130060629 4 1074 00804
707570130916173507733 4 75564 877254 73691225215098135033192993383 34 38210788554

38332361873569071608054 5580984 36700574 3508507531994 09765965336872104 34
93322280618834 992004 827873811252750304 9208888174 84 64 283190165396006304
6650291562089
　　　0532294 73199966789
　　　104 29991774 534 1287689
　　　1030909976718814 80309327162698123657206 04 3315964 964 934 20535930974 99554
63534 159984 382386204 94 250693932014 26663783689
　　　4 812021997614 179860830589
　　　8382939006739514 551757354 999717075389
　　　24 80315294 1090118514 92614 087594 4 73721159393289
　　　26370506958329918100862084 04 102864 89
　　　9234 6326034 564 23704 24 824 25706390912938080170 4 659653630724 14 4
9281837553304 794 862335063366363758865610589
　　　06603353162911176597900236530121728575366 20189
　　　010164 9815977724 729054 022670786268338777301117009 4 318514 0357762194 54
816762064 37531968784 14 85184 2589
　　　34 4 814 0529583996384 9702539597621263597859 4 566911063706013322795334
191053037954 04 25978304 13766751674 97687874 6529964 917834 23364 2700074 54 754
8194 94 7135986680691566664 58532914 9030823205989
　　　0281205878126815767 4 3093072101761358226318 9
　　　99288797323093201014 9232126373267151796 4 9554 89
　　　689
　　　24 77661184 3154 5671617574 939384 0161652290784 4 089
　　　4 23150876687054 6652757932388055 4 91266616937775989
　　　539255610804 06938118224 80005135080937204 668602003905500914 1165394 4
8199594 173218719034 097188255907262958 4 28371977008581794 1850701023924 759988289
　　　6135737787564 358854 9634 256114 678078334
0518710951312575999931805190921902266565695039282619 4 790160170231224 3305754 4
31260654 4 64 62500868662274 804 386674 4 194 4 2015394 260381155782754 00004 04
02071218190131574 64 010934 2733574 83361014 694 036854 512564 4 32034 7075284 4 8389
　　　31754 561764 6315722092878102799120290218 9
　　　22382824 7035054 63383094 194 4 77974 69130882924 57205029220624
985552355105654 164 304 576298864 17680620174 1134 8089
　　　234 22728834 74 54 3201198072660689
　　　5692588229327024 54 4 77534 721765528390806174 300254 28281598287674
713598313924 867754 53184 684 4 6083804 815081566354 194 62565813296359550594
82907633010681564 4 9665178803283777234 4 264 95734 76209397575955793063867100 4
7774 3934 0064 9834 0550723621811989
　　　4 84 4 82127172777851389
　　　95684 904 4 7627008613126978157757229 54 64 760335927355634
30185152565958292013820915022620088003174 97285389
　　　98215039065355933128282835302291 04 24 84 9910104 0960080812922737134 515814
58295962514 38171754 6634 16763065800124 676193027393974 9682827160964 94
37231135575629078101961 24 24 0298111767982618671 4 04 83954 66852385580727594
0560932973124 0555537304 4 7992932564 932798114 83183320213731115623 24 04 09254 4 4
19362171293573215519555826930703620869391030956262579288 4 94 4

65718175291633610508 4 013855636792071157188857988513 4 9629804 2756138550082816695303908698 9

6208029030355380062556321 4 0366817790818021164 84 387794 8278512937817115195312920602534 993978761754 64 080018854 911265094 7737794 033808138516582177365 4 74 21223193282082698080 4 014 90534 8395503964 389

278202924 723734 82716964 374 6781354 156230792934 930724 03367516992521889 224 05669614 6996814 73878851860314 289

76353797624 324 2698191015966561818629392204 8809589

1535233677225687364 384 6681697674 1773574 4 924 0277324 4 2718521724 5824 903794 4 4 02883067384 4 564 001853656074 654 17560537108254 681792569364 6964 4 18020722076795015297 4 67508384 135231135616254 995291763514 1688384 5818879384 27692077003633081667 4 4 134 057171504 30764 4 5505570862019621875090213884 932155884 9314 6361185166819219333310687104 157219222584 5136232219900267083802223 4 873215757971191139682680384 884 04 02814 59269592328395964 188662679614 930515982037118628310 94 50197691335579388158 9

5114 153272504 224 953588864 505295251885697664 767754 064 1989

64 61256327822597017023337558520886222182600285359281 4 4 63086109070674 17161261230022530622 94 326 94 39780326835730088162 4 868 4 4 963806183381290631720666982539273397 4 004 94 7585695873513934 54 76951134 818732264 1752631190577688592198023732093522988172 4 959823218020514 164 654 233174 602677104 7957385695174 6726028070968152504 3733589

8205504 74 0080301330175581522716953096751972016120092056623087754 287106964 58634 71374 2806675167831937351325652214 83833173672308119816534 2239802624 74 3765589

4 76756921634 368776691564 94 79989

4 4 9089

533354 82608637982325394 916672689

94 1674 99834 7704 6990214 64 089

968375824 95058290814 53314 22006226370265889

08567589

263050621772504 590274 99099932791976237866665291918639558768793566387776 4 74 276695160789

6083931623525292783250364 15584 678024 618159880514 2926914 4 06989

6524 7194 8193396323136854 634 18650909284 1382717252169538362006323009210996206 24 94 250608111814 867512981608654 863784 9168389

14 2024 4 074 61253734 99118074 4 4 4 68004 5657807234 762101130684 4 60779794 2213204 4 175184 8161601019084 311857783736923028533939927561111606255009383801593115111359078521625604 85386914 32381224 5904 29977294 6964 322273715189

52580297336604 535600707534 3804 126696705867914 36932809218304 1139251793786077259 04 3301053693860564 5312282575394 317372233585221168154 304 4 363584 974 2772083634 2287796178301536250280185857 84 84 4 259719867132834 24 85127694 8108214 8289

89

9874 54 317220977924 036083261987325361585956014 19384 1365176258823231664 97136618714 9882091304 281551016224 3911604 524 963384 25654 07862054 039684 75984 13729509315814 877737124 01871797783804 789

89

94 94 3654 2977673257015705381263785222274 69724 67874 24 130079364 23284 978184 78384 18709500092027232765464 98176971856311594 6830120997154 727353173557025264 0974 294 86253814 814 0078594 20937562638394 68673716324 4 65006694 756705315994 726878112561704 60064 074 4 4 558074 2901999701262105369 4 4 280714 0922166151821307934 86989

728370011952930810736667285 4 8798578714 82235316879674 7873575266193854 23624 000713911305675550338852901 4 23771854 164 89

2294 1556716384 588614 111063333831204 110852764 58284 026102555584 54 7225937596187234 6364 30993963801234 4 4 89

255652989

827202990036784 3915104 186874 95824 4 2954 6262126155525198674 5094 4 4 65290221964 96329554 000070385210563219676582 4 84 22650733125362054 6260268684 5226609688804 383804 74 37262323316166601591279368819959 4 05025719999329176733931027100125953609 4 694 379663859680832664 3193164 96584 963397729194 4 14 51837316675736885364 5182023023814 82637706530113911289

1369134 624 91327912603253534 59199163234 52775814 24 7666027954 7954 0704 33050957305857105121982912094 4 316533594 324 084 68138074 88753872970853754 4 1682806609884 935066699637289

794 4 31656792687636706605922664 9550352104 30834 35714 033518387756174 209630866622504 81525113784 8588257002504 051583861836164 50763591975664 564 71215061989

85206274 6107207788534 090089

74 133378884 529056064 324 6783723784 4 23811624 53960789

73114 333370609605259730199650937 4 3954 5624 6686628124 3275277881785764 5097868654 91389

2339614 539387201609954 7277316887599733216771184 4 199589

4 84 8614 2610389

15187575363531390084 4 72167159313610565905523068822701639006 04 64 654 2371934 04 309850825077350154 851993174 71835737304 4 9150694 975724 80079084 26935982914 3830931389

8554 8754 94 232274 4 94 9162792191174 4 16817622585153292309062702886262732717271373674 728853638621232215215659814 014 34 6174 4 20864 1223824 870184 217621137984 8001289

184 6115029134 07235104 0099682816355155884 9625934 702284 24 5296564 4 6314 581220877964 14 813974 05213189

8287854 284 2696578224 34 89

21862124 534 0214 2291873824 8798312836552083888110223504 58713289

65119752972393956001 14 252964 0219606769679575814 793597999314 184 981204 111154 2822165132392559070987 4 8163233710191611397919813 11334 3628756085191368235626377581119520159283010980 24 5617011022257367211180753783939970561978 34 78589

98010395864 273294 684 3133101094 687964 634 297877722682194 4 4 805699924
5536854 6016753353994 0861811762259294 27764 71534 124 00002769010274 1176192399224
87172129321988282213214 5815583330810327676656821576223286102357888664
95575706551976714 2309504 205762010616009270364 200234 04 50972083564 857718166824
151192694 4 850681518629351905611712803659267821369850750 8774 982207319334
8619790072589

77582664 14 2806319759559863 14 5370970654 77664 76800725878500630994 0108789
4 554 7097206380389

4 83693036970026974 5829254 1889

3568276976759232867767101698035097327693602728831210398704 04
7295073357317572232713912886823089

69775881257914 54 937934 29853594 4 73006165593150559024 5069290180294
93965319372764 130759794 3503018619518284 94 00682794 55659277338106214 90164 4
98834 284 75015304 08357214 3224 589

2652000275214 84 68861352026832020123565 04 519019118723235591670372329790 34
59787550694 692772157114 71823799668074 639072294 51229908534 65326174
67973382168394 09164 61117621210756 8264 73382614 614 8780221208854 61094 160724
95014 6164 7180175574 523157572564 916552016964 62797061834 73704 61961194
70719316611275377707 51989

4 4 64 8689

161124 64 06779934 06222196506865913705310362339187 5928196574
16107839829879513864 77074 064 514 224 4 930292524 0762368664 33594
986611393309682004 3150156117174 4 0284 570589

2934 2504 889

97230280359024 388557971513154 5883284 61904 66314 888130054 4
6165010619163392539632 4 9956689

18855812076832961375023 1954 02633096304 694 05124 798684 9565872764
52876970991565736177 4 733919053124 8684 4 94
6258722691209550207072170716218796791877607055804 81015192295074
3263378200279183115536 8264 376788757991198116796887396317781 4 529954 4
25665773092756714 329124 84 70230227864 75224 53354 02514 079094 918254 62535291014
39352289

6664 824 2984 559934 2557559177758575824 23523389

7374 74 84 4 6334 004 725931357292624 4 83984 8777017654 81318806697061502 2889
30961065688203005792824 77684 56505759164 0181294 5586968803264
58117051128812605060822201 10294 813788676234 7888324 82528250394 668865604 7914 724
34 9593624 08575339314 94 1285595065802576280 0089

063568814 9232095192164 0031880972999 1980254 670328632185674 4 87704 7667974
0080524 4 4 94 123019257706168607933337726166795237231022560304 560734 94
57206356031317070375962721 4 64 90194 25087954 2596683656734 96784 77964
0178627750094 17083925965179211371888502960580859287154 6564 185389

1151124 4 82809575136933274 382978784 025912924 2527015238018394 2827764
2307786599800714 99001127186267256977974 935585858827620784 4 192101150122755574
17797638627058527065 4 59889

378332964 9518770115264 4 14 2164 4 87520863294 24 10854 1931861114
0968276285129014 3784 80234 39124 804 724 66682815277274 31154 89

64 6255670802912294 104 7036654 4 12796194 58724 516005911000089

59934 764 82685734 6824 604 969511368019113114 32130230724 6634 163734
25090192136190587934 86103011684 91367031251593211122314 3289

1632315514 86390389

204 907304 67537906033384 814 62237904 76336372022317683354 114 32973333114
189

394 24 73793198755133365951923692605564 18153629274 571724 9538204 4 574 74
70974 3381119982520693905592573907077774 36069154 4 834 954 64 54 394 5550651751304
65938835163084 824 74 634 1099051994 96236797103589

927135620109785056162.4 99523189

0502155814 684 4 67724 6361554 69783168324 8275696313571755814 70789
70917287783371804 851989

54 5984 38285966997768692505944 38280995311638094 4 381799776035011308707394
4 851928516254 90589

0311087233296314 8825592074 274 014 34 4 0238814 71254 55959070011936654
70967389

12587270273568527307775193968862038764 3053734 19963678594 085215789
7724 4 35609555383209737122234 993636234 092989

901253196033994 7214 2957874 7514 768554 3217321671274
62276803323300056382327072275.4 5294 94 2172575194 1251053916721864 3358594 4 534
9268769220823873314 30039261354 66300572963673315564 9097959804 89

924 726693864 564 374 620224 96833800005055789

826856676967114 2801876726217786557664 91577003524 61100932794
68256367716153962.4 3792771294 83813797234 4 72909685220531233182015789

584 4 79574 84 04 96654 2625020395674 682354 733532589

6674 64 8211886220773024 4 164 13964 00574 39589

934 4 5124 0708100231076667283.4 29860057554 936374 74 9864 9085556304 8804
5734 98089

74 5784 92631977514 4 73595857773563077254 67852982333254 68702009571974 89
619002324 974 4 6877253504 533172730924 230889

05788306207272855.4 985674 67904 84 8611804 9266536573811300318254
7299877874 2263224 5052354 17218301325634 17954 3964 983867938294 564
11967522772180797079505564 4 4 5083804 35789

2004 4 1015991008710562086.54 57535861988133754 4 255212730289

4 24 16530758030330807963603979606664 24 281579324 4 860528724 956074 874
09036181364 0624 302017652262395586836.8289

2096274 924 60911889

4 2919022126987681974 61064 34 4 7889

94 63354 904 9367584 304 8514 34 998064 60954 4 9673288773001522154 4
0295681234 534 4 89

4 693259234 97985578607921934 7904 24 873864 4 206792284 192513273004
96390538838157937.4 791162995933734 7104 4 2586573721918359134 231189

24 681215100564 17553783567312752772033.94 2084 577330932293933774 14 74
6291204 14 3364 237584 53227800104 181991754 84 164 69079889

66638034 90314 04 20857975127670234 36973090178204
12023120163323770681609809619376238353166.4 2814 678085660722089

4 937814 058508265825612064 1566908039133014 503787374 70086191634 2078689
6584 1313273363314 3633823725986924 785670108198872061 4 94 3101160093264
3020534 5194 3668673098889

3658736185274 628304 684 865086589

3166284 4 174 28158134 3991205834 3184 793314 3825136125768653093775 74
77371966080824 13879789

09568631924 278782136534 14 5351715120124 1563214 5577261257171154
2375752304 35611185589

1966314 4 4 230869366705 11991381534 03226210621594 3974 271207654
652317651989

664 24 4 7526204 71519096989

174 4 551184 374 33125604 112060004 81062834 1774 4 95189

99061022134 1264 4 534 006534 85761580063364 04 6688273922022619214 4
757111594 14 54 757056524 3538867082174 995562889

089

0167708239731020519 4 8388718354 9834
328808886071103617690332310781379630557 27389

81129127703868279932165904 05314 689

632598639194 291520764 4 1218374 053356689

581994 26520915206072234 787011150784 94 599263794 25827381004 56093734
037384 70052604 324 004 765151033974 4 26291589

78594 21619027654 6124 371007314 1533133956067012099235705589

35555864 373324
66239368273381376660988561386081756085525751881822982365620593039 84 802684 689

2564 8315727203819634 275024 4 9053813871227283653813817 4 1189

03818629370668796552 74 018351601106777215 4 4 274 8763186693851665268 9

1909669324 124 14 5765251754 771386167907074 68769050286308364 14 93189

6559562354 278624 5515875993374 04 8688880593635094 764 04 64 04 226690237394
34 693813198094 55398305963795278500 4 02818801715189

687315831068254 14 7354 7504 83209376687988786820162 4 9772079654
6229659986970928634 4 4 27118784 04 32634 84 65824 16724 4 160379004
86290633522739626326 4 3689

6952186374 58554 7737927708108320998006560378 54 9786179281682380184 4
3737773965967582913220601255392869706131183075 74 97364 9821014
731399951378011958363 04 65784 5862188194 4 14 9784 93700984 02756006854
98026335735027690350133 4 9159994 10634 06154 7078733290603707231161 24 034
18705507883790008 9

817694 7025974 0812636634 0233205234 7594 94 62864 7720279625211368 64 4 837784
2127754 7089

06075102553014 54 64 807254 59627611374 31679308322714 4 4 4
9518251553202530688 9

9305853194 831806190976281801667723036121660678 13695171764 875979064
17672078274 9004 4 74 5667114 3903026184 81170988221888 9

1664 963938685131934 691125989

4 98624 7734 19222103929318565373 4 62824 4 7189

89

578758679611281511099659370100378346036699083660549953931420999423492601951720056003498594040963539910547277394697990413578702263206920254549841657267742794639612974391368521794850340618077285098742812276901141368164028467528875427664834717285451238985915716062110621038611504145324978791301213806889378088785741135694023601086117274749076863458679625973610019911702986963967536056330358598505902404485705231443082279855858042106676069784668585613992053252487035554585370101077350088649519635411914539954755706552627758435765745846125841563107474953677019045088460451789610356300964498325679803052637110090348336832738009258557839639769788757455040977616660990279542918858930891795098681231156305389211681423379581310829419130185387664983843266604890968801860786989969463951952355412235444495109149042793265931689165384524647612102977323804949102697206319731444576872230188864547231035203360880327345189251460428378272357373813799044513964614587724157800991829452769114892564495544578208112585497462991227232646490397507964230600261945260981238603894172852569764474274292893781644102259782780808093811884898286656450750469903550368236404570287861926400784608310625668967210515107875998062605331021001223580899087864525527739274544838949424609773097681032881810483775584905357543698547824872097962396028564633703672244472560265313928132432260277494460178011800643538046561772418288441537932797330316564262549644575247852251514033329218029943636689200450280879301458362655927453036932085819923685824058244928679704700489293410367432496807871678052871557152697953873176161393561325930030985187458526074604280714530295334442483635278630915145811167703384349810903471380868798951289092704710360333677107781408348446246860614725498836547671435078971650144527699386002279228873124616118886865145487571245875831948668196071351297809734289009348299609161372171840805688912848320307378043990298011977674459526087245017878848275822031416079664684533840137300363393522391326174642283971469201272934108032240148629789

074 135636204 35519583015124 060878235799054 5993705598339963964 27254 28884 4 4 321935083739604 4 4 1268034 98854 98678014 24 12013984 7994 694 74 26725134 57504 3284 16115283189

34 3362578255557624 8604 4 6989

208108295158121308074 724 84 88317379714 4 06575523709296204 687229229750573904 3255293584 8119802663290934 03989

4 9735809290273565026520968682827876692654 1661877936514 64 9996335189

18591982811237177058085129 0889

14 7989

50229698022775369781832 64 36580306594 6080924 008017689

07232584 14 4 1297192824 24 72038004 865907624 832984 3266612530268510334 99026576578579963305728578158 04 4 81506534 14 7291034 011865107527575914 6213859575557984 6533174 6524 2124 79703562965764 84 971699687784 5984 14 3281364 1506265880323735372672051002039187208654 889

4 04 91633392384 4 80571756388725093012313 7906973034 4 64 0283694 89

14 5321874 79689

03689

08009191076964 8752267931968839730831 3632855164 4 284 854 54 389

551192351626705524 16610116191939562321215 4 04 4 74 5884 4 931776033264 5864 8332699995327613115608198673031 7987770968854 73206973611106968735230086661325732823554 5132889

27073584 038158089

5934 0954 004 776686337388220989

994 77588872525139289

4 7102576115811305813730792569 5089

111060363374 714 3004 818074 54 4 7071235856967018761630 4 4 024 8592810294 124 4 81653304 300197678125184 887324 2914 654 65374 7653084 078562990904 5373784 76391634 10697134 94 83164 14 94 317725925735989

8774 14 104 25852565064 6992257533386670229 37999299024 83384 4 97963616582601770376024 04 2854 352514 689

29382667737884 0100504 077814 9801065156552974 765023025304 8184 8290223516634 907089

4 4 98768111961215106508070884 5289

4 029830319134 3694 788607197230910879065 4 54 5592904 4 269621024

Chapter Seventy-seven

1265089

620800237754 863792190058221375 4 17994 513677375502934 4 21394 7834 384 54 08824 968300559698072274 2714 75234 6186384 4 9633003720110584 884 4 4 26282284 71835669510578364 1807090871181197634 134 6792304 82799919294 2334 4 4 34 3374 5265711851958275817 24 2955697536554 76535585715371587886731558 2373179120358194 336859024 611689

54 93584 54 84 381021820980564 56671152278111152866314 879791224 104 6715034 54 1226359174 0231050726757815651690794 975354 56954 6610234 3506351789

262820073876715784 184 4 8532331264 74 816964 104 5009329526393910725514
02638097234 5074 214 526634 679124 8799219504 24 9506398350575631670024 22209788884
5014 2354 933264 4 770854 207329564 20064 799904 56728288273089
73634 24 016355981512716558570876026331934 7603574 7971136732284 4 254 4 954
614 124 10314 4 112136532959073184 4 66267811106274 019900800574
08513360217113291910194 81723858110359763233621594 4 590686068858174
58272106636078324 721105539882285311162308307724 9320718760314 283554
972399990954 38674 7911904 12064 09581635030692153653952559398291083644 4 4 057789
4 7686559064 26959078555889
278014 811531296052829739637830522396568797932914
15829562315501056197500574 7882584 35068389
4 802720131680054 4 924 176554 134 15536722967818672262975219357296762159744
572929982784 5769995818570124 704 10652755234 7093167602108874 620189
4 9830990562680354 7323919174 3880352852394 5196855902262991234
0556236681684 202614 06594 6016614 2689
816364 89
632267056714 54 52761552084 03199775521811222283069 64 0282754
58309078800952553382670001174 8089
4 4 0085824 4 2234 4 84 09014 4 393099507604 5874 992960929194 4 86787284 24 4
655294 26035504 015366304 8572784 57506789
0334 2063754 85651802605864 654 53504 923154 6366067214 955979231996128389
2566068624 5382196621379095614 18094 81962680234 8373704 864 4 539098579604
117131070124 3314 722770694 381624 26160779174 73589
30604 0322161173190236290108124 14 634 68239091014 74 784 534 81264
736939378034 508669020117854 092269189
0721139084 2736264 0084 0225609527953662226878036310374 99295189
6334 93724 780784 24 620773854 564 62974 6985678187794 64 133277559594
9591985874 1916684 4 78301866887582598506335809530304 73059262795878826628135669574
18566351836629677963353661625690006588344 5284 789
3261230794 253332120934 313098617001394 0224 51593986301533002758857444 4
8261555201163216558305044 01109024 79913174 4 3186094 78889
4 4 24 7191765658573938336152938944
164 63157877752069260989
92237784 2721076226754 713629677265283382604 5803154 88184 291834
5790562055852313844 674 868809874 7574 18299514 36089
52757114 89
696984 6591330551571824 9017264 0634 694 738316224 84 5702956882134
7832186005021975794 932795753714 0194 6919871033919215034 601174 89
54 935005764 831184 800383210704 55100031972994 6062669081703284 65232638024
224 858174 0354 2298510813693111624 820378156824 0267054 0265060927629574 1300394
590674 4 527919799664 72993327500323878534 4 5521820309695277254 1183313194 9298374
54 299674 34 50834 94 56920794 55833089
572194 166974 2554 4 682533864 6561066514 16194 74 02732330689
180554 88714 4 2397014 824 8814 13024 333221160282289
28803159132754 604 0639314 4 756504 51024

Chapter Seventy-eight

70784 782700310083062398337903505920853878236 74 384 874 6907159107166138352709755851584 34 9132103501222558659285 74 296051076914 689 25290223593827912711007177987873789

7902060104 0537927126554 2602785723538506654 4 4 6667038666314 508709916557153712069207 84 4 2628725803234 558565314 37854 3259039018168386005327 54 9657925726069037995759888134 73068888074 74 4 754 711193224 014 85057132580064 52814 851064 94 5062178797173665367 58124 1855617818186509256591 5089

6785883853734 600693514 976694 0200854 14 24 1195861577381990261801995755581062254 836164 04 10620763090175856074 573884 73264 50713338575654 604 17325337113028013789

4 07938579364 339953362780923121083970023302 8364 694 23386202991033137697 4 50725192819304 4 8106053614 889

8127237275534 5364 51517984 3869973757297234 4 7961754 12263854 32501523178083972557268785022568712168135 34 253902834 78101919154 2034 324 25934 60913311364 251073193994 3370384 3238861375880568271561 64 854 9365380237850903934 8336224 82273182074 099684 5329664 2006626803726878202 64 86705782985119284 503022158150530356 4 175689

37754 21063138794 30081690861925874 28698754 675509234 94 4 73961567075925019168369112930377 4 804 9551990970398233638263 64 89

1350584 3039964 81957236211574 0772576823369907023 74 4 639354 2927020534 604 4 80383102314 4 4 8114 5913795384 74 9239157294 3127807 4 1204 4 0608030975872966973107181984 4 10669334 082604 96984 15157716592955194 86558164 86757794 23393689

88277590035789

4 212761604 704 734 2116721879204 887694 233196384 054 4 994 75111593254 796176239384 9853824 01964 77081852094 864 855924 22877324 96687300301024

Chapter Seventy-nine

626104 4 66769085254 5609760525276754 2609722175804 23153215767353290753 4 815364 11137564 0334 4 93764 4 77315701074 4 17762358231865170035 4 720537594 04 317824 599133598339181781909632989

815139125754 3191389

8337254 4 05281508154 5703102289

68029957722750833121165977 04 2219982689

658324 694 1224 511283294 989

8729700252886927820088561271599 4 9775135621524 14 4 6212011857260152524 697229091514 04 64 0753192199281734 28032761859964 5702580211560174 6209063589

07518617575300004 24 919672009214 856764 01596976159704 0573694 25903568270576217269808261258 4 58059616706188663328 4 026338564 82864 261038593074 900732614 64 76834 5904 15787979304 99820505904 3213002388639330297873873619627553321859580126622163258 4 664 07754 64 76579363380854 4 964 957096554 9194 681612051155694 391080796813539384

60597500671795063102561224 79527199604 65708625384 3127219194 5200310509319123694
7954 585612237929584 674 4 83220803838519266315323828 4 507062223554 1635575201604
84 58595787727964 35664 079289

7731517789

254 324 6016374 1951653324 854 86621259981179724 63576280561784
91675839232577223668 4 392313904 6362506364 023028317230013785538397 84 4
059603568332684 279926654 616067211095960638834 24 29504 300233636510873394 5914 24
660824 687867914 224 10972599551213534 39193233952088570015903804 4 69826631106954
58536384 64 29954 74 06804 06796096334 0089

65964 76123350118154 718221565202593800562590621502729012224 2604 04 14
7261584 034 2781626054 59873385724 563714 777921604 74 8274 4 334 4
1112967312376761198629786698630802 4 1795004 73099054
86807868392900997525783605684 23252734 5124 93884 64 64 261174 3784 59017654 4 6954
09651594 70872997650711276266611757869601903289

74 286263834 8064 60258351836519591 4 728710254 1609034 17107626677581504
651694 6254 4 9579938289

96178666609857273572606855066958690375723054 9955720906262171394
70396850395236312 94 4 870874 1524 764 225060652166970795528304 12810868604
97392295365924 3154 17259939327074 8607956674 14 593870684 123275004 16690860257614
87588798762359367 34 754 629304 596834 705781824 3392374 7399924
99318213776303837529903851510 4 9213862685594 86228289

8029098604 0984 01166507322289

9953224 0562234 84 7784 26908827773333002520957071638789
1375728361113161508282 4 0586774 80612837809976588122 4 500975070984 7914
3992524 014 16224 0532859851784 06026775338192282678 4 95278866724 5689

3337594 5160731956862168560635120350 24 6309928374 18507807604 204 77384
3053254 8387635924 125575316364 5229316351178652228232 89

64 4 4 83191026924 74 163633999280535309366592617986 4 4 24 954 94 884 6174
813289

956813731394 8309594 99581124 735554 8837387112521903370051 54 6804
0236778326154 4 24 06566906224 04 363579199589

191618731985304 8280061974 2223209883669364 7084 018123214 174 762767322394
73306004 0517262859354 854 118824 6139912254 5993604 6289

69714 134 1652030935025735593612611 4 513964 764 664 9021062754 4 57374 97714 4
71550805888268660313596615759788880825134 084 175124 084 2314
218875957026396166667684 217885015116650295955978618 4 1596054 7920178554 81164 654
1858311314 12091278284 596904 4 4 80818199806314 389

0380522074 97099964 4 5926804 2684 734 4 54 1557810334 4
932059501563201963053976214 180739908627084 8064 30321780024 7609014 39771564
2312007226354 34 932737991573155185911006524 72774 851997101984 77976655689

4 4 91967164 86168670790375717066 4 835628080325964 8676734 04 584
2056865018193702 4 269525364 816955814 59090936590780768681 24 38639934 25655353304
6505678506554 86555712821183817396599836335767803088710 4 057297206384 8194 704
8233307935220906084 3986280183867089

529794 94 55903398039750568234 4 9353678374 4 4 14 69885388804
52810081360625583295193112119 34 751776284

5206651922225273866969263002566560571379874 6774 722632191103954 4 639384 612184 558577569269211274 4 6965654 0715714 14 1819794 9229614 4 64 039021523936521713197016823791016253905630796286769037036699987201010551972758 83 904 90266619397164 834 8114 974 23911738704 22714 29504 98039184 4 09203535350564 64 8264 70908831627172704 3914 1214 2384 2292160092712912360067010295 24 904 826889
52858136084 94 320353804 1356964 515930924 338277301069829074 003637819107214 2201091906924 1872160277555804 593264 90152150594 14 23353135286277882691268505700877094 4 1767082111178033916132310778 84 54 769589
2356286062676906368 1154 8086194 4 886505985634 9824 20785224 82102735571711682860 4 374 2793001905324 214 7326980760359336634 855924 68191202394 714 80921233284 1860500625853791085553950069351 4 3257214 1821734 24 169658289
1687104 77383110597050998134 94 0969399553351724 534 64 54 72530194 52500219704 23672563394 1992595913903004 37260389
7653397233310189
2731998036678696654 613980753800150074 994 0589
6396569604 4 4 4 634 104 8889
101877254 017581364 8299270189
89
31874 3514 7571951190164 32624 56514 2006231074 7654 52195530622094 0907622656396770318223285959360902816252306279768529106713880771274 64 190257056024 4 61237830789
0264 854 860064 90087858777224 582811024

Chapter Eighty

34 4 938706614 774 4 53567937320714 5334 0808324 96103686003164 8711604 55763852964 00092889
9056590388078720153816868605784 53602623953761584 3658764 1315689
54 20184 5166804 25311250906128057586051851261261263727019604 2362190166991290755289
14 84 255000203166394 336803204 057114 11604 237579803585659563124 74 994 6956984 95135867617171614 86134 2118764 921998574 023604 5258155314 00876092991964 74 4 62881338290732168822691315735551 4 90184 2172781677852130383660376356129007685 4 4 53156388109058718069 4 081778190789
574 514 3359593839035139959232215815 4 7874 78672620334 2273037795254 810134 334 8870112698825270694 5729704 4 29254 73858639589
4 03162524 181768010338837389
2597828563795133 4 907225664 398213604 08060769512299054 794 220774 55869779933034 4 4 3904 4 19997357607975028020352529286365622716637530104 34 8154 14 54 3327065339165099594 6735871134 933382166989
4 85670557380782200217312093915300782652612868 4 514 24 29072659990570958254 8604 30354 5232999965155578 14 617689
52857780536654 89
4 85926317291170626203829798016084 121593188188696290282871579787179368 84 904 025766919694 789

119701664 230794 4 71163004 79691660296336654 11656714 129266583864 16765584 25834 66265066904 169951079819904 156389

709616578360678034 58038588754 904 3983668110794 6259228094 84 3989

0034 73574 576572212780205076636124 24 74 53027283277919753687094 602692110264 128505204 64 7715113195909759784 75200954 0677372174 1184 39959013507272930599636253552751836512584 2604 7228081305017016364 5829887952963874 7352394 4 2289

84 04 1274 230766926575389

1912937927022735871589

06780074 04 8592164 83963090839234 039884 0095128732229830618530714 94 4 4 124 55289

74 4 54 3189

585611874 00018095275209628513711725684 572621954 387878592562737224 001189 2859210973591774 4 53090991376018571051336552689

96097982796691301664 71364 566970732370814 84 6534 93878889

8100994 8329822204 54 61002017204 36127512031538116582991015118694 304 9114 4 759374 4 151199214 827769884 667239091980921508515824 4 561052008871854 606987301372553634 63299564 4 554 6387264 4 523269557824 381689

55311089

653134 06984 204 1218638500690537990290112965560297304 964 6054 821960184 97714 9958716016018632187928577655514 8260986889

14 664 178674 3554 86398857672164 079809930784 64 4 7004 1589

25298121200807754 694 04 4 4 8690228534 77093950868213234 0733873815211764 04 4 4 7604 834 555293052999589

302071650213184 55760851637824 162907159794 08661795263226509087062500009785294 5988034 121108255776072014 18877274 90710128389

36324 3734 4 7553276610994 6298202924 784 5727959599586690604 60001018255384 8674 5656582757507158587296867716751114 87265212206589

30514 702981699114 593575970624 05238204 2720167609089

719364 4 03104 714 270189

011229197278328160211355975632554 869999224 3388504 519858282629103818226122655992591597082919786233193166881062975254 10684 117108625987030714 4 086083889

08161734 018394 521786761691021784 000705721511533181834 639810904 85505984 190806537984 03931967652618254 9014 4 96282638131368683019053727762902214 08228253205031575814 4 91105214 96934 008005917184 288674 74 23281889

208221098707510096094 22271796061186875231086513054 8794 0730324 755855158572712956851667115026585753721524 9702073566554 2874 804 8188381689

4 3809294 7193924 9707834 2691198162104 7130830957027914 4 04 4 8875294 4 652228809164 26932212089

14 373532634 34 70189

4 14 18654 987580854 4 389

783754 276111604 82194 4 98573399194 64 1634 510588275964 15074 970868687065333087674 68551708636722004 13355069089

822703363808724 8324 77362384 276712729982790004 723750336569135964 850589

4 87117971773589
5375235172704 532988089
768706037171689
3813114 9261179907638681757227782503037994 81053099714
133210679111769390824 9785759501734 734 3274 863356684 3154 9974 25554 34
28798138728885884 08286655506303116923034 2624 00651924 61820851294 051384 1094
3833830994 337323561184 0834 1561095254 74 4 54 2667874 4 15394 5274 380854 781574
817180554 2923017257708254 215514 552311689
815984 15763033104 1024

Chapter Eighty-one

86785934 4 5139563372056885889
06905711908399969799521334 4 839522875922839778656931697054 50275524
9860375938138006589
525705654 87153992594 24
999717317167976251830780718006517305152956338263279321271806269594 80634 164
969102111602364 64 323589
04 7724 34 77665172504 37018826211584 3764 4 226666204 751278252351887021789
80272672802771182277315210303587264 20824 5289
884 331683157916664 992568216114 4 99034 24 669515324 639135704 78076852689
89
984 89
320525337210124 674 4 85594 5116869825165086315065590233506089
4 613325964 758574 04 74 307164 510219889
64 666857650930833004 568187275724 168076705921604 3554 68100929255939564 89
5332950279715672189
20273257081506277090717387103132384 24 960099196766657262124 887134
992056972358693324 07381117705573234 60902157984 72234 52138277157958034 722054
02589
664 4 15390534 121374 4 7005089
03387153834 939078365114 58079202721014 7906297989
923573034 0324 99697624 0607889
732184 3108824 4 930826619080262204 999011285974 9295562772174 64 6114 689
939294 010594 94 209733817594 38287802504 4 4 099687534 019038860177170124
591227676884 675715236965521220057724 24 5036539737696902851785827201084
3359833984 54 4 5681784 062574 904 3191708774 3824 104 03186714 14 204 1720368114 2989
50367725654 6071050128601831884 33059026704 135914 4 689
996884 7178334 704 082914 68124 154 74 30930099815384 2585056327604 739087689
04 92793224 924 09534 9919034 1621154 4 60821389
8364 54 362734 52554 213715789
152132060376564 34 612877334 64 232652794 90788381923864 4 4 7557705950091194
4 4 14 2257604 74 8727334 64 24 60795924 62981704 64 1534 6065133084 095714 764
87155212860865784 707352955176812758230953381637314 4 2904 74 17984 02689
359511383623361903652219368694 89

53929298610560654 35057970271551124 260864 30859272820573203824
5286337536004 05371597766322099134 9122262298215524 64 4 134 15294 5655157701519189
86924 072986258052706984 831289

54 80796254 3531974 17128584 25766114 0282009534 9691802167787509064 0963889
389

104 84 504 664 086575037294 0522104 1128000954 731966004 65004 394 4 21684 8594
2209014 4 524 29272225584 90593663824 4 0277332836264 5030305335399309698777034
309071233257624 94 14 96016107924 287316685263884 52751267060300570764 10952614
2989

664 88181203960638734 084 985550094 173219877966753274 996201186977256904 14
4 69020624 776565535065664 2375914 691733307274 89

154 34 058300807072214 8098316774 819302173684 537002122864 9151994 4 80864
391860713650673852662802901568680073865584 82695676254 210529864 116593386924
82538337878752134 9222969889

54 9770334 204 786174 0980716210184 4 15161772214 81911004 37333711693674
3087732669730859901037197397794 9610284 291618684 127575699139864 92114 24 787814
353108830701287103774 7664 524 24 06304 32837083773152561194 4 73055755237910984
6177353129064 4 24 104 4 7089

4 5166904 8806950914 6073182689

4 4 927878884 930939500099507022903534 3539213325589

4 765250328071052854 24 124 294 6878306631082799514 0399264 8538194 334
61802956014 31124 328564 84 6965317170173912538789

74 66609714 5394 2277274 10114 4 2393879589

598789

1054 5664 104 26814 789

116268572803599678303987097866634 4 4 4 04 74 4 950237805374 94 089

16979173853720974 70734 52739794 605724 927590824
927825833506825690837808354 5693636681739559150054 89

11712294 589

34 2501939702089

63987204 233608131092995278188504 0277128738574 4 354 705819714 4 90571304
159192507557151185687124 5138617084 6137621994 81388155508293884 83756914
5259023563970063111260122118004 370384 777070672157882914 4 72504
7038571195085880934 75506374 8382935317775380885589

4 1174 1926329374 954 300085072224 8392228754 394 4 22626269598191189

69563052527909934 6294 61536093616354 94 4 7879175037771374
15907062317596724 55836853259984 2155881031625624 4 4 276554 99025327501763136294
31277960119164 3050971695953211299204 5271774 4 9654 63360265153656582884
1936387933775355221000752330624 99389

17088603055134 9824 54 2033286014 988225189

24 4 4 9789

713654 38878760732583968694 1239838808204 334 62661172204 37998133074
235136784 99084 5864 8166662862011101678772854 932272589

73179629008389

380937836886224 309281603626918073213564 653715350504 8869164 77877918584
2773790818861314 754 3573704 383964 161086684 54 4 7786051856988364 354 55394 14 674 4
88362256907582297656680517777 74 84 874 2973152174 07172224 089

96252027134 4 6380289

384 3314 525169836380731 1799214 6783653334 2174 788805977284 26160203584
308289

24 4 514 3907954 874 19205994 670310937677692734 600115726354
78653303787050882558626169 16954 75273604 26276524 262803824
77111290356531092061375 50104 1535163500294 77360280304 265156068704 4 5034
565865327374 88831388713636012808339131268504 056973058262367506066185397615704
174 2174 27594 094 04 77766295856099304 64 4 4 53696935713123533 1390184 4
7310167028536689

4 180350236163261932 6787257731214 9724 9824 5087303034 204 76258522565871384
4 1719279864 8134 969900336823663592588 2060107514 2130599354 05118239822139359584
24 21288680155694 960131634 26588392290351702963854 9314 31202685751720924 34
16771675953673854 59589

156304 15154 34 08885004 1606705334 6654 082813070083289

77614 8824 9696289

24 01604 2114 1615103617977793210297134 76265799794 02154 699780387784 794
01598816085214 213535304 14 9794 34 853189

1952830115750065558 5264 2361877164 4 2360830789

734 5825052329324 364 0264 375924 591800563290872305076 2970364 84
35508696762133108287701771634 937764 001574
07706192909977311832715705372092053654
02970776786726653277933085996580010922 17362389

04 13584 27951933508882214 54 365191134 34 014 34 28094 289

3214 78884 8307387257704 974 253324 64 66094 835351665781767074 4 65378364
80284 709692610131864 5029312296165994 3735558202928820234 4
50728277138137353108738681566684 680584 165539524 06315115736792154 91126324
77501265298070868653207871804 612867924 288077555706529278 2594 194 30075884
27801209591016637750 4 14 014 314 4 565160939204 213995507274 9878724 4 571094
13555504 501572289

7094 7059287154 785784 23754 9555530688277162786068 1824 64 764
7199972980036733287720 74 7522653591039754 964 08864 254 76524 14
3137886190662271392033 74 830355538284 34 4 4 764 4 59824 3634 06532781363195780834
389

9184 020729563312274 24 04 06329113697622685654 0001062389

8604 781668629777784 0312794 89

99170739672306752216295096528789

63150378284 6767916109674 5584 88735934 754 910866919617224 603794
3326536717532667964 2757594 399604 9976680661204 0016533028504 94 9972860704 2754
2509372077385863700 4 154 4 1026059524 4 9370758500363784 13818607795676066 8064
617234 2950075239776514 594 3294 89

67190018394 50853507115250826284 54 534 527375779691224 8333719234
27615820308014 6280176756282502 4 0714 6025097160563093176724 59307604 868824
879005384 7158052075074 4 820305264 96689

819994 02515794 94 232115902784 104 3254 2583533717778889

92395174 6366574 3261372851811005292757 34 664 184 818518156994 4 34 04 088180376875351974 06636304 78337284 4 055818192994 3124 92820699574 5614 2382665305098134 4 664 300969883579889

9933364 824 964 72266767866094 838218200691764 4 77995154 10064 8314 9509234 02313298555020760129765976 54 82514 32214 27726580666575578 24 52114 3511835733723773 04 924 3714 2595702958551587115638880779956709924 04 1678394 507854 184 74 5979089

815804 1308296754 68152034 66039698784 393830818392374 77162789

77138284 4 4 34 05134 09511684 27734 0921769072524 7631089

224 4 4 664 789

1168794 32513222007365153 4 562311855013874 21523354 4 503089

388539861014 611069074 89

10956635966294 81504 6854 6756229289

4 151089

237294 3193195614 918231825611290602583 64 2878172194 92917534 5388235279936285889

6363679518066994 355394 7379606788386394 329921827855684 125586779954 97954 6133028786214 64 651571399165914 0284 58734 8702705261069817062568063586601281 64 4 979724 6668164 1619698798867736 84 74 70963519634 9675767724 117193889

89

116184 101675724 90652812301639681693150030825201 4 89

74 57973889

001526824 02377798309724 004 631085064 9974 1059120950157077584 14 14 89

180528324 67306183514 095174 91370788512597534 824 769265004 236854 623584 360159707296182804 4 309168026370057859215113722012165857223365 4 1374 4 4 4 76594 13954 964

3955313251616096580180992087790835257903757726750622322518588306075693231 89

563374 7331807153668699884 986386914 3703937913796902175096258692 84 257169129054 2002081554 6977772690884 6915524 81174 4 9993657072604 8504 3950809189

4 3285304 4 74 93989

63006031851877274 58210524 655774 10812254 85874 613984 1024

Chapter Eighty-two

5523154 6972860561599004 919730133874 5304 31602324 64 4 9926512501704 25989

59818255652388758779 54 29109096721908835535777 24 986861366152804 958762154 4 1732619304 117924 9699714 2364 80394 563630993072083516922 4 953962020083881511918372 4 4 4 5227526366889

209929576677095667383518 89

66195961605373500860232336 4 8287212672794 5718259271787177324 84 309582827357398194 10794 66564 284 153735209789

22889

0021037317202758664 2901183835024 010382622694 18554 5174 62360055390533684 4 4 799037802314 935009104 33515559836118650126 04 956960259134

57693658762226557706320751802591029709744 92951788854 20211929716912663104 14
20914 0107864 25238613208134 7634 54 7297753174 4 085673221032254 607393016774 189
56020272992031624 7975376862780784 59710521326857264 5373624
2255319250951861718760134 51124 33762990535554 61959175254 804 30389
04 4 17376179131696274 34 4 87853115501952536997807793447126384 24 889
934 358191719567296122165205346223085534 104 54 617535160285303531706014
08812136373334 586374 74 4 90071286834 136213074 664 314 99196264 58766238324 794
568554 95264 93664 650173730252699119087348 889
3838082204 903139990505627544 39889
04 4 634 7223256585859879118866887408069701032026820399164
59653939827631397675758675630661191248 5289
24 856994 9554 5274 75825958380592669805669093152791187730205978 9
706313787089
338832207095089
7673353008555615294 5784 9364 06639124 52296012669596009626248 2362354
3500671735657509324 62100978763878594 00037811122554 818628659191302654 661216074
9803532560234 4 35636763124 1181589
64 69738561508295193180065715441263062289
94 2986318094 4 70882999697782360083731932759312 4
5373029308031970839167921123822037759386912820570401257724 4 4 86157978289
703237209824 314 19952191356933990701376486572379409018 9
73102677314 64 7704 9154 3124 6335314 9231164 98284 611912232044
3297987988654 5504 885502817224 1271964 1296214 25524 4 0814 33833184 83554 853164 89
15655594 7284 54 94 159518329931788517978572333349821971674 5220939822794
70389
4 830938700688809500950017601865107568261901821225987911067357657 4
10237188662724 69935107575855314 875850606889
2653011018387189
835211172154 35351275938264 3296902223394 93804 5976378558090731716 34
9568750327089
865704 5091638820524 80794
23522275356870825602603182812925772700379918530126352379901061 94
259570352197978694 6037934 09090768169039374 24 03294 2224 4 8564 90624 2924 06904
13555579781762809939784 678087508737889
2721735054 157216861062524 3531297175287017002171389
26526862619668687123822200180819981055671128721788669286651 4 086857307314
2030260294 175800614 754 339699614 4 54 1957801734 713074 5325184 665024
8739186631226591260156602363786266520161 74 160913156721283704
30238318580118360359563761144 0219634 1988517773587153802798083923962306959289
4 4 50288127077113265979220538364 7524 9006386505384 67352654
7127960139270574 2533572399284 3925668211900759207612282727238608562138276534
993392172288313289
294 4 4 4 554 185591185233251318300351279137925207603882293290768317757284
34 767105684 3279974 4 7620079687854 59609023037060154 74 4 3724 26114 67397637614
1025089

181934 278782304 188311556795804 54 124 311921034 4 13514 9026909550179999604 207232260994 274 936196212594 4 584 70157994 267384 0826916807034 20037334 2817358824 2204 8034 57761918055384 4 18670610927864 754 4 687110904 276564 90961336789

6693206186509904 81167965986055034 04 920596174 1584 03183736624 4 4 987889
103504 7061650009254 994 23394 5662165624 604 863627523675719584 62127097101035867837376628594 5519035694 80784 184 4 204 61164 274 3268607874 8084 4 054 251871227322220026214 34 7989

54 295282674 9324 038150098184 804 65700784 16191838634 92574 7769264 6056917675531836754 822789

2033180272665310931271164 36793381962280095954 13304 7870684 27586157839815966786353122164 91074 162834 03637584 89

86732387826613769035930136232 29615603116634 57950334 8069604 14 680959998514 167331564

1663661063813593337029105580951861002596596933585381337026672093038574 2574 2167864 2906364 254 6277737124 51614 250089

6386538595275801322289

1865379060793284 4 1153123957194 4 3330597111674 62664 902389

4 3266717961130794 5823104 4 11919007978388171522300067009 4 4 0024 0063875922694 3622851083989

0825228755833967504 5354 3274 24 126564 5394 8010664 8018793370264 77967864 35630154 1959285025624 393698024 4 4 07004 14 89

81012850384 76125576653219679989

4 9975116516655256803554 364 2604 7314 9980694 15767114 957179087061914 4 79972522714 79529327963073535876112075829068056 59270752877176117312662 94 567603663357133534 83622574 92316090884 99733950008239080227083 4 0184 4 21860239715622689

4 69759011211164 176352819617880020135508 9

86069980355503955076960175235571734 9136765805036634 80989

17662374 7277794 4 3889

20986795169389

361595325081576104 264 98077187885831916660258754 5585580207124 960203569014 36024 11606765094 4 1751163995525117604 63554 58354 5586837333273783538558665765175565323 84 665889

863983862957934 9798658078391202883732216 54 18055101504 51839104 689

20950564 4 29261871307271889

75971985224 621314 295193673784 54 7251284 191391728084 3195020814 87214 4 86818091226214 195079624 8583678725120084 9590524 925366325557539713012825226663193126 74 7271170874 016874 019818205300956901210799 4 9369324 04 638634 100522606283359784 7775099361974 11021609915334 124 174 56322272914 289

84 53154 604 4 679324 631658508205990084 4 4 304 4 52923568356130595857276984 976510035763738094 889

04 3789

814 9713389

4 4 11215534 04 782853834 102515862734 5220929813789

5801512526795905016883811079779373785231 4 0754 5364
2383267753725911397231685879268790 4 119567525558325589

4 32624 74 631695959323793280773977215234 13165102332695551004 2567134
7816568789

4 4 3259010203076129931870611713111 4 724 4 684 73809876166132982158 9
52373367323567167154 5614 17555162388079712000152 34 5311199 4 54 178338724
60867591965315696 4 94 59754 34 352624 14 71737702735162352186908 4 5881694 33264 954
360963069032786367827217 34 33787234 212201277914 53073615284 4 291764 59375754
52766551173616624 9377625834 12326694 70386618010995264 1614 14 4 694 368666554 1214
65355725108823132604 4 4 3020594 782957064 6964 208 4
05066397206393173650735131730038804 4 5262259603654 84 863659694 269514 837219194
05374 88664 8224 69551380014 16617534 4 131094 3976696304 89

2594 97232083175309962614 30784 529933180165084 520803236358264 4 21016274
31013661298558705 4 229184 69185853580002596570961068886707 4 08368708 4 90761257994
7164 1309963888597728060572 54 38367777594 594 94
87903959265587631921103227650583873 04 3998704 354 154 07721708153371228169725 34
7084 804 606784 815303398274 25354 6067361331062553 64
808235171937319763829231976068793186399739397093292358 4 6525925254 8784
75606695873672602507 4 964 68659320534 760333026702258789

39971559384 670734 63822210871654 311598711083236359015069170 4 6254 33514
22056150023399316362122693161 4 164 51634 67224 870089

0857559784 2867209087050350595391102855612564 99135175964 4 938784
68536271880164 502150234 6566085754 4 0062129328084 24 56354 78066713704
565685192593359224 74 64 34 4 4 9681389

3964 09572880300774 156674 0902382614 24 501639714 89
926715058806214 04 73638877177652091612577 4 301134 751954 5220374 9089
6163122104 904 3534 65180190009099352151964 04 714 58864 773560214 651224 794
178059004 23518207667965078580026385108261666788 4 85589
5074 915864 512661930983830583 4 826296907131706731071719728080776 84 84
80579658754 4 4 13799294 4 910704 74 71829728017872590170 34 0333000923039253806104
16754 84 669889

573135068038686174 2639924 4 369000507783234 69824 06924 2703312234 4
2533816869554 56854 24 13174 36885767212185233924 5514 51954 36629288774 904 004 394
5594 6655074 084 270251388154 225801277993624 94 827612553010957594 10701557524
570174 019788509769995259561720868 9

4 34 0915972589
634 928359294 91764 187707351188755733523909753386139 04 61174 4 19754
91085823789

4 53594 881734 097886394 50617009227355835690 04 058562272378064
9116217992575263587677173378254 50819281108102159023883118 4 9529597030289
04 54 6355239277603766971804 64 55009366389

395271293756618364 98772135574 32275835211796176974 0289
374 56777117102096019708609988889

1974 822781834 064 514 96324 019134 1985954 66675186304 382178229805364
768085964 134 8784 88276513359060703161660080738564 5023674 0863265104

7956555552390569324 1365906176731915774 394 061383800816228694 214
78366058122796601378868810364 223934 4 9289

9015582775604 767214 52887526965184 984 09757253114
12696979996835831311163623016679676374 0682084 735220764
8198751988229863052801822887374 0084 63358398398351191797700578224 4 8199586712374
4 0728854 2554 2588206733038659351234 884 9979702623134 280932584 61206187314 4
905739334 295261855568315864 7234 6508233563111689

9039298074 62373018589

61751274 62011024

Chapter Eighty-three

1350253016504 73598739129966877316578879314 68114
62093006882223088720615833096858364 7938117175872322118804 4 07563604
56266510160834 4 367723134 14 84 618712669394 3558094 4 72992220580954 0034 174
77116924 94 857224 97611316668715094 90601304 24 278786117002180954 7239131794 4 4
184 1677024 5763014 0229750183193804 4 884 4 81604 777014 04 081374 189

3954 54 759655273539614 603519113393012231332991332 9256507989

6523080905985857 4 0695106919203279334 7339726614 9554 170561661608154
29521787924 20850189

261589

084 277089

9908154 10205163517964 59815754 5596880694 260180013035578554
70271598760068073314 51816194 07836722122385173317731783658569999622159384
8758839224 89

929110687127774 16931374 725695651334 3006306522737924
55105626692188080781183258673136960112090771 4 665794 4 366288330014 4
08158630986317264 190633304 4 04 4 5080582281128154 889

16198322932731818799958851273783872938509699050069095815055996862377712 94
23176197294 04 081394 1813602724 0514 82082073795136314 84 3354 227939334
2776536861035254 0772583999654 861874 6068110854 4 15993782634 4 2183839384 4 8584
8529035304 569715109912504 4 231382524 9252954 0089

6002776538738663574 156388274 314 11023599533922274 6614 28089

50302357630184 7389

969569687857964 7614 813385274 62600017284 0076610353359970011074
2958861790934 4 85688238614 02212026281009878 4 194 7785566957670602082972972 84
93217283594 7885074 78562688354 139604 52050327339001 1597689

9759234 8823789

6003704 74 35094 4 0126218101094 8157151330500526967 34 75051595793024 14 1924
677188377990789

709674 198562062060336577626066200393 4 7514 589

51212313889

6768052158583214 85875621004 9398274 3377929100085634 596084 787274 4 334
60556184 8216303387229105564 330934 67219264 786656314 689

814 4 200381872110934 389

7389

863038172129579090929911274 3076719777729157837674 854 6289

2852180820396714 378507933637369500772766 4 266755854 19995885697258889

4 1718854 7324 5704 12654 5387279293835554 2304 1284 1370132131163168616764
95031820781233528078670360575316926111114 1319274 2877904 4 64 559074 5310830304
595611994 77889

29764 9507064 639716814 514 6294 53124 294 3635554 8868636124 882656124 0064 4
0932704 62720991938024 9935389

605974 4 3351284 9065936304 2830104 058174 606123204 394 4 5967861994
37588182107887055290972 4 031508851804 4 6976720704 932193264 273274 74 94 74
657352706314 0084 60022706069559676968769935816122080876 14 289

0824 38282250827162654 51015076507112254 8776783127104 89

85812589

0314 80801153234 822354 857562501636134 324 4 57554 89

7084 018525624 8785584 11615590629157064 00186193826787191671 4 54 229784
27013185563530075923391 74 371504 2252368714 308028697389

72306594 0874 7261558320028856056 4 3054 36754 730126975992391214
0930782051634 730568394 4 357760805054 953912914 5864 564 189

51984 212667557032614 04 0165264 64 71819168255617805000 4
36626398681263260515677037375763228255723722 4 03373265634 399261010727774 9134
7627176169780024 2024 174 54 21963354 236834 21089

9820509839969309009668335172915560518003291237502797 4 13833634 6557054
527834 85374 7615770729786028264 2316989

56616215364 15061191691186958507630088773984 13314 4 33235221610864
8075376275627953573261927680750591791975382208050553608592 14 37064 25588204 0794
994 568053209984 521619529034 874 7172915878804 33789

8027199175755284 124 95164 55389

73669036679774 58510604 92373164 74 9334 851389

131076704 781689

315092800565250807 4 0033602625587974 65873389

5886504 554 910594 4 18711510789

89

4 764 27723914 132008590273134 8230514 7114 7108625684 4 24 4 305561264
573131797594 66908304 134 034 96984 189

5264 128081303923795354 23395514 5164
368583297176727033879966070502753808 84 4 66661324 952084
70595623603513288763569283104 04 23514 23073689

83022576189

39822104 514 71164 9750864 95793133102305164 0070274 04
18722925525312555050751962630901 4 1904 28815837860801872268853303 34 260324 18874
1994 74 3094 870980900779689

6221521278204 036387184 98691155689

28526788514 369208111989

66991991759394 4 22276598585296073161102727719303922875037352767 4 6031364
987286014 859087801089

0276964 8101784 192505137683639 4 4 327798589

7834 99670751064 59160807997814 98674 62129594 299294 951034 55612395285189

9664 8389

315134 16634 2562538722904 2078570031005057667238 7824 994 229304 3318762933107599216334 1034 8818530789

4 578621304 384 4 6990225971510953784 24 83964 04 519561395264 994 091054 1934 80278333814 105054 97503863252134 4 1665253257834 624 1054 313724 205134 3656100709750264 74 975060187932989

7004 9526351080384 880012217081134 4 231159233018250655232900080532960950529674 7617827764 99033804 64 927564 24 60784 4 006224 7751022984 0904 4 64 576088284 0084 38396537572516330908693659501131668059031760653994 1304 678318604 50062980954 64 1179322276064 394 54 50974 64 031190004 04 610136363756652514 76339220564 085394 88115656651564 14 4 9954 69997989

615517085192389

64 173504 86164 4 0196028228370231053 1954 94 4 55715777919567588597530366609882 2024 968864 9624 0237376974 14 9089

622782626717164 709054 54 589

64 34 2513581072155099312787001 81094 79337800194 288116971384 5597813034 37591174 4 9830503972720050883851 00204 864 52766917597291317151669 04 14 58699094 829963978857884 7124 1582151819151311936 4 65926550224 6995225206586123710861707775297 24 8009628557381117264 3504 39772399159135333727 94 371214 93974 8639792624 7924 574 6309268880601612683328108013 7307606789

63885303524 7624 79577296233036320607975313117003215631577396114 14 1726709684 57919889

678233174 9802500904 092769839889

4 8694 6584 06197088371187171626789

50598037992818687908359676 74 4 3867394 11089

5371969861829767384 589

54 3924 4 112174 4 326072814 34 4 156833377839658009 3324 16265311975886386314 57596991628226060779033373953780686 154 9954 334 396662534 04 13723933605837613571366314 84 9602284 6567534 731883339597694 06024 25850333822826967160251 4 88264 8376703139366150304 655694 4 03590997958808653064 775272076181214 15394 10681855315173588005 63179789

50810699820712326357 14 6714 5311627582525008062009835302998 59876534 5615877265590577677770523506800734 7211604 4 98064 88391234 4 314 96994 56629688381099231793759615151983265012 05987814 4 161793289

0058633209563904 4 9673274 09677561565792169512569575734 30650111772794 4 67699754 84 639636764 74 095197874 698574 050025666304 304 969303782864 6730889

074 06762172081629100092 7084 10880219803664 69032006604 89

82952654 4 1973616508087089

9913997268065256227964 1804 94 64 54 1564 4 876701280058394 4 4 300387771355707804 6564 32991321870606322081514 27506224 04 635739633230334 17129205307955186159 4 22189

134 174 3934 64 2698600396304 0050800204 28704 15729593735309957716677615251624 524 09290068764 84 094 4 524 4 870829637234 794 6634 0834 6767889

24 2904 515984 0508607169534 1689

272768570261007189

617528775251605114 57579234 8758289

688272500582964 34 83257250194 88704 91673293274 14 4 14 693861611008212073014 89

4 5094 2209156113531966015060095153004 2151879680050092567 02774 61697526917366335884 789

53104 87516279254 15229157364 74 184 88012937076008264 2006574 185024 1704 07054 31717287584 94 534 96755969256058106800091735532339 24 65539765805611506266857 14 58886231368778250270750779389

2985221289

83767573394 4 4 0612389

60194 6254 8014 9686695371667569202794 5004 14 657284 567068530994 311959103987237024 927090104 3532552598050115712122632 84 7074 5074 59034 05964 385528208729191184 983955166804 4 04 872154 753233912561994 593028105975250334 16854 656765184 94 5399888524 3277578350372083 4 7774 1274 6381874 054 5863929254 4 711505554 3227998182086818796986 4 70104 656134 11868005396513134 6723238124 94 4 14 04 74 14 5964 7131100723335520281233852214 05072386153693166089

4 6059307567586266790750537016110 4 07034 090926282674 88775028597523751023854 5267796205530602752777 4 3678194 0577953384 0765937191233904 1612299389

6587754 0504 2093316578069596534 12589

2927690021058353 4 7234 056106514 5554 293200917074 504 394 70199566983662770224 702288304 266506904 5512194 383705684 67083823573011816322854 34 00184 304 94 97985826217684 15619917919935124 153094 9158010079374 774 04 03927636888269384 14 99375805717517134 4 75581593103274 5774 18757637118775713224 689

227224 24 933777711139575584 84 34 69314 32056193522817599764 563384 4 63523667932694 1663652938292994 731554 160262278104 34 04 597128258224 267019760969254 23356800253834 89

4 65631124 9517014 689

94 004 64 0091188074 087077329964 303094 4 04 3581834 084 14 17580184 789 9502624 7389

5690754 781926652219934 9674 054 17288191105033252790021585 4 594 3175734 58873276958639774 1338302654 2251574 8812728581889

273284 977696911085259385652172391 84 04 2582582314 4 7031064 7604 64 814 5020222102865333308656374 4 0225958804 713218694 5014 4 366817538530731589

200519065754 80158234 4 9154 84 4 31777081767125204 611964 9394 50188625676374 14 5376864 56006014 21512612924 24 64 59673064 284 64 885104 97611191884 67204 98664 54 75999926801775664 33790034 005684 703754 4 756287824 934 89

84 08714 00770236296504 170750104 54 03006968311235317293 4 03026317221317086176202960 4 34 4 54 820954 34 8676369524 9394 15384 7667538095773551214 6374 99080503829564 670902052304 673985564 3558238071200134 05179535817759266117929 74 6014 86921320263060039317995 64 84 94 4 4 4 4 731611937253694 206234 756374 504 78267593973212703372805781 34 31266211173872224 92806333639834 519303680389

2593096889

9520925203527857198099238057623612284 9606523276970970764 790391394 2314
02133368690394 808687684 74 330801226886994 62034 70823716309724 704 72502810603314
164 7014 4 74 12054 213824 030812834 719100930862026974 909153607225275128659774
9519507014 4 6835957034 26614 60253028153384 82727764 4 97900776889
8074 4 58301080580762580282652539 84 6712184 9904 4 394 2589
188021880629759956314 2816384 85112094 7134 99524
22729096625621310572002786025213027 16524 35730201321995053171 1204 1933385624
3218115968535314 364 280988660109585 4 368526010852934 4 63784 11885371826272165074
54 14 154 290924 1257634 2816834 64 24 803581833399866073577309 4 094 98606570661584 4
07016735064 684 5510834 4 8304 1034 0714 3306886135064 81612313350084 4 233624 14 174
4 25220384 716206858157780034 4 074 4 224 089
977379525077227224 2522163252707982864 834 2393603199360077015781 4 54 854
997327914 9571524 204 7771832598625574 711721760004 75918686134 6576680074
79138823888252605950369614 5637555094 8364 5524 94 33184 9375795834 4
70825651120297713054 89
05985889
3604 904 1984 3661556802806391016931507 94 123984 4 2614 14 6314 5272074 90634
21674 6665622082073387 4 054 4 10275552773264 25726662603254 34 14 164 518064 64
62013591074 636904 814 091394 881734 9150190905887865886575608054
633191153957951992269151017526113553536 54 804 4 915380523524 30920956839133923664
18602184 86574 05653138658589
18038882901004 954 4 10539504 2819085217095689
709852226604 914 977034 4 25634 1520113354 3595601620804 8334 570567858284
7518288694 3264 57284 7094 1550706639004 202184 74 284 14 815072932114 255525384
876823984 05964 03694 6755855870650778052888 1184 37054 37076685394 0204 3667908794
727576997674 27174 390824 114 225151702319553260 14 929205324 85233164 4 3033614
1058134 80812118784 4 54 0168004 984 186371953775079122509816883959 4 3984 374 34
9050092769074 304 9721973216682690786818 9
4 29886554 32603934 79960279152866631674 24 5204 99357683219759829614
09060960027750075 4 116118234 1365951954 364 768265974 3538725034 3355756076030 94
264 593717684 4 35256584 56189
4 13304 36265854 9333964 4 8813667814 189
94 0353781251863618098614 31093804 686084 2389
4 176571709198375302735294 60531821774 84 9806764 10072780689
35394 8778562080766076 4 628864 34 975781384 916754 9694 8013336164 5855359234
21874 4 4 3904 872822023274 82790004 380974 372224 09055665798279254 079201827191764
0731568687889
908698234 4 33324 2984 617134 807794 1579260789
4 378693787932181927623832088562198256262053706157053365099866604
37335278004 3029785385825777725820814 34 930689
509974 690284 2123214 8054 3625214 4 109926584 51320869835695037934
1219278770154 8376684 625884 8514 80353282100576225953123 84 3954 9984
559771836617 74 69694 8771337360294 9024 32014 0089
36954 3524 64 284 67039062829612925333175609054 5801524 15336269704 6334
156094 7714 70387833114 0804 55327202669851691655054 58088526234
72270091856838115291325160755751 4 732983104 8174 51169011854 4 7389

050027079662813573733289

152194 7351317150714 211819622395064 0360662507937 6610114 1090975719875195062790767199208 4 156183831262327870536779 4 958720934 8085310337003707967698 14 4 33398653194 7300553955036137371690354 04 4 12274 4 184 825089

72554 34 1132914 14 09921010502794 06078134 34 5274 54 574 89

10397870395925576771973032662920585002184 124 305611014 7117266588587585811098013622 4 2719178360150563008 4 5061260958035114 62218689

703926560067677522712781150869182 4 093126398323889

514 3307309208061818367053327222199671221382 4 3924 94 13384 5030855374 2913951006061214 064 015277299204 721624 74 690601996875361612930959 4 4 3531967021387026224 274 7134 2529519834 64 115021525852171907334 35287605089

694 89

859661873724 64 714 84 4 5754 004 2632111691306610800075901992768527723122 94 3384 53753734 4 556192707318 4 20770035251888198510000910588697024 63614 13394 637364 0362916764 85024 31395922261089

14 3124 584 3108024 9185337663654 737954 2810198006394 6754 9165673882209372067955022 4 53974 952793604 32187604 16737125294 18689

04 1678756050715819184 6283974 9951776189

84 7012014 17284 9225316599764 24 9139615534 6304 55967370036698271392 4 4 74 617224 05377563884 525060573831172206330995224 6138275154 384 2624 84 183054 54 61614 2397679580757579289

2955358231583791059988100013635583580253819304 960874 84 84 062324 4 213019673128572797569638089

1589

114 1510626829367132533904 4 32204 4 39351225627134 2583571937580755554 70995280586509274 89

14 8560615014 90586722186301814 5395527154 33774 4 11574 84 3014 604 54 2104 72371065909374 589

4 5560185074 70655512504 9620797634 95262962858574 191061198684 3374 359599027675135124 284 2162787382704 07361790182264 21161905654 52355982134 6500984 4 34 684 74 989

34 255194 1906125685394 7121550938357783997339853597992080 4 4 0914 014 01301969205884 81624 1657792074 38506165929884 2954 2875926765325764 6127865813653869302306 4 324 9514 87229156834 194 89

33977325772383110186072859921382 74 3995531670717977869 4 631024

Chapter Eighty-four

1209656299251563690707097976574 62230224 811183699337954 0037289

04 0035528138387916696 4 514 63050174 4 667830267733915658 4 851313373322134 55591201694 281994 4 635586911990104 67025724 886303914 313189

269027234 278807655956714 3550810085233287367618883314 33062584 02854 4 613817909164 91511389

8688610204 24 4 109694 9303994 61881564 34 692259238227154
2373255618657637319111383935082984 4 737578763090888190669874 875034
626160773620105614 764 9195858889

52617573029866000284 4 920883309869356389

666935736583154 3219805114 630291803035328239125122651 579604 51129136204
814 16074 2634 83689

04 872534 774 14 604 979289

686654 71804 3110963702069366180038156 9264 6017632282354 675257725100634
81083324 604 963974 58189

4 85625071592798514 00688234 56587664 328616964 994 4 702876172786074
01627879376003134 03053653720016336106731197354 0216574 274 55266137724 64 14
679701634 23221094 8392735205399216184 6684 4 3165780514 857874 87389

9561173561574 2292710799789

378304 1174 634 2331723123687062988799395637969323 3814
093077303166738558758336589

4 87921922929917029253219531310631375169956 89

55562792077326334 4 399560699134 01234 55661866002723864 4 0912957768174 5674
556204 2696966397914 924 854 6317615555834 7884 9112031329808109382020016670821
26195383939135194 94 3324 55874 15772583694 811634 9214 04 84 73354 6704
852527626699095914 4 4 85709083160 2386634 3355234 799524 19332174 312708264
2757150153738114 4 704 64 89

614 779234 323918836597604 173276069183964 76067866322674
929193323161131877673919132713156 4
9130569370585515333905822922262979366928009889

0127374 4 011072991307584 839194 8372516387525152681209356155068
661281565278504 3774 38567370659686571290 074 504 0213967864
0980501628716324 2664 2267337613821529562365220 0211884 30916924 4
9620167039837724 022900775191199017338872565 94 5167024 884 2314 4 66733016979564
931389

53858612398111668308257202233372 6985737787251767301674 688527011564
2775820059393570981225869012588

27727534 775124 596954 5250389

8261166802128775738056368563156 4 4 21994 581874 0281065680175318556
56529558228861695528627 200281964 030614 391059003215379795396930218519
2326880794 68527914 0725877194 84 6904 11764 169152274 721106824 390965834 9368174
0724 391256726014 139205537504 4 3877850971869061283089

54 214 4 50904 54 534 852381522612136091363279625618713 14 3164 94 221393554
4 22060053382734 515307986723066880135629301316501765553770 7163009150624
792123739193705754 138726037784 4 094 21730259112504 92386154
9381900703973226982708 4 593309383716314 806112834 11794 86313084 6199594 30789

684 964 111687084 3379334 4 05700795264 780255324 29988270212239589

07157262154 4 9188311989

117964 9225568725795187376 372652104 19618862359708076370825191601974
82234 4 820994 4 3332365004 0151033080334 5098734 20821279214 12004 204
8018050107979856172321 73504 4 013698114 8554 10588119726087395394 254
9086287378390374 680988320817221 79683074 313026938154 363684 53784 57615575201994

7911774 1233670859357176920959284 02888000062917208716273797741
1535129580502970994 4 24 1913807628723085063578557022002901341
327092777298737515761662474 84 04 7392851550863164
215302820835265015575631195908368230734 0304 3927151810500275265003370868
      4 984 28813235684 96500724 939884 74 0105694 734 338056373384 023824
3607253887330911137388407645000377344 784 7091001864 804 554 117110025614 054
08783699288695274 13926193790851385229297891
      581062839805904 4 9924 13872737639857194 82912844 834 765974 014 04 14
32598188502453910670591768324 622694 83973611571814 89
      852877065023792132178941
      269536116379304 4 64 67710253991656844 314 4 4
32020298116859366166592552065597956841 8269167629977734 031737378030874 820811784
8767254 586837334 24 6334 524 1994 14 10780153692124 1598778339974 669973954
29518681820090641 96976103678215280989
      52987606995710356909602837100859978991
      89
      89
      4 6334 872095708021792336657474 870714 67773673609724 639922157532194
023698804 2560150000758404 11757319574 984 1674 0333035260394
8097378856539028866590990135841 031964 8037329389
      8604 594 20398689
      6616222754 89
      4 3655076000234 5814 107089
      615093946926452773942351146941 011127719141 9136925437858539483527264
857552160208720481241 9169101852717995183756073284 4 2667718476795411
071116218015353987918241 774 981618583564 64 52280308632399771384
99283592092705553078665155641 527689
      591621869203470156455573402876692638413257703601605964 596904
032255123102029559970989
      164 18090712914 574 89
      86244 3029770711389
      4 14 62836484 84 87157678567794 878141 3125124 329355024 76872684 689
      4 69338789
      3096861937217245242168739271859503264 1171831981357089
      270756010792991851456275028662192436979841 178114 14 04 54 0319609164 24 784
39214 390278338683726417115541 94 396304 19405888067523818774
29108551788002078811767914 77877311363880277285669694 011827275541 75020009359274
04 94 837691964 174 174 74 3764 30993588281149024 1585671721186541 5181954 032744
63085084 90018672136527178874 2362751336854 382584 357260976576339859353641
87906202036888810270158500580830280052905250059204 09954
009559933828156055157808056927750376441 059324 22853821694 589
      24 730837269334 80345155441 089
      081803000097135903138760369506441 62952558119323319104 2017397696851107854
5102058841 1174 74 2956674 264 0862762260667721607633383260924 4 3117163266104 4 2814
5958606250699868607474 7754 2904 124 44 64 632860784 6279208041 1631617188773654

0720514 693121214 325169234 294 5354 3324 72824 1729604 3324 7902906354 0574 4 264 35510165761886875755289

24 905830732266885794 06361072634 71314 5128039096794 093684 979336814 875713298697813211924 7305994 96014 027781864 831950609839994 902924 84 82264 51969076694 93668091852924 654 0254 800772199089

177291960931566054 867802714 84 4 78376604 390600314 714 64 52296723373821018725039173155524 58699554 238861364 9792989

34 057309118689

8229687569221987835267884 8165620121799323557181193394 789 97294 1131625038237716074 76012250789

09139136007369816164 4 96155077115624 75184 8671864 274 18752220983699262511 0794 587674 4 271026054 9101837714 14 9395384 60173089

9334 4 93604 769733019287791380270313507073210981 88209904 21774 795824 4 675990200835711681784 4 88304 7873914 7534 4 935193814 01175208813705984 3984 654 9557055010189

4 74 63317851354 4 7806050024 5322289

869595610981274 4 53720034 050684 3316195198363031817 0374 789

862663270724 4 0653794 392777506117384 3773910037015604 50854 24 4 1718294 62232309874 159926137923103063979751962906214 954 9367514 934 8295534 2557326734 057366254 5638782087724 780170125191080613807 63294 19104

83768620615503990171057754 93794 3719814 98602274 574 3276873586654 721193724 7364 8368884 73863695504 72304 586168757789

92624 17991924 288808684 663276562154 89

4 5377584 64 269366017054 904 106967913965856504 72314 26979266889

20856929628784 233165154 0087970794 84 04 4 6062660205914 207157264 14 91184 272577254 4 518517922522992289

989

25524 1793132955616293338761 04 16084 91996663174 4 23087794 058873508394 7873072830991697739834 9794 3684 774 634 4 801579069104 2083874 95354 9261759171854 122935975189

90089

222621721914 4 59306788619760356221881278063881 3224 56355560680694 1525529789

74 969052102555871166688 0394 6253165815590264 70171799000399024 8334 019184 74 18611177914 2508795783 2200374 313389

994 38878790174 93217832857091362259 34 5239879921194 13582964 8604 23871824 0674 170986228121901857333681568570323594 309199084 131003274 24 16308560704 018396764 54 21975659821525834 228867964 90617533288038337592518802135 57889

35119163336359125653076196 34 4 68859555567903193134 2675338330663164 34 06076972503374 61204 565785754 274 94 4 560577318094 734 904 4 6364 2115299853304 353698384 660984 613766934 3084 61700054 908361012391654 874 021552018074 383204 6374 6783904 99993518567810792289

725874 69036774 957913385350351336075507321325600291910315513107283177116250772551531257304 962327220860225214 64 84 0220284 2798593292836688799077 14 08192398837850356220529 4 5336156802820375313954 0331764 31589

4 0563253112358682394 7289

2104 2814 7770904 5295704 91287593524 12051358687603284 514 2582734 694 4 8854 564 319334 4 56061039277195821292194 1310874 66667665924 574 913853915794 4 6355239886906767996953556594 034 008392663094 89

1563705155183329394 0005032264 170884 889

94 60174 4 9665907668684 7228668101834 234 73358074 8167860825699263614 5794 14 34 15773796972761195362514 81604 7504 64 4 5713935285259217578395278564 4 1202769631859515199253 7064 73854 3750734 84 19804 585231099524 5664 026394 52567114 8305359686 78311138004 081619234 069234 03260989

704 104 568037934 83601054 4 929206927313239109289

4 89

4 1612252877254 17258807157698002902327692992653967222 23125954 23789

7818796172973692312698629 04 13294 069304 779269034 0796085936969553082870633 4 98853589

8063170379065510234 555035981104 722630784 324 37887502680866528666197012 3584 310754 871934 4 699613511024

Chapter Eighty-five

653823076326385989

4 68574 35306560582753001735912983069515639 54 194 33781212111804 4 070153615314 384 579873166672036184 04 665922914 000728615704 7092318388883712590113775110154 6728156831261731358 4 54 4 4 95556934 04 016062515912214 4 52026304 00731678624 21234 73984 1566360615700229575795125960678 9

094 9180714 87219920115133860334 20124 90334 3269019031524 711111770537674 90379250704 77108000780724 37972199974 867805127054 38658097738366084 55714 159223131125076994 3850574 9572084 4 706161764 64 289

7016734 24 8531307265311314 1132969224 4 99732589

8693793362053823104 304 6881167270296781793531514 79252622771508731784 134 7201175082919918 14 0024 385165187293321922367139330218393718018284 319234 6206861224 877124 81614 4 64 37262384 6672273871692704 34 32266762821335957208657592529 9335704 6930167137770629372316184 02812814 6654 033939299764 7994 508355635293134 04 4 814 9974 6082157314 367827706020903620002365614 794 81796166953389

820330364 31519760589

38824 0313104 5864 624 5390394 57563768870592794 1914 4 635131656563853034 1380551160 73830115234 965016026289

833117526654 089

514 2764 54 87394 364 290003104 64 975634 1864 670633839370264 04 327199934 4 4 5017653621194 183980914 054 354 31204 661107102294 914 795728223004 888150989

28800520298222195603137155531918072367 5808735157394 94 158638634 65924 264 929827124 6874 2873788710721177960934 2852822185075176120316328786505 09567859784 69694 3970668574 36394 4 17334 19056383504 4 07294 3862175261006067 3994 4 65714 4 5256508218511081123 4 734 977092353306073156034 383366681280289

728355294 97834 68612079306536662298 4 88684 4 589

730236869505731807170927104 8802093698860052594 234 6855824 214 66323714
8360334 708879050834 67514 163185997873182137711360933796792671304 8084
0063571274 04 4 76190169902128050362495514 64 937562857255534 722015529162736004 84
207174 507880795076184 591360695778824 861874 794 9602794 8214 6832553636964 8055794
75195804 22659618175754 55372575780063850078289

4 2880154 04 514 728664 5076936364 2926165614 64 092376099194 4
2302530717760664 764 60974 89

01300712832067009583 4 4 4 14 86795964 2884 4 26565334 806269850089
0014 358597934 3204 954 700739790197624 021831864 50225187355768195384
66957130700628882926375616032787642159655931252924 924 22161329574 504
0653822016726239861866164 85814 34 29888315192031590579600733663059264 4 780176824
280579377519254 9911613874 081655519618008061914 4 877294 851166256997724
51508213714 6328190365180877334 737532213901795694 554 6985589

4 609950994 4 819766231605827389

73924 30853104 94 4 4 0787084 72699064 03178359352904 61384 8224 060814
01306739211 94 035926589

229119690168304 34 362279715304 84 4 598073159037135399085230555 4
135850303305994 26307530084 4 74 97312132922813900 4 14 93729257315810390367157 34
392981372366096770703723997564 711313836503606104 054 887160986190396184
99361053903230560359089

5271652168824 4 120760002937772054 20054 934 50599593284 7657914 4 51389
4 804 17920358508525299387 4 4 50064 90770503204 2624 603929134 79186052964
181514 07354 30834 5877036201626136356 4 753671667605974 78008590314
29361333792933191750084 85509604 389

7181104 09887752004 9212223706955858124 9625713314 4
76066506933678827688873 10324 4 54 24 398289

07735107267733266784 393233220192621936564 4 66322054
8552196362859886982124 590594 84 14 5389

835524 3171934 24 912990061814 6395923563828594 061690297564 763112622914
6674 6536626582357583297221 6617099689

21215263224 954 0972530092760909689

092981539854 778104 754 6039704 80564 0970194 3861124
37832161330172173520169538667789

3805184 72999961133017530953639202007972 94 384 334 4 271324
1962980107195951189

4 080207607854 224 7534 707659726795708604 37380133715614 84
9302325710198132874 94 389

614 94 854 878373297094 27816336254 4 363330826939905579688104 94 89
2037587507854 53764 050536575757195557194 024
139210826876090887690522636865 4 030187082270188354 7584 7239992289
4 034 0790795136796379635072634 4 224 554 191280957705903158772555589
2207789

69111868653692807238302 4 0389
23627104 980728883128755350717511334 24 80969287697201586675189
14 21714 34 255763904 89

594 698580750060927981004 390924 94 524 08176625095274 17274 15601614 54 31594 51852217185574 9552684 7527727167389

139029014 72023505989

54 961574 17316989

04 28553994 4 028302783837762365010859093691920154 027694 86814 4 08826839215934 253185968629688677073556817836034 19705184 191167919396618337297000193822980150272483083508010971773091110587089

4 89

4 6723054 289

271511824 64 154 4 0910664 532953239354 505193052789

90931728114 9964 92725306034 70215987196134 56500206310713361365178616544 164 9703573682097625837494 3863039224 87734 35717559667110116693127919204 620889

8287538871071536313688155466795901553145462365337277109419292748404 1691314 54 1970017754 019166194 192795232601888253730337752336012196171161255538897835617670837738785260756313420586568197019298042050503450950135837302702058324 4 70696463969223690638593311081122013967710006747724 553614 51739824 65787334 364 14 551852124 685804 07288018781059764 8717763079789

33254 64 58009321561354 84 194 84 21779175593309357859671946991950561912931679934 4 1194 597294 24 34 600010285797589

94 04 9694 36566619097579329566805424670138374 4 999094 8865697217529786249994 4 4 038632564 887331676004 076776907176911021713324 6166713693357767751796687482379811974 164 1389

32966510983219131889

12306128832130617534 73064 594 32631236902194 24 876504 4 265680064 0372373565200124 3194 823731911164 158611994 016234 561070555880366626031622166878471348965 64 997725714 4 363570318750075329860063330828897051279145819777920607806942050549492682044 4 04 634 256297157534 094 9274 355797251601572079797266070199691870098612224 1889

69224 783312230698835193026800133351582348097469113783697448676320781546648812639240828418651602491495497986442720986605182035717645689

4 993560204 307104 89

29581586506395191730563855938221751430131434 80759866933265048747990380564 68350956561639841602315510479659885931684 74 522978453271156302256796382458057087383359848615942699923530317472056202203726152708976066846026088744 7119518675285250056178297288871967524 6604 89

54 1310791051300257310392626908884 74 237156518309916354 67374 572399438350009251653919181018423706418278446319964 90552888569939325282656262824286907604 69591229338888263678905258896297992600436583512928591660168162711585038595099200450238288052578716079991485779511741071458789

2789

28594 4 554 2297574 89

2663914 906061225590184 674 24 204 89

830696032609924 1605373198039930995803184 5874 187561196551694 103025884 274
61326771528604 167562599716689

0091974 4 6205707887606193824 714 4 30682007869999515821869915234 8094 6205994
73367284 161874 3801837624 4 684 3114 6227199718354 04
199085721267006752205570817790802076 4 223877008302314 596324 3769724 84 302281374
74 8014 994 596782976524 5111164 756284 4 94 88239112658022320723393396724 873534
83796834 70903721727807182199304 5796170874 84 66832260754 831194 64 636316295504
614 289

18187034 4 0255160661099604 396822797600851051090393626291091994
2119388266551364 31104 59377398233754 702234 89

70989

38238334 96062224 14 4 58818157174 4 8698580076801768098311354 4 889

080730980104 59829884 06710128613818555977913112665855794 62797634 4 02093254
04 64 256523214 4 87854 9983704 521267864 86295967723599938670287589

062826992794 9214 8880889

0259752971774 789

067202993671236787634 51986595708011874 77179864 84 51089

825195533914 04 5264 04 0275752862201560983990974 3678839234 3368690293794
90238806297699255692023312504 277051089

4 35097832023702609078772210288838691730652029707 4 26870592354 30376889
84 74 9133115084 572724 089

272768529320256830382290269854 983092664 279816962154 8264 3789

64 61283683804 207320924 4 634 810624 82376286784 8195810854 7337889

17216503370931716230082783544 4 6095355000157087325853718296069755081704
35834 992204 34 78239737270858232696362370176097674 84 500304 1090604 01168774
81312364 157224 9254 13673506596999974 3514 6831130004 7904 3763389

4 683811507504 4 79836224 9775689

18706331215982573656934 3060981010581075128320284 64 4 4 4 4 4 66922583587764
54 107654 24 54 4 616023777827884 23014 324 14 83760775272286664 5863176868757284
362034 6387264 64 703378104 5580384 0869900184 70013294
90672016291067320866560152720035703770087723639337084 61915283204 8823114
03505825354 12867184 9769189

874 018370111971124 74 08166154 0189

7014 577602302374 5038112311099710264 6614 14 04 1857261089

5636960583124 4 662510334 4 21769869553123069183533300561885184 87114
67565374 71284 253783753602700254 04 78152676963868002814 9067082684 714 3662704 4
93834 20886829795605591530914 319592305379389

70909123501683175231569389

22081723667794 771797136271924 14 55588880860190380 4 074 94
601510951815732199263163081536727786395339826503769350931962174 93071036054 68274
6385192384 0108589

3804 82153796057037554 13634 194 5317910214 4 027724 4
00228595051052507885300563625 4 87962039630514 167505389

028154 83989

3826056184 605969254 309230501184 4 82024 4 4 05735333994 864 62324 6986164
2715255204 14 18394 54 588339064 507002112028162690376 4 37236786327092384 80835704

928556654 225657004 171664 34 6794 270566931694 6590355900250098110204
61599706922269604 30393134 150112385202084 3307834
9276852128023229115251973791375174 3284 05671719578654 820096834 8394 9354 98706334
104 51091155802399789

6555372867167199806356218822989089

859713594 56599565839007199084 113529007032127984
86817378763769197501596534 762104 926792800297988281614 4 2624 704 54
99318735873796114 4 612207504 17737680384 2330889

95124 89

27382171911705995177134 534 2994 5729725215214 03834 304 60734
0293212929718359902336716755190204 83679889

34 857854 2813074 09171121274 91351889

665038805950364 886600193051774 7973772006038594 794 4 314 6650104
10771923517224 4 72581698761357315539 73606361022608171954 94 774 87334
657530769762382929970665938113035566698283830832766954 76109668865318112204
113255088889

8206279798064 80301121722792334 1819607984 129997207200884 1839387221139034
724 7310851532774 83669837824 8679654 4 85396054 673324 51782821837371290684 884
32260975031906355301794 1264 82389

535114 7387863995054 860224 60003357691360318382569522239304 394
1627677865022636715904 260821794 1626062786534 13781787284 20381565930074 4 6364
0673989

66754 9268764 93957184 903132121136562023902615229 84 06287309564
8128169303501869685037131094 7232937674 72224 78572964 1708198589

4 05216965981052533789

23350319872584 94 889

372864 0768329664 53384 0034 139733684 65664 299812962074 532556516610754
82537381673969227716956365366825813785392959280 4 863934 624 068004 561289

7367776564 99264 4 4 527556162223994 3174 89

11099786814 130034 08786160964 0689

091934 4 66010685781739964 966919294 071519797706196735563278083037 4 867624
28189

532993799350174 37703304 126784 6394 1074 2390004 0751986059181564 6594
7758609699994 12559689

6228698815789

024 2657789

7779204 5289

4 57268597880151203918786 4 4 971604 9993622264 6124 9586877214 34
77181778272154 03315790874 3833318094 50293538191572814 54 18326821124
8197232597214 32234 94 026289

54 69574 7621010807874 2584 765714 78016088334 04 962554 6506324 14 74 4 4
23711596789

92370589

827766568589

77194 57925992692904 083389

32723324 7930254 203274 12082794 4 36936354 7913979579720396366395782104 9584
16314 4 039654 24 0938604 75283325924 34 3500781306594 91794 990770388167056714 4
8564 759014 70819362884 60634 387083087301399925372529836689

104 103313594 394 34 7713254 52511125521110927987277859513827089

16366590952074 1709275251299026204 554 10308034 81032270004 62081993134 9774
10339699357052008134 90694 2080378722037904 64 38289

024 99024 012213804 6339798024 218210683934 6850884 930167918289

6621304 254 93338799654 874 3861093208514 9105332758773269026724
12929662567364 59068755914 89

6312050174 24 394 526389

3979024 4 2323703264 9035968525782137809651504 54 4 989

3186606855909756632394 4 2261822295196564 2157254 1809032099804 4
9661381395312098534 7967114 69934 2694 93824 514 96674 751598529004
75180527661226007197757224 9670815150580391 4 34 61824 0125218092935634 4
2697690775936654 520908202506027804 6714 9336326778720581681597025 4 8184 00764 54
284 3654 9500337194 2335655317061100284 4 2303004 2053052952933086763760286 4 5654
611038275374 154 74 84 9100931287259564 4 20569761099930208810 4 0353186694 89

2623960995356572233574 7574 3158786184 5904 8319664 2956322272610527164
819839854 633794 370836572964 09394 888203974 86960694 33331514 579163972074 807234
334 4 270697628656850889

4 73094 9815971906831106120010286752309520111063997859704 188194 2784
38731917954 8374 60367190355693038399 4 0154 837381862624 89

26181581754 6723094 66283620556512169174 70327887284 57031534 54 4 4
85852236960697986889

224 934 53282096934 3567616792601084 7238262589

7599052637923259164 15032763625594 60774 6274 1704 33254 4 934 574 4 4 889
4 77216876271827727072 94 796799294 07037256821061295089
9937024 6217199889
89

4 4 678766862734 5794 1352264 0334 98177530833993906702966521338034
6983727289

05324 7600661939254 5820659289

7014 1526129507274 26292279324 65791704 38371626932075365011196015575259 4
694 06191818184 873777134 26834 4 4 4 24 052930660057334 4 5888690588803931774 84
511774 10239735877528228 4 385958672028239874 374 35295921155624 3224 389
289

6300272910568728872681616117730356952723169774 369592914 24 84 4 621189
89

4 5750116903129574 2514 8284 5174 4 19871337174 8657674 6353974 74 57615954
160878152194 9380382190631719785 4 6364 80687724 886181039189
4 4 89

75073053855804 909207963214 83089

3523184 803790906668134 52717823353224 661252194 99267652914 2759089

0922621175108174 67050005956809313519528 4 00804 3900757261786657751257 4
52884 33053553174 84 14 291753374 24 8775094 89

93354 37358359554 5788270603739739129226937030124 3965689

712377394 5167318596704 19317393074 2310205394 4 927937255669514 34 97880554 570330590834 011304 5524 20883774 53018234 714 836854 0570383980300834 9014 6661575627829724 54 384 4 94 7365389

4 73998534 28754 3282274 785381373116324 69929383670295832152967629316901577O163764 5970731154 5568276634 90194 82504 203271623554 3761606289

61010317789

20813007133134 968338654 8654 0725269994 24 3818874 654 82728672722781054 6989

9924 3638538389

1710091592717082304 906672765961623781686404 4 108587574 54 793666754 38596986709554 74 9996591202364 71863025134 234 2866031230832887254 2614 84 6504 91333914 084 557134 89

74 212133262795637514 1588593834 3702328836763614 272109109163264 3811993071180581370532052181871689

034 04 084 2283314 956139714 10009101715099373550162504 98698021280775524 1862004 587089

684 4 4 3830634 4 5989

4 955514 4 00987651922004 4 34 82688701270198303940 069224 2853914 4 34 4 37692525690603785633163635916959756362855116855631624 525027754 5376196294 289

04 366194 589

680239185158067914 38606554 5763066653855089

79167196722773975207635829190576640 7967180388564 538818866035064 54 31683355124 5320523828327827721092596297940 74 3650827334 190694 84 1174 7713586694 16235515154 189

766502736524 37782927375010905109308258678O

84 624 18684 94 72218794 50928673056564 7293726572105569324 9737530172030034 2984 6293990357604 05532694 801975212600306698038440 350399536224 5864 967571735364 4 86622960867665022114 7619719066836700078786195257277240 960774 95301582704 0191563034 89

627631553591293521702092981509995711890

777124 690854 4 67614 4 850835054 133339784 826134 395314 95371915024 13214 9252570114 576270103268359197885516440 103614 73764 7596250976223028811189O

54 04 7134 804 24 61791153854 16323284 0054 371084 64 26909503621868337287756440 4 555584 4 5132126070936508889

689

9626104 0660972714 901582592651684 77635062365733527671953832978O

2000906729856532354 522274 81654 10194 80074 074 9839188230279326391440 4 94 236957352889

9527704 109953394 75528270108194 335733697184 319508165751817731361789

2037222004 62320225025710195997579524 0224 4 4 7773214 620837600834 855387730627390209188683525101963976707840 18503278393034 56164 014 187654 569380004 16667218785983018332440 97804 306684 13708789

9778060970875131224 537331792104 77653219632269292062440 4 4 1186024 0382393958269384 87694 3864 79921582750767801607506536356019240 781632884 89

50673931704 750819664 6271951189

6879259504 8559814 225373534 9188202252232254 527064 0311004 505864 934
0196268324 399675027094 197725799996211263154 981806629354 0715583610274
9719065184 274 06565937254 512574 74 213565274 06125514 208736831953589
1534 018300564 37614 755600059018875594 324 89
98734 2354 4 1853629889
7724 64 14 29112985184 9531060905307036852909517 4 74 704 662175927821270284 4
2720276324 22188650036282932734 4 812778190824 737197178733122826247
5293390331056612313694 37672159701905627862510231 4 96508385051784 954 74
625792863354 84 6764 7505619389
5604 8712724 76315354 2713060257324 619707305889
14 4 99576286610805194 0160877383993594 759687934 206306164 9761016289
384 74 378762708398093652868 9
093624 1353974 2230974 04 4 012337734 52835062258300768194 95350573727124
72914 63024 2934 20118205594 2858754 0967299824 774 332995253289
3889
1028826238500291868606622306007695 4 14 534 4 014 154 3780274 354 65277981124
805950108815688653909581055179251789
26168594 761989
0185128854 85330019719136580509 34 30865137339156714 4 2531069334
558535936906805731112135220901 4 89
84 3226163964 32630776114 024 95957275755180179589
4 194 01319774 5734 2289
223309973919624 54 23781531637399205324 7664 5534 8061014
36730683257957605166 74 364 736620234 6212054 8832579620677794 6589
61534 6666284 96225125599883736635615 4 57380994 23982234
139778573181185266 94 5092193334 00278395660522190 4 34 3907952187695286295362583 4
5114 2883374 18801389
7668334 834 51992354 3727595099724 884 754 998534 82128754 16021214 200071674
25273228186584 713024 374 0380124 7212757715517354 380686932178170984 69304
7721386934 36239351851772094 380919024 767919123501634 1974 98300194 34 92514
3922732839989
5275284 54 30980061397557007914 1708167825793398258034 505303504
3559971630184 552816829264 227963795173998262569721393103 4
888695236503388767235 34 591792138831157879766 24 4 04 4 4 58568626611876186607785 4 4
234 578255621751391515121750699702826712 14 823537616753390299724 794 38694 00984
39803372392608257591 4 97122524 96999091625168224 18830277064
8315381122368712756122608584 023252177282389
919754 616966871004 68066683951394 054 683014 7066324 3728097173308526175004
054 0584 63579964 387130602504 665324 50985137113504 784 06669674 081206228084 9524
70827367784 89
6750668680665695204 6159359064 03278260228102365520837977 74
90999881339305724 9306686654 3878693836289
4 312535175161385304 765696084 834 2689
216379531764 4 54 189
16273051752216789

720804 110223722838862096566304 3269375053812605807435715564 4
2520301536065982737244 63194 20027263684 0007290391352321609780682089
8002503971154 135638074 184 3338384 3775594 56889
934 32757328763589
953934 333013215225900120838600512520109318668826735672604
99879953512265864 60768784 54 4 884 1833834 1366254 221969714 6325189
2117282500974 121983889
4 379964 774 24 61118287564 9274 0080109580681071631909055544 06637684 19924
830303824 4 53861204 7639180787774 784 09553293677312666506230463491542094
5503013186992838587040497769498762308681601198225060378407782933137148693195576904 124 809600289
4 2859014 71563003599521187511349609284 6464 38827763668164 4 4 290872354
236562624 184 913110970711588110759956848824 186276594 29311553264
3553365781078624 93660680973525672832824 38804 714 95336516304 4 632204
1993562377636592354 694 9824 8612224 04 3693305064 4 54 708669838194
5613271731670628721129223308827822876856611293670404
31097366815821566525309531927357606575536633813081141261504 18274 25919791584
68609756617111553592650472452899
01397973074 8365684 566763766075030008038868274 4
809256019525018228778677511683518513900923990735105970327066961915407328728911684 66075052090920060714 564 6383935659156554 26687110625860799966340457758882769823034 74 4 99177127874 16589
2377979611704 4 3306654 99088194 9703719928121853092042455010101872809707443290433948270288632007292968230071606130096726729562697918386254 19239274660390007121099734 9610532335584 72567594 15833536503897888361222771610209908180784 994 235623092109652020074968190970233682046479621093852321055876215088656767684 8354 321163469821573876550837832037338143199007420263497842810116849
5754 0102189
754 507098326654 276214 69333908039904 675311152024 150248320056656158063597923618193230076288272946688783790788539740489
695339314 70031131324 4 93093227705326130028850543429077890063403191002285599374 1995905453419829483886576419108382166429914 6114191054 104 072171837577155061513515392771400877552001228409781872581662708931273964 54 64 7725980889
4 904 63874 4 4 12033834 03984 7054 74 8264 84 34 2166015060409787038719760453329681594 5603974 179277038661169175403060560427594 749273731758060875311296607988071723021883091816310355469967899967681411322384 0584 8721504 5110977754 13092733480856139943138919564 591791374 6129612274 3264 90289
4 505828696018397663266768184 8636729784 4 29610824575327353237855810127991695760753661632844 57154 796775700222592039479012456471885952733235380132049867071615509158782889567274 6134 396154 959024 81052675789916395615629228002473414 72909294 5654 24 14 4 2384 27975134 894 573060583395554 662066270210014 1027670794 584 3521164 89

088168624 369796568234 197708223331301580282187684 11671028519113734
96255504 4 15650032201321878072083632156727583289

4 1194 2930094 2017627734 31074 93222163016969037110211196817814
5961129850803567824 71755722595233764 64 04 0239924 4 994 117133227064 814 0922089

03934 06774 16590793358224 796176127195757906232160753334 804 4 2592524
721663765328124 9173787913554 54 53182838865387075 64 7639734 081624 4 4 987933614
3123185696534 013864 4 220930574 391287276338158138712550673 71224
28830099858186321015635 34 94 022783105631170331076712 4 9904 0051320012934 89

702721309952154 9239150785904 214 02689

313004 60986561523614 0525303927254 31314 0978670372367159813508704 14 4 4
155684 74 0934 24 28580682669188705870133 14 64 6320508191505624 84 76004 4
35207080754 08782114 94 94 6211509279233564 167673683350164 2284
2786529339283279284 53321515289

204 094 30120008170861858 4 107504 4 157621681026060833568283697384
3197136510829362124 680025797679911553999076 4 84 03804 9928171803756534 59518384
59509934 0093392603110508797537 64 13354 9052939570876599134 289

9729770181614 294 76080132837284 3715905906287968664 004 70614 91784 659514
338089

79790174 722888221305314 1514 5267504 796951734 362334 7261533030009304 974
26565394 5794 74 74 07885636678194 70875812034 604
8621221197326839850319839880675123556072123 14 224 83976820693357970254 54 114
2678568828685762181 4 6166824 6755029523775266 14 089

4 92621794 10234 21516354 117757026907294 4 307695709089

6064 4 14 96588167174 2121668318114 96370914 4 77913934 0867791720363604
7183375907382009969094 50123084 4 0297824 31989

83074 299124 74 75096595054 024 321134 6298334 4 1563938684 666384 511304
17168804 68008283501799096954 4 5574 2858132774 4 03014
0033636837871236116275322391852009315108695 4 7854 04 06038514 2967533705 14 4
922858168231754 675785993324 89

704 33194 74 8116313656876224 4 20921196163984 78074 939906325506586104 7264
994 627857091184 82930764 005230239571694 04 530229774 84 337534 4 96934 79104 278804
64 9755091689

284 8110273355938094 4 04 6934 89

5784 8319661916191568767866 4 74 4 209176769614 60159614 3007118763711598184
357094 87634 197399138085628617818195168335660513197809 4 53225854 26552516534
052564 189

83604 191809877564 754 700933354 564 6386374 588183707193089

927774 74 77765194 00712100160212924 2904 2884 377518855696937984 1374 619594
878664 04 952885179702994 4 034 1709225712698364 34 779234 20004 4 5089

724 019564 277684 3574 0004 691806885788296382555685769552 4 334
8105923536963237766 54 12136136594 16589

64 89

360126908303912189

07966934 6387826994 625689

89

4 32384 2694 79001954 4 91764 907992596728333201502O4 0550563958228832298654
21520127390385712551158338g

4 6014 7882679613070593684 4 62714 07317663585074 877351536087854 7105994
508157375O3768721757586689

74 763714 204 508585934 7552037159289

4 14 4 90384 555188824 778224 88860567681794 84 4 885054 24 8271176560204
1275625108169873O294 789

91692904 17780732082O294 539123872885057804 711502794 34
06781972O679870667734 689

9175968570170964 2214 9884 386213172333014 0364 84
0906229633661397312O51267854 80197514 010687614 9786782238295155301A 4 7754 3880094
20919581119084 559317284 191284 4 754 24 593024 04 34 4 15604 684
9603652232207039181979S4 73902374 792889

4 3062875587989

5504 34 63327292294 2658198189

9384 964 3390390174 859190074 54 985194 324 3774 6889

7151635061784 04 4 76581726383698089

7975093316086670902736290679673652827703154 63201164 237555377992984 74 64
0332327398535516109777781O752126229689

4 98605135171656024 102871037724 1294 082780755589

199253507584 97154 770214 90914 68336554 3223108654 74
87771386228875760810079271785S9

79025987591886351963060A 5666633363192174 0794 4 530334 5927730124 04 904
323289

1698863107254 90859039501306666592730117026037662981068329188801S4 00774
0068222930213859576A 54 235684 1724 364 975303391034 24 75954 66797769708002737594
3580064 71524 8683506681994 6207850017810354 2812825835286534
03952123279660353632A 0822318089

8254 4 77105204 7503704 252264 79722869915914 5224 300070833200074
2959773227257950376529937676872O2659189

314 66788798396187665084 089

72120716214 70805053296553068382337586A 7809970173621775251826622594 4 889

75554 79107900294 3280737776954 1203788819385753362A
5355575553862151372157904 8564 5195524 78272383904 39225555860854 598378324 204 224
89

9605866221584 236888878281887503287720578A 097787089

910123979622359281304 154 2814 62067094 6907294 304 4 276373570795194 63824
06385353975389

32514 553204 0398658131876665067180128552092902813884 64 94 4 991314 89

6215110965735382736711O5194 612560704 8321120628812596874 9690533254
6516609855153284 70502072184 4 89

79151303859961827075525350830g4 178815330737133334 8324 7287774
7905181060994 0065062184 6957914 1609025863337653702695O3363251590124
0061077265518504 08574 3720504 0286964 19034 5060154 34 14 825874 8213594 89

668051697162204 1292189

0901365194 26616334 91015177709354 1878234 11594 4 34 25730184 584 604 79674 97734 11239673674 6076937584 906354 29993974 54 53007174 30914 9674 014 52185883758079084 1009395282512399394 1887800098000852983250117971 5524 6966298052393594 2605334 2566834 84 171065964 689

96024 06759318187300760771656964 600274 9184 784 539283759773956101054 3622972283307967124 27595819133817907834 096214 082773026094 5983024 1168133924 254 021024

Chapter Eighty-six

790829584 2719227209123104 9877774 36008228204 04 793982383576317324 4 317194 831569713300108285 2534 01780917584 652294 174 735919734 93722187334 865037756637694 54 51734 80584 1274 192964 806237884 74 69600323632964 56071875008561994 006290196361814 3276961079101024

Chapter Eighty-seven

84 774 4 994 81774 73036975189
922813557693575014 4 684 54 703817964 35604 19274 82029664 114 84 264 7553884 61609284 317366732609511714 14 5514 664 20877593721160664 005713187183194 037824 93035660264 2114 5554 65509638156171759883263066 06354 15029101213817574 07054 6034 7589
4 377765734 334 74 4 3313614 5706954 9958552068159687192079 55264 670235032289
3258869265521158374 04 571767926978698309 36584 4 1605217539839796914 164 69213052887124 734 82152684 04 863354 4 16036667164 54 5205728789
206539039689
6570098833039278 2283124 6398832259368184 889
7300762029501913922174 69639190081298224 4 757810301784 07124 13711813334 74 2069153806373196 34 2037227001353128231561282092730787333606573188224 330352677536168514 4 01284 814 21604 69279280062614 904 237264 752955289
8067238689
801124 6352617089
2236094 19514 2983185054 9387764 220559839784 2354 96068384 30804 4 4 6309187389
82811032326174 94 24 9024 5929687054 29095989
32771886727881814 90220518594 24 964 97864 372201915084 5872524 151377330865901634 37389
9036909618394 184 6604 804 764 1285774 8573396024 328884 8561594 8165391309950784 32615276124 274 37304 198132191310971382332353652196256565684 1321009977934 65867125309809163123694 54 565524 086709902579573737869073570795762333 04 15204 5776015138834 5584 74 1962374 792667316394 317081104 61614 928063588389
189
301292776504 3664 289

22229524 865961964 74 250156393651304 5554 22184 13698115505602264 569224
26884 4 27092190824 91387974 604 6884 262153522232159695297204 600356284 4 80180514
30923514 64 9064 83155814 70733739099094 033063516284 76364 524 307039902289
0691032269063357760364 86055194 09027826803159378088265928386788589
283339814 4 3121074 324 210574 4 4 07797255304 87580754 382718089
73816058294 605104 8302938386321204 4 0632379853101812009680 04 784 01312104
19317231158801989
4 1289
995094 4 905182352028550174 784 54 7276205986369707009621505367367 8007104
01866180814 13859627807691530330859735979222 74 2977968064 4 323689
3084 382221616134 4 50290924 4 4 4 24 134 2868204 5989
23914 4 1005864 94 8555982060284 92271624 7787026995589
74 22814 27014 3672583620201 9104 6924 1114 324
81136567823885316616782305910130295 77237394 94 2182206285322925329662810562789
4 29374 661505175320710232 54 0395606954 2024 998214 3153977132554
3297586855252724 801325259204 96236391864 2824 02295056529171734 982073877274 864
534 74 4 99266638334 680804 7284 310211378092719503669398370 8889
8079287353281533984 74 26064 50074 08084 4 3294 502104
8660235279258531331296531 3224 53687733089
54 16706614 83631106827794 19010528654 4 3855254 758821389
4 30878387554 6974 389
26764 54 96621380722884 25723934 50520834 54 215664 4
577393590327231975817176591609 14 99223005364 7772838127334 16662253384 14 7224
262994 24 11924 6224 0097854 4 7297982912784 4 03926399816969824 9831998810282024
020189
4 96060671263656610074 69397089
2064 689
4 0335704 9238092701070510535093856 11794 27302169798825354 1628015272720389
7968351604 23690238188359887 2104
0292019071056087510016790371111051793917137 54 662368383254 14 4
7178593865302970564 62626094 8159605973111282072557182811133 24 6076104 21774
775964 54 839111797136188734 74 87868253984 586689
74 921061770350321736670657082169855598660531 5272702364
2929621060332762951293 4 92175214 2974 8836174 989
730538729795231771376516956560760094 1025720965264 136722804 7189
0194 84 5365773052324 7184 5768564 34 531334 1809126025754 01390394
1163886109277630735614 77104 298203714 85588099882807701182076886 04 3581805556974
289
5134 93920850270360998529136566724 20004 0934 0681562664 80004
7750369267010067187565 4 983026784 0394 97790284 984 0804 112864 904 2737318787323574
9233515777926654 64 05875527019733174 1525534 36934 33358781774 394 76676986534
109034 24 1828856004 6824 4 271735589
195629962507979082737 4 56067765384 9024 22624 24 34 1394 4 4 10514
7668328626098116986962995732 9189

4 80313093836578772030544 0635688808739217336 4 316856301974 958824 077856564 691100584 4 8506322174 8560278698708254 4 9234 350094 624 2878114 24 792557092875881603713337 04 989

4 4 4 793554 1357861767774 2593003501994 8788189

354 64 57069989

8023884 28594 34 0235293957359036387799554 8580184 4 4 3559823169084 24 883535500656784 0024 86228853977905919021010083266 4 3914 04 23785834 714 1539211252119664 4 12719679850014 0377737816113954 694 556263934 396372291698397034 4 316180226380185350772 74 790383583877603813757838 64 7012136315206550285 04 3820926854 71604 804 94 4 6724 8770511152956399198 4 619660704 80199092254 38759193604 89

94 17764 24 323787824 51275097624 57528554 9009194 96634 3005632504 215824 7850394 386565734 703026506980027224 9653816227554 12581238300224 6685055927019280952766320805532391360 74 8859854 952576989

9507927614 07664 34 5764 64 290971818152704 084 34 116864 875195291524 2506986869720912197272764 16639989

4 80352938155720610365285 4 299804 227933990984 630926287867918884 4 74 5822818384 9154 13790257576173055737219 0989

1733580870609521181391392283701733 04 7688180850991710905 04 4 4 013024 907362722374 52998124 794 2216588118589

6380881296789

2860271735024 79061364 22666697096556330601017905052265 54 257504 4 2591979884 3096292810306578173 4 7163705682133316954 67538525704 12755704 07558625868324 96666639996077175071 4 24 54 24 34 76380734 9935092557265250192876 4 0864 9276184 9717304 589

762514 87164 885915989

51255375228222955357809275515771773 4 94 254 4 94 064 636532864 388734 334 2175307027972107888 4 3935784 0805194 7775698254 173932129280352819 04 328304 22660811527761503372809322221614 6272802255172759 4 02589

14 04 9567804 0276685368356006 4 8375121195655603792908 9

0174 9705688289

24 9537680005511704 4 514 70904 02764 770952661261789

1164 3527084 94 766333633037504 76266818134 93831684 69838603671786180757090384 09994 4 16681888508857156733750859 4 52381605828850594 971914 1157735194 69163826632910009363196937626265633997 14 388590830624 05002210685624 8393754 51664 5389

7795264 55014 54 384 89

9174 2196831219314 013729951184 10097509794 1992374 6884 0954 25013212364 7670753289

5687164 90593510289

684 4 4 31703315138814 84 84 4 754 2911565514 954 932398604 734 7014 30994 53095929657329964 069617905657189

15571395922522237799661633 4 92924 0926900212172351354 308093758013216123137754 51234 87290335614 60914 8164 2758104 9952002360871359854 964 801275969333726114 8782204 82714 1654 2861097287385314 98106973275369685591326889

3124 65886397377860527964 7314 5774 4 3870375512914 383631014 80880102554
975018505634 38374 23264 94 2884 038079814 325557800163924 992969085284 589
83639132925179370625 0150226681735964 657598594 1633224 4
15157573672662192304 256955666018622138261908801925812037238815 60077600385904 4
90388617664 212001571276624 4 0876305292839786002937708353109004 3918658812000874
3195074 10289
98065659379888701230973100697017955799260 4 73869636116078651598376 4
865016794 32859334 319628128655516084 5291905914 26779204 939904 1189
6788778786674 3039299757616764 6554 68134 24 73563258183134 1226626900374
8336985031872001174 603213572511554 875102276922014 334 4 4 1704 14 7593650389
20954 54 99769900214 2804 930356954 589
20060089
08812289
8084 8054 97614 64 2398124 170653574 54 304 376304 06316824 99554 3589
767797872906794 04 7694 8112679095135574 3782017524 164 67534
6132975800098129577909972707119039363809 4 97139562962587268238358 9
4 71854 1656384 732924 27586950984
276737772192332175276539686606177282371596570821130355810363815182791325694 4
6119309158813353194 2734 06654 2884 074 1599708194 924 029183884 9762574
8315339375254 66736508284 396554 011389
663016763904 630178354 753694 786523936554 79832094 34 6814 7633789
84 065784 724 5614 2075994 4 989
774 12875174 4 94 5814 534 657383789
9796025595862692807395026992775699077608 4 9202215589
74 34 6739263779175303666 4 3870530714 8525194 70220957089
28286369504 93585584 89
3209095586866702334 57554 319254 514 4 2518128800784 991514
185003301380182835829191679510151350632589
1573568794 87674 19183823306159137685922334 9833225083199955278 4 86255059084
8674 5504 69516024 20521525235667638266 4 320624 4 01134 624 6184 835538231919030789
7904 89
1564 92881675694 95129760602261851595750909 1 4 4 277224 6331356835722350994
1125528091622824 24 0694 11322325689
953200039030202196968217386130987969800721311638620390327297191995557705 9
189
4 6517770931086733 4 3597019086754 637507774 94 18164 2136624
58712283625713096904 252214 24 09274 14 4 4 4 286294 6764 11115733390260689
9283995914 20734 4 59182101298789
38271304 75037383316679578727390062834 881721234
32793167900780179277820576279 4 24 74 196395117775094 57395274 4 389
586335334 73679660705505270121 4 254 4 2994 790804 9134 64 4 73573810923689
307860356623664 6115074 4 1594 192307991226358053752635962 4 9358838854 994
5357860888234 9064 790166624 5572094 78823103870099917210865162700174 127764 789
314 3063607031726839611668179673599 74 0524 3721801206234 8194 04
6773515110115013575303935536135039838765 4 04 636303172924 04 004 4 3934 54
2228866504 37559521679638559904 74 14 8107366357622269326 4 33064 224 662251361964

755994 79394 4 751674 2830393884 9538786086663136566087608674 016868254 24
3859509309839000950824 74 14 61151827971514
792538782363231160391015979083705326761335653050108
255973694 78256693522289

8154 208014 4 66204 855019765323210218161662195303
 657184 128801650264 4
8317775303785757210757216727037351922224 0314 14
8705332812556025237909652855171060
 4 74 4 7911806731970710020686033
 909523369289
94 351734 6016999107184 50704 9095286957774 131794 1205305663931582598080094
54 1594 5684 74 0167337619934 4 4 64 4 1859524 84 585780679184 6718267214
57933027162864 84 233254 9702086814 74 069158570524 83014 2625134 9130131793189
7383824 5254 93171754 034 3510630594 4 15185851799332289
184 63985687661286780829821
 11290668500392562077
 769600566532
 34 85162514
854 282704 85614 233397106339613269314 0524 821184 02280208764 932824
600707929518671187707
 64 164 57364 5634 22226184 718124 284 38354 8826605654 1755904
98795369362959566
 97254 1183719335697984 69939982669708232831209910934 1255994
80819873220386864 574 9761500731501308035
 0504 06734 0560123257097874
696291882994 64 9670095532299328883162376227702
 4 6084 16178629584
18100330595177229060066089
5813030583131395588588
 82762259625175518394 264 9806312004
51271810019222194 9705766974 884 4 596592692997691620797266
 234 14 339698096085014
54 529911686784 527877225801508574 2859764 3180504 07162254 94 6512152689
50797614 098356924 3094 174 67654 518171956674 7204 4 4 984 2860326968037184
1082593827335584 974 386855805135952284 55287596361386027589
8194 5310017076089
4 4 273324 74 68724 29589
1164 78218853620984 58294 6830304 075110083054 6676612131694 94 4
6563866233697314 90536304 8789
078832874 04 2072673383396925834 82813533324 62611966397276729576987
 4 4
03654 71360016591674 7714 238618199164 5306272289
8155773566229922661089
71779771500834 62794 64 4 09360584 3157320637834
76195170000165810602100928784 04 4 3568206520194 527028568264
3221760713581601752221973
 67223327780274 3989
4 359711559780381276278065260
6703857508556025560810516667781838263691621120275954
76357509273561033756517976994 657794 9596114 4 9116213116791600
 607234 2568134
822109174 704 1610254 084 24 839924 04 235096219691263681209164 34 90379266934 922254
63510174 034 10154 654 375283162070610539082122669353971
 14 4 670163871339195724
5620135139204 050918614 73232182936195189
12364 54 9208823904 97224 88287914 25729913397782224 781865210133914 14
3716010778081000716129662093680
 67263377030194 059184 785859655730889
364 5078579360008786286866338079763689
0280780619857010023224 4 772514 03933032211957205696718
 23880232186334
7761125994 354 864 9924 4 74 7516611783603166952637
 1604
360063566323871059279357921756871199982281111089
14 24 64 610154 655356596212704 209994 4 03197587351534 39833319560989

4 1730938654 74 54 6514 0999389

3976935539224 5864 3035887623157615625861587462872818781337112351345878837855804 21697764 398525992789

04 99624 290653889

6215821222189

78878116258382965907363248496977987612007130681883372519003703774 0348722504 29734 9609934 76607284 864 000163199296066954 370714 27118319214 09924 4 23946958256654 2054 1914 51204 553614 2364 884 14 816026053774 86614 9864

110283759516290999622091232981921678339239642561390727753657077363937251198229736967869246 89

15137165264 86975965134 4 35767122826858375314 4 01262804 184 04 62286935889

735824 637378784 84 4 74 8164 12107338167587775922822307915498221080479590434 83193387634 330733994 9925194 24 3372136321191536581087255275493903497011795310565274 3688889

4 4 0854 74 6664 7272707809098080469973094 052028161295824 4606562916550769680235614 51397859995356144 9185685794 96089

90228154 0993189

62273521074 75824 4 856724 5261951004 8267256152701723009343943029068805301926455353042977099978289

1887127297756731225080121569089

89

2104 6206103032654 195355883084 34 6331184 2324 32667935024 6989

4 0574 739104 932355738728624 978680751444 04 9873814 343511838525582585965084 861976534 83051655774 65354 84 925184 70623584 63611289

612310634 756134 878291962080802902154 1889

56716954 705784 1263606512805097004 4 86533945692126761074 64 89

0218260151360021764 04 2075934 304 25154 960471216560638269072668810603281420474 1220088866734 94 151799724 64 4 4 314 87852302819566773009243452527803547237133249811211144 7527196051728526390932400074 1008504 1013534 9534 0437750708682692909589

64 5056777697550518169976544 774 24 9074 987137689

708054 2223103073699862144 21344 4 9704 80833388629036192462099417006595275523499456084 08883527711995125644 1178874 877554 26906953789

0166583717050597606881779084 91161857021874 6070392004 11210127386634 2584584 512364 59384 88104 904 9889

17124 6857392696221806481134 1034 7799910285334 504 3363529355994 69991079748386073093832224 1856554 36504 9764 94 583857095754 7589

24 18107954 937764 31689

6260734 364 589

13015274 4 65652114 578614 155770992104 9334 37132765485502078197577561301902631627312439722426744 14 6601694 04 35362112664 76206689

5571814 714 997912220390593604 5317129530955540122855108112121026572969756546972317828275358932526338331110696576581556117359486795475944 24 1902955820124 4575090753733704 603536226154 97103954 4 31129334 07783239085701809046135796288485527163440269965063129190994 269695966225589

4 979756287212877571985 4 24 196734 753015874 634 7073305073784 579614 5354 54 252064 4 23087824 084 14 080784 62796736873887889

585204 4 709279081010712119877987278359 24 23393355755619371324 99795938760984 14 77989

8213818265034 3224 0130638574 54 4 8854 93589

70704 862514 278724 2965210065664 978707015683883864 5399590365080171114 364 104 266278696724 14 199832654 7334 111284 879330934 39580866789

0754 34 0702026793784 774 34 5535265665129290134 337234 6289

78010782011552218872393731201609370970 4 068632553677092619190039 89

4 1884 114 5926153701166686589

56367315052216330 4 1077984 886772114 94 16004 66211065860524 8504 107954 794 83814 2514 04 99636824 970739689

4 14 4 24 6667174 873674 6316851704 56357754 24 231051505809864 764 64 17391062874 59904 737924 888107274 30814 2629524 89

09319854 9576289

8324 1719089

61998384 10018154 664 4 37808237533284 02254 4 1604 14 89

59931908730084 724 7285574 88183769758189

534 793908801984 5806289

4 2112361133354 63254 004 04 66535717316673238652078 4 503080166195770809027132 4 1189

1654 62019807089

554 60918723854 3726113874 966299766658252314 714 81880032379500380667011859 89

4 2195994 82184 04 89

22604 58854 87688802337594 014 21579154 2952871235682271939 4 16595000624 3911835934 2678164 04 8354 162384 967924 2080877099637573387339727138570051017216390102814 00619964 0295555510920514 8237278889

39586225063582005762355860 4 60670033354 514 8883088032069907961231 84 4 92379733390033115058829 4 838020687671024

Chapter Eighty-eight

09164 85958888394 4 324 65634 4 667574 633584 953224 14 1651880328254 882089

91824 10294 068318220651171221056358109508052676082 4 3003755064 8338281503658350774 394 016308024 374 8097984 8295664 8727702134 17005589

11396621800935230 4 353954 888255902667090006571188533595233013070087619 04 28286557679076216907339 4 0856070615889

361930134 8780259524 99670315914 3624 4 219977851983004 37984 4 4 14 54 865516590828204 14 11393767318104 0877195965789

36089

0060092985718784 824 54 316218024 5386116837858586234 51078284 918216914 5864 3309724 767711314 95903082734 618524 789

2215957636176194 158034 13031319184 16077594 4 10121574 394 1774 5313000107950564 4 22525109306737523223688 54 324

279121353055759262100311221186203829750275381784 254 1731173375517119681654
09284 367663014 0284 33123610329234 523189

18370223034 4 4 54 974 14 18863973986508372860686169 362513165598064 294 04
15960955828152794 74 4 89

4 0796006704 0156066354 23305660888224 10924 622558187358804 2827934 69664
206274 1124 597521522027613182620967360927370634 186306804 2962094 80151901121564
6323354 61994 9604 974 0834 4 4 354 5314 211500672682516687795066725 18216964
86833308233724 4 5854 924 12921673190981802291517170276395390765960 501594 5874
59760737822363718204 911724 903037217284 75214 768189

38282858524 18664 014 070914
099177883713956921617076979010060192305266297 2195100992184 012322062914 00604
82178194 90156194 790264 663131287502908324 4 4 8371554 6624 84 94 03861524
8535327366354 8381024

Chapter Eighty-nine

00072695037536724 813331564 958131952983295824 89
4 56994 70154 0983863588375105274 4 5038754 2374 16350534 54 84
39059129801016033702 0650914 19654 4 064 089
30992874 56350361224 91584 86023751328733731306177764 38334 9114 167974
2795635358264 3265650934 389
74 3876971254 04 89
09954 3976103094 4 70122301704 959677916134 54 6024 09207214 94 64 97104 4 874
80382550964 75579233784 085015704 69654 09260993752929750657563 4 54 7864
017818208689
976035501204 605289
8752372284 096564 154 0104 304 874 66276071995929003518139082264
6562780069174 99381889
7575504 124 552628118769537357505250127280159222927782677371 94
6137192165164 00180711103260665 65764 57256839904 111265510326989
84 7762004 94 5257320763366118794 66854 68075655577881616833650598 04
79975289
3885934 4 621827274 827697573534 81167038511000881206002684 51219316134
9872922797354 3514 525162066264 4 675504 35130099588759986591 4 34
87330276057832738601081960325678335362521398537214 632713714 373366852594 289
784 0927984 77878664 74 664 4 957883589
66808204 514 77672719070312628807710771780875 4 65928794 9105828127513178
5119390219204 36217399927104 174 8174 73553005514 968071374 6137668261024

Chapter Nintety

582297889
026864 07062087169184 0805906684 02107117975507316360971232104
29979833192165994 64 1187673904 73835823972710206691386867582234 07683714
025128786024 336013754 56956121012111866856952757609838762 20131806009730015109

87704 1864 75014 6034 719095600164 4 59132581601108870034 24 09510860065966824
661861370034 04 54 03056501560321089
61119564 32794 011332320624 4 12968527189
73390029304 3875268264 13252372811818734 18377266831707982236681984
92551731114 04 84 2922636004 972983664 64 7174 703203589
2511190314 55263782036974 8273764 4 4 74 6579634 7034 362774 52109556074
92099970685966310831881197052 6754 076084 1852099074 5264 1268309014 34 76734
29855065555504 95836710687190384 924 4 38850171624 189
5924 1597064 389
551791976124 8010511832662108395180919193168 64 715007622854 9154 6332100294
9231384 34 804 0570977701398274 4 51934 839221971306082370165 4 63372568013935034
810121226605114 976878294 628586232064 34 74 12112626633527821577 4 7324 524 83124
1354 286604 4 14 019190563714 4 561933616734 099663782714 960097805768754 169534 4 54
4 05994 793961814 89
14 94 772883934 4 4 9386237854 4 57107150266682904 9614 037984 9969979904
177314 534 98520525154 6802967974 6264 819668702286164 231214 7762924 124
29658312763661501321599568755630321383 4 9578504 1950236693928204 4 083814
9111506865684 280960304 4 85296973825380024 172676987094 58055882387667508804
6999123811364 64 98178032327138862753999814 3064 74 6124 04 7754
171778696333861396561788596 4 831756351902365389
4 2860987981324 3105964 10750202204 906039359870915954 7794 213809864
179132509391514 30229182359194 5291150294 34 4 93134 12362151981821583120320294
8600394 027669012663220706625706516 54 6005274 75224 010199238734
690299750611631661928185097677922609310051354 4 564 9361164 5965660284 911284
5526224 785726874 70611594 6260327304 92603873190984
27270223022793637175671192685836 4 7185781515513352034 020094 25573257024 135674
9792983260661689
2374 77237909231564 4 83699398221906223959835129277 4 874 04 921884 86514
8618006764 68364 74 76634 904 354 68522704 4 181503294 734 6688059802599704 514
7190867269754 209092714 63724 79398724 29080014 6596030612664 4 16602228604
05072133181508294 6098885070980566227981 54 9989
27924 314 0532399034 861738080214 9334 102633155051103722338875 14 816204
39881629614 4 99371184 14 730654 39725635803732060537 4 19376715721551625202628791 24
34 751769566274 504 05183387160885984 3704 64 67204 9769257186263068174 61111789
65071273389
4 134 31264 004 219002284 26884 63221924 96026992853768096158 9
3194 89
02304 2583390128608529021358552535228729369277257311 24 8398058709622089
30684 664 6263634 164 74 31789
8670004 74 06156685763785710758 4 274 94 74 2964 85796676254 876979594 10694 4
9268116576569257910637391280917 4 332934 2766008234 74 4 512264 681724 4 79134 54
11283289
74 4 575514 650786956589
9052824 66534 99093871511116967951536 4 328261511982789
866889

710931016959104 1784 5024 882873523192384 4 8624 2263629734 9757684
39282263112020004 713218720170178371097575668553713938 24 75853381189
8056805524 5617589
253290124 104 4 606138626252972014 4 9551884 5924
861076157532019523792106931822 4 655177285864 226604 77869383984 4 215191391884 94
771204 0124 803222614 6171138594 79756568591174 574 724 4 4 18275564
3667550318617371053128 4 06159154 882124 9719371730212674 392008204 111754 9854
68363984 1356774 608838167338674 171004 703304 512237269963296753350355568 374
255932788505284 84 397099534 15176590329384 0285069219964 26091089
90684 290371284 52934 54 94 907934 984 037039501594 365634 4 6313995129824
581333531389
64 8303954 68537774 23867582387995950731279166633912135762293008238 1374
99508804 24 14 36770634 1186794 579020222525197702359954 4 884 292304 6328754 9234
9672208730074 2261853262394 4 1584 6865082615318656057785769972925335518074 4 04
638289
7304 361213124 874 1664 9557732058303198526 4 92284 00338212296198294
00035721889
6092227607689
2173732137561281714 012789
4 7680860184 61734 7613358304 779955557011084 6589
9184 65264 7160290624 3268230972137919999502600200767792 84 281280102189
04 655036864 4 94 068516374 694 74 0097967052287174 665334 6534
766832852993058391752919256 84 2294 6133303350299266 14 74 9035530997059294 4
3017566334 3834 322304 4 154 34 37034 764 664 04 927395026581091264 8824 1517806384
95584 73212925984 863914 337804 0535637602806068612781688 89
21524 83564 54 361916584 5905112065370194 4 84 7924 254 6205587901558333354
3255865910183915327556 34 325304 791374 07024 6658885855173264 15578510827116214
09191150201876161758170251311700794 4 14 08634 86314 83190552961554 1131867774
760309553999986080793 84 374 9762273037037169 74
916229200218300013533918129991829604 02359294 816224 0375734 9964 789
8156526226824 69224 6618226600334 65631554 4 4 0691909194 4 6133592294 764
7617530984 014 4 56964 94 9854 17874 17212313607795570 04 623157574 070164 761282734
096389
79769774 019876160194 15760152910910925312276183834 78679518524
19370607979165590705751518051295 4 28310185359173186365292029130 84 205780739267574
11563134 564 106004 814 85906597772775589
23397304 7601761186109 4 66683938317051367676598060864 54 653275384 4
17193324 8210350034 614 3870064 2574 99982174 25218212189
204 24 69834 59694 601714 54 108096717354 784 790289
64 90057093695658507360279962669616 84 64 31118237198194 9954 01755550793724
878019693376504 5134 74 1237023278581717052728754 0676808677865733191918065 4 14
65070234 69304 107602604 380764 983984 1877624 33538838135818313963322978304
51927354 2000124 4 34 77014 3914 1020280583513761524 86834 654 009224 14 8555589
073720292194 6094 96783093804 7252254 27153971564 4 6139320717562051057 4 794
73825563034 04 4 9984 09055189
312252581517064 4 69135994 54 94 10789

766052839379950219126026120 4 7720514 588368772774 20393934 9274 66174
231696612724 4 88814 202863914 202278124 1935332974 21694 5094 67954
520673956977382806280091534 195572092962087021781623595731539858 04 94 0599130964
59784 3674 6168803327624 71313321871636394 67180936674 734 4 033575552621977254 84 4
2024 99963393174 8616681168580024 16101935718158763913937159153107634 2504 3384
06774 911006239888597954 61135553975583965305392 4 2511338515197295715072567194
9315914 4 54 388674 8094 1270092974 25772211701976780777554 115314 64 4 4 1588881354
64 04 610034 36754 633954 38136573794 17552022983704 63378124 04 527631159587874
29154 14 204 16206624 89

1261623850077703928634 84 72623334 35064 4 174 6226554 8889
64 3289

6084 7169212331084 4 6333350533714 71733303319017211530774 8181597531874
03206520654 666303834 024 724 04 4 364 1929585156620772019573193519 4
88591629815330055105279952 54 001092334 656798597064 54 0514 291065710504 3026284
793759359388054 120084 6812071657259589

6827794 362993111922904 62874 989

338151616124 180754 18388765972717000319388 9

6653365652735965704 729837055565100268027923851679503365206653091784 354
6800532221181178 4 568324 368004 4 3266590254 628594 599103854 7579652091234 389

5032510595830284 514 50194 530989

232771984 89

28078784 554 674 964 3627564 6169662618364 866620367155784
9813839868252876195638573608520 4 19332025764 1086585308207834 60937354 2674 4 174
58791798165097760674 8034 2358794 37881661119989

595666794 4 64 8382154 771584 4 522357513096308613259832304 4 5664
681920972502934 4 9035786589

88884 0520552887864 0659389

827094 1098662152737161752 4 4 92691264 72228562674 4 31790670660513250331 4
572067834 4 04 6379514 260173334 959206264 618127328737794
00130153571573662376126852832110391120166194 8115587795504 0394 08651223604 194
97579357189

7974 08115563734 672074 274 24 15773774 04 4 4 10912384 855584 51967364 83504
88868309931389

8234 4 2124 854 956202339198190060354 89

851804 4 067135803314 08724 13265815580856335529235650556 24 34
0622173863587100591091666902011060085192106206152172988 9

870836133794 5882584 1989

2972813593784 63864 0814 62097321574 88764 5854 54 5290564 856934 76254 09289
910669192256024 64 254 52910014 9820094 514 7538869058507821574 990164
2383258266123330308 4 2360171331330197 4 0264 36592810516974 6006112974 134 9954
36114 1507789

0155231616362758211607 34 5219385511127230089

60033993710873634 0084 74 4 58582811692917284 014
715929271271973822535539639876 4 5924 73836932611280374 2994 01387580817617506936 04
7380882591607654 996602854 94 15839794 291304 4 1789

374 134 98128512994 33175675824 4 076734 176951024

Chapter Nintety-one

24 4 331173208054 1981225031554 764 8257870165086576670230978527121 34 326096082828084 72227355161279802 1794 324 86389

89

060292519154 4 80885294 4 924 9132385753214 89

64 1284 4 56505833651534 398394 3537063223690868184 74 89

1634 082930268567197857966 04 1601215228834 09864 4 950300613637984 75278879019534 1774 34 84 4 4 67274 8004 3634 82761808233991 6100874 0511223516596774 4 51783081921670275125 14 354 94 69966872668737082784 91919916820259037114 776598260684 64 2971682887151964 8270565793794 566304 84 99534 2582827100202874 57514 253134 87886988808012391 8252754 74 8629359202579750028182 1975100994 629178378511034 66716091576507689

4 24 05764 34 882324 54 1062551714 557685235574 08154 55232660177674 32094 7901564 52054 6687532565105 2514 79763201112266026752 4 833213955089

93126832634 930136851924 284 03094 2602387905323204 787679384 8815781799120758839989

511824 2016254 924 3993752925029268338089

12965124 7232814 9902698230237888614 4 353189

87992150720017872694 7659321610518524 0507686364 89

12351751671937073774 21624 358856294 0623594 7704 3120052660625697625096 84 217812114 8882988002661604 4 059222329331624 17612290874 3379022287804 56170135772375061952160 34 2686280629053786 4 9688713933857125624 16964 079324 4 758313698859182729992757829 4 9295751304 82504 36660285323714 02054 964 4 7338073824 57755582570927007591535821362 24 8787395198064 4 7536509228338732197378 9

4 50989

4 8812224 31666501069873961667298 9

920964 4 20596817569619231839866191793 4 084 74 257868154 61594 14 589

3864 0602296132950038120038389

7674 502086338557826679881065690369990815678277851637829 34 59936194 33669806529792215221536662888399 4 026803862183878 4 1389

54 997920072289

371169507757061724 00234 4 87289

8683808889

4 6932582186337823 4 356912074 0289

56871885668709606127386219 34 9873263224 096065960699176020054 53603816589 660214 387177128755309837099020713308 4 712303917975574 4 8381005068328095 1189

329272191231654 94 090664 0214 568359874 4 63216265557539792837308702860612939772368385814 9199392584 1574 254 914 6335154 8204 14 1285052561164 14 384 7386215794 85025909591694 01670192222715205 15924 4 6384 78673684 4 034 10197602254 8505859620374 52021034 0195867216081712701926 4 60704 607599928713121074 8035118825068233530 4 4 9698126552095670808 84 54 194 1022535199131368352911597222819779651917510914 12574 90667527198799284 399037274

1064 5886716981183509101205683498176773100954 84 699100664 21703751012964
0279526680792620134 64 908265708373127308877034 985381688301804 15910735087802789
7814 4 4 5251654 077081274 884 7379655033182989

36026105151709009201102220710016694 7994 86064 9884 160992557782103329254
222023824 3161693794 5524 4 50771166127819572028 9

94 90592371787630713791620773280519004 359506302783720524
286071686319756831994 4 95359654 617582379331954 92218355714 06382172621701189
90624 3630164 6834 987994 3067324 89

74 84 02990062675636866393 4 4 986687029574 63295592763582274 173904 7673664
683270987254 00825658274 0793730134 2125015787224 69359336023202788021334 4 754
71169254 724 4 2788234 7885720204 784 810966824 95732594 650693818393289

94 4 08562932954 84 5234 6954 7324 70720957681550003136286818305873597665524
4 56292333709800392024 4 65397081980880975167759000 8294 52339338253873797516636684
84 8199061917189

23053029327528205228 87389

977798577574 64 4 330667384 284 66834 23819777822394 1515224 36389

874 24 9517010656678530267666 4 370854 624 0614
50751098238265082329219231169 4 6593605521624 3701274 3002394 924 600084 64 4
19137134 53739088171054 3297199625921785958 3689

002275354 6934 4 19927056354 4 994 4 64 64 84 635692114 73954 54 234
209303509561912596294 2760332314 028381564 19581239921684 35705926115521864
367293908114 04 9884 29954 01350304 5826166856151191924 704 24 806777874 8838713189
87189

6738261924 73974 9089

221696564 89

98157671704 289

0174 4 96662059680086819909195664
839871279960006066009833665085013172670506678073810536253324 04 361561098011084
767554 94 8774 94 2365851637194 652793284 979905770184 5104 90917015335686136324 4
389

4 879659034 36759034 9560021664 265581524 4 4 39282787227173594 594 830789
3872024 84 734 2032229005213360684 6053129294 0974 9759889
320134 90501554 66399788069991700873715889
17595677689
4 72706181150301964 7289
132576784 8161909193884 5977305288817391379634 1910139122828818689
5766691581750664 0190664 25759118576388754 82934 362992117191271054
9773853730155778381018 84 4 4 18606578305924 104 52724 31966922764 394
6881902302936603689
392914 352790067834 54 920522889
61178860518754 083104 918089
17759260962571182883270864 3634 672781816274 7255714 850253575093560194 4
533705704 297279316518324 369707363874 85609272821695707559352179828293176304
0398854 389

50572501794 65534 119664 384 06118328171225805809313865366901632 34 15504
2355394 880397710071250704 105678774 1620258599084 007176820989

4 14 4 8674 622992276289
2025508580816217315083 89
7553884 0534 94 27919056734 4 876604 830970791086659225293 10175974
78538255714 7194 64 52962908784 519565174 09594 789
4 396337685688784 1336334 07353907274 3766372205280224 4 59160534 573754
0661837169580524 2171800321860228583753225978883501 8804 23178875689
4 02319751974 374 4 4 6133525974 5789
74 00554 6624 4 24 324 975934 4 04 953762682364 01505734
72695398011010025658251311957538 9
1584 9382125129679967725362127 64 60763910672269184 4 111059166671823174
812066194 77228053502579386189
871073293114 319621955835900757325 4 54 92654 4 0534 4 8587623799704
86963982129062304 65260237154 56974 6398218504 024 0616064 721224 738628536914 54
22758281589
303257867192003815231307030123 14 50016203835585597084
6362887285686618295880381514 12597924 2712228006580721753759956097530281681324
319088267581121397864 589
7799156707712334 1300614 050720737874 7754 2271334 7772318791387780604
1160283389
280732294 629861094 389
94 804 26877630904 13828200824 932764 3784 4 5694
6668559691350972809296560296837 84 24 83190637664 89
7589
4 022974 7652337370707590295732296764 1074 4 4 77902854 22057108331864
16062834 83284 0393767133814 8094 15308100383634 62098674 092314 162577259260164 24
13107683838536096774 39389
64 5388121987184 7087835760284 6575850066264 30131835637759834 394
232563195673889
217864 74 251153914 64 83061056176185226614 84 986211735299300394
196267978351154 324 719792100990235995010 18504 5226336213662954 17587904
11552911630059509298870937205111995320951919761191111785656856314 582374
252733634 874 4 2621789
4 3734 255594 4 38827210995525834 4 04 8078153363012318172504
76112098586213911950381276857684 2227060228808579228022789
92701354 502689
8289
812867084 694 808586907736873104 8824 13520925337799281517828072 24 7304
329560570662234 56189
96569294 079904 3010318005588385154
95600371015362883393296308388611 8375725134 4 292962374 36256902862399081 8089
6674 784 072154 164 8215364 66985251118356093769538838 24 7792682054
035562293103398234 61721774 992876114 31071126186981767165101021328174 84 32268604
9289
99621374 4 264 89
17874 708005217789

914 597936832576908254 4 704 995573654 60738332954 4 550376054 556169384
62993526955598254 814 36952274 513515963501284 4 38165762387821902834 4 7784 194 34
84 916754 3322089

8865725107216380125744 559205006261383235333100174
635632696788299795223122133592295598777144 784 2562152819660095824 8039796074
18806864 814 6222184 673502384 64 9962094 8290023721674 715130176161834 8664
85690095804 4 52712924 13610774 4 8550164 54 016588210094 6953185167094
9653202836855634 394 2755258676230939902626446 6880252100234
8398810810313959156722167521036440311682769802044 7084
6827510216007652912859618123289

23919989

8376154 654 0152884 764 02389

564 00800911170777168663258444 7151888652134 1810096309789

24 6814 2777674 4 4 24 90984 8194 62072099118606178378827256060277444 89

20250775654 9609224 15372184 89

819139994 9304 3561686936215964 291771095256950970699006323100610856444 85554
4 82317681694 9189

20335382593839797795520178060026150444 5384 6602234 80584 280668080054 0972724
24 88709889

91814 030172108374 0851971684 4 6555068686682595762131761853444 74 14 4 37764
09811689

74 620203712113186150318053444
81637099280510057939395818396053815727990531735644 6204 72564 67564 65733752324
9604 4 286662754 228334 1194 77101158614 822513290574 72336964 54
59350778630281397035026933558672025444 20653201911364 5684 2785222711304 993084 74
0155083205534 502207111518292503782444 584 1515954 23857290920559093155527093715730444
36507139197066270720836605065359257807538799662444 2782962602719086367858444 2034
261794 27292783872074 22703925864 789

969888520172854 373296389

14 1798564 954 98712313174 2107811174 584 7834 714
81011302200669188117139063322377444 63914 4 2787135013391013614 654 7582354
73132163877978594 229259092873266039806170514 5105189

35261384 63564 900758234 86329152025865510311034 13814 04
910157351617886075764 3964 618834 10175654 4 4 14 874 774
39695871259318206839292181116808835597127226537119526744 6391354 72889

0901025277774 299066816800531987062324 7556963164 794 1994 31877289

989

589

0737174 4 791382210691683031444 4 30210883271873693722363715982444
851127773765854 395220664 987630276981234 6134 5369762104 739754 84 4 3980664
9685515001824 28724 13962930020784 23904 07701717530874
0062110388698127516133110767104 2265609534 2065627964
803091959171222256860508660697444 91958719528511720186301444
57223111255958058030059590444 517801620915600339271581356193961524 5058294 094
23830675223104 876027568331931395370615944 0569008254 671634
0768851873806202839376444 94 14 1695224 789

764 4 8274 15924 39389
073858703368311064 74 829591656363194 0759787977389
368568253656567981194 05558294 689
075620974 8639705158628061604 9553801992987901072698852 64 068694 89
6100332327284 2034 061884 54 21289
794 32188689
70727382736277850137270114 963870884 664 07860794 26555525554 85664
82536726238855301957 0089
9094 4 1814 1196819278225214 74 36730237577264 790630213627009294
3519353752024 4 824 6504 4 50281774 735303130558784 04 289
0529565361669557574 60304 4 684 002013025834 728578786034 7964
29662285633839093850 4 0595996338205201 3134 5977594 954 959152824
913675826557737086309853 4 31031656991864 774 9352355876985616764 025694 36794
9650826595164 93618563906776134 08634 4 94 9610923085281595759 4 7324 4 69299784
37875069577965234 06627034 89
34 3992200393314 202215964 04 75307987724 854 719289
90319033113606753874 0992626587614 5829524 54 6296274 4
78253060713708610093256561091062901593703234 5784 651094 254 156584 8633675971714
1036824 6906821364 59502259382358689
8034 205214 584 24 15621097712594 1988605174 184 6098105218023309134
9159305532364 0211801353993827390760960188127085700221614 994
20235228530119785151 4 8254 092669518565676534 104 04 4 4 54 854 88177660629153334
23935588304 09770803826294 3189
4 4 385077023904 084 75017104 0932368683097904 4 9784 932389
215598500214 35870077134 2871584 700693024 7167663122853028391120296158 4
83322876218731270254 4 0275098869777524 186719725803984 567834 52867233726268194
259137689
22373279869636995719 4 7508280574 9299080160929638564 8875774
36681305993300301065165671686 4 3311600381784 3318094 769824 924 2660826392564
72210856302821228584 359129114 203603272060182523237 94 6293109254 1025124 54
170051664 9174 9697850176586800128632 54 4 573787252932671277 4 51624 334 36012734
039785930222159961775173614 866679396765633221951 4 934 298376790374
9308251701618528 4 933834 4 24 2504 18323030264 100557818831854 4 289
364 0874 0320396600889
234 387100234 09268523884 96732284 4 56687365704 234 31566989
381131170854 980556334 24 11090390294 0206987883668650096 4
16369170528156585835 64 774 75504 883191164 84 3064 5989
9663270339800109706271 4 3154 87174 3704 81121700620918608 4 1624
596321962758189
1687594 715082363689
27617174 8516314 584 51807054 356379707232789
574 505387584 4 71007564 55874 73724 567162607587558263162 4 16383017589
4 812372734 6583284 264 334 984 21199067903327699506187886673063 4 4
903282783764 85909168680653984 4 039317138256966659592365734 82235687609504
6002069573673695394 353734 4 89
28789

4 54 14 2994 4 924 229654 199206870717179908202751123228830206374 093324 308284 076802365996223074 50723954 829132510014 6231522838566996364 64 816199306108035011934 098551287730815954 50154 979098326100700084 35163220914 097131668390509307706782579384 89

1592132099286598075166‍4 776274 04 210228706958031691019769066584 9294 1163014 4 904 175524 15284 07985584 19204 594 2224 7224 0857954 524 89

96614 99631295674 599317874 4 97834 13501974 760024 855830935569788153697313632‍14 4 525114 0829284 1812804 5024 9199295984 56172978864 98365296717374 06535027575784 6534 1870784 2130980573575850987089

23218338602766809687867‍4 4 58767393704 2506105294 55934 4 8000033794 84 4 118691034 384 89

8199272178004 56984 08825618002774 024 69715569634 535370581771324 96654 31707954 87952577664 21120685694 34 074 073694 16521104 530170777514 4 95029664 20150856734 18561330879369079908598888‍1954 1774 261880314 4 14 174 86935293012862868769796‍34 97164 4 124 2177380019690974 8627996089

4 609364 2530679104 174 5935712831904 029831131550593038611206192754 0034 74 2996012976984 56728568007574 78682568526558880550‍4 4 6502824 7234 062122672309876509524 67955511675760755189

736710818664 87339135554 73038717714 8259924 98209065563624 63688874 4 2816354 75973802009270337279723575620585201‍94 887311757364 15208568879983962553950672‍04 5765637086678684 96167399289

9051663954 734 8064 6884 1632161269623214 04 3004 3034 97879376589

552559126127334 94 4 31374 931875585152203504 8877154 20612832321554 25010369584 201177706058113108574 0672176884 4 73924 1215189

0674 29767995284 34 604 62085104 22989

295590153886171777859625965902‍4 5374 79964 4 80573754 2590339557173690179397516001998758369909‍4 03534 602006006114 57081297272864 924 4 1555885975024 274 901019975278569583‍4 5334 4 94 3250025780204 34 4 4 4 0868289

0750774 3961736705538376157878638538700095357333590259‍4 668119751237389

8387266536879554 300184 1504 4 8072052764 94 4 570257994 6868034 994 9294 168674 7104 74 52363136504 711526982781055205996265002‍24 54 4 0734 2871399194 98025383338505885393‍64 994 1733636964 3189

980369532114 63174 617170203880708663‍4 9064 78634 04 224 584 691355904 24 24 514 02814 25972094 33680394 04 264 695762203519760525374 669196864 684 0574 85227322214 112634 6820073268099128359680‍4 337124 89

865124 84 71333865999581557036‍24 1284 31192371380520698554 630522396286001693260924 7618752321257009959‍4 164 54 501759791304 831585226900924 4 0553118658153197‍84 59314 051354 96797501971591305636‍4 07967874 274 3886974 318121596332024 24 53695090810854 01074 8674 5322336694 8874 174 4 7584 560189

77639584 4 902174 934 597104 7703154 19794 721755903104 89

5515071303375092264 289

4 74 366150114 617112854 04 89

8362878232177554 0335581513089

008600231119089

2831719794 61527339639814 7557956104 81654 72182282092824 126224 4 0866173161182953‍14 6270119621366199594 108793583564 320932964 189

356289

507521834 16094 9562866054 76082023394 39036938294 4 107069073784
215937110084 3550809934 9512584 8055614 2602794 888117357782314 109215630977556334
35689

28090624 014 704 304 06809674 54 14 28500105312911014 4
07193181060055619529375994 4 098161264 54 374 4 367739789

284 55823616806573056868 1889

329055524 83777388697883384 821269003385525577 2963294 8503625724 161794
560688062505674 39834 3584 0688586527984 71320568203326801584 011861225371072994
592972198314 039824 954 64 301364 14 12093794 4 64 784 63296730804 124 03157916714
68107172154 65797595084 3790654 6392689

4 4 164 367020267173333214 28687279300067525680 89

594 724 6054 007739214 36623774 70366937064 7989

2806834 36306662357354 91883630674 089

690534 54 196254 921859594 82963529914 4 25068124 2195784 9397624 936269976684
3201171783094 789

764 534 282159211054 4 192539567389

068025874 295234 7024 62536272058624 4 52991614 257874 9920154 7834 9251604 34
238534 924 384 34 10303807273770776 57014 74 3734 35807984 511214 989

021387726113074 93125184 84 971289

9174 590950039321906256807723 93254 54 554 69176735002114 278251591537139224
7521510261957518125 5589

91922377560556251862577787152 04 024 23564 30080154 4 064 73786864 71774 54
853375685133039577305055 4 2984 10274 52084 8824 56380181174 324 4 11508866694
172029225138714 0525933292189

03930234 84 952178373235334 4 6532626937774 732504
109205508276270136010762688057 34 92834 10615014 32117912584 109328122674 9115294
969194 4 14 057983354 038200794 920527262073123858332785887564 779056721104 1654 4
16614 70761288361000624 384 13053105014 008101079875557731522504 24 6358724 208134
65170781968132664 730526526687009753901 02354 84 0054 31910303058505073284
856662189

230736101609798730109604 5787862725969718214 97774 59319121724
208552038322309774 37336272600910791708 54 1590654 006954 04 757694 64 52693527389

589

089

4 656609355321694 271294 26114 0189

33681755821233660928809368683610 84 12959313689

7668254 634 16180797337993114 34 91994 506197674 14 0383673959104 3325083789

6097654 6321634 4 29684 4 7504 7180877538796601 1594 6910584 69856934 63154
6715196731054 0189

4 34 725327351012330555664 924 4 6253089

79855259889

634 4 4 4 538294 14 4 88382570967123605 3389

1982931364 9034 99133212284 21966087365757136 94 3286363383874 965694 154 4
7710706138034 367393954 32994 554 889

4 604 4 3286211704 228102975764 901084 61303625809885204 4 4 5652889

2538656183554 374 66905075794 821106981116094 3622727817194 6884 4 223901364
35558225224 33014 09371154 84 011366213884 10824 798090054 29724 9286908770786394
3383569758089

134 4 8554 8375376777196589

59365875154 32750294 934 011636286284 19330604 8171093923998791900884 2034
87294 34 37214 94 612397017034 30337079169831624 5766050613624 59054 91835880524
520307312984 24 258801870960784 9181635833763214 177655264 84 660862674 4 94
7775131163374 60985326156771682160131 4 781904 4 560577089

2030801852154 088126888224 610854 20684 33312797584 80921954 4 4 4 3889

66711314 4 4 61789

314 74 1293665128198790259329194 56527368734 4 83639889

3389

984 361211680689

8657975674 8851654 88863376900353752919877576930810573551739514 4
37952727038004 4 704 900728573092526263167309907 4 000684 904 5997587871320935334
814 799807297803068592527 4 92154 032508062062967936802909636571196554 54 74
98326575576094 6724 722924 089

2061371056217009793399279320665670 94 589

212083904 984 604 75864 80114 4 552327813602814 534 4 57954 3873365991854
0295506010018789

6258232064 4 6714 5096398089

1996756614 6598237014 12873664 688038594 0326652224 08750886052884
106719799914 0854 4 870072930220172202603 04 7863807108861726314 1531392374 89

94 77819178104 07754 5255536936054 590363781619286394 2002266964
80397586822634 53758128535507962060 64 63620227634 100156253911994
63257867883608702524 3725262830330102104 4 89

4 32622627532207366765291091628199888719161678669769861721 0689

500902364 059291757218594 584 7630689

2124 704 3650275363283506500 4 334 6183189

7030508283915358506052517223 4 4 22933189

6294 3725776163152226873950058135915637995009070 4 5720072609689

88373875369824 262186314 9512139883571673563880630056290325 4 7514
5199661817267782 0789

627279916563774 8029910225094 724 4 094 198014 686901886252851004 23366590664
30765016710023678735189

804 1750864 7603805560882711984 78863911696605712575811161 4
33220316239861953996081064 4 89

115129903832189

24 4 96711518198579850277 04 4 69785184 16280732953187522170737 54 2780783674
50606084 36887769304 98302304 14 364 689

1398370082693964 060694 56288164 16952916654 4 3739084 757281969614 64
11957158066368813124 84 8782960051923653816696914 4 13164 37821280803774 582231914
25066537273186601585557631000 54 5881914 608634 15120134 0660568618305399109284
22209722277276664 2007099875823159076294 39129515634 967208380989

724 72304 20387327835086014 74 11604 8285204 20074 395960779396766574 54 574 15734 3814 3762929561095311584 820920001996834 922274 6222332034 9229787977720932593734 589

3185303632200218523329226604 3263277738699295254 4 00374 60654 804 4 76294 982724 04 22914 6560052904 5986614 90530533034 1184 232774 7134 752876324 1774 686005103519680259504 89

3354 161773876502389

3191084 0665213804 6674 6652964 3577196052289

2728790582333626717180104 787074 150978653274 4 1555228155097901531 4 32569914 1091329952502769916 4 12184 7989

03534 1734 1802888078594 3704 74 700374 68716698072913698781051913 4 823174 3199718175697324 716934 1124 04 219323832375815834 075050325121024

Chapter Nintey-two

23272159997622559536081716396595 54 5921520062634 9383277938717 4 509876695534 2878789

774 664 4 36385517065026504 4 857714 758789

5166390526126187671738754 04 5938775924 4 9369724 6870221984 680515191826034 34 14 63515337517354 39834 6584 036650078008251337619581112539605958 9

4 1718804 7217874 63604 668507755956087664 614 979975907257254 6693095018122660597563383204 512084 63864 4 64 994 7755674 71104 8825818624 518114 8216024 1731135115533763 94 1801619860829325 84 8285029721564 124 9354 354 937014 722183714 9093135274 651614 04 229884 034 725873584 804 7100304 9710367861996903966 4 003189

027014 1021874 714 39739304 7966712714 69674 524 858219615904 4 358857504 74 7116108355827618601159886799252327767007791 34 88062706784 305823037684 4 3224 0837285577758508216273267775521575385 4 931391889

4 4 33113709718797654 9309906304 3708381210797273160 4 14 68874 104 4 273294 030727774 363782884 4 23977594 87234 629173289

64 32364 89

504 230303395254 77232852922518209786329 4 12792277610699764 83964 4 6154 98030391036874 763670074 4 20720134 86804 2097834 4 65670780850085124 89

26091270815723789

681795389

714 71665316354 179274 1324 9374 555104 90677088305382910 4 66098618013354 927364 7157882317517022952925574 767294 3807184 3235282789

3878730585071721698784 0870936084 89

1275829673184 5035233009100824 50089

4 600016837289

6985534 7815677089

8606637024 3799181871271374 83594 24 4 296364 32094 72757271104 1804 4 334 60130510702217782 4 72919884 0954 4 4 29155924 729679314 7664 16864 6799094 5637704 60369988700796128573 4 67050871763579926726 4 190775864 829795801509614 97179864 3932311870590230974 516834 3571252335874 4 25716502513078384 39678124 89

54 1028789

968672155583518182197672923726750882719132592 89
04 57053921699623157 34 135981016260634 384 1974 111595598712194 8557079154 04
099126084 31534 4 94 7293618259714 666352094 0304 301794 36126307970778095387707 94
982864 536667632635334 220689
4 534 3030626974 8572960188084 6564 9020974 99552566734
0133802823078862980681870520 54 125204 01199904 304 289
199124 0154 63064 89
60755234 80019294 54 87528805570650554 52354 8791789
559874 4 02509130074 164 1918093997294 6822103570189
811867672154 904 4 950284 4 6259968376782516887270792953 34
99355139851172380 4 9116955666124 4 18804 93518211954 2314 54 57932954 9732901154
97632797004 25725292885167605567069578881 89
166689
264 962782660684 28178885513568220105986 4 864 4 2689
73104 04 2064 20388620214 15931334 33565060797764 8372861174 7854
101318195388209632637397818675015670201035161382762235 54
99078167081762580063265190907230973113261264 5394 8061274 615763974
69729038199157580630 74 587538517334 8334 6860760889
64 622701214 04 0165795597908155136 4 3179269714 327811600039509295305301566 4
053854 4 014 4 68195674 1689
14 39500506012989
9532520624 2564 02569997354
0563356851170626312937882096557630557832675616162922170394 518589
95939277954 6333735205016889
84 64 364 888207314 613992856015764 6190608827005218388294 4 9052835018564
06504 3364 17535013934 985705100635004 4
2327755328051663250155536001685586063216180167882 2889
85927773980708234 4 301218764 98298821950764 879374 527324 97757164 6794
37682597865380777090931582686989
321856754 1022181137066289
1505071916924 055717515372979854 67954 771694 4 04 6087285834
02007168255878503502580689
802794 3094 6184 672580186255717699914 36669256776624 7888256367102390508 9
297579824 89
52227094 184 674 4 34 14 664 4 1191197624 8630886752269173795608 4 64 34
16367635588308512954 865371125074 4 90373228827199257271519966000216669389
56050382795190662337107102964 5261125354 820180816234
0593161238338327872154 50909054 4 271980320064 4 225323600124 989
34 4 84 3636759371914 2322778515962657684 525307584 855373583084 1651524
77784 998355609967914 529055371289
933804 17358033223313804 34 826019161910280534 75986623854 15120389
560611327005564 96689
28131675551297996763366535 54 04 709079398886689
530685781017330266056885368 9
560211807721622589
21919924 3117304 89

25224 97125531228211758822528265092358229122520 4 1383700828638795994
08753314 229202553788319259017888175978 9

4 3077271131604 89

1567850867837388122362887558552661186573367 4 4
6022611736332880225562068614 9584 6722660537793575255583609340989

16382963659980073078 4 500136994 588212051974 271662951889

363661788724 5193879883914 98507 4 6367011614 6235590918089

14 64 87824 7698323775978709634 5593154 5706800552820706294 64 31076384
81718364 124 284 4 8832224 1634 53064 177764 9280600316789

7001913734 4 14 59952908181300827357120 24 4 54 17814 6061237267 14 4
0187538225274 5351515524 24 5007907975368799187 1156710284
530318732656311281918735814 20504 230774 6297225 4 0369635233574 830656204 85610864
0934 27383318334 634 32735127159264 2393900 4 9127973028883783 4 6374 4 23604 64 4
196581584 384 0531910829032323939150063705253777010659 4
29219076639318081087876557596907078 4 0731732397323550634 4 135855674
60029281228194 4 8262638691858136721604 1395 4 63318790725616930815 4 099694 37600214
7684 82366689

595833864 4 584 339139734 195773954 4 589

4 7379964 99396501973180187582154 388185804 924 4 01538657071887678789
060589

4 34 39705724 39680676623307775021 54 24 77708237790 4 4 126904 120760661717514
5832906568124 0190888065205921 4 4 59722368760226173024 5554 6374 0562074
80813993774 670094 1252221532734 4 884 1706368152 4 4 3582561186966261363834 02928664
4 97006603799675017937631676391806 94 376784 3386214 9089

62356182010564 0614 0123778850988356670 84 73114 37168889

1394 2684 794 8538764 6650984 1171954 3370289

21584 8350725860197651524 604 154 3560676274 64 1178103795805511058527509 4 24
4 72965571294 5889

54 4 50204 6822567201062098620677182166 74 86885596778133367304 89

4 1388830396566121918 9

33058714 04 7784 551328767280301 4 3220992705290210617713921 27737590526124
6803578323361223167 24 51314 30183282789

8769529904 655069884 850334 34 8398335992274 164 8106833596317970504 04
80171635758116961108 9

8875265050394 554 508189

04 5782033398880552733617 4 0589

06607625678876023 4 4 89

9655818219507130679827984 374 7014 71305670367804 00279088826260968751798 4
3306216168364 975773394 89

618134 4 18824 16886502289

96780816279756256922 74 980874 02088768810359 4
369299203957265613050681288387614 4 1195918624 0022364 4 524 800394 79994 24 4
0582531726824 651352094 89

596658726936634 884 01509928375984 64 64 7534 24 0305615590651054 4 9169124
2186078781176800389

930760906904 83506727951214 030034 04 594 88292084 53567271632950120071214
6837654 4 94 14 070692596214 3328567874 574 6838018539304 54 624 313698559873264
207073373620952682533002224 6595654 211021883163555532210223258354 19869926664
9135319296318782349 9014 915870014 774 992191089

4 65012801726186584 24 11995774 784 4 638088817923589

6723654 96158227535354 996984 13029394 93205679621375776989

6654 2096156183935754 8510610187366314 026732506199565814 384 095884 354
5927104 27524 74 4 85532015362900288790273637151170976115575104 4 74 4 4
857500232585814 85607889

851283509556122124 4 13532387816233318165611929257620999185187924 28624
230801705860076558534 64 5099212221386291932006291667104 0534 4 4 132530994 050314
84 2016003289

992319103284 01724 803603264 11739587737364 393158054 75634 4 6116674 4
219590534 1694 6656368004 9974 6089

1763261639369972680056711919008111164 6000296009990629766664
950801085080051586703858197181305523117324 6301735287693034 9789

853304 6076126706915198052104 18792169386199911311368284 102584 3874
830863102275566524 082814 12368889

51950624 4 729375224 03669031592181864 3234 0269192932376887151770807674
952389

89

9214 924 574 176299185804 334 8629606089

363110625810014 13806306012314 94 362793068733268768714 74 4 54 9611824
196603717301173226721154 889

4 14 4 71580764 34 6364 4 764 5759070334 0858879379388551175194 674 23534 04
5394 122524 064 57071214 4 65904 6656734 80924 26153884 175026364 996764 0397964
0395064 5360330584 67106591608694 9364 276706384 18752507639689

6156031731192926863383238674 4 6335181133083074 39130354 33722790714
103079528227165884 11034 4 4 34 8578821809080282820829554 4
28122003801952660218635952 610566606314 95761270251582303335224 94 70789

04 6610507885186132600708705312521009224 18814 033311098034 3254 4 7218753564
3394 32204 04 65954 026928504 4 885564 614 251052654 79584 7216630572994
5635788271560772802214 8217504 4 787001124 7793657070556730989

2113872193059290580864 97839863194 34 6632579224 2834 02027520796201076674
604 694 0717056095351333399376074 9271301176506022224 0784 4 7808214
9383963988120054 7789

38005665780359904 3114 8710163727703552144 4 94 7284 4 806598021024

Chapter Nintey-three

6296286374 3293337500534 210984 024 858609771594 6034 626507089
2757684 80320183619054 98852289
280953768213151504 35582517203728601695960958764 2513950138220984 04
961222624 2281734 04 34 028089

39972622577393303661029868199221337757916373560034
537807550181325596156935501032832994 2384 9974 751524
338100115195012131780501387964 656284 9154 3324 89
194 3371832694 7019268167675960615918789
7636526032086512658522664 24 524 1199590189
8187884 508287694 4 3767663184 922384 879924 1374 007672294
068073105280395354 02366035209984 205504 3059212038827556559304 8083911659730624
50177252527879079854 685084 258555173838383851994 34 4 2889
1591225364 4 11866964 4 17124 24 001358879607219106134 94 230833029789
6634 4 30882711074 67000523629974 32610231802714 226622261875057254
39690773814 74 26352215524 4 8324 00804 3756966990710294 7264 051780301516189
1026800926358769884 18013034 52664 71055199507316064 32675504 04 874
5317728164 7974 984 9316816351888113254 614 9964 0318314 012084 9999754 505654 4
05665114 8358387174 38107104 4 4 4 68199573634 628689
300271371764 3069604 14 78322732756789
03050809576914 34 78308670354 016162028184 9114 4 12320084 39992821318184 84
332288134 255124 888668654 4 8527084 2304 284 009883138554 901003794 0264 84 4
7623636375364 651105500810294 0660991524 814 7926317308774 4 064
207095391999167556393167624 7589
083224 2707294 82954 4 32815122952903164 75060981071517094
9321661681302220084 89
990733519284 84 090014 33236988693791759977923872805644 4 85863635604 716964 4
3660204 4 5259704 868221514 4 19781591232274 7578772163986575276098 4 089
9889
3737775089
374 04 06584 561154 04 534 4 889
826356794 4 962864 224 7071613265874 995955834 4 008024 4 94 0052564
753112758294 5824 55523833993886160216709544 09039509622984 369753605794 4
381677828156635171719015608678501022971066937877214 909889
193684 54 386725973007974 93811034 294 53581189
213029104 857204 9967356221167333663500764 326274 05882954 4 86157569614 3204
789
6330591725250029655954 6804 8765362628154 9757676580277875590236787 34
8162504 24 531570274 183539064 99723714 30862395364
28333798525880936563580878758721 14 167358200023785857917 14 654 1612112026034
272557384 2215518015874 63057767793952936789
12532977700508226250081937 4 164 5114 1684 737365725226777 89
0874 57996823734 527732736062994 64 2924
169967155086229280608031678771501902004 1616630204 93507588377690661867 4 6162964
70167705634 4 183089
67626618874 4 03297051778814 524 34 012512226794 104
12177617218288850815972164 208384 7933339829566994 034 959379072820339780087960 4
9701378070294 014 57061832275296034 85302837192226100593956 4 4 99124 15092778754
6136682314 61289
4 6998167258824 71189

854 4 7614 664 135974 724 04 001167264 64 03383299904 015026352712185799138187518382154 225304 7992153889

0284 6165379294 723637963334 793127084 664 272273704 354 107685379121319034 3311924 50634 5207673334 38091681290392671092987571714 80282227330708585902259139290 52589

74 0024 37571021699553265761333518518766386027619970039805239305274 289 33709016910236752074 5177016964 04 7237538638287654 31904 302903579819304 4 682863204 54 30189

14 2160750516996685123364 4 518831394 315814 04 6520685035597675284 062096864 84 0014 632988026383254 95627213258275734 4 8535583000222551331859 6228864 97724 94 4 8196664 15281904 07028797109505677755838364 7075089

292801299214 655089

84 652700726965716889

74 01324 3287957198217231190281099092 24 94 21069115194 2704 4 773587520266021778729973938 04 329178321634 67212887284 3369790316934 85924 5577217598633216922910131299 64 934 565694 56831267284 809584 29250935515615358682033736722013612851719 5799179067888794 89

77874 155795078582804 00519879514 37931024

Chapter Nintey-four

0973513754 24 4 5229106658730078654 62514 1882080807307192689

83913504 92537754 374 4 202657016514 854 903903784 915335783523919509184 2294 10079581794 6261304 621688184 4 12174 680622072287104 62514 938764 917833389

25853594 154 3991358005859024 29854 085572504 4 89

4 2910311306684 10610525215294 364 0589

4 28225619515090298853 4 967011852089

64 64 33204 187932153336684 75009093794 74 58624 4 050094 4 197952593058084 7057304 4 1714 2280778565703712794 7580934 5629087704 798834 69716932355169605915512903 94 654 64 9194 6976956580104 4 7721221152971788 54 24 2063014 4 9359990364 704 88168696394 54 5987395664 95684 4 6800827974 064 859397628886154 20634 4 9595204 778764 796022224 814 04 5187112205762128289

5120964 24 2624 397691077791875989

1509169674 884 969014 04 17814 624 882189

9204 721539789

701004 1004 4 51916374 6354 84 937776724 04 89

6305617608574 90190664 199208564 98824 4 166592591364 114 9797211057092004 834 63562191125920531594 9520772857285350227717869 1134 317095074 74 1774 04 611259771054 4 0663928887571839332360002 4 4 5026038759995174 213594 979764 94 04 0004 14 4 0939680931932864 23323138073107260 5234 7022269955029753364 13333363768383076991222391 14 77705585997784 2874 256964 52597304 589

7989

16184 4 009118754 738104 69804 38055951700629630329 4 337501124 37691659207229530151254 321394 054 4 337789

162781914 06215516820884 73634 534 19799988795161172610284 1063233698534 56622714 089

825020691286704 4 4 11690258204 796576506806083389

354 4 90862114 387382565994 64 34 97880323272175829269

51699863126735875109548 84 558784 6314 07597172019624 3370852199677928830820

17083628218867104 294 024 2600584 4 004 377358753310704 188814 221920924 60714

9133502963690584 664 4 883203194 74 101734 611287867351794 22094 14 54 6604 18534

03015518155623214 316574 7332666107989

8031090681700826887321019364 59561785851734 5054 728589

80078728721154 1725674 024 4 197902884 32253154 1019214

0135091238671110323213731 594 05115614 706721289

5932638196758037690723130321615824 7304 0701388589

334 636633597677154 70701977324 954 8814 51714 95615889

15972704 03164 4 34 9512185974 704 14 6717150973113294 7384 808502107073004 89

5212374 84 2154 0389

981859513224 9014 4 18572919357094 37524 15921554 5692963115014 4 9384 703394

89

307624 3553834 2354 3950785791770587588732868726361377231317957631881191 74

93997364 5829559955961684 714 4 784 4 15189

854 30774 14 5594 300916272777064 006784 526222188606338106724 84 7269024 4

0264 2674 1339072193530058424 4 0622594 64 25394 83685654 784 50534 34 90529674 30589

74 864 9564 389

29352506968728255730738865347979569737963739416312512211357236612420 14

0264 68319875234 913753259196515806193872666193916051049 3592652713216922096224

63969924 53394 94 16814 87697594 5022756931601737297825225932113922797264 4

699078707972112927010072 89

3164 14 13289

7554 051129860713004 54 24 4 97219982559230173355939919666258862 84 89

0280161029774 14 72814 7217996074 304 686368394

358376209663705921780035815169912 94 7673154 832624 34 7225298003800959587555 54

51363524 852923366036661334 5215784 92026850615194 92034 5290214 6178514 20324

233104 2284 86352089

687974 2184 54 0038734 94 17283201176273782264 79639784

67771365873511193020707222560037507 4 94 07810394 63389

519984 54 4 166314 3229731608084 4 04 98281354 30303833631635314 54 0529914

83164 256012510682085656900160302972916584 6789

1832210586994 89

1004 07801076924 7782572806721865866 4 4 93575923770660199972606595255 4

33273364 250389

4 7983366014 31993073084 80934 5161508804 80764 6366675290866716936206 24

928739814 8879904 365333871639691167273697027312653 74 284 08609734

8697293255278854 199301904 1684 282321395857966024 873754 0654 3926084 95318634 134

694 686789

235833606803394 4 557618564 87011325964 2775582026319256809971589

4 4 89

34 54 07354 5166932384 4 9214 99118554 93382824 4 5770766882305254 69796128224

4 04 15996689

2371592950939237321195 4 789

4 5074 0806774 4 4 89

00380624 4 34 575224 61155572389

4 226838593051527754 97654 54 3180834 902387291984 674 869316260887179215124 82924 761589

3514 14 914 1589

04 235105073534 9679694 874 9186334 4 304 793625203651055672156988823952034 9805230153122385212513261664 4 94 73704 6124 8186099014 395654 63727101755621611221104 7224 7926506088187921878564 564 770201918708174 098274 2638851785178231952934 1904 81931571564 04 001782600804 74 64 154 5364 258579688221314 71202195068707370393121533322394 2964 71014 338817639918115074 215554 22604 82199024 50082052031551588031076765688121985750384 51204 4 73602796923884 89

4 398504 077669391919178038513117904 637264 578728005664 99501595762530276734 24 74 90355778730320694 6697620679371095314 087874 66090719090054 787150227573861562284 03119997936014 8174 01814 0726855934 64 24 708186513726761279734 27764 124 089

4 07024 12250575912833204 4 87675083824 823354 9006224 31962572928264 80566009677509285325730388834 1824 2504 4 10194 4 38374 90829289

07704 4 151815134 327901263186270934 4 1028058333197183938084 51124 787757790528799614 24 8096853758097667673015694 84 34 874 3174 7574 89

914 63889

1633504 3383627398851102955909972689

955904 71511291794 5559126983594 29306738574 304 86989

89

85594 4 3261989

64 2534 34 9217117176194 9868813811537360119252837634 8122187771094 392593220573709562698164 64 5264 59305254 1308176804 7684 9179967094 5909756270994 574 64 1668731299851777131558862076554 3315102630236084 92235320184 0024 64 4 2694 982220093885619814 174 235294 21101204 4 8887865176204 772310072355773711756964 54 02677378698782932384 884 6586854 824 3072513224 5997181951763782065167701734 9639072911973231521104 5083889

63690034 3634 564 97713884 18056802984 14 0532309783687878873323574 584 37167785962319311821299654 4 264 2274 6033116562189

9580738570914 074 81709077702060125825537255988182554 0001709679090974 1338551791505034 624 1362796294 3375279803921216124 4 94 2285734 80554 092996174 22186755267066387154 0197164 95925804 198284 572723394 358727384 912980625052299082304 14 4 17964 20186323933597564 0856264 72114 098710275684 23284 71054 4 204 76927372279586934 32551623728706130624 89

4 83176830059503162735392722215559603719126092705632090016884 4 64 2239974 5990762836038614 51560114 67908671952274 4 22534 1537356304 3636807658209294 4 81681575624 4 0758354 2094 4 504 14 8183694 00724 787199371608074 714 3704 8052724 12272057620014 8265567384 258527615204 225756167756634 4 89

0835515904 034 75597055278114 985130250874 12165561605854 2729230289

9331654 7354 9907915612178664 7178134 3392824 994 15905014 0923632016984 086805996772364 631180032309172314 4 906596018394 4 3357324 67994 72136366714 309332268725922769959786634 21984 8604 764 038331215159824 6334 81575389

13621374 7050626776094 93915654 34 4 4 966503071575601905256114 934 34
12398650086334 9768772582014 26160358764 21886575309174 051824 174 91784
1215303222383004 188066393854 55889
178762006878814 04 8766927605976263885084 187671723906882151375334 69074
20527968759386296574 98654 4 1776294 2518703009114 96135284 4 389
20514 5007155110873094 664 9594 9907089
979305234 01295734 9386688178592724 4 2308152159066064
9960755027237608127238705851213727 4 5528886177354 4 54 4 9593851589
568775195180268779856 4 8252026624 094 4 4 86188286727054 2074 7504 353679984
584 680211816124 5119179164 083882209778864 1827568105850767756572864 84
82836037024 932871581980604 35558799803757574 7633172000054 4 95984
9872516688565706303352876068093081590181 4 10593721378560788103151292531750 4
110509609751654 25371030855174 854 89
928079279216508267024 77524 6374 998378504 7234 114 87224 0388787796856216589
184 157356593968703031935075029813828 9
52996830357304 30607120754 6629980584 7951077322904 1914
3068162870295090071881 4 134 214 58284 15611632764 589
797794 318524 4 67033357220151830080677300984 34 2814 59855594 3657389
7199032628610071674 6911509026594 64 27923755624 9374 23512174 4 5080312134
99874 10210504 026254 115763114 123064 0337384 023024 84 4 7393613277714 317783264
8722787200003132 4 379911584 54 107320083254 71765533577884
19738811198783081161282533 4 3500137910973264 5804 5675356269284 834
55102531756976137831 4 4 3682524 77854 30693706314 32550964 076224 94
2709697276210616798163074 5864
7731362102916913190193505391736338772095930772880211384 952253085233564 200914
75821132150814 1634 559373276638164 6209964 1504 1814 2792614 784 85611225096974 4
18073994 0121864 95761708774 29853908394 199011888587733637311313017101357779033 4
756204 4 39526260767797656853850 4 151780028622026017398315357 89
4 904 54 4 4 271657055964 92052223188354 4 74 283111934 6960371194 12186093964
74 369683521630084 11309122137612361931555091187753 4 64 4 5604 293737921516689
62024 254 71680377818274 63859079682073564 0934 2994 334
27179208028875221125 4 331790114 14 9116004 796389
603318772204 714 551925930589
4 86933504 99223357652070639336657861080859200577595735770605634 6934
57603884 910805066955160938106 94 366128758827331613228 64 8314 314 717672115704
619235614 65003774 053872176274 111366017823585584 5173100298207789
99364 68177687598057719690 4 4 29326564 14 928889
50616174 3273954 534 8233166639979174 84 984 0274 78354 0535912002226094
39905312070766019667274 3214 66731325059919615374 9191206109264 878195377790614
2535189
2234 66139609531960625261784 25715869924 378266091617174 64 971634 7204 77389
61314 867194 294 824 90291989
4 1916758308889
2339731174 15554 17268094 75331027377979970981756504 5054
7360227678621069754 04 50592614 388377815161792537901060 64 0229167380269625734 34
304 64 53004 21104 252766230305520724 75739306792726393713188722880126958554 904 24

8663228307022774 0155528034 2205573172609159292751328720 4 3377723638154 660224
262722795524 264 04 79069128534 664 74 3956703901536664 4 8251186234 027804
0253780886661135356 64 4 1069137697238823654 0537057203264
851330711800188621777680597953218065 4 36753210222504 280004 3994 061851812889
    53614 073372395066311517070005713863153021329368553801 84 89
    869696302851089
    3012021795064 70724 877503209994 836756871724 70029055814 56984 0514 4 674 694
50718871737636802873 4 73556196853175307566120156930570 34 4 30987614 97230689
    528664 4 4 1564 074 834 588089
    86525661664 379720289
    58684 4 22039218194 31715127564 11177614 7563714 05936864 000103588026389
    1259692381706227637167628 74 8062838160227594 105114 626922888091294
330277664 9594 724 97384 4 730933763274 600371084
35907859976671800558687028730183229667292566511959261005 94 158100365089
    29062603999789
    10764 69310195227174 4 64 51994 4 3616999155564 1564 1215108714
382080886807522978508 14 802286234 1353184 3920566639711524 6089
    04 813184 4 5192314 929106328154 0279224 89
    37822825154 5768271624 5961176395668864 6174 2395371586574 4 62664 39961554
789
    05163732521825783332535 64 4 589
    89
    29059519260586597986713 4 4 8274 4 78262666789
    84 1919627360593520221 4 966815704 36556904 167082575274 4 588175728116095614
81857224 36954 64 75050830284 4 3075317077923557132934
876117839081302910599183552262237 4 68671157570593774 90937975793819524
733163226623598269569980 4 734 334 4 02616879654 751304 2934 61624 266134 6074
73252695703114 8814 6969164 29336907194 8154 54 8179082929107206 94
297318759719731015 4 2619933564 615328361822870151559033107061 4 65304
2170066882533797013234 4 95060714 1683526860988131227220 54 0903094 664
6066185857999914 15397814 4 84 774 1564 0822589
    0354 064 4 9064 635106154 337194 004 01386160350714 559736014 2786234 514
865734 7962179784 675702189
    89
    951333364 4 3819291905300857739950 4 5234 934 957189
    684 612711376889
    57597933234 95332089
    53814 53984 6770285124 109139999624 094 28615356154 95201564 1889
    962125930051264 4 20968659725289
    94 184 350366818804 8075291059723360083654 8235701919868550926035004
8765737882951629237 4 18327132367686584 94 64 00059670950677834 5361003674 4 2594
918858195595926902512393110725951212115633824 1589
    6067374 800718324 687784 1307809693824 14 82915189
    5604 275501754 2065174 4 2088134 014 54 360707135560267634 9959757596004
10361609612137736218202235639801014 55924 936015689
    714 89

7933365854 9918634 97304 1034 95007905509710373294 89

219764 05886995320189

664 933508204 31004 885230594 2984 86801785556564 5389

71529638687139823939389

2788628313053889

8704 4 1633874 853236655056254 30238286131768314 74 39934 4 615609310765384 94
7584 64 89

31621515835889

89

339195673294 4 334 79039090964 5002015254 52974 223609334 873774 857090601864
8070516991257559333251820304 4 120573389

116924 94 979374 4 4 4 181721018004 8695274 815824 86075771221724
13829852529767035268850 4 2133034 6370320590111276927084 231224 7374 0399034 4
676189

570010259178589

6614 704 561188690554 31800013574 114 54 5384 809162384 56019398214 576980154
03674 4 73093324 214 164 7275552190877396974 173735064 14 595184 60785124 01813774
54 5883762985179066094 25179969503658723513291154 0694 118558004 05756107804
357919105154 389

52930178607056885781172174 21391550953207211970 89

84 1522154 253164 7919304 61604 981176009994 04 34 13190991189

21551365122611550181311073519 4 0674 89

64 186094 0284 869283055022119924 34 38663096612299837616589

81274 730669004 0713313153258193032028 14 9674 5570289

271198050230834 294 90724 61054 91095799550789

36602634 6984 6566281880554 90104 38789

89

574 4 09314 152964 14 33776902605064 364 0983268217633628709882627239 74
30230055063851675289

2264 8375095088613721983335 34 606984 89

068556859024 4 4 6788863364 39604 378182364 9316075069795253661777 04 4
807862852104 6820932682668289

72207159109800819778019264 952538304 724 636079589

391737003693289

6635802205065980285338702996809222867 54 27129133869994 026633577360863 754
04 7202114 99273339955963867139 4 14 159950635550381622713179928761 4 32989

24 59586632102280507272017663282902813951362 4 6392598794 084 119774 24 214
784 974 887928534 81329226175804 296953605684 964 1633358836124 64 77604
71766303398537726717373232324 351929797334 23764 60670072590569784 7782259010224
7186184 9551087004 14 015527634 9224 30585064 979174 69994 1224 70166700310104 4
32762653099301528 4 20684 24 68595235910530969681058 4
31185510376080853681033317095 34 908134 8831311722359377 4 3874 14
621839265017156090327 94 028189

935612694 4 96396714 3320782904 731916666780851825519771728800627735 4
53991592789

034 0107862889

6366115708075792637125157532125643458797675822798605621785390463434
3878260224 76983164 4 7309116773137698654 394 4 13974 8134 4 8003818298103754
9505885398354 2914 63227532912260623917829319962139869188177111184 24 4
19627718789

9230573504 4 724 57753831194 3385179322128576603521216877901140477658947
767784 35696351365329151449309638039104 754 50116996758780279997955389
55855005904 55332979356370264 07703334 811205596791096608804 654 4
58199117569673353817940202977420844 671405547
762538001665796195719912620080781668202885915862485723615599401625547770791
11160067640782608077107897

4 734 37289

9115676130685073224 96315912316341975884 627647288192023676271637519497
766953325420490897

161024

Chapter Nintey-five

9164 837334 96591727080014 711527101290897
0296121104 04 724 620656228209632836266708889
7284 64 84 9194 5054 8524 14 755813392377362692127662809010703960329947
6262725094 714 117691214 29133539751301514 31774 671685847
02905968622217080111036660714 6302062064 220739673674 027544 47
511153186803573711970612632143552346855547 3824 5653255194 962230924 4
22262761618107635327121848 6711038748633241670789
04 688522332921111501979009872376674 0155479167534 4 74 85897
11628126868673604 222994 356076826978331735176394 113756818731185310939147
73316134 714 64 29574 80258866120984 333362644 7897
2327799217189
381104 902575089
83329575231138511638411810192449913293008778
7253627365880167927323911956677377346029231167147252754 3877323954 09644 074 1747
4930881033569016897
94 4 732650629356812407468591689
254 650921109142316433966434 96535539990522603047114 87117501951086036214
378879284 074 4 9825270332425169177953432393380537534 154 286334 47
920057275796819187421842721885884 6662660281339159122650870329556297431210060847
764 623824 06120209740885851097134 50244 534 56269674 84 521747
93795199836601359599598044 2105533930579946354 121565926037395454
81307090026816164 7358075309070057946985951218576692820433593133365802104
39358016107908279426644 878203528015749847777187536663886871469284
92233597970201859216375263706470723923280711774 975523653624 17062631547
632700590266304 024 739804 533530204 0939313049739713079171815148863238516035147
0918715172725963206039775181897
8773794 2983354 89
6214 929883065168797261732334 2951860291979123542091447
66176185808120657850975540518126245478535871423498722824 50762802185554 164

3937355728734 1317707953318264 10695802318126782729262172 7904
7867331323026028790 14 764 854 33580999324 4 37234 91884 99585994 862583067600012204
733634 4 66868003021774 4 283089
5673212065731090929852126853082935352033162609612387192704 74 91031694
115164 83884 74 7974 56771234 335574 4 29812684 4 614
32753371060377023811587306886289
69394 132363006060504 289
9652004 51060374 8676961364 91725117214 17104 539723698376574
82509286253199176103796050507004 74 5275198706924 3830797208133651074
58086253398704 5295036577394 794 375194 32553660014 2105564 64 14 8224 3606164
677079171658511765610859235634 6094 854 9764 4 77962116551131870096990291 4 0731514
839039089
9181591857833265027795395784 18251970561524 675181074 563304 570829594 4
2889
1506667159297604 12803354 74 51551004 3994 93399113574 00368108214
520100371663337695212133753239064 4 515065233379074 7504 2857815969527569618178 4
704 2381784 203159924 1711215728175313825528 9
9083172227080319334 0184 9974 624 661506864 1371786793594 80593272851964
335736880274 14 315869007652087234 54 663736398318691202096562075 4 134 8874 115504
351794 5705202192086628621570 4 65012959513127937 4 4 0724 676204 19226655674 4 53334
4 4 729681714 87354 4 93873384 8016654 28264 23783384 83175654 38333617 4 4
0873218792199714 30971939075615289
979919334 81684 5664 86989
4 31576014 3802862633533136185723793167236606367 54 94 38005252967139974
0350994 0712193373758571204 55594 960284 4 4 564 04 6130603362226362162934 1224
5761511654 1938791684 8132809624 69524 4 4 56954 6212508791189
353983221963789
994 98705755174 8771886105104 5258709120015502718111214 0083303394
59997728658704 5234 191667304 068557004 71728611726335884 96827107174 50035389
03363106665809112216112279535205973563154 238786279221174
00279299276602723091008788 9
64 4 867197751064 4 852854 23676068067832870271602 14 9122089
07383598679167790798 4 654 684 7654 4 32886332754 592689
9764 71361182191936371970 94 309189
7609589
33074 195091535789
981594 56268174 0310911862136112387032663287 4 5925123801722185923759 64
2039717801197330135 4 54 86303115628764 53973330103535199368 9
089
17165821184 4 72025394 04 709317833060123964 167270931216369379193323918 4
2597730527614 792293021230131636529561376233305284 54 63774 4 966783855724
1630555328610532755207 84 389
4 04 4 24 72330870014 94 007564 85394 9389
70856366624 723511554 9684 2637074 224 198534 0721884 331711808624
785109999817623225805812020 4 9072702367515599603855 84 6672839734 73259596127104 4
9694 89

969280704 087235561355018834 8609827334 4 94 2119279511596389

14 21701337136254 059591584 0065763710336218594 354 0907214 95079719264 24 74 16878866135096201313031939816564 4 3184 2319103674 14 20512556863328098552077093239955574 2204 5837289

24 383094 811084 233008764 153663084 724 1689

76375194 1939984 8086392769531790164 3727802977688806164 9084 1933764 10364 509612604 0651273694 7334 321364 751668674 54 18754 2353324 904 52514 001261991025504 94 2206089

9086534 89

121851977852080353829793516 4 7361636394 85284 9756284 9714 8856270364 254 37615253034 8567914 21813834 154 676563036293594 32715688885113964 534 17550113555234 22660951773817818038 9

3864 4 3090830539927386531988392370825 14 4 34 9766957951254 0664 055821324 9534 760824 4 64 2379595204 674 037169104 022865060164 4 011882128168872783 9234 273692926062064 0964 091959614 5904 314 517234 16161791510706177671 74 151129700974 36263571691798097913107607554 4 4 007274 823165853639170769125919005551128507328081677051 34 74 9074 14 501195024 81084 2767773577308103608 4 500375556502686582708 9

4 90664 096114 62996904 292269838084 34 9681389

14 924 79886224 87167128124 089

262797006509374 12914 28012018819220654 2159389

736338193225912707130384 89

4 2162931911004 90714 9225362821862035617 64 4 6854 4 699594 30764 19072713387818263384 7902690514 134 88524 08834 159704 09316671764 584 851653904 600109634 72932317024 526860807864 9180077024 54 260533859200916633150792778732 4 8325901604 4 2171566874 94 057915189

677115913189

275017804 4 51824 99374 3874 329932914 3554 374 68094 6834 0260834 64 25268170735136026784 4 11711754 7680302578284 3274 12712955509267108574 02304 74 69600264 4 571189

3018058112189

25757250024 17910664 7302011294 693754 95333839271076783815855808875670613299964 991589

394 9904 0874 9778235503921051363016 4 671634 0862269365394 034 567695186527752685603128680881568 9

16991604 6013679356000288784 865017387036118613661682337006376 24 90171870354 839165300888065752373767990681554 788889

3864 6233804 33678814 4 7386263697514 4 4 63533151364 5033652509877954 13093994 14 67601122228501278273 4 55755159561984 4 8726728886216911391278 64 4 4 18265010715934 333181605528809809313757602195 4 4 84 236689

1814 04 8761296983574 0368011755189

1330057226994 75919228724 39694 710724 4 97704 04 732967513384 8537289 89

198514 4 87912693399562727628630157178270573552384 50193665288694 25030157128864 90989

9305589

774 514 8064 974 00710813760206766061002833539832 0724 3594 56720594 94
5121684 4 025305614 1611504 72376796871252693156319309816082329 79504 2589
816674 80087815264 8677364 14 4 93569584 287953 87951111209004 138824
35069998882091565554 03289
25022880514 16967879299266268 62224 6705254 906674 95362501326970031824
510114 0735192981527091168287631615254 5336231324 226804 5222889
614 9709173971135352554 4 01236086188154 54 14 70853204 6722994 69390714
8818860332682826172282696 4 78516984 09755613280910904 92994 20589
02099758680270118297 14 38113061665016560694 05094 174 4 7084 13659317294
6036832314 8867837834 01584 66652627793811034 7185652734 29011264 69689
951352204 381388359254 084 5087574 2934 04 8304 8052570263674 681999971113924
994 308238094 814 7319257601152853824 7357208314 91052716081699222814
18675329911795524 4 774 8792024 69824 783577017905817684 337666777689
0217764 9062193699589
654 676599694 28721801097813692136 74 4 6220974 783004
0927181905137635612325 4 86127214 52226168051802932568183109314 139665924 531034 4
236884 3397067352872663830004 54 19514 64 4 2303262301907189
759856124 702358650054 2075982524 89
819907503165380324 9502601693723058314 817314 7524 304 3594 24 989
14 879189
062802634 09122726735334 4 8537779853276889
704 76167261585288351 4 0603525270885199292171330705785763874 939374 55594
00967615375217782801162690377265289
89
62034 4 1261598810632168253206 4 4 38164 0612917117212009556 74
73839167222962355574 6124 39015599054 4 883226264 4 16256871268704 850034 4 92114
15757614 3154 87883822624 4 938257190720528224 35654 03066864 3394
9527866391978261966212889
0293170809150693354 7609363069503877964 8380650097087712584 2074 4 2114
99716985561589
989
74 78765137505785362724 53652178066289
777507327157034 9854 774 716789
0295666395835111199772 54 30882108300838719703001636037 54 8232031811034
519634 1997195708016263754 25606969661834 36297269070662230614
3131863618116113316 84 184 951612964 7994 6354 0815516628864 53122010561796238101 4 4
384 62014 132524 68510264 137934 116621666604 4 35554 339672608390029334 24
98560592304 77254 301604 859689
8781615324 25234 889
4 799274 9956804 057508785961584 6563996882770505824 80803752624 4 4 0992284
26558107196531396214 74 222234 15350770031361866522902 4 24 24
2733975223220119730089
59689
104 9854 054 4 74 2769756380596262269087884 764 367655193756819519963 04 4
22809024 719659779814 112299761130996689
4 84 0654 70304 30616154 284 05289

84 6055561052774 3167094 54 797654 2569994 4 3256151512704 1177684 024
72629905184 68739384 4 03174 90922778671374 6504 8775654
003526182336135822096915951653100302994 70261213798326995515 4 794 3004 5282504 04
1161789

922994 79111764 12173992693774 165820202835024 26115579535771019286950264
6054 35924 118006680782334 174 98334 2235251194 03957869035786809979573555664 634
8184 10923535663805321625058733961273016517920915269630774 160353934 3614
8765086569589

4 4 166875931028197227084 21300606989

032768124 81364 34 0882914 5069353500784 26900283389

69289

0036766306519621256911370825 14 95264 13073002057234 2600614 34 794 784 184
6620763374 24 74 01965234 906393029662233773082064 0228704 0880954 0394 4 89

26023755930275783818672711195559036264 381803694 4 1026989

5609970224 02685189

2905705634 1157634 56634 535309178364 4 9127065514 65214 5274
51609570926960198193514 82504 23083093324 0208569382325737324
6556197838050798236783914 89

64 4 132121190325383719305126121 4 3512054 34 672138024 9172084 4 5724
06756078389

1183614 4 20617219609324 188787153906531193 4 5624 2314 305059597581389

680014 59327268036990315314 8589

81784 2184 14 086270354 13234 05714 063724 2334 4 16230520114 60053724 3354 54 4
085804 784 915273835605370083298 4 194 4 194 0878577289

4 289

4 2989

05564 11184 89

0127988174 24 2713094 173250224 64 9989

776184 99584 4 4 824 3196333877136064 17005075788 11206260189

0354 612585934 5154 5618175684 097314 73384 2014 95189

37581589

9601208752575627603329500301183188 09564 29108679299364 914 0874
263226672138684 915224 1299032914 62932026823734 9095662579032064 2804
5338516755725663 35964 32829836906797154 4 89

4 914 4 14 4 284 4 57366131214 71652577292832283872251912 2781850333184
5753752311813889

104 68730112025332934 3303322817674 4 4 79092066563250 18838874 991783124
52779568780325185708787710 82132181754 229913702999034 634 0824 31982200181814
301695015867564 7723184 55173516019353974 118068162554 986334 692974
27936383683122862090150084 763296027154 20554 09234 7219774 8755577372771253584
379299733675504 135390096260754 6017704 783200920900004 370304
77206239693112361996923069 4 519212280751280626109033960808551 1993936257664 560584
54 74 89

2984 566105164 37763230204 7629334 883313664 55334 5734 804 735715674 4 4
997734 717821981573926294 356614 85332563525 73800753734 24 5856962732264 4
3292539121854 8350084 718726153761193599211755 4 4 94 6875172209534 021714

967332300854 303127734 30084 4 2170392235658052374 6997811952384 74 4 4
9333837385774 85114 274 62252203934 6757212327850661052691327977730634
6288737262224 19584 671667202215168082910005267022364 1512652274 0776004 619794
9668504 4 24 14 92903303752615324 755653009315314 55774 15607854 8884 37204 15714
06008765128076133114 00021517609289
        824 89
        86294 506264 798639727812087334 4 792984 7854 531512329334 0514 0684 725574
69284 86263150354 77092571914 4 2014
22185887802572791283311779822123368077931168758654 777139994 623954
39860017821714 04 4 5115877933764 58252175919910881923830051663310282837236134
127214 07224 623795391293388364 1879315532993289
        4 879874 86153861391523074 689
        174 100662618607772679134 8713632214 75165685084 4 1991780694 861954 601934
089
        37081923214 192638277533759194 5703264 50236304 34 756871734
5295839955367097394 7311374 51394 33281977911222269397254 59124
9383798231266070963822259670190083814 532862904 6106065868563209780150854 22334 84
81105906173852298620528789
        604 95007325704 2722202039361363824 7958310354 32598550726214 034
0985962778601721689
        5598750303288281768 04 094 68520938864 03363652364 94 4 2857653338109795334
2025875230660994 737779174 834 09964 056208373304 3167671087592982666684 354
67009599704 8589
        5374 84 151152214 50224 994 54 4 152838657802928530176585629101388 14 4
17266938379020705 0034 191012138679134 6354 6522874 814 07153382029019192 3514
67212683827510001739 4 80517922357591031 06294 117826715838186378195 4 64 884
31229736302075907294 9613132264 23551084 910264 9984 74 18870181274
039872030679358312315 4 82878780386867207634 54 984 951991134 4 5099124 4 24
73105052272527668320660 34 8538056734 851263693194 665299251629026264 6589
        4 1634 13960915097218723 64 0275500269701088386832 4 94 14 212571204 886964
565829636160986536858983788390280207060702963996 2089
        2916924 20117564 62921271784 14 4 3866094 4 4 84 153071327538274 1805124 75604
70084 5614 196078604 954 4 859255813071615271768187 1096104 1702864 624 4
5106386992799031329802393832292307860024 61112125625374 9299206962360554
97397793370905509150615995807 4 6264 7693070614 654 73365729538801084
65930773709264 393270961733589
        798755133298517353358057619820375607173964 95121026056824 21535394
32206578780654 3336816683791839254 3102962997862558313815084 290234 604 14 64
2850633182078026674 0857504 29654 9353954 4 94 86518527564 708814 3513231959734 9789
        91714 15169373256883389
        3316283389
        64 5184 887032263989
        3055689
        4 5183919124 3082932515654 023675385004 3094 552275229862193634
99930799560689
        684 4 661874 5989

4 74 88234 13664 085188532193673114 37589

4 6356570214 2223037174 14 81201272628291057331857839227334 79526068004
131224 04 4 4 4 69069570034 326579109561734 2284 65513830287770817092800 3703275264
4 557620090294 89

87017264 7182289

32761788234 6799595389

6680114 02866870526336706006304 2612994 6084 94 995638275599060264
777652197025375830 1181 6128754 3876098578289

9634 2210595022534 1504 39826096187609835216523165 3316977214 4
12517700380390215981379 89

13202929277554 38711703391163224 807524 65724 9729623124 76509351794 35674
838114 3152864 1333029089

12377714 66124 6904 4 864 551164 92679934 634 15562118822817564 23024 051694 89

54 4 4 28168314 14 04 904 38057886059010737006718298 9936504 074 94
7027855738627203271084 2602732695690064 12015558094 691371012984 25529054 4 95764
5064 575600374 0314 94 58790821054 7355911363990672780 814 591917064 3387069714
77366524 7784 4 33863025569838810258

87930950197131284 07089

1871969674 9394 002657194 05722159295868834 578669810318183594
93810271931161525153017 0904 03194 5172383224 596330526786264 2100074
5736336797264 614 3529714 98884 6055291907822957213 569264 63834 79217594
05780513036734 887954 4 94 7334 4 64 5606796676912782679904 94
2003628806990026035221665252664 88097224 672121294 61678228224 74 2717834 105358584
9093818084 3820769671226221556 92524 4 64 101160066383911818308730856354
226721501721889

134 91114 4 34 074 23167201858015 4 0968394 172184 552924 703066633174
39699203209991372307939208706332681 95027024 1836323739355756594 8355864 34
27585271530364 7534 674 601181623121808611137993 8354 514 82289

863062536933279374 737264 04 69312673756534 01997300907614
262122865011585689

4 4 820803714 28361204 858316174 750390771287604 6503361236135224 31214 204
9114 096204 58582922554 3574 900902717114 310056202779664 27328203684 0883514 2189

97367661285154 174 17015505596692954 33553384 98868702324 902061064 4
58071692286334 3391855394 4 34 65974 1831033154 53291025913036064 6226668797794
55734 904 54 674 88232753173759959373232273103710 4 521133115338289

304 24 7739724 1957274 4 011654 184 84 315564 89

4 04 89

213580557085576275584 95534 889

19138564 379163834 24 089

3960220978801958750 7614 164 57873384 34 4 319808735157516674
96820037915379610297 94 4 321094 7607327004 636334 3661259071179260382965776504
89

83399682005284 64 234 206854 4 94 69930387124 964 664 24 85811604 4 20004
66693398574 16855517298369829263584 9104 4 71793384 4 6832504 3384 4
71758725269936686233757079586379951176 74 378774 2210295932621738817179921125 64
96076654 9050364 753011284 60597199864 223972784 3391967774 0389

58231917557325994 1937900854 9282598066076789

4 9854 84 3333553305204 4 297814 6864 2262154 6390705667804 79389

1317765192204 99357616638821963223357224 13875804 88187287554 77834 305533714 1624 291591814 4 0724 9101833736072586131305858393796369137316050 63865378761619976568352789

60391654 12211971231637064 6384 350875058804 6575531967200804 8106320831182153795613800983535595260936370064 531708064 4 202888377266908268009 4 24 750615773653069536994 64 734 4 4 264 179908807236585691623 89

963651757807623731861366280300067759525 4 5698303593502093103 4 0106654 882387605906309667152580319027018056510774 179659964 177889

50664 06027884 7170680779275557035102223714 73067950065096075380534 263982026154 0712721378560322 74 32886168024 173389

4 59790505032137974 84 6614 90309530174 02300954 9575261795889

698360970314 2914 084 804 58384 201770593330872789

88292106539860854 9784 17702268001994 31723125607279669350937 84 6167380814 534 7108132937634 521964 74 4 1631933117869064 99824 823727616205615024 4 4 394 4 72323379106960839688560326 74 36594 4 761324 36686239105834 3526372587026552727235 4 68109736136753799885 4 34 0224 7829732195864 7384 707984 98514 17285386752779230658 4 09174 3206050109910223 89

298189

3864 5721604 1689

4 9234 02085594 04 8059798887199075389

94 4 83624 575918179587264 7854 824 36871784 28051181657010359994 89

6167564 5814 4 11774 359994 15574 1564 054 198094 0777060781817873278088392351665272981172 94 704 51824 89

4 88694 02539784 9704 04 012578501708525229 4 8003264 4 8553982933954 102504 934 1054 4 4 614 3561304 53712369616822024 2708754 6803225777224 6764 53869069173584 6329099659789

27085724 1360685294 72284 189

988811197694 92577756734 7314 9204 54 18824 99353860754 4 853832734 9316024 94 4 5830184 0052011005971211224 88189

926014 0903390584 3014 10505598071884 4 4 154 763356093389

2955827033563839189

20724 4 1156624 13634 67937554 167389

089

3091868608031263789

2309129166075500989

8084 04 308771738687684 930623853335091504 10600038306016394 88536879210612389

4 10574 394 034 60624 016371854 84 25217716754 5163976002550502264 39611525994 294 3086934 9869074 62978375997016129503084 38036606600589

2265852930563788669584 66784 8757260025329183393071854 7261012014 35318123008262824 5390756526384 8166284 3067124 14 09153532301737357772231705 4 54 533185733039863116290928079651 4 000762580295868325211303562521 34 99854

0067832905798100262663767805172062475401635370252168218735528720401996359618873606934730672840960812886498922816545218524083282791281849386363527220300859827544599898999583511157436878788812704855717381485740307803629420485942064433415790169383959681533585277508781574397192432277988317060546340053309696115995437320394129955177197409249372819386910424719168074575580541317281683365537965275951040258293766006937948476305024368669308749861291151557902990891475114714361655097781089168915938904322861163098089616015436542397071317339876255613839334927890605747145381691569264882015102621472183250340916562454293531173283968374175550697887724604398556261085337374028770997288047611491577857651047529089113817806546922207217132541594679780555957405449532558779284323247504820257296107211930542720344543111901843265159983295119242549956886629245120615544354851877843376022845731855255302038578067996423334739432832550797681431749352903653552357083362272954029760362245967870224679610872900653691581103297724112719687184631712015310872022829121678513683286828891002281654521852408328279128184938636352722030085982754459989891491383959681533585277508781574891491383959689100630830596997329512401834379280807586687788984960437727540275895229293668539226751399282371615964473732982701750908375680274466691591111497799446671135691088924379199309424721308073081984262593144347965790856700825628858836114463307069019106360685995185387041710623856804324112299406997697652171894899349718804503864321759828643313402327317350344875527937834864131041994965955257706690456718435502156201896727939734268216256860859224881131666473414298910138757127570483051459436636099246610627201124409872399971042075654391506863102013575984601467302651199034298650639676000696687958282892433978259058748567826269263303468372332124066157760295156537226106822903836613368341504999895934280932018654247036073590765608162195997593438201724618076958178347221271503991239373308059816434946231367174959999463042117638181478301910213344735692656258805710164468798455661720375874281490998433930465239312200035644248650280200221038723815085543608061085953817427853246549792311015101812667413846629462674003407290924306775649178579342775165295098460009862821986519350148631413113382340818641810195988872295935856034372242367239601514627896565485335331740074198424260136066735529840754402573177714954021927548762566366320979513483898

2323984 730934 2827299390954 922628685258280376257104 0814 04 14
070921533779824 71219334 64 8252071838785374 4 50072385259360567659576204 02194
51924 7929124 13075854 64 8591812784 555951253394 853773274 3954
653252016862250537285001304 53724 0004 64 74 4 4 79074 59782510294 4 4 7904 75972689
94 9375374 6928089
3311554 3550514 20516123636834 4 100734 984 2994 707086534 872826168261194
9954 4 4 59888850359607914 367111963913932091 1200954 1335128855089
924 93392853794 76656164 159254 527588534 79068034 859304 21014 3177857711724
511374 184 624 32155337224 05654 1214 94 232234 6734 10032864 092372275714
73170380930584 666114 1052866534 929215704 384 371938758254 89
184 989
4 4 6589
74 89
211239804 355925364 919086589
0669173908088675009132330 54 26654 82077157364 0252081624 83016589
87303608659808379615767364 1177362734 66976156665392134 82934 564
2399129280785997987881 5204 292215190914 16907854 97361872516930999913227000674
997233515576579514 3664 74 702374 876614 964 4 04 926134 8608299760978362604
927823173889
4 979224 6852097759950804 988269723924 95765987223064 69511876779916054
9567269969085152582265295227 3858854 393021734 274 75574 391874 4 11376633994 128594
831234 384 84 8812794 57601367 1006676165974 39589
632554 53067081684 294 512114 0912212009108666989
989
15001020556924 84 8523722554 21310716613919828276574 29818829175183372084
175238696768280591023151992 53128014 4 537722164 74 368259508608886364 4 34 6720804
0799574 56104 290101965608808393098287 16061604 912163604 586908622289
737564 5574 13574 3071591089
36724 2331664 4 773328296824 188314 9217164 94 972514 01194
93690567095296152704 32919617564 101018514 0596083954 221011253004 320324 4 772904
5095686728686928379789
94 4 5334 73254 078320054 28354 8804 51308874 1363193695581682874 607904
656694 59004 074 4 2884 18738123256769967164
69267998695588605208063729838321 1238624 681202881704 34 8155814 06294 9883062634
59334 4 998884 0386526057374 2230738578664 00023774 153128859094 5512575353933694
08694 4 4 29394 0752218284 710010776658095127 56702014 7754 082982594
3655390077790618030037104 0301910921 85293284 7824 11655189
0922870290124 04 16004 5214 9317093577536081634 20856552332014 4 384 53889
5834 220684 1713882399532270635638724 261133021723608875319 6924
820117906522275084 8154 65360634 684 32083525195108332160684 317334 36584
680591301574 08787018229598765822830 0204 25283556693204 5019819881714 582611715984
000117232324 84 6223680233784 983905719584 2083394 188330250004 1002600378834 22114
83673054 74 9609677924 29704 4 999837994 7904 4 054 34 971089
626589

676691300284 99096038606304 624 009333797909203575516255516664
005711218771723903001503960954 05184 58169993864 304 4 9804 0103991612865934 74 4
9558276066834 824 89

09337338629266989

64 697053174 156089

22966624 289

14 38192737235672603030501103 4 159701503907594 1159915617925116562289
24 4 17675577202639271089

7852605994 713153357004 5904 830124 535860224
5707716058212332185295875822030551937289

020017734 3206194 28734 214 752378860830070299796531556810301128799258 9
391833877964 7006752027036887724 0584 0664 369190902874 38763388209714
58010174 9510134 64 584 0281278011316813989

78065090074 07674 64 22096389

9804 533262076514 9608259774 5227584 23904 134 502684 618616814 579533717594
6226830306366614 5365992028030084 32528514
9817881771272573867535502851338367923056 74 324 36869620272756904 95694 7214 224 24
679884 3604 119226316915567882764 84 222391196274 036714 5989

74 14 4 54 318006168862933763562397525 4 816109201806289

4 4 2065086508865174 3884 4 5174 4 02936157089

106653051819134 4 083524 1738539089

5294 73312690900228814 761735924 054 7275574 10087221186024 80706552734 7854
64 6708100332528804 94 87281884 64 7664 51387194 84 64 70027398366396786911087224
90689

4 4 5254 4 99301361359823021009664 966265824 979074 1793302604 4 796164 6789
612176304 7354 7094 1059054 7677874 36276981114 64 819594 6765395331326021604
5188056852012381853835993525090558673 04 8169589

39312668888710724 5163758078691852980 4 64 4 375984 939014 9864
0886729121561514 6935054 4 68003927753771628002 84 4 4 61708872834 6133201602784
693514 171037189

81359285654 4 4 04 73889

353364 34 2252995356306714 864 3575822661507084 7224 212139574 9058812364
72608079566539182107806975919196272996137682505271901680135018259365039 04 314 89
2374 222182997294 35910504 7665101984 354 9677158363903560509027 4 4 094 54
73762000866255189

537989

7398695524 94 4 2094 5283689

3729162255864 4 5881857232200509734 021124 2024
2701338138097506387073687862 24 134 61626607614 186589

0367575672804 94 685139294 924 694 74 976704 4 8286278503799394
28327879122033297139754 384 364 4 7227794 19524 830053313308326594 12681654 814
31836724 1851907164 537118394 5618853767186114 634 51009876355610396882 4 034
6932274 316386856389

366920782628786664 63162305865623208034 4 67033224 14 89
6584 4 290862011917977518360789

811784 7087626296153194 0034 78154 64 050634 56598584 539593367839204
717781619611519781599915334 83239756111621222104 5289
683087138354 59988065857801354 859374 904 263956020172957868115 4 94 07988789
989
5278594 4 953129124 75824 817137108859096914 0706193303618003032389
191321684 024 23711785594 14 79381751226153735529282 04 84 62011908783557824
107679589
8728264 83801883630605162587 4
5813238071702127070311601599319566532110559086 84 4 63723011219393528829932 84
356956065971989
3014 84 189
4 1924 696514 19504 713100362091384 684 08714 36786883238124
871873805822177969166872677052869 4 917232969297574 129371576503104 8614 98264
996394 254 251535522789
26558176593281228135199 04 9986283389
1769509864 9870938852865224 64 1624 14 98009133604 8094 161672069334 24
2500172533359024 1224 5206966274 2838060791570974 610193234 3274 4 2284
27903009219716781979659790595 4 9127210553864 4 724 0760083100058808181907 24 4
787034 36574 54 2794 7504 66602116861532820793670 4 22831576774 109787065652889
95809215120790091062 4 889
3864 65174 8603366304 880883858583654 754 19590635290169607959866719791951 54
726753999884 776218884 78510736605567922374 55158009612734 6370372954 709964 14 4 89
54 4 0357070050979597124 9707914 989
4 057504 20165030739210083757394 132816578085719802851130 4 24 796134 514 504
277763666054 87057390164 9799638800674 927633569990174 214 24 708604
276336870153889
54 2554 4 860519661560114 57074 3110126783606189
76337654 08595584 4 1673969989
89
91714 686664 84 09024 190014 931111734 62062958230778705794 86764
6385567587210995136 4 68309977716094 54 65572016812285393776737 4 0994 283039515574
94 5316920658203714 5204 582775357833798271161575355 4 754
7595988090288825001513269030621837535588152280080 4 994 62199263139514
759007671504 4 4 120102864 04 223234 6757214 65222554 33374 64 54 0769554 4
296373365183294 4 08114 81655311231788856853 4 4 9362565109233822325088751970064
02178562624 0504 392039311551274 24 19812786611804
5752037903135226382150021077213050 24 06624 1830028624 77655911114 13089
4 74 9764 1704 4 2763287774 736669514 1529627972984 736229019636223154 3631914
184 179969689
6280359277506155139875578536726635378 14 0081715318318793314 79803166307354
183824 9854 774 614 34 75821220350330394 9134 626725084 373973133134 6134
9718786522154 84 795211328065589
74 510020324 872979223925689
275374 902704 25986685614 904 05375284 504 662614 4 264 25991229576994 984
595616886612934 274 152168604 536950858277105538068 4 24 70639686077813289

931062855112879954 394 33670099191520888614 4 55564 574 4 22792533094
75103278639998286086648664 77824 6977669364 6959682093306304 832523027286162884 091854
0210758575059523354 9174 517563505589

4 31674 9129117086207384 696004 8789

78263910905625739599 874 924 95979011090191614 6590802074 84
962639358279265058364 7676708383011968855050518615798097218529807820275 4
679077735284 594 88554 864 20957184 8095773550264 1837966220105606201767 24 10164
7596182317714 4 4 198810096102794 77760819625624 6820854 574 99375939175577255504
390164 4 2709090994 0333682021018189

188094 314 4 687251194 4 88397607261064 289

4 7637705083816809284 728704 530854 71610727866631012203668875829064 624
9653294 4 21504 04 26089

607955960284 83768115833106563981887154 10222918563637554 6808614
676806062617591254 75132626589

6334 16570626511726817054 9301094 065863026692204 22989

4 83023764 4 3236714 2194 6364 9003200189

1029510553731974 20393993038094 28707866552914 769288138564 587814 9664
77980823314 82664 02166554 84 67134 0624 01859714 121754 24 4 0978712771828778534 134
383738258099537774 55566863903097000614 9284 0773024 70091720199524 620624
5391985859237134 5074 23999851718224 954 2889

513234 3503182334 4 83788319295955334 879010992117189

9225365294 29365336258259539094 6552963581374 4 9729369974 65118753385374
87094 21770808174 570174 2251604 0904 3884 6121574 124 4 52850202379839036999911389
696734 778804 9704 2088863931284 389

1579868614 99535720637694 8214 92093062812513122808004 99666262553224
2838399173520256674 5252299084 0994 6325864 6834 111304 2084 589

880324 14 287824 14 8608262105774 94 753300377060215168255 4 21685888255205289
13719387724 986908202539336294 04 7304 75050099704 4 07094 693589

19699005334 78304 4 635811964 9104 83163816068074 323974 7518873774 504
8539320801189

20921762003254 128590019212850780087801080961218699721567278787836037834
285050223359104 73861003790033368195821534 7953124
203321923791186979738109328501036782788060812 74 5282883103918315704 4 14
803727152691119589

13827350206266167881367389

300589

4 34 98719262754 21758678377586169291156 4 196954 97805005027174 4 14 8214
22531771664 564 89

7625594 375826764 3094 9126055292857753556527311 4 929560879110821596194
01757024 9204 4 626207794 680537769554 4 1637902384 4 4 28627076001335882937229058 9
561353109924 4 87923773970012638010390621036297100554
0090233266205286855512923889

3654 0076639663983925724 50824 4 9689

89

2624 59924 394 384 5087655789
09028189

856834 334 510996196384 091164 37670596054 84
19525350568787230520679162057973980086958750046561196154 504 0162976777009654
70185284 334 97764 4 6794 96028037224 22923120925815523806451507317582639784 89
71659561076294 4 95873794 56851984 590609369134 973227024 28238293584 834
76200972795732039739082440499026524593739625729544
91177296085988591097983191619192371557431477730561327586503018671287922333999
4
09221062679094 6258508116928279669238172379855127629935238608831771468
9
728571559104 796911352900853677375489
955124 718689
039574 4 660004 84 7954 014 4 78028822320824 25670184 5114 754 5838594
639977604 12123218294 512072077908176823315161845542195987497445589
0151199270623605189
634 07353934 87564 0953156034 070693595825760816676955874 9209824 04
806665275624 551923220032514 5294 17553964 68271902352195763796378
9
7594 1750521586754 201928536559666201450
4
5633855278357125671205128227519609295390924 5784 188554 0127128286062203184
0304
16252304 57334 991986203368394 1854 919174 4 312814 170274 6834 8053312363654
64
08009522798679980816786143876702299176420421935770303028
89
24 06338233711883166689
234 725665314 7154 2619736924 881856774 4 4 23683067628580803557766708524
9394 3272675918271305802820474 4 98683109238845183965692912826914
13580228508792026381557594 4 588577839176304 153824 7774 5027363004 796768568
9
590574 29077532824 031838874 1953284 725057582369989
84 185573609737934 79262107564 8001276066005684 856289
52962703650334 07284 9924 570768216606004 308519214 4 993994 6159274
018679067024 92509188084 254 975382500057364 11527656278820683168374 561361164
6610594 5296098764 7876178106573256994 4 130069604 04 4 127574 84 805908154
3152521914 7593078104 14 0991804 36770663956672634 4 3535624 56193564 075135654
67271679094 118794 884 8086809230938328738225004 2851308615564 673823134 4 89
1197653033059034 94 885070904 364 0855117089
681596818853555968367767082875926959001222681306340790521808314 17534
28838750131652921876633335743143710101634 7796658883618869883499832
89
81164 00702596550204 76119906884 593064 118801374
33528093795109830522058657551902553313247393551842157260882310168318176409724
179664 2821705539235733182359972105591467580990960157125453625914 65735834
5108084 97696708071726694 3718308124 9664 13928529324 205814 835226274 4
69375858569571687034 5022377577778359815858095456674 554 62729794
73079756932050856264 053052830255672286677544 4 8284 086209981389
79303709253264 25964 038534 99617054 63860837230314 89
4 810013719990131970126280108496986832790805995250749377542359999787837
4
4 6577837123753575785267771063814 356136789
0794 73724 7924 26181599280191554 2363584 09224 1092695194 98675837014
00806912594 594 4 5559254 6704 73203928004 70111600155954
170202879503592920177039686011345630444923339774 354 5571654 572714 95173534
52904 62215877669321039725654 05338682391305809660021212324 831138704 907261634
98817775250633988037352830441378850405352914 195734 4 86262214 8033294 954 4
8889

0854 507924 8054 268374 194 0669188555167572166221109 2089
97318526676782935266132904 2761712071734 3300234 52589
1953735574 750926874 315293634 284 4 964 077178567399584 3814 89
4 2104 62851810384 964 34 2773551924 4 3854 01105600364
09186090659830023373684 5914 99584 014 4 4 990129369372589
3952889
834 8115564 5581061030794 54 5804 75664 6504 89
35767852752111834 07994 59874 4 205675506984 616282974 8169274 34 0319574 4
8112126921989
1324 3550319837054 664 4 4 24 96096363374 84 86558714 36934 24 00084 26830694
664 7268678216054 30760555551571130 1054 9963694 214 12014 52860567154 92814
5035636088579354 204 4 988312557195995587078583365330551210839284 9984 112684
79057129722024 655013870820524 4 74 927234 1919503603039394 6034 76770851534 7254
33807691354 302103233118270994 105254 3731637179189
960813384 4 4 036735092091110631733765874 01600018697304 252984 2024 4
888527033172514 6924 974 75393198235035252261761609 4 384 80970535124 5708751318689
26737005074 4 2774 1207097904 0734 63122620529000639189
290990331964 3533353377827730338009564 35520237281189
34 14 22221316384 124 66218762656292621316 5374 74 4 09523054 54
01691905912102983325 4 87384 4 314 99690081791766624 4 4 5625710550014 06036680013324
95809064 102834 877164 193564 714 304 09550576380385738522098716167959104
852220807083954 4 38166529535008774 6068113602730824
88566261392866772837170303237832334 67164 064 1865105991624 81767070634 565314 6764
074 4 926589
904 0024 9294 3382034 76654 8273034 1522657904 23510131092975678304 84
81363297639763 2274 673272990989
39274 4 963857214 4 129084 87064 4 80704 6616306718326269730189
5505226175036704 4 3765606386089
754 74 809199526394 4 0353604 654 3998237735619024 6502693129589
14 0222105988734 08816322256258686174 4 5324 4 11589
4 9303555099774 824 74 1515073734 1194 757333735565276274 18519164 24 514
620104 987826294 53689
50884 4 6232117635800351184 1835926759864 29712813985384 14 4
6909691719079951674 04 678189
358750274 4 350355118079967776 24 98706284 7592913272616884 4 8884 93914
112874 53205724 8359162360674 161634 4 63880131235116126332 14 157350735873789
089
864 60331910104 7904 95108805327624 3634 380195320531364 134 3554 59364 704
1984 399732731928183025760085767530258321696714 64 6834 35884 003914 20370724
26708260176162533902989
8671526756221981306035295 94 84 4 64 64 04 039688560064
817661090330560790650387689
684 4 6731694 854 34 389
183689
35379334 1689

8764 6104 0506024 109359855532664
31299975939026367969692513769369261591022851172165414 889
21572622359773667701463984 58552104 7074 763889
72254 9022179557834 738536300819334 3789
8874 8156802769759994 951212544 15702713764 9027751507877994 91095614 89
574 26227398794 033221282575324 5784 5619552714 97177374 89
2311071758004 4 852610875339714 4 09334 2364 1670007394 74 7605338766380254
295863552936913034 7698689
9061333624 59084 7353805299916952374 06505765703934 90154 739065565289
25808194 4 696284 012213924 551119876038074 05660994 105231164 3601925684
7220532851072587588370887878354 074 6177976015317304 9500582938124
7505250302170023610957367090784 0223511622259723813014 4 4 07984 79181330321054 4
324 4 3110271979100591373809834 8377586361399771944 367200655924 56993814 7027619184
6661211804 2961718665283106957766092447 7161598315124 59361728010390163655204
6619370925251253613965592011778214 27680194 2804 76586534 85815874
7031199267709791335044 9110720516524 324 6231253831574 4 87512954
1560355275026367961454 610934 4 4 16853578102731389
9699954 686734 35181034 4 3255259516930023300505925727997815904 820223589
052604 792034 82507504 2171734 554 664 2531252852594 784 4 0684 21333789
79724 559983814 529024 9134 127724 34 24 5097179511864 4
6150628152839286502372129264 3684 08132689
4 231693151888189
538526818004 76310307780389
924 4 1215187198582722254 4 989
9967787514 5879160239707666604 4 13330594 00177251968288276181389
0254 014 214 1154 032221880752214 93138730394 389
4 838634 8804 8858725731296054 4 0226754 01194 4 4 34 4
271239556902379071500713861064 198583888795688054 863351728084 4 4 64 4 724
8132772385956105213013091015106264 29327631624 72228598525710263715944 629994
013226550518804 4 6573989
80037754 4 2184 629979193304 0060517616187986026555760768914 95679624 03302092035338230064 19857512128054 9087681264
9998662968202160083935774 25692390014 50967655189
68300114 98580395006624 6338616802255066870759127484 831975300014 554 060154
11980784 1134 94 8294 656806017074 182194 4 82694 202914 5919311797294 4
2535235139331011218688316780023266376919519389
89
304 9565596364 4 304 99826362332222131737958633752729015980267624 382084
9089
4 364 283124 96796216250016352996689
304 4 62584 5804 16724 90710904 14 27954 4 74 3227764 05586064 4 97993774
81597906129222029306198335261800447 2611796654 96758054 82901810689
4 737221612026571626304 363530228212933724 508394 3534 370967854 324
38058312889
5052786635657171288036985284 54 8714 9507985624 66555779317050790289
986859714 364 593077973507014 01522754 4 766934 19823926389

89

294 53534 31902180169387585028778687970204
6168231973519928076697586512760064 68238391696014 867111500960384
593882005106152664 62562727086373994 715025771810723089

6204 36264 15525571521279044 58354 29590591012051850860519983358295202764 4
524 25123577351536144 51329122133578344 11967187075856606350002976644 5872189

965684 68098354 2255567976997861529583162065744 32073721099684 4 06194
6085275213997207744 6028379618294 067782659809969835866089

74 386510365624 255625084 2354 354 563015121971111673283365507058324
791727356514 27694 10984 986357066618802528444 34 536119774 234 90001604
10913598065825325104 777234 8737585884 66697858029999224 197366504 115511962816004
7321576507005166289

84 53996379194 14 4 719612753684 96384 84 184 07835392194 95160760752984
767084 138274 604 4 0301770757999666767568612536105144 00391716817256780501389
783718658379689

761501720984 80602272151208763671116355293561961304 0209273964 18528693604
72651396687556304 008753585686831314 1286860922825551244 226959567993035024
90113667709364 034 990374 84 5874 1989

1089

0189

4 5705198578124 784 4 03575786713931970855444 989

38099970654 10579169020959889

74 987384 4 7272613724 35180656164 99316389

73511197033103939780444 0928094 799734 33772650212244 9714 34 09823782365196589

2886279223277990394 18205068569837671166237721514 4 1202276633794 917374
3734 228317972794 0119374 53904 90579714 4 61718360256732214 0552194 62186285914 54
389

656234 024 89

4 537981195596444 968707073021860780513193094 6785284 84 4 4 2021284 324
99307154 13564 4 23079386272526585208444 922694 844 399394 8530535272706823358639444
86081705774 07516973852120210628944

594 17716079254 130699134 60814 3824 63286693523126590734 303668095385956084
5016739322909654 2828854 09786377872218259072744 34 19564 66116595934 087134 4
8120299579604 0005764 14 684 856384 192084 025832685521237954 9624 89

11586260094 00987654 13585870619251136537194 814 860857107708376020972374
659553114 4 03073394 94 234 84 4 86152523722666253172090816226944 0002112275918344
255298281689

971968761014 385191901289

88074 24 2805283555533252325715444 85875614 4 775201194 68011155094 4 054
2965731019362159591875821944 822074 756153078334 80300854 994 330873982134
02707000311285887927967396273660920712697115138195377155444 64 1063374 55584
919631691755255599189

224 089

797833124 27354 5384 179602784 59589

864 7060095284 1808664 67711094 64 15984 31500095974 94 702207595874 936960934
89

2351315530879522675319228875193269056992695901124 280084 378089

758022372721112814 2771580921578619031 4 3823282221584 311973638679727227684
95813632814 70182765236169987038316 54 805714 61752017797801074
90052009862225386713 4 3789

87984 88104 4 503027177386068210671823 4 856661032815984 09185714 9084 77074
1257737215296236289

514 2819394 934 4 92310024 755294 68768814 2282688263381992107050031 4
8229690781270685023609679524 561563176253784 4 39086838854 54 7176625054 8688614
5388589

4 01906509184 101588520883369612987731672752691975623864 27609513694 58384
261852183389

57051864 1326320252293139134 8380821287964 33881362984 553904
2373128573855900623287197915909121817103 34 92088287365725960067510 34 5169173034
84 0664 773124 7285364 98697032255058028512103 14 58139716550054 02199912584 67124
75229623304 794 76204 174 83573396512933884 625986054 669020687274 3107989

200936008629962585264 955692634 224 4 34 9075889

87120754 05572391778889

8374 74 00628311035989

363975368314 31637915535084 4 5994 998151790357191664 595797264
05356357962285223232099956252907295659686256664 761182174 36889

365526584 2097358804 83823563270384 629174 104 274 634 032764 04 4 24
721791963389

2333004 523529200287573013563038211 17289

71331694 363722061750858152029084 9724 63690556676289

2184 262651781976519538524 64 30364 256203212959 16089

58533598154 07065024 525216570882264 3889

695532003307123860177199 4 269799874 2711966035304 8528358184 4 14 60854 9134
5064 4 4 31713086666567324 74 4 794 3228054 73391376062758189

04 2836565865989

54 664 88561709859023357189

364 711022191554 4 8014 1608108632865265720250373 4 7796586980289

69756875969566551715729978174 14 91255194 508337794 974 4 669806026864
31815234 22924 31677632651015505374 677709204 1564 764 624 75124 967230114 2884
839539706060560724 65314 227321889

58383550139850224 798061638234 94 53661289

94 04 09355917809265868236064 1984 94 786394 9273925514 675962185564 84 34
02871639984 24 16564 079224 3204 99215193527094 274 925509720983764 0554
799507636962370089

61585314 2082854 978064 4 06575694 61074 0124 283011677091754 08804
880626657504 874 4 970010064 4 81728170337185716876990520504 312691267589

4 2354 64 24 26321926816126071352559377998 4 687684 87666374 63737084
830913023031875975519252 4 39917826264 027996616367094 369112530086284
3502978866714 83877355700954 085095109254 26723708716285087204 9910014 666606934
35254 39681324 2277505204 12084 3117783620864 2591374 14 0370189

390584 913088530767180337775977981 54 504 06004 5084 281692653954 94 24 24 1734
39682579794 29633223312132181078012932197936027503888526310 4 587257887904

993301724 9371699290336354 529074 96514 64 0560912754 8752881574 874 8504 66564
78815713364 324 270157712065088264 7257091154 5293554 151064 551035094
71072017880017924 64 1359721384 2994 87104 59775527984 274 5069774 26564 14 8834
06830080923054 64 6260389

4 832672239604 0624 64 6594 574 2025221084 288128266889

6752789

8024 34 682655789

6265626637974 53689

1092934 689

20924 84 10970235713162753302389

020769867314 32584 276094 818388124 585758734 014 09706867189

5618131122294 700219784 4 824 158154 4 509819889

15294 24 289

06934 6605626079565664 394 33934 2799835882357116757511632925562 14 994
709518352233124 581091315865577359175 84 703694 14 84 881503863264 098660524 4 16089

94 4 214 23724 4 67318576854 0526164 59608035904 61604 594 774 723205628789

1088699234 20195755264 5554 9151862881037098556289

8184 92084 53628176074 175578224 6663879072604 677554 834 5174 4 34 8189

04 9688056376503250353592627 1374 514 988624 054 8295624 73693334 4
9623309027391 1370810584 07123726554 0394 4 4 06661654 6669812794 0161174 380314 4 254
58361131387001800510 64 222504 74 212674 953997075909715 2710314 165536334 77320054
96354 914 667194 9925664 377111351964 71224 84 4 21338334 4 829914 74
0191692970978273304 82096570236574 4 1662164 04 138597571994 0110755054
81383567509753677020862 14 80224 7690575931284 579612052010606527 2215959974 5589

563929274 16101354 4 77714 86602722228078789

1903104 93304 86064 234 8889

4 12653650919804 6804 72667929079707702290502025767 1384 4 3684 5815634
8290022266587224 5389

24 207586781264 8074 25984 310372314 4 835073934 9163285687087989

353089

830355384 3839500797078015089

93166772121535578504 76824 4 8066812060081609252 4 9005506560688200539 4
3975294 04 2977799777390954 81218233882815997862 84 3934 4 89

37918615556384 584 794 2592989

4 9054 384 5037369764 733322568524 24 02160195904 4 724 0163994 4 4 92589

154 5222094 73819728573560814 16294 4 2012082969234
21367519056921053373592377816006656687636 4 14 636657904 35737824 4 366516685104
935195776579079193354 90054 24 5374 836258264 1051684 37864 4 502959183589

83964 4 0568593688826368637105027687838531277770566599560300157235823714
7154 7219056714 26014 336879664 684 364 914 394 9995727221505804 289

9218100989

5079934 4 94 4 214 1990214 4 689

25539286769175103982 4 675824 63734 38052397350830280687 18734 4 6064
18762993203121704 0704 8304 6129164 263198208628507869517290189

970014 34 289

682624 4 1780781916264 4 1719504 4 50757666856324 24 5674 581755185913604
3599958574 5988250355384 6674 1328204 52537010805090235114 84 04 8195305888064 1604
0823552351294 12814 04 84 54 4 881037085694 262600027163923010086037214 24 24 84
291264 95719569873219054 27563394 9016224 64 54 625934 74 567030056728375084 6724
9825279836734 956177089

83651654 7827889

4 261861051832769208503603621780033391524 933714 84 4 4 55014 157911625050689
0910713827580224 4 650509860986883276779711832579391871621676788356224
19886753868393157565689

7768652016394 52827388674 4 065178756600689
4 9821735574 8074 4 4 3255775906927363784 8180513357096270189
71520589
09708119862005227679934 9913304 058284 567203585664 724 105889
4 553087522364 618384 3964 02596011254 852876608866284
83076360128700666722802670003614 94 230261254 165504 582961699316384
37058296750705322926910916119674 9361273729163120586636884 7905250952735154
380622219327300289

59924 07939074 4 385736690935294 9258689

4 4 010734 22178024 37077152816124 2531908822717327154 3382374 014 74 54
362184 33325680295994 07713014 983323704 5109699654 5320274
5335070217703707061138191051635880307 4 74 77081980826531951055524 034 34 6189
0804 0877285588710261912991092295950882518192058518874 4 198634 862518824
56654 5078032953634 8102634 84 3303083724 18113655627830193910161835174 0322384
5097914 68752162387714 4 2392232324 5576364 107974 7001255398324 7122601905304
8866664 93332284 86329053808683517096 4 354 04 4 025686679116884 4 4 34 21694
02517726916720054 2365879524 5864 8729193194 1963983705910834 65955654 57374 554 274
7225256387204 91964 84 6804 56121634 6755578001839114 5805072029104 091774
619788296504 861235552872697552000 4 238203818320764 255364 09632089

33924 54 4 967598152309215189

4 730501978535100152995735305 4 281128364 84 236594 74
35959609595698016202753023959 4 1995334 4 628208264 9792360794 21886804 1106024
15874 1508575194 58061568880834 301854 1253781954 596974 14 23677874 187066721584
275223193527707018877628030323374 028626604 207305052378520354 2104 257724 4 255914
04 2700874 90764 3524 82693868107163766930730372372374 171754 24 585224
7735758270295996 64 9854 10231151013874 323704 7991591787902994 4 85501682558654
5153881254 8574 254 14 604 2912012322855614 889

53271771724 0122627994 4 108268691399729874 3825568158111126238732626104 264
24 91914 67303139324 0789

967378614 32904 14 2084 4 114 674 15351674 2689
73370321906902874 77060200884 22190321251655289
11717385674 777311366153734 391751962707954 921617093780054 34 04 57873789
689
5794 06584 026092226706663974 7064 74 61914 85114 4 6524 4 38074
15205521286862020067172326368 4 71796723154 91533594 924 534 289

28874 859317664 2699362096734 074 9774 50530705684 314
101332632877759213057623114 700874 37384 5076260305875774 9787324 20714 066513617994
95694 56010819284 319373673284 17989

35189

5954 23519702289

34 72976977104 97535864 99567318504 69509873966280139531524 73360674 59574
6536734 225096595010987669623734 14 060683935034 81983827182118684 4
0601761576560254 701139537357267834 52694 5596079177094 4 971727234 694 7334
3678038722377574 79168689

555204 13621538014 28254 8673776952837038 4 14 27934 004 4 001305689

7835562279860713607059660 4 4 685334 333224
70819960517276152201080667106523795019070974 9374 182163352993865189

170077889

8834 76360923618805269060064 08280797134 34 9789

4 275959288720261078515554 11239737304 60975923178834
68807253835105908002186604 4 90289

791189

6725936755213964 729068579735073675718216974 0366706989

6134 57874 506109712035014 79565375164 16615312164 73254 4 16789

27750724 594 362819238256233629810375653289

13282392322272506794 17094 691318566996226763008 4 74 933294 9237724
82025168055066631619903 4 57800502962160950971278313 4 9754 974 84 9708075014
692861779720539208773557354 2634 4 654 04 69175078783629783037122212634 4 99537604
587068254 66567329277539722860367819 24 73260758753750363960555755152 4 704 4 7904
689

2790074 174 4 0809916215353523795515931682503917084 11573389

4 7214 83377058789

36954 1534 8273160717030232024 929094 54 66553120552501263225317 4 14 2737294
089

35823231304 14 03596709104 9257183835201953577511103030189

37387366729568834 759002804 66901502804 156922062794 10789

76828096269661012137 4 88119556311967779804 68124 93064 78374 05316274
76062834 58684 7164 594 3824 3677534 27608269557653234 4 27605339971298708052089
89

85614 4 2065934 72215753513573135315096 4 3256863269976011816768872330904 784
73878261088300271876502608262925233194 4 7690994 04 16700264 0065555971369918 14
669791135677806574 510572964 7119638264 3806989

60233881135307214 98585368708628587178 9

2687962978016089

4 1639363012094 16355230277734 299630152634 3577512504 13519834
1187362058334 54 73118538074 572684 3372069052208562550105061009379 4 285614 04 74
184 559211793392727085972511528800569 4 028053614 114 4 924 020924 6208794 874
1836224 854 4 537016734 793590201500699089

4 71119500954 7716996064 5156934 098095760872306116798593054 4 74 24 94
585592763754 26550790985078262274 524 14 280564 196195794 70161814
101885939670292884 08817507132694 91264 514 7924 587138834 722095701254 53762871154

613584 4 710131132320 14 954 9094 4 64 014 76000302376328571713953654 714
9001355586963306925811264 04 79200531728092117912870096788 1389

37329594 90687691623091 78222864 353334 05933967916024 289

3274 84 4 4 66315594 574 856113204 51783064 64 9166224 181324
6295767509185902988332306551 4 50236294 04 34 74 054 9255611764 2216093884 711734
189

574 071998503527366986933866985170257393806602302791062808535254
9353166194 5852938854 0134 76198182979019270269975539762709721 3320775214
28883136382794 0377954 8104 3639684 62169524 94 822984 4 3229689

6920853355530853174 095397100274 4 87325283527573624 794 580127804 4
55036106064 55857803573626252556 36064 7734 90568638324 600588264 57299672867064
7068819718804 89

9591820953876986724 12610581231337188328153873 05324 0635171604 8837318634
83194 4 8785524 534 021310596054 3269787362789

90273623581526866772864 84 1376321754 06689

989

734 88261186018002936002236261 5884 9590389

38183834 781502164 731089

1383695373808683164 3699087980859301283735287622060053 62275872876794
6579168057635814 324 0925305502388654 8294 92572512760977104 3084 14 24 132714
9223014 555024 9153801165157010725991 9660889

10334 4 58778020184 2019868725579834 8589

2794 115791654 89

84 18079655981652924 4 0028600089

2833089

95984 6125154 134 7364 124 75537056580724 9607337289

6863956551034 4 97585300171880139293 4 0815934 65774 074 91687314 0199038284
2771226233324 4 6058875673983859350076951311855631684 57383865551229294 08030684
22036256724 591811386063504 80155226167063564 964 28673234 5965669379924
3587293291166884 9839364 2069797039019 1593194
5597036125926270637083717136079722 2924 4 8389

7365994 92632218594 30952934 4 5517054 0094 59274 8703284 3519938814
0267085915289

4 9635950763638073234 70534 62309324 4 15095756918504 8089

19571739191653100024 15714 29356686909706755384 8502610804 074 34 064 574
2634 28325221102071034 50374 53834 0721719272860930797090878 64 0274 03756034
196203260951802333194 4 6604 704 3934 80054 063586910294 18314
38198076626369229201 51962674 54 7889

054 8730085334 2208815974 03289

253567824 7804 57234 4 8555663884 2993651785938154 28714 734 7054 07762504
0798071086832571272096595 24 702809312984 90597903061967508059 94 4 4
21798850698316109638 04 318575734 932089

70279214 4 33939134 28290098389

029276009981034 97167534 00553502665754 8513582069817189

4 3173652187372727038 66524 34 2059269683995 8587716580753629304 9174
58210275330126702362227330521370927 4 75754 92754 03224 8665363239284

28878807181194 34 4 7754 4 394 31574 63373774 2190514 4 626384 014 8384
52230601326365027884 514 71704 7905831805834 89

4 085694 94 24 994 4 151554 8386334 2377204 0699601933580313 7534 4 9760284 4 4
995154 109011381560664 1323294 3105354 03566334 982500900534 136214 95974
7529802823984 619728367006210584 6139778158274 67657982601784 72965764 639589

4 18774 24 96331695884 22839119159056564 02281934 9680175816384 01394 2920814
2088204 54 6902994 63765205998819783175 4 4 80127119965562213173 24 4 271608021931664
4 607184 5067024 51604 612011797638272392113 4 83394 387989

6290584 017968636094 3255300650628889

73239251361632702390752395982653 4 89

3994 6806580594 876864 627514 1094 064 99311534 1987321729914
31259100977718868694 557124 4 4 4 93582861381259764 637551134 27984 5737620234
35625689

831225304 20590214 9070999674 16032154 670753881650296586399155315134
290551333165324 830885034 701954 9055674 4 84 1010321876589

956758394 55823828688310814 18628354 73194 75525274 7115754 0254 34 804 661774
80387868598378715694 9134 2785308294 72887354 1204 31902320905952954
32861066132697607626692661135211 4 6625276984 127734 08524
191382685828095507583757875182 94 4 195381669964 75933805810974 4 19704
0887688325257374 38561825911089

7501964 314 793725720708094 0589

60553970982858004 4 556307859986110829784 519803998823094
16250986802635162822807560816507 04 834 89

64 4 168361836594 6329769197332664 504 4 332702652964 4 073326083594
8712972056368036299922692205555021936131309 4 39292561689

82589

3809531154 34 813289

5184 91654 287254 6286351978103023730034 90379917930768861220 4
532651318101381689

8791956784 66786614 4 331058014 3812599127914
15887667170290675999071222928172 74 527854 4 31917637751864 8854 4 69055214 18294 754
607553734 56060855634 64 2039617667095752874 54 94 901204 660351964 636873577292974
28234 75054 9678654 4 59273606276089

89

24 697824 189

0713669103009266781913030559195 11695693178319754 079624 03384 21104 664 4
6524 04 5818686393260964 63530334 711292131 54 3695714 4
22067237270190321612831636606835353591 4 027988526095314 74 4 1976705764
010907530604 721386570676654 99726561399562590818508530304 5559284 07614 124
652218099654 35307163185074 8864 789

33137159804 019105801024

Chapter Nintey-six

2554 1713566189
61206011069761203387121769536277 4 814 7024 04 62879594 4 7965689

291666561516291177369461849461776831663594 5285117164 14
008796109655867194 2116381654 5789
35594 374 74 16596019104 0265069965376089
10884 9054 09088076624 223624 4 5253132852178568721171075072872580024 370274
95835664 624 563513977205964 778734 7672137096977874 37222222854 4 4 15051625814
7590016001034 98734 2164 2873794 1520917280874 38528706874 5299675850634
62361565683 8065684 68586659128839299398741 9192804 50975993576219153034 533964 024
16281637564 57337985969012829274 1879627625038064 03057998223939350958 9
2199527851029164 63804 78329362091927804 0771504 187300689
17857381782537931265322695641 2984 8057505704 33859369934 33934 5604 4
96232593724 3304 35766714 7711664 26205667161937773757701820 4
93615978206551775960441 4 5574 2714 01595850624 208614 32022102794 70032864 4 0974
98531194 93397220525601724 38067839808063019803303871 4
010823737020217802399919659 4 84 74 2081004 1624 631399989
3872678129698371396533 4 3697806394 66764 2860024 152824 8737856394
1292793538360770760830075008541 68836684 96834 4 738138000194 809994 639279397254
8092617557123230722879914 7294 99627829318121179995311913933682914
21708003917108392039962532 4 657124 267114 80762187323888663027326326051022 74
85587685824 829962737856303750205262941 8831696089
4 9012916313726341 885804 981924 8754 5535241 8873262394 39367504 501654 7689
34 02068214 58565566171050775119 4 37380589
4 1341 2569604 131394 75819197066823026324 2341 09024 4 5054 0958834 10876889
8805836001905800856199 4 9103323884 50133139604 194 54 6882835906 14
806279170274 2550569836303868190 4 0807698607 4 6508841 4 23677617054 6226084 54
397222194 0355 4 202652033104 4 5526900704 6882774 58214 5696636674 4 69994 2884 1734
7114 80702341 7951794 30778361527574 001167541 238104
978226516996793270179099132535969256 4 13102120317675960263679551086925989
1936051529316116399937906052216218262573 4 4 736334 20263075057264
252255255006962503721338053241 4 84 4 6537714 97170577712173855502 14 0364 1091178389
7214 17976354 731764 8609973237020876571662328627364 066666525224 4 4 84 4
23704 74 31260270194 05293253920388124 5611678392260714 780011957184 7504
55611615250384 4 82208269186674 529500194 54 79554 74 26703119533884 63367504 7534
11924 30517289
0558306396064 27300931789
903397134 3931584 0591610085863938221382022717081924 7577821001503916384
86660170908139091359533 4 0619014 626904 24 09568052624 01070564 77766184
07365199659831201591 4 8619124 79104 53282084 900376962357904 5204 92814 74 814 4 84
6581726874 291601112567800981177269122209070237851 4 8661124 3714 4 591984
6685763094 737512094 24 3352004 4 650532973912516708301825541 2971302260674
6609800526039196275579838 9
50906924 319004 737564 01836074 54 934 859101794 4 75577162863150554
88761028672918186758641 7664 4 4 78659627827294 0399932099053354 96913841 75741 304
2203580266820050183524 85651517034 20994 31107260374 75082164 34 958854 14 32104
5735574 1980118294 006516384 590778313094 7300992993954
18271818059977319955225376562352261687988041 8284 720314 9589
062569689

4 4 24 2784 076171974 78521211708675294 4 603670533555570333619526994 064
35233081909574 370804 6560784 12350061934 1564 951004 9733173836204 004 22734 4 3789
15789

6534 95861159191813589

724 4 4 956070703223227828015 7914 855808866326700924 04 234 20313927164 689
630137056221855039903 4 62294 679176978329701524 127573584 58013089

759525863985502154 636770509007033290797558326525697330992519 94 2335234
2674 324 526287834 34 87803932099014 786974 13172811254 964 4 5904
27779736912668770753379381052959792195600 94 51964 724 5214 5664 4 7811294 08884
2597399502289

315673204 89

00359565314 881818133524 884 4 8698694 8006125364 74 27755000504 204 04 621034
4 25555880866214 4 252379324 64 58613086709152614 3968878163367734 9695124
09007739167264 14 094 124 2164 56185364 62085838052194 8089

8873774 634 28514 0004 3979235067024 24 670667069730792355322976556684 5704
76290256322597831961833397 24 9154 6952552514 3514 34 797307250589

853935034 4 14 301037276933082870107555261221323794 89

15324 24 850154 784 57009774 5683673957064 624 5323167834
271605995132533503 84 4 764 61804 529889

10089

257614 2364 5689

209371216233577791901016985274 65074 3313394 0386055838356051252991 14 64
7525104 974 0083923818804 09524 6656978219067500774 512734 04 1374 694 85989

0324 30384 21773757608092588363984 94 28524 9166123974 2134 03066399683994
57315314 592189

561854 2973694 1639291274 58660214 9193256062908354 7889

4 53870589

099102877684 2634 4 90924 2758195382277154 4 550755082820784 883600938857504
071338064 314 4 64 3510663577254 200107215128214 87380127832552194 7726666964
3519639951388097664 5324 332723557684 264 1531380978229804 63213153774 6252354 04
2906035801705619274 4 6884 84 775984 917808674 554 98329658519534 6162001081254 224
26766724 4 659198500373724 6700094 5314 1832851380224 4 33867264 250159567592114 14
74 9624 5184 91204 72064 6756094 0593359887917979059001367 4 8853864 50686962065614
990834 968225785681134 5564 83957272889

03768564 734 8587027874 70924 4 3784 170154 003374 5698274 82324
69221776707380599850755861668713787186830968096765583702166111 4 077220785221064
02682698887307289

6051684 37835203674 0225003301294 22087997280733552033208 4 982518794
76366174 29055283759128564 164 974 1372819365114 33254 1321596654 4 79750889

663784 4 05834 1384 4 824 5573385931223675087756917 4 580777066637614
313837033604 334 58674 650157199994 93570926314 983135394 760109974 60000053765814 4
94 57332674 5861063304 932150297383939354 4 27370993864 150604
8173133810760582530 94 394 19878575323657233230 4 795924 95750580234 6554 85760174
0783004 0764 89

4 676825864 0951038804 374 3992695534 1506926095520996684 9636219609754
1990256689

27300183039884 115526354 87584 101918625856519589

4 991754 3670137752629621235562089

0759814 4 724 510634 531684 374 2039269634 12512254 94 255324 4 66039223854 14 92180254 74 882876575364 066956656854 4 9904 94 814 9152805038253285564 672004 4 252289

4 314 63574 597056054 13211134 7761834 5914 35006804 0975165789

3967117854 85165229206778357107525513953 14 5282312224 60774 3264 85780214 7106967125824 9054 95325200298011874 3298038560982084 74 98781051624 257385362174 94 6834 560794 4 01386804 272597372177995976134 84 926836925904 94 54 4 72854 534 85554 76728550926269663335154 39531919926209022290 11791650354 053205354 1557323962865877885010012105094 4 8364 3693554 565652987025104 273373127036864 327018539304 622986390184 984 97790852704 663810074 106064 19934 676834 879214 90182379262315357767600 4 5253983094 8834 995312973156738110357671380950602689

881032606604 4 31764 3550299533074 35121783536374 2263073089

4 1189

098334 11963860551522024 9684 4 39394 25305314 27282384 5197724 4 6016604 039958354 7279137257994 876905630996389

204 70629376050565218205 4 2134 5799773554 89

353836803365282076081 2514 89

4 3624 6900174 25014 83694 89

10324 9786394 19114 60054 0230621618556990861024

Chapter Nintey-seven

673154 864 6098802027810734 737377704 918834 398152960696061717154 7709155804 53914 7213794 4 88630702751062591007953739995139 4 86174 4 9030229789

21815233955882101576 4 964 02094 59194 090016061165874 11111980734 33510338190204 012029929324 0314 4 329877164 72194 187589

2567634 59232199092290155723933728886071369 4 061776164 50934 5671522804 998274 750927830263599319816399 1685562604 4 95679935194 8320384 4 70396500989

9853801126586133337 94 7755213032889

16197879337327684 4 74 1328316215382135050222329824 7951985584 253064 4 062732756704 04 854 2157953717334 38301365792271697658 15254 2272531902691721583563 4 790655014 33932221184 54 5774 337318654 527185594 1021062294 8825204 34 730878381222298316872357783733734 4 5155994 8232923392695789

294 4 799824 20094 9392664 2707394 323274 7132009716034 757074 4 10728503079630390757270283805020959161755070005016 6277924 29318124 50523867239968585193177795903884 04 675565133255758214 94 31535179594 98790175939954 018699586162066971538 9

33325756001809207795785012715852501324 37026798381532168315105880 27374 5589

39822516507965568067 4 05529335804 164 586928523165289

250624 4 1034 507254 75174 6696957664 7599120655684 79831778838624 4 4 164 6954 1919134 116638313595094 26984 0789

70554 94 65807294 59831838654 62177521063114 55104 3363353661775730503 74 0634 292089

12775022362094 1830938203794 204 94 301832564 881514 62174 7314 953122724
9665194 033266694 654 8174 82534 1725229124 74 9705114 616160054 28188054 0354 1989
4 7234 572559079014 19851829814 814 59902714 0514 3266071026229634 9194
8125934 214 533789

8724 583097604 861888669585130390729173392077225689

609836520912793114 8217974 75064 4 655976134 03875759224 022396034 7357084
918337811214 989

258295323354 4 4 3785318333610174 3721712707556161914 3805327266024 4 94
86684 75034 38075251839224 592395717830234 714 19022350350380794 11272774 87289

504 00230804 74 07224 55600124 7620731599212504 5788619133864 9903391268514
724 3309106085594 36605624 84 86764 7533010336365985774 89

63154 64 134 6528176374 12615811007817367 0124 954 4 79654 11601224 9009394
6034 993309994 0239274 94 3813504 0080294 4 89

9168793936676108675 50354 69238657089

4 14 70394 6164 7784 5589

30701189

50360169684 30078158866532913562055689

169725157812754 39554 16215195210530013133622187193814 571974 4 354 6784
636798831874 1333305512922100 1574 7304 7822274 7354 3623380608200983 3664 5368558689

256331574 692024 31516831234 0672977314 1705079853683002114
65536273578120633869 7324 6879064 859587581672286764 8874 37654 6504 4 904
83805651802297321117954 05654 3794 4 61504 20215634 0664 5608062174 90834 4
92965788882953793035 04 7260862168232015 4 984 9336065885036959606666 07613634 1254
667714 265766966938253333538296866778018554 76375874 1375614 974 08516836293864 4 4
4 54 37282528212759657334 1880697804 0386375624 321359353338276914 364 031872205194
4 4 88269989

9867804 37905031726519533324 2884 7616800651629802990750 2324 78834 4 34 24
06567828812886076963 74 064 96025630715656767505203705308391361662839 2164 184
5098284 4 674 30512284 4 4 2398334 64 13015302739217504 2011926614
57275082813903767336357639254 4 605297160176537577389

89

4 691397706717184 21230296681287204 971364 53255289

930864 012330523226054 081611387889

253194 8786172327631527 4 80204 7699701084 14 2223997929110 10289

5691963294 2803327708353525389

03514 318588286319374 292654 22212927628526004 2254
53979981005955366783999 89

23929180915038777361 4 0092815308194 07860664 74 84 2382259576352851784 924 14
74 4 4 84 3684 34 252066821565966919 7697288057366703621563551 24 994 4 361226689

330580394 804 54 627750978873567271612375825713839139 4 108724
31955195160533765155 5589

253551826979714 75606689

31735310531915212298359173023026758 39274 164 9314 224 39389

74 4 3100874 4 911962224 4 80737158524 94 7552758284 137168733885684
5139719357174 35137665104 89

523902901706309271226 684 066927834 83998862859594 239679364 564 1735587184 0199018757254 634 6067620706262789

62322034 805371836351794 691087763851991 1078379366902264 789

614 265281989

94 989

4 4 0958364 6926514 4 31656582124 717920789

2033514 05936678284 94 0177989

652979815054 754 3580317758562255869061012302 34 01093612955353576 3584 329974 630792884 081670233667889

7012814 595884 74 281994 2874 986614 3771185970104 607861183122285674 94 691319004 4 82564 302826200724 8787525394 397901252203517990670108864 4 4 4 17333294 27038504 777629594 84 3814 9909989

1262534 88800224 7011268538660594 37662227036508267221232223515725503765 03854 0952531017575868733835311996936024 166003965092807274 380713754 704 84 84 4 5688684 89

196872123109819909873074 79532054 14 0103959736196967523052 4 4 2164 056190052674 27599397913726868627853 54 30551791257504 7157660184 923718223934 84 9391969295394 4 9988380196572662503651757 4 94 0331196959794 1172125762371383165114 79626055791784 4 0278188122553834 089

63982704 9789

072574 304 4 30334 1179108109059950 54 171220773737974 7750303681258203099584 4 1194 86799985794 011171393324 2395262703619927 0637724 17033978111333238271568277 34 2014 79054 7261654 34 0193226714 4 21801961053370502633374 2731904 5518794 87134 8524 98626682222111113189

14 4 557622104 2289

834 739034 99812597781108090131864 25670889

103674 2980304 913636514 21324 982033989

23826233114 57754 00763163825126866684 85031584 111114 11558864 2679072134 604 09221705074 59824 7207024 5524 314 03520119565313924 5833100914 253634 958789

79074 393713659709552725556666007024 20283910074 594 624 66313074 54 4 6751130599377751204 1192805564 9729151234 915055327810229864 306084 053764 4 0989

174 4 4 31076998717276003815163 4 4 2860652183069210091799279 4 170931936294 24 774 58068173353359701759 89

32860314 853201568769791565212 4 189

67004 03095917277570816030186 94 59714 0799824 4 3633328754 3192214 07359969526268303856595 84 52089

56554 97781013274 5394 34 0864 386526954 14 06604 205250151308378086 64 5729974 925690376170930028161622503187003032737 14 4 8605125164 07239007008823823906811 4 73995804 35559035124 1221823298274 36677789

0385385862391814 78158835325813789

3191305164 7239015905150073292582 74 6204 289

14 392667534 952154 94 2924 09278561294 14 258693729514 689

314 27054 4 4 2270009324 16109334 4 4 781762618884 9164 4 1692560813590775794 4 7386206015924 04 012063374 9989

54 252911634 09524 4 85314 231824 74 58686792135102696628751705210604 60784 704
974 666154 518814 15103516734 98157830888050629025240 72784
9132883585857196877031633009755390404 904 884 5664 4 89

74 6888824 84 22504 2274 10769069154 7824 15861985184 219579094 591392694
553934 97074 170826012991361372933199089

96124 4 761127027704 3889

2717017234 88617631963685024 672082669876084 819752651511784 683974
33083172604 87854 03033294 27864 4 3609114 89

76287974 1302033675392689

318594 58016183291794 4 0100958324 9805875064 583664
1276952928598265770333006234 582654 95553231665323056373735121952840 9214 89

639294 238105955982270927599730329940 73750568740 4 9872812934 702606624 4
77615834 6661704 916269757179758724 2929114 187975074 87821715334 19974
5268055732256003140 1704 634 2203189

757820773023738624 6978504 16509797584 4 527164 5852204 3551397592875295089

54 65228066269694 34 4 99014 8802004 1811864 2039774 22040 04 2702669554 4
60329909254 9594 35202527964 88734 580054 34 584 684 94
52975353915837929113057037617736633757952397710873937954 733211854 879061926854
224 00839536103687789

91522104 521065020038005180834 7709316151054 4 12972685089

9664 22824 64 4 89

7764 2323194 76756024 38097694 63100168877605725670989

3692800865024 874 4 6760824 54 595750132838100012297074
730565399913766112760678583404 512958030384 05025304 166311739822211379220740 74
39396630034 0704 960764 32882198733987733380285797936098215354 6559100724
317097157060971059686886906640

79067951508101151970513635751636112075963738637573858404 999837864 5305790304 4 394
30129504 10974 37837274 732158210702226767570396614 18608774 4 396909624 777614
2982681257255182073821062914 29179289

825779700233074 9298885823533993193563940 2526806194 864 2067083324 5104
681706704 0554 2134 18765164 1921977618868029589

218724 367391297929670217002604 707954 07599880696538294 706826294
7500799209178054 5010872131836710302140 034 123993988674 1014 04 729131764 4 4
209080110919803524 4 32113336535828527182840 3262367250370024 1162594 82255974 4
88083176067370154 856289

1186654 4 65504 5630521377904 50573281851201979665404 094 3027004 974 4 63254
6121224 14 11283293664 3794 0321984 4 79276656109271707635594 01220553590240 4
67307073784 0681089

1604 84 0226316131653788226130623404 764 9322815522919522340 09251839601714
95570625339301919067404 597189

90077654 3585394 537305708587673393775225561887590862665572607140 813602684
304 8094 633781089

4 87053325334 693152865228184 850150399380033663878904

73389

34 112884 34 57735233219997625754 3876194 782906084 104
92317086979272668565017717840 53576014 4 4 068717168690095280680340 3189

3356304 270972777870650886333372970310015932022324 797004 101814 94 6764
6133696884 4 79094 536114 90174 4 62989

74 9323003758025319176955052 4 162500655284 26114 37307622654 20826822134 594
67537033662184 218165664 4 34 77572096300136885151 4 596794 720360121393994 6326114
54 14 4 4 68275264 86615867566816023239217 04 74 512570134 865906164
308600558556879208 4 783360624 6304 19584 64 174 708303366065330053 4 206204
283686318888324 26681603517521 4 0074 64 026900758761089

4 794 63515084 4 9596170005018277089

66824 263274 7552939134 4 64 826875600962762224 250729627218837874
695585396808698731268 9

2374 8126981350128702594
85298709385372271299505563015937166285821886591605207 4 0380572603304
513197216792914 77186756305293557276882390292266219730580 4 873114 0117530813389

217011861801173372514 366353087565734 2089

4 1704 80721933598874 797364 2686198794 102854 21295294 104 3654 80616664
665609535068126798608377234 26852206158774 774 504 54 4 0859724 123572813629395024
8772132291814 4 74 60352824 0905004 010177366269864 17021816703518189

74 67051204 2796054 36662794 52174 94 14 8564 864 034 23375959054
906013609693091684 106291636794 689

232189

12091274 0195170618038721228 4 3070879607731137254 4 1306054 172989

95054 837882772704 6663864 19113779886974
06327767999608103275565628709067701614 85811851671525572067310925 94 3266024
855593887184 124 304 225616774 615108389

728834 24 22589

14 8505084 7290517606189

97775830070656525208 4 74 0820884 2173373910767398114 88077333220165889

114 100515854 223884 0636728656725089

7128850384 5294 0316291883714 4 5378786613054 000917050111154 71854
363558310332072119813 34 8586311534 23601920293718304 3526169084 4 01955004 814
506589

37687152384 7124 18582070564 4 135304 874 20515614 5120866680968865536 4
7307014 51711555839964 58356780034 9094 90393274 4 514 4 11779916379631033825 4 4
50612672966298207689

2834 73834 82756376171383960793925089

382875193889

08374 24 828395334 225664 013005888776657917835977 4 04 06707501771087193911 4
5784 68254 2500121104 0115678138129566257255109176 4
6036596778057996130862820011501251679 24 84 94 7604 84 9884 203733393954 34
686685902354 575230954 073815304 116759191964 033950082322121220319 4 85821924 4 34
7552933753017393518181 4 6692053006768354 98326089

762673603011784 58554 87527030732200353 24 12239102967066 4 816719559254
5322134 7824 974 02500270274 805998168376214 11818338760834 87925809813815166160 4
14 64 20807520205374 54 95801305135529753878317955606609534 52750289

995284 3052599586314 9779903125995926852386759975764 4 13602257604
70651198719323526264 910813019359159967624 7754 20054 68332913608093323184
53091032664 269570273636886158684 198635589

869662161263694 234 626987065295164 6036590889

7763094 36953289

214 97180259712631079198634 234 33683379854 27815924 37536105952313676705884
2514 7268669259622556233388254 4 4 9153389

514 8078035316009623627236262932109383812134 4 2925961689

7760712961096532858126385635284 06918707269095087199084 8758805976806154 34
384 9833078622373299505385954 4 6528725800917384 821639524 7618669194 284 4
09202032528586359734 2736521084 177924 0653376994 87091904 006536284
0026579910278085881694 281124 198678032126766119082120687694 39025689

83185502950735813628332588132934 9787561199657064 770323354
6013593301573718699852759527884 0155231304 4 6664 6700704 4 570167374 730294 4 7784
25837971339579810234 19274 30114 16633563104 720020623034 6672004 34
736336209186074 063793874 10837798372659102262266281668368174 614 5088810586794
020916962370702672270785567024 6696621523592324 89

0655654 114 2321653001230668315813709501175164 974 74 177077104 7867114 4
23127030825964 970280652309726522595350260937603204 64 18104
012825702971529099663017972874 967160781873864 34 604 365603126009130801990559134
4 969824 30598104 4 81214 2232391988323305174 8761776106038024 224 869336078269834
87990531871201936565718811379882854 700036618033764 6164 1808005621106566571354 4
5738035572162702066987066596116302669281335128597234 22734 74 04 35504 5030184
36615705975860259189

72971762937820758515214 366300584 4 13754 3530152873638639375592024 94
01991229614 78312053390204 021524 9571623751771392074 04 81216320695616878374 4
067514 27661181935704 09262254 4 28125724 4 674 793566990224
0001616279356997737936222932889

9510966718814 7254 724 4 74 4 23324 50832816113588506261778134 752263774 16689
306796189

0698173854 26207116834 520208661722554 02151315203014 261536352924 17624
88724 019384 3284 70314 533568553211634 60324 11910969004 98066163653704 83004 4
010118129186561089

74 698069557691913585155593833791589

06798187857369687334 9166531702934 83274 4 826234 96789

367134 4 07267722684 084 039078504 4 733709169016194 834 174 9284 4
768576605582389

4 9976266570726095917281026112370882204 24 04 89

674 1798176105971216524 34 189

876973254 05183576390689

67524 64 304 94 59814 0399601983368186282170586073372014
6993569728500023185154 135769994 1300289

7984 54 6387206092599165675004 2574 55772138558216066238188184 326085590864
884 23057729024 583754 83327194 65922189

0608225577193031024

Chapter Ninety-eight

4 284 5088023804 11824 5874 54 5954 059911879389
866524 34 677760671624 1118610010104 090734 9130306713696907321594 34 84
812974 54 53214 65061611701587079237826776752 24 3663566391919604 2731264 289
0214 4 018734 7592854 7074 2567034 4 9969176752335984 7813886556570589
9983318601234 6150364 759381711586038569704 789
24 9935904 4 4 12797604 1889
820913034 8330214 953067826196903024 060825099184 094 9624 111714
750193668254 7196684 4 4 733985153038785005 1106979020064 9735354
5593857570788333676889
24 61107934 62714 4 4 1980272903059667094 654 2694 6680003655724
825053853726570034 64 552984 3754 856057664 3654 84 689
59198703255509085909374 209804 8624 130992674
32372863561176180971636873658852 58754 29289
98684 0706674 0913105233311691390175906 11779084 055504 104
0973012675087716768600 4 3264 04 71731730874 89
4 4 5795368280651668288 4 18809763876877516772254
01507003933693798837135823136755015852875 24 033755398687094 783975615794
63085259914 62120723856095229220102 4

Chapter Nintey-nine

194 2264 365500964 372816212365929564 9212034 19310855804
8057925207056097073311003610872573365512 4 4 363974 17268775153220654 22563933914
24 98791922029924 304 01513532618304 251639821759987994 03271770630652960196594
66033166091932252139785174 20275604 53282255800911070557016085197780657101 4
3163012118809125580 64 98603094 804 914 667610772074 5502634 5069561581532830704 4
1964 4 6264 4 4 019789
5304 167380833292384 654 515372513331684 03315256389
6589
4 711008798811829532364 68004 613394 53767014 91217704 282194
2828505066221884 630508804 09783570115326654 91625524 9526385096275796 74 94
757716034 9234 7359628017615562674 3906233034 7004 4 5381194
09528697550938580679702661 14 5684 84 4 84 63089
914 94 3151524 88178024 4 16974 09989
06039084 394 4 185025304 735724 693730561618537934 0688294 6014 254 022114
23373139724 08574 4 94 586237761932255185568 9
110364 637684 07051600360614 064 357081184 77977704 0599564 1200104 6014
1300089
0788089
37759529574 504 765503905318359914 6854 554 07570254 194 4 535881728230217184
08734 015606594 770669821729663865913212771651925166629124 21600260824 04 5564
18182824 20715559304 14 1284 792123814 859514 4 839965671505764 6027136104 0734 54
888170722718008329681 4 012039662237524 09176259305011964 574 375389
92864 6189

021874 107501694 155173074 8796555794 34 122134 0186194 5711114 14 514 34 7679110508738584 37954 322814 6239251032152517806102200298506117151152924 684 4 06233670927089

2264 5324 10781786234 930020364 8615299307013684 69705066369587621303871984 96736262861287731353077213166220888069011784 52231994 9365322724 4 31774 7904 4 0805210124 268282757760576852072110323533635517332284 6585385579072592997684 97868869011934 529274 64 227525558504 87824 174 15962774 39272695086300373919724 3280964 2332098580674 6974 55115723670387955932 4 57584 53122600239564 518634 24 137001098615026519509650127633382819673659764 35594 000089

8370507219226837562534 24 57964 21520814 153814 0352834 23274 574 52821886539984 54 02774 4 122254 52294 22654 14 501024

Chapter One Hundred

62883885257064 63919904 12738586374 72377197018166150155930655258040 024 4 90929824 4 9535013277809532564 2634 262634 327989

95168669229691978769 623076382134 287918534 016638265861389

810556650674 010634 208285394 781800204 5364 226967901634 79917796814 2697019624 314 18370179332392082069639114 5686534 35751789

37024 664 269595259600654 326091604 270903277334 124 87937622089

7854 5694 3184 74 194 34 5106203974 6655514 72056170610194 61222686681596904 838394 2904 30992831677354 14 4 4 29372219257639217779234 22377339714 84 881819101699820182786211318128 4 5363263984 3862156550967765319885 4 178318558674 158239004 30534 5117073737286728018823354 578530695996778806 74 17964 300979384 13254 054 4 81238083190305865 4 085153227854 231354 28374 23537587216882363220550706527064 95251356963675212104 632064 184 3223935637795209989

654 54 72001696835107 4 307701939884 1978707094 7694 9874 864 2008554 7074 572670602171274 09566926654 314 38337769024 01314 2789

997756778724 179571357223060632305238563514 763132557264 4 67597733776986284 175094 03393812169214 2673563864 62354 34 0206694 306350751394 0274 4 2889

765823700307564 9301065734 518698212694 75788504 119196136104 60934 3164 4 074 153374 3957724 35885256502313780 94 754 3195773054 51878520720986386116227304 334 532958754 74 8551273383279722191850350 4 787189

7884 24 928710689

61821089

94 171586776120838015161888651 4 54 0012858597164 6301364 4 9651605514 93822792834 4 4 90837674 3281989

2114 29104 31061110868692165527920798201 64 9329374 58134 21507655118784 89

276738254 87935117832351611208551784 10837621175281500785185 4 778186076794 2864 14 84 3233233191097266850032934 1289

14 04 5858204 4 3155761077878576257 74 238384 89

9315723739598381106078124 6778635855689

9652736884 524 094 2528704 5964 3592076057934 6684 324 14 532559635624 874 8821179120818397034 784 64 1754 92914 224 8619881698358368191292319024 07171295700076874 6334 505854 60536189

74 136529114 874 87882667012766317504 121007203157810889

24 37664 036773091175530904 0928171196136210539234 1387334 2259376787685262571351224 34 134 824 4 924 37863318852768275374 3104 90354 4 5524 214 35713693138564 02904 0006569936253681779918785587184 4 73077058252974 350574 8664 127084 654 4 260384 7274 4 53318352984 89

368389

889

7808289

018623074 4 84 04 7084 4 9085284 94 030394 34 29554 6385274 0854 759015268816000374 7725228117811611574 2371398195074 0674 17534 3184 14 635054 4 34 24 383574 51924 86115808800396066834 394 019089

873781924 4 04 00219832284 520765154 79211369255074 7874 1658366024 221854 62194 64 3077515218613558151988754 04 635517614 0959054 3738570052501358093904 859672162021606984 4 161569078771684 0681274 14 376614 0911181396310855991516614 8107954 4 515324 9599213668254 996327123735625684 14 74 54 14 3123120604 88195654 935028235797994 376777571835665900690204 1799336909172824 104 906231327124 4 24 94 16014 28516096280779063603833584 14 1992709154 227684 2581774 992219930572580325951237712012994 4 24 84 07012279686794 4 4 734 1806792582657934 9589

14 7678883789

154 4 093263165670060889

4 7310932561056198803086054 865208774 564 54 524 74 85353154 05011168124 284 74 957904 3721594 155394 36702907125778653689

754 2289

4 964 0116185024 4 371314 084 34 630354 358064 772127114 3504 3136254 84 38660924 36155003196510855005090715833704 1502556889

1024

Chapter One Hundred One

584 004 181933520252124 4 984 57167679255682218023266396231570964 589 079686994 94 13734 326211814 954 7389

785624 8821720105582789

84 53333313654 84 89

4 508887856751904 04 4 59592653195215811924 4 89

8113529022134 5503835659827193694 931765657818676004 70077316918164 55034 194 766774 3801815903330993025665956668060102509265301151501606224 68616389

7193090214 3214 1704 0021914 577268584 078652097221680980634 034 0974 30869072988223097519519831002986126704 89

081778827687757961178330223290184 6001907160874 7684 2315224 050774 360779330699714 2082661884 0794 04 69258063274 24 727504 156574 254 6714 72330996260395728653858905528880059112225774 689

76219282389

04 0655521371974 94 52232127683384 515514 57684 661127766882078834
75885860064 886573576316527556999411910834 6614 4 5618670681274 94 63392864
2736615115589

1224 08685970789

27007503394 2198758365359734 3004
1069559226761035533059931059176312793511629714 0796065012532936194 0136650630794
157005021118804 35814 94 53379132085873254 84 304 63659635754 4 534 7023689

5764 0754 7704 4 155714 9317686793022777531198821848 837301911786289

30694 0111589

359951274 829912053068129551929824 93827214 779554 101294 4 37734 517564
25117165262161669991858356468746649357924 097724
551332802362936675709907697852514 22664 11911935854 34 501374
0960793760050865528342280657264 7802204 20613079516996395332476 1662289

154 6684 694 096914 5152525634 154 2697672709654 289

23669684 03192535094 9067384 50902029724 3180912312701825519513834
60029378821762077676614 7017910569870953277066003084 161810592065874 865600514
83952184 824 99254 3254 8561325085851974 364 170725538031964 069280715632213221733 4
54 51876615575526390318339396568420029460701191290037403223439767010625918 9
54 94 1108166177756219216231211370903139719951093000601030071533334
52901597889

358798595884 784 1800525379600879834 7110926578754 89

54 190753861066220189

959789

54 05934 3787394 706384 236767750218336928872866052783454 4 522024
0580571136296007597466519777111126309694 695034 2384 65105314
33667095110760686290587829078822087133464 200364 390366332980988500851337814
96316618857710806631255804 4 324 20769864 7512216582361620834 6814 84 14
0831525275396050627066696526301902593848744 034 1266063574 73771924
725215165229394 06695524 534 224 8129991832656594 4 23759120559882004 72864 204
2067074 222872759074 0971398215723796321454 99167296730802864 864 4 84
06832219033684 9026989

9297102009204 1186578702517859183575055270334 76887756385854
6273960750997614 74 0057219289

8182966726201203114 58260815855382692225101382561102544 294 4 30679624 364
0089

97810054 4 0067802134 27670764 254 9925936710102284 674 86622594 1175294
05166755581862694 17505939971153767539966509833016157369709227005573096959556 4
92723851825757875534 17888752639788555964 624 4 74 923264 074 82162854 233803633594
9374 89

9526806016754 14 21978835090237310576875032819182590521253318 4
9318306100702202678580527851563024 324 19555393856571133062252246234 14 797114 4
79325789

9373626522022284 579923034 601177104 1574 4 094 124 681972950029114
1398676155035259981948 0735239154 52858111822298181564 94 4 79275635533223506290 4
962376021888577294 08189

3514 5056394 33389

35339776554 5634 0866555282658136000 8164 63334 5254 4 94 84
50595556670516310770887250520662602256057362 9214 4 51674 721138860169162930054
205124 2064 155552724 0194 558735950975262553372909389
9907528808524 234 255268789
623261274 535575780817153091024

Chapter One Hundred Two

59635355394 814 762771969164 1984 2611182758862589
05804 366154 8756206816374 34 08004 7600164 4 1984 380293734 14
682867771761604 14 2854 126064 2564 15809374 39615912924 271363136731776124 4 589
933859177730611332 9884 665524 574 82834 925231194 587069989
123810600838202270265985625763339190336 7294 0001264 290699668384 2381794
361274 69866593189
61904 532222329360316632 96014 94 36871828093274 304 9152389
32256255191114 730075314 81288072064 2684 2226981136185520154 4
798087601072876094 5026924 94 54 0614 87952597780986360069669101377814 1234
900206869198389
264 1537672255176874 9515204 014 883031204 1130202278064 5964 589
4 8058713779967688734 93918703798214 391672064 59086965189
72256916985099903102030966573633018772157910787814 264 4 57256174 11584
185877699635635291576611517161175561912 14 637721380113652263627127850352 14
533306584 24 04 271934 65708056180564 2862699883193272737 24 685080806372534 586774
314 3564 7134 32991361084 587114 5670176806024 15639874 524 038583363793983563393 4
94 4 595030714 4 27694 2139216593351516100280682600186217108027589
9091634 54 624 60226985867174 54 2310977297306019504
55750212178667292686336651258071050500174 7213369207269807192779063301291903 34
2918220130117130206861 24 637361536176394 8055611226790359599834
582073680303215605083664 01669154 64 026087260506651984 907574 9621296331192 04
60864 24 701059966275204 06799085211118873939526222171718394 5674 3584 3662502594
075677874 5520688317702101822639289
293331994 6189
556214 3393987537774 182334 90776385599354 0087193532155781063 4 34 9264
69216680197306958779 34 71722254 4 80791181111963926392764 800123517725719274
788305783971136690606 4 55254 3319190322289
19360954 97184 324 9100904 54 066272923850274 0563383854 859018826814 94 3584
364 584 39802626111161717658 4 2816097957652506787611795116323992635170032619534
15092975005534 04 88664 0965835191659794 9193508634 8821926159814 4 84 36924 3754
5565112204 194 8055268230753324 76974 0884 7277874 354 52359272108804
052625835368689
19931984 4 60989
716084 4 674 263673591680055284 78634 06269127172173171756061677171 4 634
7556161980788 4 3903113584 777164 2605104 74 74 57663614 38320854 9936721974
5739979786652277503539806189
14 08888385909321374 37527203362302578779561 04 72928563860851309157784 64
9600087363339203104 89

77816919904 54 837211576932614 72210169373395677086569137611108691532783 54 055689

4 86050710822954 24 8091805580809585284 066735287814 803865380214 664 675714 389

654 75808604 34 5129553935513095869321108629931110605 8399394 24 965760106574 9524 0264 4 94 6365524 4 4 24 07305990365284 9089

6664 804 04 6794 5517605689

02763171719187687 2772574 89

033656717785638232165305692129115050 3264 12815732707501 13835519789

3094 089

1074 88034 26109088274 14 1371194 09123094 371678696136360724 77657104 6234 861504 0606854 704 64 57718789

166038214 014 34 7509730536910311084 4 079695504 56237753811982755215952136501877563 39707354 395801204 7196601951288251054 5033173051621634 109051819226052554 6312264 3553225929574 75728820016262708082 3604 24 4 4 59035813619904 59604 4 916754 0375537272061819889

99514 7771614 932760797999354 0532317930374 3527584 9954 2681718721374 73000259335615361921111292616389

162184 695669562033564 97059650933237168855 18784 2033304 18075030665055606251 74 160505262331664 091925223825887095 52189

028812957505217116559791713082534 04 6084 33079774 654 768816669196814 4 7689 73284 839179217767764 27103215174 524 4 7950735880763289

054 1673160318119261024

Chapter One Hundred Three

17003817775659611825654 15251809679876026 1634 30172783703279617329250813 4 704 7654 85765605901072767352138 54 59827689

2987332975832994 4 68536565991927 2027231284 19689

66632593594 7726672235001137195 0264 673084 4 92628609598526205224 0952182235920031 4 70698269779266722504 236559291924 92054 350354 4 4 239094 08805762010504 65309269773134 94 1085727997638011304 9279739865584 1989

8876583320159334 396104 6875079635201784 72987317304 4 084 2726696584 0609618054 654 656319302505014 9598884 0192508559631880923328014 73038791291957958251012920 4 37765334 74 1089

1807580724 712724 0276166629686262222231660704 4 875229214 7150714 61596077335123827216691 54 55272913078876136704 00334 4 77105207700594 289

9727117736591924 2991321208097064 89

631255884 391194 4 264 24 834 5550207274 615226720992564 4 5652834 67989

94 9066034 174 13684 76155773134 4 0734 69800379804 214 1226713203724 6532107321735737604 9193206275564 676654 903913028689

9780152779120272 4 7510532924 59552739864 206624 529571800868091573355539701965129 31004 832314 704 13504 94 2935965118265724 04 98204 4 313975670314 705370985061314 615599154 5967908038206332711270539764 389

4 61306833524 669156764 4 4 80584 790531856264 957839354 54 6836297097508864 0725578236692990650812706 4 3207674 253904 3688571381094 074 5855659674 181134

8102672978012876597705816267284 57561593281266064 575328698356754 1694
37335171869154 4 94 2980395328095625329671764 74 2784 192171054 9638534 14
28321986214 86189

5267914 8304 004 54 23024 3724 4 624 94 276958818851304 78794 805150924 022184
72726874 3260289

6204 8598568318074 375214 86290992133913992180695380744 3634
7110623021020239908016649 283121979039310889

89

0286812774 4 9139877816012369634 9353837904 83373886164 97398864 24 08564
038860012173560371256630282 4 193284 4 1393715260355025536500684
69137995125330157088169317619805957660961132814 53624 863814 374
7081376099733927934 0713871021835604 4 3794
655957632108597263805611317386277996186628281065800063606056696516050027 54
63200064 28383399004 7068610621589

78013591870802388375 7689

557911171327021871913861244 6092285094 66217880091235664 6714 25284
5813168832334 3861702634 54 531063573268617 14 17326825210992719583249078323219289

804 85122982303379378592697226931 9589

5033354 126067763684 519202799011294 35132900852589

604 906134 817684 6124 4 81858634 5267324 94 4 123950337024 289

552856674 5576377654 8313039154 4 90724 174 4 69903334 89

6301032696085126 4 053688782221214 62152194 23825090781889

4 0264 35367515689

104 4 885683292128360258157 4 8009984 5832054 87653084 0824 256135089

359722960318588388503835818566 4 4 1215386708767601248310104 630844 74 4
32188014 4 790933674 74 6884 4 78564 14 8174 4 5909124
5398103230088592063710156358756516 4 30959611273964 0158617697813 14 08795073714
2883177604 36689

8196264 134 7500697194 056519504 550516774 239794 019689

986252789

00852374 4 580732886706974 177396357254 50609854 234 56789

85204 25073228607094 2026394 84 182866925660616654 4 4 07204
5775683939323122654 078124 7831666880180301 84 22504 520053551868684 8505584
5308525384 9754 261205794 305353308074 77508264 960885294 4 5572785003 44 1395589

379335051184 0302252987061629150596 4 22599960058564 89

57233653179869136696994 4 278665789

12525684 62604 14 79811086568557173907213307 89

331085259033331137185877287034 9262790271567329168662716674
9081993182583166832828500157570780161193169221931514 754 937755159804 654
092839991094 9374 20103717085608605881785 4 4 9005704 104 13604 04 3513764 24 689

981526806092554 011234 65329504 34 91805374 77356166667104 6929830956789

203164 8206393173922124 84 05512034 78063211131681337322 4 0632164 554
1558823784 609194 2738088502838312362266 54 974 4 30055809989

8299574 2584 32353764 2986314 656350552835604 770907574 732826367704
39630979234 65629794 934 4 5664 139608514 64 371303932136774 2124 70904 4 5272154
068792154 263064 25972602920189

94 65529811514 2612604 90076386714 173023572727683904 15597234 506666938664 605882920124 7114 4 178831782234 82153389

1876058363276181819 4 33227695553112581904 84 75174 629056200134 689

964 4 0716198232054 34 7184 6110205113155509302268251074 9199014 960817856260510885903658 4 74 5150376384 915134 00032951639910621924 05572830081035217619796168322139816924

08357639556211657126112192905087163255258558 64 9616638254 1935914 8218187619592329205699550637 64 58182685575221152787011802994 3354 674 153627620774 97854 054 1333031363354 236824 101084 64 76374 906388527984 14 900764 64 69764 854 0094 7963589

54 9754 614 4 81376369705916356998368119875250 54 79306935320757076678014 84 4 77014 24 71624 19081668224 90074 207111864 88154 77289

171865359677653957993350334 2728214 6054 16964 9600984 70697958559264 304 2870363664 713071314 7823306115764 199132224 2064 609989

88307626858360555274 09904 784 676107604 24 1784 21506285175573529996 4 7862552954 283674 29870664 5794 3375801014 074 0211618614 4 84 32976574 4 2634 28528704 7785563083096314 3527878304 194 501970294 657577773281674 68580874 5393160393725331589

92805794 34 6314 0873586086177882633 4 92774 6151184 91165513068184 671367734 882334 10851364 0394 7939208876886336339 4 6138235834 4 794 081569610914 29387734 71389

34 2377361910964 60564 24 4 4 74 77908207604 96602713561689

54 1064 4 4 8321365980829389

097296189

1211834 2914 90616389

638610693752089

534 688398334 4 4 67189

82124 34 780723874 074 57697554 5074 3684 674 7135024 8588183996655681963 4 4 52881194 1833172636825050611864 900394 125520574 571203603557802514 1904 35267183721921384 829905803224 69584 24 3231589

84 4 3251039654 4 353505354 322921674 704 0778614 684 8597625574 4 61535118800314 30569954 92784 71674 54 4 97269761283933251838197222328360707522781292813010 65694 126294 8730634 26883733818174 217060864 754 8276394 24 23914 0275321804 29519034 116351704 698074 233515560578575624 509992532017874 9963664 04 734 770389

855873065076038709977318 4 312810989

789

8820854 355955094 325390237189

52168202334 4 24 5572575307879263398550901 64 5594 237339662522335164 8750589 55694 21729724 4 89

5998825089

232112034 79589

4 154 654 6030378786175915716613988693268737 4 9684 73054 965329378214 7564 81057938082853005324 4 7080506569294 2234 001095934 8294 614 53907889

06616264 0215013073533003319207 4 563726377077099939992288621224 324 8802062634 850888530360107234 3689

0136064 275814 252839878594 917997961121963 79757651924
5218670960880921371119775000878159304 3072934 4 883930957574 15924
137528597779729189

34 5385050803831986774 59002518657917 2370808574 164 297153807884
0607130686803619824 19715774 76389

5072534 684 04 56919275953193722370229015580065607604 73854 7359904 4
7799674 874 99697694 27137668695533195125337764 09858709668386 3263926164 94 5608684
14 0374 5684 207194 0595070174 30354 691821509004 664 9399855174 1389

3851975731215682616228622318810967 2974 7606013028331193716114 0874
727067625585677751199566674 86151964 912970193318084 994 1096181392964 92789

360902125354 4 3327375064 260624 2994 12032736255824 4 174 9834 5094 73094 534
36615907284 163193683075719798068231535737155571 8161221567879364
250138871170232755557793022667858031999308108305 7630765233205074
00139390958079016377176292592837 64 874 790177274 12567819055556 2180504 87674
699114 083997791937654 2320623374 717324 70336976335792589

1515260315614 03332127284 9194 4 184 3715069655208754 24 505989
5678796130331164 628399634 64 604 220901061057794 58151

Chapter One Hundred Four

[REDACTED]

Lightning Source UK Ltd.
Milton Keynes UK
UKHW051056240621
386081UK00006B/271